THE FOLLY OF WAR

THE FOLLY OF WAR:

American Foreign Policy
1898-2005

Donald E. Schmidt

Algora Publishing
New York

ISBN: 0-87586-382-5 (softcover)
ISBN: 0-87586-383-3 (hardcover)
ISBN: 0-87586-384-1 (ebook)

Library of Congress Cataloging-in-Publication Data —

Schmidt, Donald E.
  The folly of war: American foreign policy, 1898-2005 / Donald E. Schmidt.
    p. cm.
  Includes bibliographical references and index.
  Contents: Prologue: a critical review of America's wars — The Spanish-
American War — World War I: Europe stumbles into war — World War I:
America's first European crusade — World War I: the armistice and the treaty
— World War II: the infamy of Pearl Harbor — World War II: America's
second European crusade — World War II: a Soviet victory — The origins of
the Cold War: the longest war — The Korean War: the great reversal — The
Persian Gulf war: punishment of aggression — The war on terror: the contrived
war — A presidential conversation in the West Wing.
    ISBN 0-87586-382-5 (soft cover : alk. paper) — ISBN 0-87586-383-3 (hard
cover : alk. paper) — ISBN 0-87586-384-1 (ebook)
  1. United States—History, Military—20th century. 2. United States—
Foreign relations—20th century. 3. United States—Foreign relations—2001- 4.
United States—Military policy. I. Title.

  E745.S33 2005
  327.73'009'04—dc22
                                2005000218
  Front Cover: Peace protester flies kite with anti-war message in sight of
American B52 bombers at RAF/USAF Fairford airbase in Gloucestershire,
March 16, 2003. B-52 bombers have been based here ahead of a possible war
with Iraq. With Iraq on a war footing, U.S. President George W. Bush headed
for an emergency summit on Sunday with close allies Britain and Spain that
could start the countdown to an invasion. REUTERS/Peter Macdiarmid
  Image: © Reuters/CORBIS

Printed in the United States

To my wife, Annette,
whose support and assistance in this project, as in my life,
have been indispensable.

TABLE OF CONTENTS

PREFACE

It was a crisp, clear day in January 1991, a day that beckoned us to go outside and enjoy the beauty of a Southern California winter. But there were grades to be assigned and outlines for next semester to prepare; the aesthetics of the day would have to wait.

Momentous events were transpiring across the continent in Washington D.C. as the Congress debated President Bush's decision to intervene in the Iraqi dispute with Kuwait. As a college history professor, I was vitally interested in the Bush decision to send troops to the Persian Gulf. Most of my colleagues were opposed to any such military venture. I gave some grudging support to the President, although even at that time I would have preferred to see the Gulf States and other regional powers deal with the problem.

My office door was open and a colleague stopped to chat, the conversation quickly veering to the impending war. My colleague, we will call him Dick, expressed strong opposition to the military conflict and I made some weak comments in support of the President.

Dick curtly retorted: Would you want Dave (my son) to go to Kuwait and die for this cause?

I made another inconsequential response as Dick left.

But, Dick's sharp question struck me like a thunderbolt. Was this a war that would merit giving up the life of my precious son, David? My only son?

I closed my office door and sat staring out the window — deep in thought, terribly disturbed by the prospect of such a tragedy. In all my reading in American history, in all my studies of war, that question had never occurred to me. But why not? The more I thought about that comment, then and over the next decade, the more I became convinced that every citizen ought to be asking (and answering) this very personal question — but we generally avoid it.

Is this a war that is so important that you would be willing to give up the life of someone who is most dear to you?

Answering this question should preface any war for policy makers as well. I wonder if President George W. Bush considered this question in 2003 as he sent Americans to Iraq to die.

For the sake of freeing the Iraqi people (or whatever other objective has been attached to this war, in hindsight) would you, President Bush, be willing to sacrifice the life of one of your daughters — Barbara or Jenna?

Most people regard history as mythology — simply a fable to be read for entertainment and to confirm their pride in their nation and its heroes. For these people, history should soothe and comfort, not confuse. Anything that conflicts with this view is too unsettling. For others, history is a critical examination of the past to learn from mistakes and successes. These readers analyze history, relying on accumulated facts and the use of logic. They are willing to draw appropriate conclusions, however unpleasant and unexpected they may be. If this is your view, please enjoy reading my account of America's 20th-century foreign policy.

My own perception of war has never been the same since Dick made his rather acerbic comment at my office door. This book is written in the hope that all who read it will thoughtfully consider that question, now and whenever this country proposes to go to war: Is this war worth the life of your child?

Chapter 1. A Critical Review of America's Wars

Governments and peoples do not always take rational decisions. Sometimes they take mad decisions, or one set of people get control who compel all others to obey and aid them in folly.[1]

Winston Churchill.

The Changing Face of Warfare

War is as old as man's search for food and shelter, having been pursued by the earliest human civilizations in the Middle East and Africa. Some writers attribute mankind's war-like tendency to a territorial imperative from our animal nature, something resembling packs of dogs scrapping over a forest glen. The historian Joseph Schumpeter describes war as an animal-like response, devoid of reason.

> [N]on-rational and irrational purely instinctual inclinations toward war and conquest play a very large role in the history of mankind... numberless wars, perhaps the majority of all wars — have been waged without ... reasoned and reasonable interests.[2]

Far from being the calculating and coherent efforts portrayed by American leaders, war erupts from "the most secret places of the human heart, places where self dissolves rational purpose, where pride reigns, where emotion is paramount, where instinct is king."[3] The 18th century French dramatist, Beaumarchais, commenting on the nature of mankind said, "Man differs from the animal in eating without being hungry, drinking without being thirsty, and making love at all seasons."[4] It might be added that Homo sapiens — the "thinking" animal — often makes war when there is no need for it or when it cannot be "won."

---

1. Winston Churchill, *The Grand Alliance* (Boston: Houghton Mifflin, 1950), p. 603.
2. Joseph Schumpeter's treatise on imperialism quoted in Norman G. Finkelstein, *The Holocaust Industry* (London: Verso, 2000), p. 52.
3. John Keegan, *A History of Warfare* (New York: Vintage Books, 1994), p. 3.
4. Quoted in Will Durant, *Our Oriental Heritage* (New York: Simon and Schuster, Inc., 1935), p. 45.

For whatever reason, mankind seems to love war; the human species is the only one that systematically and enthusiastically kills members of its own species in large numbers. In the 20th century — the bloodiest century in history — tens of millions of people have been killed by other human beings in episodes of organized state violence! Consider the forthright testimony about war from some who lived the life of a warrior:

General William Tecumseh Sherman — "I am tired and sick of war. Its glory is all moonshine.... War is hell."[1]

General Colin Powell — "War is a terrible thing with unpredictable consequences. Many people are going to die."[2]

Leo Tolstoy — War "is not a polite recreation but the vilest thing in life, and we ought to understand that and not play at war."[3]

During the several thousand years of recorded history, mankind has made advancement in abolishing a number of barbaric practices — slavery, dueling, infanticide, suttee, human sacrifice, clan vengeance, lynching and personal vendettas. It is time for humans to take the next step: warfare should be abandoned, as it is mankind's greatest remaining Folly.

War is organized murder by government action. What we are not allowed to do as individuals, we can do to others in the name of patriotism. If in a fit of rage, John murders his neighbor, John will go to prison. But, if John joins the Army and travels to a foreign land, he is allowed to kill hundreds and his reward will be public adulation. The Italian statesman, Camille Cavour, recognized this phenomenon when he said wryly, "If we did for ourselves what we did for our country what rascals we should all be."[4]

This book is written with the expectation that it will raise in the reader's mind doubts — serious doubts — about the rationality of military conflicts and the capacity of modern war to solve problems in international relations. It is not the work of a pacifist, as it seems obvious at this time that nations need to maintain a military force. There is wisdom in the old Roman adage: "If you desire peace, prepare for war." But at the dawn of the 21st century, it is disturbing to see the US fondness for war, the public's gullibility in believing their president's facile justifications for war and the masses naiveté about how carefully presidents have considered the alternatives to war. Further, the public makes all-too-easy assumptions about what it means to "win" a war. When questions are raised about United States military adventures, Americans pour scorn on the critics, berating them for failing to join the team. Indeed, those who question American wars are derided as lacking in patriotism, even being "anti-American."

If the legitimate roots of war originated in the need to protect the family encampment from raiders, it has now grown to such immense destructiveness as to bear no relationship to its perceived benefits. Killing an interloper at the family cave door is quite different than using steel, fire and atoms to incinerate entire cities. The ritual of war has grown far beyond what is necessary; the loss of human life and material property, the enormous costs to all sides, the Aftershocks — the unintended consequences of war — raise questions about the prudence and wisdom of modern war. Daggers, swords and pistols are markedly different weapons than laser-guided missiles and nuclear bombs.

---

1. Keegan, p. 6.
2. Jean Edward Smith, *George Bush's War* (New York: Henry Holt and Company, 1992), p. 249.
3. Paul Fussell, "The Culture of War," in John Denson, ed., *The Costs of War: America's Pyrrhic Victories*, Second Expanded Edition (New Brunswick, NJ.: Transaction Publishers, 2003), p.420.
4. Richard J. Barnet, *The Roots of War* (Baltimore: Penguin Books, 1973), p. 13.

As World War I loomed in Europe, Jean Henri Dunant, the founder of the International Red Cross, foresaw the dreadfulness of modern war. Dunant predicted that all the modern conveniences — railroads, telephones, autos, airplanes — would be lent to the hounds of war. He warned, "Ah, war is not dead! If it has changed its form, it is only to become more terrible. Everything that makes up the pride of our civilization will be at the service of war."[1]

Modern war — total warfare of democratic industrial states — had arrived; war in the 20th century would be vastly different from the monarchial wars of earlier centuries. In the 17th and 18th centuries, monarchial armies frequently engaged in harmless maneuvers, even returning home with no casualties. Daniel Defoe comments about earlier warfare: "Armies of fifty thousand men of a side stand at bay within view of one another, and spend a whole campaign in dodging...or observing one another, and then march off to winter quarters."[2]

But modern total wars have passed out of the stage of gallant poses and artful military maneuvers; they are deadly struggles among competing nations with the populace whipped to an emotional fever pitch. It is more than war — it is a lethal crusade. World War I was the prototype for this irrational carnage: "People were deluged by a barrage of propaganda inciting them to hate the enemy, to believe in the righteousness of their cause, and to support the war effort without complaint or criticism."[3]

Americans have come to believe that democratic societies are synonymous with peace. However, the reality is that existence of democracy has intensified war. In order to raise money, produce immense supplies of weaponry and recruit a citizen army, the people must be enthused about the pending military venture. After the president has decided on war, he turns the propaganda machine on the populace to elicit their support. The military crisis is always portrayed in black and white shades of a melodrama: Uncle Sam is a bright, shining, benevolent Good Samaritan; the enemy is a dark, sinister, grasping monster. With such a stark contrast drawn by the White House, the people don their war bonnets, let out a full-throat cry, and then march off to slay the evil one who threatens democracy and freedom. In this heightened emotional state, the US seeks annihilation of the enemy, but never compromise. The old restraints of war are cast aside and there is talk of unconditional surrender — total war.

Once the fighting has begun, all discreet, rational purpose is lost as the nation begins the dance of death. Any and all political objectives once thought important are subsumed in the rage and fury of killing. John Keegan, author of *A History of Warfare*, describes this descent into primitivism during World War I:

> The war's political objects — difficult to define in the first place — were forgotten, political restraints were overwhelmed, politicians who appealed to reason were execrated, politics even in the liberal democracies was rapidly reduced to a mere justification of bigger battles, longer casualty lists, costlier budgets, overflowing human misery.[4]

The bloodiest battle of the Napoleonic Wars, Borodino, outside Moscow where Bonaparte lost 28,000 men, gave a foretaste of modern total war. Men by the thousands played

---

1. Walter Wallbank et al., *Civilization: Past and Present*, 5th Edition, Vol. 2, (Chicago: Scott Foresman Company, 1965,) p. 438.
2. Hans-Hermann Hoppe, "Time Preference, Government, and the Process of De-Civilization," in John Denson, ed., *The Costs of War*, p. 488.
3. Wallbank, *Civilization: Past and Present*, p. 439.
4. Keegan, *A History of Warfare*, p. 21.

their unthinking role in the military slaughter, never asking why they were there, what purpose was served and how long their service would be needed.

> Men stood silent and inert in rows to be slaughtered, often for hours at a time; at Borodino...the infantry...are reported to have stood under point-blank artillery fire for two hours, during which the only movement was the stirring in the lines caused by falling bodies.[1]

Surgeons performed two hundred grisly amputations during the night after Borodino, all done without antiseptic, anesthesia or analgesia. History does not provide a record of the pain the men endured, the success rate of the operations or the misery of the survivors over the course of their disabled lives.

During the Vietnam War, a US military officer inadvertently described the totality, depravity and insanity of modern war when he commented: "We had to destroy the village in order to save it." This comment exposes the folly of modern war — maiming, blinding, burning, destroying, and killing in an indiscriminate manner.

Honorable and thoughtful men have over the centuries made efforts to restrain the engines of war. *Just wars* were defined in ancient times and codified by early Christian writers. *Just wars*, the only acceptable wars, were defined as conflicts that passed the following tests:

- Was the war waged by legitimate authority?
- Is the cause just?
- Are the intentions positive and the goals clear?
- Have all alternatives to war been exhausted?
- Are there reasonable expectations of success?

In addition, the Christian Church restricted the manner of fighting: Holy days must be observed (such days constituted several months of recess from war each year), no fighting on the Sabbath, civilians were to be immune from the killing, sanctuaries were provided in hospitals, churches and monasteries. Safe havens abounded in time, person and place for the subjects of the realm.

The political theorist Niccolo Machiavelli eroded these restraints when he provided an apology for war in the 16th century. The Italian writer weakened the *Just War* theory with his argument that wars are legitimate when waged for "reasons of state," a vague concept at best. To Machiavelli, national sovereignty provided all the justification needed to go to war; a *Just War* was any war a sovereign chose to pursue. As the power of Church leaders succumbed to the authority of the state, and Church restrictions on war weakened, Machiavelli's concept of state amorality became the norm. With secular national power flourishing, wars by the 20th century were unrestrained. Military conflict could now be pursued for any reason announced by a national leader, pursued every day of the year and damage inflicted upon all the enemy population — including civilians in their homes, schools and workplaces — with any means at the nation's disposal.

As the 19th century rolled into the 20th century, nations sought limits to the horrors of war; fire and chemicals, machine guns, cannons, airplanes, submarines all gave reason to find a check to what could be done during military conflicts. Conferences were held at The Hague in the Netherlands and in Geneva, Switzerland at which nations subscribed to the limitation of weapons and pledged to restrain their conduct. Peace Pacts were solemnly signed affirming that the signatories would not use war as an instrument of national policy. The League of Nations

---

1. Ibid., p. 9.

Charter included a stipulation that all national conflicts would be resolved by peaceful means, generally through arbitration. The United Nations attempted to reign in the Machiavellian basis for war by incorporating into its Charter the League of Nations arbitration requirement and the outlawing of war from the Paris Peace Pact of 1928.

Today international law allows war only for obvious self-defense purposes or under the auspices of the United Nations peacekeeping apparatus. It is constructive to apply these prevailing legal restrictions to America's wars in the last half of the 20th century. The US wars in Vietnam and Iraq (2003) are obvious violations of the United Nations Charter as they were not pursued for self-defense nor were they authorized by the United Nations. The Korean War and the Kuwait War of 1991 were given tacit United Nations approval, but in the case of the Kuwait War, this approval was obtained with considerable financial "bribery" of nations by the United States. In the case of Korea, the inexperience of the fledgling United Nations and the dominance of the United States determined the vote of the organization.

A nation that marries itself to war has a fickle partner. In the 19th century, the US fought two small wars — in 1812 and 1846 — losing fewer than 5000 men as the young nation defeated threatening foes along its coast and across its borders. But its 20th-century wars have cost enormous sums of money and meted out deadly consequences to hundreds of thousands of fighting men and their families, yet rarely improved the nation's security. Since the fall of the Berlin Wall and the end of the Cold War, the US has fought 8 significant military campaigns — in 14 years. The United States has been on a treadmill of defense spending and military adventures, frantically searching for an era of peace and order, but never finding it.

With the tradition of aversion to wars bequeathed to us from the Founding Fathers and the ideals of Woodrow Wilson pointing the way toward collective security rather than Machiavellian amorality, the US has within its bosom the potential to lead the world out of the horror of war. John Keegan, the historian of warfare, sounds an optimistic note about the future of wars: "There are grounds for believing that at last, after five thousand years of recorded war making, cultural and material changes may be working to inhibit man's proclivity to take up arms."[1]

AMERICA — THE EXCEPTIONAL NATION

Herman Melville wrote in his novel *White Jacket* that "we Americans are the peculiar, chosen people — the Israel of our time; we bear the ark of the liberties of the world."[2] That comment on the American character echoed the words of Governor John Winthrop of Massachusetts as he predicted, in 1630, a unique future for the newborn colonies:... for wee must Consider that wee shall be as a Citty upon a Hill, the eies of all people are upon us.[3]

And in the 1960s, in the midst of national self-doubt during the Vietnam War, National Security Advisor McGeorge Bundy expressed similar sentiments in a more plebeian manner: the

---

1. Ibid., p. 56.
2. Loren Baritz, "American Exceptionalism," in Jeffrey Kimball, ed., *To Reason Why: The Debate About the Causes of U.S. Involvement in the Vietnam War* (New York: McGraw-Hill Publishing Company, 1990), p. 316.
3. Walter A. McDougall, *Promised Land, Crusader State* (Boston: Houghton Mifflin Co, 1997), p. 17.

United States, he said, is the "locomotive at the head of mankind pulling the caboose of humanity along behind."[1]

Since the 17th century, the inhabitants of the middle latitudes of North America have perceived that something special is taking place here. Whether as a colonial "City upon a Hill," or the instigator of the "world turned upside down" in 1776, colonists and their successors supposed themselves to be uniquely blessed. When the Founding Fathers gathered at Constitution Hall in Philadelphia during the summer of 1787, Thomas Paine saw the product of their labors as the "noblest, purest constitution on the face of the earth." He rhapsodized that these United States had "it in our power to begin the world over again."[2] Two hundred years later, the document produced that summer is, in fact, the oldest written constitution in existence, a successful model of self-government for the world to behold and emulate. The economic, political, technological and demographic successes of the United States are a marvel. Most don't say it — although President Lyndon Johnson did, and Secretary of State Madeleine Albright essentially did — the United States is number ONE!

> LBJ's comment was: "We are the number one nation and we are going to stay the number one nation."[3] And Albright's: "If we have to use force, it is because we are Americans. We are the indispensable nation. We stand tall. We see further into the future...."[4]

What would Americans do with this special gift? In the wrong hands, American exceptionalism could inflame into rank arrogance and a self-confident drive to conquer nations in the name of "freedom, democracy and progress." But the Founders of the United States foresaw this possibility and would have none of it. Unlike the French revolutionaries rampaging around Europe in the 1790s, Washington, Adams, Jefferson and the other Founding Fathers envisioned a nation that was content with being merely exemplary. Where wickedness existed in the world, nations would have to correct the evil themselves; America would set an example, but would not launch crusades. Those men who founded the nation and bestowed appropriate ideals on the culture had modest ambitions. This American exceptionalism "was not *to do* anything special in foreign affairs, but *to be* a light to lighten the world."[5]

As early as 1783, the Continental Congress passed a resolution affirming traditions of neutrality and anti-militarism in foreign affairs. Congress vowed that the thirteen states "should be as little as possible entangled in the politics and controversies of European nations."[6] Utopian temptations were in abundance, but America would channel its idealistic energy into domestic reforms. Colonial Americans had watched in the 17th and 18th centuries as England and France fought dynastic and territorial wars, most of which seemed unimportant to European subjects and remote from colonial interests. Colonial citizens and their governments learned to avoid large standing armies, excessive taxation and invasions of their liberties (such as the draft), choosing instead to concentrate on improving their experiment in self-gov-

---

1. Barnet, *The Roots of War*, p. 115.
2. McDougall, *Promised Land, Crusader State*, p.19.
3. Barnet, *The Roots of War*, p. 3.
4. Sandra Mackey, *The Reckoning: Iraq and the Legacy of Saddam Hussein* (New York: W. W. Norton, 2002), p. 358.
5. McDougall, *Promised Land, Crusader State*, p. 20.
6. Justin Raimondo, "Defenders of the Republic: The Anti-Interventionist Tradition in American Politics," in John Denson, ed., *The Costs of War*, p. 67.

ernment. To become a player in the European game of war would endanger their own interests and entice Europe into North American affairs. Thus, when President George Washington delivered his Farewell Address to the nation in 1796, his words reaffirmed a colonial tradition of avoiding involvement in European politics. The great rule of conduct was simple:

> It is our true policy to steer clear of permanent alliances with any portion of the foreign world.... Taking care always to keep ourselves by suitable establishment on a respectable defensive posture, we may safely trust to temporary alliances for extraordinary emergencies.[1]

These cautionary words about avoiding involvement in world politics are said, by some 20th century US leaders, to have been eclipsed by modern transportation and communication. They assert that the rapidity of modern travel and communication demands US participation in foreign disputes. But, on the contrary, the American tradition of abstaining from foreign quarrels is based on a unique *attitude*, not on a geographical position or the existence of a telephone cable. The fact that an e-mail travels instantly across the planet is irrelevant to the issue of whether the US pursues a policy of neutrality or one of global hegemony. And note, Washington's counsel is to avoid entanglement with "any portion of the foreign world," the adjacent lands (Canada and the Caribbean) as well as the distant climes (Vietnam, German or Iraq). For centuries, Sweden and Switzerland were warring nations terrorizing much of Europe; more recently they have pursued a benign policy of neutrality. Their role reversal has nothing to do with a new position on the map; it has everything to do with their new attitude on war. Human beings make policy, not geography or technology.

On the occasion of the nation's 45th birthday celebration, July 4, 1821, Secretary of State John Quincy Adams delivered an oration emphasizing the modest nature of American exceptionalism. Adam's words became, along with Washington's Farewell Address, the Holy Grail of American neutralist foreign policy in the 19th and early 20th centuries:

> America does not go abroad in search of monsters to destroy. She is the well-wisher to the freedom and independence of all. She is the champion only of her own. She will recommend the general cause by the countenance of her voice, and the benignant sympathy of her example. She well knows that by once enlisting under other banners than her own, were they even the banners of foreign independence, she would involve herself beyond the power of extrication, in all the wars of interests and intrigue, of individual avarice, envy, and ambition, which assumed the colors and usurped the standards of freedom.... She might become the dictatress of the world. She would be no longer the ruler of her own spirit.[2]

In the cogent words of Walter McDougall, America was to be a Promised Land, not a Crusader State. Prophets of the Promised Land abound in early American history: Washington, Jefferson, Alexander Hamilton, John and John Quincy Adams, James Madison and James Monroe. Henry Clay, expressing the spirit of the Founders years later advised that we Americans "should keep our lamp burning brightly on the western shore, as a light to all nations...."[3] And that's all!

President Grover Cleveland, in his first inaugural message in 1885, reaffirmed the neutralist tradition when he proclaimed, "the scrupulous avoidance of any departure from that foreign policy commended by the history, the traditions, and the prosperity of our Republic."

---

1. McDougall, *Promised Land, Crusader State*, p. 46,47.
2. Ibid., p. 36.
3. John Denson, "War and American Freedom," in John Denson, ed., *The Costs of War*, p 8.

American neutrality, Cleveland asserted, rejects "any share in foreign broils and ambitions upon other continents and repelling their intrusion here. It is the policy of Monroe and of Washington and Jefferson — 'Peace, commerce, and honest friendship with all nations, entangling alliances with none.' "[1]

Opponents of the neutralist tradition, led by Franklin Roosevelt, derided this policy in the 20th century by referring to it as "Isolationism," thereby suggesting an ostrich-like stance of ignoring the rest of the world. This pejorative term is a clear and deliberate distortion of the original concept of neutrality. Under the neutralist banner from colonial times until the 20th century, America carried on a lively economic, cultural and diplomatic exchange with the world. As "Isolationist" Senator William Borah remarked: "In matters of trade and commerce we have never been isolationist. But in all matters political...we have been isolationist."[2]

It was the genius of the Founding Fathers to guide America's exuberant idealism into domestic policy — improving the experiment in self-government. They recognized the danger of allowing this messianic urge to soar across the oceans and intrude in foreign affairs on every continent. Neutralism, non-involvement in foreign quarrels was their restraint on incipient and explosive American idealism.

THE AMERICAN CRUSADE AGAINST EVIL

Since the formation of the nation-state system in the 17th century, international relations had been conducted through the prism of realism. It was assumed by kings, prime ministers and presidents that each nation would arrange its affairs of state according to its own tangible national interests: physical security and economic necessities would be the guiding star, and national power would be the means of its success. To realists, it was irrelevant what ideology motivated another nation, whether it was a democracy or monarchy, what political principles a foreign leader espoused, whether a nation committed aggression or violated human rights. Nations judged others in foreign affairs according to whether actions were clearly threatening to their interests, not whether the actions were evil or good in the abstract.

But all this changed early in the 20th century when President Woodrow Wilson began teaching his lessons on idealism. To Wilson, the son of a stern Presbyterian preacher, American foreign policy should reflect the moral and legal principles that guide domestic life. It has been said by idealists that America should not keep two sets of books — one for domestic matters and another for foreign affairs. International relations, in the hands of idealists, would be dedicated to the eradication of evil behavior in the world; nations that practiced humanitarian, Christian precepts would be rewarded with the favor of Washington D.C. The Sermon on the Mount would replace national self-interest and power; America, the exceptional nation, would teach the world how to behave. But to do this, America would have to shed its traditional policy of neutrality; America would have to become a Crusading State, rather than merely a Promised Land.

The Crusading State that emerged one hundred years ago was stimulated by the rising religious fervor of Protestant evangelism. Evangelism gave religion its aggressive, crusading inclination, sending missionaries to the four corners of the earth, urging temperance and prohi-

---

1. Justin Raimondo, "Defenders of the Republic," in John Denson, ed., *The Costs of War*, p. 73.
2. McDougall, *Promised Land, Crusaders State*, p. 149.

bition of alcohol, abolition of slavery, promoting female suffrage, child protection laws and assorted other ameliorative measures. The Anti-Saloon League, an arm of this fervent Protestant movement, announced its world crusade in 1917: "With America leading the way, with faith in Omnipotent God, and bearing with patriotic hands our stainless flag, the emblem of civic purity, we will soon bestow upon mankind the priceless gift of World Prohibition."[1]

(Sexual purity was also of paramount importance as evidenced by General John Pershing's directive to the American Army in France during the First World War. Pershing cautioned that "sexual continence is the plain duty of members of the AEF (the American Army) both for the vigorous conduct of the war, and for the clean health of the American people after the war." Pershing attempted to get the French authorities to close brothels wherever American troops were fighting, but to no avail. So the God-fearing general forbade American troops to travel into any French controlled area. Surely, the American draftees did not realize that celibacy would be part of this idealistic crusade in Europe. It is interesting to note that the "virtuous" General kept a mistress in Paris at that time.)

American values were to be carried to foreign lands, not only by missionaries, but also by diplomats, the military and businessmen. American "imperialism" would be of a unique variety — it would conquer the minds and hearts, not national territories. America was interested in ideas, principles and values, not ports, mines or cities. America's military would be a unique fighting force — carrying an evangelical message to the "heathens" of the world. As President Johnson prepared America for war in 1965, he asserted this new imperialism: "Because we fight for values and we fight for principles, rather than territory and colonies, our patience and our determination are unending."[2]

American foreign policy has been laced with religious-based moralism throughout the 20th century; America fights wars to assure the triumph of right over wrong, not merely to defend its national interest. In an earlier time, American Founding Fathers would have ignored the military rumblings taking place in far-off Poland, Korea, Vietnam and Iraq. But because of the tutelage of Woodrow Wilson, America busied itself about perceived aggression and "evil" dictators everywhere in the world, all in the name of righteousness. A Presbyterian journal urged a holy war early in the 20th century, saying: "And if it be the will of Almighty God that by war the last trace of this inhumanity of man to man shall be swept away from this hemisphere, let it come."[3] The current president, George W. Bush, exemplifies this Protestant evangelical fervor. As a "born again" Christian, Bush believes that he is an instrument of God and characterizes international relations as a Biblical clash between the forces of good and evil. Following the terror attacks in September 2001, Bush stated that he was "chosen by the grace of God to lead at that moment."[4]

Since 1898, US presidents have fought numerous wars in the name of stopping aggression and to remove dictators from power. Wilsonian idealism has imbued Americans with the belief that aggressive military moves anywhere on earth, being evil, must be stopped, even when America itself is not directly threatened. Over the century America's warrior children have died around the globe. And the Army of George Bush II stands astride Iraq in 2005, having trium-

---

1. Murray N. Rothbard, "World War I as Fulfillment: Power and the Intellectuals," in John Denson, ed., *The Costs of War*, p. 258.
2. Loren Baritz, "American Exceptionalism," in Jeffrey Kimball, ed., *To Reason Why*, p. 325
3. Thomas A. Bailey, *The Man in the Street: The Impact of American Public Opinion on Foreign Policy* (Gloucester, Mass.: Peter Smith, 1964), p. 204.
4. www.belief.com/story/121/story_12112.html.

phantly destroyed the evil of the dictator Hussein, while the multitudes chant hosannas and sing God Bless America!

America has sought a world without aggressors much as Jason pursued the Golden Fleece in ancient mythology, with all the obstacles and eventual futility of the quest. And there is good reason for the inability to eliminate aggression. National borders are not sacred, inviolate or permanent. Only those societies, like America's, that have overdosed on the pious rhetoric of Woodrow Wilson, would readily sacrifice human lives to combat the mere violation of a national border. From time immemorial nations have "adjusted" borders, sometimes, unfortunately, in military conflict. Border disputes that led to American military conflicts in Eastern Europe, Korea, Vietnam, Kuwait, and in the Balkans have not enhanced US security or wellbeing, and are better dealt with by the nations involved or by the United Nations. For half a century, presidents have rhapsodized about our duty to "teach aggressors that aggression doesn't pay." But the anti-aggression lessons have fallen on deaf ears. The well-intentioned effort to stop all aggression smacks of a utopian dream, the perception being that the world should accept all existing borders as legitimate and unchanging. But the reality is to the contrary. As nations evolved, their borders were established in whimsical, even irrational ways. The borders of Iraq and Kuwait were drawn in 1922 by British diplomats for the advantage of the British Empire; the requirements of the Iraqi people — their history, their ethnic, religious, and economic needs — were not considered. The boundary between North and South Korea was drawn haphazardly and hurriedly by Americans in the summer of 1945, with little or no awareness of Korean history or economic conditions. The boundaries around Germany in the 1930s, which Hitler found so offensive, were drawn by spiteful, vengeful French and British officials in 1919, many of whom later admitted that there would need to be "border adjustments."

Nations will resort to arms when their national interest determines that such activities are necessary. The most pertinent lesson that the world has learned from the United States is that America went to war in the 18th and 19th centuries on several occasions to "adjust" its own borders — against the Indians, France, Britain, Mexico and Spain. And there was no moralistic superpower scolding from afar or interfering in these border adjustments.

America persists, however, in applying the anti-aggression "lessons" of World War II. As American military power was thrust into every corner of the globe during the last century to stop aggression, tensions flared, alliances harden and battles escalated. Local struggles in Asia, the Middle East, and Europe were inflamed, not diminished by American intrusion. Rather than providing amelioration, Uncle Sam irritated the situation. American presidents seem unable to allow local conflicts to simply burn themselves out.

Rather than learning the anti-aggression lessons of World War II, the United States might have learned a more fruitful lesson from World War I. In the fateful year of 1914, a local squabble between two Balkan powers escalated unnecessarily into the horrid tragedy of the First World War. As the world emerged from the folly of World War I, mankind perceived the lesson that the Great Powers should avoid becoming involved in local quarrels. In the summer of 1914, when Russia, Germany, Britain and France overreacted to a minor crisis between Serbia and Austro-Hungary, an insignificant local spat became an international cataclysm.

The lessons to be learned from the two Great Wars of the 20th century are absolutely opposite each other. World War I tells the Great Powers to stay out of local quarrels; World War II says the Great Powers should become involved. The record of the last half-century indicates that American foreign policy is following the wrong lesson.

Just as the Founding Fathers suspected, American exceptionalism turned militant without the restraints of a neutralist foreign policy. American presidents invade other nations with impunity, pronounce America to be the enforcer of United Nations sanctions, proclaim that all nations should establish democratic governments based on the American model and even conduct trials of captured foreign leaders. (A notorious example is when President George H. W. Bush sent military forces into Panama, "arrested" a former Panamanian president, Manuel Noriega, in his home nation, then brought him to the United States for a trial. He languishes in a US prison even now. The resulting military carnage in Panama took 1000 lives in that Latin nation.)

Nineteenth-century humility in American leaders has given way to twentieth-century arrogance. It has come to be expected that America should have a foreign policy position on all foreign issues. What does the White House think about — the Bosnian crisis, the Palestinian situation, the Chinese human rights record, the North Korean nuclear program, the Iranian religious situation, and on and on! One may well ask: What is the Peruvian attitude on the Palestine question? How does Denmark stand on the China-Tibet border question? And what are the Salvadorians going to do about the Korean nuclear program?

American leaders in the 20th century frequently said that Great Powers have great responsibilities, implying that American interventionist actions are inevitable and ameliorative. But, in fact, these interventionist decisions are choices made in Washington by men in power. There is nothing inevitable or automatic about any decision of foreign policy. When Japanese "aggression" reared its head in Manchuria in 1931, President Hoover refused to take military or economic action to stop it, deeming it irrelevant to American security; several years later President Roosevelt began the road to war in the Pacific with severe reprisals against Nippon for its aggression in that same area. America's different response in 1931 compared to 1939 had nothing to do with the imperatives of Great Power responsibilities. FDR made a decision that was at odds with those made by Hoover, and war came to the United States in Asia as a result. In 1895, President Cleveland rejected congressional efforts toward war in Cuba; in 1898 President McKinley obliged the "war party" and the Spanish-American War flared.

When Arab terrorists killed 240 American Marines in their barracks in Beirut, Lebanon, President Reagan discreetly withdrew the American forces from the Middle East. However, when Arab terrorists cruelly struck America on September 11, 2001, President Bush flailed wildly for several years across the Middle East — from Afghanistan to Iraq, slaughtering tens of thousands. It is interesting to note that during a 1984 presidential debate, Walter Mondale chided Reagan for not taking reprisal against the perpetrators of the Beirut bombing. Reagan calmly responded that when the people responsible were found they would be dealt with, but Reagan saw no reason to just throw American military might around killing innocent people. In this regard, Bush is no Reagan.

Some American presidents succumb to the lure of "Great Power responsibilities," others prudently abstain. For the war leaders — FDR, Truman, Johnson, Nixon and the Bushes — the enormous power of the United States seems to confer wisdom and virtue. They seem to reason that because America is strong, it is therefore wise. The inevitable result of portraying the enemy as total evil is to perceive oneself as absolute good. Senator William Fulbright said it well in his book, *Arrogance of Power*:

> [P]ower tends to confuse itself with virtue and a great nation is peculiarly susceptible to the idea that its power is a sign of God's favor, conferring upon it a special responsibility for other

nations — to make them richer and happier and wiser, to remake them, that is, in its own shining image.[1]

As long as historians and politicians tell the American people that its foreign policy adventures have been successful and honorable, there will be no general reassessment of the American war policy. America has taken to heart the statement of Francois Voltaire: "God is always on the side of the heaviest battalions." Richard J. Barnet in *The Roots of War* captures the dilemma when he says: "Power and self-righteousness are constant companions."[2]

After one hundred years of chasing the rainbows of Wilsonian idealism, after a century of bloody and largely fruitless wars, with the United States needing to pour its resources and talents into its own domestic problems — education, family disintegration, crime, medical coverage — it is time to return to the modest goals of those who laid the foundation of America.

> The world may be full of wickedness and inequity, prey to tyrants and false messiahs of various political hues. But it has always been so and no doubt always will be until man achieves a degree of moral perfection that has not been known upon the earth.... It is now time for us to turn away from global fantasies and begin our perfection of the human race within our frontiers.... America's worth to the world will be measured not by the solutions she seeks to impose on others, but by the degree to which she achieves her own ideals at home.[3]

THE ILLUSION OF VICTORY AND THE AFTERSHOCKS OF WAR

According to conventional wisdom, America "won" World War I and World War II; but just exactly what did it win? And, the United States "lost" the War of 1812 and the Vietnam War; and just exactly what was lost? Modern wars are about more than casualties in the battlefield, documents of surrender and celebratory speeches. A surrender document received from the "defeated" Germans at Compiegne, France in 1918, or in 1945 from a prostrate Nazi regime does not tell us much about the future security and well being of the United States. History lessons taught in American schools and colleges convey the idea that American wars in the 20th century have been valorous and triumphant, with one exception — Vietnam. With these hopeful lessons fixed firmly in mind, another generation of Americans sally forth in search of another "successful war," trapped in their illusion of victory.

The mindlessness and the foolishness of military adventures are readily seen in the *Mayaguez* incident in 1975 during the presidency of Gerald Ford. An American merchant vessel, the *Mayaguez*, was captured by Cambodian renegades off that nation's coast. The Cambodian rebels incarcerated forty crewmembers, whereupon President Ford within two days sent a rescue team to free the imprisoned American sailors. In the tragic rescue effort, forty-one American Marines were killed. Concisely, forty-one Americans died in the process of rescuing forty Americans! The Ford administration hailed the venture as a success and the public swooned over the President's resolute military action. Secretary of State Kissinger justified the hasty venture

---

1. William J. Fulbright, *The Arrogance of Power* (New York: Random House, 1966), p. 3.

2. Barnet, *The Roots of War*, p. 262.

3. Ronald Steel, *Pax Americana* (New York: Viking, 1967), quoted in H. W. Brands, *What America Owes the World* (Cambridge, England: Cambridge University Press, 1998), p. 255.

because the capture of US Marines raised questions of international perception of American *"resolve and will."*[1] How nonchalantly politicians and diplomats send young men to their deaths.

It is a fair question to ask whether it would still have been a "success" had sixty or one hundred Americans died in the rescue of forty Americans. On behalf of the forty-one military men who died, one can ask whether all means short of war were exhausted before the Marines were precipitously sent to the rescue. Could some diplomatic deal have been made, some concessions granted, some exchanges obtained, some patience displayed that would have secured the release of the 40 men without the expenditure of the lives of forty-one heroic men? What is a "fair price" to pay for displaying diplomatic resolve, military muscle and spawning military heroes — and presidential "greatness"?

The magnitude of the tragedy is painfully revealed when it was learned that the government of Cambodia had immediately ordered the renegades to release the American crew. At the moment the American Marines were engaging the renegades in battle, the captured crew had already been released unharmed! President Ford and Secretary Kissinger had "pulled the trigger" in haste; forty-one young Americans had died needlessly. Serious, thoughtful people did not question American power, resolve or will. But they did question the judgment and prudence of American leaders!

Wars are often fought in which the costs are too great for any advantage gained. Over two thousand years ago — in 280 BC — Pyrrhus, a cousin of Alexander the Great and a king in Greece, sent his Army into Italy where he crushed the Romans. But Pyrrhus's loses were staggering and soon afterwards his monarchy declined and he died. For two thousand years scholars have reflected on a Pyrrhic Victory — an apparently successful military campaign which led directly to a long-term political collapse. Pyrrhus's foolish victory has been replicated many times over the centuries by a long line of presidents, kings and generals who have gone to war, returned "victorious," then found that the costs of victory were too great. General Douglas MacArthur is said to have expressed the view that "There is no substitute for victory," but the General did not elaborate on the nature of "victory" in a modern war, or whether a Pyrrhic victory was better than abstaining from war, or whether there are more useful ways to resolve conflicts than by war.

Concepts like military victory and defeat have little meaning in a dynamic modern society. Great Britain fought two costly World Wars in this century and "won" both — with American assistance. But, because of the immense financial costs and the upheaval created in world politics, Britain lost its vaunted empire and world leadership slipped from its grasp. Winston Churchill trumpeted that he was "not elected to preside over the liquidation of the British Empire," but it was just such a misfortune that occurred to Britain nevertheless. Looking back on 1914 as British leaders stumbled into the Great War, then through the bloody months of the war as the enormous casualty list mounted, it occurred to British leaders that the war was a tragic mistake; yet they launched no serious effort to obtain a negotiated peace. At the end of the 20th century, after hundreds of thousands of deaths and a near-bankrupt British treasury, the leadership of "Little Britain" must reflect sadly on its Pyrrhic victories of World War I and World War II.

---

1. Gerald Ford, *A Time to Heal* (New York: Harper & Row, 1979), p. 276.

Germany, on the other hand, is deemed to have lost two horrid World Wars, yet the eighty million German citizens today are among the most prosperous and contented of souls and their nation is the rock upon which European unity is based. England and France emerged from the two World Wars so decimated of men, so deprived of finances, and so drained of spirit that a humiliated and twice-beaten foe, Germany, emerged by the 1950s as the greatest power in Europe.

As the Cold War materialized out of the confusion of World War II, American prophets and sages often wailed that, "The United States always wins the war but loses the peace." This dictum beautifully captures the simplistic and distorted American notion about triumphant military adventures. Americans see themselves as slow to anger and hesitant to enter a war, but when sufficiently provoked, the nation becomes enraged and smites the enemy "hip and thigh." And before the Vietnam fiasco, it took pride in the knowledge that, in the 20th century, the United States always received the surrender of its foes. Then, somehow in the years after each war, the victory would turn sour as events occurred that called into question the perceived victory. The American perception was that the generals won the war, and then the diplomats lost the peace.

Nearly two hundred years ago the Prussian military officer, Karl Von Clausewitz, wrote the classic work on military strategy, *On War*, in which he stressed the importance of political issues during a war. To Clausewitz, wars were fought for a *political* purpose, not just to destroy the enemy on the field of battle. The object of war might be to obtain a seaport, or a naval base, a slice of territory — some tangible concession. Military victory was the means to acquire the end product. Thus, war was too important to be left solely to the generals. As Corelli Barnett points out, to Clausewitz, "War is a political activity and ... therefore political consideration should rule its conduct from start to finish."[1]

However, to the average American watching the progress of a war, there is nothing more disturbing than seeing the generals and admirals restrained by politicians in the White House or interfered with by the State Department. "Turn the military loose" was the angry cry heard across the land as President Truman fired General MacArthur for advocating a wider war in Korea, or when President Johnson placed restriction on bombers in Vietnam. The indiscriminate terror bombing of cities during World War II and the atom bombs dropped on Japan were met with glee by military-obsessed Americans. "Destroy the enemy root and branch," then the diplomats won't be able to dilute our victory. Smash the enemy; demand "unconditional surrender" to ensure the enemy will not revive. And all the while, wanton destruction of war devastates lives, destabilizes society, creates new conditions and sows the seeds for the next war.

Modern war, with its awful destructive weapons and a culture that allows their unrestrained use, is like a violent earthquake; destruction is spread capriciously far and wide. "Aftershocks" — the unintended consequences of war — rumble across the planet:

- The Spanish-American War was a quick military victory for the United States, but the Aftershock — the Philippine insurrection — cost America 4200 more lives and entangled America in Asian affairs for a century. The source of American troubles with Japan before Pearl Harbor can be traced to the unanticipated Philippine insurrection in 1898.

---

1. Corelli Barnett, "Solid History, Shaky Theory," *The American Conservative*, January 13, 2003, p. 38.

- World War I caused a gigantic upheaval across Europe and into the Near East. The disintegration of the Russian, Turkish and Austro-Hungarian Empires — Aftershocks of World War I — fomented revolutions and national uprisings on three continents. Such turmoil spawned the likes of Hitler and Stalin and eventually the Aftershock called World War II.
- As World War II was the Aftershock of the First World War, the Cold War was the Aftershock of World War II. The great battle between Nazi Germany and communist Russia for control of the heartland of Europe — Eastern Europe — was a struggle that the Western nations could not win. Disappointment in the West about communist Russia's control from the Baltic to the Balkans stirred animosity, and finally more war.
- In the midst of the furor over communist North Korea's invasion of South Korea, President Truman sent a military contingent and financial aid to Vietnam. The Aftershocks of the Korean War reverberated into Southeast Asia.
- President George H. W. Bush's moralistic crusade against Iraqi aggression in the Persian Gulf in 1991 drew American troops into the Holy Land of Saudi Arabia, infuriating the Muslim faithful. The Aftershock of the Gulf War against Saddam Hussein was the tragic terror attack on America on September 11, 2001.

As America pursues a "peaceful" society through war, Aftershocks stimulate new crises, leading inevitably to a new war. America's constant search for greater security and peace always creates another evil which has to be expunged. Perpetual war is pursued for perpetual peace.

America began the 20th century as a relatively peaceful nation, content to develop its vast natural resources and ensure a bountiful life for its citizens. However, at the beginning of the 21st century, Americans can look back on a bloody century of wars, with over 600,000 of its young men and woman sent to early graves and its financial resources diverted to weapons of war. But perpetual war has not produced perpetual peace. There was always a new devil to destroy:

> Each time [a war was entered] Americans were assured this war or this intervention would help bring a peaceful and harmonious world. The results were exactly the opposite. Perpetual wars brought death, destruction, and a loss of liberty for the American people.[1]

Modern wars are dreadfully expensive, awful in their destructive capability and doubtful in their capacity to produce the desired results. With millions of deaths, financial catastrophe, and the unknown Aftershocks lurking, it is fair to assert that all 20th-century wars have been Pyrrhic victories; there have been no winners. No modern war is really ever won, especially with nations possessing nuclear capacity. What in the world does it mean to win a war in the nuclear age?

Robert Southey's bitter and poignant poem, "The Battle of Blenheim," captures the futility and foolishness of military conflicts. The Battle of Blenheim, fought in 1704, brought the Duke of Marlborough the status of hero, at the price of 41,000 dead in a remote Bavarian village.

> They said it was a shocking sight
> After the field was won;
> For many thousand bodies here
> Lay rotting in the sun;

---

1. Jacob G. Hornberger, in Richard M. Ebeling and Jacob G. Hornberger ed., *The Failure of America's Foreign Wars* (Fairfax, Virginia: The Future of Freedom Foundation, 1996), p. X.

But things like that, you know, must be
After a famous victory.
And everybody praised the Duke,
Who this great fight did win.
'But what good came of it at last?'
Quoth little Peterkin.
"Why that I cannot tell," said he,
"But 'twas a famous victory."[1]

LIES, DECEPTION AND EXAGGERATIONS

"We are talking about using military force, but we are not talking about a war." Thus spoke Secretary of State Madeleine Albright in 1998 before the students at Tennessee State University after the Clinton administration bombed Iraq. Such dissembling is an insult to the Framers of the Constitution who made no distinction between war and military action. Surely the people of Iraq who felt the sting of American explosives — bringing death and destruction — would fail to see the difference between "using military force" and "war."

Presidential lies, deceits, and exaggerations during the Vietnam War are legendary; Presidents Johnson and Nixon were properly condemned for their misdeeds. But the trail of presidential sins stretches back over the entire century. "When war is declared, truth is the first casualty."[2] It has been so since President McKinley took America into its first foreign war in 1898, and continues to the Iraqi war of George Bush in 2005.

Democratic self-government and war are unhappy companions. When the Founding Fathers set about to create a self-governing society, they recognized the necessity of discouraging easy entrance into wars. To limit war, they offered a system in which the nation would go to war only when the Congress, after extended debate, voted its approval. The attributes of a democratic society have nothing in common with a war-like society. Democracies require a cool, rational debate on issues, tolerance of diverse viewpoints, recognition of a legitimate opposition and sanctity of individual choices. During peacetime Congress reigns supreme and the president presides over a docile, modest military force.

However, a culture of war requires the opposite; the president asserts dominance over the Congress and public debate ceases in deference to the president's war. The military force becomes inflated and resources are diverted to "defense." Dissenters are reviled, censored and even jailed for treason. Individuality retreats to make way for servility, and discussion warps into conformity. A society based on volunteerism is transformed by the military draft. Having failed to sell their war to the public and gaining too few enlistees, presidents use the naked power of government to conscript young men for the war, placing them in harm's way against their will. The ultimate power of government is not the power to tax and spend; it is the power to go to war — to decide issues of life or death. Alexis de Tocqueville saw this dilemma early in American history when he wrote in *Democracy In America*: "Foreign politics demand scarcely any of those qualities which are peculiar to a democracy; they require, on the contrary, the perfect

---

1. *The Battle of Blenheim,* by Robert Southey (1774-1843).
2. John Denson, "War and American Freedom," John Denson, ed., *The Costs of War, p.3.*

use of almost all those in which it is deficient."[1] The Frenchman Tocqueville, an expert on European culture and an observer of the frequent wars in Europe, counseled the new nation about the baleful effects of war: "All those who seek to destroy the liberties of a democratic nation ought to know that war is the surest and shortest means to accomplish it."[2]

The American people express great pride in having the world's oldest democracy, yet they have never reconciled the bloody, destructive use of force with the noble purposes of self-government. Thoughtful people were dismayed at the use of atom bombs on Japanese civilians in 1945; most Americans, however, cheered their deaths. What does the terror bombing of enemy homes, schools and workplaces do to the consciences of citizens of a democracy? George Kennan has written of his concern on this matter: "It is essential to recognize that the maiming and killing of men and the destruction of human shelter and the other installations, however necessary it may be for other reasons, cannot in itself make a positive contribution to any democratic process."[3]

The savagery of war must be concealed from the people, else they turn down the next offer of military conflict. During the Kuwait War in 1991, newsmen filmed footage for television of an Iraqi soldier being sliced in half — literally ripped in two — by fire from a United States helicopter. The Pentagon refused to allow the footage to be shown on television, saying, "If we let people see that kind of thing there would never again be any war."[4] Precisely!

Presidents and politicians of the "war party" can depend upon court historians to spread the good news — the American military always wins a smashing victory against the evil, dreaded foe. American generals and admirals appear as Supermen, arriving just in the nick of time to save civilization. Yet, in truth, most of America's military victories in the 20th century have been exaggerated:

- In the Spanish-American War, the United States fought a small, backward European power whose navy consisted mainly of old wooden-hulled ships. Spain was hardly a worthy foe.
- In World War I, the United States Army fought only the last few months of the war and was largely unprepared for battle, contributing little to the military outcome. Yet, most Americans have been taught to regard General Pershing's Army as tipping the balance of power.
- World War II in Europe was a Soviet Union victory over Germany, although even now the United States citizenry refuses to acknowledge this fact. Germany experienced 90% of its military deaths fighting Russia in the Eastern Front.
- In Korea, America was victorious in driving North Korea out of South Korea, but was defeated at the Yalu River border and driven back by China.
- And the world knows that Vietnam — tiny Vietnam — threw the United States out of Southeast Asia in the 1970s.

America's military history in the 20th century has been gloriously inflated. Boastful and uninformed politicians brag about America's military triumphs, and craven historians, fearful of a public backlash, confirm the false news that America is militarily invincible.

---

1. Barnet, *The Roots of War*, p. 308.
2. www.mises.org/freemarket_detail.asp?control=124.
3. George Kennan, *American Diplomacy* (New York: Mentor Books, 1951), p. 77.
4. Paul Fussell, "The Culture of War," in John Denson, ed., *The Costs of War*, p. 421.

As American presidents edge the nation closer to the abyss of war, and as the public shows reluctance to oblige the presidential caprice, the commander-in-chief becomes the "liar-in chief." A harsh judgment? Consider these morsels from America's 20th-century wars that will serve as appetizers for the Folly of War:

- When World War I erupted in Europe in 1914, President Wilson pursued a fraudulent neutrality and concealed the truth about the Lusitania. The President deceived the people.
- In October 1941, as FDR maneuvered the nation into World War II, the President told a startled nation that he possessed a German Nazi map of the Americas showing Nazi plans for armed conquest of this hemisphere. The maps and plans — as FDR knew — were bogus. The President lied to the people.
- The USS Greer was an American destroyers that President Roosevelt, claimed was attacked by German submarines in the north Atlantic in the fall of 1941. The attacks were actually provoked by the actions of the American Navy — on orders from the President. The President lied.
- In the early stages of the Cold War, President Harry Truman deliberately "scared hell out of the American people" by telling them that Soviet communism was on the march in Greece. The President exaggerated and lied.
- A civil war in Korea in 1950 was presented to the people as a Moscow-instigated case of aggression. The President deceived and exaggerated.
- President Bush distorted Saddam Hussein's actions in 1990, rushing troops to the Persian Gulf to stop the alleged aggression against Saudi Arabia. This distortion by President Bush has been the source of profound anguish for the US, as the terrorist group, al-Qaeda, now seeks revenge for desecrating the Land of Two Shrines, the land of Mecca and Medina. The President tragically deceived.
- President Bush, the younger, has joined his father in the Annals of Presidential Liars with his tall tales about Saddam Hussein's Weapons of Mass Destruction (WMD more likely translates as Weapons of Mass Disappearance). More than two years after the invasion in 2003, no evidence of weapons of mass destruction has been found.

The American road to war in the 20th century is strewn with the lies, distortions and exaggerations of presidents. Students of history can search the annals of presidential statements in the 19th century and will find no such inflated, deceitful rhetoric. The problem that confronted 20th century presidents is that they were taking America into wars which were unnecessary; thus they had to stretch the truth in order to obtain support. President Madison in the War of 1812 and President Polk in the Mexican War did not have to stretch the truth; British gunboats were in the Chesapeake Bay and hovering off the coast in 1812, and Mexican troops in the 1840s were around and across the US border. Madison and Polk needed no compulsory draft nor did they need to embellish the truth.

Elections have afforded presidents a golden opportunity to "create history." On several occasions during the 20th century, presidential elections have occurred as war clouds loomed. In each case the president told the people what they wanted to hear — that there would be no war — then reversed course. Wilson's campaign slogan in 1916 "He kept us out of war," then the reality of 1917, "He took us into war," has become standard campaign tactic – FDR, LBJ, Nixon and the two Bushes all deceived the electorate about going to war.

"Elections by panic" — frightening the public into thinking that they are poorly defended and that the "enemy" is on the verge of attack has also become a standard on the campaign trail. Prior to the 1988 presidential election, Vice-president George H. W. Bush gave Soviet leader Mikhail Gorbachev warning of the American "cry of wolf." Bush cautioned that the Soviets should not take too seriously the "empty cannons of rhetoric" booming from America.[1] In this candid admission, the future president is conceding that American presidents find it convenient to use inflammatory and dishonest rhetoric during campaigns. But the "cannons" are not empty. The verbal shrapnel falls on innocent, believing citizens. President Bush seems unconcerned with the impact of these provocative words on the electorate, or with the possibility that such bombast may provoke a war. Over the century democratic leaders have "energized" the populace, then found it impossible to tame the aroused beast.

There is always a "GAP," an insufficiency of some military weapon, that will result in America being threatened, invaded or bombed — a missile gap, a first-strike gap, an infantry gap. It seems never to occur to the American electorate that they are being toyed with as though they were little children. A "bogeyman" always is ready to get them if they don't watch out. None of these weapon GAPS existed; all were contrived to elect some president or to inflate the military budget. Since World War II, the American defense establishment has always been several times larger than its closest competitor; yet, for some, there is always too little.

In the midst of the run up to the Iraq war in 2003, White House spokesmen for President George W. Bush and establishment figures in the institutes and universities asserted that "we have to accept the president's words justifying the war." But after a century of the Folly of War, with presidential lies, deception and exaggerations abounding, thoughtful people are no longer inclined to give the president the benefit of the doubt. It is now more rational to believe that the president is not telling the truth.

LEASHING AND UNLEASHING THE DOGS OF WAR

The genius and humility of the Founding Fathers are best seen in their modest use of the military, indeed, their aversion to war itself. Despite the fact that they had spent a decade at war against the British and had become famous pursuing the military arts, they were reluctant to use armies to radically change society, and they saw in war the greatest horror government can impose upon the citizenry. While the American Revolution was the first of the great national revolts in the last two and a half centuries, it did not become the proto-type for others in the manner of using warfare to accomplish social change. As revolutionary fervor gripped other nations — France, Germany, Russia and China during the last two hundred years — it became commonplace in those nations to use the military to uproot social classes, re-distribute property, execute thousands of dissidents — in short, to militarize society. Napoleon, Robespierre, Bismarck, Hitler, Mao Tse-tung, and others, dressed in military uniforms bedecked in war ribbons and medals, had created a military society. Their own political birth was in the military; their lives would be lived in that fashion, and at their deaths they would be remembered for their military exploits. But not the American revolutionary leaders. They were more interested in "clogging rather than facilitating war."[2] It was their intention to "leash the dogs of war."

---

1. George H. W. Bush and Brent Scowcroft, *A World Transformed* (New York: Alfred A. Knopf, 1998), p.5.
2. Doug Bandow, "The Power to Declare War," in Ebeling and Hornberger, *The Failure of America's Foreign Wars*, p. 13.

The experience of the Founding Fathers in dealing with the British government and their reading in political history informed them that war-making powers were abused by past monarchs and executives. James Madison wisely observed that "War is the true source of executive aggrandizement."[1] George Mason, a Virginia delegate to the Constitutional Convention and one of the prime movers of the idea of a written Bill of Rights, argued that the executive "is not safely to be entrusted with" the war-making power.[2] Alexander Hamilton, a military aide to General George Washington during the war against Britain and no shrinking violet on executive power, nevertheless expanded in *The Federalist* on the dangers of war-making in presidential hands. The Constitution does not think it wise to delegate "so delicate and momentous" a task as war-making to "the sole disposal of a magistrate as the president."[3]

Thomas Jefferson, though not a delegate at the convention, caught the same spirit when he said, "We have already given...one effective check to the dogs of war by transferring the power of letting him loose."[4] That check to the "dogs of war" was to prohibit the president from taking the nation into war. Only Congress, the people's body, could take the nation to war. On this crucial matter, there was near unanimity. Article 1, Section 8 of the United States Constitution states simply and directly that "Congress shall have the power... to declare war."

But the executive was placed at the head of the military establishment, creating a civilian head of the military to forestall any "man on horseback" — a general on the loose — taking over government. The president would have an army, but he could not unleash it. Hamilton stated that the president's authority was:

> in substance much inferior to it [monarchs]. It would amount to nothing more than the supreme command and direction of the land and naval forces... while that of the British King extends to the declaring of war and to the raising and regulating of fleets and armies; all of which by the Constitution would appertain of the legislature.[5]

Military adventures, more than any other government activity, bloats the bureaucracy, inflates taxes and burdens posterity with debt. The president did not have the power to legislate, nor would he have the power to take the nation to war. The question was not only a matter of life and death, but also the basic nature of government. James Madison's thoughts are important:

> Of all the enemies of public liberty, war is, perhaps, the most to be dreaded, because it comprises and develops the germ of every other. War is the parent of armies; from these proceed debts and taxes; and armies, and debts, and taxes are the known instruments for bringing the many under the domination of the few.[6]

But, can the president "make war" without an official declaration of war? The subject came up in the discussions at the Constitutional Convention when Pierce Butler, a South Carolina delegate, suggested that the wording of the proposed Constitution allowed the pres-

---

1. Ibid., p. 19,20.
2. Ibid., p. 13.
3. Ibid., p. 14.
4. Ibid.
5. Ibid., p. 12-13.
6. Ralph Raico, "American Foreign Policy -The Turning Point, 1898-1919," in Ebeling and Hornberger, ed., *The Failure of America's Foreign Wars*, p. 54.

ident the legal ability to make, or start a war, thereby bypassing Congress. In other words, Butler suggested that *making* and *declaring* were different; one belonged to the president, the other to Congress. Elbridge Gerry from Massachusetts immediately complained that he "never expected to hear in a republic a motion to empower the executive to declare war."[1] Butler's motion was rejected by the convention. The Founding Fathers considered the words "make war" and "declare war" to be synonymous. And so it had been until President Harry S. Truman broke the tradition, sending American troops into the Korean War without a declaration of war by Congress.

What about repelling a sudden attack? Must the president convene Congress, request a declaration of war and wait for the congressional debate to proceed before responding to an enemy attack? Obviously not! The president has the inherent power to respond to a surprise attack, using military force against such an enemy. Roger Sherman, a Connecticut delegate, commented on this when he exclaimed that "the executive should be able to repel and not to commence war."[2] If, at the height of the Cold War a missile attack had been launched against the United States, no one would have split hairs about how an American president should respond.

However, the Founders were so concerned with limiting presidential war powers they even withheld from the executive the power of reprisal — the power to punish a nation for an attack. Hamilton expressed such ideas in *The Federalist* when he said the commander-in-chief could "repel force by force.... Anything beyond this must fall under the idea of reprisal and requires the sanction of [Congress], which is to declare war."[3]

Recent presidents and their supporters frequently argue for an expansive view of the president's ability to use the military in combat. To buttress their argument they point out that past presidents have used military force over 200 times, all without a declaration of war or approval by Congress. Historical precedent has been set, they assert, for a generous interpretation of the war declaration clause. But according to constitutional scholar Edward Corwin, those two hundred incidents were minor "fights with pirates, landing small naval contingents on barbarous coasts... the dispatch of small bodies of troops to chase bandits or cattle rustlers across the Mexican border and the like."[4] The following examples show the rather inconsequential nature of these two hundred incidents:

1859 — 200 soldiers cross the Rio Grande in pursuit of a Mexican bandit. No casualties.

1948 — Marines sent to Jerusalem to protect US Counselor office. No casualties.

1963 — Marines deployed off the coast of Haiti. No casualties.

(Some of these two hundred incidents did, indeed, prove tragically harmful to American men, for example, the disastrous bombing of the United States Marine barracks in Lebanon in 1983.)

---

1. Bandow, "The Power to Declare War," in Ebeling and Hornberger, ed., *The Failure of America's Foreign Wars*, p. 13.
2. Ibid., p. 16.
3. Ibid., p. 17.
4. Ibid., p. 18.

The Constitutional Convention debates, the plain words of that document and historical precedent provide no aid and comfort to the recent views justifying the presidential war-making of Truman, Johnson, Nixon, or the two Bushes. Yet, since the Korean War, or "police action," presidents have argued successfully for the power to make war without the interference of Congress. Secretary of State Dean Acheson's comment in 1950 represents the current "informed" thinking on this matter: "Not only has the president the authority to use the Armed Forces in carrying out the broad foreign policy of the United States and in implementing treaties, but it is equally clear that this authority may not be interfered with by the Congress...."[1]

President George H. W. Bush went further in his assessment of presidential war making when he launched Desert Storm in 1991 against Iraq. The President averred: "I have an obligation as president to conduct the foreign policy of this country the way I see fit."[2] When questioned as to whether he was planning to ask Congress for authority to go to war, the President snapped: "I don't think I need it."[3] President George W. Bush has asserted the same expanded presidential prerogative in the 2003 preemptive war against the regime of Saddam Hussein.

Prior to the 20th century, presidents had always deferred to Congress on the question of going to war. In 1812, 1846, and 1898, Congress gave approval to presidential requests for war. Even though Presidents Wilson and Franklin Roosevelt maneuvered the nation into a situation of *de facto* war, those presidents still allowed Congress the opportunity to vote "No" in 1917 and 1941. But since Truman's action in the Korean War, presidents have asserted the authority to take the nation to war, without congressional action. There have been no formal congressional declarations of war since 1941.

One of the purposes of the congressional declaration of war requirement was to spread the decision about going to war among a number of people. In Europe, a single person, the King, decided on war; in America the representatives of the people were to conduct a rational discussion and come to a collective decision. However, a study of 20th-century wars shows that one person — the president — now decides this momentous question. The American people should be disabused of the idea that grand councils of state over long periods of time carefully and rationally determine whether this nation should go to war. This is not the case. Presidential whim, presidential prejudices, presidential emotional piques — any of these may be the singular factor in deciding for or against war. Wilson's blatant pro-British bias, FDR's sentimental affection for China, Truman's hot temper, Johnson's domineering personality, Nixon's dark brooding ways, George H. W. Bush's patrician sensitivities, and George W. Bush's pious sanctimony — these govern whether our young people live or die at war.

So, now at the beginning of the 21st century, we have come full circle. A colonial revolt in the 1770s against arbitrary British government resulted in reforms to "leash the dogs of war," and for one hundred and fifty years it was a successful experiment. But since the Truman era of the Korean War, and now in the Bushite era of the Persian Gulf wars, we have returned to the ways of monarchial war making. Our president-kings have unleashed the dogs of war, as they do not feel bound to ask Congress for permission to go to war. The comments of two much-admired

---

1. http://www.cato.org/pubs/pas/pa071.html.

2. Smith, *George Bush's War*, p. 4.

3. Bandow, "The Power to Declare War," in Ebeling and Hornberger, ed., *The Failure of America's Foreign Wars*, p. 14.

presidents on the matter of going to war provide encouragement to those who admire the old ways of the Constitution. First, General Dwight Eisenhower:

> When it comes to the matter of war, there is only one place that I would go, and that is to the Congress of the United States...I am not going to order any troops into anything that can be interpreted as war, until Congress directs.[1]

And, lastly, the elegant prose of President Abraham Lincoln:

> Kings had always been involving and impoverishing their people in wars, pretending generally, if not always that the good of the people was the object. This our Convention understood to be the most oppressive of all Kingly oppressions: and they naturally resolved to so frame the Constitution that no one man should hold the power of bringing this oppression upon us.[2]

THE FOLLY OF WAR

For several centuries nations had cast their foreign policy in the realist mold — policy was based on a nation's perception of its national interests sustained by its power. However, idealists, motivated by the awfulness of modern war, conceived of foreign policy being based on moral and legal principles, eschewing military power and relying instead on collective security and the peaceful settlement of disputes. Concisely, realists such as Theodore Roosevelt glory in the use of power to sustain American interests and assume that other nations will act correspondingly. Wilsonian idealists, on the other hand, are guided by their notion of morality — doing what is right — with reluctance to use power, demanding that other nations also follow in the straight and narrow pathway.

The struggle between realists and idealists consumed much of the early 20th century and by century's end had produced a monster. America has created a new and unique equation in international relations: a hybrid that I will label *Militant Idealism*. Taking moralism as their standard from idealists and borrowing the instruments of power from realists, America has refashioned itself into a lethal, crusading military state. In creating this hyperactive combination, the United States has loosened the restraints of power from national interests, placing power in the service of a universal message — to remake the world in the image of America. We have combined the most perilous of Teddy Roosevelt's militaristic realism, and the most intrusive of Wilson's notions into a new breed — militant idealism. We have armed ourselves to the teeth to carry freedom, democracy and human rights to every corner of the world. Instead of proclaiming ourselves the beacon on the North American continent and arming only for narrow legitimate national self-defense, we have become a crusading knight, plunging here and there on a zealous quest to ensure that the abstractions of right and wrong — as we see them — prevail everywhere.

In 1906, President Teddy Roosevelt received the Nobel Peace Prize for producing a Far East settlement based on spheres of interest and balance of power between Japan and Russia. But presidents since Wilson have been constrained from such diplomatic maneuvering because it was seen as a violation of the idealist moral code for nations. Americans came to regard the

---

1. Ibid., p. 20.
2. Ibid., p. 12.

frequent shifting of the balance of power system with its border adjustments, cynical diplomatic deals and temporary alliances as abnormal, illegal and destructive of the world's order. presidents, governed by the creed of Militant Idealism, sought to prevent these gradual shifts in the tectonic plates of international relations by freezing borders in place and discouraging any backdoor deals among national leaders. Any outbreak of hostilities, no matter how small, no matter how remote, was deemed to be of concern to the United States.

During the 19th century, America pursued a policy of neutrality with respect to conflicts overseas. Local powers were allowed to deal with local conflicts, and it was understood that if nations far distant from the dispute intervened, the contagion would likely inflame and spread. Peace and its associated conditions, freedom and human rights, were divisible. America did not feel threatened at every shooting of a border guard somewhere on earth.

But with the 20th century, the *Militant Idealists* proclaimed that a threat to peace in a remote village was a threat to peace in America. Peace had become indivisible. All conflicts had international ramifications, thus the United States was obligated to intervene. And because the United States knew what was right and had the necessary power to affect a change and to correct wrongs, it would intervene — anywhere and everywhere.

The long period of the Cold War (1946-1990) gave impetus to the image of the United States as the guarantor and protector of western civilization. For nearly fifty years, the European chicks stayed under the American mother hen's wings for fear of the Russian hawk. Nine presidents — from Truman to Bush the Elder — grew accustomed to directing international affairs from Washington. American dollars flowed freely into foreign economies, United States troops provided the guard at the frontier and American armaments reached deep into the heart of every military machine. Prior to the War on Terror and the invasion of Iraq, nearly a quarter of a million American troops were guarding the ramparts in nearly 130 foreign countries. Sales of American arms totaled over 40% of the world trade in armaments. And by 2003 the United States annual defense budget was as large as the rest of the world combined. After so many decades of American hegemony, it greatly disturbs Washington to see national independence creep back into world affairs, as when France, Germany and Russia raised objections to the American war on Iraq in 2003. The mother hen is losing control of the chicks as they range farther from her skirts.

Built into Cold War thinking around the world is that America will always take care of any incidents — in distant Korea or Vietnam, the jungles of Liberia and arid wastes of Somalia, the cities on the Rhine or the Persian Gulf. Nations do not need to bother about their own defense — Uncle Sam will come to the rescue. Nations around the world are encouraged by this relationship to spend their public money on things other than defense. Regional defense arrangements are only permitted if the United States is a member, and, of course, can then exercise a veto over the group's actions. (The United States has vigorously opposed the creation of a European Defense System, fearing that the United States controlled NATO will be eclipsed.) The Persian Gulf states could have created a defense system in the 1980s to contain Iran or Iraq, but they didn't, because they knew that America would spend its own lives and money to deal with any problems. Early in the Cold War, the following dialogue occurred in Burma between the Burmese War Minister and a British diplomat:

> Burmese: We don't want a mechanized army. What Burma needs is plenty of soldiers with a gun and a handful of rice, who can walk anywhere.

Briton: That's all very well for tracking down bandits and to keep internal order. But how would that kind of army stand up to invasion?

Burmese: You mean from China? We couldn't hold out long against the Chinese Communists. But if they invaded, you British would be right back to fight for us.

Briton: Not so fast. We aren't prepared to come.

Burmese: Well then, you're still clever enough to make the Americans come.[1]

"Clever enough to make the Americans come!" Much of the tragic story of America's 20th-century wars is contained in this incriminating statement. Militant Idealists will ride to the rescue.

Repeatedly, Great Britain has become overextended internationally, then enticed American presidents to assist them in defending their inflated ambitions. Presidents Wilson and Franklin Roosevelt were beguiled by Winston Churchill before World War I and World War II and in both cases exaggerated the threat posed by Germany to America. President Truman fell for the British appeal to defend the imperial position in Greece in 1947, although he dishonestly told the American people that the intervention was prompted by Soviet communist aggression. Even Vietnam and the Persian Gulf ventures smacked of British Empire complicity and intrigue.

Throughout the 20th century American foreign policy has been dedicated to the proposition that people should be allowed to form their own governments and be free of pressures from aggressive imperial powers. President Wilson's call in 1917 for "national self-determination" rests heavily on the American conscience nearly one hundred years later. To that end, the aggressive designs of a variety of nations — Germany, Japan, Italy, the Soviet Union, Iraq — were opposed by American military might, with thousands dying to defend the right of countries to create their own government.

But American leaders never squared up the facts; the anti-aggression campaigns were hypocritical. In the years preceding World War II, the Western allied powers possessed a much larger colonial empire than the Axis: Great Britain, France, the Soviet Union, and the United States controlled over 800 million people, while the notorious Axis — Germany, Japan, Italy — controlled less than 200 million. But never would an American citizen hear complaints from Washington D.C. about the loss of freedom and the subjugation of people in *British*-India, or *British*-Hong Kong, *British*-South Africa or *British*-Ireland. German conquests were evil; British conquests were just in the nature of things.

Whether in Greece and Turkey, Iraq and Iran, the north Atlantic and the south Pacific, America foreign policy has served the interests of the British Empire throughout the 20th century. Defending the British Empire was regular American policy; destroying the empires of Britain's competitors — Japan, Germany, Russia — was standard fare in Washington. And in the process of defending the British Empire, America began to emulate British foreign policy. Nineteenth century American presidents used Washington, Jefferson and John Quincy Adams as their role models; 20th century presidents imitated British Prime Minister Winston Churchill who saw his role as defender of the British Empire. Earlier presidents followed the ways of neutrality in world affairs; recent presidents pursued the role of the pseudo-imperialist.

---

1. George A. Lundberg, "American Foreign Policy in the Light of National Interests at the Mid-Century," in Harry Elmer Barnes, ed., *Perpetual War for Perpetual Peace* (Caldwell, Idaho: The Caxton Printers, Ltd., 1953), p. 590.

American 20th century foreign policy has *not* been deliberately rapacious and predatory like most imperial conquerors. Rather, it has been motivated by a sincere though deluded effort to improve the world. Its troops have been sent abroad for protection, not predation; its monetary aid offered to improve the lot of natives, not to enslave their workers. Wilsonian idealism raised the issue of the awfulness of modern war, but then the nation morphed into the world's greatest military machine — Militant Idealism had arrived. Early in the century there were promising efforts to replace war with non-military means of resolving conflicts, but these attempts fell victim to the gigantic military budgets of mid-century.

Once Americans identified themselves as the savior of civilization and as the purveyor of moral standards, it assumed a "take no prisoners" approach to war — unconditional surrender, unrestrained use of weapons, no diplomatic compromises. Just "Total War," with America becoming an avenging angel. The price for conducting foreign policy on the basis of abstract moral principles is the impossibility of distinguishing among individual cases. Any crisis at the other side of the world is dealt with the same as a conflict on the nation's own border. Relatively insignificant problems (Vietnam) cannot be distinguished from more serious matters (Cuba). In the abstract, Saddam Hussein is the same as Adolf Hitler. There are no shades of gray, no subtle nuances, no deals to make: "Once having identified the problem of security as a death struggle with an enemy out to 'bury' you, and to 'rule the world,' it is hard to defend moderate or conciliatory strategies for resisting such a menace."[1]

Thus, one hundred years after the first salvo was fired in the war against Spain, and eight decades after the deceit of the Lusitania, sixty years following the tragedy of Pearl Harbor, half a century after Truman stumbled into the Cold War and Korea, forty years since President Johnson lied the nation into Vietnam, thirteen years after President Bush thrust American power into the sensitive area of the Persian Gulf, the citizens of America find themselves more vulnerable to physical attacks than at any time in their history.

Self-evaluation only comes on the heels of a military defeat. But the bitter cup of Vietnam has been diluted by the "ecstasy drugs" administered by the various occupants of the White House. Americans have been deluded into thinking that the World Wars, Korea, the Cold War and the Persian Gulf wars were all successful ventures. Vietnam was just an aberration, says the establishment. The official tale continues: hundreds of thousands of servicemen who died in America's 20th-century wars did not die in vain, but laid down their lives as heroes defending freedom.

A century after Protestant enthusiasts laid the groundwork for America's good deeds in the world, and after Woodrow Wilson called the nation to carry out its exceptional mission, American combat soldiers step lively to the stirring strains of *Onward Christian Soldiers*. That revered old hymn combines the elements of religious vigor and a martial spirit, a fitting anthem for US foreign policy in the 20th century — Militant Idealism.

A nation which excuses its own failure by the sacred untouchableness of its own habits, can excuse itself into complete disaster.[2]

---

1. Barnet, *The Roots of War*, p. 271-272.
2. Kennan, *American Diplomacy*, p. 65.

Chapter 2. The Spanish-American War: The Great Hysteria

Remember the *Maine* — To Hell with Spain

The battleship *Maine* lay at anchor in dock #4 in Havana harbor, having arrived there Tuesday morning, January 25, 1898. Since the ship's arrival, the crew on board the *Maine* had been uneasy. They had not been allowed off the ship during the three weeks in port, and tension was beginning to build. The night of February 15 was routine, except for the unusual humidity for this time of year. The sun had set at around 18:30 hours (6:30 p.m.), and as the clock moved past 21:00 hours, lights in the berth areas were extinguished, and men sought fresh air on deck where the lights of Havana could be seen. A newly arrived passenger liner, the *City of Washington*, lay nearby, occasioning an unusual number of "lighters" ferrying passengers and cargo between ship and docks. A group of sailors stood admiring the scene and enjoying Cuban cigars, one of the treats of this duty. Captain Charles Sigsbee, the skipper of the ship, was in his cabin and had just completed a letter to his wife. As he placed the letter in an envelope, a dull explosion struck the ship, followed by a second violent blast that appeared to come from the bowels of the earth. The great ship seemed to be turned upside-down as the bottom keel was blasted upward into the main deck. Smoke, fire and debris mingled in the air; on what remained of the deck, blood, human remains and cries for help overwhelmed the senses. It was 21:40 (9:40 p.m.) February 15, 1898; the destruction of the *Maine* ushered America into the violence, brutality and folly of the 20th century.

Captain Sigsbee immediately sent a message to naval authorities in Washington D.C. urging caution about making a judgment on what had happened and who was responsible for the blast:

> *Maine* blown up in Havana Harbor at nine-forty tonight and destroyed. Many wounded and doubtless more killed and drowned.... Public opinion should be suspended until further report....[1]

---

1. Ivan Musicant, *The Banana Wars* (New York: Macmillan, 1990), p. 6, 7.

But most people were rash, like the newspaper magnet, William Randolph Hearst, publisher of the New York *Journal*, and did not suspend judgment. Shortly after the explosion, Hearst received a telephone call from his newspaper office and was told of the tragedy:

"Good heavens! What have you done with the story?" he asked.

"We have put it on the first page, of course," was the response.

"Have you put anything else on the front page?" Hearst queried.

"Only the other big news you saw," came the reply.

"There is no other big news. Please spread the story all over the page. This means war!" announced the publisher.[1]

The headline in the *Journal* the next day was:

THE WAR SHIP MAINE SPLIT IN TWO BY AN ENEMY'S SECRET INFERNAL MACHINE!

As usual, future president Theodore Roosevelt also rushed to judgment with the opinion that "The *Maine* was sunk by the act of dirty treachery on the part of the Spaniards...."[2] As the emotional outburst spread across the country, children were heard to shriek, "Remember the Maine," with their fathers adding, "to Hell with Spain." Women wore ribbons in their hair emblazoned with "Remember the Maine," and that phrase was even found stamped on peppermint candies. Photos of the magnificent ship were everywhere; there was a child's toy ship that would "blow up" when a string was pulled. Some measure of this angry fury is understood by those who first heard the news of the Japanese attack on Pearl Harbor, or more recently, the terror attacks on the Pentagon and World Trade Center, September 11, 2001. It was a defining moment in the lives of nearly all Americans. Many years after the horrid event, the watchman at the White House remembered President McKinley pacing the floor in a daze muttering, "The *Maine* blown up! The *Maine* blown up!"[3]

The *Maine* was the first of a new class of battleships recently constructed by the United States. Commissioned into service in 1895 after seven years of construction at a cost of $2,500,000, it was the first battleship designed and built entirely in the United States and with all domestic components. The *Maine* was the first truly All-American ship, and the country was justly proud. Certainly, it was the wrong ship for the Spanish to have blown up — if, indeed, the Spanish had done that terrible deed.

The explosion killed most of the 329-member crew of the ship; 266 men lost their lives in the blast and the remains of many sailors were never recovered. The wounded received medical attention mainly by Spanish authorities, with local hospitals and medical staff taxed to their limit. A newspaper correspondent described the tragic scene:

Men that I took by the hand are this morning dead or will be helpless cripples for the rest of their lives. In cots were a sailor with his face half blown away and another with both legs so badly fractured he must lose them. At the end of the ward was a lusty Marine crying, "For God's sake let me die!" The Spanish doctor's were dressing the face of a fireman. "There is something in my eyes. Wait and let me open them." Both eyes were gone.[4]

---

1. Peggy and Harold Samuels, *Remembering the Maine* (Washington D. C.: Smithsonian Institution Press, 1995), p. 120-121.
2. Samuels, *Remembering the Maine*, p. 146.
3. Robert Farrell, *American Diplomacy: A History* (New York: W. W. Norton, 1959), p. 198.
4. Samuels, *Remembering the Maine*, p. 114.

The Mayor of Havana and Governor General Ramon Blanco, the Spanish administrator of the island, showed their compassion on behalf of the Spanish government by visiting the fallen sailors and arranging for the burial of the dead. For many Americans it was a confusing scene: the Spanish "murderers" were showing sympathy and providing basic necessities for the dead and injured Americans.

Some thoughtful Americans began asking questions about why the ship was sent into Havana harbor in view of the strained relations between the two nations. For some weeks early in 1895, the McKinley administration had considered the idea of resuming the friendly exchange of warships with Spain to reinforce normal relations. The decision had been made that the Spanish would send a warship, the *Vizcaya*, to New York City, and the United States would send the *Maine* to Havana. With some demurring within the McKinley administration and only lukewarm approval by the Spanish authorities, the *Maine* sailed into Havana harbor late in January.

Newspapers in Madrid, Spain, were angry: "We cannot suppose the American government so naive or badly informed as to imagine that the presence of an American war vessel at Havana will be a cause of satisfaction to Spain or an indication of friendship."[1] Spanish opinion held that McKinley's decision to send the great ship into a hostile harbor was a "sop to the American jingoes" who wanted a show of force; it was to be "a gloved fist, not an open hand." Even the American press recognized some danger in the venture. Hearst's *Journal* opined that "It will be almost a miracle if there is not some friction between the American sailors and the Spanish troops."[2]

Why, then, did President McKinley send a prize ship into a potential trap — a hostile harbor, possibly mined and surrounded by Spanish guns? The former President Grover Cleveland had specifically rejected such an adventure just a few years earlier. Was McKinley playing to the jingoes in his own party? Was he too weak to resist the pressure of those, like Theodore Roosevelt, who wanted a showdown with the Spanish, or of Senator Henry Teller of Colorado, who expressed the view that America should fill Havana harbor with its ships? Or was he positioning the ship to provide shelter to Cuban-American citizens in the event that the Cuban civil war flared? Or, perhaps, even sincerely hoping he could mend fences with the potential belligerent? The answer to these questions was unclear to contemporaries, and it remains uncertain yet today.

The men on board the *Maine* recognized their precarious situation immediately upon entering the harbor. One sailor said, "You would have thought we were at war," and another commented, "We had the decks cleared for action and every man on board expected there would be trouble."[3] Although the Spanish were seemingly hospitable when the great ship berthed, another sailor complained, "We can't go ashore here, the Spaniards would kill us."[4] On board ship there was a heavy night watch with 25% of the crew assigned duty. Visitors were scrutinized carefully and followed on any tour of the ship. Sentries and guards were everywhere. "We are standing watches every night and are keeping a good lookout for every small

1. Ibid., p. 64.
2. Ibid., p. 71.
3. Ibid., p. 62-63.
4. Ibid., p. 72.

boat...," wrote seaman Andrew Eriksen, who later died in a Havana hospital as a result of the blast.[1]

However, to avoid antagonizing the Spanish port officials or offending the citizens of Havana, some of the standard Navy safety precautions had to be modified, concealed or even disbanded. Sentries were on watch to observe any action around the waterline, but no nighttime patrols on the water were used and no searchlights were turned on at night, except to show guests how they operated. The harbor bottom was never dragged for mines or wires that might lead from submarine mines to the shore. Sentries were instructed to remain hidden so as not to offend the Spanish. The McKinley administration had thoughtlessly placed the *Maine* in a dangerous situation, but denied the crew adequate precaution for its safety. It was a show of muscle, but the craft was deprived of the necessary means for survival. Two hundred sixty-six young men lost their lives in the waters of Havana harbor because they trusted their commander-in-chief to make prudent decisions on their behalf.

One week before the destruction of the *Maine*, an incident that became known as the de Lome Letter occurred in Washington D.C. Dupuy de Lome was an experienced diplomat who was posted by Spain as ambassador to the United States. On February 8, the New York *Journal* printed a letter that de Lome had written to a friend in Cuba about the American president. The letter contained a number of uncomplimentary references about McKinley, including the statement that he was "weak and a bidder for the admiration of the crowd, besides being a would-be politician who tries to leave a door open behind himself while keeping on good terms with the jingoes of his own party."[2] The substance of the comments were not in themselves original or rare in America; Teddy Roosevelt had made similar disparaging remarks about the President, at one time saying that McKinley had "the backbone of a chocolate eclair."[3] But it was another matter entirely for a Spanish diplomat to make such charges, even if it was a private communication. The McKinley administration made the most of the incident for a week, then on February 14, with de Lome's resignation in hand and an official apology from Spain, the issue was put to rest. The next day the *Maine* blew up and American-Spanish relations never recovered.

In 1898, the American people and leaders were emotionally inflamed and truculent, using the *Maine* incident as a reason for war. However, by the 1930's the American people were remorseful for misidentifying the culprit and to that end President Roosevelt sent an official apology to the Spanish government. As one historian lamented in the 1970's:

> We are no wiser seven decades after the event. At the time, people believed what they wanted to believe. Today, official Spanish culpability seems unlikely. The America rush to condemn Spain appears to have been a lapse into irrationality.[4]

This "lapse into irrationality" had caused thousands of deaths, widespread destruction of property, poisoned relations between Spain and the US, spawned an American empire that required tending and thrust American power into the world where it remains to this day. False lessons with disastrous consequences were learned by the American in their first modern war.

1. John Weems, *The Fate of the Maine* (New York: Henry Holt and Co., 1958), p. 48.

2. Musicant, *The Banana Wars*, p. 12.

3. Ibid., p. 14.

4. Samuels, p. 284

Lingering in the American heart yet today is the thrill of "doing good," of protecting the little guy and coming to the rescue of those in distress. These lessons, learned well and applied throughout the century, spawned many unintended and tragic incidents.

The United States conducted two investigations into the causes of the explosion on the *Maine*, one of which examined the hull of the ship enclosed by a cofferdam. Both inquiries found that the ship had been destroyed by a mine placed along the ship's hull, but a second explosion in the ship's magazine did the greater damage. Recent speculation about a coal bin fire seems unlikely inasmuch as the fire alarms on the ship were functioning and the coal on board was not the type to combust.

The culprits were most likely Weylerite officers, eager young men associated with the anti-American General Weyler. Captain Sigsbee had received an inflammatory flyer from the Weylerites just weeks before the explosion. "The moment of action has arrived....Death to the Americans.... Long live Spain! Long live Weyler!" warned the flyer.[1]

CUBA LIBRE — AMERICA EDGES TOWARD INTERVENTION

The Cuban civil war had been surging across the island sporadically since 1868, mostly in the unsettled and poor eastern area of the Spanish colony. Cuban rebels had been restive under the rule of Spain and hoped to emulate the independence movement of other Latin American republics. American soil was always a safe haven for insurgents, and Cuban rebel centers developed in Tampa, New York, New Orleans and Key West. From these protected enclaves, Cubans raised money for their cause, staged parades, influenced news stories and developed caches of weapons. These immigrant insurgents and their American followers pressured the administration of President Ulysses S. Grant to send warships into Cuban waters and give warning to Spain, some even urging American annexation of the tropical isle. But President Grant merely expressed sympathy for the rebel cause and declined to involve the nation in a Caribbean war. United States disinterest in the rebel cause and the Spanish suppression of the insurgency combined to quiet revolutionary ardor by 1878.

But in the mid-1890s the civil war flared anew, this time aggravated by a severe economic depression that struck the island's plantation economy. Sadly, American tariff policy had exacerbated the struggles in Cuba. In 1890 the McKinley tariff had placed Cuban sugar on the "free list," permitting Cuba to export sugar to the American sweet tooth without having to pay any tariff. With this stimulus in the early 1890s, the Cuban economy thrived; more land was brought under sugar cane cultivation and with a booming American market, sugar prices soared. The Cuban economy was based on two products — sugar and tobacco — both of which depended heavily upon the American market and the benevolence of the Congress to permit duty-free shipping to the American consumer.

But in 1895, pressure was building in Congress to give protection to domestic sugar producers, and to that end a new tariff bill was passed which removed Cuban sugar from the free list and assessed a substantial tariff. The world economy was already shaky; this act to protect homegrown sugar caused world sugar prices to drop, striking a fatal blow to the Cuban

1. Weems, *The Fate of the Maine*, p. 54.

economy. On the back of America's new perfidious tariff policy, the rebel drive for independence moved into high gear.

Lacking arms, money, technology and sophisticated leadership, the peasant movement depended upon guerrilla warfare to survive. Guerrilla armies, living off the land, used "scorched earth" tactics to intimidate landowners and to deprive the enemy of sustenance. With only 40,000 rebel troops against 150,000 Spanish forces, the Cuban rebels "hit and ran," burning villages, fields and railroads as they moved. To defeat a guerrilla force a conventional army like the Spanish would need a ten to one advantage, numbers not available to a nearly bankrupt Spanish Empire. Spanish troops, frustrated by their inability to capture the rebels, sought vengeance on the farmers. Both sides treated the countryside as General Sherman treated Georgia at the conclusion of the American Civil War. A future United States general, Frederick Funston, who volunteered with the Cuban rebels for a time, describes the scene: We "scoured the country, taking from the miserable people the last sweet potato, ear of corn, or banana that could be found."[1] He admits to burning farms and plantations to wreck the economy. The Spanish, ensconced in the larger cities and port towns, were better supplied but were equally guilty of such savagery. The American press reported only the depredations meted out by Spain's hapless Army.

In February 1896 there arrived in Cuba a new, tragic force in Cuban politics — Spanish General Valeriano Weyler. Weyler was expert in counter-guerrilla warfare and immediately set out to cut off the rebels from supplies. Wherever guerrillas raised their banner, whether in Vietnam in the 1960s, Greece in the 1940s, or Indians in the American West, their defeat could be engineered only by denying them access to food and weapons. General Weyler began a program of building forts and enclosures, herding the peasantry into these fortifications, often to their great objection. Weyler's opponents dubbed them "concentration camps," but they were nothing more than frontier stockades used by Americans in the American West, and later in the "strategic hamlet" program while fighting guerrilla forces in Vietnam. Americans who were sympathetic to the rebel cause were given plenty of fodder for newspaper stories about the cruelty of the Spanish. Weyler was dubbed "Butcher" Weyler by the American press and newspaper barons in the large cities found one of their first modern news scandal.

The newspaper business was going through a virtual revolution in the 1890s as new printing methods were developed and new ideas on mass circulation were evolving. Two New York City newspapers, the New York *Journal* of William Hearst and the New York *World* of Joseph Pulitzer, have come to symbolize a new type of journalism. These aggressive journalists sought out a story rather than waiting patiently for government officials or citizens to bring a story to the fore. To that end, Hearst sent the noted American artist-writer Frederick Remington to Cuba to report on the carnage. When Remington cabled that "Everything is quiet. There is no trouble here. There will be no war," Hearst shot back, "You furnish the pictures and I'll furnish the war."[2] (Hearst always denied this story told by Remington.)

Joseph Pulitzer, a Hungarian émigré, seemed to be the instigator of the new sensational journalism. In 1883 he purchased *The World*, a small eight-page paper with a daily circulation of 15,000. By 1898 *The World* had become a force in American life with a circulation of 5 million weekly. On the three days following the explosion in Havana harbor, the *Journal's* daily circu-

1. Musicant, *The Banana Wars*, p.7.
2. Ibid., p. 7.

lation ballooned to 1.6 million. The new journalism found that headlining tragic news, even inflaming the story, resulted in jobs and profits and the journalists became players in the great game of politics.

The New York *World* headlined, "Blood on the roadsides, blood in the fields, blood on the doorsteps, blood, blood, blood." Pulitzer urged American government intervention: "Is there no nation wise enough, brave enough and strong enough to restore peace in this blood-smitten land?"[1] Around the tragic events of 1898, "yellow journalism" was born.

Assassination was in the air in the 1890s and would very soon strike the American president, William McKinley. In September 1897, the Spanish Prime Minister, a man closely allied with General Weyler and the hard line on Cuban rebels, was assassinated. A new more liberal government sympathetic to Cuban independence came to power in Spain, and Weyler was shortly replaced with an old Spanish don, General Ramon Blanco. The new government also vowed to dismantle the forts and camps constructed by Weyler and to pursue a policy of limited autonomy, though not independence for the island. Even if the Spanish government and General Blanco were sincere about a new policy toward the rebels, it remained to be seen whether the American press, the jingoes in the Republican Party and the nation at-large could be patient enough to allow time for the reforms to take place.

The pro-Cuban movement in the United States in urging *Cuba Libre* saw the Cubans following in the footsteps of colonial America, attempting to throw off the yoke of imperial oppression, and developing a democratic movement on their island. Even today, the American people continue to have aspirations about democratic movements across the globe, seeing American foreign policy as a useful tool in spreading these ideals. But the effort at democracy failed in Cuba, as it has failed in most areas of the world, because it is not possible to export a sophisticated Western concept, like democracy, into a native culture. The ingredients that have gone into the creation of democratic societies were centuries in the making and these ideals cannot be exported to another culture as though shipping television sets or cars across the ocean. The American expectation that democratic rights can flourish in a turbulent land like Iraq or Cuba is a delusion. As Americans continue to nurture the democratic dream, a situation is created in which aspirations and expectations are never met, frustrations set in, and American leaders use this to provoke the public to sally forth in war against another misbehaving child.

The Republican Party platform of 1896, on which McKinley ran successfully, urged the United States to take a more active interest in quelling the rioting and killing on the island, to achieve belligerency status for the rebels and to work toward democracy and independence for the island. Republicans were afraid that if the Cuban struggle were not resolved, Democrats would campaign in the next election with the dynamic slogan, "Free Cuba" and "Free Silver." President McKinley's State of the Union message in December 1897 emphasized the humanitarian theme, saying that the "concentration camp" policy of Weyler was "not civilized warfare" but "extermination." The President threatened intervention: "When that time comes, that action will be determined in the line of indisputable right and duty ... to civilization and humanity, to intervene with force."[2]

---

1. Ibid., p. 9.
2. Ivan Musicant, *Empire By Default* (New York: Henry Holt and Co., 1998), p.115.

An active American military involvement in Cuban affairs had been rejected by the Grant administration twenty-five years earlier, and by the Cleveland administration immediately preceding McKinley. America's more active role in the Caribbean was well underway, with the sponsorship of the Republican Party, when the battleship *Maine* sailed for Havana.

McKinley Concedes War to the Jingoes

The sun had begun to shine on Spanish-American relations by the end of 1897. General Blanco was toning down the "concentration camp" policy and the Spanish government in Madrid was working towards concessions in Cuba, even considering a new relationship between Cuba and the mother country on the order of what came to be the British Commonwealth of Nations. Spanish agencies began sending food and medical supplies to the impoverished Cubans and European governments asserted pressure on the rambunctious United States to allow Spain time to achieve reforms. In his State of the Union message in December 1897, the President warned that the upheaval on the island could not continue, but the Spanish ambassador commented in a letter to his government at the end of the year that "the political situation has never been better since May 1895 and I am informed by the McKinley administration, all motive for irritation has disappeared."[1]

Then, like thunderbolts across the sky, came the de Lome Letter incident on February 8 and the sinking of the *Maine* on February 15. Three weeks later on March 9 at the urging of President McKinley, Congress passed the Fifty Million-Dollar Bill, a huge appropriation for defense — or as some said for offense. Spanish officials were stunned by this hostile action in preparation for war. Spain hastily agreed to discuss compensation for the *Maine* and to remove the hated camps, even allocating funds for aid to victims. Perhaps most significantly, a military truce idea was broached with the Cuban rebels, a major step in that it would give recognition to the rebel groups for the first time. McKinley countered with a proposal that required any negotiations to be conducted by the good offices of the United States, a proposal the proud Spanish were loath to accept. Through March and April the two sides continued their diplomatic sparring, with proposals and counter-proposals floating across the Atlantic through cables. As Spain came to accept an American demand, McKinley would up the ante; Spain seemed unable to move as rapidly as the United States expected. Madrid never did catch up, for it had to be cautious of restive Spaniards who would not accept a complete capitulation to the upstart Republic in North America. Spain was caught between a war-mongering America and a potential revolution at home.

On March 31, the Spanish made what turned out to be their final concessions: an armistice would be granted on April 9 ending the Cuban civil war, Spain would immediately abandon the camps, submit the issue of the *Maine* to arbitration, and place the issue of Cuban-Spanish relations in the hands of the Cuban parliament. The American ambassador to Spain, Stewart Woodford, cabled McKinley on April 10 that he felt a satisfactory solution could be achieved in short order: "I hope that nothing will be done to humiliate Spain, as I am satisfied that the present government is going ... as fast and as far as it can. You will win the fight on your

---

1. Samuels, *Remembering the Maine*, p. 10.

own lines."[1] The Catholic Pope and other European governments were optimistic about the new positions. Spanish newspapers saw hope for peace if America restrained itself: "It now lies with America to show whether she will cooperate with Spain for peace or whether she wishes to provoke a quarrel."[2]

But the Republican jingoes were too much for the President. Roosevelt's friend, Senator Henry Cabot Lodge, caustically referred to the truce proposal as a "humbug armistice."[3] Teddy Roosevelt was furious at McKinley and while leaving a meeting at the White House was heard to comment: "Do you know what the white livered-cur up there has done? He has prepared two messages, one for war and one for peace, and he doesn't know which one to send in."[4]

President McKinley, a sensitive man and one allied with the peace or business wing of his party, was caught in a vice. The Congress, the press, the jingoes and the public were clambering for war. During the height of the drama while talking to a friend, the president broke down and cried, so his friend later wrote, "like a boy of 13."[5] The President said he had slept no more than three hours a night for the last two weeks. One wonders how the resolute Grover Cleveland would have dealt with this pressure, or the phlegmatic Calvin Coolidge, or the generally pacifist Hoover?

On April 11, 1898, the President delivered a modified "war message" to the Congress, in effect washing his hands of the affair. McKinley affirmed that "the Executive is brought to the end of his efforts" and "forcible intervention of the United States as a neutral to stop the war is justified on rational grounds." He suggested that it might be time to "use the military and naval forces of the United States as may be necessary for these purposes."[6] The presidential message concluded with an appeal to Western civilization: "In the name of humanity, in the name of civilization, in behalf of endangered American interests which give us the right and the duty to speak and to act, the war in Cuba must stop."[7]

Congress voted on the war authorization proposal without the knowledge that Spain had essentially accepted all American demands and was prepared to move dramatically toward Cuban independence. But with the President concealing from Congress the March 31 concessions by Spain, the elected representatives of the American people voted to go to war. On April 19 the American Congress adopted a four-part authorization for war that stipulated that Spain must immediately grant independence to Cuba and remove its military forces, or the US would be used to accomplish these purpose. War was officially declared on April 25, but because the United States Navy had blockaded Cuba on April 22, the war resolution was post-dated April 21, 1898. With virtually all Spanish concessions in hand, and while the European nations were pleading for peace, the United States chose instead to engage in the Folly of War.

The United State Army was unprepared for war, having only 25,000 regular troops, making it the 14th largest in the world, ranking just after Bulgaria. Now it was up against a

1. Patrick Buchanan, *A Republic, Not An Empire* (Washington D. C.: Regnery Press, 1999), p. 157.
2. Samuels, *Remembering the Maine*, p. 231.
3. Farrell, *American Diplomacy: A History*, p. 199.
4. Ibid., p. 200.
5. Ibid.
6. Musicant, *The Banana Wars*, p.15.
7. Julius Pratt, *A History of United States Foreign Policy* (Englewood Cliffs, New Jersey: Prentice- Hall, Inc., 1972), p. 202.

Spanish force of 150,000 regulars and 40,000 volunteers. Eventually, the United States Army ballooned to 250,000 as volunteers poured in, most of whom were clothed in winter blue for a summer war in the tropics. Troubled by poor planning, tropical diseases, spoiled food, transport systems that were inadequate and lack of housing, the United States Army went to war. The unreality and amateurishness of it all was captured in the comment of one government official who asked, "But what if it rains?"[1] This is a startling expression of naïveté and light-heartedness about the tragic and real consequences of war. The young men were not going to practice tent pitching on a Boy Scout camping trip but to war, to kill and to be killed. So what if it rained!

WAR TO FREE CUBA BECOMES WAR TO CONQUER THE PHILIPPINES

To assuage American guilt and proclaim its virginal innocence, the Congressional declaration of war included the Teller Amendment, announcing to the world that the United States would not annex Cuba. The New York *Sun* stated the war aims well: We are fighting "for human lives and liberty of human beings, for *Cuba Libre*; not for an extension of the United States territory."[2] The psyche of the nation required that we justify the war against Spain as a righteous crusade, to do good in the world, not to merely acquire territory. And the nation held to that commitment; Cuba was not annexed. But the Philippine Islands — that was another matter.

The "innocent war" against Spain to free Cuba lasted only 107 days and cost 385 American lives in military combat. The war to subdue the Philippines, which unexpectedly grew out of the war in Cuba, would last three years and cost America 4200 of its sons. The American public, after jubilantly going to war against Spain, fell into a bitter three-year argument over the fruits of their victory; should we stay in the Philippines, or just go home? Without design or calculation, America found itself fighting native people in the Philippine Islands, thousands of miles from Cuba's shores. Going to war is much like entering a dense uncharted jungle. One never knows which trail to take, and soon the labyrinth is overwhelming; the traveler never knows where he is, or how to escape the tangle.

The route into the Philippines began with some inadvertence. On February 25, ten days after the explosion on the *Maine*, Assistant Secretary of the Navy Theodore Roosevelt took it upon himself to cable instructions to his friend, Commodore George Dewey, commander of the United States Pacific Fleet:

> Keep full of coal. In event of declaration of war, Spain, your duty will be to see that the Spanish squadron does not leave the Asiatic coast and then offensive operation in Philippine Islands.[3]

To the exuberant Roosevelt, it was a rewarding time as he readied the Navy for war. In his diary the day the order went to Dewey, he noted: "the Secretary is away and I am having immense fun running the Navy."[4] Secretary of the Navy John Long, upon returning from a day off work, was stunned by the actions of his impetuous assistant: "Roosevelt has come very near

---

1. Musicant, *The Banana Wars*, p. 17.
2. Pratt, *A History of United States Foreign Policy*, p. 199.
3. Musicant, *Empire By Default*, p. 193.
4. Gary Nash, *The American People* (New York: Harper and Row, 1986), p. 672.

causing more of an explosion than happened to the *Maine*. The very devil seemed to possess him yesterday afternoon."[1]

The orders to Dewey by the impulsive Roosevelt were not countermanded, as such action by the Pacific fleet was consistent with American strategic plans. Dewey did advance to Manila the night of April 30 where he bombarded the decrepit Spanish fleet the following day. When the black smoke of battle had lifted, Dewey saw all seven Spanish ships sunk or sinking with the loss of 400 Spanish sailors. Dewey had lost one man — from heat stroke. This was "a military execution rather than a real contest."[2] Commander Dewey cabled McKinley for troops to control the harbor as Spanish guns loomed from the city. Though McKinley confessed that he didn't know "within two thousand miles" where "those darned islands were,"[3] the President sent sufficient troops to conquer the capital city. But the tangle of war soon enveloped the American troops. Filipino rebels, led by Emilio Aguinaldo, made the same demands of the United States as their Cuban brethren made to the Spanish — Freedom for the Philippines. During June 1898, Aguinaldo and Filipino leaders wrote a constitution and organized a government to rule the islands when Spain left. The American government disregarded these actions and a war to Free Cuba turned into a War to Subdue the Philippines.

Hostilities between the Filipinos and their new American "conqueror" began in the winter of 1899 and continued until a truce was signed in March 1901. Eventually 60,000 American troops were sent to the Philippines to control the hundreds of inhabited islands. To pacify these inhabitants, the United States military instituted a program of rounding up natives and placing them in "camps" to provide protection from rebel guerrillas and to control their activities. It is ironic that finding itself in a guerrilla war, the United States used the same tactics of pacification that were used in Cuba by the hated "Butcher" Weyler. The concentration camp order from American General Franklin Bell ("Butcher Bell"?) informed the natives,

> of the danger of remaining outside these limits, and that unless they moved by December 25 from outlying barrios and districts with all their movable food supplies ... to within the limits of the zone established at their own or nearest town, their property will become liable to confiscation and destruction.[4]

As the Philippine insurrection flared into intense warfare, the frustration of the American administration showed in this statement from the Secretary of State:

> This government has known the Philippine insurgents only as discontented and rebellious subjects of Spain, and is not acquainted with their purposes.... The United States, in entering upon the occupation of the islands as a result of military operation in that quarter, will do so in the exercise of its rights which the state of war confers, and will expect from the inhabitants... that obedience which will be lawfully due...[5]

It was dishonest for the Secretary of State to allege that the United States was "not acquainted with their purposes," for rebel leader Aguinaldo was befriended by United States officials before the war, and American authorities had returned him to the islands in a calculated effort to aid in the struggle against Spain. Thus, the United States had used rebel leaders

---

1. Nash, *The American People*, p. 672.
2. T. Harry Williams, *The History of American Wars* (New York: Alfred A. Knopf, 1981), p. 331.
3. Ferrell, *American Diplomacy: A History*, p. 206.
4. G. J. A. O'Toole, *The Spanish War: An American Epic-1898* (New York: W. W. Norton, 1984), p. 395.
5. Walter Millis, *The Martial Spirit* (Boston: The Literary Guild of America, 1931), p. 252.

and the rebel cause to defeat Spain, then turned against them, claiming ignorance of their desire for independence. One American who didn't buy into this dubious argument was the American consul in Hong Kong, Rounceville Wildman. He cautioned:

> I wish to put myself on record as stating that the insurgent government of the Philippine Islands cannot be dealt with as though they were North American Indians, willing to be removed from one reservation to another at the whim of their masters.... The attempt of any foreign nation to obtain territory or coaling stations will be resisted with the same spirit with which they fought the Spanish.[1]

For years political leaders, like Teddy Roosevelt and Henry Cabot Lodge, and intellectual leaders, like Captain Alfred Mahan, had been urging upon the nation a policy of imperialism for political, military and commercial purposes. Until the war over Cuba broke out, the business community had rejected the arguments of imperialist, fearing the disruption of war more than any advantage gained by colonies. Early in 1898, Roosevelt shouted at political boss and McKinley confidant Mark Hanna that America "will have this war for the freedom of Cuba ...in spite of the timidity of the commercial interests." [2]

With the Spanish War raising emotions in America, the imperialists were ready to take advantage of the military upheaval to acquire new islands — from Spain there would be Puerto Rico, Guam Island, Wake Island and then the Philippine Islands. Midway Island already had been acquired; Hawaii would be annexed, and later an inter-ocean canal would be located in the isthmus of Central America. Great Britain had ports around the globe — like stepping stones — for the servicing of its fleet. Coal-burning ships under full power emptied their coalbunkers every five days and thus were tethered to their ports. With the new additions to its empire, America's new ocean fleet would be able to steam unaided throughout the Pacific Ocean and Caribbean Sea. Captain Mahan's concept of the national struggle for survival would bear fruit, as the new Republic controlled key sea lanes and ports, asserted naval supremacy and developed foreign markets, projecting America's greatness across the planet and, as the imperialists argued, guaranteed continued prosperity and security to America — all done under the guise of protecting democracy and human rights.

When the "Philippine revolutionary" war was well underway and Americans were debating the merits of imperialism, President McKinley delivered a speech in 1900 to a group of expansionist-minded Methodist ministers. This *ex post facto* explanation of why the United States was fighting in those South Sea islands is interesting for its rather unassuming manner, although some feel that the President was dissembling. This speech shows the valiant effort by Americans to explain their actions in a moralistic manner. Here for the first time we hear the arguments of the *Militant Idealist:*

> The truth is I didn't want the Philippines and when they came to us as a gift from the gods, I did not know what to do about them.... And one night it came to me this way — (1) that we could not give them back to Spain — that would be cowardly and dishonorable; (2) that we could not turn them over to France or Germany — our commercial rivals in the Orient — that would be bad business and discreditable; (3) that we could not leave them to themselves — they were unfit for self-government — and they would soon have anarchy and misrule over there worse than Spain's was; and (4) that there was nothing left for us to do but to take them

1. Leon Wolff, *Little Brown Brothers* (Garden City, N.Y.: Doubleday, 1961), p.112.
2. Dale L. Walker, *The Boys of '98: Theodore Roosevelt and the Rough Riders* (New York: Tom Dougherty Associates, 1998), p. 63.

all, and to educate the Filipinos, and uplift and civilize and Christianize them, and by God's grace do the very best we could by them, as our fellowmen for whom Christ also died. And then I went to bed, and went to sleep, and slept soundly, and the next morning I sent for the chief engineer of the War department (our map-maker), and I told him to put the Philippines on the map of the United States, and there they are, and there they will stay while I am President.[1]

In a speech before the United States Senate in March 1900, expansionist Senator Henry Cabot Lodge eloquently stated the imperialist arguments:

I believe we are in the Philippines as righteously as we are there rightfully and legally. I believe that to abandon the islands, or to leave them now, would be wrong to humanity, a dereliction of duty, a base betrayal of the Filipinos who have supported us.... The argument in favor of the retention of the Philippines seems to me so overwhelming that I should regard their loss as a calamity to our trade and commerce.... The taking of the Philippines does not violate the principles of the Declaration of Independence, but will spread them among a people who have never known liberty.... In a policy which gives us a foothold in the East, which will open a new market in the Philippines, and enable us to increase our commerce with China, I see great advantage to all our people....[2]

Senator Lodge's speech bristles with self-righteous language: duty, liberty, legally, rightfully, humanity. America will take the Philippines — for the sake of the Filipinos, for the sake of humanity, for western civilization. The imperialist's arguments are a foretaste of the Militant Idealism that will emerge from President Woodrow Wilson's World War I crusade. Providential destiny was driving the new American imperialistic spirit said one American commentator:

It is the Anglo-Saxon's destiny to go forth as a world conqueror. He will take possession of all the islands of the sea. He will exterminate the people he cannot subjugate. This is what fate holds for the chosen people. It is so written. Those who would protest will find their objections overruled. It is to be.[3]

World conqueror? Exterminate? Subjugate? Chosen people? The language is that of a ruthless Oriental potentate or perhaps a German Nazi. But, no. They are the thoughts of a mild-mannered Kansas journalist — William Allen White — closely associated with the reform movements in America. Militant Idealism was forming in the American soul.

The presidential election of 1900 and the debate over imperialism were won by the Republican Party, with McKinley receiving a larger share of the vote than in the previous election against the same Democrat candidate, William Jennings Bryan. The futility of the anti-imperialist crusade was seen when Bryan, an ardent anti-imperialist, advised the Democrats in the Senate to vote in favor of the Treaty of Paris, which included a clause allowing the annexation of the Philippine Islands.

Although fighting a losing battle, the anti-imperialists, through the Anti-Imperialist League, raised issues relevant throughout the next century as the United States expansion continued. Some comments from their camp are:

- To impose our sway upon them against their will, to conquer a nation of Asiatics by fire and sword, was the abandonment of every principle for which this country has stood.

---

1. Nash, *The American People*, p. 675.
2. Henry Cabot Lodge, "The Philippine Islands," in Theodore P. Greene, ed., *American Imperialism in 1898* (Boston: D.C. Heath and Co., 1955), p. 71-73.
3. Arthur A Erich Jr., *Progressivism in America* (New York: New Viewpoints, 1974), p.189

- My patriotism is of the kind which is outraged by the notion that the United States never was a great nation until in a petty three months campaign it knocked to pieces a poor, decrepit bankrupt old state like Spain.
- Imperialism is hostile to liberty and tends toward militarism and evil from which it is our glory to be free.
- The serious question for the people of this country to consider is what effect the imperial policy will have upon them if we permit it to be established.

Upon hearing that America had killed 8,000 Filipinos in the first year of fighting, Andrew Carnegie, a fierce opponent of imperialism, wrote a sarcastic note to President McKinley "congratulating" him on civilizing the Filipinos. About 8,000 of them have been "completely civilized and sent to Heaven," Carnegie snarled.[1] And a parody of Rudyard Kipling's poem to imperialism, "White Man's Burden" came out this way:

We've taken up the white man's burden
Of ebony and brown;
Now will you tell us, Rudyard,
How we may put it down?[2]

During the Cold War, Americans heard a great deal about the "domino theory," an idea that suggested that if one nation fell to communism that event would inevitably put pressure on its neighbor, causing that nation to fall, and soon there would be a cascade of nations falling to the enemy. William Graham Sumner cleverly created the "ultimate domino theory," showing the fallacy in the concepts of Mahan and Roosevelt to be eventual "world conquest."

We are told that we needed Hawaii in order to secure California. What shall we now take in order to secure the Philippines? No wonder that some expansionists do not want to "scuttle out of China." We shall need to take China, Japan, and the East Indies, according to the doctrine, in order to "secure" what we have. Of course this means that, on the doctrine, we must take the whole earth in order to be safe on any part of it, and the fallacy stands exposed. If, then, safety and prosperity do not lie in this direction, the place to look for them is in the other direction: in domestic development, peace, industry, free trade with everybody, low taxes, industrial power.[3]

President Theodore Roosevelt, in 1907 during his second term in office, had second thoughts about the venture into the Far East. He came to consider the acquisition of the Philippine Islands as the "Achilles Heel" of American foreign policy and expressed the view that the islands should be divested "at the earliest possible moment."[4] Teddy, the great militarist and imperialist, had changed his mind after three years of bloodletting, 5000 American lives, over 100,000 Filipinos lives and monetary costs in excess of $150 million. Roosevelt now decided that the effort to subdue the Philippines was a mistake. The Folly of War was exposed.

---

1. Nash, *The American People*, p. 676.
2. Wolff, *Little Brown Brothers*, p. 271.
3. Joseph R. Stromberg, "The Spanish-America War As Trial Run, Or Empire As Its Own Justification," in John Denson, ed., *The Costs of War*, 2nd. ed. p.201
4. Richard Hofstadter, "Manifest Destiny and the Philippines," in Theodore P. Greene, ed., *American Imperialism in 1898*, p. 70

THE FOLLY OF WAR

The Spanish-American War should never have been fought; there was no provocation that demanded an urgent military resolution. A diplomatic solution was in the offing, but the American public was in an emotional frenzy over the sinking of the *Maine*, and the leadership of the Republican Party took no ameliorative action. Indeed, key individuals in government and in the media fanned the flames of war. It was a tragic and shameful episode in American history, and one that would typify America's response to foreign crisis in the next century. Repeatedly, we have misjudged events, proclaimed our intention to "do good," gone off to war and killed. Then, later, sadly we find ourselves entangled in a thicket of problems that were never anticipated. Some would claim that America is doing evil in the world; but this is not evilness, it is folly.

During the summer of 1898, late in the war, John Hay wrote a much-publicized letter to Colonel Theodore Roosevelt expressing his great satisfaction with the war:

> It has been a splendid little war; begun with the highest of motives, carried out with magnificent intelligence and spirit, favored by the fortune that loves the brave. It is now concluded, I hope with that fine good nature, which is, after all, the distinguishing trait of the American character.[1]

This is a very revealing letter between two American militarists, congratulating themselves on destroying the colonial realm of a decrepit Spanish empire while Madrid was attempting to offer diplomatic compliance to the overwrought young nation. It is instructive to analyze the comments of John Hay.

- *"It has been a splendid little war…."* yet costing 385 American lives in Cuba while fighting the Spanish. In addition at least 2,000 more died from disease, food poisoning and accidents as a result of sending an ill-prepared army off to war. And perhaps we should include the 266 young sailors who died aboard the *Maine*. John Hay might even acknowledge that we should also include the 4,200 who died conquering the Philippine Islands, for a grand total of over 6,800 American dead! The Spanish and Filipinos dead in the adventure totaled over 200,000. Over two hundred thousand people killed in a war that should never have been fought… Wars cost money as well as lives; freeing the Cubans was not cheap. The diplomatic historian, Samuel F. Bemis, calculated the monetary costs of the entire affair with Spain thus:[2]

The War against Spain	$250 million
Philippine Insurrection	$170 million
Purchase of Phil. IS.	$20 million
Veterans Benefits	$1000 million
Total Costs	$1440 million

Indeed, *It was a splendid little war!*

---

1. Musicant, *The Banana Wars*, p. 6.
2. Samuel F. Bemis, "The Great Aberration of 1898," in Theodore P. Greene, ed., *American Imperialism in 1898*, p. 91.

- "*...begun with the highest motives....*" namely, to seek revenge on the Spanish for a deed they most likely did not commit. The best evidence we have about the cause of the sinking of the *Maine* is that a mine triggered the catastrophic explosion. A fair assessment of who did the sabotage would lead one to believe that the Spanish government was disinclined to take such an act, but young officers who were followers of General Weyler would have a motive. The American people panicked and rushed into war, encouraged by an irresponsible press and led by Republican officials with ulterior motives. Ten years after the fateful explosion, a New York congressman commenting on the fickle American public, observed, "The day after the ship was sunk, you could hardly find an American who did not believe that she had been foully done to death by a treacherous enemy. Today you can hardly find an American who believes Spain had anything to do with it."[1] Richard Hofstadter scornfully asserts that "Evidently McKinley had concluded that what was wanted in the United States was not so much the freedom of Cuba as a war for the freedom of Cuba."[2]

- "*...carried out with magnificent intelligence and spirit....*" although one does wonder about the intelligence of sending one of America's finest battleships with a crew of innocent young men into a snake pit like Havana harbor in 1898. It was not an intelligent venture, but one of great risk that failed. Leaders who risk American lives and ensnare the nation in tragic journeys should be criticized, not praised. The wife of Lt. Commander Richard Wainwright, the executive officer of the Maine, was likely expressing his feelings as well as hers, when she commented about sending the ship to Cuba: It was "a foolhardy thing to do. You might as well send a lighted candle on a friendly visit to an open cask of gunpowder."[3] As the historian T. Harry Williams concludes about the Spanish-American War, "the United States entered it without having a clear idea of the policy aims it expected to achieve."[4] The venture was an emotional outburst, rather than a carefully crafted, rational foreign policy.

- "*...favored by the fortune that loves the brave....*" and certainly any man who entered the arena of battle shows courage, but Spain was hardly a formidable opponent for the young giant, America. The United States had a population of 75 million; Spain had 18 million people. The United States was the premier industrial nation in the world; Spain had an antiquated industrial plant. The battle in Manila Bay was a lop-sided contest, as Spain's seven ships included two armored cruisers and five wooden hulled vessels. Spain had thirty-one guns to Dewey's fifty-three with larger bores. If the schoolyard term "bully" has an appropriate application in international affairs, it would apply here. A vigorous young tough is seen beating up on an old, declining nation for little or no reason, except to show off its might and satisfy an angry misguided public, thereby fulfilling the dreams of a coterie of American expansionists. Spain was complying diplomatically, although slowly, with every demand McKinley was making, and had enlisted the good offices of the Vatican and other European nations. The American ambassador in Madrid was frantically cabling words of patience to Washington, but to no avail. When the United States had gone to war against Britain in 1812 and Mexico in 1846, there had been a vigorous debate and a divided vote in Congress on the

---

1. Samuels, *Remembering the Maine*, p. 257.
2. Hofstadter, "Manifest Destiny and the Philippines," in Theodore P. Greene, ed., *American Imperialism in 1898*, p. 58.
3. Samuels, *Remembering the Maine*, p. 86.
4. T. Harry Williams, *The History of American Wars*, p. 317.

war declaration resolution. The congressional resolution declaring war against Spain passed without a dissenting vote. To dissent in the face of this emotional assault would indeed have demanded more "bravery" than possessed by any member of Congress.

- *"...that fine good nature which is, after all, the distinguishing trait of the American character."* John Hay concluded by applauding the quality and benevolence American leadership. The intention of the American public in foreign policy is today, and generally has been, altruistic and humanitarian. McKinley spoke of a virtuous trait in the American character when he addressed the Methodist ministers and explained why he chose to annex the Philippines: "There was nothing left for us to do but to take them all, and to educate the Filipinos, and uplift and civilize and Christianize them, and by God's grace do the very best we could by them...." Because America viewed itself as an exceptional nation, it had a duty to others, something which Germany, France or even Great Britain could not comprehend. Richard Olney, Secretary of State under President Cleveland, expressed the concept of American exceptionalism well: "The mission of our country is ...to forego no fitting opportunity to further the progress of civilization." And another statesman intoned: "... with God's help we will lift Shanghai up and up, ever up, until it is just like Kansas City."[1] There were those like Roosevelt and Mahan who spoke of American military power and commercial advantage, but they usually couched their words in the tone of an idealist, ever mindful of the America public's need for doing the good deed.

Much has been written about how the yellow journalists caused the war with Spain by their lurid and exaggerated depiction of Spanish treachery. But if yellow journalism fanned the flames of war, we must look elsewhere for the origins of the fire. The Hearst and Pulitzer presses only blew hot winds across already smoldering embers. This war was not provoked by arson perpetrated by Hearst and Pulitzer, or by Mahan and Roosevelt, but was more of a spontaneous combustion in the hearts and minds of the American people. The press and political leaders do not manufacture basic cultural values and traditions; they can only offer a program of action, some of which is accepted, others rejected. The accepted ones are those ideas that are compatible with existing values and traditions in a culture. Imperialism and territorial expansion were in the air, and the American people, ever mindful of their exceptional nature, chose to take advantage of that burst of energy to civilize and Christianize "the little brown brothers" as their duty to God. The eminent historian, Richard Hofstadter, dismisses the American talk of God as mere hot air: "Where contemporaries heard the voice of God, we think we can discern the carnal larynx of Theodore Roosevelt."[2]

Hofstadter's skepticism about the religious basis for America's outward thrust fails to credit the deeply held spiritual beliefs of the exceptional people. From the time of the Puritans in the colonial days, to the Methodist ministers listening intently to McKinley's sermon about converting the Filipinos, God has been at the center of American political life. To the average American, God's hand was seen at the Battle of San Juan Hill and at the Normandy invasion in World War II, just as God's plan is now being worked out in the Middle East by another

---

1. Nash, *The American People*, p. 668.
2. Hofstadter, "Manifest Destiny and the Philippines," Theodore P. Greene, ed., *American Imperialism in 1898*, p. 66.

devotee of Christ, President George W. Bush. The yellow journalists' depiction of events and the Roosevelt clique of expansionists found the pious and exceptional American people receptive to their appeals.

There was much talk among historians, politicians and journalists about America flexing its muscle in the world for selfish national advantage — for raw materials, for trade and markets, for profits. But from the perspective of the early in the 21st century, having witnessed America going to war on a number of occasions, it is quite apparent that, as a people we require some transcendent value before we enter the bloody arena. Our public mission is to uphold the ideals of civilization against malevolent foes in each war — Imperial Germany, Nazi Germany, militaristic Japan, Communist Russia and its "stooges", and currently the brutality of Saddam Hussein. Our quest is not one of earthly aspirations — oil, tin, rubber, ports, canals, and allies. We are on a mission for all of humanity. Admittedly, the mission has often lacked success, but the altruistic motive is sincere.

If the basic instincts of the American people are decent and humanitarian, the same cannot always be said about the behavior of America's leaders, including President McKinley. Repeatedly he took unwise and provocative actions. He sent the *Maine* into the dangers of Havana harbor, short-circuited negotiations with Spain, concealed Spain's concession from the Congress and public, inflamed the crisis with a large defense appropriation, sent the Navy into the Philippines, then waged a war of conquest in the forlorn land. In these and other actions, McKinley frustrated debate and prejudiced a diplomatic solution. His actions depict not a weakling, but a conniving, resourceful leader who was determined to have his own way.

There was a joke making the rounds during McKinley's presidency: "Why is McKinley's mind like a bed? Because it has to be made up for him every time he wants to use it."[1] McKinley had a reputation of being unsure of himself and relying on others for advice, but some of that was a pose that McKinley assumed that served to disarm his opponents. His actions in taking the nation to war suggest a more devious, even deceitful person than is widely believed. Certainly he did not have the forceful personality of his predecessor, Grover Cleveland, who repeatedly rejected congressional moves toward war over Cuba. When a delegation from the Congress called on President Cleveland and told him, "We have decided to declare war against Spain over the Cuba question," Cleveland refused to fight. "There will be no war with Spain...while I am President," he firmly retorted.[2]

William McKinley kept his ear to the ground to sense the public mood, and to this end took a tour of the nation during the summer of 1898. (Congressional leader Joe Cannon observed that the "President's ear was so close to the ground that it was full of grasshoppers."[3]) The President discovered that the nation was thrilled with the war in the Far East and wanted to annex the Philippines. Perhaps he also heard the shouts of the upcoming political campaign, for 1898 was a congressional election year. From Sen. Henry Cabot Lodge of Massachusetts, came the advice that "if war in Cuba [between the rebels and Spain] drags on through the summer with nothing done we [Republicans] shall go down to the greatest defeat ever

---

1. Ibid., p. 62-63.
2. Herbert M. Levine and Jean Edward Smith, *The Conduct of America Foreign Policy Debated* (New York: McGraw-Hill, 1990), p. 100.
3. Musicant, *Empire By Default*, p. 614.

known."[1] A historian sarcastically assessing McKinley's plight said: "Better a foreign war than an internal upheaval; better that Spain should be ejected from Cuba than the Republicans be ejected from Washington."[2] By such a measure, a Republican electoral victory was worth 6,800 dead American military men.

Theodore Roosevelt cast a long shadow across all the events in the year 1898. After President McKinley's untimely death in 1901 and Roosevelt's ascension to the presidency, the Age of Roosevelt was ushered into American life. Or perhaps it would be more apt to call it the "Cult of Napoleon," for both displayed personal instability and megalomania, glorification of the military, and desire for conquest.

Theodore Roosevelt was thirty-nine years old when war was declared. He immediately resigned his post as Assistant Secretary of Navy and organized a group of cowboys, celebrities and college athletes into the famed military contingent, the "Rough Riders." Roosevelt's wife, Edith, had major surgery in March and experienced a difficult recovery, during which time she told her husband that "she did not want him to enlist if war came."[3] It is seldom noted that at the time of his going to war in Cuba, Roosevelt left his wife, still frail from surgery, and five children at home, including one year old Quentin. The military adventure turned out well for the ex-cowboy, for he gained fame at the Battle of San Juan Hill and came home something of a war hero. But what was a thirty-nine-year-old man with an invalid wife and five children doing charging around in a tropic isle looking for a gunfight?

(The panic caused by the supposed attack by Spain on America and the exuberance of men to volunteer for service even touched my own family. My grandfather, George Schmidt, a 28 year old father of a two year old boy (my father) and an expectant wife, volunteered for an Ohio rifle regiment in July 1898. George was in the service until March 1899 guarding the ramparts, while my grandmother delivered their second child in October 1898 without his attendance. Such, it seems, are the imperatives of war.)

Humility, prudence and discretion were not part of Roosevelt's personality. Earlier in the year he had overstepped the bounds of his position in the Navy Department at a time when the Secretary of the Navy had taken a day off. He had given orders to his friend, the naval Commander George Dewey, to proceed to Manila harbor in the event of war against Spain. Upon returning the next day to the Navy offices, the Secretary of the Navy commented that "the very devil seemed to possess him yesterday afternoon."[4] Being somewhat possessed of the devil was a constant condition of the future American president. His daughter once said that "My father wants to be the corpse at every funeral, the bride at every wedding, and the baby at every christening."[5] The British diplomat Cecil Spring-Rice observed that throughout his life Theodore acted "about six years" of age.[6] The biting criticism, even ridicule from contemporaries, was vicious. Henry James, the writer, commented that "Theodore is insane."[7] Henry Adams saw him

---

1. Nash, *The American People*, p. 672.
2. Thomas A. Bailey, *A Diplomatic History of the American People*, 7th ed. (New York: Meredith, 1964), p. 461.
3. Kathleen Dalton, *Theodore Roosevelt: A Strenuous Life* (New York: Alfred A. Knopf, 2002), p. 170.
4. Musicant, *The Banana Wars*, p. 13.
5. Doug Wead, *All the President's Children* (New York: Atria Books, 2003), p.107-108.
6. Caleb Carr, *The Alienist* (New York: Random House, 1994), p.3.
7. Dalton, *Theodore Roosevelt: A Strenuous Life*, p. 9.

as a "drunk," commenting: "Theodore is never sober only he is drunk with himself and not with rum."[1] A once budding friendship with Henry Adams (the grandson of John Quincy Adams) had turned sour and Adams commented that Teddy was "a damn fool and he has become a damn nuisance."[2] Historians are continually fascinated with Roosevelt's comment: "Speak softly and carry a big stick." This maxim became something of an aphorism of Roosevelt's character, yet he never spoke softly in his life.

But Teddy possessed more than a hyperactive personality. In the air throughout the world was the smell of gunpowder and explosives, and like many young men of that time, Theodore's nostrils flared at the thrill of battle. Combining social Darwinist thought about the "survival of the fittest," with Otto von Bismarck's "blood and iron" ideas, and Rudyard Kipling's call to "Take up the White Man's burden," Roosevelt glorified the military virtues and the new role for America in world affairs. Theodore founded a dynasty that might be called a warrior caste: Americans Henry L. Stimson, Dean Acheson, John Foster Dulles, and the Englishman, Winston Churchill carried the torch of good deeds and bore the scars of battle through many decades of the 20th century. In the Roosevelt-Churchill tradition, these men and many others carried a heavy moral burden: never "shrink from power," carry out the "obligations of power," bear the "burden of power."[3]

President Roosevelt believed that "All the great masterful races have been fighting races," and "No triumph of peace is quite so great as the supreme triumph of war." The United States must not relax its guard and become "an easy prey for any people which still retained those most valuable of all qualities, the soldierly virtues."[4] He confided to Senator Lodge in 1895: "What the country needs is a war."[5] He valued war for its own sake for he was "very sorry not to see us make the experiment of trying to land ...an expeditionary force [in Cuba], if only for the sake of learning from our blunders."[6] Future President Taft commented that Roosevelt "is obsessed with his love of war and the glory of it. That is the secret of his present attitude. He would think it a real injury to mankind if we would not have war."[7] "Cowardice in a race, like an individual, is the unpardonable sin. The diplomat is the servant, not the master of the soldier,"[8] apparently forgetting that in America the civilian controls the military.

If Americans, then and now, heard such incendiary, militaristic talk from a German leader, it would be seen for what it was, and a sharp eye would be kept on the "fascist." But the words are from "Teddy" and he was our first hero of the 20th century and all is forgiven. Self-delusion was all around, and by the end of the 20th century, the American people would be masters of illusions about their wars.

By 1901, the Filipino insurgents had laid down their arms and America stood astride the Caribbean Sea and the Pacific Ocean like a colossus. President Theodore Roosevelt sat on the

1. Edmund Morris, *Theodore Rex* (New York: Random House, 2001), p. 82.

2. Ibid, p.103.

3. Richard Pfeffer, ed., *No More Vietnam? The War and the Future of America Foreign Policy* (New York: Harper and Row, 1968), p. 49.

4. Hofstadter, "Manifest Destiny and the Philippines," Theodore P. Greene, ed., *American Imperialism in 1898*, p. 60-61.

5. Walker, *The Boys of '98*, p. 27.

6. Musicant, *The Banana Wars*, p.10.

7. Denson, "War and American Freedom," John Denson, ed., *The Costs of War*, p. 33.

8. Walker, *The Boys of '98*, p. 76,77.

American "throne" in the White House and America was ready for world leadership in the new century — the American Century. The crown jewels of the American conquest were the Philippine Islands, giving America access to the trade of nearby China, or so it was hoped, and affording America a noble opportunity to bring "civilization" to the natives.

But the Philippines soon became a diplomatic and military liability, the Achilles' heel of American defense, as Japan used it as a hostage against American foreign policy in the Far East. Through the first few decades of the 20th century, the United States had to make concessions to the Japanese in order to protect America's place in the islands. Finding defense of the islands difficult because of the distance from the main Navy base at San Diego, and disappointed with the monetary results of the fabled China trade, the United States soon realized that a new venture into Asia would be required.

To that end, Secretary of State John Hay issued his famous Open Door Notes in 1899 and 1900, hoping to keep the imperialist forces of Europe from slicing China into slivers of colonies, as had been done recently with Africa. The issuance of the Open Door Notes thrust America even deeper into Asian affairs. Now the exceptional nation was to become the protector of China; America had become an Asian power with major responsibilities and privileges. By 1941 those responsibilities lay heavily upon the Americans as the United States and Japan, both new expansionist powers, repeatedly clashed over dominance in the Far East. On December 7, 1941, the Japanese answered America's Open Door Notes and its presence in the Philippines with bombs at Pearl Harbor and the Aftershocks of the war of 1898 crashed across the Pacific.

The Spanish-American War presents a microcosm of America's 20th-century wars. The scenario for each war follows a similar pattern:

> An international incident unleashes public rage and panic over a perceived insult or imagined threat to America. The President takes actions that exacerbate the situation rather than moderating the issue. Hoping to capitalize on the event, presidents calculate how the incident can be used to his political advantage in the upcoming election. The President and his assistants portray the potential adversary as a depraved monster threatening democracy and our freedoms. The American nation, seeing itself as a modern day Sir Galahad, plunges headlong into war, even though little or no war planning has been completed, nor is there any rational assessment of how this incident relates to the true interests of the United States. The forthcoming war is always presented as a "good deed" rather than a venture serving the selfish interests of the nation. The public and the leadership seem oblivious to the Aftershocks of war — dangerous and unexpected events that are triggered by the military action, which destabilize the region and instigate unforeseen dangers to the United States. Later upon sober reflection, the nation experiences remorse and sorrow at what it has done. Billions of dollars are appropriated to rebuild the devastation caused by the American military, but no appropriation can replace lost lives. This is the Folly of America's twentieth-century wars.

Chapter 3. World War I: Europe Stumbles Into War

The six-car motorcade bearing Austrian Archduke Franz Ferdinand and his wife Sophie left the Army camp outside Sarajevo at 10:00 AM Sunday morning, June 28, 1914. On this warm, sunny day the royal couple basked in the friendly welcome provided by the townspeople. The couple was attending a reception at the city hall, then going to a museum and to a luncheon at the Governor's home. As they drove along Appel Quay, the main street, they followed the river into town, unaware that seven assassins of the Serbian terrorist group, the Black Hand, were waiting to murder them.

When the motorcade approached a bridge, the crowd lining the street began to cheer. Taking advantage of the noisy, emotional moment, one of the terrorists, Nedjelko Cabrinovic, pulled a bomb from his coat pocket, struck the fuse against a lamppost and hurled it at the royal couple. Cabrinovic's aim was true, but Franz shielded Sophie and the bomb bounced off the Archduke's upraised arm, falling to the street behind the royal car. It exploded, injuring several bystanders and members of the motorcade. After pausing a few moments to attend to an officer who was the most seriously injured, the motorcade continued toward the city hall without obtaining additional security. The remaining assassins did not avail themselves of the opportunity to continue the attack, whether out of fear of reprisal or surprise at the turn of events. Festivities at the city hall went as planned, but the Archduke decided not to continue to the museum or to the luncheon, choosing instead to visit an injured officer at the hospital.

But in the morning's confusion, the driver of the lead vehicle was not informed of the change in plans. As the motorcade retraced its route along Appel Quay, the lead driver turned onto Franz Joseph Street, following the route toward the museum as originally planned. Shouts rang out: "What is this? We've taken the wrong way!"[1] The driver of the royal car applied his brakes, stopping directly in front of Moritz Schiller's food store. A tragic mistake!

---

1. S. L. A. Marshall, *World War I* (New York: Houghton Mifflin Company, 1964), p.11.

After seeing Cabrinovic's bomb explode on the street, the other would-be assassins had dispersed, resigned to the fact that their mission had failed. One of them, Gavrilo Princip, crossed Appel Quay and entered Franz Joseph Street to purchase food and drink at Moritz Schiller's store. After finishing a drink and loitering in the store for awhile, he walked to the street where, to his surprise, five feet away from him was the automobile bearing Franz Ferdinand and Sophie. Presented with such an opportunity, Princip did not fail. He pulled a gun from his pocket, stepped toward the defenseless couple and fired two fatal shots. As the motorcade raced away from the scene, Franz pleaded with his wife: "Sophie, dear! Don't die! Stay alive for the children!"[1] Sophie had been shot in the abdomen, Franz in the neck; both were dead within minutes.

Archduke Franz Ferdinand and Sophie were visiting Sarajevo, Bosnia to review the troops in that troubled area of the Austro-Hungarian Empire. The occasion was not only a State visit but also a vacation that would coincide with their fourteenth wedding anniversary. Because Bosnia was a newly annexed frontier province of the Empire, Sophie could ride in the same automobile as her husband and sit with him on the reviewing stand. Sophie Chotek von Chotkova was born into a family of lesser nobility in the Czech lands of the empire, and because of her "lowly" birth, her marriage to Franz, the heir to the throne of the empire, was morganatic. Sophie could not become the Queen and their three children could not be part of the Hapsburg lineage. At all State functions, her non-royal social position dictated that she never ride with her husband, nor sit with him at the same level, nor even enter a room with him. The occasion of their summer visit to Sarajevo, the ancient city along the Miljacka River, was to be a festive time, with the strictures of court left far behind and fond memories of their fourteen years together.

Archduke Franz Ferdinand, a nephew of the Emperor Franz Joseph, had become heir apparent to the throne upon the death of his father in 1896. Shortly thereafter, Franz fell in love with Sophie and requested permission of the Emperor to marry. Franz Joseph refused and a yearlong battle ensued that resulted in the morganatic arrangement, but the struggle left Franz Ferdinand a reclusive, embittered man. His short temper and rudeness to his staff and his innovative schemes about reforming the Dual Monarchy alienated him from most of royal society. Friendless, immature and spiteful, he wandered through the social life of the Empire alienated; "he was the loneliest man in Vienna."[2] The future monarch took up stag hunting and became something of a modern day Nimrod, the legendary Biblical hunter. "By the age of thirty-five he had shot his thousandth stag; by forty-six he had bagged five thousand. In Sarajevo, at the age of fifty-one, the hunter became the hunted."[3]

Franz Ferdinand was a moderate on the Empire's ethnic policies, as he was a "Slavophile," desirous of accommodating the Slavic minorities. The Archduke had toyed with the idea of expanding the Dual Monarchy to a Triple Monarchy so that German, Hungarian and Slavic nationalities would be equally represented. At other times he talked of creating a federation of a dozen or more ethnic regions, each exercising some autonomous powers. This made

1. Ibid., p. 11-12.
2. Ibid., p. 8.
3. Ibid., p. 8.

him a select target of the Black Hand, for Franz Ferdinand's policies would be ameliorative and would undoubtedly disrupt the Serbian aspirations of absorbing Bosnia into a Greater Serbia.

Sarajevo was the capital of Bosnia, a province south of Austria that until 1878 had been ruled by the Turks. In 1908 the Austro-Hungarian Empire annexed the ancient area, but many Serbians of Slav ancestry residing in Bosnia desired their land to be part of a Greater Serbia. Vienna and Belgrade, the Serbian capital, were engaged in a vigorous tug-of-war over the province. For decades vitriol had poured across the borders separating the two nations. "Serbian nationalism was a savage thing, born of centuries of oppression, and therefore ugly with accumulated hatred and suppression of ambition," as one historian observed.[1] The hatred of Austria was so intense in Belgrade that a secret terrorist organization, the Black Hand, had been formed under the direction of the Serbian chief of military intelligence. In the summer of 1914, the Black Hand had decided to assassinate the Archduke. To accomplish this evil deed, the Black Hand recruited seven young men, the most infamous being the eventual assassin, Gavrilo Princip.

The assassination plot was a poorly kept secret and the Serbian governmental leadership soon learned of the effort. Fearing the consequences on Serbia of a royal assassination, the Serbian Prime Minister assigned to its ambassador in Vienna the task of discreetly informing the Emperor's government what was about to transpire. The ambassador informed the Austro-Hungarian Finance Minister, that "Some young Serb might put a live rather than a blank cartridge in his gun and fire it" when the Archduke arrives in Sarajevo. The Austrian Minister failed to grasp the subtle hint, merely responding with a shrug, "Let's hope nothing does happen."[2]

Some measure of the ineptitude of the men directing the affairs of Europe at that time can be gleaned from this tragic episode. The Austro-Hungarian Empire, already brimming with discontented Slavic minorities, compounded its woes by annexing the rebellious province of Bosnia, thereby creating enmity with Serbia and Russia. Russia, a nation that envisioned itself as the "mother of Slavs," had formed a close and protective relationship with the new Balkan state of Serbia. The annexation of Bosnia necessitated Austria deploying hundreds of troops in the region and operating a secret police system to track terrorists, none of which provided adequate protection for the visiting royal couple. Upon being discreetly told by the Serbian Ambassador that an assassination effort was planned, the Emperor's government incredulously ignored the warning. The Archduke and his entourage toured Sarajevo with minimal armed protection, at Franz Ferdinand's insistence, and when a bomb was thrown at the royal motorcade, nothing was done to bolster security. Then, the final impossible twist when the driver, uninformed of the change in travel plans, turned the wrong way directly into the path of the waiting assassin, Gavrilo Princip. The standard of government within the Dual Monarchy has been described as "absolutism mitigated by sloppiness."[3] "Sloppiness" is surely an understatement.

After the assassination, Gavrilo Princip was attacked by an angry mob of bystanders and nearly killed by his own gun, saved only by the intervention of police. For several days, Bosnian

---

1. L. C. B. Seaman, *From Vienna To Versailles* (New York: Harper & Row, 1963), p. 177.
2. http://www.gwpda.org/comment/sarajevo.html
3. Marshall, *World War I*, p. 25.

Christians and Muslims rioted in Sarajevo, expressing their anger and frustration at the horrid deed of the Serbian. During subsequent interrogations, Princip was uncooperative, refusing to divulge any details of the plot or provide any information about the Black Hand. Eventually a court found him guilty of the assassination; as he was just twenty years of age, he was sentenced to only 20 years in prison. Princip died of tuberculosis in prison four years later, ironically in the same year the Great War ended.

IMPERIALISM, ARMAMENTS AND ALLIANCES

The Great War, or World War I, grew out of the assassination crisis of 1914, with the Central Powers (Austro-Hungary, Germany and Turkey) arrayed against the Entente Powers (Russia, Great Britain and France). Theobold von Bethmann-Hollweg, the German Chancellor in 1914, summarized what he viewed as the basic causes of the Great War; ever since this has been standard historical dogma:

> The imperialism, nationalism, and economic materialism, which during the last generation determined the outcome of every nation's policy, set goals, which could only be pursued at the cost of a general conflagration.[1]

And so, for nearly a century in every high school and college textbook, in every television documentary, in every movie, and every newscast, it is proclaimed that IMPERIALISM, NATIONALISM, and we might add, the ARMS RACE caused this war. Thus the war was inevitable, caused by fundamental conflicts among the great powers. But on closer examination these prove to be simplistic explanations.

Each of these "culprits" describes basic conditions of life that prevailed across many decades and, therefore, tells us very little about why the war occurred in the summer of 1914. Imperial conflicts had been around for fifty years and no general war had resulted — until 1914. National rivalries, as a cause of war, tell us nothing as they exist all the time. The build up of armaments sometimes flares into wars, but at other times produces a stable balance of power. Imperialism, national rivalry and the arms race are descriptive, but they tell us little about war causation. Some historians, anxious to produce a grand theory of war using institutions, policies and conditions that are, in their view, out-of-favor, spin a fascinating and apparently coherent tale about war causation. Imperialism, arms races, nationalism all are somewhat disreputable in the political culture of the historian; therefore they must have caused the war. And, it is argued, wars can be abolished if we discard imperialism, arms races and extreme nationalism. It is a neat package of political propaganda, which the historian presents as truth to the gullible.

Imperialism had been pursued ardently by the Great Powers in the last half of the 19th century as Africa and the Far East became "ripe" for development. Britain emerged as the preeminent colonial power with its empire, at its zenith, claiming over 20% of the globe's surface and over 20% of the world's people. It is astonishing to realize that Queen Victoria ruled over 440 million subjects! Britain's greatest rivals in the imperial scramble were its World War I *allies,*

---

1. Niall Ferguson, *The Pity of War* (London: Penguin Books, 1998), p. xxxviii.

France and Russia, not Germany. France and Britain fought numerous battles across Africa, particularly in Egypt and the Sudan, as France attempted to weave an empire from the Suez to Gibraltar, and Britain had plans for a tier of colonies reaching from Cape Town to Cairo. Russia and Britain clashed in South Asia, in and around Turkey, Persia, Afghanistan and Pakistan. For decades Britain was busy killing Russians and Frenchmen — British allies in World War I.

If a general European war had broken out in 1882 or 1895 when serious imperial crises had flared, the combatants would surely have been Britain and its archrival France, or Britain and the Russian Bear. As historian Niall Ferguson commented: "...if we are to explain why a war eventually broke out in which Britain, France and Russia fought on the same side, imperialism is unlikely to provide the answer." [1]

England and Germany did have some squabbles in Morocco and in the old Ottoman Empire. Germany's aspiration to build a railroad from Berlin through the Balkans to Baghdad in present-day Iraq — the Berlin-to-Baghdad railway — created friction with London, as Britain zealously guarded its position in the Persian Gulf. But this squabble was resolved on June 15, 1914 when an Anglo-German agreement was signed in which Germany agreed not to build the road past Basra in Iraq and to recognize British needs on the nearby Euphrates River. The Morocco crisis had flared earlier in the century, but after 1911 was quiet. Nearly all of the imperial disputes between the two nations had been settled before the war broke out. Sir Edward Grey, the British Foreign Minister, admitted in 1911 that it did not matter very much whether we had "Germany or France as a neighbor in Africa." [2]

Actually, the tapering off of the imperial quest overseas seems to have created greater pressure on the European scene. Far from being a cause of war, the acquisitions of colonies tended to be a "safety valve" for the Great Powers. As long as the diplomats were active in Africa, the Middle East and Asia, they were distracted from inter-European conflict. Italian diplomats busied themselves with dreams of empire in Abyssinia or Tunisia. As long as the French pursued their goal of empire across northern Africa, their hopes of revenge against Germany over the debacle of the Franco-Prussian War abated. For Russia, dreams of pushing westward into Europe and southward into the Turkish Empire were placed on hold because of the Czar's aspirations in Manchuria and Central Asia.

Britain, with its extensive colonial empire, sought to turn the other Great Powers away from imperialism toward Europe; in this they were especially successful with Russia. In 1902, Britain signed a treaty with Japan, thereby warning Russia to limit its ambition in the Far East. Within three years the Japanese had defeated Russia in the Russo-Japanese War. Facing revolutionary fervor at home, trounced in the Far East by the upstart nation of Japan, thwarted in their ambition of expansion into Central Asia, Russia turned toward the European Balkans. After the French defeat in the Nile Valley, France also turned its attention to European matters. British diplomatic machinations eliminated many of the imperial competitors around the globe, but created tensions in Europe. One historian saw the situation in this way: "It is hard to avoid comparing the British to careless picnickers who, thinking to light a little fire on which to cook themselves a modest meal, find they have started a whole forest fire." [3]

---

1. Ibid., p. 42.
2. Ibid., p. 68.
3. Seaman, *From Vienna to Versailles*, p. 153.

The fabled arms race before the Great War is also overblown. Since the days of Queen Elizabeth I in the 16th century, it had been English naval policy to possess a Navy at least twice as large as the world's second largest fleet — one fleet to protect its homeland coast and another to protect its empire. By 1900, Germany had begun a vigorous naval upgrade program, as the German Navy was only seventh in the world, a status deemed unbefitting a Great Power. Kaiser William II envisioned building sufficient capital ships to protect German overseas colonies and permit Germany to play some role in an expected war between Britain and Russia. But the German naval program ran into financial constraints and was largely abandoned many years before the Great War. A German publication admitted the failure of the German dreadnought venture as early as 1908: "Boxed in between France and Russia, Germany has to maintain the greatest army in the world.... It is obviously beyond the capacity of the German economy to support at the same time a fleet which could outgrow the British."[1] By 1909 Anglo-German relations had turned a corner with the new German government under Chancellor Bethmann-Hollweg. German-British imperial rivalry had diminished and the naval race was abandoned. "Bethmann-Hollweg sought to achieve a gradual rapprochement with England by reducing the naval competition, which domestically meant limiting [Admiral] Tirpitz's still decisive influence on Reich policy."[2]

For ten years, between 1898 and 1908, there had been a "battle of the dreadnoughts," as Germany pushed the British toward innovations in battleship armor, gunnery and propulsion. Then the naval race became dormant as the Kaiser's Navy quietly accepted its second place rank. On the eve of the Great War, the two great navies seemed resigned to their respective roles. One historian concluded that "Anglo-German relations appeared almost serene, with the British Navy in late June (1914) paying a call on the German fleet at Kiel."[3]

When the Great War erupted, Germany had 17 capital ships and Britain had 29; along with the 17 ships of the French fleet, Britain was able to maintain the historic ration of 2:1. There was one signficant naval battle during the war, the Battle of Jutland off the coast of Denmark in the North Sea. The world two greatest navies blasted each other for two days and nights. As the smoke cleared over the sea, the British Navy controlled the waters and the German fleet never again emerged to do battle. As historian Naill Ferguson asserts, "Indeed, so decisive was the British victory in the naval arms race, that it is hard to regard it as in any meaningful sense a cause of the First World War."[4] The German fleet was inactive until the fall of 1918 when it was asked to make one last desperate effort against the vaunted British Navy. At that, the despondent sailors mutinied, making a tangible contribution to the eventual collapse of the German government in 1918.

British wartime propaganda depicted Germany as a militaristic nation and many historians have obediently furthered the myth. The American public even now believes the British World War I propaganda that the Germans were closely related to the rampaging, barbarous Huns. Some correction of this distorted view can be gained from the following statistics:

---

1. Ferguson, *The Pity of War*, p. 85.
2. Andreas Hillgruber, *Germany and the Two Wars* (Cambridge, MA.: Harvard University Press, 1981), p. 19.
3. Samuel R. Williamson, "The Origins of the War," in Hew Strachan, ed., *World War I: A History* (Oxford, England: Oxford University Press, 1998), p. 14.
4. Ferguson, *The Pity of War*, p. 83.

NUMBER OF MEN UNDER ARMS

	PEACETIME TROOPS	WARTIME TROOPS
Russia	1,445,000	3,400,000
France	827,000	1,880,000
Germany	761,000	2,147,000
Austro-Hungary	478,000	1,338,000

Prior to the war, the armies of the major Central Powers — German and the Austro-Hungarian Empire — were 50% as large as the combined French and Russian armies, and after the war began, the Central Powers had forces equal to only 60% of their opponents.[1] In 1914, Britain's expenditures on its Navy was twice as large as Germany's.[2]

Militarism also could be measured by the percentage of men in arms. The figures for 1913-1914 are revealing.[3]

MILITARY PERSONNEL AS A % OF POPULATION

France	2.3%
Germany	1.3%
Britain	1.2%
Austro-Hungary	.9%
Russia	.8%

Germany spent less of its Gross National Product on armaments than the Entente powers.[4]

DEFENSE SPENDING AS A % OF NET NATIONAL PRODUCT

Germany	3.5%
France	3.9%
Russia	4.6%

The point could even be made that Germany was more "democratic" that Britain, certainly more so than Russia. Despite the fact that Germany still retained the trappings of a monarchy in the person of William II, a freely elected legislative body with widespread suffrage governed the country. France, who had created the first republic among the Great Powers, provided the most open voting system.[5]

---

1. Ferguson, *The Pity of War*, p. 92-93.
2. Laurence V. Moyer, *Victory Must Be Ours* (New York: Hippocene, 1995), p.371
3. Ferguson, p. 95.
4. Ibid., p. 443.

PERCENTAGE OF POPULATION ELIGIBLE TO VOTE

France	29%
Germany	22%
Austro-Hungary	21%
Britain	18%
Russia	15%

Anti-militarist sentiment, or pacifism, was expressed most ardently in the Socialist political parties across Europe. Here again the picture of militaristic Germany is flawed. In no Great Power was the anti-war Left as strong as in Imperial Germany.[1]

SOCIALIST PARTY VOTES IN LAST ELECTION

Germany	35%
Austro-Hungary	25%
France	17%
Britain	6%

While Germany had a relatively democratic form of government, in the area of foreign and military matters the Emperor, the military staff and other elites played a larger role than the political parties or the public. The blundering brusqueness of Kaiser William II caused alarm across the continent, and the agitation of Pan-German groups always caught the attention of neighboring states. Nevertheless, "nowhere was the anti-military Left stronger than in Germany, which had one of the most democratic of all European franchises."[2]

The legendary Chancellor of Germany, Otto von Bismarck, had created the European alliance system after the German wars of unification in 1871, and with the master's touch he made it effective in providing stability and peace. Great Britain remained aloof from the alliance system prior to 1900 as it practiced "Splendid Isolation." Therefore, the alliance system involved five powers — France, Germany, Italy, Austro-Hungary and Russia. Bismarck's dictum for Germany was to "try to be at three in a world governed by Five Powers."[3] This strategy was critical for Germany, as it could easily be surrounded and outnumbered by hostile states.

The Bismarckian alliance system that existed as the Great War began did not reflect the master's touch. Britain had joined the system, increasing the membership to six, and on the eve of the war, the Turkish Empire replaced Italy in the Triple Alliance. Germany, the leader of the Alliance, was now surrounded — east and west — by the Entente powers, and had exchanged a reliable partner, Italy, for a decrepit one, the Turks. Bismarck's rule of not being surrounded by

5. Ibid., p. 29.

1. Ibid., p. 29, 30.

2. Ibid., p. 30.

3. Walter Wallbank et al., *Civilization Past and Present*, Volume 2, p. 415.

three other powers had been breached. In any war, Germany would have to fight both Russia and France.

Triple Entente — France, Britain and Russia

Triple Alliance — Germany, Austro-Hungary and Italy (replaced by the Turkish Empire when the war began)

Alliance systems reflect existing diplomatic relationships; they do not, in themselves, create crises. Claiming that alliance systems cause wars is somewhat like blaming a mirror for one's disheveled appearance in the morning. Alliances, rightly created and wisely managed, contribute stability to international affairs and provide protection for a nation's perceived interests and values. The crisis of 1914 was created, not by the alliances themselves, but by mismanagement of these relationships.

These alliances were not defensive pacts, like the famous Cold War NATO alliance, which legally obligated all participants to come to the aid of any member who was attacked. Such defensive alliances automatically trigger war. Neither the Triple Alliance nor the Triple Entente required that members come to the aid of the others in the event of a general war in Europe. Germany could have abstained from an Austrian war in the Balkans and Britain could have chosen not to come to the assistance of France or Russia if the cause was not right. The dominoes did not have to fall. But, the dominoes did fall — the alliances snapped into place — because inept, clumsy leadership of the Great Powers foolishly pushed the dominoes over during negotiations in July, and Europe stumbled into war in August.

NEGOTIATIONS IN JULY — GUNS IN AUGUST

In the modern era, the assassination of a national leader by another state has rarely been tolerated. Agencies of the United States government used assassins (mainly against Fidel Castro) in the early days of the Cold War, but in the 1970s, by executive order, the practice was forbidden. During the 19th century any assassination of a royal figure would have been dealt with by all royal houses; such an attack would be seen as threatening to monarchy in general. Henry Kissinger, an authority on the Metternich era of mid-19th century Europe, says that Russia in those years would have approved of Austria's punishment of Serbia for its complicity in the assassination of Franz Ferdinand.[1]

The Serbian government, encouraged by the military, had been fulminating against the Austro-Hungarian Empire for years: propaganda in schools and newspapers, organizing anti-Austrian parades, promoting terrorist activities, and now the tragedy in Sarajevo. Emperor Franz Joseph and his government responded vigorously against Serbia for its involvement in the assassination of Franz Ferdinand, for as the Emperor said "The crime against my nephew is the direct consequence of the agitation carried on by Russian and Serbian Pan-Slavists whose sole aim is to...shatter my empire."[2]

1. Henry Kissinger, *Diplomacy* (New York: Simon and Schuster, 1994), p. 211.
2. Wallbank et al., *Civilization Past and Present*, p. 419.

On July 23, 1914, nearly a month after the assassination, the Austrian foreign ministry delivered an "ultimatum" to Serbia to be accepted within 48 hours. The Austro-Hungarians disclaimed any efforts to obtain Serbian territory and expressed those assurances in diplomatic notes to Serbia and Russia at that time. The demands contained in the ultimatum were:

- dissolution of organizations that engaged in anti-Austrian agitation.
- cessation of anti-Austrian propaganda in schools.
- dismissal of government officials accused by Austria of complicity.
- arrest of two cabinet officers for aiding in the plot.
- trials of the accused.
- a public apology by Belgrade.
- a joint Austrian-Serbian investigation.

Serbia initially vacillated, hoping that time would cool the ardor of Vienna and the issue would pass. But the plot thickened when it was learned that the Serbian government had assisted one of the Black Hand assassins in his effort to flee prosecution. The Serbian Prime Minister knew that if a joint inquiry was launched Austria would learn of the Serbian cabinet participation. Belgrade decided it was better to shield the truth and attempt to bluff its way through. "Thus, Serbia's policy throughout the July crisis would be apparently conciliatory, deftly evasive, and ultimately intractable," which "guaranteed a definitive confrontation with Austria."[1] The Serbian response was unacceptable to Austria and, despite mediating efforts by Germany and Britain, Austria mobilized its troops and declared war on July 28.

Two days later, July 30, Russia began its fateful mobilization across the vast border with Germany and the Austro-Hungarian Empire. "No other actions in the crisis, beyond Vienna's resolute determination for war, were so provocative or disturbing as Russia's preliminary steps of enhanced border security and the recall of certain troops."[2] In the days before the war, the Russian border pressed against Germany, extending some five hundred miles from Konigsberg in the north to Krakow in the south. Alarmed by the hasty, provocative Russian action, Germany began its own mobilization.

Today the act of mobilization does not sound ominous, but one hundred years ago mobilization was the equivalent of launching intercontinental ballistic missiles. If one nation took the first step, the other nations would be obliged to follow immediately. The mobilization of the nations began, ominous and determined, like the motion of a giant pendulum: Serbia — Austria — Russia — France — Germany — Great Britain. By early August, a tragic general war — an unexpected and unnecessary war — had come to Europe, the first in one hundred years.

Contemporaries saw the war develop like falling dominoes, one after the other the nations went to war as though no one had the personal will or diplomatic ability to stop the conflagration. But why had this localized incident festered into a general war? There had been other localized wars in the preceding fifty years — the Crimean War, the Franco-Prussian War, the Russo-Japanese War, frequent Balkan Wars — none producing the domino effect and a general war. During the Crimean War (1853-1856), Prussia (Germany) "stood aside" as Britain, France and Turkey fought Russia. Why in the 1850s did Prussia not take up arms, but in 1914 it went to war? In the Franco-Prussian War (1870), when Prussia occupied the French coast on

---

1. Samuel R. Williamson, "The Origins of the War," Hew Strachan, ed., *World War I: A History* p. 16.
2. Ibid., p. 20.

the English Channel, Britain "stood aside." Great Britain had always been sensitive about the presence of a military force across the channel, yet took no hostile action against Germany in 1871. Why was Germany's occupation of the channel coast in 1914 cause for declaration of war, but in 1871 there was no war?

Otto von Bismarck, the Chancellor of Germany until 1890, had once commented that all the Balkans (Serbia, Bosnia, etc.) were not worth "the bones of a single Pomeranian (German) grenadier."[1] Wars occurred frequently in southeastern Europe as the Turkish power waned and others rushed in to fill the gaps. There was a Balkan War in 1912 as the young nations in the area ripped chunks of territory from the old wounded Ottoman Empire, and another in 1913 as the victors quarreled among themselves about the spoils of war. But neither had caused a general war, and each was over in a few months.

But in 1914, "The dynamite in the Balkan bomb was the involvement of the major powers," as one historian concluded.[2] In the previous wars, the Great Powers had used restraint and allowed the local belligerents to resolve the conflict. Alliances existed during those earlier campaigns, but the treaty obligations were interpreted in such a way as to prevent escalation. If that pattern had been followed in 1914, the Austro-Hungarian Empire would have administered a beating to Serbia, and that would have been the end of it. There would have been no World War I, and no World War II.

A critical question then is: Which of the Great Powers violated the unwritten rule of restraint? The answer to this question, as determined by the victors in World War I, was Germany, as the Treaty of Versailles assigned Germany and its allies the responsibility of causing the war. But the historical record shows that Germany was making efforts to moderate Austrian vengeance against Serbia, although those efforts were tardy and eventually ineffectual. Indeed the German attempts to slow down Austria's mobilization were ongoing when the Russians announced their ill-fated general mobilization. "It was the hasty Russian general mobilization...order on July 30, while Germany was still trying to bring Austria to accept mediation proposals, which finally rendered the European War inevitable."[3]

What responsibility do the major powers have for this conflagration?

SERBIA. While attempting to create a Greater Serbia, the Serbian Slavs were active in terrorist activities in Bosnia and adjacent regions of the Austro-Hungarian Empire. Members of the Serbian cabinet and military participated in the plot to kill the Austrian Archduke. The Prime Minister knew of the plot to kill the royal couple three weeks before the ill-fated Sunday, but the Serbian government made no attempt to stop the assassination effort, and only weak efforts to warn the Emperor. Such actions have traditionally been a *casus belli*. Years before the assassination a Serbian diplomat had confided to the British Ambassador to Belgrade: "We live in the hopes of getting something for ourselves out of the general conflagration, whenever it takes place."[4]

AUSTRIA. While an assassination was considered a *casus belli*, the Austro-Hungarian government in its ultimatum made severe demands on Serbia for the purpose of fomenting a war in the region to crush Pan-Slavic activities. The Emperor Franz Joseph did not know the extent of

1. Crane Brinton, *Modern Civilization: A History of the Last Five Centuries* (Englewood Cliffs, NJ: Prentice Hall, Inc., 1957), p. 586.
2. Wallbank et al., *Civilization Past and Present*, p. 419.
3. Sidney B. Fay, "Origins of the World War," in Dwight E. Lee, ed., *The Outbreak of the First World War* (Lexington, Mass.: D. C. Heath and Company, 1970), p. 19.
4. Ferguson, *The Pity of War*, p. 147.

Serbian government involvement at the time of the "ultimatum," but it was apparent that Serbia was creating a poisonous atmosphere in and around Bosnia. The Emperor's government, acting in the tradition of a Great Power, decided to administer a lesson to the vitriolic Serbs. But it was not the Emperor's intention that the war would spread across Europe. "Austria desired to provoke nothing but a local punitive war while the plans of France and Russia envisaged a general European conflict."[1]

RUSSIA. Aspiring to be the "mother Slav" state, Russia encouraged Serbia and by indirection Serbian terrorist actions. While posing as the leader of the Pan-Slavic movement, Russia also was furthering its interests in acquiring the Turkish Straits. The Russian general mobilization on July 30, while negotiations were progressing, is now widely considered the point at which the crisis became a general war. Russia and perhaps its military ally, France, are most responsible for fomenting a general war. Had Russia allowed Serbia to be punished by the Austro-Hungarian Empire, the military events of 1914 would be known merely as the "Third Balkan War."

FRANCE. The French, with revenge against Germany ever in mind, for real and imagined grievances, poured gasoline on the fire by encouraging Russian mobilization and Serbia militarism. France saw a general war as the vehicle to regain the lost territories of Alsace-Lorraine and to reduce the power and influence of Germany. To that end France and Russia engaged in joint military negotiations resulting in the precipitous Russian mobilization.

GERMANY. The government of Kaiser William II initially gave full support to the Austrian ultimatum, granting a so-called "blank check." However, later in July Germany attempted to moderate the Austrian demands on Serbia with Kaiser William II telling the Emperor that the Serbian compliance was satisfactory. These efforts were in progress when the Russian general mobilization occurred.

BRITAIN. After making efforts to mediate the Balkan conflict, the British deepened the crisis when it declared war on Germany. The ostensible purpose of the British belligerency was the moral-legal issue of Belgium's neutrality being violated by the German invasion, but it is now recognized that Britain, if necessary, would have themselves used Belgium territory as an invasion route into Germany. The British knew a good propaganda issue when they saw one. And, as previously mentioned, on other occasions, Britain looked the other way when Belgium neutrality was breeched.

The German invasion of Belgium was the last straw in the drama of the summer of 1914. After the mobilization of both France and Russia, Germany was presented with a dreadful choice. The Reich was surrounded by enemies; its strategic plan called for a quick thrust westward into France, then after a victory west of the Rhine, wheeling the army eastward to face the slower moving Russia. But the key to victory was the lightning move against France, a difficult campaign because the French had constructed heavy fortifications along the French-German border. German contingency war plans developed years before called for an "end run" around these defensive fortifications through "neutral" Belgium and Luxemburg. Because the neutrality of Belgium had been created by a treaty among the Great Powers in 1839, any incursion into that nation might be met with opposition from England, France and others.

On August 3, Germany made a formal request of Belgium and Luxemburg, asking for permission to travel through the two nations for purposes of invading France. German officials gave a commitment to withdraw their forces upon entering France and to provide all their own provisions; the territorial violation would be, the Germans assured, only temporary. The Belgium government rejected the German request; King Albert of Belgium contemptuously retorting "Belgium is a nation, not a road." In order to reach France, Germany would have to invade its neighbor; Belgian troops were waiting and British propagandists jumped into the

1. Harry Elmer Barnes, "Summary Statement of the Revisionists Position," in Dwight E. Lee, *The Outbreak of the First World War*, p. 14.

fray. It is seldom noted that neutral Luxemburg complied with the German request and there were no untoward incidents. And, the neutral status of Belgium had previously been severely compromised by unneutral actions by the government in Brussels when it concluded secret military agreements with France and England. The German-Belgium border was studded with fortifications, while all was quiet on the French border.[1]

(The Belgian monarch's indignant comment about his nation not being a road for German transit should be seen in contrast with the monarchy's rape of the Belgian Congo, now known as Zaire, where massive atrocities, well-documented, did occur. Some estimates are that 10 million natives were killed and dissidents were punished with their hands being cut off. Belgium has been seen as a hapless victim of German aggression, but its behavior in the Congo belies Leopold's concern for international ideals. Chapter Four, "World War I — America's First European Crusade," will recount the exaggerated tales of German atrocities in Belgium.[2])

The peace of Europe was doomed when the British declared war against Germany, ostensibly over the violation of neutral Belgium. German officials from Kaiser William II on down had acquired reputations for brusque talk and German Chancellor Bethmann-Hollweg was heard to remark that the 1839 treaty that guaranteed Belgian neutrality was a "scrap of paper." That gruff comment would come back to haunt the Germans.

Sir Edward Grey, the British Foreign Secretary, recounted a poignant moment when a friend stopped by to visit on Monday, August 3. The Great Powers had mobilized for war, and the next day German troops would invade Belgium on their way to France. Sir Grey remembers:

> We were standing at the window of my room in the Foreign Office. It was getting dark and the lamps were being lit in the space below on which we were looking. My friend recalls that I remarked on this with the words: "The lamps are going out all over Europe: we shall not see them lit again in our lifetime."[3]

THE FOLLY OF WAR

World War I was the first war fought among democratic, industrialized nations; it was the first modern war, and the first war that required a total effort of nations. In the past, wars had been fought between armies and navies, with casualties falling upon those who had purposely chosen the military career, or somewhat later, conscripted into battle. Deaths among non-combatants were uncommon. Cities — homes, work places, schools, religious buildings, hospitals — were not targeted by armies, nor was the citizenry involved in or inconvenienced by the war. With some exceptions, such as the tragedy called the Thirty Years War (1618-1648), civilians went about their business unmolested and unconcerned. Wars were the hobbies of kings, aristocrats and military professionals. Communications being primitive and popular participation limited, news about the war front was sparse and interest low. Often warriors were hired from neighboring countries, notable mercenaries were the Hessians of Germany who had been employed by the British during the American Revolution. Most professional soldiers or

---

1. Thomas Fleming, *The Illusion of Victory: America in World War I* (New York: Basic Books, 2003), p. 50.
2. Fleming, *The Illusion of Victory*, p. 49.
3. Wallbank et al., *Civilization Past and Present*, p. 423.

mercenaries brought their own weapons to the battle; many rode their own horses. The weapons industry was not far advanced.

However, all this changed with World War I. In modern war, deaths of civilian out-number uniformed troops, and wars are fought in people's neighborhoods with weapons more lethal than Napoleon ever imagined. Success in modern war depends on popular support: massive propaganda to sell the war, higher taxes, extensive government regulations, expensive debt programs to pass on the cost of war to the next generations, immense production of metal, fabric, chemicals and food. War often creates prosperity — for those who survive. Vast numbers of men were conscripted or volunteered in the Great War — over 65 million men donned the uniforms of the belligerents; over 8 million did not return home. War now would involve all citizens and would absorb the total energies of the population. The generation of souls who went to war in 1914 could only hope that "success" in war would balance the destruction it wrought.

This was the first war in which democratically elected leaders conducted affairs of state. Previously, diplomacy had been managed by appointees of the crown or by royalty themselves. Metternich, Bismarck, Cavour, Palmerston, diplomats of the 19th century, were steeped in statecraft; they knew how to weigh dangers, to obtain advantage, to measure motives, to broker compromises, to avoid slaughter. They were responsible to their own class and to the monarch. They recognized the horrors of war and successfully steered the European states away from a general war throughout the 19th century.

The modern democratic leaders, untutored in compromise, unsure of proportions, tuned only to the cheers of the multitude, adept at looking to the next election, brought a novel and perilous touch to international relations. The leaders of 1914 had more reach than skill, and brought a foolish, disastrous war upon the world. The French President Raymond Poincaré, German Chancellor Bethmann-Hollweg, Austrian Foreign Minister Count Leopold Berchtold, British Foreign Minister Sir Edward Grey, all exhibited a reckless nonchalance, caring more about their own political ambitions or "national honor" than the collective health of Europe.

It is soothing to hear the words of a real statesman, Lord Aberdeen, who as British Prime Minister, counseled Her Majesty about restraint at the time of the impending war with Russia in the Crimea:

> No doubt it may be very agreeable to humiliate the Emperor of Russia; but Lord Aberdeen thinks it is paying a little too dear for this pleasure, to check the progress and prosperity of this happy country and to cover Europe with confusion, misery and blood.[1]

The notion that national leaders are invariably emotionally mature, capable and knowl-edgeable is not well founded. Many are simply bewildered, confused and uninformed. Consider the comments of British Foreign Secretary Lord John Russell, who in the 1850s advised aggressive action against the Russian Bear before it was "too late." Sir John's thoughts on geog-raphy are instructive. He suggested that "if we did not fight the Russians on the Danube we should have to fight them on the Indus."[2] Lord Russell was proposing an extreme of the "domino theory," as the Danube River runs through southeastern Europe and the Indus River drains the mountains of Pakistan into the Arabian Sea. This comment brings to mind President

---

1. Seaman, *From Vienna to Versailles*, p. 25.
2. Ibid., p. 24.

William McKinley's remarks about not knowing within a thousand miles where the Philippine Islands were, while at the same time approving a war to acquire them for the United States imperial collection.

Malignant or at least befuddled leadership had more to do with fomenting the disaster we call World War I than the usual suspects — imperialism, armaments, and alliances. Leadership either connived to bring about a general war, or was overwhelmed with the task of finding diplomatic solutions to the problems. "What made war inevitable in 1914 was a failure of human intelligence, human courage and human goodwill. The men of 1914 let the war happen not because it was inevitable but because they could not think of anything better to do."[1] Great Britain's decision for war on August 4 was the final stroke ensuring military catastrophe. The British government was divided on the question of war, with a majority of the Cabinet and the ruling Liberal party opposed to involvement. However, Germanophobes in the party, led by First Lord of the Admiralty Winston Churchill and Prime Minister Herbert Asquith, created a public clamor over the German invasion through Belgium, resulting in the party caving-in to the public demands for war. Other British leaders, such as Cecil Rhodes and Joseph Chamberlain, were known to be in favor of a German-British alliance, and had their group been in office, Britain would not have gone to war. The British decision for war in 1914 was entirely dependent upon which element of the Liberal party dominated the Cabinet. Wars are not the consequence of any inevitability, but result from the personal decisions, even whims of men in office. Whoever is in office becomes the decisive element. Ralph Waldo Emerson once said that there really is no "history," only biography.

In the immediate pre-war years, Germany was a contented power having no territorial demands on the European continent. Germany had abandoned its naval rivalry with Britain some years before and any imperial disputes had been soothed. Attesting to this new amity, the future British Prime Minister, David Lloyd George, acknowledged on the eve of the Great War, "Relations with Germany are infinitely more friendly now than they have been for years."[2] Another British leader said that Germany had "no interests sufficiently at variance with our own to be likely to lead to a quarrel."[3] Even as late as June 27, 1914, the British Foreign Office was of the opinion that "the German government was in a peaceful mood and...very anxious to be on good terms with England."[4] All these comments were made in 1914 — the year the Great War began.

Indeed, the monarchs of Britain and Germany were cousins, grandsons of Queen Victoria, and for years an Anglo-German alliance was seen as a possibility. That these two nations fell into war is simply a sad story about how they fell victim to foolish choices of government leaders, mainly Herbert Asquith, Sir John Grey and Winston Churchill. The British cabinet chose to go to war after the German Army invaded Belgium, and during the occupation of Belgium spewed poisonous rhetoric and inaccurate facts as they condemned German behavior. Germany did cruelly execute several thousand Belgian citizens in attempting to quell rioting, and their troops destroyed the beautiful university town of Louvain. And, of course, there is

---

1. Ibid., p. 177.
2. Ferguson, *The Pity of War*, p. 87.
3. Ibid., p. 45.
4. Ibid., p. 70.

always the callous comment by the Chancellor about a "scrap of paper." But the British depiction of German war aims and military tactics were tragic distortions.

Britain's own military plans had long ago determined that in the event of war with Germany, Britain would violate Belgian territory and occupy the channel ports. If Germany hadn't invaded Belgium, Britain would have done so. British propaganda depicted the German invasion of Belgium as a dreadful moral-legal transgression, yet Britain would have taken the same action. "For British propaganda the violation of Belgian neutrality was the ace in the pack and it was played *ad nauseum*."[1] Spewing propaganda far and wide about the "scrap of paper," the Louvain tragedy, crucified Belgian babies, and violated nuns, the British marched off to war to do battle with "barbarous Huns" from Germany, all the time speaking loudly so that moralistic Americans, across the Atlantic Ocean, might be influenced by the lurid tales of "Hunnish barbarism."

The issue of Belgian neutrality had surfaced before. In 1887, as France and Britain were squabbling over imperial booty, sparks flew between France and Germany. Britain passed the word to Germany that an invasion of France through neutral Belgium would be acceptable. If Belgian neutrality meant nothing in 1887, why did it mean everything in 1914? The fact is Britain went to war in 1914 simply to prevent Germany from securing control of the English Channel. It was a security issue, not a moral-legal matter. But democratic nations find it necessary to hype their wars, to portray them to the multitudes as moral crusades. For the British this exaggeration was critical for obtaining American support, as the Americans were well known for their tendency to moralize foreign issues.

In the process of creating a moral Armageddon, the British spawned a mythological picture of German war aims. The "barbarous Huns" were out to establish a "German hegemony over Europe," and would annex France, Belgium and part of Russia, then take any colonies they wished in Africa. British security would be jeopardized by a German victory that would make the Huns "supreme over all the Continent of Europe and Asia Minor," warned the hysterical British Foreign Minister Sir John Grey.[2]

For centuries, France, the Catholic Church and other political elements in Europe had successfully prevented the unification of the German people. When Prussia finally unified the Germanic areas in 1870, France, England, Russia and others found it difficult to accept the new, powerful nation dominating the center of the continent. The French were even jealous of the fecundity of Germany. As the military historian Samuel Marshal comments: "In France, the birth rate was falling, in Germany it kept rising. Already outnumbered, France was bound to feel alarm."[3] When an economic miracle resulted before 1914, and Germany became the strongest economic power on the continent, the irrational fears of France carried them away. Some statistics on basic industry will illustrate the cause of British and French anxiety.

1. Ibid., p.231
2. Ibid., p.169
3. Marshall, *World War I*, p. 16.

COAL PRODUCTION (units of production)[1]

	Britain	France	Germany
1875	99	11	28
1913	287	40	273

IRON AND STEEL PRODUCTION (units of production)[2]

	Britain	France	Germany
1875	6	1	2
1913	8	2	14

In the 20 years prior to World War I, Germany had far outstripped the British and French economies.

PERCENTAGE INCREASE OF THE ECONOMY[3] 1893–1913

Russia	97%
Austro-Hungary	91%
Germany	84%
Italy	83%
France	60%
Britain	40%

The recently united Germany was an amazing success story, content with its newly found unity and economic well being. The German leadership had no need to plunge Europe into war in 1914. There had been more advantageous times for a German offensive. "Had Germany really wanted war, no more favourable time could have been found than during and after the Russo-Japanese War (1905-1906)."[4] Russia was weakened, Britain and France were engaged in disputes across Africa, and the German naval program was underway. But Germany had no need for military success against Britain, as London's desperate economic and demographic plight was manifest. As the historian L. C. B. Seaman says, the leaders in Berlin "could not help assuming that the decline of England would be as inevitable and as uninterrupted as their own ascent to prominence. They would wait, therefore, for destiny to work itself out."[5]

Relative to the Entente Powers, Germany was not a heavily militarized society. It had fewer troops in peace or wartime, a lower percentage of population in arms, half as large a fleet

---

1. Wallbank et al., *Civilization Past and Present*, p. 399.
2. Ibid., p. 399.
3. Ferguson, *The Pity of War*, p. 44.
4. Erich Brandenburg, "Conclusion: the Causes of the War," in Dwight E. Lee, ed., *The Outbreak of the First World War*, p. 8.
5. Seaman, *From Vienna to Versailles*, p.143.

as the British, and spent less of its gross national product on defense than either France or Russia. Further, Germany was the first nation to develop political parties, the first to begin a social welfare program for its citizens and a leader in the development of public schools and universities. It had a thriving democratic society early in the 20th century and its political leadership was in the hands of the Socialist party which eschewed warfare. There was a saying in the 19th century that captured the various temperaments of the Great Powers: England ruled the sea; France ruled the land; Germany ruled the air. This was an observation about the British Navy, the French Army, and the German universities where research led the world.

But, the Entente Powers were restive, looking for prey. Russia had narrowed its search for booty to the Balkan area, and France, falling far behind Germany in industrial production, was looking to gain success in the international arena. Historian Erich Brandenburg's comment about the Russian Empire can describe the French troubles as well: "It was thought that the only way to save the threatened existence of the [Russian] Monarch [or the French Republic] was to give proof to the world of its vitality by administering an exemplary chastisement to this dangerous neighbor [the Austro-Hungarian Empire]."[1] Both Russia and France were spoiling for a fight.

Great Britain was also feeling hard-pressed by the economic success of both Germany and the United States. The island nation was in relative decline economically; it was heavily dependent on its colonies and the United States for food and other raw materials. Bitter political quarrels washed across the islands as the Irish demanded independence and the upstart House of Commons sought to clip the wings of the aristocratic House of Lords. "The enormous and unprecedented power which the United Kingdom had enjoyed between 1815 and 1865, and which the mid-Victorians had thought part of the natural order of things, was everywhere threatened."[2] Things were changing across the face of Europe and the old, status quo powers — Britain, France and Russia — were anxious, even truculent.

Beset by domestic unrest, having a divided ruling Liberal party, the British leadership vacillated in July 1914, then panicked choosing war over peace in August. During the July negotiations Prime Minister Asquith could have given early notice to Germany that it would side with France and Russia if Germany declared war, or Britain could have warned France and Russia that England would remain neutral in any general war. Either of these actions would have used the vast power of Great Britain to slow down the rush to war. But in the hour of crisis, Britain did neither. Diplomatic Folly had led Europe into a savage unnecessary war. The lights in Europe had indeed gone out.

---

1. Brandenburg, "Conclusion: the Causes of the War," in Dwight E. Lee, ed., *The Outbreak of the First World War*, p. 8.
2. Seaman, *From Vienna to Versailles*, p. 137.

Chapter 4. World War I: America's First European Crusade

The Last Voyage of the *Lusitania*

The *Lusitania*, the great ocean liner that was the pride of the British Cunard Steamship Line, was being loaded at Pier 54 in lower Manhattan for its 202nd crossing of the Atlantic Ocean. It was Friday, April 30, 1915, the day before the scheduled sailing date.

Thousands of miles away along the North Sea coast at its Emden, Germany submarine pen, the *U-20* slipped silently, ghost-like, out of its port. The *U-20* commander, Lieutenant Walter Schweiger, headed the small, deadly craft northward into the North Sea toward Scotland, then around the British Isles to the south coast of Ireland. It was heading for a rendezvous with destiny in the cold waters of the Atlantic Ocean off the southern coast of Ireland.

On Saturday, May 1, the *Lusitania*, loaded with 1959 passengers and crew, was nudged out of its berth by tugboats at the foot of 14th Street. When the *Lusitania* left port a crowd always gathered to watch, for the ship was immense; the *Lusitania* and its sister ship, the *Mauritania*, were the only ocean liners to have six full decks and outfitted with four funnels. It steamed past the Statue of Liberty and the familiar skyline of the Battery at the foot of the island-city. This would be the last Atlantic crossing of the *Lusitania*; its demise would eventually bring America into a European war for the first time.

The great ship held the speed record in crossing the Atlantic and with that feat returned the *Blue Riband* award to the British. Its huge turbine engines produced a speed of twenty-five knots allowing it to make the crossing between New York City and Liverpool in five days. But on this crossing, the Cunard officials had ordered six of the boilers closed for economy reasons. The arrival in Liverpool would be on Friday, May 7. The journey would not be completed; the *U-20* would meet the *Lusitania* off the Old Head of Kinsale, near Queenstown, Ireland.

The Atlantic crossing was uneventful until the ship reached the southern coast of Ireland. Late in the day, Thursday, May 6, the radio room in the *Lusitania* received the first of four messages from the British naval center in Queenstown (now Cobh), Ireland. The message warned of enemy submarines lurking in "Torpedo Alley," the area just south of the Irish coast. Captain William Turner ordered all lights to be extinguished at dusk and the lifeboats prepared. Confidently, Turner sailed the *Lusitania* into the German-declared war zone. The *U-20* came to the surface at about 12:45 p.m. Friday, May 7, and the commander climbed the steps to the conning tower and swept the horizon for any prey. Visibility was clear and the sea was calm. While eating his lunch, suddenly in the distance, he saw a streak of smoke; soon funnels appeared — four funnels! The *U-20* had the *Lusitania* in its sights!

Schweiger quickly made calculations about the speed and direction of the liner and shouted, "Prepare to dive." Shortly after 3 p.m. the *U-20* was in torpedo range of the ocean liner. Amazingly, at just the right moment, the liner turned starboard, offering a perfect target. With his eyes glued to the periscope, Schweiger calmly counted down:

Eight hundred meters ....
Seven hundred fifty meters ....
Seven hundred ....
Fire!![1]

The torpedo hissed as it struck the water, the twin propellers driving the 300 pounds of TNT at over twenty knots. The *U-20's* torpedo was heading straight for the starboard of the ship just behind the first funnel. From the logbook of the *U-20*, in Schweiger's own words, the awful moment is described:

Torpedo hits starboard side right behind the bridge. An unusually heavy explosion takes place with a very strong explosive cloud. The explosion of the torpedo must have been followed by a second one [boiler or coal or powder?].... The ship stops immediately and heels over to starboard very quickly, immersing simultaneously at the bow... the name *Lusitania* becomes visible in golden letters.[2]

Eighteen minutes after the torpedo struck, the ship gathered itself for its final dive to the bottom of the ocean carrying with it 1198 souls, including 128 Americans. And the world wondered what had become of human decency and civility. Questions arose immediately about the events surrounding the sinking of the *Lusitania*:

- Why did the British allow the ocean liner to sail into "Torpedo Alley," an area where U-boats were known to be lurking?
- Why was the ship traveling so slowly and not running a zigzag course?
- Why did the British Admiralty not provide a destroyer escort into Liverpool?
- Why did the ship sink in only 18 minutes? (The Titanic, which had sunk several years before, took three hours to sink even though it had a 300 foot-long gash in its side.)
- Why did many people on the ship believe that there were two torpedoes, when the U-20 logbook showed only one was used?

The day of the disaster, Lieutenant Schweiger wrote in his logbook:

It is remarkable that today there should be so much traffic despite the fact that two large steamers were sunk south of St. George Channel yesterday. It is inexplicable that the Lusitania was not routed via the North Channel (that is northward around the Irish Isle).[3]

---

1. Robert Ballard, *Exploring the Lusitania: Probing the Mysteries of the Sinking that Changed History* (New York: Warner Books and Madison Press, 1995), p. 81,85.

2. Kenyon C. Cramer, *The Causes of War: The American Revolution, The Civil War, and World War I* (Glenview, Illinois: Scott Foresman and Company, 1965), p. 155.

3. Patrick O'Sullivan, *The Lusitania: Unraveling the Mysteries* (Dobbs Ferry, NY: Sheridan House, 2000), p. 93.

Unbeknownst to Schweiger and the German high command, the British had deciphered the secret German naval codes and were privy to communications between the German naval officials and its ships at sea. On April 30, British Intelligence intercepted signals showing the U-20 moving toward the path of shipping from America to England. As Patrick O'Sullivan says in his book, *The Lusitania*, "Destiny had allowed [the Admiralty] twelve days in which to decide what measures could be taken to safeguard one of Britain's greatest liners."[1] But the British Admiralty gave the *Lusitania* no specific notice of this increased submarine activity in "Torpedo Alley." Why?

In the months preceding May 7, the Admiralty had taken prompt and resolute action to protect most British and neutral shipping in the war zone around the British Isles. A catalogue of maritime incidents early in 1915 shows considerable success of the Admiralty in protecting shipping:

- In January 1915, two Cunard liners were sent to the port at Queenstown to await destroyer escorts rather than allowing them to sail unescorted through "Torpedo Alley."
- In February two steamers were diverted to port as a precaution; one of the steamers carried a cargo of mules. One does wonder at the British government providing more protection for army mules than for 1959 people on board the Lusitania.
- In March the Lusitania was provided destroyer cover around Liverpool when British Intelligence intercepted German signals showing U-boat activity in the Irish Sea.
- And again in March the Lusitania was detained in port for several days until destroyers determined that submarine activity had diminished in the area.
- On May 1 the Gulflight, an American ship, was torpedoed off Land's End, England with the loss of three Americans.
- On May 4 the Orion, the Gloucester and the Jupiter, all British warships sailing in submarine-infested waters, were either diverted to safe areas or given destroyer escorts.
- On May 5, two days before the Lusitania tragedy, the U-20 sank three ships and attempted to sink another, but the ship escaped to Queenstown.
- During the first week of May three British warships were given destroyer escorts and ordered to divert away from the sub-infested southern Irish coast.

With knowledge of intense submarine activity in the path of the *Lusitania*, why did the Admiralty not provide a destroyer escort? There were four destroyers available on May 7 at Milfordhaven, Wales on the Irish Sea, and two Q-ships, merchant marine vessels refitted for war, at Queenstown. Why no escort for the *Lusitania*? And why was the ship ordered to travel at reduced speed through this dangerous area, and why was the ship not zigzagging through the channel? Or why, as Schweiger suggested, was the ship not sent northward around Ireland where there was little submarine activity?

The British Admiralty assigned blame for the disaster on the actions of Captain Turner. First Sea Lord Sir John Fisher said, "I hope Captain Turner will be arrested immediately after the enquiry, whatever the verdict."[2] Winston Churchill, the First Lord of the Admiralty, chimed in that Turner should be "pursued without check."[3] The British government and the naval

---

1. Ibid., p. 84.
2. Ibid., p. 115-116.
3. Ibid., p. 116.

authorities proclaimed their innocence. Investigative tribunals in London later placed sole responsibility on the U-boat commander and, of course, the German government.

Captain Turner did bear some responsibility as he disregarded standing orders to sail in mid-channel where deeper waters would inhibit submarine activity. Instead of sailing 70 miles off shore, the *Lusitania* was only 12 miles from the lighthouse on the Old Head of Kinsale. And yet the Admiralty had not told Turner that since he had left New York City a total of twenty-three ships had been sunk by U-boats in the waters around the British Isles. There were a total of five messages sent to the *Lusitania* in the two days preceding its sinking. During the enquiries, Turner and the Admiralty refused to divulge the contents of those messages for reasons of national security. While at war with Germany, this was a prudent action, as any divulging of the contents of messages would have revealed that Britain had broken the German naval code. But after the war the messages should be available for historical research. In recent decades several historical sleuths have combed through the records of the British government to locate these messages, but to no avail. Critical records are missing from the files and other files show evidence of deletion. It does appear that someone has covered his tracks!

There has always been a suspicion that the *Lusitania* was "set up" by the British to create an international incident. As Great Britain was maneuvering the United States into a wartime alliance, Germany became the culprit. By loading passenger liners, like the *Lusitania*, with munitions, German submarines were attracted to the vessels and were tempted to sink the passenger liners. If Germany took the bait, the world would condemn the act as "Hunnish depravity." If the submarine allowed the vessel to pass, the munitions would put German soldiers into their graves. Winston Churchill had trapped the Kaiser.

Patrick Beesly has chronicled the story of British Naval Intelligence during the Great War in his book entitled *Room 40*. Beesly points out that "no effective steps were taken to protect the *Lusitania*" and concludes:

> unless and until fresh information comes to light, I am reluctantly driven to the conclusion that there was a conspiracy to put the *Lusitania* at risk in the hopes that even an abortive attack on her would bring the United States into the war. Such a conspiracy could not have been put in effect without Winston Churchill's express permission and approval.[1]

Winston Churchill was keenly aware of the benefits of such a conspiratorial action. On previous occasions Churchill had expressed his hope that America would become entangled with Germany and the most likely venue would be in the Atlantic Ocean. One week prior to the sinking of the *Lusitania*, he wrote to the President of the Board of Trade that it is "most important to attract neutral shipping to our shores, in the hope especially of embroiling the United States with Germany."[2]

The logbooks of the *U-20* show that Schweiger fired only one torpedo, yet many survivors claimed to have heard two distinct explosions. Available evidence today indicates that the second and greater explosion was inside the *Lusitania*, the cause of which has generated a controversy. Three theories have been advanced to explain the second, and presumably, greater explosion.

---

1. Quoted in Ralph Raico, "Rethinking Churchill," in John Denson, ed., *The Costs of War*, p. 332.
2. Ralph Raico, "Rethinking Churchill," in John Denson, ed., *The Costs of War*, p. 332.

There is evidence that the *Lusitania* was carrying explosives that were detonated by the torpedo. A manifest of the ship's cargo was filed with the United States Customs Office in New York on May 1. It does not show that there were any high explosives in the cargo. According to the manifest on file, the ship was carrying mostly non-contraband items and some contraband — rifle cartridges, shrapnel shells and fuses, none of which would have caused a violet, destructive explosion. However, ship manifests were often incomplete and evidence has recently been found that the ship carried aluminum powder, a high explosive.

Historian Robert Smith Thompson has found proof of deceit practiced by President Wilson in this matter. As President Franklin Roosevelt maneuvered America into World War II a generation later, he was looking for lessons from the Wilson presidency about how to cover his tracks. In his search, FDR discovered "a packet that, in 1915, President Woodrow Wilson had ordered concealed in the archives of the Treasury Department. The packet contained the bill of lading, undoctored, of the British ship *Lusitania*.... When the British published the bill of lading, it contained only civilian goods, the original, however, as Wilson knew, listed contraband."[1]

This incident is a grave indictment of President Wilson as it evidences his effort to conceal material information from the public. If the American people had known that Britain was running high explosives under the cover of a passenger liner, it is doubtful that Wilson could have convinced the citizenry to enter World War I. With that, the entire history of the 20th century would be changed.

The United States Congress had foreseen the potential for foul play on the high seas when it legislated the Passenger Act of 1882, which states that "no vessel could legally sail with any explosives likely to endanger the health or lives of passengers...."[2] Any United States official responsible for a violation of this law resulting in death could be found guilty of manslaughter, punishable with a ten-year sentence. Thus, if there was any collusion between American customs officials and the British Navy, it could have, and should have been dealt with as a serious crime. Now, with the revelation that President Wilson knew the *Lusitania* was carrying illegal and dangerous explosives, yet deliberately took action to suppress this information, it appears that Woodrow Wilson himself had committed a critical violation of the law.

Another perspective on the second explosion is provided by Dr. Robert Ballard who recently used underwater submarines to inspect the carcass of the ship lying in 295 feet of water on its starboard side. Ballard claims that there is no hole in the forward magazine where any explosive cargo would have been stored.

> One thing we are sure of: if any contraband had been stowed away in the magazine, it didn't explode. We were able to inspect the entire exposed area of the magazine and it was clearly undamaged. If it held munitions, they were not the cause of the secondary explosion that sank the ship.[3]

Then what did sink the great liner, for a single torpedo would not have caused the *Lusitania* to sink in 18 minutes? Ballard poses a novel idea. "Any torpedo would have struck the *Lusitania* [coal] bunkers...After the voyage from New York, the *Lusitania's* coal supply is getting low.

1. Robert Smith Thompson, *A Time For War: Franklin Delano Roosevelt and the Path to Pearl Harbor* (New York: Prentice Hall Press, 1991), p.198.
2. O'Sullivan, *The Lusitania*, p. 117.
3. Ballard, *Exploring the Lusitania*, p. 194.

By now she carries more coal dust than coal. Layers of the stuff form thick carpets in the bunkers."[1] When the torpedo struck, a thick cloud of coal dust would have risen, forming a highly volatile cloud that could have been ignited by a spark from the first explosion. Ballard concludes: "The result: a massive, uncontrollable explosion, a tidal wave of fire that rips through the ship's lower deck, and blasts its way through the side of the hull."[2]

Ballard's investigation is interesting, but it will not be the last word on this mystery. The ship is lying on its starboard side; thus, any physical investigation of that side is limited, and the starboard side is where the torpedo struck. Our knowledge of the magazine in that area of the ship will be incomplete until the ship is hoisted out of its watery grave.

There is circumstantial evidence that the bottom of the starboard side of the ship was indeed blown out, contrary to what Ballard asserts. A 6,000 pound shipment of fur pelts carried by the Lusitania was found floating in the area of the ship's wreckage. Those pelts were blown out of a hole somewhere in the ship's bottom or starboard side. Further, there is a large, unidentified object lying at the bottom of the ocean near the wreckage. Could that be the cargo of high explosives — cases of aluminum powder — that were blown out the starboard of the ship along with the fur pelts?

Lastly, Diana Preston has developed convincing evidence that ruptures in the steam lines running from the boilers of the great ship, or possibility boiler explosions themselves, accounted for the second explosion. Her research shows that these internal blasts were the most likely cause of the Lusitania's rapid sinking.[3]

This is a tragic story for the nearly 1200 people who died in the sinking and hardly less so for the survivors who had to live with this nightmare the rest of their lives. The responsibility for this tragedy lies with the British government. Churchill, not Schweiger, is the villain in the Lusitania story.

Technical arguments over the cause of the second blast should not cloud the basic issue: the British, with America complicity, were running contraband material across the ocean in passenger liners, endangering unsuspecting travelers and, with diabolic intentions, ensnaring the United States in the European war.

Even if there were no high explosives, but only non-explosive weapons of war, such action was in violation of established law and neglectful of simple human decency to transport contraband in passenger liners. Additionally, the British Admiralty's Q-ship program — cruisers disguised as passenger liners with concealed deck guns and standing orders to ram U-boats — created a situation in which the Germans were bound to lose whatever action they took. If they sank the ship, they would be condemned by world opinion, for the world did not know about the Q-ship program. If Schweiger had surfaced and allowed the Lusitania's passengers and crew to leave the ship in lifeboats, the submarine would have been rammed. If he simply left the liner alone, it would deliver its deadly and illegal cargo to the British Army for the killing of German youth on the front lines.

Torpedoes from U-boats often misfired, went astray or proved to be duds. But this missile fired perfectly and the commander's aim was true. It is no consolation to the dead or to

---

1. Ibid., p. 194-195.
2. Ibid.
3. Diana Preston, Lusitania: *An Epic Tragedy* (New York: Walker and Company, 2002), p. 501.

those who mourn them to know that Commander Schweiger had fired his *last* torpedo. The *U-20* was heading home![1]

BRITANNIA WAIVES THE RULES

The European nations had long observed limitations on how wars were fought, giving respect to a more civilized age. Rules of war had developed in the 17th century as part of international law and were the subject of periodic conferences. In 1856 an international conference was held in France with the resultant Declaration of Paris attempting to codify the rules of war. The so-called Cruiser Rules regulated the relationship between neutral and belligerent ships on the high seas:

1. Merchant ships, whether flying a neutral flag or the flag of a belligerent, were obliged to stop if confronted by a ship (a cruiser) from a belligerent nation.

2. The crew of the cruiser must be allowed to board the vessel and inspect its cargo to determine if it was carrying contraband — illegal goods.

3. Contraband was defined as munitions, that is weapons or goods that could directly aid an enemy war effort. This definition lacked precision and was, therefore, the subject of debate and even litigation. All non-contraband goods, such as food, were legally traded by neutrals during wartime.

4. Any captured ship carrying contraband became a "prize of war," subject either to destruction or confiscation.

5. The safety of the crew and passengers must be provided if the ship was to be destroyed on the high seas. Lifeboats were used or the crew was taken on board the cruiser.

6. To be afforded such protection, merchant ships must abide by several regulations: ships must fly flags of the home country (no false flags), they must not be armed and they must stop when confronted and not use any hostile or evasive actions.

The purpose of the Cruiser Rules and the Blockade Rules (to be discussed later) was to allow neutral nations to continue trade relationships even during wartime. The United States, often a neutral during European wars, was the main beneficiary of these rules.

Great Britain was a notorious violator of the Cruiser Rules, as they controlled the high seas and selfishly saw no reason why their naval power should be limited. To the British, the Cruiser Rules were the same as baseball's rule against pitchers throwing a spitball; the rule applies only to those who choose to obey it. Winston Churchill, as First Lord of the Admiralty, put into operation a scheme to evade the Cruiser Rules as soon as war broke out. The British Navy requisitioned all merchant ships and reconstituted them as "Q ships," so named because the work was done at the Queenstown, Ireland port. Freighters and passenger liners were molded into warships, complete with concealed deck guns, new names, dummy funnels, altered deck configurations and false flags. By this action, Churchill turned the entire British merchant fleet into a disguised auxiliary of the Navy, a gross violation of international law. German naval officers soon realized that every British freighter was a warship in disguise. A wisecrack of the time was: Britannia not only ruled the waves but also waived the rules.[2]

---

1. Cramer, *The Causes of War*, p. 155
2. O'Sullivan, *The Lusitania*, p. 37.

The British leadership was always a step ahead of the Germans as the two belligerents vied for America's attention and friendship. To combat the U-boat menace, the British Q-ship program proved to be a crucial factor in obtaining American support for the cause of England. Churchill claims that he knew in 1914 that the U-boat would be the deciding factor in the outcome of the war. It appears that Winston was gloating about the pending battle on the Atlantic Ocean when the naval chieftain said, "The first German U-boat campaign gave us our greatest assistance. It altered the whole position of our controversies with America. A great relief became immediately apparent."[1]

Indeed, merging the Navy and the merchant fleet began at the time a ship was built. In the case of the *Lusitania*, the British government provided the Cunard Steamship Line with low cost financing for construction of the *Lusitania* and its sister ship, the *Mauritania*. Each year the *Lusitania* was in operation, Cunard received a financial subsidy from His Majesty's government. The *Lusitania* was constructed with its boilers below waterline, provisions for twelve 6-inch guns and an amazing speed of 25 knots. It was a cruiser in disguise, ready for conversion in wartime to a full-fledged warship. By the fall of 1914, Britain was flaunting the rules of the high seas. "The effect of Churchill's new policies meant that all merchant ships including Q ships and neutrals were indistinguishable in view of the misuse of flags, a policy which caused massive loss of life and played havoc on the high seas."[2]

Early in the war there were instances of German U-boats surfacing and attending to the safety of the crew before destroying merchant vessels. The U-boat's "reward" for observing these rules was that it was rammed by the vessel, or a deck gun would appear from under a cover spewing shells into the thin skin of the submarine. The U-boat commanders soon learned to ignore the rules and shoot first. Winston Churchill's Q-ship program had created this dilemma; but in the court of world opinion, Germany bore the guilt.

The German "shoot first" policy became the fate of the *Lusitania*. The week of the sinking of the *Lusitania*, the *U-20* had come upon a small cargo ship and provided for the safe escape of the crew before torpedoing it. Schweiger could have allowed the passengers and crew of the *Lusitania* to escape in lifeboats, but because of Churchill's Q ship program, the danger from ramming or from deck guns was too great. The *Lusitania* captain had, in fact, been ordered by the British Admiralty to ram any U-boat that surfaced; a cash bonus was offered for any successful attempt. Knowing of the Q-ship program, Schweiger took the safe way for his crew and thereby changed history.

(Schweiger himself did not survive the war as he went to his death in *U-88* when it ran into a British mine off the coast of Jutland in the North Sea. The *U-20* ran aground off the coast of Denmark, remaining there until after the war when it was destroyed.)

In addition to the Cruiser Rules on the high seas, there were also rules that might be called the Blockade Rules. According to international law, blockades of enemy ports were legal only if they were done in accordance with the prescribed rules. Blockades had to be "close," that is picket ships or mines had to be within the three-mile limit at the mouth of the enemy's harbor. There could be no picket ships or mining on the high seas, for the open oceans belong to

---

1. Cramer, *The Causes of War*, p. 135.
2. O'Sullivan, *The Lusitania*, p. 37.

the world's merchant fleet — even in wartime. Blockades must be precisely at the port of the enemy.

However, German cannons placed at harbors could hit targets 10 or 12 miles away; these long-range guns made a "close" blockade unhealthy. So instead of conducting a blockade at the enemy ports, Britain mined the English Channel and the North Sea, thereby making it dangerous for any ship, neutral or belligerent, to travel to any port in northern Europe. Any ship navigating successfully through these mined seas could still be captured by a British warship, taken to a harbor in England and detained for days. Additionally, the British arbitrarily and illegally expanded the list of contraband goods that could be confiscated: cotton, copper, rubber and oil were now forbidden. Shipping anywhere on the European continent was hazardous, time consuming and costly for neutrals, either from illegal German or British actions.

World War I saw the introduction of a number of military innovations — long-range cannons, submarines, airplanes, wireless telegraph, the tank, machine guns and notoriously, poison gas. These weapons changed the nature of warfare, making it more deadly and uncivilized. The submarine destroyed the Cruiser Rules, and long-range cannons eliminated the Blockade Rules. "Necessity knows no law," said a World War I diplomat and that was certainly true of the clash between the old rules of war and the new weapons of war. Wilson, a man of strong principles, and many other Americans anxious to retain the traditional limits on war, demanded of the belligerents more restraint than they found possible to give.

Neutral in Thought — Biased in Action

At the outbreak of the war, President Wilson proclaimed American neutrality. Speaking on August 4, 1914, Wilson urged his countrymen to "be impartial in thought as well as in action, [we] must put a curb on our sentiments as well as upon every transaction that might be construed as a preference of one party to the struggle before another."[1]

Wilson's reference to "every transaction" was significant, for in August the State Department advised American banks that loans to any belligerent would be "unneutral in spirit." However, in October 1914 the State Department sent a secret memorandum to two large banks, Morgan Bank and National City Bank, advising them that loans to belligerents could be made. The policy of "strict neutrality" was a public pose that the Wilson administration struck for only a brief period. Neutrality was never a consideration for the "House of Morgan." Thomas Lamont, a Morgan bank official, confessed his "sins" thusly:

> Those were the days when American citizens were being urged to remain neutral in action, in word, and even in thought. But our firm had never for one moment been neutral: we didn't know how to be. From the very start we did everything that we could to contribute to the cause of the allies [Great Britain].[2]

As the new military weapons shattered the old rules of war, all nations suffered. The submarine campaign took a frightful toll on Britain; by 1917 the British were losing five ships every day and the nation was down to six weeks of food. The British blockade of Germany was

---

1. Irwin Unger, *These United States: The Questions of Our Past* (Englewood Cliffs, NJ.: Prentice Hall, 1992), p. 678.
2. Patrick Buchanan, *A Republic, Not An Empire*, p. 203.

causing widespread hunger, even starvation on the continent. Germany, like England, needed to import food for its largely urban population. United States exports to Germany were nearly eliminated in two and a half years, dropping from 12% of the United States total export trade to less than 1%. But American exports to the British Isles thrived, though harassed by the U-boats, and its share of total exports to Britain rose from 25% to 33%.[1] The dramatic distortion of American trade with the two belligerents can be seen in this table:[2]

	Central Powers	Allied Powers
1914	$169 million	$825 million
1916	$1 million	$3,000 million

Such an immense increase in purchasing by London and Paris could not be paid for in cash; American banks, notably the banks of J. P. Morgan, provided loans to the British and the French in staggering amounts. "By the time America went to war in April 1917, US banks had extended $2.3 billion in cash and credit."[3] The burgeoning trade with the Allies derailed the emerging American depression in 1914, as farmers and city workers alike prospered from the new international commerce. But in the process the neutrality policy was shattered. In the 1930s Congress investigated the relationship between United States loans to the Allies and the eventual American entrance into the war. The Nye Committee Report [Gerald Nye, R, ND] was a damning attack on Wilson's supposed neutrality. Its conclusion in part said: "Loans to belligerents militate against neutrality, for when only one group of belligerents [Britain] can purchase and transport commodities the loans act in favor of that belligerent. They are especially unneutral when used to convert the country into an auxiliary arsenal for that belligerent that happens to control the sea...."[4]

The Wilson administration applied relentless pressure on Germany to cease its illegal U-boat action. In August 1915, Wilson elicited from Germany a pledge (the *Arabic* pledge) to sink only ships that were given proper warning and provision for safety. In May 1916, the President extracted another pledge from Germany (the *Sussex* pledge) which gave assurance that the U-boats would henceforth strictly abide by the Cruiser Rules as long as Britain abided by the Blockade Rules. Wilson presented this to the American people in a devious manner, alleging that the *Sussex* pledge was a significant triumph against German U-boat deprivations, but slyly neglecting to point out that Britain had not modified its illegal blockade and mining.

Indeed, Wilson saw the British and German violations as distinctly different in nature. The British violations were merely delaying or destroying cargo, while the Germans were killing people. This wanton disregard for human life came to epitomize, for Wilson and many others in his administration, the depravity of German leadership. This erroneous perception of the "Huns" soon swept across America. "The undersea warfare of Germany against non-combatants and neutral commerce on the high seas came to symbolize the aggression of the Central Powers."[5] And as historian Samuel Eliot Morison argues: "No citizen of a neutral state lost his

---

1. Cramer, *The Causes of War*, p. 128.
2. Nash, *The American People*, p. 730.
3. Buchanan, *A Republic, Not An Empire*, p. 203.
4. Cramer, *The Causes of War*, p. 124-125.

life as a result of the British blockade and all neutral cargoes seized were paid for at war prices."[1]

Increasingly Wilson and most Americans saw the war zone that Britain had established around Europe as a necessary inconvenience. No US ships ever ran through the continental blockade, challenging British picket ships or deliberately ramming through British mine fields. Because the US merchant fleet respected the illegal British blockade, there were no American deaths. But American and British vessels did ram their way through the German "blockade" around Britain, encountering U-boats and their torpedoes, with the result that nearly 200 US citizens, mostly on the *Lusitania*, lost their lives.

Germans were killing Americans; the British were not. This important fact was true, but Morison and others failed to point out why this was so. Americans were treating the British and German violations in an unequal manner. The United States challenged the U-boats by carrying cargo to the British Isles or traveling on British ships into the German-declared war zone, but they respected the mines and picket ships of the illegal British war zone around the continent of Europe. Americans were dying not because the Germans were wicked, but because the Wilson administration refused to treat the two war zones in an equivalent manner. The influential magazine, *New Republic* asserted that: "No American lives would have been lost had we acquiesced in Germany's policy as we have in Britain's."[2] President Wilson treated the two belligerent war zones differently, then complained that Americans were being treated wrongly only by Germany. President Wilson talked the platitudes of neutral rights, but the substance escaped him. The intellectual dishonesty of the president eventually led to America's declaration of war against Germany and the deaths of over 125,000 young men in Europe.

Actually there were only three American lives lost on American ships (the *Gulflight*) prior to 1917. About two hundred American passengers were killed while traveling on British or French vessels. This situation prompted Secretary of State William Jennings Bryan to urge Wilson to prohibit Americans from traveling on belligerent ships into the war zones. Bryan argued that Americans traveling on British ships were guilty of "contributory negligence." The Congress passed a joint resolution recommending that Wilson enforce such a restriction on American travelers, but Wilson refused to be guided by this reasonable policy. Angered by the President's obtuseness, Secretary Bryan resigned from the State Department in the summer of 1915.

William Jennings Bryan became the leader of those Americans who preferred a policy of actual neutrality, rather than the bogus Wilsonian neutrality. Referring to the British blockade that was starving people on the continent, Bryan challenged Wilson's intellectual honesty: "Why be so shocked by the drowning of a few people, if there is to be no objection to starving a nation."[3] (There is evidence that 750,000 Germans died of starvation as a result of the illegal British blockade.)

---

5. David Trask, "The Entry of the USA into the War and its Effects," in Hew Strachan, ed., *World War I: A History*, p. 240.

1. Samuel Eliot Morison, *The Oxford History of the American People* (New York: Oxford University Press, 1965), p. 851.

2. H. W. Brands, *What America Owes the World*, p. 70.

3. Buchanan, *A Republic, Not An Empire*, p. 200.

At another time Bryan called attention to the British practice, initiated by Winston Churchill, of loading people and contraband together on passenger liners, like the *Lusitania*, and running them through the war zone around the British Isles unattended by destroyer escorts. Bryan put this reckless, inhumane British practice in perspective: "Germany has a right to prevent contraband from going to the Allies, and a ship carrying contraband should not rely upon passengers to protect her from attack — it would be like putting women and children in front of an army."[1]

After the sinking of the *Lusitania*, Teddy Roosevelt decided that war with Germany was inevitable and so advised the President. Secretary of State Bryan attempted to stem the hysteria and presented another view to the president:

> We [the United States] unsparingly denounce the retaliatory methods employed by Germany, without condemning the announced purpose of the Allies to starve the non-combatants of Germany and without complaining of the conduct of Great Britain in relying on passengers, including men, women and children of the United States, to give immunity to a vessel carrying munitions of war.[2]

There is considerable evidence that the *Lusitania* was sent into a war zone as "bait" to provoke trouble between the United States and Germany. It was sailing in violation of both American law and international law and custom; innocent passengers were callously sent to their deaths. Many in the country were mesmerized by the British propaganda; Bryan was not. Bryan, "The Great Commoner," a very decent man whose values were formed in the 19th century, was appalled by the 20th century practice of using human shields in wartime. He did not live to see the bombing of Hiroshima, London, Dresden and Tokyo and the wanton destruction of millions of civilians.

"He Kept Us Out of War"

The Democrat Party nominating convention in 1916 in St. Louis was a gigantic, electrifying peace rally, as Woodrow Wilson struck another insincere pose for neutrality, and delegates cheered hopefully that he would honor the slogan, "He Kept Us Out Of War." By the time the convention keynote speaker had begun his oration, it was clear that the delegates wanted to hear reassurances that the nation would not go to war. Martin Glynn, the keynote speaker, had the crowd on its feet as he recounted incidents in American history when presidents had refused to engage in military actions. Citing an incident when President Grant refused to take the country to war with Spain over Cuba, Glynn shouted, "But he didn't go to war," and the crowd roared. Citing similar experiences with Lincoln, then Harrison, "But he didn't go to war." The crowd was hysterical. Warming to the task, Glynn turned to earlier Chiefs, and for each the chant: "He didn't go to war." Glynn concluded:

> This policy may not satisfy those who revel in destruction and find pleasure in despair. It may not satisfy the fire-eaters and the swashbuckler...this policy does satisfy the mothers of the

---

1. Morison, *The Oxford History of the American People*, p. 852.
2. Ralph Raico, "American Foreign Policy — The Turning Point 1898-1919," in Ebeling and Hornberger, ed., *The Failure of America's Foreign Wars*, p. 68.

land, at whose hearth and fireside no jingoistic war has placed an empty chair...It does satisfy the fathers of this land and the sons of this land, who will fight for our flag, and die for our flag.[1]

The leader of the peace movement, William Jennings Bryan, who had resigned as Secretary of State because he felt that Wilson was leading the nation into war, now succumbed to the oratorical theatrics of the convention. The "Boy Orator" proclaimed to the enthralled delegates: "My friends, I have differed with our President on some of the methods employed, but I join with the American people in thanking God that we have a President who does not want this nation plunged into this war."[2] William Jennings Bryan was onboard the Wilson campaign and the Democrats had their campaign slogan: HE KEPT US OUT OF WAR!

The President's own views on neutrality and military preparedness reversed between 1914 and 1916. Wilson's State of the Union message delivered to Congress in December 1914 was true to his August neutrality statement. He rejected increases in the defense budget because this would signal that "we had lost our self-possession" as the result of a war "whose causes cannot touch us, whose very existence affords us opportunities for friendship and disinterested service...."[3]

Throughout 1915, Wilson was buffeted by pro-war or "preparedness" groups centered around Republicans like Roosevelt, presidential nominee Charles Evans Hughes, and Senator Lodge. Senator Henry Cabot Lodge, Republican of Massachusetts, was forthright in arguing for an immediate commitment to the Western powers and was candid and honest in asserting that, in his view, geopolitical conditions had changed since the early days of the Republic when Washington and others had counseled against involvement in European wars. The junior senator from Massachusetts said that the "ocean barrier which defended us in 1776 and 1812 no longer exists. Steam and electricity have destroyed it."[4]

With these pro-British arguments and actions swirling around him and concerns about his vulnerability in the 1916 election, by the fall of 1915 Wilson cast his lot with preparedness. Wilson had convinced himself to pose as the watchman on the tower warning of doom. The words of the Old Testament prophet Ezekiel rang again, this time from the White House: "But if the watchman see the sword come, and blow not the trumpet, and the people be not warned...his blood will I require at the watchman's hand."[5] President Wilson began to proclaim from the ramparts that the German "Huns" were at the gates (even though the German Army couldn't get to Paris) and American defenses should be raised. In the summer of 1916 the President asked Congress for a large increase in defense spending, creating a Navy second to none. The Big Navy Act envisioned a 10 year construction project building dozens of ships, which when completed would bring to an end the centuries-long British dominance on the high seas. Wilson's conversion from neutrality to preparedness was complete by 1916, and he was edging toward and alliance with his beloved Great Britain – just as the slogan "HE KEPT US OUT OF WAR" rang across America.

Wilson came into office in 1913 as a Jeffersonian democrat, proclaiming the evils and dangers of big government, vowing to return the nation to the days of rugged individualism and

---

1. Buchanan, *A Republic, Not An Empire*, p. 186.
2. Ibid., p. 187.
3. Kissinger, *Diplomacy*, p. 45.
4. Buchanan, *A Republic, No An Empire*, p. 183.
5. Morison, *The Oxford History of the American People*, p. 853.

small government. But in the fall of 1916 desperate for the votes of the Progressive reform party, Wilson abandoned his principles and his aversion to big government, adopting the entire reform party platform involving extensive federal government action. A French Protestant King once proclaimed that "Paris was worth a mass," thereupon he converted to Catholicism. In 1916 Wilson found that "Washington D.C. was worth Progressive reforms" and proceeded to prostitute his small government principles.

Using the campaign slogan, "He Kept Us Out Of War" as the final "sweetener" Wilson went into battle with the war-Republicans. GOP nominee Charles Evans Hughes joined Roosevelt, Lodge and other Republican imperialists from the Spanish-American War to assert that "there is no isolation in the world of the 20th century."[1] A Republican victory would lead to war; supposedly, a Democrat victory was a vote for peace. The Democrat election campaign slogan of 1916 was effective:

YOU ARE WORKING — NOT FIGHTING!

ALIVE AND HAPPY — NOT CANNON FODDER!

WILSON AND PEACE WITH HONOR?

OR, HUGHES WITH ROOSEVELT AND WAR?[2]

On the strength of the peace vote from the reform-minded West and Midwest, Wilson won a close election. Sadly, five months later, on April 2, 1917, Wilson asked the Congress to declare war on Germany. The election campaign of 1916 was more about political maneuvering with deceiving slogans than about reality. The American electorate was essentially defrauded in the 1916 election. They voted for Wilson and Peace; they got Wilson and War. The president confessed in a private moment of candor that he couldn't control the flow of events. "I can't keep the country out of war. They talk of me as though I were a god. Any German lieutenant can put us into war at any time by some calculated outrage."[3] But the truth be told, it wasn't the actions of a German lieutenant that took America into war; it was the political opportunism and duplicity of the American president.

A "calculated outrage" was soon in coming, but it was at the hands of the German Chancellery and the General Staff and it came in two forms — Unrestricted Submarine Warfare and the Zimmerman Note. On January 9, 1917 Kaiser William II, Chancellor Bethmann-Hollweg and the military leaders met to discuss measures to resolve the grim situation in which Germany found itself. Their military campaign had bogged down in France, and with French and British divisions outnumbering German divisions by 190 to 150, the possibility of Germany being invaded by the Allies on the western front was looming. The demoralized German Navy was bottled up at its home port at Kiel. Food was so scarce as a result of the illegal British blockade that people were actually starving or so weakened by malnutrition that they died of disease. British war production was in full swing and the American trade and financial advantage was beginning to be felt. The military staff urged the Kaiser to unleash the submarine fleet on

---

1. Justin Raimondo, "Defenders of the Republic: The Anti-Interventionist Tradition in American Politics," in John Denson, ed., *The Costs of War*, p 86.

2. Unger, *The Questions of Our Past*, p. 688.

3. Nash, *The American People*, p. 735.

shipping into the British Isles. Hindenburg advised the Kaiser that "Things cannot be worse than they are now. The war must be brought to an end by whatever means as soon as possible."[1]

Kaiser William II signed the fateful order: Unrestricted Submarine Warfare would begin February 1, 1917. The *Arabic* pledge and the *Sussex* pledge be damned! The Chancellor, who had opposed the decision, was slumped in his chair alone in the room following the meeting when an aide entered and asked what was wrong. He said disconsolately, "Germany is finished."[2] On February 3, as a result of the new submarine campaign, Wilson severed all diplomatic relations with Germany, although not yet asking Congress to declare war.

The second bombshell was dropped on March 3 when the contents of the Zimmerman Note were revealed. The British had intercepted a coded diplomatic message from German Foreign Secretary Arthur Zimmerman to President Carranza of Mexico suggesting a German-Mexican alliance in the event the United States entered the European war against Germany. The German offer was enticing as it promised the return of Mexico's lost territories — Texas, New Mexico and Arizona — if Mexico would attack the United States. Additionally, Mexico was urged to seek an alliance with Japan and offer Nippon the newly acquired islands of Hawaii. To the preparedness and pro-British crowd, this was all too good to be true. Germany was sinking American ships in the Atlantic resulting in American deaths and concocting land grabs with the unstable Mexican republic on the United States border.

It needs to be emphasized that the German offer to Mexican was contingent upon an American declaration of war against Germany — it was inoperative unless that occurred. If America remained on the sidelines, as it had in all previous European wars, American had nothing to fear from the Mexican Army, an Army that was nearly non-existent anyway. But the pro-British and preparedness groups made much of this purloined message with its emotional implications for war.

On February 26, President Wilson requested that Congress authorize the arming of the merchant fleet, mimicking the illegal actions of Churchill with his Q-ship program. Wilson's request was for authority to "employ any other instrumentality or method to protect [the merchant vessels] on their lawful occasions."[3] Stalwart peace advocates would have none of that; Senators Robert LaFollette and George Norris led a filibuster which successfully rejected the request, for which they earned from Wilson the sobriquet, "a little group of willful men."[4] It is astounding that a professor of American government would denigrate the constitutionally proscribed actions of the Senate. Angered by the Senate rebuff, Wilson on his own ordered the arming of the merchant fleet; American freighters went forth to do battle with over 100 U-boats of the German Navy, without the blessing of the American Congress. Between March 12 and March 21 five United States ships were sunk by submarines resulting in the tragic loss of American lives.

The Unrestricted Submarine Warfare strategy was initially an amazing success for Germany. In January Britain lost 49 ships, and in February 105, then in March 147. Fully 25% of all shipping going to Great Britain went to the bottom of the ocean. If this toll continued with

---

1. Buchanan, *A Republic, Not An Empire*, p. 206.
2. Ibid., p. 207.
3. Morison, *The Oxford History of the American People*, p. 859.
4. Cramer, *The Causes of War*, p. 157.

both Britain and Germany unable to import sufficient food, London and Berlin would have to negotiate peace terms.

Wilson came to the rescue of England just in the nick of time. On April 2, 1917 President Wilson, the "peace president," became the "war president" as he asked Congress to declare war on the German Empire. The gravity of the occasion hung heavily on the devout Presbyterian man. The day before his war declaration address he confided to a newsman his concern about the future of America. In retrospect these thoughts seem prophetic as American society turned ugly during the war. "Once lead this people into war, and they'll forget there ever was such a thing as tolerance."[1]

Politician eloquence was at its finest as President Wilson solemnly addressed the hushed and respectful members of Congress and the people of the United States:

> Neutrality is no longer feasible or desirable when the peace of the world is involved and the freedom of its peoples, and the menace to that peace and freedom lies in the existence of autocratic governments backed by organized forces which is controlled wholly by their will. We have no quarrel with the German people. We have no feeling toward them but one of sympathy and friendship....The world must be made safe for democracy.

> With a profound sense of the solemn and even tragical character of the step I am taking and of the grave responsibilities which it involves, but in unhesitating obedience to what I deem my constitutional duty, I advise that the Congress declare the recent course of the Imperial German government to be, in fact, nothing less than war against the government and people of the United States; that it formally accept the status of belligerent which has thus been thrust upon it; and that it take immediate steps not only to put the country in a more thorough state of defense, but also to exert its power and employ all its resources to bring the government of the German Empire to terms and end the war.

> It is a fearful thing to lead this great peaceful people into war, into the most terrible and disastrous of all wars, civilization itself seeming to be in the balance. But the right is more precious than peace, and we shall fight for the things which we have always carried nearest our hearts, — for democracy, for the right of those who submit to authority to have a voice in their own governance, for the rights and liberties of small nations, for a universal dominion of right by such a concert of free people as shall bring peace and safety to all nations and make the world itself at last free. To such a task we can dedicate our lives and our fortunes, everything that we are and everything that we have, with the pride of those who know that the day has come when America is privileged to spend her blood and her might for the principles that gave her birth and happiness and the peace which she has treasured. God is helping her, she can do no other.

The United States was officially at war when the Senate voted 82-6 and the House of Representatives voted 373-50 to approve Wilson's request. America prepared to go on its first crusade in Europe. William McAdoo, Wilson's son-in-law and Secretary of the Treasury, caught the President's evangelical mood when he told Wilson: "You have done a great thing nobly! I firmly believe that it is God's will that America should do the transcendent service for humanity throughout the world and that you are his chosen instruments."[2]

The six dissident Senators expressed their distress not only at the decision to go to war, but also because the President was conducting a moral crusade; his goal was not simply the defense of the nation, but a revolution in international relations. Senator William Borah complained: "I join no crusade. I seek or accept no alliances; I obligate this government to no other

---

1. Morison, *The Oxford History of the American People*, p. 858.
2. Murray N, Rothbard, "World War I as Fulfillment: Power and the Intellectuals," in John Denson, ed., *The Costs of War*, p.251.

power. I make war alone for my countrymen and their rights...."[1] These maverick Senators introduced a resolution in support of the once sacrosanct principles of neutrality and non-involvement in European quarrels, policies initiated by Washington, and followed assiduously throughout the early years of the republic. Despite invoking the names of Jefferson, Adams and other giants of the past, the motion died. In April 1917, the United States abandoned the proven counsel of the Founding Fathers and marched off into the unknown world of European politics behind the President-Preacher Woodrow Wilson. Militant Idealism was replacing the neutrality of the early century.

HE TOOK US INTO WAR

Imagine the following scenario —

Heinz Metzler was elected President of the United States in 1912, the first man of German ancestry to be so honored. Metzler was a devotee of German culture, having been raised on the stories of the brothers Grimm and other German folk tales. Later in life he was an avid reader of noted German writers — Goethe, Schiller, Hesse — and as with all German-Americans, he was proud of the musical masterpieces produced by Beethoven, Mozart, Bach and Brahms. Metzler had been a university professor, writing extensively on German culture and history. Even though he was a man of letters, he regarded German industry as the leader in several areas — chemical, pharmaceutical, automobiles, optics and others. His family's dedication to education was a direct result of the German emphasis on quality education, as Germany had pioneered the idea of education for all children from kindergarten through the gymnasium (high school). Although it was not widely known, political parties had developed in Germany as early as the 1860s, and it was in the land of his ancestors that the first social welfare programs evolved, later copied throughout the industrial world. Some of his political opponents in America often hurled slurs at Germany, asserting that the "Huns" were an aggressive, belligerent nation, but Metzler rebuked them by pointing out that it was Great Britain, not Germany, that ruled the oceans, and it was the English, not the Germans, who had conquered over 20% of the globe as evidenced by the British Empire. He chided his critics, pointing out that the British Empire was acquired at the point of a gun, and that Germany, by contrast, had only a small collection of colonies. When war broke out in Europe in 1914, Metzler took a firm stance against the illegal British blockade as well as the illegal use of submarines by Germany. He rigorously enforced the US policy that forbade American citizens from traveling on any belligerent ship into both European war zones, and he enforced the legislation that forbade US banks making loans to either belligerent. As a result of Metzler's leadership, the US remained true to the legacy of the Founding Fathers of the republic; America did not go to war in Europe, and non of her young men died in the killing fields of France. The European war ended in 1918 with a compromise peace — no victors and no vanquished. None of the belligerents were completely happy with the outcome, but none were reborn as resentful and hateful nations seeking revenge.

Fantasy? Yes, of course. A very different scenario, in fact, played itself out in the early 20th century. But this scenario does illustrate the point that "personality makes policy." Which

---

1. Walter McDougall, *Promised Land, Crusader State: The American Encounter with the World Since 1776*, p. 136-137.

president is in office has more to do with whether the nation goes to war, or remains at peace, than any objective criterion. Some presidents give us high taxes, some offer bargain basement taxes. Some presidents offer belligerency and war, others give us neutrality and peace.

Woodrow Wilson was the descendant of stern Presbyterian stock from the British Isles and his entire life seemed to be a stage upon which Wilson acted out his role as a strict, moral Calvinist; a missionary sent from England to recreate the British culture in the wayward American colonies.

> As a Princeton undergraduate, "Tommy" Wilson drafted classmates into games and clubs so that he could play the leader and indulge his love of things British. In war games he fancied himself a British squadron commander, in political clubs a British minister swaying Parliament with his rhetoric. He kept a portrait of the crusading Christian Prime Minister William Ewart Gladstone on his desk....[1]

After having failed at the study of law, Wilson turned to the academic field of political science and distinguished himself with the publication of an analysis of American government, *Congressional Government*. This popular book criticized the American constitutional practice of separation of powers and checks and balances; Wilson thought the British parliamentary system better. His convictions about a League of Nations were derived from British Liberal Party notions about the dangers of nationalism, and he borrowed the phrase "a war to end all wars" from the British socialist pamphleteer, H. G. Wells.

After the resignation of Secretary of State William Jennings Bryan in 1915, Wilson surrounded himself with Anglophiles — his personal aide Colonel Edward House, the new Secretary of State Robert Lansing, and Robert Page, the United States Ambassador to Great Britain. The President confided to his press secretary that he was having "unneutral thoughts" one day: "England is fighting our fight and you may well understand that I shall not, in the present state of the world's affairs place obstacles in her way when she is fighting for her life, and the life of the world."[2]

It is indicative of Wilson's intense pro-British bias that he would equate the English way of life with the "life of the world." It is also interesting to note that this is the same war which Wilson had described in 1914 as a struggle "whose causes cannot touch us," and had asked all Americans to guard against favoritism in every thought and action. War psychology, governed by personal bias, was at fever pitch by 1917 in the mind of Woodrow Wilson.

While serving as president of Princeton University, Wilson undertook to eliminate the Greek fraternal organizations on campus. An acrimonious battle ensued between Wilson and the Greek fraternities and sororities, with neither side giving in. A university official one day attempted to secure from Wilson a compromise; the colleague suggested that there were two sides to the issue. To that effort at mediation, Wilson retorted, "Yes, the right side and the wrong side." There was no compromise that day. Commenting on the President's fierce individualism and his self-righteousness, Cecil Spring-Rice, a British politician, said: "He consults no one and no one knows what he is going to do next. He believes that God had sent him here to do something and that God knows what. This may be pleasing to God but not to Congressmen or ambassadors."[3]

---

1. Ibid., p. 126.
2. Ralph Raico, "American Foreign Policy-The Turning Point, 1898-1919," in John Denson, ed., *The Failure of America's Foreign Wars*, p. 67.

Wilson's sense of righteousness caused him to go out of his way to antagonize people, even at the height of an election campaign. Just prior to the election of 1916, he received a telegram from a pro-German group criticizing his policy of approving loans to England and France, permitting munitions to be sent to Britain and suggesting a more balanced treatment of Germany. Instead of learning from the note or just ignoring the message, Wilson sent a hot letter back saying: "I would feel deeply mortified to have you or anybody like you to vote for me. Since you have access to many disloyal Americans and I have not I will ask you to convey this message to them."[1]

To the virtuous Wilson, any dissent over foreign policy was "disloyalty," and later it even became treasonous. At one time Wilson had expressed concern that war would bring intolerance to American society, and it certainly had — in the president himself! When the United States entered the war, Wilson became an angry man using the power of government to stamp out dissent. One doubts that Wilson would have rebuked Thomas Lamont of the Morgan banking group for his comment that, "From the start we did everything that we could to contribute to the cause of the allies." David Lloyd George, the British Prime Minister had insight into the man when he observed, Wilson "believed in mankind ... but distrusted men."[2]

But the pro-British bias existed throughout the American culture, not just in the White House. As Patrick Buchanan wrote: "The most important fact of the twentieth century, it has been said, is that America spoke English. A cultural affinity and common Anglo-Saxon heritage helped us identify with the English...."[3]

The Anglo-American ties were numerous and pervasive — language, literature, education, law, politics, finance, trade, travel. This British cultural advantage was supplemented by a monopoly of news from the war front. When the war began, the British Navy severed the transatlantic cable running across the Atlantic between Europe and America, thereby ensuring that all information received in America came through London. For the British the channels of propaganda were open; the "Huns" were cut off from America.

The eminent British historian and jurist Lord Bryce authored a report on *Alleged German Atrocities* (1915) in which he asserted that the "Huns" had committed terrible atrocities in Belgium while hurrying through on their way to France — rape of nuns, babies pierced by bayonets, hands of boys cut off, priests hung upside down on church bells their heads performing the work of the clapper. The pro-British *New York Times* ran a banner headline:

GERMAN ATROCITIES ARE PROVED

YOUNG AND OLD MUTILATED

Yet none of the alleged human rights abuses were proven. No witnesses or victims were named in the report. The noted American attorney, Clarence Darrow, traveled to France in 1915 where he offered a large monetary reward for evidence of any mutilation. He found no takers. After the war, researchers attempting to examine the Bryce Report were told that the files had vanished — like the victims. The cultural bias of America allowed these fantastic stories to be

3. McDougall, *Promised Land, Crusader State*, p. 130.
1. Buchanan, *A Republic, Not An Empire*, p. 188, 189.
2. McDougall, *Promised Land, Crusader State*, p. 126.
3. Buchanan, *A Republic, Not An Empire*, p. 193.

believed; only later after the war did a more sober American public come to acknowledge that the stories were largely fabrications.[1]

The trumped-up stories of atrocities in Belgium by Germany may have had their origin in actual human rights abuses in the Belgian Congo, an imperial enclave of Belgian King Leopold and his successors. Historian Thomas Fleming summarizes the tragedy:

> The Congo's blacks had been routinely starved, beaten and shot for trivial offense while being forced to labor endless hours as slaves to extract millions of dollars in rubber and ivory for their Belgium masters, chief of whom was King Leopold II. For many years, the royal family literally owned the Congo, making and estimated billion dollars out of its exploitation. Behind a screen of unctuous lies about bringing Christianity to the dark continent, an estimated 10 million natives had died....[2]

William Jennings Bryan's resignation from the State Department was a godsend for Britain as the new Secretary of State, Robert Lansing, was ardently pro-British. Lansing saw the war not as an unfortunate diplomatic blunder by European statesmen, but as an Armageddon; a struggle for the soul of civilization requiring an unlimited number of human casualties. Lansing asserted that German success:

> would mean the overthrow of democracy... the suppression of individual liberty, the setting of evil ambition...,and the turning back of the hands of human progress two centuries....[3]

The influential columnist Walter Lippmann editorialized in the *New Republic* (February 1917) that Germany was a dire threat to the Atlantic community of nations. He warned that:

> [If] Germany won, the United States would have to face a new and aggressively expanding German empire which had made Britain, France, and Russia its vassals, and Japan its ally....a German victory in 1917 would have made the world unsafe for the American democracies from Canada to the Argentine.[4]

Nearly a century later serious historians continue this British line of propaganda. David Trask asserts that "The choice of which side to join reflected the nation's natural opposition to expansionist powers in Eurasia."[5] The statement provokes an obvious question: if America finds the expansionism of Germany to be threatening, how does it excuse the expansionism inherent in the British Empire? The colonies of the British Empire did not benignly fall into London's lap, but were acquired through bloody wars. Irish patriots were in armed revolt against Britain at the time of the Great War; no German colony or province was in revolt. If America were truly distressed about aggression, expansionism and denial of self-government, they would have had it out with the British, Belgium and other imperial masters long before this. Historian David Trask elaborates on this theme: "Like Great Britain and other insular nations the USA had a vital interest in preventing hegemonic enterprises by any land power in Eurasia."[6]

It is a common theme among realist writers in Britain and America to pronounce the "Realist Rule" — no hegemony allowed, except, of course, Anglo-Saxon hegemony. Seldom do

---

1. Fleming, *The Illusion of Victory*, p. 53, 54.
2. Fleming, p. 49.
3. Unger, *The Questions of Our Past*, p. 686.
4. Cramer, *The Causes of War*, p. 144.
5. David Trask, "The Entry of the USA into the War and its Effects," in Hew Strachan, ed., *World War I: A History*, p. 240.
6. Ibid. p. 239

these realists explain exactly what it is about a land power in the Eurasian continent that is so distressing to the Atlantic powers. Bourbon France was a hegemonic power in Europe for centuries, while Great Britain thrived, and the colonies remained neutral. One does wonder how these prophets of doom would regard the European Union of today? The EU is the most dominant economic power, and potentially the greatest military power in European history. And America lives on, apparently oblivious to the danger!

The issue here raises a point about how humans go about choosing sides and justifying war. The American alliance with Britain evolved in the citizenry's mind at a visceral level; instinctively the British were regarded as "family." America and Britain share a common language and political culture, and "mistakes" that the British made were ignored or explained away, as one would do with an eccentric uncle. This family relationship was bolstered by the commanding British propaganda that floated daily across America.

But the human mind prefers to make "rational" calculations about such matters, therefore, America, it is explained, came to dislike Germany because the Huns were "expansionists" or Germans were violating American rights. Humans are the only animals that are capable of "rationalizing their prejudices." We think we go to war based on clear, reasonable provocations, but the reality is we are driven by hidden urges. The exigency of wars produces this dilemma in leaders and ordinary citizens; war psychology warps minds. But from the vantage point of the 1990s it is difficult to understand why competent, professional historians are still responding to these same simple, primitive instincts as they write our history. John Turner, another pro-British historian, enlightens us on politics in Europe:

> In central and Eastern Europe, mass politics had had relatively little impact on the structure of government. The German government was dominated by the Kaiser and his court. The chancellor and his ministers, appointed without reference to the Reichstag, ruled with the help of a powerful aristocracy, an efficient bureaucracy and the army. The political parties had little influence.[1]

The larger point being made here is certainly true. Western European democracies were further advanced politically than anywhere else in the world. But on the specific question of foreign policy, on war and peace, on the deployment of troops and disbursing of navies, there is little difference between nations, like the United States, and less democratic societies, like Germany in 1914. The German Kaiser and his staff had a near monopoly over foreign and military matters; but the same can be said about these matters in America and Britain. In July 1914 the ruling majority Liberal party in Britain was opposed to war, but Prime Minister Asquith, with the aid of two cabinet members, Grey and Churchill, took the country into war anyway. In America, Wilson's pro-British biases created a condition in which the United States was essentially at war with Germany by the end of 1916 through actions of the president — the Congress and the political parties were largely irrelevant. When President Wilson asked for a declaration of war, what choice did the Congress have after submarine warfare resumed? Even in the western democracies, the conduct of foreign policy actually remains at the stage of monarchy — whatever the leader wants, the legislature and the people accept.

Regardless, by 1917 it had become clear that "Most Americans had come to believe that the Great War... was a struggle to protect western democracy against the spread of German

---

1. John Turner, "The Challenge to Liberalism: The Politics of the Home Front," in Hew Strachan, ed., *World War I: A History*. p. 164

militarism....",[1] this being so in no small measure due to the actions and rhetoric of President Wilson. Germany contributed to its own demise by clumsy attempts at sabotage and espionage in America. Two German agents were expelled from America due to their efforts to sabotage munitions plants. And, in the most spectacular case, the Austro-Hungarian ambassador to the United States, Dr. Constantin Dumba (yes, Dumba) was caught fomenting illegal strikes at American munitions works. An American newspaper couldn't resist waxing poetic.

> O Constantin Theodor Dumba,
> You'd aroused Uncle Sam from his slumba:
> That letter you wrote,
> Got the old fellow's goat —
> Now his path you'll no longer encumba.[2]

"The Great War spawned the most spectacular advertising campaign to date. Its product was justification of war."[3] The British knew their quarry well. Americans thought in terms of "right and wrong," so the Germans were portrayed as the devil. Americans had a tendency to remain out of European quarrels, so the war would be portrayed as an international threat. Movie stars and other celebrities acted as shills for the war effort. Charlie Chaplin, Mary Pickford, Douglas Fairbanks drew immense crowds to hear appeals for Liberty bonds. Speaking before a crowd of 30,000 on Wall Street, then later in Washington D.C., Chaplin said:

> This very moment the Germans occupy a position of advantage and we have to get the dollars. It ought to go over so that we can drive that old devil, the Kaiser, out of France.
>
> The Germans are at our door. We've got to stop them. And we will stop them if you buy Liberty Bonds! Remember, each bond you buy saves a soldier's life — a mother's son! — and will bring this war to an early victory.[4]

The frenzied propaganda even reached into American homes — into the children's nursery; toddlers were not too young to catch the anti-German spirit:

> This is the house that Jack built.
> This is the bomb that fell on the house that Jack built.
> This is the Hun who dropped the bomb that fell on the house that Jack built.
> This is the gun that killed the Hun who dropped the bomb that fell on the house that Jack built.[5]

THE FOLLY OF WAR

Historians have been preoccupied with the question — For what reasons did America enter the war? — a question that assumes the United States should have entered the war if for the correct reasons. However, they should first ask the question: Why didn't America stay out

---

1. Cramer, *The Causes of War*, p. 119.
2. Buchanan, *A Republic, Not An Empire*, p. 202.
3. J. M. Winter, "Propaganda and the Mobilization of Consent," in Hew Strachan, ed., *World War I: A History*, p. 216.
4. Ibid., p. 223.
5. Ibid., p. 219.

of the war as had been the practice for over a century? Could the United States have remained neutral in the Great War? Was there some way that America could have avoided going to war — a war that eventually took the lives of over 125,000 of its young men?

The United States had gone down this road before in its history; there were signposts guiding the way. The road to peace was bumpy and the journey required patience and persistence. America's leaders would have to display a willingness to accept less than the ultimate. Wilson proved incapable of such suppleness of thought or personal flexibility and instead chose the path to war.

In the 1760s the colonists had tangled with Britain, the mother country, on a number of issues, and often resorted to economic pressure on Britain — colonists simply refused to trade with England or to abide by English tax laws. These efforts to resolve differences short of war were sometimes successful and established a model for later use.

Three decades later, during the 1790s, the Atlantic waters roiled with disputes between the United States and Britain, later with France. With patience and dedicated negotiations, the United States avoided war with the two European giants. President John Adams was proud of how he maneuvered the ship of state away from war, despite vigorous protests by his countrymen. As Adams said, he had "steered the vessel...into a peaceful and safe port." Later he told friends that of all his accomplishments he took the greatest satisfaction in shielding his nation from war. He wrote to a friend saying, "I desire no other inscription over my gravestone than: Here lies John Adams who took upon himself the responsibility of peace with France in the year 1800."[1]

But the best lessons on how to handle quarrels in the Atlantic are afforded by the issues that arose during the Napoleonic Wars (1803-1815). In 1806, the British instituted a blockade of the European coast from Germany to France; Napoleonic France reciprocated, declaring a war zone around the British Isles, a familiar story for students of World War I. Shaken by the denial of traditional rights of neutrals to trade in wartime, the United States under the presidency of Thomas Jefferson applied economic pressure in the form of a series of embargoes on France and Britain to force their adherence to international law. America, then a small nation of 7 million settlers, intended to force compliance with the law by withholding its money. Although some of the embargo measures were ineffective and were unpopular with some coastal areas of the nation, it is important to remember that the embargo measures did eventually work. By April 1812, the British relented, removing their illegal maritime practices. Unfortunately, three days before the British capitulation, the United States Congress declared war on Great Britain. The British ship carrying news of the repeal of the illegal war zone action passed, in mid-Atlantic, the American ship carrying the declaration of war. Because of inadequate communications across the Atlantic Ocean, the War of 1812 occurred, and history forgets that the embargo worked. By 1917, the United States was a mighty nation of nearly 80 million people and the greatest economic power in the world. If it threw its financial and economic weight around, Britain and Germany might capitulate. With resourcefulness, creativity and patience President Wilson could have achieved an honorable peace, as had Adams and Jefferson; Madison in 1812 would also have avoided war with modern communications. President Wilson's neutrality proclamation of August 4, 1914, should have been supplemented by these measures:

---

1. McCullough, *Promised Land, Crusader State*, p. 567.

- All loans to belligerent nations are forbidden. (Actually, Wilson did this, then secretly rescinded it two months later.)
- After the belligerents created their respective war zones early in 1915, the United States prohibits American citizens and American vessels from travel to the European continent or to the British Isles. This was put in effect briefly prior to World War II. Today governments commonly restrict travel of citizens into areas of great danger.
- All trade in munitions with any belligerent nation is strictly forbidden. (Wilson did place an embargo on all weapons shipments to Mexico when that nation experienced revolutionary times.) The United States Bureau of Customs would enforce this at the various ports. Not only was trade in munitions illegal by international law, but selling weapons at a profit to belligerents is a dirty business. Companies engaged in such nefarious actions were aptly named "merchants of death."

These actions would have been met in some quarters by opposition and would have produced economic hardships. But it is the responsibility of the national leadership to take action that is in the best interest of the nation at large, not a few bankers, "munitions makers" or farmers who were taking advantage of the war to grow rich. When war clouds gathered in Europe twenty years later in the 1930s, some of these measures were adopted under the name of "Cash and Carry," that is, belligerent nations trading with America would have to pay cash (no loans) and carry goods across the Atlantic on their own merchant vessels. Had these measures been taken in 1914, the world may never have heard of the sinking of the *Lusitania*.

An alternative approach would have been for the United States Navy to convoy American freighters and passenger liners into both war zones, confronting the German subs and the British blockade. In doing this, America would have defied both belligerents, treated each the same, and created a crisis in which either one or both may have abandoned their illegal actions. It is possible, also, that such an action might have provided an opening for Wilson to act as a mediator in the war, a role he desperately wanted to perform. America did not take prudent steps to avoid war in 1917 because the nation and its leaders had become impatient, arrogant and truculent. Instead of using economic and diplomatic pressure, the country turned quickly to war. The cause of this confrontational, impatient behavior is rooted in the nation's sense of its own exceptionalism and its supreme confidence in its own military might. However, instead of recognizing this cultural arrogance, American leaders often claimed that objective conditions in the world had forced American involvement in European wars.

Senator Henry Cabot Lodge asserted that the age of steam and electricity had minimized or eliminated the Atlantic barrier between Europe and the United States, making neutrality no longer feasible. The Senator was wrong then, and those who use this line of argument today are wrong! Just because an e-mail can fly across the continent in seconds and a jet aircraft can transport people across oceans in hours, does not mean that border clashes in the Persian Gulf or along the Rhine are any more pertinent to American safety than in the days of the Pony Express.

America's tradition of avoiding wars and remaining outside debilitating alliances in Europe was a policy choice that 19th century American leaders made. It was not something imposed upon them merely by the physical presence of an ocean or the remoteness of Europe. Even today Switzerland, Sweden and other European nations make choices to abstain from European wars and intrigues, even though their borders touch warring nations. These choices have nothing to do with territorial remoteness or proximity. There was no more inevitability of

America going to war in Europe in 1917 than in abstaining from war in 1798 or in 1807. The choice for or against war was in the hands of Adams or Jefferson or Wilson. Adams and Jefferson rejected going to war; Wilson accepted the invitation.

Traditional historians have written volumes on the questions of why American went to war, offering many divergent theories. Motivations propelling the United States into war abound: munitions maker's avarice, opposition to German expansion, international banker's cupidity, balance of power theories, and neutral rights defenders. Though interesting, none of these adequately explains the American slide into war.

The Munitions Makers and Bankers theory — Thomas Lamont, an official with Morgan banks, confessed to working for British interests; after issuing millions in loans to the British, one can readily understand the banker's position on the war. Senator Frank Norris excoriated the "rich man" for triggering the war. Bankers, Norris fumed, "concealed in their palatial offices on Wall Street, sitting behind mahogany desks, covered with clipped coupons...coupons tainted with mothers' tears, coupons dyed in the life blood of their fellowmen."[1] Dupont Chemical, General Electric and other manufacturers of weapons and munitions did have an interest in protecting their trade relationship with the Allied Powers, although most of these companies were diversified enough to shift to other areas of trade should neutrality be observed. The truth be told, there were as many businessmen who were neutral as were pro-Allied. Neutrality allowed them to make profits without great risk. "The international trading and banking fraternity...remained international in outlook and was alarmed at the prospect of war."[2] The large and diverse American business community was divided on the question of war.

Balance of Power advocates — Some Americans perceived Germany as a military threat rather than an evil force. These realists, led by the columnist Walter Lippmann, wanted America to come to the aid of the Atlantic allies, England and France, in order to prevent Germany from dominating the continent, thereby changing the existing balance of power in the Atlantic world. They perceived American national interests as being intertwined with Britain, and any foe of Britain's was a foe of ours. However, this realist idea was not commonly discussed in 1917, only later receiving considerable publicity when Lippmann's book *US Foreign Policy: Shield of the Republic* was published in 1943. President Wilson was an ardent opponent of realism in foreign affairs and would not himself have been swayed by such talk of power and national interest. Giving a speech in Mobile in 1913, the president-scholar said it is a "very perilous thing to determine the foreign policy of a nation in terms of national interest. It is not only unfair to those with whom you are dealing but it is degrading regards your own actions."[3] In the 1940's and 1950's the balance of power theory was in vogue and was used extensively to describe the American response to Germany in the 1940's and the Soviets during the Cold War. But to apply this idea to World War I involves transmuting 1950 notions back to 1917.

The Neutral Rights school — The struggle over neutral rights in the Atlantic dominated international affairs for two and a half years. When the American declaration of war came in April 1917, it seemed to be provoked by the illegal German Unrestricted Submarine Warfare campaign. Millions of Americans were well educated about the nuances of the Cruiser Rules

---

1. Justin Raimondo, "Defenders of the Republic: The Anti-Intervention Tradition in American Politics," in John Denson, ed., *The Costs of War*, p. 89
2. Samuel R. Williamson, "The Origins of the War," in Hew Strachan, ed., *World War I: A History*, p. 13
3. McDougall, *Promised Land, Crusader State*, p. 130

and the Blockade Rules. Many historians in later years asserted that the defense of neutral rights was the motivation not only for the American people but also for the president. But neutral rights was not the abiding issue for Wilson, indeed the entire neutral rights matter was an artificial one. Wilson talked the talk of neutral rights, but his actions betrayed any real commitment. His neutrality proclamation in 1914 turned into a fraud, he concealed the British complicity in the Lusitania incident and he badgered the Germans about neutral rights, but winked at British transgressions. And when the war came to the American shores, Wilson disregarded neutral rights just as the other belligerents. In 1917 in an effort to prevent German-boats from leaving their pens on the north coast of Germany, the United States Navy mined the North Sea between Norway and Scotland. In taking this highly illegal action the US prevented neutral nations from using the high seas, precisely the same violations of international law that the US had complained about for two and a half years.

None of these commonly discussed "causes" of the war adequately explain the dilemma the United States found itself in by 1917. Decisions about international loans and trade made by the President in 1915 and 1916, combined with Wilson's personal bias towards all things British, determined that America could never be truly neutral. By 1916 Wilson was looking for ways to blame America's growing belligerency on Germany. Decisions that were made early in the European War made it nearly impossible for America to accept the defeat of Great Britain. The American economy became so closely tied to the British, with massive loans and extensive trade, that an economic recession would have resulted should the British war efforts have been unsuccessful. Richard Hofstadter observed that the Germanophobe of Wilson and his advisers "caused Wilson to make legalistic discriminations on behalf of the Allies and intensify American economic involvement with them; and in the end he became a prisoner of his own policies."[1]

America's leadership at the turn of the 20th century was divided into two distinct groups, sharply at odds on issues of diplomacy. The older group of neutralists adhered to the dictum of Washington and believed that foreign war would not only jeopardize American lives unnecessarily, but also divert energy and money from reforming American life. America could better spend its money and efforts improving the republic than going forth to slay monsters. Opposing this traditional group were the Imperialists of 1898, men who had gained ascendancy during the heady days of the war with Spain when America acquired an empire in the Caribbean and the Pacific. Their goal was to project the power of the US into the world.

Dr. Woodrow Wilson, professor of political science, desired to teach America a new lesson in international affairs, as his ideas fit into neither of these two groups. Wilson wanted to de-emphasize national rivalries and to stress the common bonds of all people, regardless of national boundaries. Wilson, the country's first internationalist president, saw the United States rising above its role as just another nation, assuming leadership in a world association of nations. The realist concepts of national interest and balance of power were vestiges of a more primitive stage of development, as Wilson saw it, and the neutralist program of the Founding Fathers was too passive, narrow and restrictive.

The American role in world affairs was "not to prove...our [national] selfishness, but our greatness." [2] There was a decisive missionary quality about Wilson's beliefs as he suggested that

---

1. Richard Hofstadter, *The American Political Traditions* (New York: Bantam Books, 1948) p. 263

the American purpose was to protect the liberties and rights of the *world's* people. Wilson eventually came to believe that the "security of America was inseparable from the security of all the rest of mankind,"[1] a vision that has possessed American presidents from Franklin Roosevelt to George W. Bush. In his State of the Union message in December 1915, Wilson depicted a noble vision that America had an obligation to stop aggression and root out evil everywhere on earth.

> [B]ecause we demand unmolested development and the undisturbed government of our own lives...we resent, from whatever quarter it may come, the aggression we ourselves will not practice. We insist upon security in prosecuting our self-chosen line of national development. We do more than that. We demand it also for others. We do not confine our enthusiasm for individual liberties and free national development to the incidents and movements of affairs which affect only ourselves. We feel it wherever there is a people that tries to walk in these difficult paths of independence and right.[2]

As 20th century presidents sent troops into battle around the world — Iraq, Kuwait, Vietnam, Korea, Normandy, and Iwo Jima — their inspiration was the stirring words of President Wilson's war message to Congress in April 1917: "Neutrality is no longer feasible or desirable when the peace of the world is involved and the freedom of its peoples, and the menace to that peace and freedom lies in the existence of autocratic governments....The world must be made safe for democracy."[3]

When war erupted in Europe in 1914, Wilson pronounced America to be a neutral nation, thereby following in the tradition of 19th century presidents. Consistent with the beliefs of the Founding Fathers and the European idealist, war was considered a disruptive force, while peace was the cornerstone of a good society providing a curative and uplifting influence. But Wilson soon became trapped in his own pro-British bias and action and was forced to revise his attitude toward war. As Wilson moved America closer to the Allied side, he had to confront the possibility of war against Germany; somehow war had to be made to appear palliative. At one time Wilson regarded war as "organized murder" to obtain national advantage. But by 1917 he announced that a "war without victors or vanquished," a "war to make the world safe for democracy," a "war to end all wars" had redeeming qualities. War for the greater good on behalf of humanity, was a noble gesture. "When men take up arms to set other men free, there is something sacred and holy in the warfare."[4]

A fateful marriage was thus created for future Americans: foreign policy would be based on moral and legal principles backed by the military might of America — Militant Idealism. No longer would the United States be the neutralist nation of George Washington, nor would it pursue Teddy Roosevelt's self-serving nationalist imperial policy. And Wilson had forsaken the pacifist idealism of the 19th century. In the 20th century America would perform the work of an avenging angel, of a crusading knight to all the world.

The "exceptional" nation was going to take on the responsibility for the welfare of the world, very much as missionaries for Christianity went to the four corners of the earth with their story of salvation. The old European idealism had been based on a humanistic approach combined with distaste for war, even a dash of pacifism; Wilson's idealism would have Prot-

---

2. Kissinger, *Diplomacy*, p. 47
1. Ibid., p. 47
2. Ibid.
3. Morison, *The Oxford History of the American People*, p. 859
4. Nash, *The American People*, p. 729

estant evangelicalism as its basis and would glory in war to rectify the evils of the world. The Presbyterian minister's son would lead a regeneration of international relations and introduce the world to Militant Idealism.

The idea of America simply being *A City on the Hill*, a beacon for all to see, was outdated. Wilson had a more active role for the Stars and Stripes. "We are the mediating nation for the world and we are therefore able to understand all nations."[1] Wilson affirmed that it had always been the mission of the United States to carry the good news of democracy to the world's people:

> We set this nation up to make men free, and we did not confine our conception and purpose to America, and now we will make men free. If we did not do that, all the fame of America would be gone and all her power would be dissipated.[2]

Decades later, Secretary of State Madeleine Albright in the 1990s echoed and amplified Wilson's comment when she said:

> If we have to use force, it is because we are Americans. We are the indispensable nation. We stand tall. We see further into the future.[3]

The Great War was a truly memorable event providing the United States with an opportunity to revolutionize international relations. Wilson envisioned himself as a savior who, in the words of Robert Wood, a leader of the National Conference of Social Workers, could supervise a "great humanizing process through which all loyalties, all beliefs must be wrought together in a better order."[4] America thrust its power outward in 1898 when it undertook an effort to spread the benefits of American reform to colonies in the Pacific and Caribbean. The events of 1898 were the opening chapter in America's new journey into world affairs. But in 1917 the United States began playing in the major leagues; Spain, Cuba, and the Philippine Islands were just the rookie league.

> But a truly fateful step took place with America's intervention into World War I. The American government decided that it was time to end the endless series of European wars, once and for all....Through American intervention, the world would finally be made safe for democracy. It would be the war to end all future wars.[5]

Thus the US purpose was noble, but the goals remain out of reach yet today. It has been a bloody, dangerous century of wars, and nearly one hundred years after Wilson's crusade the United States is no closer to the elusive, utopian goal of universal peace in a democratic world.

In 1898 young, bright, energetic men followed Teddy Roosevelt into battle and admired his patriotism and his imperialist quest. America needed to flex its muscles and stretch its wings across the seas. It was thrilling to see the Stars and Stripes unfurled in foreign lands and watch the respect afforded the new, powerful, conquering nation. Then in 1917, another generation of young, bright, energetic men followed Woodrow Wilson into battle, not for selfish national purposes but for the betterment of mankind and to demonstrate their own personal

---

1. Ibid
2. Kissinger, *Diplomacy*, p. 50
3. Sandra Mackey, *The Reckoning: Iraq and the Legacy of Saddam Hussein*, p. 358
4. Murray N. Rothbard, "World War I As Fulfillment: Power and the Intellectuals," in John Denson, ed., *The Cost of War*, p. 269
5. Jacob G. Hornberger, Preface, in Ebeling and Hornberger, *The Failure of America's Foreign Wars*, p. x.

rectitude. Roosevelt saw foreign policy as power utilized in the national interests; moral purpose was not of primary concern. Wilson's religious-based idealism foresaw international relations as a moral crusade without considering the finite nature of American resources, or the willingness of the world to accept the Gospel according to Wilson.

Woodrow Wilson's Militant Idealism, the belief that American foreign policy should be governed not by what is important to the national interests, but by what is morally and legally "right" for the world buttressed by a crusading army, has been the most significant idea in 20th century foreign policy. When America goes to war against Hitler, Saddam, the communists or any other evil, the country is expressing its Wilsonian idealism. Unfortunately, we are nearly all Wilsonians today, nearly one hundred years after Wilson taught his lessons.

CHAPTER 5. WORLD WAR I: THE ARMISTICE AND THE TREATY

SLAUGHTER IN THE TRENCHES

The leaders of Europe stumbled into war in 1914, unaware that their diplomatic blundering would result in nearly 10 million military men and 5 million civilians being killed. Did the slaughter in the trenches result in a "better world" for the survivors?

Private David Sutherland was killed on May 16, 1916. His platoon commander, who carried his body from the battlefield, wrote a poem to the dead man's father:

So you were David's father,
And he was your only son,
And the new-cut peats are rotting,
And the work is left undone.
Because of an old man weeping,
Just an old man in pain,
For David, his son David,
That will not come again.[1]

For the disabled survivors the torment cf a lifetime of being blind, crippled or deranged may have been worse than death. There were 41,000 British amputees and in France 100,000 men were totally incapacitated. Germany suffered over 2 million permanently disabled men, many of whom could be seen for years walking the streets and lying in the gutters of that nation. The French population, in relative decline since the time of Napoleon, experienced a tragic dip, falling from 16% of Europe's total population in 1880 to under 10% at the end of the war. Having entered the war only in the last year, the US suffered comparatively less. One hundred and twenty-five thousand young Americans were buried in Europe. Over 40,000 were treated for war neurosis, or "shell shock" as everyone called it. Many of those young men

---

1. Ferguson, *The Pity of War*, p. 438

remained in hospital care for the next sixty years, their lives completely wasted. Someone once said that the living envied the dead; this may have been true of those disabled in the Great War.

The following table shows the enormity of the human toll experienced in the World War. "In four and a quarter years of mechanized butchery an average of around 6,046 men were killed every day."[1]

	Mobilized	Killed	Wounded	% Killed and wounded
Russia	12 million	1.7 million	5 million	55%
France	8.4	1.4	4.3	67%
Britain	8.9	.9	2.1	34%
Italy	5.6	.7	.9	28%
USA	4.4	.1	.2	8%
Total	42.2	5.2	12.8	43%
Germany	11 million	1.8 million	4.2 million	55%
Austria	7.8	1.2	3.6	63%
Turkey	2.9	.3	.4	24%
Bulgaria	1.2	.1	.1	20%
Total	22.9	3.4	8.4	52%
Grand total	65 million	8.6 million	21.2 million	46%

The vicious slaughter reached its apogee in 1916 at the Battle of the Somme and the Battle of Verdun. The Battle of the Somme was the worst defeat in Britain's long military history, decimating an entire generation of young men of the leadership class. By the summer of 1916 the war had dragged on for two years with each side desperate for a victory. British General Sir Douglas Haig conceived a plan to punch a hole in the German lines at the River Somme near the French-Belgian border. General Haig's scheme was to use his artillery along a 20-mile front to destroy the German artillery positions, then send in waves of infantry to break the German lines. The bombardment by British cannons lasted eight days, and at 7:30 AM Saturday, July 1, over 120,000 untrained volunteers marched forward in orderly ranks, each carrying 66 pounds of equipment and a single weapon. This "New Army" of Britain was composed of hundreds of thousands of volunteers, mostly from the British upper class. Tragically, the eight-day bombardment had failed to destroy the German machine guns and light cannons; the "New Army" marched in orderly rank to their annihilation. In the first two hours, 20,000 British soldiers died. A sergeant serving in the "New Army" describes the carnage:

> I could see to my left and right, long lines of men.... By the time I had gone another ten yards, there seemed to be only a few men left around me; by the time I had gone twenty yards, I seemed to be on my own.[2]

The sergeant himself fell injured shortly after.

The machine gun was a devastating weapon; each machine gun could do the same damage as 50 infantrymen with rifles, and six machine guns could hold up a brigade. The British assault at the Somme gained nothing! Not an inch of ground was taken. The Battle of the Somme

---

1. Ibid., p. 436
2. Neil Heyman, *World War I* (Westport, Ct.: Greenwood Press, 1997), p. 41

is remembered as the single greatest day of human slaughter in world history. Over 20,000 young Brits died at the Somme in an hour or two; another 40,000 fell wounded. The Germans lost only 600 men in the battle.

Verdun was an ancient fortress city in the east of France, only 50 miles from the German border. Attila the Hun had once found military glory there in 450 AD; Wilhelmine Germany hoped to recapture that glory in 1916. The German siege began in February and lasted ten months; from winter snow to winter snow the battle raged with the French grimly hanging on to their fortress. It was the longest continuous battle in military history. The dead totaled three hundred thousand, with France losing over 160,000 and Germany 140,000.[1] No fortifications changed hands; no ground was gained. This was the war that Winston Churchill called the "glorious delicious war."[2]

German university students mobbed the recruitment offices when the war began, even though they were exempt from conscription. After a meager two months of military drill, they were formed into two armed corps and sent into battle at Ypres in Belgium where they faced experienced British regular troops. The slaughter was predictable.

> The result was a massacre of the innocents, of which a ghastly memorial can be seen to this day. In the Langemarck cemetery, overlooked by a shrine decorated by the insignia of Germany's universities, lie the bodies of 36,000 young men interred in a common grave, all killed in three weeks of fighting....[3]

Democratic societies depend upon an adequate flow of information enabling the public to make correct judgments about government policy. During the war the British press failed to serve the people, as newspaper reports offered little accurate information about the results of battles or casualties; the typical news reporter concealed the fact that the war was going nowhere. British war correspondents "protected the high command from criticism, wrote jauntily about life in the trenches, kept an inspired silence about the slaughter, and allowed themselves to be absorbed by the propaganda machine."[4] So the Great War progressed with the people oblivious to the problems at the front and intimidated into submission by the charge of "traitor" should they question the endeavor. The democratic spirit is crushed during war — no discussion, no debate, no dissent.

The leaders of the Great Powers took eagerly to their task, sending more and more young men into the trenches, knowing that only half of them would return to normal life. Having stumbled into war, they became absorbed with the idea of winning at all costs.

> Once plunged into war, the leaders of Europe became so obsessed with fratricide, so maddened by the progressive destruction of an entire generation of their young men, that victory turned into its own reward, regardless of the ruins on which that triumph would have to be erected.[5]

By January 1917, the two sides were in a dance of death, each side gripping the other and refusing to let go. Germany introduced poison gas in 1915; the Allies minimized it with gas masks. The British innovation called the tank was negated by the German impregnable fortifi-

---

1. Ian Ousby, *The Road To Verdun: World War I's Most Momentous Battle and the Folly of Nationalism* (New York: Doubleday and Company, 2002), p. 6,7
2. Gretchen Rubin, *Forty Ways to Look at Churchill* (New York: Ballantine Books, 2003), p. 94
3. Keegan, *A History of Warfare*, p. 358-359
4. Heyman, *World War I*, p. 14
5. Kissinger, *Diplomacy*, p. 219

cation called the Hindenburg Line. The German unrestricted submarine warfare was thwarted in 1917 by convoying merchant ships. Two exhausted behemoths struggled to hold on until the bell tolled the end of the struggle.

THE ARMISTICE — NOVEMBER 11, 1918

Then, suddenly, America entered the war. The US Army did not immediately turn the tide of battle, for it was only the 17th largest in the world. With 130,000 regulars and 70,000 national guardsmen, the United States ranked behind Portugal in size of its armed forces. However, conscription was legislated in 1917 requiring all men ages 21 to 30 to register, and eventually the American military forces ballooned to four million men. The American Expeditionary Force (AEF) was of "no practical military value as far as fighting in France was concerned. It was scarcely enough to form a police force for emergencies."[1] The AEF would not be combat ready until 1919, a year after the war was over.

President Wilson insisted that the United States was an "Associated" power, not an Allied power. This was an important distinction, as many Americans wanted the young nation to distance itself from the self-serving, land-grubbing war aims of the Allied powers. The United States went to Europe to "make the world safe for democracy," not to pillage and loot. To emphasize this point, the American military forces were not integrated into the European Allied armies. The American government insisted that the doughboys fight separately and have their own separate military front. The Secretary of War, Newton Baker affirmed this policy when he wrote, "It was necessary at all times to preserve the independence and identity of the American forces so that they could never be anything but an instrument of policy of the United States."[2]

And so, America fought alone. In the fall of 1917, troops of the American Expeditionary Force saw combat for the first time, and by early summer 1918 several hundred thousand troops of the AEF were in place. But, they were poorly trained and inadequately equipped for battle. The Allied commanders had hoped to integrate the Americans into the existing lines, using them as replacements for the war-weary French and British. Instead, by the fall 1918 the AEF was engaged in a bitter fight on its own in the Meuse-Argonne region; the battle did not go well.

> As [British General] Haig and others had feared, inexperienced commanders and staff proved inefficient, and the tactics of "open warfare" which Pershing insisted upon, were inappropriate in the area under attack. The vastly outnumbered [German] defenders poured murderous fire on advancing waves of massed [United States] infantry. The outcome amounted to a severe check if not defeat while the allies achieved victory elsewhere.[3]

Mobilizing a huge army involved time and organizational skills. By the fall 1918 there were two million men in American uniforms mostly draftees, but it was not expected that efficient battle operations could be performed for another year.

1. David Trask, "The Entry of the USA into the War and its Effects," in Hew Strachan, ed., *World War I: A History*, p. 242
2. Ibid., p. 244
3. Ibid., p. 251

By early 1918, it was clear that the German submarine offensive was not going to bring Britain to its knees. Germany at that time was in a precarious situation. There were murmurs of revolution as the shortage of food worsened. Even though Germany had defeated Russia in the eastern front, military reserves were depleted. In the spring, General Ludendorff, now in command of the German Army in the west, persuaded Kaiser William II and the political leaders to make one last push toward Paris — a spring offensive that may be the last gasp of the fatigued German Army. The spring offensive thrust violently at the French capital, but by July it had gained no ground. The German Army watched hopelessly as fresh American troops arrived in large numbers. Strangled and starved by the British blockade, out-produced by the industrial might of the Atlantic powers, facing an ever-growing Associated Army, the German war effort was near collapse.

Late in September, the Central Powers position was broken in the Balkans when Bulgaria, a German ally, sued for peace and the Turkish Army was routed. In October, the Austro-Hungarian Army was destroyed by the Italians. On the Western Front the British forces finally broke through the Hindenburg Line early in October and began marching through newly-liberated Belgium.

Besieged all around, Germany sent a message to President Wilson asking for a ceasefire and peace terms based on his generous offer of a "fair" negotiated peace, called the Fourteen Points. Inasmuch as Germany did not make the same request of Britain and France, the appeal was interpreted as an attempt by Germany to split the Allies diplomatically. Wilson and the German staff held sporadic trans-Atlantic talks for three weeks, to the consternation of the excluded Allied powers.

President Wilson's response was to inform the Germans that "if the United States must deal with the military...and monarchial masters of Germany, it must demand, not peace negotiations but surrender."[1] Wilson, the idealist, was pressuring Germany to abandon the Hohenzollern monarchy that had ruled the German states for three centuries, and to establish a republic devoid of any element of Prussian militarism. It was very clear that Germany could only have a peace based upon the Fourteen Points *if* it removed its military and monarchial rulers. Germany promptly complied with Wilson's demand; General Ludendorff was dismissed and Kaiser William II abdicated on November 9. The German State began to operate as a republic with no monarchy for the first time in its history. Germany had complied with the American demands and expected to participate in a negotiated peace, not a surrender.

The end of the German war efforts was approaching. The Austro-Hungarian Empire asked for peace terms from the Allies on November 3. On that same day the German High Command ordered its fleet to sea, confronting the British Navy in what would have surely been a suicide mission. The German sailors, sensing disaster, mutinied, killing several officers and returning the ships to port. Food riots were widespread in German cities and the Army was in full retreat in France. The war had been fought on the Western Front entirely outside of German soil. Now, to avoid the ignominy of being invaded, the German leadership asked for a ceasefire based on Wilson's Fourteen Points.

It was a dramatic scene in the Compiegne forest northeast of Paris on a frosty November morning in 1918. Here, in a railway car on a deserted rail siding, the German representatives

---

1. Marshall, *World War I*, p. 447

approached French military commander Marshall Ferdinand Foch. The Frenchman did not make it easy for the Germans:

FOCH	What is your purpose? What do you want of me?
GERMANS	To receive an armistice proposal.
FOCH	I have no proposal to make [implying that the war would continue].
GERMANS	We are here to hear your armistice terms.[1]

The Germans persisted and terms were eventually spelled out:

- German evacuation of all occupied territory.
- Germany stripped of its Army and Navy; cannons, guns, vehicles, planes, U-boats and ships to be surrendered to the Allies.
- German evacuation of the left bank of the Rhine River as well as the right bank 25 miles deep into German territory.
- German repudiation of the Treaty of Brest-Litovsk with Russia; German troops withdrawn behind pre-war borders in the East.
- Forfeiture of the German East African colony.
- The blockade of German ports remained in effect for an indefinite period.

Gasps were heard from the German delegation as the severe French armistice terms were read. Realizing the precarious situation of their retreating troops, Germany asked for an immediate ceasefire. The request was rejected. It was November 8; the Allies had decided to await the numerically correct date of November 11, and to have the ceasefire and the armistice announced at the eleventh hour on that date. Thus, World War I would end in the eleventh month on the eleventh day at the eleventh hour, satisfying some hidden psychological urge of the French military leaders. But the troops would not be told; fighting and slaughter of the innocent would continue. How many unsuspecting soldiers went to their death in the interim? It was quite obvious from this playing with dates and time that the French were not inclined to be magnanimous.

The tragedy is that Germany complied with the Americans request to abandon its centuries-old monarchy, then did not get an armistice based upon the generous terms offered by Wilson. President Wilson's promise to engage in a negotiated settlement with the new German republic was dashed when vengeful France took control of armistice arrangements.

Germany also expected that with the armistice the blockade that had caused so much suffering to German families would be lifted. But, tragically the blockade was maintained until the summer of 1919 and even extended into the Baltic Sea after the armistice, depriving the Germans of a meager supply of seafood. This final angry act by the Allied forces was spiteful and cruel, as it contributed to more starving children and civilian deaths, embittering the German people. The blockade was removed and food allowed into the stricken nation only when the Treaty of Versailles was signed seven months later in June 1919.[2]

The Allied refusal to remove the blockade, the severity of the armistice terms, the delayed ceasefire, the trickery over the terms of peace, the failure to grant a negotiated peace, the

---

1. Ibid., p. 450
2. Estimates of civilian deaths as a result of the British blockade range up to 760,000, which may be an inflated number. The illegal blockade did cause starvation as well as malnutrition over the four years of war. Such suffering caused an untold number of early deaths from disease.

haughty attitude of the French infuriated the Germans. This misbegotten treatment created a smoldering fire that would erupt into an inferno twenty years later. Imagine the actual scene at a German prisoner of war camp in November 1918:

> Fifteen miles from the Austrian border near the little town of Traunstein lay a great barbed wire compound confining thousands of Russian prisoners. News of the armistice made little difference to the garrison; the routine of guarding continued in the deep snow. Corporal Adolph Hitler did his accustomed stand in the wooden sentry box that night. What went on in that dark mind, how he brooded, whether he already plotted and planned to avenge the defeat of Germany, is not of report.[1]

WILSON'S CONFESSIONAL VS. THE EUROPEAN BUFFET

On the morning of November 11, 1918, President Woodrow Wilson made a jubilant victory announcement to the American people. The president's message said, "The Armistice was signed this morning. Everything for which America fought has been accomplished. It will be our fortunate duty to assist by example"[2]

Certainly, the significance of this statement was lost for most Americans; they were simply overjoyed that the long brutal nightmare was over. What did the president mean when he said that America would "assist by example?" Wilson had allowed the ship of state to run aground on the shoals of a European war; that misadventure could not be undone. Wilson surely realized the tragic detour America had taken in going to war in Europe; he was now straining to find a suitable role for the exceptional nation to play at war's end. It may be that Wilson even had personal regrets about his venture in the trenches of France and was looking for salvation at the peace conference. How could the loss of over one hundred thousand American servicemen be justified?

In his victory message the President also expressed satisfaction that "Everything for which America fought has been accomplished." Did that mean that "the world had been made safe for democracy?" And, even more hopefully, that the Wilsonian prophesy, "this is a war to end all wars," would come true? In February 1918, the President had warned the Allied powers that in this war, "There shall be no annexations, no contributions, no punitive damages."[3] And later in the year he gave assurances to Germany that any settlement would be based on his non-punitive peace terms — The Fourteen Points.

These visionary statements were calculated to raise the expectations of the American people, as well as cautioning the Allies that the conclusion of this war would not be business as usual. Wilson wrote to his confidante, Colonel Edward House: "When the war is over we can force them [the Allies] to our way of thinking, because by that time they will, among other things, be financially in our hands."[4] Thus, in Wilson's mind, the United States would control the peace conferences through the debts incurred by the Allies.

---

1. Ibid., p. 455
2. Ibid., p. 453
3. Wallbank, *Civilization: Past and Present*, p. 446
4. Kissinger, *Diplomacy*, p. 224

To force their hands, in December 1916, Wilson called for the Allied powers to disclose their war aims; he invited them to the "Wilson confessional." But, from across the Atlantic came some dissembling and considerable silence; Britain and France were not interested in confessing to the world, or to Wilson. Seizing the initiative, President Wilson addressed Congress in January 1918, revealing his Fourteen Points for the first time. His concluding comments in that address about the place of Germany in the post-war world are especially significant:

> We grudge her [Germany] no achievement or distinction of learning or of enterprise such as have made her record very bright and very enviable. We do not wish to injure her or to block in any way her legitimate influence or power. We do not wish to fight her either with arms or with hostile arrangements of trade if she is willing to associate herself with us and the other peace-loving nations of the world in covenants of justice and law and fair dealing. We wish her only to accept a place of equality among the peoples of the world...."[1]

Having observed four years of total war and the slaughter produced by modern weapons, Wilson perceived the urgency of ending the Folly of War. If the American entrance into the war had been a mistake, perhaps, somehow Wilson could recover his losses by transforming international relations. Wilson's sanctimonious personal behavior should not blind us to the wisdom of his insight about the need to end the practice of modern warfare. The president's own peace proposal contained no recriminations, no War Guilt clause, no reparations, no stripping of German economic substance, no unilateral disarmament, no slicing off of chunks of German territory. Although the United States entered the war as a belligerent against Germany, the young nation was an Associated power, a position that afforded the nation the opportunity to mediate the peace. In this, Wilson was following in the footsteps of a Nobel Peace Prize recipient, President Theodore Roosevelt, who mediated the Russo-Japanese War. Having no permanent friendships or animosities, with no entangling alliances, with a hand of conciliation for all, the United States would regain something of its 19th century role as the Promised Land, not the Crusader State. George Washington, Thomas Jefferson and John Quincy Adams would have been delighted with Wilson's efforts to re-capture America's past foreign policy.

To the Congress and the nation on January 18, 1918, the president divulged his vision of a fair and just settlement of World War I. His Fourteen Points were as follows:

1. Open covenants openly arrived at, nullifying any secret treaties.

2. Freedom of the Seas — so neutral nations will not be dragged into wars to defend their rights on the High Seas.

3. Free trade and equal access to markets — ending trade barriers.

4. General reduction of armaments — by all nations.

5. Impartial adjustment of colonial claims — with special consideration to the wishes of colonial people.

6-8 German evacuation of Russia, Belgium and France.

9. National boundaries of Italy established.

10-13 Self-determination of the people of the Austro-Hungarian Empire, Serbia, Romania, Montenegro, Poland and Turkey.

14. The creation of a League of Nations to keep the peace.

---

1. Ibid., p. 225

President Wilson's proposal was the most ambitious program for revolutionizing international relations since the creation of the modern state system in 1648. It was a philosophical statement — a program of goals and objectives, not an operational manual. It has provoked derision from those who claim to be "hardheaded realists," for they say it lacked an awareness of how national power and interests govern affairs of state. But just how is that so? Free and open global trading is now the mantra of nearly all nations, and national leaders would never consider making treaties in secret anymore. Britain objected to the freedom of the seas clause and the idea of interference in their colonial empire. But, by mid-century the British didn't have to worry about their empire; it was gone! And the world is a better place not having to deal with the constant British interference with freedom of the seas. National power and interests would remain extant, but restrained in Wilson's world. Can anyone deny that the world would be a safer and more stable if all armaments were reduced and all nuclear weapons were abolished?

A centerpiece of the Wilsonian program was self-determination, allowing people to create their own ethnic-based nation, rather than have national boundaries drawn by "statesmen" in the foreign affairs offices in Paris, London or elsewhere. Although drawing national boundaries along ethnic lines is a task fraught with complexities, how else would the new state lines be drawn? It would not seem an improvement to have Prince Metternich, Otto von Bismarck or Catherine the Great emerge to do the drawing of national borders.

Wilson's noble aspirations clashed with the land-grubbing wartime aims of the Allies. All Allied powers had harbored the desire for "territorial adjustments" prior to the war, although all had muted these dreams in order to display their innocent disinterest in such advantageous objectives. During the war, in secret conclaves, all Allied powers had cut deals to ensure at the war's end they would gorge themselves at the "European buffet." The "secret treaties" of 1915 and 1916 gave assurance that their appetites would be satisfied. The table was set and the lunch counter appeared thusly:

Russia — Annexation of Constantinople and the Turkish Straits

Italy — African colonies, Austrian Tyrol, Adriatic Coast of the Balkans

France — Alsace-Lorraine and Greater Syria

Britain — Palestine, Kuwait, Greater Iraq and German colonies in the Pacific

Japan — German colonies in China and the Pacific

These mercenary deals were kept secret from the world until copies of the documents were found in the Russian czar's vaults by V. I. Lenin's revolutionary government. Lenin gleefully divulged these selfish deals to the world in 1917. To the communist world this confirmed their belief that World War I was a "capitalist-imperialist" venture and nothing more. Indeed, to any fair-minded person, the Allied hypocrisy in allegedly fighting a war against the evils of "German imperialism and autocracy" was revealed for all to see. After the diplomats had fumbled their way into this conflagration, the war had far more to do with Allied desire for territory than for the protection of their "way of life." Britain's sanctimonious cries about Germany invading Belgium were now exposed for all to see — mere hypocrisy. London, more than Berlin, was after loot.

The "secret treaty" war aims, as originally conceived, were actually quite modest, as they were arranged early in the war in 1915 and 1916, before the nations' blood turned hot. Towards the end of the war, as the terrible slaughter sunk in, the stakes had increased. Great Britain by

1918 developed a virulent case of Germanophobia and sought to weaken and dismember the "Huns," rather than merely re-establishing a balance of power on the continent. To this end Germany was to lose its battle fleet. Russia also increased its demands, as it wanted to annex all of Poland. France, who always saw a united Germany as a menace, grasped the opportunity to permanently eliminate the unified German State on its eastern border. The French goals were to create a buffer area along the Rhine River, disarm their neighbor and demand financial compensation from the losers.

The scramble for territory even among the Allies became intense as claims began overlapping with claims, personality clashing with personality. The erstwhile Allies, Italy and Serbia, nearly came to war over competing claims along the Dalmatian coast. Japan and the United States saw differing needs in China. Britain and France eventually came to disagree over how much Germany should be weakened. The British-French dispute became personal when George Clemenceau accused Lloyd George of telling false stories about him. Lloyd George, possessed of a quick temper, accosted the elderly Frenchman, grabbing him by the collar and asking for an apology. Wilson, always the "peacemaker," stopped the scuffling but Clemenceau was deeply insulted. Reverting to an early age when dueling settled such manly conflicts, he asked Lloyd George to step out on the "field of honor." The Tiger offered the Welshman a choice of pistols or swords! Even during peace discussions among the victors, there was quarreling. It was a bad omen. The clearest indication of what a German post-war world would look like after a victory of the Central Powers was the Treaty of Brest-Litovsk imposed by Germany upon Russia. The German Army was victorious in the eastern front by the winter of 1917-1918, as the new revolutionary nation, soon to be known as the Soviet Union, dropped out of the war. In January 1918, Lenin, the Soviet leader, agreed to disastrous concessions to Germany, losing 66 million people and over 500,000 square miles of territory, nearly all of European Russia. German annexations from old Russia were astounding: Finland, Estonia, Latvia, Russian Poland, and a protectorate over the Ukraine were established. Russia ceased to be a European nation, as their border was moved back towards Asia where they had been three hundred years before. Germany stood astride Eastern Europe like a colossus in early 1918.

President Wilson had attempted to re-capture his lost honor and ensure the purity of the cause by offering a confessional for the greedy European powers. But in the end, all supplicants had failed to appear; they were gorging themselves at the European buffet.

THE TREATY OF VERSAILLES — 1919

The Paris Peace conference, the most famous peace conference in over one hundred years, convened with 37 nations represented. But in reality, the proceedings were governed by the leaders of the United States, France and Great Britain: President Wilson, Premier Georges Clemenceau, and Prime Minister Lloyd George. The new German Weimar Republic, was not allowed to participate in the conference, despite the fact that Wilson had committed the Allies to a negotiated peace. The Weimar Republic had been created prior to the Armistice at the express insistence of the American governments. But, in the winter of 1918-1919 with the Allied blockade still in place, and Germany receiving handouts from benevolent nations like America, and with its new republic functioning, a peace treaty was dictated to the German nation. This would be a victor's peace — a *Diktat*. American General Tasker Bliss, who was assisting the President during the conference, wrote to his wife that "the wars are not over."[1] General Bliss was right; there would be a twenty-year hiatus, then it would resume in a more dreadful form.

World War I was a tragedy at each stage as it unfolded: the diplomats were unable to avert a catastrophe in the summer of 1914; the generals in the wartime years were unable to conclude the war in a conventional manner, and in 1919, the statesmen were unprepared to create a workable peace for a new European world. Qualities of the statesmen — vision, creativity, benevolence, empathy — escaped the politicians of that age. Perhaps the ugliness and horror of war so erodes the sensibilities that an intelligent vision cannot follow in war's wake.

The conference and the resulting treaty were the result of a six-months long tug-of-war among three contending forces: the Frenchman Clemenceau, abrupt and dictatorial whose hatred and fear of Germany knew no bounds and who wanted to dismember the German state; Wilson, the idealist, whose hope was to create a new international order with German involvement; and Lloyd George whose views wavered from his recent political campaign slogan of "squeezing Germany until the pips squeak," to later a concern that France would weaken Germany too much.

Those portions of the Treaty of Versailles dealing with Germany show the astounding success of the Frenchman Clemenceau, as Germany was dealt with in a severe manner. Germany was stripped of territory in the homeland and all overseas colonies, disarmed, humiliated, blamed for the war and forced to pay war costs of the western Allies. President Wilson's rhetoric about treating the Germans as equals in the family of nations, and of not injuring them, or of not creating harmful economic conditions, had been discarded. The punishment meted out on Germany is as follows:

- Seven million Germans were sliced from their homeland and placed in surrounding nations. Germany lost 13% of its pre-war territory.
- All overseas colonies were given to the Allied powers. (Imperialism was "evil" unless it was Allied imperialism!)
- The German Army was disarmed. It was allowed only 100,000 troops and its use of weapons was severely restricted. Tanks and heavy artillery were forbidden.
- The German Navy was disbanded. (The fleet was to be taken by the British but as it sailed into Scapa Flow in Scotland, the astonished British watched helplessly as the German sailors scuttled the entire German fleet.)
- There would be no German air force.
- All German rivers and canals were to be internationalized.
- The Rhine River towns of Cologne, Koblenz, and Mainz were to be occupied by French forces for 5-10-15 years respectively.
- The Right Bank (east bank) of the Rhine River was to be de-militarized thirty miles inland into Germany.
- Germany was assessed reparations for the cost of the war, even including paying for pensions of French veterans. The total bill came to over $30 billion.
- Germany was assigned the moral and legal responsibility for World War I in the War Guilt Clause of the document.

The French were relentless in their efforts to reduce the German presence along the Rhine River. Essentially, Clemenceau had hoped to create a neutralist Confederation of the

---

1. Marshall, *World War I*, p. 468

Rhine, thereby forming a buffer state between France and Germany. The Allied occupation of the industrial areas known as the Saar and the Ruhr, the occupation of the river towns and adjacent areas all suggested a re-creation of the old 19th century Rhine Confederation. Clemenceau argued that France needed a zone of safety against the Germans, very much as Britain and America used the oceans as its zone of safety. Clemenceau asserted: "To ask us [France] to give up occupation [of the Rhineland] is like asking England and the United States to sink their fleet of battleships."[1]

The post-war conferences that dealt with the breakup of the German, Ottoman and Austro-Hungarian Empires had the daunting task of creating new nations in place of the defunct Empires. The map of Central and Eastern Europe, plus much of the Near East, had to be redrawn. Utilizing Wilson's concept of ethnic self-determination, the delegates drew boundaries for over one dozen nations; with the stroke of a pen countries from the Baltic to the Persian Gulf were brought into existence — from Finland and Estonia in the north to Kuwait and Iraq in the south. The spontaneity and the power exercised giddied the mind. There had been nothing like it since the creation week (4004 BC ??) at the dawn of written history.

The geopolitical forces of Eastern Europe had changed in the space of a few weeks. While before the war Germany, on its eastern border, faced the formidable Russian Empire, now it rubbed shoulders with several smaller, weaker nations, all of whom faced an uncertain future. The whole of Eastern Europe took on the appearance of a precariously balanced column of dominoes, trapped between Germany and the Soviet Union. These new or reformed nations, from the Baltic Sea to the Mediterranean Sea, would eventually be at the mercy of national revivals in Germany and the Soviet Union. That revival would arrive in less than twenty years.

Poland, newly created after a 150-year interruption, was especially vulnerable as it contained three million Germans and was granted 260 square miles of German territory. In order to provide Poland with a seaport on the Baltic Sea, a corridor was sliced through German-Prussian lands. This Polish Corridor gave Poland a seacoast town, but in the process dismembered Germany, leaving East Prussia separated from the main body of Germany. This unwholesome arrangement would last twenty years — until 1939 when World War II began.

Wilson received the hosannas of millions of European citizens, as they saw him as the George Washington of their newly-created nations. Poland, Czechoslovakia, Yugoslavia all would go through their own revolutionary wars and conduct constitutional conventions, all in a few glorious months, thanks to the Wilsonian idea of national self-determination. It was fully expected that each Eastern European nation would replicate the American experience, arriving on the scene fully equipped with perfectly formed borders and a functioning democratic system. It was not to be. Not only was there no tradition of democratic self-government in the area, but the intermixture of people made the principle of national self-determination impracticable. As one historian pointed out:

> It was impossible to draw boundaries to conform to national lines. More people than before 1914 lived under governments of their own nationality but many of the dissatisfied nationalities in the old empires became dissatisfied minorities of the new states.[2]

---

1. Kissinger, *Diplomacy*, p. 234
2. Zara Steiner, "The Peace Settlement," in Hew Strachan, ed., *World War I: A History*, p. 301

This idealist effort was really an attempt to apply classic liberal American notions in a region of the world where it fit poorly. The dilemma created for Poles trapped in Germany is illustrated in this lament by a young Polish-German boy:

If I say my prayers in German, my father beats me.
If I say my prayers in Polish, my teacher beats me.
If I don't say my prayers at all, my priest beats me.[1]

The financial impact of the Treaty of Versailles on Germany was onerous. The $32 billion reparations bill charged to Germany, most of which went to France, would mean that Germany owed France $5700 every minute for decades. Some accountants calculated that the final bill would not be paid until 1988! Reparations assessed against Germany for damage caused during the war were bloated to include not just reparations for destruction of the French and Belgium countryside, but pensions for war veterans of the Allied armies. The infamous War Guilt Clause and the bloated reparations bill combined the worst of the idealist's moralism with the realist's vengeance, as the concept of moral guilt was paired with the French desire for revenge. It was a potent and destructive package, one that would haunt the world for years to come.

But, the wherewithal to easily make such payments had been taken from the Germans. Much of Germany's pre-war coal and ore mines were stripped from them and given to France and Poland. Germany needed 110 million tons of coal yearly to operate its industrial, utility, and domestic plant, but the emasculation of their industry left them with only 30 million tons. Repayment of this reparation bill was a financial impossibility — and so it was not paid in full. Still this reparation bill would be a small down payment on the financial costs of that horrid war; the total bill for World War I came to over $200 billion.

In late April 1919, German representatives were invited to Paris to review the Treaty. The housing accommodations provided by the Allied powers were common, Spartan dwellings surrounded by barbed wire fences. In view of the severity of the treaty, perhaps the lodging was appropriate. Germany was to receive a copy of the Treaty on May 7, the fourth anniversary of the sinking of the Lusitania. Upon reviewing the Treaty, the German delegation was stunned by the harshness of the document and insulted by the War Guilt Clause, for it assigned the sole responsibility for the war on the Central Powers. The controversial clause read:

The Allied and Associated Governments affirm and Germany accepts the responsibility of Germany and her allies for causing all the loss and damage to which the Allied and Associated Governments and their nationals have been subjected as a consequence of the war imposed upon them by the aggression of Germany and her allies.[2]

The German delegation balked at the severity of the terms, but the ever-present blockade and the specter of a resumption of the war left them no recourse. They contented themselves with verbal outrage at the ignominy: "It is demanded of us that we shall confess ourselves to be the only ones guilty of war.... We are far from declining any responsibility...but we energetically deny that Germany and its people...were alone guilty...."[3]

On June 28, the fifth anniversary of the assassination of Archduke Franz Ferdinand, the signing ceremony took place. (The Allies were obsessed with the significance of dates — the

---

1. Wallbank, *Civilization: Past and Present*, p. 412
2. Ibid., p. 448
3. Ibid.

numerology of: November 11, the Armistice; May 7, the *Lusitania* sinking; June 28, the assassination). The final ceremony took place in the Hall of Mirrors of the Palace of Versailles. Prior to signing the document, the leader of the German delegation spoke to the assembled delegates while seated. His comments were bitterly critical of the duplicity of the Allies in offering a negotiated peace in 1918, then confronting Germany with a *Diktat* in 1919. Clemenceau and the other Frenchmen were deeply offended by the German's performance, inasmuch as he remained seated during his verbal response. Clemenceau and the others took such informality as a personal insult. Only later was it revealed that his legs were shaking so violently that he could not stand.

As the Germans departed the hall, one was heard to say, "What will history say of this?" To which Clemenceau retorted, "It will not say that Belgium invaded Germany."[1] Deeply offended by it all, the German foreign minister refused to sign the document. It was an ominous start to the post-war peace of Europe. An American delegate placed the scene in historical perspective:

> When the Germans had signed and the great Allied Powers had done so, the cannon began to boom. I had a feeling of sympathy for the Germans who sat there quite stoically. It was not unlike what was done in ancient times, when the conqueror dragged the conquered at the chariot wheels. To my mind, it is out of keeping with the new era which we profess an ardent desire to promote. I wish it could have been more simple and that there might have been an element of chivalry, which was wholly lacking. The affair was elaborately staged and made as humiliating to the enemy as it well could be.[2]

The exclusion of Germany, Austria-Hungary and Russia from all treaty proceedings cast the Treaty of Versailles as a "victor's peace" rather than a revolutionary document to form a new Europe. Much of the world — including the Allies — came to see it for what it was: a punitive document framed by illegitimate winners that fostered vengeful losers. The Folly of War.

WOODROW WILSON — MAN OF PEACE MAN OF GOD

President Wilson was the first president in the nation's history to deliver a war declaration message in person to the Congress, earlier presidents — Madison, Polk and McKinley — having sent their messages to be read by congressional officials. After delivering the message to the joint session and the crowded galleries, his words were greeted by thunderous applause and profuse congratulations. The Congress and assembled guests were ecstatic at his eloquence and thrilled with the challenge of war. But Wilson, silent and thoughtful, was stunned by their jubilant reaction. To his secretary he confided his thoughts: "My message today was a message of death for our young men. How strange it seems to applaud that."[3]

Wilson was a sensitive man who realized the awfulness of the decision he had made. More than most, he recognized the need to de-emphasize armaments and even eliminate the

---

1. Marshall, *World War I*, p. 474

2. Wallbank, *Civilization: Past and Present*, p. 449

3. Robert E. Osgood, "Ideals and Self-Interest in American Foreign Relations," in Jerald A. Combs, ed., *Nationalist, Realist and Radical: Three Views of American Diplomacy* (New York: Harper & Row, Publishers, 1972), p. 332.

scourge of modern war. The old European system of the balance of power had outlived its usefulness as weapons had become too powerful. The President envisioned an international system in which negotiations replaced military power and national interests would be subsumed in a community of interests. Wilson lectured that "There must be not a balance of power, but a community of power; not organized rivalries, but an organized common peace."[1]

The Fourteen Points were the American expression of faith in a world where decent men could live together in peace and dignity, and where both small and great nations would feel secure. Wilson hoped that America would remain true to its own values — doing the right thing, being concerned with others, adhering to a moral compass. This humanitarian impulse was to be directed toward reform of the international system. Henceforth, national disputes would be mediated in the League of Nations, rather than on the battlefield, and if nations transgressed, a League of Nations police force would intervene.

The quest to eliminate violence had been the hallmark of all decent societies. Wilson was simply taking that issue to the international level when he asserted that, "Peace is the healing and elevating influence of the world and strife is not."[2] If violence could be eliminated on the personal level, the neighborhood level, and the level of cities and states, why not at the international level? By now, it is taken for granted that personal violence, or violence perpetrated by family upon family, or clan against clan must not be tolerated; but removing war from the international agenda would be a challenging effort, and Wilson faced derision from skeptics.

In an address to the Congress on Armistice Day, November 11, 1918, Wilson spoke of the divine vindication of universal principles and a call to greater duties ahead. Later he spoke of the nation's universal duty: "We are about to give order and organization to this peace not only for ourselves but for the other people of the world..."[3] But, the nobility of his vision was marred by the flaws in his character and the plebeian nature of his mind. As with so many intellectuals, he could envision the large picture and describe the abstract, but could not create the operational plan, nor could he utilize others to aid in its development. His intellectual and personal difficulties began at home as a boy.

The greatest influence on his life was his father, Dr. Joseph Wilson, a Presbyterian minister who Woodrow later referred to as "that incomparable man." Thomas Woodrow Wilson — Tommy —was a sluggish learner as a boy, having trouble reading until he was eleven, but the Reverend was relentless in demanding excellence from the slow pupil. A severe Calvinist atmosphere surrounded the young boy as he learned that the Christian life was a constant struggle against evil; no compromises were tolerable. Surrendering to others forces was a sign of weakness, as was any personal introspection. Wilson's father lectured against a close evaluation of one's actions. "In short, dearest boy, do not allow yourself to dwell upon yourself...."[4] or one might add, on any analysis of others. Years later, during a discussion about the "causes" of World War I, Wilson's comments astounded his listeners: "With the objects and causes of the war we are not concerned. The obscure foundations from which its stupendous flood has burst

---

1. Kissinger, *Diplomacy*, p. 51.

2. www.allthingswilliam.com/presidents/wilson.html

3. Robert E. Osgood, "Ideals and Self-Interest in America's Foreign Relations," in Jerald A. Combs, ed., *Three Views of American Diplomacy*, p. 332.

4. John G. Stoessinger, *Crusaders and Pragmatists: Movers of Modern American Foreign Policy* (New York: W. W. Norton and Company, 1979), p. 9.

forth we are not interested to search for or explore."[1] This is an astonishing statement for a former university professor! But, it was recognized early that the young Wilson had an ordinary mind and he was encouraged not to analyze. He was guided by an indomitable moral compass from a higher Authority. Logic, facts, analysis, reevaluation all were shunned; revelation was the only true guide.

As a young man Wilson took up the study of law, but lacking an analytical mind, he abandoned in that endeavor. Instead, he pursued an academic career and with the publication of his book, *Congressional Government*, secured a political science teaching position at Princeton University. In 1902 he was appointed president of Princeton University, but eventually ran afoul of Deans who opposed some of his plans. Wilson turned minor academic disputes into crusades; his antagonistic personality and his indomitable will created numerous confrontations. Eventually his call for an opponent's resignation backfired and he was asked to leave the presidency.

Wilson's contentious nature did not deter the Democratic Party bosses from asking him to run for governor of New Jersey, an office that he won in 1910. Two years later he received another promotion when he became the presidential nominee of the Democratic Party. Due to a split in the Republican Party, Wilson was elected president in 1912 with only 42% of the national popular vote.

Wilson came to the White House with only two years of experience in practical politics and government. No other major world power so casually elevates a novice to national leadership. Wilson had spent seventeen years as a college teacher, an occupation that involves conducting "autocratic" lectures to impressionable, compliant youths. He then spent eight tumultuous years as a college president, a tenure that ended with his forced resignation. Whereupon he was elected governor of New Jersey, a position he used to gallantly fight the big city bosses; a mere two years later he was President of the United States. None of the phases of his life prepared him for the intellectual and personal demands of being an American president who would revolutionize international relations.

His indomitable spirit, sense of megalomania and personal commitment to a religious experience is illustrated by his insensitive comment to his own supporters after the successful 1912 election: "I wish it clearly understood that I owe you nothing. Remember God ordained that I should be the next president of the United States."[2] (George W. Bush would make similar comments of his "providential" election in the year 2000.)

Wilson saw himself as an emissary of God and woe to anyone who interfered with God's mission. The history of the exceptional nation — the United States — and the career of Woodrow Wilson had become intertwined, each giving evidence of the unfolding of God's plan. The centuries old concept of the "divine right of kings" was being revived in the American republic. To the astounded European diplomats in 1919, he claimed to be able to improve on His plan. Wilson instructed: "Why has Jesus Christ so far not succeeded in inducing the world to follow his teachings in these matters? It is because he taught the ideal without devising any practical means of attaining it. That is why I am proposing practical schemes to carry out His aims."[3]

---

1. Ibid., p. 13.
2. Ibid., p. 10
3. Ibid., p. 21

Wilson brought dozens of academics and bureaucratic experts with him to Paris in 1919, but made scant use of them. He refused to show his draft of the League of Nations covenant to anyone prior to his "revelation" of the plan at Versailles; apparently he wanted to be Christ's sole messenger. If his mind plumbed the theological depths, it only skimmed the surface of intellectual questions. His Fourteen Points pointed the way to a better world, but they offered little in the way of specific guideposts. John Maynard Keynes, the famous economist, commented on the President's intellectual failings:

> But in fact the President had thought out nothing.... He could have preached a sermon on any one of them [the Fourteen Points] or have addressed a stately prayer to the Almighty for their fulfillment; but he could not frame their concrete application to the actual states of Europe.[1]

What friends and adversaries saw as just plain stubbornness, Wilson perceived as dedication to the Divine Will. Once the President's mind was made up, it could not be changed. He frequently lectured Clemenceau and Lloyd George during the Paris conference, only to be "interrupted" with questions based on facts or logic. Interrupting the professor during a "lecture" strained relationships and Wilson responded by snapping, "Logic, Logic! I don't give a damn for logic."[2] He repeatedly compared himself to Christ, finally causing the exasperated Clemenceau to growl, "God had only Ten Commandments. Why does Mr. Wilson need Fourteen?" When advisors suggested that Clemenceau needed to discuss a matter with the president, Clemenceau replied: "Talk to Wilson? How can I talk to a fellow who thinks himself the first man for two thousand years who has known anything about peace on earth."[3]

Wilson's perception of himself as the emissary of God began to interfere with his emotional balance. When the United States delegation arrived in France, the President informed them that their nation was on an anointed mission, and he was the only leader who had a mandate to lead. "The men whom we are about to deal with do not represent their people,"[4] observed the President. In fact, Wilson's political party had just suffered a defeat in the congressional elections of November 1918, losing control of both houses of Congress. Wilson was a "limping" lame duck president. On the other hand, Clemenceau was just reaffirmed as Premier by a four to one vote in the French legislature, and Lloyd George's party had just won an overwhelming election victory. Wilson was losing touch with reality.

(There is evidence that Woodrow Wilson was in fact suffering from an illness at this time. Wilson experienced some fourteen bouts of emotional and physical collapse — indigestion, headaches, throbbing eyes, paralytic arm, leg pains, nervousness, temporary blindness, — which debilitated him during eight of his adult years. His irrational comments and confusion on many issues at the Paris Peace Conference may, in fact, have been caused by a nervous breakdown.)

John Maynard Keynes was a member of the British delegation at the Paris conference, and after observing Wilson in discussion with the other leaders came away unimpressed with the president's ability. Keynes commented that, "His mind was too slow and unresourceful to

---

1. John Maynard Keynes, "The Economic Consequences of the Peace," in Theodore P. Greens, ed., *Wilson At Versailles* (Boston: D. C. Heath and Company, 1957), p. 30.
2. Stoessinger, *Crusaders and Pragmatists*, p. 22.
3. Marshall, *World War I*, p. 468.
4. Harold Nicolson, "Peacemaking, 1919," in Theodore P. Greene, ed., *Wilson At Versailles*, p. 39.

be ready with any alternative."[1] Wilson would raise objections, dig in his heels and assert divine thoughts. But he was up against men with razor sharp minds who were accustomed to rigorous intellectual exchanges in parliaments. Wilson never could find a middle ground, never could offer a useful compromise or never save a plan from disaster. In the world of Woodrow Wilson, it was take it or leave it. When he presented the Treaty of Versailles to the United States Senate for their rejection or approval in 1919, this sense of absolutism was evident as he spoke to that august body. His final comment to the senators was: "The stage is set, the destiny disclosed. It has come about by no plan of our conceiving, but by the hand of God who has led the way. Accept or Reject."[2]

THE WAR AGAINST AUTOCRACY

Ardent supporters of American involvement in the war never failed to spout propaganda about the "autocratic" Prussian military regime, always presenting World War I as a struggle between "autocracy and democracy," in Secretary of State Lansing's words. Lansing despaired that Wilson might not grasp the fact that "German imperialistic ambitions threatened free institutions everywhere."[3]

But if it is true that the war was a struggle about freedom, the United States, when it entered the war in 1917, began fighting "fire with fire," using Prussian tactics at home to defeat the Prussian autocratic state overseas. During America's crusade to rid the world of autocracy, it undermined its own civil liberties. In striking against German militarism, it created a military society with the Conscription Act of June 3, 1917, which registered all men between the ages of 21 and 30, eventually drafting nearly three million. Whether the young man agreed with the goals of this war or not, did not matter. Uncle Sam decided that all young men who were physically fit would be required to offer their lives for their country. Over 125,000 young men did not return to a hero's welcome and to enjoy the fruits of their victory; they were buried in France. Governmental action of drafting young men for a war is in itself an act of desperation and failure. Any war that is clearly justified needs no government draft. Men whose country is actually threatened will respond enthusiastically; they will not need to be commandeered. It is only when a government pursues foreign adventures of doubtful value and cannot sell its war to the people, that a draft — forced conscription — becomes necessary.

So, the war against "autocracy" had come to the shores of America. Rose Stokes, an ordinary citizen, wrote a letter published in the Kansas City *Star* in which she enthused about munitions makers and bankers, condemning their war profits and expressing her dissent from the war. Rose's letter to the newspaper said: "No government which is for profiteers can also be for the people, and I am for the people while the Government is for the profiteers."[4] Rose was

1. John Maynard Keynes, "The Economic Consequences of the Peace," in Theodore P. Greene, ed., *Wilson At Versailles*, p. 30.
2. Stoessinger, *Crusaders and Pragmatists*, p. 24.
3. Robert E. Osgood, "Ideals and Self-Interest in American Foreign Relations," in Jerald A. Combs, ed., *Three Views of American Diplomacy*, p. 313.
4. Ronald Shaffer, *America in the Great War: The Rise of the War Welfare State* (New York: Oxford University Press, 1991), p. 16.

arrested, tried and sentenced to ten years in prison; the judge scolded her and affirmed that free speech is only for words that are "friendly to the government, friendly to the war, friendly to the policies of the government."[1] President Wilson urged the Justice Department to begin legal proceedings against any publication critical of his war policies and specifically selected the Kansas City *Star* for prosecution on the grounds of ... TREASON.

Such ignominies were not isolated cases. The famous author Upton Sinclair was arrested in California for reading the Bill of Rights, and in New Jersey, the Leftist activist and founder of the American Civil Liberties Union, Roger Baldwin, was arrested for reading the United States Constitution, both at an anti-war rallies. The Socialist politician and anti-war leader Eugene Debs spent three years in prison for protesting the war in a speech. (Debs ran for president in 1920 and while in prison received nearly one million votes.) And the war in America against "autocracy" continued:

> A Wisconsin official received a thirty-month sentence for criticizing a Red Cross fund-raising drive; a Hollywood producer, a ten-year sentence for a film that portrayed atrocities committed by British troops during the Revolutionary War. All told as many as 8,000 to 10,000 Americans faced imprisonment, official suppression, deportation, or mob violence during the war.[2]

The American darling, Teddy Roosevelt, continued the assault on democratic liberties when he asserted that Senator Robert LaFollette, founder of the Progressive Party and opponent of the war, should be hanged for treason. Wartime hysteria turned rampant as Americans forbade the teaching of the German language in schools and warmed their hands in winter to the burning of books by Germans or about Germany. So emotionally distraught did they become that German measles became Liberty measles, sauerkraut was known as Liberty cabbage. The glorious classical music of Mozart, Beethoven, Bach, and other German composers was banned in public performance.

(These hysterical actions have been the subject of derision throughout the century as citizens in the calm of peacetime reflect on the panic-stricken actions taken in 1917 and 1918. But the smugness of calmer times turned once again to hysteria in 2003 as Americans, angered at France's reluctance to approve of the war against Iraq, began calling French fries "Freedom fries.")

Mobs ruled some city streets. Robert Prager, a German-American youth in St. Louis, was seized by a mob of youths, stripped of his clothes, wrapped in an American flag, and marched through the city streets. Robert was eventually murdered in the streets of St. Louis by the inflamed mob, simply because he had a German surname. Prager's murderers were tried but acquittal of any crime. This heinous act was deemed a "patriotic murder," therefore excusable during wartime.

The public hysteria that accompanied the war prompted the Congress to legalize public anger toward Germans. In the summer of 1917, Congress passed the Espionage Act meting out fines of $10,000 and 20 years in prison for obstructing the draft, aiding the enemy by making false reports to aid the Germans or inciting rebellion. Later, the Congress passed the Sedition Act that prohibited disloyal, profane, scurrilous or abusive remarks about the American form of government, the flag or the uniform of the military. These laws prompt one to ask a pertinent

---

1. Ibid., p. 16-17.
2. Bruce D. Porter, *War and the Rise of the State* (New York: Free Press, 1994), p. 273.

question: Could a political candidate conduct an election campaign in opposition to Wilson's war? Would such a campaign in the midst of war be disloyal, rebellious, obstructionist? Is an anti-war candidate aiding the enemy? When war is declared, democracy dies.

With increased demands for food around the world, Wilson's government instituted meatless and wheatless days. A national government board took control of the railroads and another board regulated wages and hours of workers. The income tax was begun as a wartime measure and the coffers of the government bulged, the treasury swelling 400% in two years. From a pre-war low of 6%, the highest income tax rates were quickly raised to 77% by the end of the war. Still the government needed more money for the war effort, and to that end sold Liberty Bonds to patriotic Americans. Celebrities campaigned for the government's war effort, using their fame to sell the war and its war bonds. Charlie Chaplin's tawdry appeal bears repeating: "The Germans are at our door. We've got to stop them. And we will stop them if you buy Liberty Bonds! Remember, each bond you buy saves a soldier's life — a mother's son! and will bring this war to an early victory."[1] German Army officers would have been astounded to learn that they were at "America's door", for they were actually finding it impossible to get to the door of Paris, France.

William McAdoo, the Secretary of the Treasury and Wilson's son-in-law, had a more ominous view of the Liberty bond drive: "A man who can't lend his government $1.25 per week at the rate of 4% interest is not entitled to be an American citizen."[2] Perhaps had the war lasted a bit longer, those who failed to buy Liberty Bonds would have been tried for treason. The "War to make the world safe for democracy" had turned on itself. As the sociologist, Robert Nisbet said, "the West's first experiment with totalitarianism...came with the American war under Woodrow Wilson."[3]

THE FOLLY OF WAR

President Wilson faced a series of dilemmas between 1914 and 1920 that he was unable to resolve to his personal satisfaction or for the benefit of the nation. Even an adroit statesman might have found a happy resolution beyond his reach; but Wilson, with a rigid temperament and an obtuse mind, failed abjectly. The dilemmas were:

- Neutrality crisis in the summer of 1914 — The President's first response to the war in Europe was to proclaim American neutrality, but before the summer was out Wilson began backtracking as he allowed and even encouraged loans to and trade with Britain that eventually entrapped America.
- British-German tug-of-war in 1914-1916 — President Wilson stressed that the United States would hold both sides "strictly accountable" for adherence to neutral rights, but this was a fig leaf to conceal his and the financial community's actual support for Britain. He never pressed the British on the issue of neutral rights as he did Germany. His deceitful actions in the Lusitania sinking have been noted.

1. J. M. White, "Propaganda and the Mobilization of Consent," in Hew Strachan, ed., *World War I: A History*, p. 223.
2. Nash, *The American People*, p. 744.
3. Robert Nisbet, *Twilight of Authority* (New York: Oxford University Press, 1975), p. 183.

- Belligerency crisis of the spring of 1917 — When Germany forced Wilson's hand in the spring of 1917 with its Unrestricted Submarine Warfare campaign, America could have responded to the German grievance with naval power only to protect American shipping rights in the Atlantic Ocean. Instead, the President sent an unprepared Army to Europe to engage in combat, subjecting the troops to casualties that served little significant military purpose. By separating the American Expeditionary Forces from the experienced Allied troops, the President exposed the raw draftees to murderous attacks by battle-hardened German forces.

- Armistice crisis of the fall 1918 — When German peace feelers were sent directly to Washington in October, bypassing the French and British, Wilson was able to initiate peace talks on his terms, a hopeful development. But by November, the French undermined this effort and imposed a draconian armistice upon Germany. Wilson never again gained control of the peace talks.

- Treaty of Versailles crisis of 1919 — Wilson entered the diplomatic arena at Versailles with a vision for the future, but no operational plan. His goal of a world with restraints on national war-making power was honorable; but his personal inability to engage in meaningful negotiations doomed his plan.

- United States Senate and Treaty crisis of 1919-1920 — Again, Wilson found it impossible to compromise and his beloved child, the League of Nations, died stillborn on the floor of the United States Senate.

- Struggle to save democracy in America in 1917-1920 — Wilson's pathos reached the depths as he attacked the civil liberties of anti-war protestors at home, harassing, restraining, arresting, convicting and imprisoning those who disagreed with his war policies. The "war to make the world safe for democracy" turned the United States itself into an ugly, autocratic society.

When the war was over, the American people recognized the futility of this crusade, removed the Democratic Party from office and vowed never to return to Europe with its military force.

With the American Navy providing naval convoys across the Atlantic and the inexhaustible supply of industrial material and finances, an Allied victory was assured. Germany soon recognized that the American entrance into the war was turning the tide and asked for peace terms. But because of his own personal inadequacies, Wilson was unable and unwilling to make diplomatic use of this advantage. In April 1917, after the American declaration of war, British Foreign Secretary Lord Arthur Balfour came to Washington to discuss wartime strategy with the President, fully expecting him to withhold American forces, finances and supplies until certain benign peace terms were agreed upon. Balfour was astonished to learn that Wilson was not interested in making the use of American troops conditional upon American peace terms; Wilson expressed an interest only in winning the war in a military sense. Even when the Pope circulated a peace proposal in 1917 that would have concluded the war with "no victors and no vanquished," Wilson failed to respond. At every stage along the way, Wilson chose not to use the power and influence of America in any diplomatic way.

Instead of threatening the Allies by withholding loans and credits, or by cracking down on illegal munitions sales to Britain, or by an embargo against all belligerents, the President was content with simply throwing moral salvos across the Atlantic. The original idealist philosophy that Wilson espoused rejected the use of national power to achieve material goals. Thus, Wilson's idealism prevented him from forcing compliance from friend or foe. Having rejected the normal tools of international relations, Wilson was forced to use an unprepared Army to achieve a chimerical although noble goal — the end of all wars. Wilson always played the preacher, never the diplomat.

Wilson's actions were more like an Old Testament prophet than a modern statesman. President Wilson himself admitted to having a "one-track mind" and that track was always hurling moral thunderbolts, rather than discovering a workable solution. The famed diplomat and writer, Sir Harold Nicolson, observed that, "The collapse of President Wilson at the Paris Peace Conference is one of the major tragedies of modern history."[1] Wilson's unfortunate collapse actually began in 1914 and continued through the peace conference. Out of this mélange of emotional confusion, religious self-righteousness and pressures of the war, emerged the embryo of Militant Idealism.

Wilson's personal inadequacies were compounded by political sniping of his opponents. As the President was preparing to leave for Paris, Teddy Roosevelt launched one of his patented salvoes at Wilson:

> Our allies and our enemies, and Mr. Wilson himself, should all understand that Mr. Wilson has no authority whatsoever to speak for the American people at this time. His leadership has just been emphatically repudiated by them....[2]

While this attack by Roosevelt was vicious, foolish and unfounded, Wilson did present a delightful target to his opponents. He announced in 1914 that war was a calamity and no concern of ours, then in 1917 took the country into a war to save civilization. He piously proclaimed American neutrality, then undermined his own decisions with pro-Allied policies. He pontificated about the dangers of militarism, then built an immense Navy and began a conscription effort. He propounded a generous peace among "equals," then helped to mold peace terms that were a vengeful *Diktat*. He deluded himself that colonial mandates were not annexations, and that civilian damages for reparations could include veteran pensions. He imagined that there was no duplicity in promising Germany that there would be general disarmament following the war, but then disarmed only Germany. He warred on German autocracy, then created his own autocratic state in America. He staked all his dreams on the League of Nations, then suffered a debilitating illness that dashed all hopes for success. He wore the garb of an academic through much of his life, but chose instead at a critical moment to don the vestments of a Priest-Politician.

Post-war settlements should reflect the military realities that exist at war's end. When the Napoleonic Wars ended in 1815, the Army of the Russian Czar was camped in Paris and it was obvious who had won the war. Even so, in that war, the victorious allies allowed the French to participate in the formation of a new European map. When the Franco-Prussian War ended in 1871, Germany occupied Paris and justifiably dictated the peace terms from the Palace at Versailles. As the German Army walked triumphantly through the streets of Paris, no Parisian doubted who had been victorious.

But in 1918, the armies of France, Britain and the United States never set foot on German soil during the war; the "victorious" Allies never marched through the streets of Berlin, Munich

---

1. Harold Nicolson, "Peacemaking, 1919," in Theodore P. Greene, ed., *Wilson At Versailles*, p. 37.
2. Samuel F. Bemis, "The First World War and the Peace Settlement," in Theodore P. Greene, ed., *Wilson At Versailles*, p. 10.

or Frankfurt. It was not apparent to the German people that they had been defeated in battle. Yet, when the vengeful French had finished with the armistice and Treaty, it reflected not a close victory but an unconditional surrender. What France couldn't win on the battlefield, they stole at the peace table. And this foolish exploitation was accomplished primarily because of the looming presence of the United States. The European Allies used American financial power to "win" the war, then crafted a treaty that was out of balance with the military realities. Wilson had allowed America to be "used." Twenty years later, as America watched nervously from across the Atlantic, the Paris Peace settlement came unraveled. Illegitimate winners squared off against a vengeful loser.

As John Keynes pointed out, Wilson could preach a sermon and offer an eloquent prayer, but he could not lead the nation wisely into war, nor could he discover the path to a lasting peace. Keynes commented bitterly:

> The demon that Woodrow Wilson vainly fought was within himself. Tragedy, if it be not noble is not tragedy, and no one will deny to Woodrow Wilson the elements of nobility. Yet ...the very essence of statesmanship lies not in the grim endurance of preordained defeat, but rather the wisdom to know when to take occasion by the hand and by yielding the shadow to substance.[1]

Derisive comments swirled around the President about the Treaty: "a mere scramble for loot," "This is not peace; it is an armistice for twenty years." We are in for a high period, followed by a low period. Then there will be the devil to pay all around the world."

Herbert Hoover was in Paris when the first copies of the Treaty were distributed. He said he awakened before dawn, saw the Treaty and in consternation walked the streets of Paris. When he came upon John Maynard Keynes and General Jan Smuts from the British delegation, he found company in the two men. Hoover commented that, "We all agreed that it was terrible and we would do what we could...to make the danger clear."[2]

Throughout the years of war, Wilson was outmaneuvered by the Europeans; the final ignominy was the overly harsh strictures on Germany. At the end, Wilson played his final hand in the form of the League of Nations, for he hoped it would lead the way out of the vortex. The Covenant of the League of Nations promised "to guarantee international cooperation and to achieve international peace and security." Article X was the key to the League's peacekeeping ability. It stated:

> The Members of the League undertake to respect and preserve as against external aggression the territorial integrity and existing political independence of all Members of the League. In case of any such aggression or in case of any threat or danger of such aggression the Council shall advise upon the means by which this obligation shall be fulfilled.[3]

The League was incorporated into the Treaty of Versailles; they were tied together like tree and vine. Those Senators who regarded the treatment of Germany either too harsh or not harsh enough voted against the Treaty and the League. Some Senators who were determined to follow the tradition of neutrality opposed the Treaty and the League. Some Republicans smelled blood in the water and opposed the Treaty and the League simply because Wilson was a Dem-

---

1. Stoessinger, *Crusaders and Pragmatists*, p. 26-27.
2. Marshall, *World War I*, p. 474.
3. Wallbank, *Civilization: Past and Present*, p. 447.

ocrat, although many Republicans before the war had participated in the "League to Enforce Peace" which endorsed a league concept.

After losing so many battles along the way, Wilson decided to make his last stand on the Treaty and the League; on this he refused to compromise. The president hurled down the gauntlet to the United States Senate: "Accept or Reject." An amendment to the Charter of the League, reassuring several Senators about certain passages, would have gained the necessary votes for passage; Wilson refused to amend. His close friend and aide, Edward House, who Wilson said had been "the only one in the world to whom I can open my mind freely," was summarily dismissed and banished when he suggested that a compromise was in order.[1] As he was lying in bed convalescing after his stroke with the debate raging in the Senate, Wilson's wife urged that a revision in the text be offered. Wilson demurred in a touching, pitiful scene:

> He turned his head on the pillow. He took her hand. "Little girl, don't you desert me; that I cannot stand. Can't you see I have no moral right to accept any change in a paper I have already signed? It is not I who will accept it; it is the nation's honor that is at stake." his eyes were gleaming. "Better a thousand times to go down fighting than to dip your colors to a dishonorable compromise."[2]

World War I was the first great venture of America into European affairs and by nearly any measure it was a disaster. But, it is important to note that Woodrow Wilson failed because of the kind of man he was, not because his basic vision for a better world was flawed. His hopes for a world without war have become even more vital in the nuclear age. President Wilson should not be held entirely responsible for the eventual development of Militant Idealism, as he initially made efforts at reducing the scourge of modern arms.

It has been said that compromise is the art of the possible; Henry Clay is noted in American history as the Great Compromiser. Woodrow Wilson never tried to do the possible, for that was not "revealed" to him. He relied on hurling jeremiads from his White House perch, interspersed with buoyant optimism: "I have seen fools resist Providence before, and I have seen their destruction as it will come upon these again — utter destruction and contempt. That we shall prevail is as sure as God reigns."[3]

Europe and the world would have been better off had America remained on the sidelines in the Great War, allowing the two warring groups to negotiate a more agreeable compromise peace. Germany had been victorious in Eastern Europe and the entire Western Front had been fought on French-Belgian soil. Germany had never been invaded and the draconian peace terms imposed by France did not reflect the realties of the war. Out of this volatile mix came the anger and fury of Nazism and the false promises and terror of Communism in Russia.

---

1. Stoessinger, *Crusaders and Pragmatists*, p. 10.
2. Ibid., p. 26.
3. Ibid.

CHAPTER 6. WORLD WAR II: THE INFAMY OF PEARL HARBOR

AIR RAID, PEARL HARBOR — THIS IS NO DRILL

The Japanese convoy was steaming rapidly southward toward the Hawaiian Islands, heading for the United States Naval, Army and Air Force bases on the island of Oahu. The Japanese armada, consisting of six carriers, three cruisers, eight destroyers and assorted other vessels, had reached a point 250 miles north of the Islands. The morning light had not yet pierced the darkness of the North Pacific when swarms of maintenance men began readying the planes for their appointed tasks. The six large aircraft carriers slowly turned into the wind for easier take-offs. The first wave of planes was to launch at 6:00 AM — there were nearly two hundred torpedo planes, dive-bombers, and bombers. A second wave of bombers was on its way an hour and a half later, 360 aircraft in all. At 6:00 AM Commander Mitsuo Fuchida donned the traditional white headband and climbed into the lead plane. The battle flag was hoisted, whipping in the wind. It was Sunday morning, December 7, 1941. A day that would live in infamy, although perhaps for the wrong reasons.

Two hours earlier, the United States Army radar station located at the northernmost point on the main Hawaiian Island of Oahu had been opened by Privates George Elliot and Joseph Lockard. Radar was an innovation for the United States, and on the Island it was operated Sundays only from 4:00 AM to 7:00 AM. The British had already had operational radar for a year, but the Army on Hawaii had just recently received five sets, of which only one was fully operational; no technicians were provided for service or instruction. Radar, here, was a training device, not a warning system. London was protected by radar; Pearl Harbor was not.

At 7:00 AM the Army truck assigned to pick up the two privates had not arrived, so they decided to remain at the site. At 7:02 AM Elliot spotted some echoes on the screen; as he watched in amazement the screen filled with dots. At 7:06 AM the planes on the screen were 137 miles north of Oahu. When informed, the Fort Shafter information center expressed no alarm about the news, passing it off as an anomaly of the new system. The two privates continued to watch the screen: at 7:15 the planes were 92 miles north — at 7:25 they were 62 miles out — at

7:39, 22 miles north of the site. At 7:40 AM the Army truck arrived to take the two to "chow." Elliot and Lockard were riding to breakfast as Fuchida's lead plane swept overhead, southward toward Pearl Harbor.

Commander Fuchida caught a glimpse through the clouds of the lush green carpet below. This brought him up abruptly; the destination was approaching. He would have to give the long-awaited signal: "Surprise" or "Surprise Lost." He still hadn't received a report from the advance patrol planes, so he played a hunch; it would be "Surprise." He fired one shot out of his cockpit with his revolver, which meant that the torpedo planes would go in first before the smoke clogged the harbor, followed by the dive-bombers. As the planes peeled off to their assigned positions, Fuchida, thinking that his first pistol shot was not seen, fired again. But two shots were the signal for "Surprise Lost," indicating that the dive-bombers were to go first and soften the enemy before the torpedo bombers. Organization and plans vanished as both bomber squadrons jockeyed for positions to blast "Battleship Row."

Death reigned supreme over Oahu for two hours as the Japanese bombers had their nearly unmolested way at Pearl Harbor, Hickham Field, Schofield Barracks and other military installations. "Battleship Row" came under attack by torpedo planes just before 8 AM as seven low-wing planes took aim with 1000-pound explosives slung under each craft. The crew of the USS *Maryland* was preparing for morning colors when tragedy struck. On the foremast of the great ship was Seaman Lawrence McCutcheon, a seventeen-year-old from California. At about 7:52 AM, Lieutenant Jinichi Goto led the torpedo planes in the first attack on "Battleship Row." Racing in from the Diamond Head side of Ford Island, Goto took aim at the USS *Oklahoma*, which lay adjacent to the *Maryland*. Goto's torpedo slammed into the *Oklahoma*, then as his plane flew past the *Maryland*, he fired his machine guns. At that instant a bullet tore into Seaman McCutcheon's heart, killing him instantly; McCutcheon was the first casualty of the Pacific War.

At 8:10 AM the forward powder magazine of the battleship USS *Arizona* exploded killing most of its crew, entombing many in the bowels of the ship. Since that day, the USS *Arizona* has rested in the harbor at Pearl, a permanent memorial to the men who gave the ultimate sacrifice for their country. At the Arizona memorial, visitors can still see oil from the stricken ship bubbling up to the surface forming a small slick on the water; it is a touching scene, as it appears the ship is weeping for its human losses.

The fleet was on "low alert" that morning, but several ship gunners fired back at the attacking planes. Over 3000 rounds of ammunition were fired, destroying twenty-six Japanese aircraft and killing about fifty enemy aviators. Unfortunately, many unsuspecting civilians were killed in neighborhoods around Pearl Harbor by stray shells from anti-aircraft guns of the United States Navy. Heroism of American servicemen was not absent that morning as over one hundred medals were subsequently awarded. The actions of a gunner named Smith on one of the destroyers became famous, inspiring a World War II song. Smith's ammunition hoist jammed in the middle of the fight, and Smith was heard to cry out: "Oh, Lord! Oh, Lord! Make this ammunition hoist work just this once." His appeal for mechanical assistance from on High was heard; spotting a Japanese midget submarine, he destroyed it. The name of the famous World War II song: "Praise the Lord and Pass the Ammunition."[1]

---

1. Robert B. Stinnett, *Day of Deceit: The Truth About FDR and Pearl Harbor* (New York: Simon and Schuster - Touchstone, 2001), p. 245,247.

This was the first attack on American soil by a foreign nation since the Mexican War in the 1840s, and never had so many Americans been killed on the homeland in one day. There were 2,273 military personnel killed and 1,119 wounded. Nearly two hundred aircraft were destroyed and sixteen warships were never used again, but several of the battleships sustained only minor damage and were soon returned to service. Of the one hundred and one warships in the harbor, only sixteen suffered major damage. Fortunately, all three United States aircraft carriers were on maneuvers in the Pacific Ocean. It was a major tactical blunder by the Japanese to target the battleships rather than the carriers, as the carriers would play a more critical role in the Pacific War. And the Japanese also erred in not concentrating their fire on the oil storage facilities, the electric utilities, the dry docks and repair shops. Had these been targeted, the United States Navy would have had to withdraw from the Islands and return to San Diego, delaying recovery for months.

Throughout the 20th century, the Pacific Fleet had been based at San Diego, but in October 1940 President Roosevelt decided, against the judgment of naval officers, to move the base to the Hawaiian Islands. The commander of the Pacific Fleet, Admiral James O. Richardson, had two meetings with FDR during which he vigorously protested moving the base to the middle of the Pacific Ocean. Richardson expressed concern for the safety of the crew, the lack of fuel storage facilities and repair shops and the scarcity of housing and leisure activities. The Admiral asserted that the fleet was vulnerable to an enemy attack based over 2000 miles from the United States mainland, and only 3400 miles from Tokyo. Far from being a deterrent, the fleet would become a tempting target. At their last meeting on October 8, 1940, FDR was finally candid with Richardson as he disclosed his real motive in placing the Pacific Fleet at mid-Pacific. FDR said: "Sooner or later the Japanese would commit an overt act against the United States and the nation would be willing to enter the war."[1] The President was tempting the Japanese, or was he provoking them?

Admiral Richardson was equally blunt with the President: "Mr. President, senior officers of the Navy do not have the trust and confidence in the civilian leadership of this country that is essential to the successful prosecution of a war in the Pacific."[2]

Richardson was especially critical of the Naval Chief of Operation, Admiral Harold Stark, who went along with the President's plans. To Richardson, the Naval Chief was "professionally negligent" and derelict in carrying out orders when those orders were dangerous to the mission of the United States Navy.[3]

On February 1, 1941, Admiral Richardson was relieved of his command and replaced by Admiral Husband Kimmel. Admiral Kimmel was not next in line for promotion, but FDR selected him over several others because of his sterling reputation for energy and competence. Perhaps FDR also hoped that this favoritism toward Kimmel might earn the President some support among dissident naval officers. All senior naval officers recognized the precarious position of the fleet in mid-Pacific. Upon taking the command, Kimmel asserted that he was "in the firm belief that the Navy Department would supply me promptly with all pertinent infor-

---

1. Stinnett, p. 11; James O. Richardson, *On The Treadmill to Pearl Harbor* (Washington D. C.: Naval History Division, Department of the Navy, 1973), p. 427.
2. Stinnett, *Day of Deceit*, p. 10; Richardson, *On The Treadmill to Pearl Harbor*, p. 435.
3. Stinnett, p. 12.

mation available and particularly with all information that indicated an attack on the fleet at Pearl Harbor.[1]

It was well known in the Navy that FDR was "playing with fire" in placing the fleet at Pearl Harbor rather than in the more protected base at San Diego. Because the Navy was under-manned, this FDR tactic was like a prizefighter leading with his jaw. On December 7, 1941 the respective naval components of Japan and the United States were:[2]

	JAPAN	USA
Carriers	11	3
Battle ships	10	9
Cruisers	41	24
Destroyers	129	80
Submarines	67	56

The United States was outgunned in every naval category, the Japanese having over eighty warships more than the United States; in capital ships the Japanese had a fifty-one to thirty-three advantage. The military commander in Hawaii bombarded Washington D.C. with requests for more warships, more planes, more men to carry out his assigned tasks, but to no avail. As war clouds gathered over the Pacific in early summer 1941, Admiral Kimmel sent an urgent message to Washington listing the shortages at the base: trained officers, crew, combat pilots, carriers, fighter planes radar, and more.[3] Instead, Kimmel was astounded to receive an order from Washington to transfer from his fleet to the Atlantic over two dozen ships, including three battleships.

On December 16, 1941, one week after the disaster at Pearl Harbor, Admiral Kimmel was relieved of his command and demoted to Rear Admiral. The Army commander, General Walter Short was also relieved of his command. Subsequent investigations would reveal that Kimmel and Short did not deserve such a fate.

Across the Pacific Ocean, General Douglas MacArthur, the commander of the American forces on the Philippine Islands, received notice at 3:00 AM (8:00 p.m. Hawaiian time) that Pearl Harbor had been attacked by Japan, and as the Japanese forces swept across the Pacific Ocean — Midway, Wake, Guam — it was obvious that the Japanese had launched a general attack on all American and allied bases. However, when Japanese bombers arrived over the American air bases at Manila, the B-17s were still bunched on the airfield making easy targets. All B-17s were destroyed. With nine hours notice of the attack, General MacArthur had taken *no* action to protect the planes. MacArthur — the American military hero — was not demoted nor relieved of his command. Apparently, Admiral Kimmel and General Short were scapegoats enough. FDR did not want to tackle General Douglas MacArthur.

Prior to the attack on the morning of Sunday, December 7, readers of the New York *Times* were comforted by a reassuring article about the readiness of the United States Navy. Secretary of the Navy, Frank Knox said:

---

1. Ibid., p. 12; Husband E. Kimmel, *Admiral Kimmel's Own Story* (Chicago: Henry Regnery, 1955), p. 79.
2. Buchanan, *A Republic, Not An Empire*, p. 292.
3. Walter Millis, *This Is Pearl, The United States and Japan* (New York: William Morrow, 1947) p. 86.

I am proud to report that the American people may feel fully confident in the Navy. In my opinion the loyalty, morale and technical ability of the personnel are without superior. On any comparable basis, the United States Navy is second to none.[1]

"BUT THEY KNEW, THEY KNEW, THEY KNEW"

Shortly after 8:00 p.m. Sunday evening, December 7, members of President Roosevelt's cabinet began arriving at the White House for an emergency meeting. As the meeting room filled, the somberness of the occasion was seen in the ashen, drawn faces of the nation's leaders. One cabinet member commented that the President was "deeply shaken" as he divulged what he knew of the disaster at Pearl Harbor.[2] Later in the evening a group of congressional leaders attended another meeting and FDR repeated the tragic story. After the president concluded his remarks, Senator Tom Connally (D, TX) rose to speak, his face showing rage. "How did they catch us with our pants down, Mr. President?" The President looked stunned and contrite as he answered. "I don't know, Tom. I just don't know."[3]

Others were puzzled over the fact that the fleet and planes were all bunched together, making an easy target for the Japanese. Secretary of the Treasury Henry Morgenthau commented to friends that Secretary of War Henry Stimson was so stunned he just kept repeating: "...all the planes were in one place. They have the whole Fleet in one place — the whole Fleet was in this little Pearl Harbor. The whole Fleet was there.... They will never explain this. They will never be able to explain this."[4]

The public's outrage and fear was diluted by puzzlement. How could this happen? How could our military forces be caught so unaware? Colonel William Friedman, whose military intelligence group had deciphered the Japanese diplomatic code, was distraught, muttering over and over to his wife: "But they knew, they knew, they knew."[5]

Unlike most Americans, Friedman was aware that the United States had broken the most secret of the Japanese diplomatic codes. Whenever Tokyo sent coded messages to its embassies around the world, the United States was "listening." Seldom had a nation possessed such an advantage as war clouds gathered. Eight decoding machines, called Purple, were eventually built to automatically decipher the "Magic" messages, as the decoded messages were called. Four Purple decoding machines were kept in Washington D.C., two for the Army and two for the Navy. Three machines were sent to London for Britain's use, and one was sent to the United States military base in the Philippines for General Douglas MacArthur. The main United States Fleet in the Pacific at Pearl Harbor did not receive a Purple machine, although Admiral Kimmel had asked for one in April when he first discovered its existence. On April 22, 1941 the Office of Naval Intelligence (ONI) commented on its refusal to provide a Purple machine to Pearl Harbor:

---

1. John Toland, *Infamy: Pearl Harbor and Its Aftermath* (Garden City, New York: Doubleday and Company, 1982), p. 304.
2. Ibid., p. 13
3. Ibid., p. 13-14.
4. Ibid., p. 14.
5. Ibid.

I thoroughly appreciate that you would probably be much helped in your daily estimates if you had at your disposal the DIP [diplomatic code]. This, however, brings up matters of security, et cetera, which would be very difficult to solve.... The material you mentioned can necessarily have but passing and transient interest as action in the political sphere is determined by the Government as a whole and not by the forces afloat.... In other words, while you and the Fleet may be highly interested in politics, there is nothing that you can do about it. [1]

The naval officers in Washington D.C. essentially told Admiral Kimmel that he was not to be trusted with highly classified material, although the British and General MacArthur were apparently "more responsible." It is amazing to realize that London and the Philippines were given advantages that were denied to Hawaii. If, as the ONI asserts, the "Magic" messages were of transient interests and concerned marginal political information, why was a Purple machine provided to MacArthur, and more importantly, why were three Purple machines given to London?

With the benefit of the Purple decoding machines, and other decoded messages, what did the Roosevelt administration know before the attack on Pearl Harbor? Did the Japanese catch us "with our pants down," as Senator Connally commented? Or was it true that "they knew," as William Friedman said? What specific facts were known by the United States government by the morning of Sunday, December 7, 1941?

What did we know and when did we know it?

On January 27, 1941, Secretary of State Cordell Hull received a surprising message from the American ambassador to Japan, Joseph Grew. Grew's message said that Dr. Ricardo Schreiber, the Peruvian minister to Japan, had reported to him that Japan was plotting an attack on the United States if a diplomatic solution to problems were not reached. The message from Grew said: "Japanese military forces planned in the event of trouble with the United States, to attempt a surprise attack on Pearl Harbor...."[2] The Office of Naval Intelligence (ONI) in Washington D.C. informed Admiral Kimmel on February 1, 1941 that they found such rumors to be unfounded, reassuring the Admiral that the ONI "places no credence in these rumors.... Furthermore,... no move against Pearl Harbor appears imminent or planned for the foreseeable future."[3]

Dusko Popov, a British agent known in the spy business as "Tricycle," had passed along to the F.B.I. during the summer of 1941 a detailed plan of the proposed Japanese air raid on Pearl Harbor that he had obtained from German military intelligence. Popov was traveling aboard a steamer in the Atlantic Ocean on December 7 when the ship captain announced that Japan had attacked the American base in Hawaii. Popov was not aware that the surprise attack was a disaster to the United States; therefore, he was enthusiastic over his part in exposing the secret plot. Later he reflected on his thoughts: "It was the news I had been awaiting.... I was very, very proud that I had been able to give the warning to the Americans four months in advance."[4]

In late October, a third story was circulating, this from a Korean source inside Japan, that asserted Japan planned to bomb Pearl Harbor. The reliability of this source was high, inasmuch as it came from within Japan and from Koreans who had good contacts. The message was received on October 28, 1941 and Sidney Hornbeck the number three man at the State

---

1. David Kahn, *Code Breakers* (New York: Macmillan, 1967), p. 25-26.

2. Stinnett, *Day of Deceit*, p. 31.

3. Ibid., *p.* 32.

4. Dusko Popov, *Spy Counter Spy* (New York: Grosset and Dunlap, 1974), p.190-191.

Department and a long-time confidant of Cordell Hull, took it seriously. However, no action was taken and Pearl Harbor was not notified of the story.

Three warnings from knowledgeable sources over the space of several months should have alerted Washington to the likelihood of an attack. In addition, US officials were aware of the Japanese penchant to launch surprise attacks. The Japanese had begun all their recent wars with just such a tactic: 1894 against China, 1904 against Russia, and 1914 against Germany in northern China.

By the fall of 1941, as diplomatic negotiations between Japan and the United States collapsed, Washington should have been on alert. In the ten weeks preceding the attack there were numerous specific indications that the military bases at Pearl Harbor were to be attacked. The warning signs revealed by "Magic" and other decoded messages were clear and specific; they began to toll ominously:

- On September 24, the Bomb Plot messages began. "Magic" messages revealed orders from Japanese Foreign Minister Toyoda to Japanese agents in Hawaii to create a grid in Pearl Harbor where the main American fleet was berthed. Presumably this grid was for targeting bombs. The initial message ordered:

  > The waters [of Pearl Harbor] are to be divided roughly into five sub-areas.... With regard to warships and aircraft carriers, we would like to have you report on those at anchor, tied up at wharves, buoys, and in docks. If possible we would like you to make mention of the fact when there are two or more vessels alongside the same wharf.[1]

- On September 29, the Bomb Plot messages continued, informing the Japanese agents in Hawaii that "The following codes will be used hereafter to designate the location of vessels...."[2]

- The Bomb Plot messages were expanded; twice-weekly reports on all ship movements in the harbor were requested and all military and strategic installations were to be scrutinized.

- On November 22 a message from Tokyo to its diplomats emphasized the dire straits of the doomed diplomatic negotiations: "This time we mean it, that the deadline (November 29) absolutely cannot be changed. After that things are automatically going to happen."[3]

- Between November 15 and December 6, 129 radio intercepts of the Japanese convoy steaming across the Pacific Ocean toward Pearl Harbor were made by American military intelligence. For years, historians believed that the "lost" Japanese convoy which attacked Pearl Harbor observed strict radio silence on its voyage across the north Pacific. But author Robert Stinnett in his book, *Day of Deceit*, reveals that there were dozens of radio messages passing between Tokyo and the fleet, and among the ships in the convoy. Thus, the famed "lost fleet" was not lost at all.

- On November 28, the Office of Naval Intelligence facilities located the "lost" Japanese fleet as it was steaming eastward across the north Pacific toward Hawaii. ONI reported that "at least six, possibly eight Jap units [carriers] were operating between Hawaii and the Aleutians and clearly indicated that a force was to steal out on a secret mission...."[4]

---

1. Stinnett, *Day of Deceit*, p. 102.
2. Ibid., p. 104.
3. Charles C. Tansill, *Back Door To War* (Chicago: Henry Regnery, 1952), p. 647.
4. Stinnett, *Day of Deceit*, p. 194.

- On November 30, the Japanese Ambassador to Berlin was ordered, in a coded message deciphered by a Purple machine, to inform the German government that war was imminent. The message read:

  > Say very secretly to them [Germany] that there is extreme danger that war may sud-
  > denly break out between the Anglo-Saxon nations and Japan through some clash of
  > arms and that the time of the breaking out may come quicker that anyone dreams."[1]

- During November, Colonel William Donovan, head of the World War II intelligence service (forerunner of the CIA), recorded in his personal papers that a German diplomat, Dr. Hans Thonsen, relayed the story to him that the Japanese were going to attack Pearl Harbor in November or December. Donovan was personally close to FDR and saw him several times in November. It would have been unthinkable for Donovan to withhold this information from the president.[2] (Both William Donovan and the British spy Dusko Popov received confidential information from German intelligence agencies about Japanese plans to attack the United States at Pearl Harbor. This perfidious behavior toward Japan reveals not only the flimsy nature of the Axis Pact, but also how far the German intelligence service was prepared to go in undermining Der Fuehrer.)

- On December 1, the USS Lurline, a passenger liner of the Matson Steamship Company, was traveling to Hawaii from San Francisco when radio operator Leslie Grogan picked up a faint radio signal coming from the northwest. Suspicious as to why a radio signal would be coming from that isolated area of the Pacific Ocean, Grogan continued to monitor the errant sounds. He finally concluded that it was a Japanese code and passed the information on to military officials in Hawaii. Grogan entered the following in his logbook:

  > The Japs are blasting away on the lower Marine Radio frequency — it is all in the Jap-
  > anese code, and continues for several hours.... So much of the signals reaching us on the
  > SS Lurline were good enough to get good R.D.F. [Radio Direction Finding] bear-
  > ings)...The main body of signals came from a Northwest by West area [from Hawaii].[3]

- On December 3, "Magic" messages revealed that the Japanese embassies and consulates around the world were ordered to begin destroying their codes, a prelude to war.

- On December 4, a military intelligence facility in Maryland picked up the famed "East Wind Rain" message on radio. The story of the "Winds" message is as follows: On November 19, the Japanese Foreign Office sent a coded message to its embassies that in case of war with the United States a fake radio weather report would include the verbal signal "East Wind Rain."[4] A military intelligence radio tower picked up this message on Thursday before the December 7th attack. Simultaneously, from the Dutch East Indies an American Army attaché reported the same information to Washington D. C.

- The Dutch Army in the Dutch East Indies intercepted a coded message sent by Tokyo the week of the attack informing diplomats that an attack was being launched on Hawaii. General Hein Ter Poorten, commander of the Netherlands East Indies Army, and Brigadier General Eliot Thorpe, United States military attaché, sent this

1. George Morgenstern, *Pearl Harbor: The Story of the Secret War* (New York: Devin-Adair, 1947), p. 190.
2. Thompson, *A Time For War*, p. 383.
3. Toland, *Infamy*, p. 279.
4. Thompson, *A Time For War*, p. 388.

information to the United States War Department in Washington D.C. and received an acknowledgement. Still unsure of Washington's receipt of the message and cognizant of the critical nature of the news, three more messages were sent each to a different recipient. Thus, just days before the attack, the United States government received four messages from reliable sources in the Dutch military service informing them that a Japanese convoy was sailing toward Pearl Harbor.[1]

- On December 6 at 10:40 AM, the State Department received a message from the US ambassador in London marked "Triple Priority." The message announced that there was a large Japanese armada sailing southward past Indochina towards the British naval base at Singapore.

- On Saturday December 6, Captain Johan Ranneft, a Dutch naval officer, visited the Naval Intelligence Office in Washington D.C., where he was told by the Director of ONI that a Japanese task force was traveling eastward from Japan in the direction of Hawaii. The Director of ONI pointed to the spot on the map indicating where the Japanese Armada was located. The point was northwest of Hawaii.[2]

- On December 6, Japanese agents in Honolulu reported to Tokyo that there were no reconnaissance balloons in the harbor to protect the ships and there were no torpedo nets in the water. The message, received in Washington D. C., concluded: "I imagine that in all probability there is considerable opportunity left to take advantage for a surprise attack against these places."[3]

- On December 7 at 9:00 AM, the final part of a long message from Japan announced that diplomatic negotiations with the United States were finished and a final declaration from Tokyo was to be delivered to the United States government at precisely 1:00 p.m. Sunday, December 7. Upon reading the message, Admiral Stark gasped: "My God! This means war. I must get word to Kimmel at once."[4] For Colonel Rufus Bratton of the military intelligence service, the 1:00 p.m. delivery time was ominous. There were three possible points of attack: the Panama Canal, but the deadline would be noon at the canal; the Philippines, but the deadline would be around 3:00 AM; and Pearl Harbor, where it would be dawn. Bratton raced upstairs to Army Chief of Staff George Marshall's office, but the Chief was at home taking his usual Sunday morning horseback ride. In Washington D.C., it was business as usual. But at mid-Pacific on the Hawaiian Islands, thousands of young servicemen awaited their fate.

By Sunday morning, December 7, 1941, the United States government had an impressive array of information, even an overwhelming amount, at its disposal, that would indicate a Japanese attack was to be launched against the Pacific Fleet at Pearl Harbor. All of this information was available to the intelligence offices of the military services, to the State Department, and to the White House. President Roosevelt, Secretary of State Hull, Secretary of War Stimson, Secretary of the Navy Knox, General Marshall, Admiral Stark — all these men and others had received many of these clues about an attack. But none of this was available to Admiral Kimmel and General Short at Pearl Harbor. Officials in Washington were fully informed; the commanders of the American military base in the middle of the Pacific Oceans were left uninformed.

---

1. Toland, *Infamy*, p. 281-282, p. 290-291.
2. Stinnett, *Day of Deceit*, p. 42.
3. Toland, *Infamy*, p. 6.
4. Morgenstern, *Pearl Harbor*, p. 269.

During the summer of 1941, Captain Alan Kirk, Director of ONI had forwarded several "Magic" messages to Admiral Kimmel, but when Naval Chief of Staff Stark and others heard of this, the flow of information was stopped and Kirk was transferred out of that position. Concern was expressed that there might be a breach of security if the pipeline to Hawaii continued. In view of the fact that Britain had three Purple decoding machines and there was one on the Philippine Islands, one can only wonder why a flow of "Magic" messages to the fleet at Pearl Harbor would jeopardize the security of "Magic." Some cynics complained that FDR was acting like the "President of England" rather than President of the United States.

FDR Schemes to Provoke Japan

Negotiations between the United States and Japan had, in actuality, ceased in November; by the weekend of December 6-7 the two sides were merely play-acting. Japan formally severed diplomatic relations on December 6 with its Fourteen-part message delivered at 1:00 p.m. Sunday, December 7 to the American Secretary of State. The long message was an angry summary of the tangled American-Japanese relationship over the years. The first 13 parts were decoded by 9:00 p.m. Saturday, December 6, and President Roosevelt's copy was taken to him at the White House at 9:30 p.m. Saturday evening. A military aide knocked on the door and was greeted by the president's friend, Harry Hopkins. As the president glanced over the note, angry and threatening phrases jumped out at him:

> While manifesting this obviously hostile attitude these countries [the United States and its European allies] have strengthened their military preparations perfecting an encirclement of Japan, and brought about a situation which endangers the very existence of the empire....

> The American Government, obsessed with its own views and opinions, may be said to be scheming for the extension of war. It is exercising ... pressure by economic power [which] should be condemned as it is at times more inhumane than military pressure.

> ...for the past hundred years the countries of the Far East have been compelled to observe the status quo under this Anglo-American policy of imperialistic exploitation.... The Japanese Government cannot tolerate the perpetuation of such a situation....

> The [American] proposal menaces the Empire's existence and disparages its honor and prestige. Therefore viewed in its entirety, the Japanese Government regrets that it cannot accept the proposal as a basis of negotiations....[1]

As FDR finished reading the message, he dropped the papers, looked at Hopkins and said: "This means war."[2]

The President's subsequent actions seemed strangely passive in view of the eventuality facing the military forces in the Pacific. The President called no war council meeting nor did he send an immediate, urgent warning message to the American bases in the field. He continued to visiting with Hopkins, but did make one telephone call, that to Chief of Naval Operations Harold Stark. Stark had gone to the theater and the President chose not to have the Admiral paged for fear of causing alarm. Apparently, there was no effort made to reach General Marshall.

---

1. www.yale.edu.lawweb/avalon/wwii/p3.htm
2. Toland, *Infamy*, p. 319.

Thus, the night passed with neither the head of the Army, General George Marshall, or the chief of the Navy, Admiral Stark, being made aware that the United States had just received a threatening war message from Japan.

Perhaps FDR's equanimity displayed his relief that the war with Japan was finally here. Roosevelt's plans for a war with Japan were actually initiated a year earlier in October, 1940 when Lt. Commander Arthur McCollum, head of the Far East desk of the Office of Naval Intelligence, had written an *Eight Action Memorandum* envisioning ways in which the United States could provoke Japan into some war-like act. McCollum's memo suggested:

- Moving the main naval base to Hawaii.
- Sharing bases with imperial powers — the British and the Dutch — in the Far East.
- Increasing aid to the Chinese government which was fighting Japan.
- Sending submarines and cruisers to naval bases in the Far East.
- Obtaining Dutch agreement to stop oil sales to Japan.
- Embargoing all trade to Japan in collaboration with Great Britain.[1]

These proposals were discussed by civilian and military leaders, approval and implementation began immediately. Moving the naval base from San Diego to Hawaii was the first step taken, an action that was contrary to the judgment of Navy leadership. The other actions were put into operation during the next several months. The provocative attitude of Roosevelt can be seen in his decision as early as October 1940, to embargo trade with Japan and to terminate the sale of petroleum to that Asian nation — even before Japan took any action to warrant such a drastic measure. In other words, after 1940, FDR was looking for an excuse to put Japan through the economic wringer.

McCollum's measures were actually rather meek compared to some schemes concocted by FDR. The President mulled over an idea with Admiral Richardson in 1940 of stringing a line of warships across the Pacific, in effect blockading Japan. The Admiral, already at odds with the president, told the Secretary of the Navy that he objected to the scheme, as it would provoke war and lead to needless loss of life.

Early in 1941, FDR broached the scheme of sending aircraft carriers to a Russian Far East port and provocatively traversing Japanese territorial waters en route. Admiral Kimmel was appalled at such an inflammatory move and told the president: "If we have decided upon war, it would be far better to take offensive action...let us choose a method which will be more advantageous to ourselves."[2]

The President went beyond talking about pranks when he actually instituted the "Pop-up Cruises," with this FDR began "sticking pins in a rattlesnake." "Pop-up Cruises" were designed to stir the wrath of the Japanese by sending warships into and around Japanese territorial waters, hoping to create an incident. (FDR was Assistant Secretary of the Navy under President Woodrow Wilson in 1915 when the Lusitania incident occurred. FDR may have seen the "Pop-up Cruises" as having the same potential for involving the United States in war as had happened with the Lusitania incident.) In March of 1941, and again in July, a flotilla of American ships was sent into waters adjacent to the Japanese homeland islands; no incident resulted, although the Japanese registered complaints. The most dramatic of these forays occurred on

---

1. Stinnett, *Day of Deceit*, p. 8.
2. George Morgenstern, "The Actual Road to Pearl Harbor," in Harry Elmer Barnes, ed., *Perpetual War For Perpetual Peace* (Caxton, Idaho: Caxton Printers, Ltd., 1953), p. 361.

July 31, 1941 at a particularly tense time in Japanese-American relations. American ships were sent into the Bungo Straits, a waterway that separates the two Japanese islands of Kyushu and Shikoku and is essentially an inland sea, somewhat similar to the English Channel to Great Britain or the Great Lakes to the United States. President Roosevelt confessed his motives in these ventures: "I just want them to keep popping up here and there and keep the Japs guessing. *I don't mind losing one or two cruisers,* but do not take a chance on losing five or six."[1]

President Roosevelt was playing "Russian roulette" with the American Navy! Knowing of these provocative actions by FDR, it is clear that the President was not seriously negotiating with the Japanese in 1941. He wanted war, not a compromise.

There were more schemes emanating from the devious mind of Franklin Delano Roosevelt. Early in December 1941, FDR ordered a schooner, the *Lanikai*, to be outfitted with several concealed deck guns and a Filipino crew. Lieutenant Kemp Tolley was to be in charge of the *Lanikai* cruise and he was given sealed instructions to be opened only after he left port in the Philippines. The instructions were to sail westward toward the coast of Indochina, ostensibly searching for a fictitious downed American airplane. Two other small ships were given similar missions in the seas of Southeast Asia during that time. The vessels were all at sea on December 7 when the Japanese attack occurred; all were immediately recalled to port. It became obvious that the crafts were sent on "suicide missions" into the path of the Japanese Armada sailing towards Singapore. FDR was prepared to sacrifice the lives of three American naval officers and the Filipino crews in order to provoke an incident that would start the war. Had these missions accomplished the President's purpose, it is easy to imagine FDR using his mellifluous radio voice to tell a fabulous and distorted tale to the American people about the cruise of the *Lanikai* and the "treachery" of the Japanese.

PEARL HARBOR WAR PLANS AND WAR WARNINGS

While FDR schemed to involve America in a war with Japan, Admiral Kimmel and his counterpart in the Army, General Walter Short, were essentially operating a "training base" in the middle of the Pacific Ocean, undermanned, poorly equipped and exposed to any surprise attack by an enemy. Despite the vulnerability of the fleet and the American people's disdain for a foreign war, FDR pressed on with his war plans.

Early in 1941, American, British, Canadian and Dutch war plans (ABCD plans) were formulated in secret for the eventuality of war in the Pacific against Japan. The American plans (Rainbow-5) envisioned American support for the European colonial possessions should Japan launch an attack into South East Asia. Rainbow-5 designated the United States fleet to engage in belligerent actions against Japan when the Japanese Navy penetrated a line that approximated the northern edge of the Dutch East Indies. It was clear that Allied leaders expected war would begin when Japan attacked the Dutch East Indies to secure petroleum and other raw materials.

It is significant to note that these secret military plans sanctioned by FDR committed the United States to go to war when one of the European colonial holdings was attacked — not

1. Stinnett, *Day of Deceit*, p. 9.

when America or its possessions was attacked. Further, no congressional leaders were consulted nor, of course, did FDR seek congressional authorization for going to war. None of these clandestine machinations were public knowledge until after World War II. One wonders what startling yarn FDR would have concocted had the Japanese only attacked European colonies in South East Asia rather than Pearl Harbor. But as will be shown, FDR had devised a plan to prevent this eventuality.

Therefore, no specific plans were developed in Rainbow-5 for the defense of Hawaii from air or naval attack. The military establishment's public position was that the vast reaches of the northern Pacific Ocean presented a forbidding barrier for attack, and the shallow waters of Pearl Harbor were thought to be an adequate safeguard against any torpedo plane attack launched from aircraft carriers. Chief of Naval Operations Stark told Kimmel: "It is considered that the relatively shallow depth of the water limits the need for anti-torpedo nets in Pearl Harbor."[1] If one is to take the civilian and military leaders in Washington D. C. at their own word, Marshall and Stark, working with inside information about Japanese strategy and with no time pressures, had failed to predict an attack at Pearl Harbor. Yet Admiral Kimmel and General Short — essentially flying blind — were disgraced and dismissed from their command because they failed to anticipate the attack.

The Army and Navy commanders in Hawaii had developed local operational plans that delegated to the Navy responsibility for long-range reconnaissance and to defend the islands in the event of an amphibious attack. The Army was to conduct short-range reconnaissance, defend against air attack, as well as guard against sabotage. Because of the shortage of planes, each branch of the service would borrow planes from the other. The main military base in the Pacific did not have sufficient men or equipment to carry out adequate defense of the base. Meanwhile, FDR continued to "stick pins in the Japanese rattlesnake" and to throw a protective mantel around the shoulders of the European colonial powers. An ultimate aircraft patrol of the Hawaiian Islands necessitated a reconnaissance of 800 miles in radius, 360 degrees around the Islands, twenty-four hours a day. This routine task would require eighty-four planes each day; crews and planes could only be used for such arduous duty every third day. Neither service had 250 planes for long range patrol. The Army base in Hawaii had twelve B-17s, but by the fall 1941, six of these had been stripped of parts and sent to MacArthur in the Philippines. At the end of October, the Navy received fifty-four Catalina flying boats that were ideal for long-range patrol, but they were not shaken-down for flight, nor did they arrive with spare parts. This major military base in the middle of the Pacific Ocean simply did not have adequate men or material to protect itself in such an exposed position. This fact was well known by all military and civilian leaders and was the primary reason why Admiral Richardson and other Navy leaders had objected to moving the base to Hawaii where it was exposed to enemy attack.

The United States was just beginning to produce equipment for war in 1941. Between February and December 1, 1941, 1,900 planes were produced, but 1,750 were sent to Great Britain. If Hawaii had received just ten percent of these crafts, a full-time reconnaissance around the Islands could have been conducted. In that same ten-month period, 5,500 anti-aircraft guns were produced in America; Pearl Harbor received seven! The remainder went to Britain in the Lend-lease program of FDR.

---

1. Morgenstern, *Pearl Harbor*, p. 82.

A partial reconnaissance could have been conducted in the area directly north of the Islands where a Japanese attack would be most likely. Admiral Kimmel did conduct war games in the northern approaches three weeks prior to the attack and would have expanded these efforts had he not been ordered back to Pearl Harbor by his superiors in Washington. This astounding development was discovered by Robert Stinnett while perusing the files of the Pearl Harbor investigations. The story as it unfolds is known as the "Vacant Sea" orders and will be discussed more fully in a subsequent section.

Under these restrictive conditions, Kimmel and Short made the decisions to continue training the crew and conserve their equipment, so that when war came, crew and planes would be prepared to carry out the joint military war plans assigned to the base. There was no air patrol around the Hawaiian Islands before December 7 — as ordered by Washington.

Possessing no Purple decoding machine and having insufficient men and material for a long-range patrol, the base was vulnerable to attack from air or sea. The military chiefs in Washington D. C. had an obligation to provide timely information to Kimmel and Short. But the messages that were sent were sparse and inadequate.

On October 16, when General Hideko Tojo replaced Premier Konoye as Prime Minister of Japan, Admiral Kimmel was told to take "due precaution" and make "preparatory deployments."[1] This meant that when war came, Kimmel was to conduct operations in the central Pacific to protect the British supply lines. On November 24, Kimmel was told that Japan might make a surprise move in any direction, which meant little at Pearl Harbor as the attack was expected in Southeast Asia. Then, on November 27 came the noted "war warning" message from Washington:

> This dispatch is to be considered a war warning. Negotiations with Japan looking toward stabilization of conditions in the Pacific have ceased and an aggressive move by Japan is expected within the next few days. The number and equipment of Japanese troops and the organization of naval task forces indicate an amphibious expedition against the Philippines, Thai, or Kra Peninsula, or possibly Borneo. Execute an appropriate defensive deployment preparatory to carrying out the tasks assigned in [Rainbow-5].[2]

All of these war warning messages from Washington were sent to EVERY military base, and therefore had no special significance to Hawaii. Kimmel and Short instituted the planned "sabotage alert" that involved bunching the planes and ships for easier protection. General Short radioed to General Marshall: "Report department alerted to prevent sabotage."[3] The military bases on Hawaii hunkered down to preserve their limited planes and crew in anticipation of carrying out the war plan assignments in the far reaches of the Pacific Ocean.

Early Sunday morning, December 7, the Army and Navy leadership in Washington D.C., General George Marshall and Admiral Harold Stark, failed to take advantage of one final opportunity to inform Hawaii of the pending attack. By 9:00 AM Sunday morning in Washington, it was apparent that Japan was going to launch an attack on Hawaii at 1:00 p.m. Sunday — dawn on the Islands. When Stark and Marshall discussed a last minute warning at noon Sunday, an hour still remained before the first wave of bombers descended upon Pearl Harbor. But, instead

---

1. Ibid. p. 224.
2. Toland, *Infamy*, p. 7.
3. Irving L. Jones, *Victims of Groupthink* (Boston: Houghton Mifflin Company), p. 232

of using instant telephone communication, Marshall sent a message by RCA and Western Union. It arrived by messenger after the attack.

THE SCRAMBLE FOR CHINA

During the late 19th century, the central government of China was collapsing, creating a power vacuum and a scramble by the European powers to carve that nation into pieces, as had been done in Africa. Britain, Germany, France, Portugal and Russia all sent military forces and commercial agents into the ancient "Middle Kingdom," often threatening to annex seacoast ports. Chinese citizens, unhappy at the prospect of being "acquired" by foreign powers, staged multi-year revolts against their own government; they wanted the "foreign devils" out and a viable Chinese government in power.

Because of Japan's proximity to China, the Japanese had the most to lose when the Manchu government of China finally disappeared; thus Japan began to assert itself aggressively in the Far East. Between 1894 and 1919 Japan fought three wars on the mainland: with China, with Russia and with Germany, each one achieving many of Japan's goals. Having acquired Taiwan, Korea, the Shantung province and commercial rights in Manchuria, by 1920 Japan stood astride the Far East as the strongest power. Japan, not the Western powers, was filling the power vacuum in China.

Japan had often been compared to England, in that both nations were island kingdoms off the coast of a major continent, heavily populated, lacking natural resources and food and therefore dependent on overseas trade. Being great emulators, the Japanese began copying the British style — a large navy, colonies or economic rights in distant lands and a belligerent style in foreign affairs, which included prominence on the adjacent mainland.

America was accommodating to Japan's expansion early in the century, with President Theodore Roosevelt being especially supportive. Roosevelt mediated the peace conference that ended the Russo-Japanese War in 1906, making sure that Japan's interests were well protected. He also supervised an agreement (the Root-Takahira Agreement in 1908) which gave approval to Japan's expansion into Korea and its eventual annexation of that peninsular nation. Roosevelt advised his successor, President William Howard Taft, that Japan had vital interests in the area of Korea and Manchuria and the United States did not. In a letter to President Taft in 1910, Theodore Roosevelt counseled:

> It is...peculiarly to our interest not to take any steps as regards Manchuria which will give Japan cause to feel...that we are hostile to them.... Alliance with China, in view of China's absolute military helplessness, means, of course, not an additional strength to us, but an additional obligation which we assume." [1]

The northern area of Asia was the Japanese sphere of interest and the United States should not stand in the way. Being a realist, Roosevelt pointed out that American power in the area was limited: "[A] successful war about Manchuria would require a fleet as good as that of

---

1. Charles C. Tansill, "Japanese-American Relations: 1921-1941," in Harry Elmer Barnes, ed., *Perpetual War For Perpetual Peace*, p. 269.

England, plus an army as good as that of Germany."[1] For all his bellicose behavior, Roosevelt was circumspect in using American military power where it would be ineffective or intrude into other nation's sphere of interest. For Teddy, there would be no war with Japan over issues in the Far East. The turn of the century American Open Door Policy that espoused a free and independent China in which equal trade opportunities were provided for all nations was interpreted in a loose manner. The idealism of the Open Door policy took a back seat to the realities of the Far East.

During World War I the United States signed another agreement with Nippon in which America gave Japan a "green light" in north China, the agreement stating that "territorial propinquity creates special relations between countries, and consequently, the Government of the United States recognizes that Japan has special interests in China...."[2] During the Twenties, the United States continued to encourage Japan to dominate the northern area of China, as Japan provided a stable government and such dominance was deemed more acceptable than European imperialism or incursions by communist Russia.

The worldwide depression in the 1930s struck Japan with a fury, driving Nippon on a frantic quest to expand its markets in Asia. Most industrialized nations, at this time, resorted to economic nationalism to protect their economies. America imposed severe tariffs on foreign goods, and the imperial powers — Great Britain and the Dutch — reinforced their imperial policy by imposed severe quotas on Japanese trade. Japan was in a perilous economic situation as it was a nation of seventy million people crammed into a land only the size of California but with a paltry resource base equivalent to the state of Arkansas. With Western markets closing, Japan sought economic self-sufficiency in northern Asia. Food, iron ore, coal and other raw materials flowed into Japan while workers, finished goods and capital flowed back into Manchuria. After thirty years of development, the port city of Darien was more Japanese than Chinese, and Mukden, the capital of Manchuria, looked for leadership to Tokyo not Peking. Geopolitical strategies of filling the power vacuum in Asia now merged with critical economic concerns.

To this end, in 1937, Japan announced its Greater East Asia Co-Prosperity Sphere, a program, as Japan said, of "Asia for the Asians" — with Japanese leadership, of course. The Japanese leaders envisioned an Asia guided by Tokyo with no European colonial masters. Japan likened this to the American Monroe Doctrine, which they saw as a policy of "America for the Americans" with United States leadership. Such comparisons were confusing to Americans, as the enlightened nation viewed its own actions as providing liberty and prosperity, while Japan's actions were deemed aggressive and reminiscent of gangster behavior. The two Pacific giants saw themselves through very different eyes.

The first sign of tension between Japan and the United States came in 1931, as the economic depression swept Asia, when Japan annexed Manchuria, a rebellious and mineral-rich area adjacent to Japan's colony of Korea. President Herbert Hoover was offended by the Japanese action, commenting to his cabinet that "The whole transaction is immoral...outrageous."[3] But Hoover, a Quaker and something of a pacifist, cautioned about the United States becoming

---

1. Buchanan, *A Republic, Not An Empire*, p. 247.
2. Charles C. Tansill, "Back Door to War" in George Waller, ed., *Pearl Harbor: Roosevelt and the Coming of the War* (Boston: D. C. Heath and Company, 1953), p. 17.
3. Richard Hofstadter, *The American Political Tradition* (New York: Bantam Books, 1948), p. 308.

involved. He believed that the squabbling in Manchuria was merely a dispute between local powers, and Japan had legitimate concerns about the growing power of communist Russia leering at strategically important and mineral-rich Manchuria from across the border. Besides, China was too large for any nation to swallow. Hoover asserted: "Neither our obligations to China, nor our own interests, nor our dignity require us to go to war over these questions."[1] President Hoover might have added that the Manchurian Incident was provoked in part by Chinese guerrilla bands disrupting legally acquired Japanese economic rights in the area. America leaders had recognized that Manchuria was an autonomous region of China, only loosely linked to Peking. When Manchucko was created by the Japanese in 1931, the British and Soviets were preparing to recognize the new state and sign a non-aggression pact with Japan, but drew back when the United States made a fuss.

Hoover's Secretary of State Henry L. Stimson was a solid champion of China and a moralist who saw the actions of Japan as aggressive and evil. Hoover tolerated the Secretary's moralistic sermons to Japan about proper international etiquette. But when Stimson began talking about using all means short of actual use of armed forces, the President cut him off. Hoover restrained his Secretary of State, saying that such action "was simply the road to war itself."[2] As a concession to the idealistic Secretary of State, the "Stimson Doctrine" was issued, saying that the United States would not "recognize" any border changes brought about by force and violence. With that moral salvo, Stimson was harnessed and the issue was quieted.

The fate of China took a distressing turn in 1937 when fighting in Peking between Japan and China turned into a full-scale war. The Japanese Army quickly overran the Chinese coast and thrust into the vast river valleys, pushing the Chinese forces far inland. Roosevelt came to the aid of the Chinese people with financial grants and military supplies, much of it assisted by the famed Flying Tigers, American pilots who volunteered for service. Chiang Kai-shek, the titular leader of the Chinese government, was encouraged to pursue military victory against Japan, inasmuch as China was receiving vast economic supplies and vigorous verbal support from the United States. By 1940 Japan's war in China had bogged down as Chiang Kai-shek and Roosevelt maneuvered to stop the Japanese advance.

THE ROAD TO WAR: 1940-1941

Japanese-American relations deteriorated rapidly in 1940 after World War II began in Europe. Secretary of State Cordell Hull believed that Japan had embarked on a steady fixed course of conquest that would eventually reach American shores. He characterized the Japanese as "thieves" and "highway robbers."[3] Secretary Hull was being alarmist for Japanese foreign policy was certainly not on a "steady fixed course," but instead showed a large degree of pragmatism and flexibility, and during 1941 was more open to negotiations than the United States.

---

1. George Morgenstern, "The Actual Road to Pearl Harbor," in Harry Elmer Barnes, *Perpetual War For Perpetual Peace*, p. 317.
2. Charles C. Tansill, "Back Door to War," in George Waller, ed., *Pearl Harbor; Roosevelt and the Coming of the War*, p. 26
3. Cordell Hull, *The Memoirs of Cordell Hull*, vol. 1, (New York: Macmillan, 1948), and p. 270- 271n.

From the 1890s until 1940 Japan had directed its expansion into Korea and Manchuria where it clashed with Russia (the Soviet Union later) and the remnants of the Chinese Empire. But after Germany defeated France and the Netherlands in 1940, Japan turned southward toward the colonies of France and the Dutch — Indochina (Vietnam, Cambodia and Laos) and the Dutch East Indies (Indonesia). As the Harvard historian, Samuel Eliot Morison, said, "The Japanese warlords...now planned to swing south...and Japan had to risk fighting Great Britain, France, the Netherlands, and the United States, which between them controlled the coveted territory."[1]

This turn southward triggered a vigorous response from the United States. As long as Japan's aggression was directed toward the Soviet Union (Russia) or the Chinese warlords in north China, the United States response was muted, at times even supportive. But in 1940, when the Japanese directed their "aggression" toward the colonies of the European allies, American came down hard on Japan and was unyielding in its pressure. This newfound hostility and moralistic condemnation of Japan's acquisitiveness is puzzling. Japan had been conquering and annexing territory for forty years. If the American opposition was based on idealism, ideological consistency demands that *all* aggression be denounced — that would include the rampaging of Japan in north Asia prior to 1940, as well as British, French, and Dutch imperialism throughout the world. British imperial subjects were laboring in British South African mines at seven cents a day and in the jungles of British Southeast Asia for less than that. Idealists with moral principles as their guiding star do not have the luxury of picking and choosing the sins that they oppose.

The only sense this selective condemnation of aggression makes is that American leaders were hypocritically using the rhetoric of Wilsonian idealism to stir up the American public for a war against Japan on other grounds. In reality, Roosevelt believed that a war against Japan was useful, not so much because of Japan's evilness and aggression, but because Japan was now linked to Germany through the Axis Pact, and for FDR, Hitler's Germany was the paramount threat. As Japan attempted to control China and cast covetous eyes on Southeast Asia, so much the better for FDR's war against the Axis partners in Asia. Given Roosevelt's attitude, Japan sought a negotiated settlement in vain.

The first hostile action by FDR against Japan was the partial embargo in 1940. This action was taken when Japan moved into Vietnam in July to occupy several airbases and ports, ostensibly to cut off the Chinese supply lines from Burma. Then a year later in July 1941 when Japan occupied the rest of Indochina, the United States froze Japanese assets and cut off all trade with Japan, including the precious commodity of oil. A total embargo on trade is usually a prelude to war and the American military leadership urged FDR not to disrupt the flow of oil to Japan. President Roosevelt was made aware of the serious consequences of an oil embargo when Admiral Richmond Turner, Navy Chief of War Plans, cautioned him that:

> It is generally believed that shutting off the American supply of petroleum will lead promptly to an invasion of the Netherlands East Indies.... Furthermore, it seems certain that, if Japan should then take military measures against the British and Dutch, she would also include military action against the Philippines, which would immediately involve us in a Pacific War.... Trade with Japan should not be embargoed at this time.[2]

---

1. Samuel Eliot Morison, *The Oxford History of the American People*, p. 1000.

The economic sanctions imposed on Japan by the Roosevelt administration in the summer of 1941 created economic devastation in Japan. Imports were reduced by 75%; food and other vital supplies became scarce and unemployment soared. The nation had only a few months' supply of oil and the approaching winter without adequate heating oil was a serious concern. The lack of oil was also taking a toll on the Japanese military machine; Japan would either have to secure a new source of oil or capitulate to the United States. Roosevelt even closed the Panama Canal to Japanese merchant vessels, adding time and expense to all Japanese shipping plans. As Foreign Minister Togo said, "Economic pressure of this character is capable of menacing national existence to a greater degree than the direct use of force."[1] FDR was putting Japan through the economic wringer and he would not let up.

In this atmosphere of extreme tension, three months before the attack on Pearl Harbor, the Japanese prime minister, Prince Konoye, the leader of the "Peace Party," requested a summit meeting with FDR. Konoye, desperate for a deal, told the President to name the date and the place for a meeting. The Japanese Prime Minister had prepared a ship to transport governmental leaders to the summit and had arranged to have a group of moderate military leaders accompany him. When Cordell Hull objected saying that the Prime Minister could not control the Japanese Army, Konoye gave assurances that he would bring the Army leaders. When Hull demurred because the Emperor would not be there, Konoye said the Emperor would be in constant touch by a direct telephone line. When Hull objected that an agenda had not been agreed to, Konoye said he would oblige. In Tokyo, the American Ambassador Joseph Grew was also urging FDR to meet with the Japanese leader. Grew had been told personally by Konoye that he was supported by critical Army officers and was prepared to order the suspension of all military activities in China and Indochina. Ambassador Grew wrote in his memoirs:

> We in the Embassy had no doubt that the Prime Minister would have agreed at his meeting with the President, to the eventual withdrawal of all Japanese forces from all of Indochina and from all of China with the face-saving expedient of being permitted to retain a limited number of troops in North China and Inner Mongolia.[2]

FDR rejected the offer of a summit meeting with the Japanese. FDR wanted immediate, not eventual, withdrawal from China, and all the indications are that the President preferred war over peace at that time. Ominously, Prime Minister Konoye was replaced in October by General Hideki Tojo, a general who was the leader of the "War Party." Japanese preparations for the attack on Pearl Harbor began in earnest.

In November, the Japanese submitted their final proposal to avert war. It was essentially an offer to return to conditions of the summer of 1940 — Japan would begin withdrawing its troops from Indochina in exchange for rescinding the oil embargo. This offer was stillborn, for the United States had committed itself to the cause of Chiang Kai-shek in China. FDR would not abandon Chiang, nor would he remove the embargo until Japan withdrew entirely from the mainland of Asia. Japan wanted to roll back the clock to 1940; the United States wanted to return to before 1931.

---

2. George Morgenstern, "The Actual Road to Pearl Harbor," in Harry Elmer Barnes, ed., *Perpetual War For Perpetual Peace*, p. 328.

1. Morgenstern, *Pearl Harbor*, p. 148.

2. Buchanan, *A Republic, Not An Empire*, p. 289.

The Chinese government of Chiang Kai-shek was heavily indebted to the United States; at any time America could have forced China to the negotiating table for peace talks with Japan. Conversely, the Roosevelt administration had Japan in a headlock and could have brought Japan to a peace conference. Instead, FDR chose to continue aid to China and bring pressure on Japan until Nippon capitulated — or until a general war broke out. At the Roosevelt war cabinet meeting on November 25, the President brought up the imminence of war in the Pacific. As Stimson recalls, the President warned that "we were likely to be attacked, perhaps [as soon as] next Monday, for the Japanese are notorious for making an attack without warning and the question was what we should do. The question was how *we should maneuver them into the position of firing the first shot* without allowing too much danger to ourselves."[1]

The following day, November 26, Roosevelt determined the manner in which he would "maneuver" them into firing the first shot; Cordell Hull sent an ultimatum — a final order — to Tokyo. Hull, the Wilsonian idealist, donned his best preacher's garb and delivered a sermon to the recalcitrant Japanese. The ultimatum essentially demanded that Japan must abandon all its economic and military possession in Asia, returning to the Japanese homeland. Further, Hull demanded that Japan grant recognition only to Chiang Kai-shek and that it publicly repudiate the Axis Pact. This ultimatum was a dramatic attack on the Japanese, as Hull was determined to wipe out forty years of change in Asia. Upon sending the message, Secretary Hull acknowledged the severity of his terms, saying to Secretary of War Stimson: "I have washed my hands of it, and it is now in the hands of you and Knox, the Army and the Navy."[2]

The US ultimatum of November 26 ordered the Japanese to turn the clock back decades, only then would FDR resume shipments of oil. With this ultimatum, negotiations were over. Upon receiving the 10-part message, Prime Minister Tojo cabled to the Japanese Ambassador in the United States that he would send a reply shortly and "the negotiations will be de facto ruptured."

THE BACK DOOR TO WAR

For over sixty years, establishment historians have rallied around Franklin Roosevelt, maintaining that no word of the Japanese "sneak attack" on Pearl Harbor ever leaked out beforehand. It is claimed that Franklin Roosevelt, his cabinet and the military leadership simply could not have known the Japanese Armada was heading to Hawaii. One can look far and wide among high school and college textbooks and never discover any facts about the numerous warnings available to Washington D.C. before the Pearl Harbor attack. Gary Nash in his widely used college textbook misinforms the unsuspecting students:

> There was no specific warning that the attack was coming against Pearl Harbor, and the American ability to read the Japanese coded messages was no help because the [Japanese] fleet kept radio silence.[3]

---

1. John Denson, Preface, 2nd ed., *The Costs of War*, p.xiv
2. Henry L. Stimson and McGeorge Bundy, *On Active Service in Peace and War*, (New York: Harper and Brothers, 1948) p. 389.
3. Nash, *The American People*, p. 828.

But as has been shown, FDR, Marshall, Stark, Hull, Stimson and other military and civilian leaders in Washington should not have been caught unaware that an attack on Pearl Harbor was coming. The Purple decoding machines had provided ample evidence of a pending attack; other sources supplemented these "Magic "messages. The evidence is impressive:

- Three independent reports from substantial sources within the Axis alliance, beginning in January 1941, had been received by the Roosevelt administration during the year; each warned that Japan planned to attack the base at Pearl Harbor.
- The Japanese habit of launching a war by a surprise attack on the enemy's military facilities was known and discussed by top United States officials.
- The Bomb Plot messages indicated that the Japanese were preparing a "bomb grid" of Pearl Harbor. FDR apologists have often commented that these messages could have predicted sabotage, rather than an air attack. Hardly! The messages made specific references to "torpedo nets" in the water and barrage "balloons" over the harbor. Saboteurs don't worry about these. The December 6 Bomb Plot message referred specifically to a "surprise aerial attack."
- The Japanese Armada heading for Hawaii was not "lost", but was being tracked across the ocean. Five different sources corroborate this — the USS Lurline, Ranneft's testimony, the ONI plotting, the Dutch Army reports and dozens of radio intercepts from the Armada itself.
- Bill Donovan, the wartime head of intelligence, says in his diary that German military intelligence sources told him in November of the planned attack. These German sources also informed Dusko Popov, the British spy, of this attack.
- The 1:00 p.m. Sunday December 7 deadline coincided with dawn on the Islands.

Immediately after World War II, a few historians associated with the pre-war Isolationist movement made the charge that FDR had engaged in a treacherous scheme to deliberately allow Japan to attack the Pacific fleet, then placed the blame for the disaster on Admiral Kimmel and General Short. They also alleged that FDR had deliberately goaded the Japanese into war in the Pacific in order to induce the American public to support a war in Europe, thus the aptly named "Back Door to War" theory. This theory is partly supported by the facts: Roosevelt did prod Japan unmercifully in 1940 and 1941, refusing their efforts at compromise. He schemed, goaded and pressured Japan, finally getting his war.

His efforts at creating an incident with Japan are well documented and undeniable. His belligerency toward Japan began in the fall of 1940 with the McCollum Plan, and by 1941, against the advice of naval officers, he had moved the Pacific fleet to Hawaii, a provocative and vulnerable site. "Sooner or later Japan would commit an overt act," FDR told people. He schemed to send warships into Japanese waters deliberately baiting Japan, saying "I don't mind losing one or two cruisers," unmindful of the likelihood of deaths resulting from such adventures. The "Pop up Cruises" and the Lanikai suicide mission all testify to a diabolical nature in FDR. By disposition he was a conniving, deceitful man; more of a "Fox" than a "Lion.

The mind, even of a skeptic, hopes that the Roosevelt administration was operating more in the realm of blindness and incompetence than in conspiracy and control. And consider the unlikelihood of a conspiracy to allow an enemy attack. Roosevelt would have had to enlist several others in this devilish scheme. Certainly George Marshall and Harold Stark, the heads of the Army and Navy, would have had to go along with such a conspiracy. Others in the military and civilian departments would need to be enlisted. Roosevelt could not have pulled off such a caper by himself, and the more people involved in the deceit and cover-up, the more unlikely its success becomes. Such a treacherous action by numerous top American officials seems implausible.

The trail of evidence about a Japanese attack was spread over a year; time had the effect of lessening the impact of each message. Some of the "Magic" messages were not decoded promptly; some appear more significant later than at the time. Individuals who read the messages were busy with other matters and devoted too little attention to what came to be telltale signs. All top government officials were very dismissive of the competence of the Japanese. Franklin Roosevelt himself was a careless student, rarely doing his homework. He was notorious for disregarding reports prepared for his review and for bypassing established chains of command. He cherished a personal tidbit from a friend more than documents from the State Department. It is likely that the President treated information about Pearl Harbor in the same way he did his other business, which is to say carelessly. The American leaders should have known that the attack was coming, but perhaps they never added it all up. In much the same way, in 2001 Muslim extremists provided Washington D.C. with numerous warnings that an attack against the United States was in the offing. But again the warnings went unheeded. For this author, and many other "revisionists," this explanation fit the facts — until the fateful discovery of the "Vacant Sea" order.

On November 25, 1941, the day — the exact day — the Japanese armada left its home port for the deadly mission, Rear Admiral Royal Ingersoll, Assistant Chief of Naval Operations, ordered all shipping — merchant and naval — to vacate the entire Northern Pacific Ocean. Thus, just as Kimmel began a reconnaissance in the area, United States Naval officials ordered Kimmel to return to Pearl Harbor. Rear Admiral Richmond Turner of the Naval War Plans Office in Washington D. C. explained the reason for such an order: "We were prepared to divert traffic when we believed that war was imminent. We sent the traffic down via Torres Strait [the South Pacific], so that the track of the Japanese task force would be clear of any traffic."[1]

The last statement boggles the mind! "So that the track of the Japanese task force would be clear of any traffic." In one short sentence, it becomes obvious that the Roosevelt administration knew that a Japanese task force was headed for Pearl Harbor and that Washington wanted the attack to occur. The "Back Door to War" theory is confirmed in its entirety.

From decoded Japanese messages, the United States government knew that Tokyo would attack the American base on the Hawaiian Islands only if they had achieved absolute secrecy. Should the attack fleet be noticed on its eastward voyage, the armada had been ordered to return to its home port. President Roosevelt had schemed for eighteen months to provoke an attack and now, on the verge of achievement, he did not want the attack to be abandoned. Such is the origin of the "Vacant Sea" order.

Some, in defense of FDR's "Vacant Sea" order, have argued that these orders were not devilish, but merely an attempt to keep the American fleet away from the Japanese homeland and to avoid any impression that the United States was launching an attack on Japan. FDR, it is said, wanted the Japanese to fire the first shot. But this defense doesn't hold up. When Kimmel's war game-reconnaissance mission was cancelled in November, the fleet was operating about

---

1. Stinnett, p. 144 Records of the Vacant Sea orders can be found in the Pearl Harbor investigation records complied during eight investigations. See Stinnett's footnotes on p. 359.

200 miles north of the Islands, nowhere near the Japanese homeland. The Hawaiian Islands are 3400 miles from Japan; the Japanese would not become alarmed at the United States fleet operating within 200 miles of its home port and still over 3000 miles from Tokyo. Furthermore, the "Vacant Sea" order applied to all shipping — merchant, commercial and military. Cruise ships and freighters were not allowed in the North Pacific after November 25. On November 28, a Russian freighter heading from San Francisco Bay to the Kamchatka Peninsula was diverted to a port in Oregon where it lay at anchor for five days, awaiting the passing of the Japanese armada. The United States Navy — in Washington D. C. — was directing traffic in the North Pacific to aid the Japanese fleet! Had the "Vacant Sea" order been defensive in nature, Washington would not have diverted freighters out of the area. The "Vacant Sea" order is the clinching evidence on the issue of "Did they know?" Not only did the Roosevelt administration know the attack was coming, they provided assistance to the Japanese.

It is clear to all but the most devoted FDR-lovers that the President was looking for an incident that would involve the United States in war. Secretary of Interior Harold Ickes wrote in his diary: "For a long time I have believed that our best entrance into the [European] war would be by way of Japan."[1] The President obviously shared this sentiment. It was a gamble but like all the world leaders at that time — Churchill, Stalin, Hitler — FDR strode across history with bold strides.

It has been suggested by some — notably the author John Toland in his book *Infamy: Pearl Harbor and Its Aftermath* — that FDR did indeed know the attack was coming and allowed it to occur. However, he did not anticipate a crushing defeat, only a naval and air battle at Hawaii. According to Toland, the United States Navy would inflict a stinging blow to Japan, the air fleet would harry Nippon's crafts, and Japan would slink back home, or so FDR thought. But why FDR would have such an exalted view of the United States Navy in 1941 is difficult to imagine. He knew that the Navy brass opposed placement of the fleet in mid-Pacific because of its weakness, and he knew that the United States was completely outgunned by Japan's Navy. Perhaps more slovenly thinking by the President.

The ineptitude of the Roosevelt team creates an ideal target for "Back Door to War" theorists. Political and military leaders in Washington seemed strangely out of touch with events in the Pacific. All eyes in Washington were on the weekend of December 6 and 7, as it was anticipated that the Japanese would, once again, begin a war with a quick strike against an unsuspecting enemy. As the Purple decoding machines clanked out the final Japanese "Magic" message Saturday night, where were the military leaders of America? When FDR announced to Harry Hopkins Saturday night at 9:30 p.m. that "This means war," why didn't he immediately call a "war council?" Why were the military leaders not available during that critical weekend? It was not business as usual for the Japanese Fleet, nor for the thousands of unsuspecting servicemen killed by the "surprise" attack. Admiral Stark placed himself out of touch Saturday night by going to the theater and FDR chose not to bother him. Sunday morning as the Japanese Armada bore down on thousands of unwary American boys at Pearl Harbor, General of the Army George Marshall was taking his usual horseback ride. Each American leader seemed to

---

1. Thomas Fleming, *The New Dealers War: FDR and the War Within World War II* (New York: Basic Books, 2001), p. 17.

wear on his back that weekend a large sign that read: "DO NOT DISTURB !" It appears that this unavailability was by design.

Suspicious actions following Pearl Harbor add fuel to the fire of conspiracy. Following the Japanese attack, General Marshall ordered a lid put on the whole mess, saying to his military associates in Washington: "Gentlemen, this goes to the grave with us."[1] And why are there no government records of all the reports about the Japanese Armada being tracked across the Pacific? All five of the sources that tracked the Armada across the Pacific — the Lurline, Ranneft, the Dutch, the ONI tracking, and the radio intercepts — were found by researchers from the original sources. However, all records concerning tracking the Japanese Armada have been removed from government files.

Several weeks after the attack, the parents of seventeen-year old Lawrence McCutcheon, a seaman on the battleship *Maryland* who was the first death in this war, received the following message in the mail from the United States government:

> The Secretary of Navy desires to express his deep regrets that your son Seaman Lawrence McCutcheon was killed in action in defense of his country.

Over the course of the next several weeks, 2273 notices were sent to the families of servicemen killed at Pearl Harbor on December 7, 1941. Teddy Roosevelt said that his foreign policy was governed by the saying: "Speak softly but carry a big stick." Franklin Roosevelt may have adopted the slogan "Act boldly but go unarmed".

Admiral James Richardson, fired by FDR because of his opposition to placing the undermanned and under equipped fleet in Hawaii, was embittered at the President after the attack, asserting: "I believe the President's responsibility for our initial defeat in the Pacific was direct, real and personal."[2] General William Brougher, commander of an American division of troops on the Philippine Islands, was indignant about the loss of 20,000 troops when the Japanese overran the lightly defended outpost. General Brougher angrily said: "Who had the right to say that 20,000 Americans should be sentenced without their consent and for no fault of their own to an enterprise that would involve them in endless suffering, cruel handicaps, death or a hopeless future."[3]

President Roosevelt's lame response was that the military leaders had misinformed him about their level of preparedness and had he known the "truth" he would have "stalled off the Japs." The facts are to the contrary; FDR is once again not telling the truth. Admiral Richardson was relieved of his command of the Pacific Fleet because he protested placing the fleet in mid-Pacific due to its lack of strength. Further the written records show that General Marshall, Admiral Stark, and other military leaders persistently argued for a less confrontational approach to the Japanese because the American military was unprepared for war. Instead of babying Japan along, FDR grabbed them by the throat.

---

1. Toland, *Infamy*, p. 321.
2. Fleming, *The New Dealers' War*, p. 46.
3. Ibid., p. 46.

THE FOLLY OF WAR

Negotiations with Japan took on an aura of unreality during the months preceding December 7 as FDR looked for an incident that would provoke war, even taking actions that cleared the North Pacific of shipping allowing the Japanese armada to have an unimpeded shot at Pearl Harbor. The President was not seriously searching for a solution to the United States-Japanese conflict and he made the most of every opportunity to inflame relations between the two antagonists. The exceptional people were being reeled in; Militant Idealism was the hook. The Axis Pact and the Nazi map of the Americas would be the stage upon which FDR played out his drama.

In September 1940, Japan, Germany and Italy signed an agreement that has become known as the Axis Pact. This alliance pledged each signatory to support efforts to create a New Order in Asia and Europe, and to come to the assistance of each other should a member be attacked by a nation not then at war. A separate clause exempted the Soviet Union from this coverage. Therefore, the Axis Pact took dead aim at the United States, saying essentially, "leave us alone or we will all war against you." When the Pact was made, the European war was going well for Germany, and Japan did a little "piggybacking" on those early German victories. Within a month of signing the Pact, Japan secured from Vichy France permission to use airfields and ports in French Indochina, Germany encouraging this "southern strategy" of Japan.

To Cordell Hull, the Axis Pact was an "agreement among gangster aggressors for dividing up the world." FDR, ever ready with proof of the diabolical nature of the Japanese regime, introduced a secret "Axis map" depicting a globe divided among the Axis powers, with even Latin America apportioned to the "gangsters." The secret Axis map was revealed publicly at a White House dinner the evening of October 27, 1941 and was the subject of instant nation-wide news coverage. The President commented during the dinner on the "secret map":

> Hitler has often protested that his plans for conquest do not extend across the Atlantic Ocean. I have in my possession a secret map, made in Germany, by Hitler's government — by planners of the New World order.... It is a map of South America and a part of Central America as Hitler proposes to organize it.[1]

The President concluded by saying that German plans would reduce the fourteen Latin American republics to "five vassal states...bringing the whole continent under [Nazi] domination." For the news media, this was the story of the week. For the American public, it was a shock to learn of their vulnerability, and the possibility of Hitler rampaging on their continent.

FDR well knew that this was false information. Adolph Berle, a State Department official, had told him that British agents in America had designed and were circulating these fraudulent maps. Berle advised the President to be cautious as "we have to be a little on our guard against false scares."[2] Unable to rouse the American public for war in Europe with accurate facts, Roosevelt lied — deliberately lied — to the people in an effort to inflame them against Germany and its Axis partners.

By the summer and fall of 1941, Japan had begun to sour on its relationship with Germany, as its Axis partner lost the Battle of Britain, abandoned plans to invade England and

---

1. Thompson, *A Time For War*, p. 357
2. Ibid., p. 360.

its blitzkrieg sputtered and began to die in Eastern Europe. Prince Konoye, when discussing a summit meeting with President Roosevelt, let it be known that he would consider quietly withdrawing from the Axis Pact. But when the United States required a public repudiation, the opportunity was lost. FDR always made too many demands on Japan. Roosevelt was not looking for a solution to the troubles with Japan.

It seems clear that the Axis Pact was a godsend to FDR as it enabled the President to link Japan to Nazi Germany. Americans were inherently reluctant to involve themselves in another war in Europe, but they could be enticed into going to war for the defense of the Philippines and China — two old favorites of the Republican Party. Thus FDR was able to tie the "tin can" of Nazi Germany to the "cat's tail" of Japan. Whatever Tokyo did, the clatter of Hitler was not far behind. Had Konoye repudiated the Axis Pact, there was no other game for FDR to play?

The best hope for a negotiated settlement of the Far East conflict was a proposal for a summit meeting with Konoye and Roosevelt in the fall 1941. Not only was the Japanese Prime Minister prepared to abrogate the Axis Pact, but he also verbally committed to a phased withdrawal from Indochina in exchange for gradual resumption of trade with America. In the offing was a return to the *status quo* of a year earlier. It was the last chance for the moderate leader Prince Konoye; when the summit effort failed, the "War Party" of General Tojo took over.

Why did FDR refuse to meet with Konoye in September 1941? The President took great pride in his ability to charm world leaders, traveling far and wide during World War Two — Casablanca, Cairo, Tehran, Yalta, Newfoundland — to meet prime ministers, presidents, and dictators face-to-face, even extending himself to confer with Joseph Stalin. But he refused to meet with Japanese Prime Minister Konoye! Instead of taking control himself, he turned the Japanese matters over to Cordell Hull, who promptly derailed the negotiations.

Cordell Hull, Henry Stimson and others moralists in the Roosevelt administration were confident they saw clearly what Japanese foreign policy goals were. But historians have debated this issue for decades. Since the 1890s, Japan had attempted to obtain economic rights and defense bases in and around northern China. As Japan pursued these goals they received approval from America, although in 1931 Henry Stimson inflicted a scolding on them over the Manchurian Incident. But beginning in the summer of 1940, Japan turned its attention toward Southeast Asia — Indochina, Singapore, the Dutch East Indies (Indonesia) — and with that change, the United States began to tighten the screws. This change in direction by Japan coincided with the German defeat of France and an increased desire on the part of FDR to enter the European war. For forty years America had looked the other way as Japan had its way in Asia; by 1940 FDR determined to stop the conquests — or at least to provoke an incident that would draw America into the larger war.

When Japan moved its military forces into French Indochina after France was defeated in Europe, Roosevelt took severe economic measures against Japan. To the Japanese their occupation of Vietnam was an innocent move and they asked how this action differed from the American occupation of Danish-owned Greenland and Iceland after the collapse of Denmark. When Cordell Hull fumed about the Japanese economic and military intrusion into Manchuria, the Japanese wanted to know if this was different than American incursions into Mexico, Cuba, Haiti and the Dominican Republic over the past several decades. And as previously mentioned, the Japanese saw their Greater East Asia Co-Prosperity Sphere as resembling the American Monroe Doctrine. This type of thinking even caught the attention of an American official in Asia who cabled to the American Secretary of State in 1927 that: "We cannot oppose Japanese plans in Manchuria ethically in view of measures we have taken in our correspondingly vital zone — the Caribbean."[1]

American leaders in the 20th century were completely caught up in the notion of American exceptionalism; FDR's refusal to negotiate seriously with the Japanese is clear evidence of this arrogance. In this mental condition, Presidents are blind to the rank hypocrisy of American actions. The United States was holding Japan to a higher standard of conduct than it expected of itself or its allies. America was scolding Japan, then winking at the imperial ventures of Britain, France, the Dutch or its own conquests. The Japanese were and are great emulators and had learned their lessons well from Great Britain, France and the United States. In 1933, while the Manchurian Incident was still foaming, Japanese Foreign Minister Matsuoka made this succinct, wry comment, "The Western Powers taught the Japanese the game of poker, but after [Japan] acquired most of the chips they [the Europeans] pronounced the game immoral and took up contract bridge."[2]

By the fall 1941, the United States was making impossible demands on Japan. Militant Idealism had replaced strategic prudence and the Roosevelt administration harassed Japan, demanding that it disgorge its conquests and abandoned its evil ways. To ask that they withdraw from Indochina, China, and Manchuria immediately before the embargo was lifted was not truly negotiating — it was a tacit declaration of war. In posing as the champion and defenders of Nationalist China, the United States was assuming a military task that it could not possibly accomplish. Controlling Japanese expansion on the mainland of Asia was beyond the military capability of any nation. Certainly the mothers and fathers of American servicemen would not condone an American invasion of the Asian continent. It was "realistic" to attempt to block Japanese expansion into the islands of the Pacific, as the United States could fashion a navy equal to that task. But not the continent of Asia. As the historian Paul Schroeder said, "The plain fact is that the United States in 1941 was not capable of forcing Japan out of China by means short of war and was neither willing nor ...able to throw the Japanese out by war."[3]

During the Manchurian Incident in 1931, Theodore Roosevelt's Secretary of State, Elihu Root, had cautioned his friend, Henry Stimson, then the chief of the State Department, that the United States was getting in over its head in Asia. Referring to his own agreement in 1908 with Japan which granted Nippon special rights in the area, Root warned about "getting entangled in League [of Nations] measures which we have no right to engage in against Japan."[4]

Instead of backing Japan into a corner with the oil embargo and offending them with distortions about the Axis Pact, or haranguing them with Hull's sermons on international etiquette, FDR should have stalled, bought time and displayed patience, all the time waiting for Germany's fortunes in Europe to decline, meanwhile building up American military force. Germany's military fortunes peaked in 1942, shortly after Pearl Harbor. By late 1942 the United

---

1. Charles C. Tansill, "Back Door to War," in George Waller, ed., *Pearl Harbor: Roosevelt and the Coming of the War*, p. 23.
2. Ibid., p. 31.
3. Paul W. Schroeder, "The Axis Alliance and Japanese-American Relations," in Jerald A. Combs, ed., *Three Views of American Diplomacy*, p. 411.
4. Charles C. Tansill, "Back Door to War," in George Waller, ed., *Pearl Harbor: Roosevelt and the Coming of the War*, p. 26.

States would have been producing sufficient planes, guns and ships to be able to keep for its own use more than the 5% to 10% that it was actually doing in 1941. As Thomas Fleming says in his book *The New Dealers' War*:

> ... had FDR been determined to avoid war with the Japanese, he would have conducted American foreign policy quite differently.... He would not have tried to starve the Japanese Navy for oil. And he would have settled down to some hard and realistic dealings with the Japanese, instead of letting them be deluged and frustrated by the cloudy and unintelligible moralism of Cordell Hull.[1]

There are ardent defenders of FDR who, like the historian Basil Rauch, applaud him for standing "On the Rock of Principle" and refusing to back down when facing the gangster Japanese. The so-called "Rock of Principle" is the Open Door policy — a policy of a free and independent China, open to trade by all nations. But this somewhat naive, idealistic notion was tattered and torn by the Thirties. Since 1900, the United States had facilitated Japanese expansion into Korea and Manchuria, looking the other way while Britain expanded and continued its imperial policies in the Far East. Then after World War II, FDR even accepted Soviet advances throughout the region. Showing his ultimate hypocrisy over the Open Door in China, Roosevelt, without China's approval, gave Stalin immense areas of China as a reward for the Soviet weeklong war against Japan in August 1945. The sad fact is that Roosevelt cynically used the Open Door policy in 1941 to provoke a war against Japan; a gullible, idealistic public and a compliant, obsequious historical community fell in line.

The Open Door policy also raised hopes of the fabled China trade; for a century American theorists of expansion, with their business allies, had fostered the idea of a "mother lode of riches" coming out of China. Conversely, dismal tales of economic depression were told should the China trade and investment opportunities be closed to America. The gloomy tales were untrue: the China trade was, in fact, closed to America for 25 years, from the late 1940s until Nixon began to pry open the door to China in the 1970s. Yet America experienced a massive boom from World War II until the oil shocks of the Seventies. The American public is so inattentive that year after year the White House recites arguments that are absurd; few hold the perpetrators to account. From the vantage point of the year 2004, the economic implications of the Open Door policy have been a massive fraud. Efforts to enforce the policy have resulted in thousands of needless deaths of American and Asians.

Other historians admit FDR's mistakes and recognize that he maneuvered Japan into an attack, but argue that presidential deceit was necessary in view of the Axis threat. John Toland takes this view, as does the eminent diplomatic historian, Thomas Bailey. According to Bailey, "Franklin Roosevelt repeatedly deceived the American people during the period before Pearl Harbor....He was like a physician who must tell the patient lies for the patient's own good."[2]

The political implications to the American system of government of this defense are frightening. What Bailey and others are saying here is that it is perfectly acceptable that a president lies to the public, and takes the nation into war without a rational debate. This is essentially the "Fuehrer principle," the hated notion of Nazi Germany that people should "follow the leader" wherever he went. Using the tactics of Hitler, FDR lied the nation into war. One sus-

---

1. Fleming, *The New Dealers' War*, p. 47-48.
2. Thomas A Bailey, *The Man in the Street*, p. 13.

pects that this is merely a political cover for the beloved Democrat president. Would these same historians be so forgiving if George W. Bush, a Republican, lied the United States into a war?

The American public, FDR reasoned, would more readily accept a war in the Pacific than return to Europe where memories of the fiasco of World War I were still fresh The Japanese were more easily manipulated than Germany. Nippon would be FDR's foil. Franklin Roosevelt, who many historians rate as the nation's greatest president, even took action to facilitate the attack.

The war in the Pacific was avoidable and unnecessary. Had the United States displayed patience rather than belligerence, the war could have been averted, and the thousands of deaths that came with this needless war would be wiped away. Even on the eve of the Pearl Harbor disaster, after months of Roosevelt's anti-Axis distortions and propaganda, the American people still showed an amazing resistance to the fables from the White House: Gallup polls show that the number of people in support of a war never exceeded 19%. The Japanese attack on Pearl Harbor saved FDR's pro-war plans.

In the long term the greatest casualties in this episode were truth and the integrity of the American presidency. For if the American people cannot be entrusted with decisions about war and peace and must be lied to like children, what remains of the democratic process? Franklin Roosevelt replaced a system of popular, constitutional government with a monarchy, one in which government decisions reside solely in the "royal executive." In his war declaration message to the Congress on December 8, President Roosevelt said that December 7, 1941 would be a day that would live in "Infamy." And indeed that is so. But after a closer look at the events leading up to that war, much of the Infamy resides in Washington D.C.

Chapter 7. World War II: America's Second European Crusade

The Revolt of the German Generals

The battle of Stalingrad during the winter of 1942-43 was a disaster for the German Army, an ominous warning for their military effort across Europe. The German campaign against Stalingrad was launched in August 1942; five months later the starving, frozen Wehrmacht was thrown out of the city by a Russian counterattack. During the battle for Stalingrad, Germany lost 350,000 men; on January 31, 1943 the German Field Marshall surrendered. Chancellor Hitler and the generals knew that this was not just an ordinary military defeat. This was a forewarning that Germany would lose World War II. And this was the signal for a renewal of the revolt of the German generals.

Hitler and his generals had never been friendly and the relationship deteriorated as the war proceeded. Hitler failed to consult them about conscription, a subject close to their hearts as Army officers had always been selected by the largely Prussian general staff. Hitler's conscription order in 1935 threatened to overwhelm the Army with Nazis, thereby destroying Prussian control. The Prussian military, like its counterparts in the United States, France, Britain and Japan, were reluctant to engage in adventuresome military forays. And when Hitler sent troops into the Rhineland in 1936, and when the Fuehrer prepared for the union with Austria and at other critical occasions over the next few years, the cautious general's advice was disregarded. Throughout the war, Hitler relentlessly tightened his grip on war strategy.

The Abwehr, the German military intelligence agency, was a nest of anti-Nazi Prussian officers. Prior to December 7, 1941, the Abwehr had made repeated attempts to inform America of the pending Japanese attack on Pearl Harbor, but to no avail as the United States ignored the warnings. When the military campaign in Eastern Europe began to flounder in 1942, Hitler shoved aside the military chiefs to manage the war himself. At the battle of Stalingrad, Hitler refused to stage a tactical retreat, an action resulting in the destruction of the German Army. Military officers began to desert the Nazi leadership; even the renowned General Erwin

Rommel forsook his military oath of obedience, saying, "I believe it is my duty to come to the rescue of Germany."[1] Beginning in 1943, the generals made repeated efforts to assassinate the Fuehrer, the most dramatic being Colonel Claus von Stauffenberg's attempt on July 20, 1944. But there were earlier attempts; unfortunately all went awry.

After Stalingrad, as the reality began to sink in that Germany could not win the war, General Henning von Tresckow approached Field Marshall Guenther von Kluge to join the conspiracy against the Nazi chief. Kluge agreed to cooperate and plans were made to invite Hitler to Kluge's headquarters near Smolensk. A bomb made by the Abwehr officers was wrapped as a gift of liquor and plans were made to place it aboard Hitler's airplane on the return flight to Berlin. The bomb was to be detonated by a vial of corrosive acid, set to explode 30 minutes after the plane took off. As the plane was preparing for take-off, General von Tresckow asked a member of Hitler's traveling party to take a "gift of liquor" to an old friend in Berlin. A coded message was then sent to General Beck, the leader of the conspirators in Berlin, that all was well and to prepare for the take-over of government. Unfortunately, the airplane heater in the luggage compartment failed to operate, and as the plane gained altitude, the vial of acid froze. A member of the conspiracy in Berlin retrieved the package before the plot was discovered. All the conspirators survived to plot another day.

A few weeks later, General von Tresckow enlisted Baron Rudolph von Gersdorff as a volunteer to blow up Hitler and himself with a suicide bomb at an exhibit of captured enemy weapons. The bomb was fused and von Gersdorff escorted Hitler on a planned hour-long tour. Inexplicably, Hitler hurried through the exhibit in five minutes, leaving the surprised von Gersdorff with a live bomb on his body. Baron von Gersdorff rushed to the men's room and defused it in time. Once again the Fuehrer escaped, but the Prussian generals continued to pursue their quarry.

Captain Axel von dem Bussche witnessed a massacre of Jews in Eastern Europe and was so revolted by the episode that he volunteered to be a suicide bomber. New uniforms had been purchased for the German officers and Hitler was planning to review them. Bussche, who was to escort Hitler through the exhibit, wore one of the uniforms with a bomb hidden inside. He planned to set the fuse, jump on the Fuehrer and blow both into oblivion. At the last minute, Hitler postponed the visit and before another "rendezvous" could be scheduled, British bombers destroyed the demonstration hall.

Three attempts on his life and Hitler was unscathed, even oblivious to what was transpiring. But surely Hitler's luck would give out on the fourth attempt. As Germany's fortunes in war flagged and as Hitler's mind veered more and more away from reality, the military officers were joined by other anti-Nazi figures. "By 1944 something like a grand coalition of political and military conservative opponents of Hitler had taken shape, culminating in the attempt on his life in July."[2]

On July 20, 1944, Colonel Claus von Stauffenberg flew to Hitler's retreat known as Wolf's Lair in East Prussia. The Abwehr had prepared two powerful bombs to be used during a mid-day conference. Stauffenberg planned to blow up the German leader with the bombs hidden in his briefcase. By 11:30 AM Stauffenberg was in a briefing room preparing for the 12:30

---

1. Fleming, The *New Dealers' War*, p. 371.
2. Sebastian Haffner, The *Meaning of Hitler* (New York: Macmillan, 1979), p. 59.

p.m. meeting with Hitler and a staff of two dozen officers. Because Stauffenberg was handicapped from a war injury and had only one hand and that with just two fingers, he had assistance in fusing the bombs. He and his aide, Lieutenant Werner von Haeften, went to a nearby men's room to prepare the bombs, but they only had time to fuse one before they were called to the conference. The bomb in the briefcase was set to go off in 15 minutes; things had to flow smoothly.

The military briefing took place in a wooden hut because a more formal room generally used was too hot for the sultry July day. The meeting was just underway when Stauffenberg entered the room and seated himself immediately to Hitler's right along a wooden table. The briefcase was placed under the table alongside a table leg. By the time all of the introductions and preliminaries were concluded, Stauffenberg had only a few minutes remaining. He excused himself, leaving his cap and belt on his chair making it appear he would return. Outside he conferred briefly with two confederates and made arrangements for the car that would return him to the airport. At just that moment there was a deafening explosion. Stauffenberg and Haeften left hurriedly for the airport and then to Berlin where the Army takeover was to occur. The size of the bomb and its proximity to Hitler seemed to assure that he would be killed. At the instant of the explosion, Hitler was leaning over the table studying a map. There was a flash of yellow and blue flames and an ear-splitting bang.

> Windows and doors blew out. Clouds of thick smoke billowed up. Flying glass splinters, pieces of wood, and showers of paper and other debris flew in all directions. Parts of the wrecked hut were aflame. For a time there was pandemonium. Twenty-four people had been in the briefing room at the time of the explosion. Some were hurled to the floor or blown across the room. Others had hair or clothes in flames. There were cries of help. Human shapes stumbled around — concussed, part-blinded, eardrums shattered — in the smoke and debris, desperately seeking to get out of the ruins of the hut.[1]

Several officers died or were wounded, but Hitler survived. He was stunned and shortly made his way through the wreckage, beating his hands against the flames on his trousers and attempting to douse the flames in his hair. His jacket was torn, the seat of his pants was gone, his eardrums were punctured and his arms were injured. His valet came rushing to his side, and the Fuehrer said "Someone has tried to kill me."[2] Actually the Prussian generals had tried to kill him several times. None of them successful.

Stauffenberg arrived in Berlin confident of the success of the assassination attempt. But when the Prussian Guard went to arrest Joseph Goebbels, the Nazi propaganda chief called Wolf's Lair and discovered that Hitler was alive. The Prussian Guard then turned on the conspirators and before the night was over Stauffenberg and three others were killed; Stauffenberg shouted "Long live Germany" as the bullets tore into his body. Tresckow, Beck, Kluge, and Erwin Rommel, the Desert Fox of Africa fame, all committed suicide to cheat their executioners. Over 7000 people were arrested in the next few days. Military resistance to Hitler died with this valiant effort.

The Soviet Union expressed pleasure at Stauffenberg's assassination attempt and broadcast a statement to the German Army in support of the conspirators: "Generals, officers,

---

1. Ian Kershaw, *Hitler: 1939-45 Nemesis* (New York: W. W. Norton, 2000), p. 673,674.
2. Ibid., p. 674.

soldiers! Cease fire at once and turn your arms against Hitler. Do not fail these courageous men!"[1]

However, reaction in London and Washington D.C. to the heroic efforts by Stauffenberg and the other Prussians was muted, even discouraging. Although American intelligence agents had learned of the plots and had informed FDR, he gave no verbal support nor did he pass the word to the generals that a surrender deal would be offered if their mission was successful. Prime Minister Churchill made a rather frivolous comment that there was "a very great disturbance in the German machine."[2] This lack of support for the assassination efforts of the generals was largely due to the Allied policy toward Germany of total defeat and "unconditional surrender." It didn't matter to the United States whether Hitler or the generals were in power; Germany was going to be crushed. No surrender terms would be offered to any German government.

The western press commented unsympathetically on the German generals' revolt. The leftist magazine *Nation* regarded the plotters as the vanguard of Prussian militarists and "Junker chiefs" who were just out to save their own skin. The New York *Herald Tribune* was happy to see the Fuehrer survive and saw the execution of conspirators as "doing a large part of the Allies work for them." The *Herald Tribune* continued, saying these aristocrats who ran the Prussian Army were the "personification of German arrogance" and "the chief exponents of [the] master race."[3]

Informed people knew that it was not the Prussian elite that pursued racial theories, but Hitler himself and the Nazi Party. The Prussian generals, by and large, were aghast at such human savagery. Adolf Hitler, born of lower class parents, was a man of the streets and the Munich bar halls. The Prussian elites had little in common with such a disreputable character. But the American leaders, media and public were still suffering from an overdose of anti-German propaganda doled out by the British in World War I. It is ironic that Woodrow Wilson and the other western leaders forced the removal of the Prussian generals in 1918, weakening that traditional group in German life. Therefore, when it came time to find a strong force to overthrow the Nazis, the generals were too weak to accomplish the task. Western understanding of Germany was distorted and out of focus, hardly knowing who their enemy was. Their minds were so clouded they didn't know that Stauffenberg, Rommel, Beck and the others were attempting to overthrow the Nazis and aid the Allied cause in the only way they could.

HITLER'S FOREIGN POLICY

"Hitler was out to conquer the world!" All Americans, then and now, believe this to be true, and therefore, American involvement in the European war is deemed necessary. However, the facts are to the contrary. Adolf Hitler and the Nazi Party provided a road map of their foreign policy for the world to read. *Mein Kampf*, Hitler's bizarre and disturbing story of his life

---

1. Ibid., p. 424
2. Fleming, *The New Dealers' War*, p. 423.
3. Ibid., p. 424.

and personal beliefs written in the Twenties, delineates what he foresaw as the proper German foreign:

- Abrogate the Treaty of Versailles.
- Develop an alliance with Great Britain.
- Unite in the Fatherland all Germans who were "lost" in adjacent nations.
- Acquire living space (Lebensraum) for Germany in the East of Europe.

The Treaty of Versailles had humiliated Germany; *Mein Kampf* and statements by the Nazi leadership obsessed on the hated Treaty. German obligations to pay billions in reparations to the Western Allies in compensation for war costs and damages were a lingering sore spot. The schedule of payments set up in 1921 required Germany to divert 6% of its national income to reparations, a financial burden roughly equivalent to the adjustments required of the industrial world as a result of the "oil shocks" of the early 1970s. With American assistance in the Twenties, this burden was reduced, then early in the Thirties the payments ceased altogether. By the mid-Thirties, Germany once again had the largest economy in Europe. More serious than the monetary costs was the psychological stigma of the reparation issue, for it was indelibly coupled in the German mind with the hated "War Guilt clause" and the *Diktat* of the Treaty of Versailles.

The Treaty also placed severe restrictions on Germany's ability to wage "wars of aggression" or even to defend itself. The disarmament clauses of the Treaty forbade Germany from having a motorized air force (thus the famed gliders of the inter-war years) or to build capital ships for a navy. The Army was limited to a constabulary force of 100,000 soldiers. Further, three key German cities along the Rhine River were occupied by Allied forces, and Germany itself was prohibited from placing any military force in the German Rhineland area.

By 1930, the French-British occupation of the Rhineland ceased when their troops were removed. In 1935, Hitler began building a military force, announcing that Germany would no longer abide by the Treaty's disarmament restrictions. On March 7, 1936, the German Army marched into the demilitarized Rhineland in defiance of the Treaty. German citizens lined the streets and waved gleefully as their Army marched past, but the generals were in consternation as the newly-formed Army was in no condition to resist, had France chosen to enforce the Treaty. The Western allies watched these events with resignation, as most saw the necessity in correcting the injustices of the Treaty.

German unification was only fifty years old when the Treaty of Versailles became effective in 1919. The nations of Europe were still bewildered, some even hostile, towards the powerful German State stretched across Central Europe. The Germans recognized their own geographic vulnerability; Russia in the east was their prime adversary, with France in the west, still smoldering with resentment, a close second. Rivalry with Russia and France were geopolitical facts of life, therefore German foreign policy looked upon Great Britain and Italy as "natural allies." In *Mein Kampf* Hitler explains his reasoning: "The [German] coastline especially was unfavorable from the military standpoint for a fight with England; it was short and cramped, and the land front, on the other hand, is disproportionately long and open."[1]

Germany has no mountain ranges for defense as have Italy and Spain, no great body of water to insulate it as Britain and America, no vast stretches of land that can swallow an

---

1. Adolph Hitler, *Mein Kampf*, (Boston: Houghton Mifflin, 1943), p. 617.

opponent, as Russia. Germany is vulnerable by land and by sea and must arrange its allies in accordance with geography. Hitler's conclusion was: "I have already designated England and Italy as the only two states in Europe with which a closer relationship would be desirable and promising for us."[1]

This alliance policy looked promising in 1935 when the Anglo-German Naval Treaty was concluded, stipulating that Germany would limit its Navy to only one-third the size of the British. Germany would undertake no "dreadnought" building program; no German surface fleet would disturb His Majesty's maritime dominance. Hitler would foreswear an overseas colonial policy and concentrate on the continent of Europe. Having no large Navy and no overseas colonies, Germany would pose no threat to England. In a conversation with his generals early in the war, Hitler still had kind words for the British Empire, likening it to the Catholic Church in providing stability to the international scene, and claiming that "all he wanted from Britain was that she acknowledge Germany's position on the continent."[2] Great Britain, it had been hoped, would be Germany's ally, not its adversary.

Reclaiming the "lost Germans" was a popular theme in the nation and among the ten million Germans "trapped" in surrounding nations. Wilsonian "self-determination" was in the air and the Nazi leaders breathed deeply of its nationalistic aroma. The demographic scorecard of "lost Germans" looked like this:

- Six million Austrian-Germans ready to be absorbed into the Reich.
- Three million Sudeten-Germans just across the border in Czechoslovakia.
- 350,000 Germans in Danzig on the Baltic Sea at the head of the Polish Corridor.
- Millions more trapped inside Poland, Hungary, the Ukraine and other nations.

The issue of living space (Lebensraum) was the most controversial and adventuresome element in Hitler's agenda. Many Germans believed the nation was becoming overpopulated (Germany was the most populous nation in Europe, other than Russia). Further, Germany lacked materials for industry and because of the "starvation blockade" during World War I, Germany needed more land for growing food — land for food, oil and ores, land for spreading out its burgeoning population. Lebensraum! The Germany of pre-World War I sought to solve these dilemmas by acquiring overseas colonies, an action that offended England. Nazi Germany would solve its resource problems at the expense of Russia and the nations of Eastern Europe. Theirs would be a continental policy, not a colonial policy. The strategy is clear; the enemy is Russia:

> Everything I undertake is directed against Russia. If the West is too stupid and blind to grasp this I shall be compelled to come to an agreement with the Russians, beat the West and then after their defeat turn against the Soviet Union with all my forces. I need the Ukraine so that they can't starve me out as happened in the last war.[3]

Therefore, German foreign policy as prescribed by Hitler included an assortment of spices:

---

1. Ibid, p. 664-665.
2. Charles C. Tansill, "The United States and the Road to War in Europe," in Harry Elmer Barnes, ed., *Perpetual War For Perpetual Peace*, p. 162; Liddell Hart, *The German Generals Talk* (New York: William Morrow and Company, 1949), p. 135.
3. Roy Denman, *Missed Chances: Britain and Europe in the Twentieth Century* (London: Indigo, 1996), p. 65.

- A helping of theories from "geopoliticians" who suggested that any nation that controlled Eastern Europe would be a world power.
- A dash of Pan-Germanism that hoped to preserve the German Volk and shepherd millions of Germans back into the Reich.
- Some hatred and fear of Russian communism, portending the Cold War.
- A large scoop of resentment about the Treaty of Versailles.

The German Weimar government (1919-1933), which preceded the Nazi regime, had pursued much the same foreign policy without Hitler's intensity and eventual savagery. Nazi foreign policy in the Thirties and Weimar foreign policy in the Twenties differed more in degrees than in kind. Beginning in the early Twenties, the West began "appeasing" the Weimar government, making concessions to Germany:

- France withdraws its troops from the Ruhr industrial area of Germany.
- The Locarno Treaty recognizes Germany as an equal partner in settling disputes.
- Reparation totals are reduced and payment schedules extended.
- Germany is admitted to the League of Nations.
- Troops of the Western allies withdraw from the Rhineland ahead of schedule.

None of the above concessions caused any great uproar in the diplomatic halls of Europe. Concessions (appeasement) continued during the early Nazi years (1933-1938):

- The disarmament clauses of the Treaty are abrogated.
- The Saar area votes to unite with Germany rather than with France.
- The disarmament clause dealing with the Rhineland is scrapped.
- A naval treaty with Britain is concluded.
- The union of Germany and Austria is completed.
- The Munich conference grants the German-populated Sudetenland of Czechoslovakia to Germany.

For twenty years the Western nations tacitly, and sometimes openly, agreed with Germany that the Treaty of Versailles was too harsh and consistently sought ways to ameliorate or eliminate the restrictions. Western leaders had concluded that if Versailles were abrogated, Nazism would lose some of its force. Lord Halifax, the British Lord President, agreed with this philosophy when he told Hitler in 1937 that "possible alterations might be destined to come about with the passage of time," but these changes "should come through the course of peaceful evolution...."[1]

A spirit of conciliation was sweeping Europe in the mid-Thirties as even the French let it be known to German leaders that they would not be opposed to changes in the map of Europe. A German diplomat reported to Hitler that the French Premier "considered a reorientation of French policy in Central Europe as entirely open to discussion." And there would be "no objection to a marked extension of German influence in Austria obtained through evolutionary means," or in Czechoslovakia "on the basis of reorganization into a nation of nationalities."[2] The vindictive French leadership in 1919 — Georges Clemenceau and Marshall Foch — would never have understood this new conciliatory French attitude.

---

1. A. J. P. Taylor, *The Origins of the Second World War* (Greenwich, CT.: Fawcett Publications, 1961), p. 134.
2. Ibid., p. 134-135.

With considerable agitation from the Austrian Nazi Party and some badgering from Berlin, the union of Germany and Austria was completed in March 1938; a national plebiscite later confirmed the union by a 99% vote.

In the fall of 1938, attention turned to the Czechoslovakian borderlands with Germany in the Sudeten Mountains, the famed Sudetenland. There, several million Sudeten Germans, plagued by persistent discrimination in employment, language, welfare, and in elections, agitated for union with their Fatherland. They eventually found success at the Munich conference in September 1938 when Germany was granted a border adjustment at the expense of Czechoslovakia.

Often overlooked in the turmoil over the Sudetenland, was the budding military alliance between the Czechs and the Soviet Union in 1937. Russian military attaches were swarming through the Czech state and twenty-five airfields large enough to accommodate Soviet bombers were under construction.[1] The French, always ready to stir the pot, had a hand in forming the alliance. In Berlin, age-old German fears of encirclement were revived. Russia was moving westward to thwart Hitler's eastward thrust. In June 1938, Hitler had reassured his ever-cautious generals: "I shall only decide to take action against Czechoslovakia if, as in the case of the occupation of the demilitarized zone and the entry into Austria, I am firmly convinced that France will not march and therefore will not intervene either."[2]

France's armies didn't march, nor did Britain's. Even the usually bellicose Churchill made hopeful comments about the possibility of Hitler following in the footsteps of men who began their careers with "frightful methods" then later "have been regarded as great figures whose lives have enriched the story of mankind."[3] British Foreign Secretary, Anthony Eden told his constituents: "Nobody will quarrel with the Government's wish to bring about appeasement in Europe. Any other intention would be as foolish as it would be wrong."[4]

When Prime Minister Neville Chamberlain returned to London from Munich with the document he claimed would ensure "peace in our time," FDR telegraphed him, "Good man."[5] American leaders, contrary to standard history accounts, were supportive of the Sudetenland border adjustment. Sumner Welles, American Undersecretary of State, made a radio address in which he asserted that FDR had encouraged the Munich settlement "to halt Europe's headlong plunge into the Valley of the Shadow of Death." Welles concluded: "Europe escaped war by a few hours, the scales being tipped toward peace by the president's appeal."[6] President Roosevelt said he was "not a bit upset over the final results," and later wrote the Canadian Prime Minister about his support of the Munich settlement, saying, "I can assure you that we in the United States rejoice with you and the world at large, that the outbreak of war was

1. David Irving, *The War Path, Hitler's Germany, 1933-1939* (New York: The Viking Press, 1978) p. 46, 61-62.
2. Taylor, p. 162.
3. Buchanan, *A Republic, Not An Empire*, p. 257.
4. Ibid. p. 257-258.
5. Nicolas John Cull, *Selling War: The British Propaganda Campaign against America Neutrality* (New York: Oxford University Press, 1995), p. 21.
6. William Henry Chamberlin, *America's Second Crusade* (Chicago: Henry Regnery Company, 1950) p. 99

averted."[1] The German Fuehrer caught the ebullient spirit when he said, "I have no more territorial demands to make in Europe."[2]

As the American and European world celebrated the Christmas season in 1938, they found happiness and contentment in the knowledge that the world was at peace. The harsh Treaty of Versailles was being repealed bit by bit by the European powers, and Germany was more content with its place in Europe than at any time since before the Great War. But one year later Europe was at war, a war more terrible than the First World War. What caused this about-face? Two events shattered the tranquility of Europe. One was the disintegration of the Czechoslovakian State, and the other was the crisis over Danzig and the Polish Corridor.

THE ROAD TO WAR — CZECHOSLOVAKIA AND POLAND

In September 1938 on the day after the Munich conference, Poland annexed a coal-rich area of Czechoslovakia filled with Poles known as Tesin. Then in March 1939, Slovakia, always restive as the junior partner in Czechoslovakia, chose to secede, an action encouraged by Germany. Hungary joined the feast taking a chunk out of the truncated Czech State along its border. Carved up like a Thanksgiving turkey with only a rump state left, the Czech leadership appealed to Germany for protection and Hitler was only too happy to oblige. Six months after the Munich settlement, Czechoslovakia ceased to exist as an independent nation. A true and accurate picture of the collapse of the Munich agreement would show that it was not Hitler alone who undermined the deal. Poland, Hungary, and Slovakia played leading roles in the dismemberment of the Czech State. "The German dictator instead of snatching his victuals from the table, has been content to have them served to him course by course."[3]

In the West, the public held a view of Czechoslovakia that bordered on fantasy. The notion was prevalent then, and remains so even today, that the Czechs were hard working, tolerant people who had the only democracy in the area and if left alone would have pursued an idyllic multi-national life with civil rights for all. The reality, however, was that the Treaty of Versailles had created an unstable nation, filled with turbulent minorities striving to be released, and the Czech leadership provided little civil rights protection for Germans, Poles, Slovaks and other non-Czechs trapped within the nation. It was a nation ready to implode; Hitler and the Czech neighbors only needed to give it a nudge.

The concessions of the Munich conference that were popular around the world in the fall of 1938, by the summer of 1939 were reviled. "Appeasement" entered the language as a pejorative word and America "learned" that making concessions only whets the appetite of marauding nations. In 1938, the Munich Conference was everyone's child; by 1939, it was an orphan. A culprit for the disappearance of the Czech states had to be found: the culprit became Nazi Germany.

---

1. Charles C. Tansill, "The United States and the Road to War In Europe," in Harry Elmer Barnes, ed., *Perpetual War For Perpetual Peace*, p.154.
2. Taylor, *The Origins of the Second World War*, p. 181.
3. Michael Jabara Carley, *1939: the Alliance that Never Was and the Coming of World War II* (Chicago: Ivan R. Dee, 1999), p. 71.

The last straw on the road to war was the dispute over the city of Danzig and the issue of the Polish Corridor. The Treaty of Versailles had designated Danzig as a "free city" belonging to no nation; it was governed by a League of Nations commissioner, although its foreign relations and economic status was largely controlled by Poland. Danzig, formerly a German city, was separated from Germany by the Polish Corridor, a narrow neck of land which allowed Poland to have an outlet to the Baltic Sea. This Polish Corridor also separated Germany from German East Prussia creating an additional indignity for the Germans. Danzig's population was 97% German, however, the Polish Corridor was largely Polish. This arrangement, a legacy of the Treaty of Versailles, was a geographic, economic and political monstrosity.

There were two different but related issues that created the final crisis in 1939: the German claim for the return of Danzig to the Fatherland, and the German demand that the Polish Corridor be modified to allow more economical transit between Germany and German East Prussia. Polish authorities harassed motorists with legal and physical roadblocks, making the two-hour trip across the Corridor a nightmare for German travelers. Germany asked for the creation of a German operated railroad and a highway, thereby bypassing the Polish obstructions.

The return of the "lost Germans" would be nearly complete with Danzig's addition to the Fatherland, but the Polish government, reflecting on the recent plight of the Czechs, refused to make any adjustments to the Corridor that would accommodate either of the German demands. The destiny of Europe hung on the fate of 350,000 Danzig Germans and the German request for a 90-mile long road and rail line — a "German corridor across the Polish Corridor" — linking East Prussia to Germany and providing Germans a reliable national road to Germany. This simple, somewhat harmless issue, became the spark for mankind's most destructive war.

In March 1939, Germany was encouraged that its demands about Danzig would be met as Lithuania agreed to Germany's annexation of the German-populated city of Memel. Certainly, Hitler thought, the Poles would be as reasonable as the Lithuanians and the Czechs. But as the Danzig crisis flared in 1939, the British unexpectedly vowed to draw the line against any further annexations or Treaty adjustments. Western governments had always acknowledged the folly of separating Danzig and East Prussia from Germany with the geographic freak called the Polish Corridor. Shortly after the Treaty of Versailles was signed, British Foreign Secretary Austen Chamberlain mimicked German Chancellor Bismarck's dismissal of war in the Balkans when he said, "For the Polish Corridor, no British Government ever will or ever can risk the bones of a British grenadier."[1]

Even a confirmed German-hater like Winston Churchill hinted that Poland was not worth saving; six months earlier the Poles had hyena-like feasted on the dying carcass of Czechoslovakia. Former Prime Minister Lloyd George suggested that any defense of Poland by the British would be "hare-brained."[2] The first Polish Prime Minister, Ignace Paderewski believed that Danzig would eventually return to Germany.[3] President Roosevelt in 1933 told the British that he supported the return of the entire Polish Corridor to Germany.[4] Even after the German

---

1. Taylor, *The Origins of the Second World War*, p. 57.

2. Ralph Raico, "Rethinking Churchill," in John Denson, ed., *The Costs of War*, p. 336.

3. Overy and Wheatcraft, *The Road To War*, p.2.

4. Arnold Offner, "The United States and National Socialist Germany," in Patrick Finney, ed. *The Origins of the Second World War* (New York: Arnold, 1997), p. 247.

invasion of Poland in 1939, FDR was sending peace missions to Europe in an attempt to pacify Hitler. These efforts by various FDR emissaries were designed to provide guarantees to Berlin about their demands in Poland, even offering sweeteners about colonies in Africa.[1]

The West had no illusions about Poland, seeing the Slavic nation as a greedy revisionist power; illiberal, anti-Semitic and intolerant. Foreign Minister Joseph Beck was widely regarded as menacing, arrogant and treacherous. In the midst of the crisis over Danzig, the Polish government closed German schools, encouraged anti-German demonstrations and arrested German nationals sending many fleeing across the border.

But as the Danzig Germans shouted and marched, and Hitler stormed around posing as their liberator, and as Polish leader Beck dug in his heels refusing even to discuss any border adjustment, the British cabinet panicked in the face of an aroused British public. Furious at what he saw as a personal betrayal by Hitler who had promised no more demands, Prime Minister Chamberlain disregarded the Foreign Office caution and issued a blanket endorsement of the intransigent Polish position on March 30. In a fit of emotional pique, Chamberlain thereby reversed established British foreign policy. Great Britain would come to the defense of Poland should Germany force the issue or attack. The British cabinet warning to Germany read in part:

> If ...any action were taken which clearly threatened their independence, and which the Polish Government accordingly felt obliged to resist with their national forces, His Majesty's Government and the French Government would at once lend them all the support in their power.[2]

Another ominous turn in British-German relations occurred a few weeks later in April 1939 when Chancellor Hitler renounced the 1935 naval agreement with Britain and began a building campaign of capital ships that was to peak in 1945.[3]

Some historians today speculate that the British guarantee was not intended to preserve the Corridor or the free city status of Danzig, but merely to slow down Hitler's march to the East, as well as soothe British public opinion. Indeed, Sir Horace Wilson, aide of Prime Minister Chamberlain, proposed as late as August 1939 a British-German understanding that suggested a "full-bodied political world partnership. The offer would have involved acceptance of German demands over Danzig and the Corridor.[4] British leaders were confident that war would never come over such an insignificant issue as Danzig. This idea suggests that the West was prepared to grant Danzig and the Corridor to Germany, but on terms that the West would determine. This was a high-stakes gamble, one which depended upon the unstable Polish leader Joseph Beck and the mercurial German Fuhrer; a gamble that failed and had horrid consequences.

The pre-war summers of 1914 and 1939 had their parallels: both brought tragic and unnecessary wars to the world, simply because diplomats thought they could walk the tightrope over the turbulent waters of an international crisis. The world in 1939 again discovered that the tightrope act was more perilous and it was too easy to lose ones balance and stumble into war.

---

1. Frederick W. Marks, *Wind Over Sand: The Diplomacy of Franklin Roosevelt* (Athens, GA.: The University of Georgia Press, 1988) p. 153-156.
2. Taylor, *The Origins of the Second World War*, p. 205.
3. James Compton, *Swastika and the Eagle* (Boston: Houghton Mifflin, 1967), p. 144-145.
4. David Irving, *The War Path, Hitler's Germany, 1933-1939*, p 232

As spring rolled into summer, government leaders had second thoughts about the Western guarantee to Poland. The British Ambassador in Berlin counseled that "the Poles were utterly foolish and unwise" in refusing to treat with Germany.[1] Lord Halifax, the astute British Foreign Minister, questioned the guarantee to Poland and the French government was quite convinced that it was a mistake to not involve the Russians. The Russian Army, after all, was the only military force strong enough and available to confront the German armed forces. Despite any misgivings, in the fateful summer of 1939, Britain and France came to the defense of a nation which they had believed did not deserve a defense and over an issue — Danzig and the Corridor — that they believed was not worth defending. Such is the Folly of War.

On September 1, 1939, German troops crossed the Polish border and swiftly took the Corridor, Danzig and more; seventeen days later, as prearranged with Germany, troops of the Soviet Union occupied the eastern portion of Poland. Poland, which had been partitioned three times in the 18th century, now was partitioned a fourth time. The earlier partitions were agreed to in advance by the Great Powers and resulted in no war. But in the democratic age, the passions of the people had to be considered. British public opinion was enraged against Germany; the British government, reluctant as they were to offer a defense to Poland, had to comply with the "man in the street," or see the government fall. The fourth partition would be met with mankind's most destructive display of military equipment and death.

Great Britain and France declared war on Germany on September 3 in defense of Polish independence, yet before fighting had even commenced between the Great Powers, the Soviet Union jumped upon the hapless Poles from the east. If the West opposed Hitler because of his illegal, immoral, aggressive actions, then ideological consistency would dictate another declaration of war against the Soviets, even more so when the Russians also invaded their neighbor, Finland, then gobbled up Estonia, Latvia and Lithuania in 1940. But the Western Powers ignored the aggression committed by Stalin. Britain and France directed their fear and their angry moralism exclusively at Hitler.

And a strange war it was, as Britain and France, following their September war declaration, hunkered down glumly behind their defensive positions — for Britain, the English Channel and for France, the "impregnable" Maginot Line, a series of defensive positions along its border with Germany. The Western allies' assurance of defending Poland resulted in no defense at all, either against the depredations of Russia or Germany. The British instituted no blockade of the German coast and the French failed to invade the Rhineland. It was a Phony War and a hollow British-French guarantee granted by governments propelled by emotions, yet paralyzed by ambivalence. Over the next few months, Germany waited for a peace offer from the West, for Hitler's foreign policy envisioned war only on the Eastern front. But by May 1940 no offer had arrived, whereupon Germany attacked France, the Low Countries and all nations facing the North Sea and English Channel. France's military power had to be eliminated before Germany launched its attack against Russia, and Britain's expected occupation of Norway had to be thwarted.

Hitler still held out hope for an accommodation with England, but when the Battle of Britain broke out in the summer of 1940, this fierce air war over England and the English Channel spoiled the German hopes for an early British peace offer. There was much talk of a

---

1. Overy and Wheatcraft, *The Road To War*, p. 15.

German invasion of England — Operation Sea Lion — but with few landing crafts or ample destroyers, and an inability to control the skies over the Channel, the invasion was more of a negotiating ploy than military reality. The outnumbered British Air Force held off the swarms of German Luftwaffe, thanks to radar and superior aircrafts. On September 17, the German Fuehrer publicly announced a delay of the planned invasion of England.[1] Then on October 12, British intelligence intercepted a confidential message from Hitler to the German generals ordering the military to abandon the invasion of the British Isles.[2] The Luftwaffe continued the relentless bombing of British cities for months, but it was all a ruse. Germany was faking a western move while preparing to invade the East. By October 1940, Germany had lost the air war over the British Isles; England was now secure as Germany turned its attention eastward towards communist Russia. Churchill triumphantly announced in the fall of 1940: "We were alive. We had beaten the German Air Force. There had been no invasion of the island."[3] In June 1941, Germany launched its long-awaited offensive into the east of Europe for Lebensraum.

ISOLATIONISM AND AMERICA FIRST

Stung by the disappointments of World War I, the United States under Republican leadership in the Twenties and early Thirties veered away from Militant Idealism towards its 19th century policy of neutrality. President George Washington's words uttered in his Farewell Address had renewed meaning: "The great rule of conduct for us in regard to foreign nations is — in extending our commercial relations — to have with them as little political connections as possible."[4]

The label "Isolationism" was a pejorative term attached to those who opposed American intervention in Europe. The term Isolationism lent itself to caricatures of an ostrich with its head in the sand, unaware of and unconcerned with what was transpiring around it. Used in this manner, it was an insult to Washington, Jefferson, the Adams and all 19th century Americans who regarded a limited, neutralist United States foreign policy as wise. Opponents incorrectly depicted Isolationists as refusing to have any commercial, diplomatic, cultural or financial relations with the rest of the world. Instead of debating the merits of a neutralist foreign policy, opponents choose to distort, defame and deceive.

The obvious facts are that during the "Isolationist" Twenties, as well as earlier, the United States carried on a rich relationship with the world, even while it rejected "entangling alliances." The United States did not join the League of Nations or the World Court, but its commercial ties with the world were expanded and it entered into numerous treaty arrangements, including disarmament agreements and treaties which outlawed the general use of war. World War I reparation issues were resolved, international finances were strengthened and world trade blossomed. American foreign policy was devoted to the narrow defense of America,

---

1. Churchill, *Their Finest Hour* (Boston: Houghton-Mifflin, 1949), p. 337.
2. Thompson, *A Time for War*, p. 284.
3. Churchill, *Their Finest Hour*, p. 626.
4. Ralph Raico, "The Case for an America first Foreign Policy," in Ebeling and Hornberger, *The Failure of America's Foreign Wars*, p. 22.

rather than securing democracy, liberty and social uplift for nations all over the world or bustling about in European quarrels.

As storm clouds of war gathered in Europe in the late 1930s and as the Roosevelt administration policy heralded intervention in Europe, a group of Americans devoted to "America First" organized in 1940. The America First organization was a politically diverse group; included were socialists (Norman Thomas and Sinclair Lewis), conservatives (Herbert Hoover and Robert Taft), Progressives (historian Charles Beard and Senator Gerald Nye), famed aviators (Eddie Rickenbacker and Charles Lindbergh), and future United States presidents Gerald Ford and John Kennedy). The group eventually claimed 850,000 members in 450 chapters. Its membership petition read: "We demand that Congress refrain from war, even if England is on the verge of defeat."[1]

American foreign policy should be a "City on a Hill" showing the beacon of liberty and self-government to all, but it will not be the rescuer and patron to anyone. The American Founding Fathers would have been charter members of this organization. The America First platform was straightforward and concise:

- The United States must build an impregnable defense.
- No foreign power or group of powers can successfully attack a prepared America.
- Only by remaining out of a European war can America preserve the vital elements of democracy.
- "Aid short of war" to Britain and France weakens American national defense at home and threatens to involve the nation in war abroad.

The popular support for the platform is seen in a Gallup poll of September 1940 in which 88 percent of Americans agreed with staying out of a European war. By October 1941, that number had dropped to 65 percent, still substantial support.

The Isolationist movement's greatest success was in enacting neutrality legislation designed to apply the "neutrality lessons" of World War I. The Neutrality Acts passed by Congress in the mid-Thirties stipulated the following:

- Embargoed all shipments of armaments to belligerents. America would not supply guns and ammunition to warring nations.
- Prohibited the arming of American merchant vessels. The United States would not become involved in a shooting war in the Atlantic.
- Banned travel by American citizens on belligerent vessels. No more Lusitanias.
- Prohibited loans and credits to belligerents. America would not finance Britain's war.

America First efforts were devoted to building American defenses and at the same time lessening American commitments overseas. Charles Lindbergh, who became a leader in the movement, lamented that FDR had maneuvered the country into war-like situations by 1941: "We are at war all over the world, and we are unprepared for it from either a spiritual or material standpoint. We haven't even a clear idea of what we are fighting to attain."[2] Militant Idealism was the sworn enemy of America First.

The America First leadership ridiculed the idea that Germany posed a military threat to America. The German Luftwaffe was unable to control the skies over the English Channel; how

---

1. Sheldon Richman, "The America First Committee," in Ebeling and Hornberger, *The Failure of America's Foreign Wars*, p. 110.
2. Toland, *Infamy*, p. 20.

would it be able to fly cover for an invasion of North America? Again Lindbergh's comments: "I do not believe there is any danger of an invasion of this continent, either by sea or by air, as long as we maintain an army, navy, and air force of reasonable size and in modern condition, and provided we establish the bases essential for defense."[1] The Isolationists war hero emphasized his point: "[N]ot a single squadron of trans-oceanic bombing planes exists anywhere in the world today...."[2]

Lindbergh was correct; Germany had lost the Battle of Britain by the fall of 1940. Yet the British government continued to raise alarm about a German invasion; had the British leadership told the truth about the German abandonment of the planned invasion of Britain, they would have played into the hands of the Isolationists and undermined FDR's panicky talk of German "world conquest."

America First had its greatest strength in the American heartland; its support in the Northeast was weak, even though its birth occurred at Yale University. (Gerald Ford was an early supporter of the group, but dropped his membership when it appeared that his association with "Isolationists" would cost him his job as a football coach at Yale University. Americans would later recognize during his presidency that President Ford had a weak commitment to the principles of neutrality.) The link between the British Isles and the Northeast of America was strong; ties of culture, finance, shipping and trade kept the two areas tightly bound. Members of America First believed that Great Britain was directing traffic in the American State Department and even in the White House. Senator Burton Wheeler complained that "The only excuse we would have for war with Japan is for the purpose of protecting the British Empire."[3] And a publication of America First noted that the United States "never raised a finger for China in all her four years of war [1937-40] until Britain's Eastern [Asian] Empire became involved [1940-41]."[4] Americans could reasonably ask: Were American boys going to Asia to save India for the British and Java for the Dutch?

President Roosevelt and his interventionist compatriots did not regard America First as a legitimate American organization, but instead saw it as an "appeaser fifth columnist" organization and a sympathizer of Nazis and Fascists. To an election eve crowd in 1940, FDR said, "We must counter the agents of dictators within our country,"[5] an obvious reference to Isolationists. Roosevelt's view of Charles Lindbergh was even more caustic and untrue; he told Henry Morgenthau: "I am absolutely convinced that Lindbergh is a Nazi."[6] After Pearl Harbor, America First disbanded its activities, joining with interventionists to fight in the war. Charles Lindbergh asked for a commission in the military, but out of spitefulness, FDR denied the request. Had the president acknowledged Lindbergh's contribution, FDR would have been constrained in his continued vilification of the group's leadership.

As a prelude to the meanness of the McCarthy and Watergate periods, FDR used the FBI, the IRS and other government agencies to harass and punish members of the America First organization. The President took credit for defending the nation against these dangerous domestic

---

1. Wayne S. Cole, *Roosevelt and the Isolationists* (Lincoln, Nebraska: University of Nebraska Press, 1983), p. 416.
2. Ibid., p.417.
3. Ibid., p.498.
4. Ibid., p.499.
5. Stinnett, *Day of Deceit*, p. 26.
6. Thompson, *A Time For War*, p. 241.

enemies when he said: "Let us no longer blind ourselves to the undeniable fact that the forces which have crushed and undermined and corrupted so many others are already within our own gates. Your Government knows much about them and every day is ferreting them out."[1]

Indeed the President did ferret them out; he used wiretaps, opened their mail and in numerous ways snooped on his opposition. One of the President's main tormentors, Father Charles Coughlin, saw his magazine banned from the United States mail and his radio program cut off the air by the Federal Communications Commission.[2] On January 6, 1941, FDR spoke to the nation about the "internal danger" from America First, which the President referred to as "dupes" of the Nazis: "The first phase of the invasion of this Hemisphere would not be the landing of regular troops. The necessary strategic points would be occupied by secret agents and their dupes — and great numbers of them are already here, and in Latin America."[3]

As a young aviator in World War II, future President George H. W. Bush commented that these Isolationists who tried to keep America out of war actually "flew escort for the very bombers that attacked our men."[4] In other words, George Bush considered the Isolationists to be *traitors* to their country — Robert Taft, Norman Thomas, John Kennedy, Herbert Hoover — all traitors! War does bring out the nastiness in people. Years later as president, George Bush would follow the lead of liberal, interventionist Democrats, like Wilson and Roosevelt, as he raced to the defense of Kuwait in the Persian Gulf, far from the shores of America. And his son, George W. Bush would prove even more adventurous in his preemptive war against Iraq in 2003. The Bush family from New England was part of the establishment elite of the Northeast with strong emotional ties to Britain. To them the limited foreign policy of traditional America was foolish, even traitorous.

The major historical studies of America First have been done by historian Wayne S. Cole. He categorically rejects the assertion that the organization was "traitorous" or in any way lacking in devotion to America. Cole asserts that:

> They barred Nazis, Fascists, and anti-Semites from membership, and tried to enforce those bans. The committee used orderly democratic methods in desperate efforts to keep the United States out of the wars raging abroad. The committee's position on foreign affairs was consistent with traditions extending back to the beginnings of America's independent history and before.... The America First Committee was a patriotic and honorable exercise of democracy in action at a critical time in American history.[5]

Although basically unsympathetic to the Isolationist cause, Wayne Cole maintains that Roosevelt went too far in his attacks on the group. Roosevelt and friends:

> demolished the isolationists in a spirit of triumphant self-righteousness that left no room for compassion, empathy, or sadness — then or later. Not only was the one great power of isolationism shattered, its public image was so tarnished that "isolationists" became [then and later] a smear word used to connote much that was evil and even subversive in America and foreign affairs....[6]

1. Buchanan, *A Republic, Not An Empire*, p. 293.
2. Fleming, *The New Dealer's War*, p. 114.
3. Buchanan, *A Republic, Not An Empire*, p. 293.
4. Ibid., p. 276.
5. Wayne S. Cole, *Determinism and American Foreign Relations During the Franklin D. Roosevelt Era*, (Latham, Md.: University of America, 1995), p.40
6. Cole, *Roosevelt and the Isolationists*, p. 530.

These same FDR supporters would later become inflamed and aghast at the antics of Senator Joseph McCarthy in the 1950s as he employed many of the same verbal hysterics used by interventionists against the America First organization. Franklin Roosevelt taught several generations of political leaders how to hate and denigrate their opponents.

ROOSEVELT MANEUVERS TOWARD WAR

Franklin Delano Roosevelt was thirty-one years old in 1913 when he was appointed Assistant Secretary of the Navy by President Wilson. Thus, he had a ringside seat as Wilson maneuvered the United States through its "phony neutrality" stage of World War I. As war clouds in Europe churned on the horizon in the late 1930s, FDR showed that he had learned his lessons well from Wilson, his mentor, and from Teddy Roosevelt, his cousin. Wilson taught him that America should arrange its foreign policy based on idealism — to make the world safe for democracy, human rights and other moral abstractions, as well cementing an attachment to Britain. Teddy stressed the importance of military force, especially the Navy. Thus, in President Franklin Roosevelt's view, the United States was to ferret out all international political and social abuses, using its military might to achieve noble goals and always remain attentive to the plight of the British. Nazi Germany, with its warped political principles and its alleged military threat to Britain, must be stopped. As Walter Lippmann's influential book of 1943 asserted, Britain was the "Shield of the Republic." The arguments of the Isolationists were more than foolish — they were dangerous. Militant Idealism was on the march.

When World War II erupted in Europe in September 1939, President Roosevelt immediately began evading and weakening the neutrality laws. During the next two years, his increasingly belligerent stand fell into four mini-campaigns to achieve intervention:

- strengthening the US military power in preparation for the war against Germany and Japan.
- conducting the phony presidential election of 1940 during which FDR posed as the man of peace while edging America toward war.
- establishment of Lend-lease and related aid programs for Britain.
- conducting a naval war in the Atlantic Ocean in 1941 against Germany.

As early as 1938, Roosevelt was laying plans for strengthening the military. The US Ambassador to Russia, William Bullitt, returned to Washington D.C. in October 1938 and recounts a "bull session" with FDR. According to Bullitt it was more like an "all night session as fraternity brothers" than a thoughtful planning session. At that time, FDR "in a fit of enthusiasm, had decided to produce military aircraft in overwhelming numbers."[1] Panicking the Congress with tall tales about the number of aircraft Germany possessed, FDR slipped an inflated defense appropriation through Congress, most of which was destined for Great Britain rather than America's military bases.

In October 1940, FDR sought and received from Congress permission to spend $17 billion on a new two-ocean navy and to build 50,000 airplanes for American defense — or as the Isola-

---

1. David Fromkin, *In The Time of the Americans — FDR, Truman, Eisenhower, Marshall, MacArthur — the generation that changed America's role in the world* (New York: A. A. Knopf, 1995), p. 366-367.

tionists claimed, for defense of Britain. At FDR's initiative, Congress created the first peacetime draft; six and a half million young men were to register for military service. As an act of presidential authority, Roosevelt called the National Guard into duty and authored legislation that would allow him to seize industrial plants for war production. America was preparing for war and there was little doubt on whose side the United States would fight.

When the presidential election in November 1940 took center stage, Roosevelt was prepared for his role as he had been an "understudy" to President Wilson during the election of 1916. In that election, Wilson's campaign slogan was, "HE KEPT US OUT OF WAR," although he had actually taken measures to engage the nation in war. FDR applied his lessons well as he campaigned on the ambiguous promise never to send American boys into a "foreign war." Roosevelt and his political operatives decided that deceit during the 1916 election had worked; perhaps a gullible public could be fooled again. Shortly before election day the president roared his duplicitous promise to voters: "While I am talking to you, mothers and fathers, I give you one more assurance. I have said this before, but I shall say it again and again and again. Your boys are not going to be sent into any foreign war."[1]

On November 3, FDR announced that "The first purpose of our foreign policy is to keep our country out of war."[2] Charles Lindbergh couldn't have been more emphatic. But all this rhetoric was merely a verbal show; FDR never intended to remain on the sidelines of a war involving Great Britain. FDR's speech writer, Robert Sherwood, says that FDR confided to his staff that he was playing with words and toying with the American people: "Of course, we'll fight if we are attacked. If somebody attacks us, then it isn't a foreign war, is it?"[3]

As FDR maneuvered the nation into an Atlantic and a Pacific war, an incident would surely occur that would inflame the public. Roosevelt would find his "Lusitania" or his "Maine." He would have his war, even if it came about through trickery and deceit. Roosevelt was not an honest man, but at times he could be truthful to confidants. To Secretary of the Treasury Henry Morgenthau he confided during the war that he personally was less than forthright: "You know I am a juggler, and I never let my right hand know what my left hand does...and furthermore I am perfectly willing to mislead and tell untruths if it will help win the war."[4]

With the successful election campaign behind him, Roosevelt turned his attention more directly to aid for Britain. In January of 1941, just two months after the election in which he vowed to avoid "foreign wars," the president sent his assistant, Harry Hopkins, to England to confer with British Prime Minister Winston Churchill. Hopkins told Churchill of the President's resolve to aid the British in defeating Germany.

> The President is determined that we shall win the war together. Make no mistake about it. He has sent me here to tell you that at all costs and by all means he will carry you through, no matter what happens to him — there is nothing that he will not do so far as he has human power.[5]

---

1. William Henry Chamberlin, "Roosevelt Maneuvers America into War," in George Waller, ed., *Pearl Harbor: Roosevelt and the Coming of the War*, p. 2.
2. Chamberlin, "Roosevelt Maneuvers America into War, in George Waller, ed., *Pearl Harbor: Roosevelt and the Coming of the War*, p. 2.
3. Robert Sherwood, *Roosevelt and Hopkins* (Harper & Brothers, 1948), p. 191.
4. Fleming, *The New Dealers' War*, p. 26.
5. Winston Churchill, *The Grand Alliance*, p. 23.

Actually, Roosevelt's commitment to the British was established before the European war began. In June 1939, King George VI and his wife visited Washingont, at which time FDR assured the royal couple that if he saw a U-boat, he would sink it at once and wait for the consequences. The discussion extended to aid to England, with an embryonic lend-lease program discussed. In September 1939, he initiated correspondence with Churchill, when Winston was the head of the Admiralty, bypassing the more neutralist British Prime Minister.

Neutrality laws, including an embargo on armaments, passed by Congress in the mid-Thirties were designed to ensure a true position of neutrality if war in Europe erupted. However, in October 1939, FDR requested that Congress repeal the arms embargo and replace it with a "Cash and Carry" law. Against the determined opposition of Isolationists, FDR was successful and Britain began buying armaments from the US, paying cash (no loans) and carrying the goods in its own vessels. The US was now the arsenal of Great Britain, just as in World War I. Involvement in a European war was creeping closer.

In the fall of 1940, there occurred one of the momentous events along the way to American entry into World War II. The Destroyer Deal marked the passage of the United States from a neutral to a passive belligerent in the European war. Throughout the summer of 1940, Winston Churchill pleaded with FDR to give England fifty destroyers, as German U-boats had sunk half of the British destroyer fleet of one hundred. Churchill's frantic cable in July sounded the alarm: "Mr. President, with great respect I must tell you that in the long history of the world this is a thing to do now. The worth of every destroyer that you can spare is to be measured in rubies."[1]

The President was constrained by public opinion and by the fact that the Congress would reject such an unneutral action. FDR would need congressional approval if the United States were to simply give military equipment to another nation. But perhaps a "trade" could be worked out. If US naval officers would testify that the nation needed more naval bases in the western Atlantic Ocean, then any trade of British bases for American destroyers could be snuck past an unsuspecting nation and Congress. As plans were being worked out, FDR held a press conference at which time he said that he was holding conversations with the British about acquiring air and naval bases in the Atlantic. When a reporter asked what the United States was giving in exchange, he replied dishonestly: "I don't know what the quid pro quo is going to be. The emphasis is on the acquisition of the bases for the protection of the Hemisphere."[2] Over the Labor Day weekend, while the nation's attention was diverted, FDR announced that the Destroyer Deal had been completed: "It is over; it is all done," he told reporters. When reporters persisted asking for details, the President responded that it involved "all kinds of things that nobody here would understand, so I won't mention them. It is a *fait accompli*; it is done this way."[3]

The Destroyer Deal was passed off to the public as a transaction to aid America with new military bases, instead of a benefit to Britain. And in his best patrician pose, FDR explained that the details were too complicated for ordinary voters to understand. In this incident one can see

---

1. Stoessinger, *Crusaders and Pragmatists*, p. 40.
2. Ibid., p. 41-42.
3. Richard M. Ebeling, "Hard Bargain: How FDR Twisted Churchill's Arm, Evaded the Law and Changed the Role of the American Presidency," in Ebeling and Hornberger, *The Failure of America's Foreign Wars*, p. 117.

Roosevelt's verbal obfuscation and dishonesty at its very worst. Winston Churchill privately referred to the Deal as a "decidedly unneutral act;"[1] indeed it was a disaster for US neutrality. It violated treaties and conventions of international law to which the United States and Great Britain had agreed.[2] From a practical standpoint, the bases that America received were of little military value; they were remote from the military action and duplicated existing bases.

The Isolationist Senator Gerald Nye asserted that this "behind the back action" by the President would place the United States "in the middle of war as an actual belligerent."[3] Senator Arthur Vandenberg of Michigan affirmed that FDR was engaging in hypocrisy which tries to cover up all these things as being purely "peaceful" and always "short of war." Despite vigorous criticism by Isolationists, the President sent fifty destroyers to replenish the British Navy, ignoring the Congress, leaving the Isolationists to fume and thoughtful people to wonder.

By the winter of 1940-41, FDR was secure in the presidency for another four years, and his efforts at aiding the British became more bold. The "Cash and Carry" legislation of 1939 was deemed unsatisfactory and was replaced by a forerunner of the post-war Marshall Plan. Lend-lease was a program of American military aid to Britain, the Soviet Union and other belligerents; with this action, the US was financing the war against the Axis. Originally a seven billion-dollar aid program, it was reminiscent of the financial entanglement that had developed between the United States and Britain before America's entry into World War One. (The very term "Lend-lease" was, like much of FDR's action, deceptive and deceitful. These supplies going to the belligerents were neither lent nor leased. They were outright gifts from the US taxpayers to foreign governments — never to be returned or repaid.)

Opposition from Isolationists remained strong and determined, but the measure passed both Houses of Congress with ease and was popular in the nation, the thinking being that aid to Britain would result in the US avoiding direct participation in the war itself. However, to Senator Robert Taft the measure would "give the President power to carry on an undeclared war all over the world." And to Norman Thomas, it would lead to "total war on two oceans and five continents."[4] Isolationists of both the Left and the Right were opposed to this Roosevelt maneuver.

By the summer of 1941, the nation was engaged in a massive rebuilding of its defense and supplying Britain as well. There remained only one more effort — to create an incident in the Atlantic between American ships and the German Navy.

In April, US military forces occupied the Danish colony of Greenland, and in July Iceland was taken over. These actions allowed FDR to thrust American naval power into the mid-Atlantic. Using these naval bases, FDR could more easily protect shipping into the British Isles and harass German U-boats. Although the Lend-lease Act had forbidden the use of American naval vessels in "convoys" to protect British shipping in the Atlantic, FDR was determined to buttress the British Navy. Again the verbal deceit of FDR is evident as his devious mind decides that a "patrol" is different than the forbidden "convoy." The President announced to his cabinet that he was going to institute "patrols" in the western Atlantic to the 25-degree longitude (2000

---

1. Kissinger, *Diplomacy*, p. 388.
2. Charles C. Tansill, *The Back Door To War*, (Chicago: Henry Regnery, 1952), p. 598.
3. Cole, *Roosevelt and the Isolationists*, p. 374
4. Chamberlin, "Roosevelt Maneuvers America into War," George Waller, ed., *Pearl Harbor: Roosevelt and the Coming of the War*, p. 6.

miles east of New York City) and to report to the people. Upon hearing Roosevelt's dissimulation, Secretary of War Stimson corrected the President, interjecting, "you are going to report to the British Fleet." Stimson noted in his diary: "I wanted him to be honest with himself. To me it seems a clearly hostile act to the Germans...."[1] In addition to being honest with himself, it would have been fitting for Stimson to suggest to Roosevelt that he be honest with the nation.

In the summer of 1941, in defiance of congressional law, FDR ordered the Navy to convoy British ships halfway across the Atlantic Ocean, thereby relieving the British Navy of that duty, and creating the likelihood of American clashes with German U-boats. The President was candid in admitting that he was goading Germany, looking for an incident to provoke a war. When Roosevelt met with Churchill in Canada during August and drafted the Atlantic Charter, secret documents recently obtained reveal that FDR told the Prime Minister that he was looking for an incident to justify hostilities against Germany. Churchill recounts that "he [Roosevelt] was obviously determined that they should come in [to the war]...The President said he would become more and more provocative. If the Germans did not like it, they could attack American forces. Everything was to be done to force an incident."[2] FDR's "Shoot on Sight" orders to American vessels on October 8 were designed to snare an incident with a German U-boat. But fighting a war with the United States was not on Hitler's agenda and he took actions to avoid any maritime conflict with America. Despite the pleas of Admiral Rader to unleash the sixty U-boats in the German fleet, Hitler refused to authorize an "unrestricted submarine warfare" campaign, as had the Kaiser in World War I. The German leader specifically ordered German submarines to refrain from attacking any passenger liners — there would be no Lusitania scandal. He issued orders to U-boat commanders to avoid engagements with American naval vessels unless fired upon first, and to remain east of the 25-degree longitude line in the Atlantic Ocean, thereby avoiding contact with the American "patrols."[3]

But it was not always possible to determine the national identity of a ship during the nighttime or in the fog-shrouded North Atlantic Ocean. A confrontation involving the USS *Greer* and a U-boat fueled the fire for which FDR had been waiting. The President's fireside chat to the nation on September 11 gave FDR's version of the *Greer* incident:

> The Navy Department of the United States has reported to me that on the morning of September fourth the United States destroyer *Greer*, proceeding in full daylight toward Iceland, had reached a point southeast of Greenland. She was carrying American mail to Iceland. She was flying the American flag. Her identity as an American ship was unmistakable.

> She was then and there attacked by a submarine. Germany admits that it was a German submarine. The submarine deliberately fired a torpedo at the *Greer*, followed later by another torpedo attack. In spite of what Hitler's propaganda bureau has invented, and in spite of what any American obstructionist organization may prefer to believe, I tell you the blunt fact that the German submarine fired upon this American destroyer without warning and with deliberate design to sink her.

---

1. Henry L. Stimson and McGeorge Bundy, *On Active Service in Peace and War* (New York: Harper and Brothers, 1948), p. 367.
2. Ralph Raico, "The Case for an America First Foreign Policy," in Ebeling and Hornberger, ed., *The Failure of America's Foreign Wars*, p. 27.
3. Frederic R. Sanborn, "Roosevelt Is Frustrated in Europe," Harry Elmer Barnes, ed., *Perpetual War For Perpetual Peace*, p. 216-217.

This was piracy — piracy legally and morally.... [I]t would be inexcusable folly to minimize such incidents in the face of evidence which makes it clear that the incident is not isolated, but is part of a general plan.... Hitler's advance guards — not only his avowed agents but also his dupes among us — have sought to make ready for him footholds and bridgeheads in the New World, to be used as soon as he has gained control of the oceans.[1]

The actual *Greer* incident was starkly different than the story FDR told the American people. The following is an account given shortly after the incident to the Senate Naval Affairs Committee by Admiral Harold Stark, Chief of Naval Operations.

At 8:40 AM on the morning of September 4, 1941 the USS *Greer* was notified by a British airplane that a submerged German U-boat was in the path of the destroyer about ten miles ahead. The *Greer* raced to the location using its sonar detection equipment and while tracking the U-boat began relaying the information to British airplanes. At 10:32 AM a British airplane began dropping depth charges on the location of the U-boat, but was unsuccessful and withdrew. The *Greer* continued tracking the submarine until at 12:40 P.M. the U-boat ceased fleeing, turned on the *Greer*, and fired a torpedo that missed. The *Greer* counterattacked with depth charges and the U-boat responded with torpedoes. The entire episode lasted four hours during which time the *Greer* pursued the fleeing submarine for over three hours. The U-boat attempted to avoid the American vessel, but was relentlessly pursued by the American craft.

President Roosevelt gave the public a fictitious and deliberately inflammatory account of the *Greer* incident for the express purpose of inflaming American opinion against the German nation. War psychology was building; anger was being fueled for war and emotional distortions were being created. The public was being reeled in by a cunning president.

Despite the provocation by the *Greer* in pursuing the German U-boat, Hitler again sent orders to his Atlantic fleet to avoid maritime incidents with the American fleet. On September 17, Hitler ordered U-boats to leave American vessels alone even if they were convoying British merchant ships, except in the areas immediately around the English ports.

For the first time in the naval war of the Atlantic, American blood was shed on October 17 when the destroyer USS *Kearney* was torpedoed. On the previous day, the *Kearney* and four American destroyers had raced to the scene of a British-German battle near Iceland. The *Kearney* indiscreetly placed itself directly between German and British ships and was struck by a German torpedo launched at a British vessel in the heat of battle. Eleven young American seamen were killed in the blast and the *Kearney* limped back to Iceland. And once again President Roosevelt falsely informed the public about the incident. At a Navy Day celebration in the national capital on October 27 FDR's deceit was at its worst:

We have wished to avoid shooting. But the shooting has started. And history has recorded who fired the first shot. In the long run, however, all that will matter is who fired the last shot. American has been attacked. The U. S. S. *Kearney* is not just a Navy ship. She belongs to every man, woman, and child in this Nation....[2]

The President then proceeded to tell the startled guests about the aforementioned bogus Nazi map of Latin America that showed their alleged diabolical preparation of conquest as well as plans to destroy all vestiges of religion in the New World. Implying that the America First Committee was in league with Nazis, FDR asserted that "The Nazis have made up their own

---

1. James MacGregor Burns, *Roosevelt: The Soldier of Fortune* (New York: Harcourt Brace Jovanovich, 1970), p. 140-141.
2. Ibid., p. 147.

list of modern American heroes. It is, fortunately, a short list. I am glad that it does not contain my name."[1] The president concluded his histrionics:

> Our American merchant ships must be armed to defend themselves against the rattlesnakes of the sea. Our American merchant ships must be free to carry our American goods into the harbors of our friends. Our American merchant ships must be protected by our American Navy. In the light of a good many years of personal experience, I think that it can be said that it can never be doubted that the goods will be delivered by this Nation, whose Navy believes in the tradition of 'Damn the torpedoes; full speed ahead'.[2]

The naval war in the Atlantic resumed on October 31 when the United States destroyer USS *Rueben James* was torpedoed while escorting a convoy to Iceland. Tragically, 115 sailors lost their lives that day in the cold Atlantic Ocean and the nation was outraged. Upon hearing the news of the sinking of the USS *Kearney*, German Chancellor Hitler remarked: "President Roosevelt has ordered his ships to shoot the moment they sight German ships. I have ordered German ships not to shoot when they sight American vessels but to defend themselves when attacked."[3]

For those who are skeptical of Hitler's sincerity in these remarks, consider this directive to German U-boats from Berlin found in German government records after the war and dated November 13, 1941: "Engagements with American naval and air forces are not to be sought deliberately; they are to be avoided as far as possible...If it is observed before a convoy is attacked that it is being escorted by American forces, the attack is not to be carried out."[4]

Within a few weeks the United States was attacked by Japan at Pearl Harbor and war came to the Pacific. On December 9, the President delivered a radio address to the American people making a powerful indictment of all the Axis powers:

> Your government knows Germany has been telling Japan that if Japan would attack the United States Japan would share the spoils when peace came. She was promised by Germany that if she came in she would receive the control of the whole Pacific area and that means not only the Far East but all the islands of the Pacific and also a stranglehold on the west coast of North and Central South America. We know also that Germany and Japan are conducting their naval operations in accordance with a joint plan. Germany and Italy consider themselves at war with the United States without even bothering about a formal declaration.[5]

On December 11 Germany declared war on the United States and the long agony of uncertainty was over. America was at war against Nazi Germany, Fascist Italy, and militaristic Japan. President Roosevelt had defeated the Isolationists; now he had a greater battle against the Axis Alliance.

THE FOLLY OF WAR

One of Roosevelt's biographers characterized him as "a Lion and a Fox," but a fair assessment of his presidency would see more cunning and craftiness than the majesty and

---

1. Ibid., p. 148.
2. Ibid., p. 148.
3. Tansill, *Back Door To War*, p. 614.
4. Ibid., p. 614.
5. Fleming, *The New Dealers' War*, p. 34-35.

courage of the King of Beasts. The dishonest statements of President Roosevelt about world affairs should be reprehensible to all Americans — Isolationists and Interventionists alike. A democratic society cannot function properly when the political leadership engages in massive distortions of the facts. The behavior of FDR was unprecedented in presidential history. One cannot imagine Presidents Grover Cleveland, Herbert Hoover, Calvin Coolidge, or any other pre-FDR president engaging in such duplicity. His actions set a new sordid standard for subsequent Chief Executives; Harry Truman, Lyndon Johnson, and Richard Nixon all served in Washington during FDR's presidency or were influenced by the unethical, unscrupulous culture established during his thirteen years in office. FDR's distortion of international affairs is appalling; his lies are legion:

- He promised in 1940 to keep America out of "foreign wars" while cynically scheming to provoke an incident that would involve the nation in war, thus making a farce of the sacred democratic election process.
- He distorted the Axis Alliance into an evil and aggressive plot to destroy America and its way of life, when in fact it was a defensive arrangement, much like the American Cold War organization called NATO.
- He falsely claimed that Germany had plans for world conquest, when in fact, Hitler had deliberately created a foreign policy that was designed to avoid antagonizing the British or Americans.
- He falsely alleged that Japan and Germany had made joint military plans, when in fact no joint talks were conducted and no military plans were ever developed.
- He falsely claimed that he had a map showing Nazi designs on Latin America and that Hitler had hatched a program to eliminate all religion in the New World. The phony map had been drawn by British espionage agents operating in the United States. It was a bogus map and FDR knew that.
- He concealed the real reason behind the illegal Destroyer Deal in a fog of confusion about the need for more American bases in the Atlantic Ocean.
- He blatantly lied about the Greer incident, disguising the fact that the Greer was provocatively tracking the German U-boat and radioing its position to a British airplane.
- While posing as a man of peace, FDR shamelessly goaded Japan into war in the Pacific, then disguised facts about the Japanese armada and its attack on Pearl Harbor.

The honor of the presidency and the integrity of the election process were both damaged seriously and have not yet recovered their pre-Roosevelt integrity. Roosevelt's mentor, Woodrow Wilson, prepared the way for FDR by maneuvering America into World War I. But Wilson largely deceived himself; Franklin Roosevelt deceived the American people. Jim Farley, a Roosevelt confidant, found Roosevelt's lying too much to tolerate. Said Farley to his president: "Boss, you've lied to me and I've lost all faith in you."[1] The historian Robert Dallek expressed his concern about the effect of FDR upon subsequent political leaders: "...the President's deviousness also injured the national well being over the long run. His actions in the Greer incident created a precedent for manipulation of public opinion which would be repeated by later Presidents in less justifiable circumstances."[2]

---

1. Ibid., p. 75.
2. Robert Dallek, *Franklin D. Roosevelt and American Foreign Policy* (New York: Oxford University Press, 1979), p. 289.

Perhaps the saddest tale about this matter is that American historians, the men and women who know the details of FDR's conduct, rate him as the greatest president in the 20th century. Nearly all of them "play dumb" about his mismanagement of the Pearl Harbor disaster and his persistent efforts to embroil America in a war with Japan. Nor is there any mention of the deceitfulness practiced by the President concerning German policy or actions. One can only conclude that American historians are so dedicated to the liberal Democratic Party program that they find it unbearable to expose the flaws and tell the true story of the man who founded the modern Democratic Party. This tells us something about the intellectual honesty of the history profession. Henry Ford once said "History is bunk." And so it can be!

Despite his Dutch surname, Roosevelt was predominantly a Yankee whose ancestors came to America from England as early as the 1630s. The Roosevelt and Delano families were well-established in baronial homes along the Hudson River Valley when the American Revolution erupted. James Roosevelt, FDR's great grandfather, was a Tory during the American Revolution, thus he fought against Washington and the other American revolutionaries. James Roosevelt never wavered in his support of King George, but due to the benevolence of the Founding Fathers, James Roosevelt's wealth and social position were preserved.

One branch of FDR's family enriched themselves on the fabled China trade in the 19th century and young Roosevelt was steeped in tales of the Orient. FDR's grandfather Delano spent thirty years in China as a consular official and businessman, building the first telegraph and starting the first steamship line on the Yangtze River. Sumner Welles, a confidant of FDR, describes the family ties to the Orient: "The President's mother had lived in China as a small girl and the President repeatedly told the story of the business dealings of his family in the China trade of the early nineteenth century."[1] When some of Roosevelt's advisors counseled him to abandon his moralistic and unfounded attacks on Japan in 1940 and 1941, FDR replied: "I have always had the deepest sympathy with the Chinese. How could you expect me not to go along with Stimson on Japan."[2]

It was the British Navy that had protected American trade in Asia; much of the Delano family wealth depended on the goodwill of British Imperial policy. As Franklin watched Britain struggling to retain its empire in the years before World War II, and as Winston Churchill made appeals to him on behalf of the British Navy, FDR could not resist. FDR spoke grandly about freedom of colonial people, but he could never reconcile those noble thoughts with his affection for the British Empire. American foreign policy was shaped by Roosevelt's personal memories of China and the benevolence of the British.

By the time Franklin was a young politico in the Wilson administration, his pro-British bias was well established. His education had been received in private academies and colleges — Groton and Harvard — which emulated British elite schools. He loved the American Navy in the same way his English counterpart, Winston Churchill, loved the British fleet. And like Winston, FDR admired military exploits. He confided to a friend during World War I: "It would be wonderful to be a war president."[3] America had come to the rescue of England in 1917; America would come to the rescue in the 1940s once again. Anything else was unthinkable.

---

1. Sumner Welles, *Seven Decisions That Shaped the World* (New York: Harper, 1951), p. 68.
2. *Hofstadter, The American Political Traditions*, p. 343.
3. Fleming, *Illusion of Victory*, p. 254

Thus, American foreign policy was shaped largely by the personal whims and reminiscences of the president, not by thoughtful, rational calculations concerning the needs of the American citizenry. There is no record of extensive high-level conferences held and carefully reasoned papers written on the subject of American involvement in a European or Asian war. There were no groups of experts established to study the question of the nation's response to the crisis in either Asia or Europe; no ExCom group of the type that served President Kennedy so well in the Cuban missile crisis. The nation just slid into war based largely on FDR's personal feelings.

Franklin's famous cousin Theodore Roosevelt dominated American politics for the first two decades of the century; Franklin always found it difficult to outshine his cousin. Several incidents during Franklin's tenure as Assistant Secretary of the Navy suggest the shallowness of FDR and illustrate that he was capable of some unseemly grandstanding. During the height of the panic about German espionage in 1917, the young Franklin Roosevelt said that he was the target of an assassination attempt, claiming, without proof, that a bomb had been sent to his office. (There had been an attempt on TR's life in 1912.) In 1920, perhaps in an attempt to embellish his record during World War I, he asserted that "I committed enough illegal acts to put me in jail for 999 years,"[1] maintaining that on his own he had prepared the Navy for war in 1917, without the knowledge of Secretary of the Navy Daniels or President Wilson. The young Assistant Secretary surely remembered the tales about his hyperactive cousin, Teddy, ordering Commodore Dewey to set sail for the Philippines when a war broke out in Cuba, an action taken without the Secretary's knowledge. Franklin was pretending to follow in Teddy's footsteps. And his braggadocio continued. He claimed to have written the Haitian constitution, which he hadn't. And he said that he had governed a couple Latin nations, which he hadn't.

Franklin Roosevelt's tendencies to embellish facts for his own electoral benefit are illustrated in his use of a bogus document concerning the condition of women in the newly-created Soviet Union. The fake document decreed that women would henceforth be "property of the whole nation.... Men citizens have the right to use one woman not oftener than three times a week for three hours." FDR campaigned for the Vice-presidency in 1920 speaking to women's groups and posing as a champion of feminism who would fight through the League of Nations to stop such sexual indignities.[2] It is not recorded whether Roosevelt knew the document was false; one suspects it would not have mattered.

During his presidency, FDR frequently used special emissaries to pursue investigations or to make personal contacts, many of whom worked a cross purposes with each other. His inclination to bypass established authority using numerous personal aides predates his tragic paralytic affliction. Secretary of State Cordell Hull was often excluded from meetings dealing with foreign affairs. Harry Hopkins, his personal confidant, was sent on diplomatic missions, bypassing State Department experts. The State Department had provided the President with a wealth of information to be used during the Yalta Conference with Churchill and Stalin in 1945. The material was not consulted until the eve of the meeting, then generally disregarded. His management style was unusually disorderly and haphazard. Henry L. Stimson attests to the chaos around the four-term president, suggesting FDR was a sort of Mr. Moonbeam:

---

1. Christopher Andrews, *For the President's Eyes Only* (New York: Harper Collins, 1995), p. 76.
2. Ibid., p. 79.

> Conferences with the President are difficult matters. His mind does not easily follow a consecutive chain of thought but he is full of stories and incidents and hops about in this discussion from suggestion to suggestion and it is very much like chasing a vagrant beam of moonshine around a vacant room.[1]

FDR privately supported the Munich agreement, then raised the ire of Americans by condemning any compromise with Germany. He urged Poland to give Germany its due in the Danzig and Corridor issue, then turned on the Germans for taking what the Poles refused to grant. Thus he encouraged Hitler to seek Treaty revisions, but then told the Western allies to resist Hitler's aggression. He offered to hold a summit meeting with Japanese Prime Minister Konoye, then scuttled it a critical time, resulting in Konoye's replacement by Tojo. He told British King George VI that America would enter the war when the first bombs fell, then did nothing of the sort for two years. When the war began in 1939 he urged all sides to refrain from bombing cities, then turned on the citizens of Germany and Japan with a ferocious assault on their cities from the skies. He took the US into war to save Manchuria from the Japanese and Poland from Germany, then casually turned them over to the Communists at war's end.

The President is known for his consummate political skills in dealing with Congress and his marvelous speaking skills in marshalling the energies of the nation. But the world of international diplomacy requires more than the talents of a raconteur and the personality of a chameleon. Roosevelt showed little consistency of strategy or vision of policy as he steered the ship of state through difficult waters. Roosevelt was considered an intellectual lightweight in his early days; he remained throughout life a man who relied on good humor, delightful stories and personal charm. He was, in this regard, truly a man of the frivolous Twentieth century.

Had World War II resulted in a stunning and lasting victory for the United States, one could overlook the foibles of FDR. But such a victory eluded America. Thus Roosevelt's polices resulted in a tragic, destructive, unsuccessful war, for the foundation of his thinking was flawed. He claimed that his actions would avoid war; they did not. He claimed that a simple military victory over Hitler and Tojo would secure the future for the United States; it did not. "The ideas upon which he rested his case from 1933 to 1945 proved to be a veritable bed of sand. The rain fell, the floods came, the winds blew and beat against the house, and it fell."[2]

The Founding Fathers had constructed a Constitutional system that, had it been followed, would have prevented a man such as FDR from taking the nation to war by his own actions. Congress was to be the judge of whether and when the nation sent its sons into battle to die; but the Founding Fathers certainly never anticipated a conniving president like Roosevelt. Congress did approve a declaration of war in December 1941, but few understood how FDR had maneuvered the Japanese and Germans into war-like actions. By 1941, America had come full circle: a revolution in 1776 to rid the people of an arbitrary monarch now saw an arbitrary and dishonest president duplicating monarchial behavior.

Apologists for Roosevelt fall back on the argument that the dangers inherent in the German and Japanese regimes justified a dishonest response; the threat was too great and the American people were not facing reality. Leaving aside what this argument says about democracy — the people's right to know and their power over policy — was Nazi Germany a real military threat to the United States? Were FDR and Churchill right about the German

---

1. Ibid., p. 86
2. Marks, *Wind Over Sand*, p. 276

menace — or were the Isolationists correct? Some facts about German foreign and defense policy are known:

- THE WRITINGS AND SPEECHES OF NAZI GERMAN LEADERS — *Mein Kampf* describes a German foreign policy based upon continentalism, a policy that would avoid war with the Atlantic community. German ambitions lie to the East of Europe, not in the West. Nazi leaders considered communist Russia — not Britain or America — to be the true enemy.

- THE ACTIONS OF NAZI GERMANY UNTIL SEPTEMBER 1939 — Between 1935 and 1939, Germany annexed or set up puppet states in Austria and portions of Czechoslovakia and Poland. These actions, although disruptive to European tranquility, were directed into Eastern Europe; this was a Drive to the East, not into the West. If the Western nations felt threatened by Germany, they could have built a defensive wall at the Rhine and in the Atlantic Ocean, presenting a united front against an imagined future German "Drive to the West."

- GERMAN DEFENSE SPENDING — In 1938, the last peacetime year, Germany and Great Britain were spending the same portion of their nation's gross national product on defense — 15%. The German defense budget declined somewhat in the next two years, giving proof to the contention that the war over Danzig was not expected to be a general war. The peak of German defense spending was projected to be in 1943, not 1939.[1]

GERMAN-BRITISH-FRENCH MILITARY FORCES — 1939[2]

	Germany	Britain	France
Battleships	5	12	5
Cruiser/Destroyers	23	259	90
Carriers	0	6	1
Submarines	46	38	59
Bombers	1180	536	186
Fighters planes	1179	608	549
Troops	800,000	220,000	800,000

Other than in air power, the British-French forces were significantly stronger than Germany. President Roosevelt falsely claimed that Germany had 6500 airplanes, while in fact, Germany had about one-third that number. Either FDR was depending on faulty espionage, or he was deliberately inflating the numbers to frighten US citizens. Given FDR's frantic search for entrance into the European war, one would suspect this was a deliberate falsification.

- GERMAN-RUSSIAN MILITARY FORCES — Soon after Germany launched its invasion of the Soviet Union in 1941, its military forces were decidedly inferior to the Russians. Eric Nordlinger comments that "By late 1941, Germany's early advantage [in the invasion of Russia] had lost their sway outright. Soviet superiority in troops, tanks and

1. Taylor, *The Origins of the Second World War*, p. 286.
2. Robert Goralski, *World War II Almanac 1931-1945*, (New York: G. P. Putnam's Sons, 1981), p. 89.

planes became dominant."[1] Operation Barbarossa — the invasion of Russia — was destined to be a German failure. The following figures are for late 1941:[2]

	Germany	USSR
Tanks	3,300	20,000
Airplanes	2,800	10,000
Troops	3.4 million	4.7 million

Americans are regaled in books and on television with tales of astounding Nazi military successes in Europe. However, an analysis of the German military campaigns shows that their vaunted military machine won a few easy victories against inferior opponents early in the war, then Germany was militarily finished. The German military campaigns were in this order:

1939 — Invasion of Poland — Won

1940 — Invasion of the West (France, Belgium, the Netherlands) — Won

1940 — Invasion of Eastern Europe and the Balkans — Won

1940 — Battle of Britain — Lost

1941 — Invasion of the Soviet Union — Lost

Germany was victorious in 1939 and early 1940; but was defeated by the British Air Force in the fall of 1940 and was trounced by the Russian Army by early 1942. Germany was thrown out of Moscow early in 1942 and crushed at Stalingrad by Christmas 1942. Germany had been defeated in the West by the fall of 1940 and in the East by the winter of 1942! The first signs of a military disaster for Nazi Germany occurred at the time of the Pearl Harbor attack. "When the disaster of the winter of 1941/42 broke, the Fuehrer...realized that from this point of culmination onward...no victory could any longer be won.[3] Little of these encouraging realities of the war were presented to the people — then or now. If these facts had been public knowledge in 1941, the United States military role in World War II would have been diminished, or eliminated altogether.

US troops did not enter the battle in Europe until well into 1942. Before their military force had any effect, Germany was in decline and on the run. Germany's blitzkrieg campaigns were very effective against small nations, like Belgium and Greece, but completely ineffective against heavily armored forces like the Russians. The Blitzkrieg was "lightning war" with tanks in flying phalanxes, dive bombers as flying artillery supporting motorized troops, and all coordinated by radio; the German blitzkrieg raced through the opposition. The French were defeated in 1940 because they prepared to fight trench warfare as in World War I; German motorized divisions and air force swept around and over the defensive fortifications, capturing Paris in six weeks. But German strategy depended on a quick war; they did not want to get into a battle of factories and banks with the West or with the Soviet Union.

By the winter of 1940-41, as FDR searched for an entrance into the war in defense of Britain, the Germans had already lost the Battle of Britain. There was no likelihood of a German invasion of the British Isles — if there ever had been a chance of that happening. Britain con-

1. David Gordon, "A Common Design: Propaganda and World War," John Denson, ed., *The Costs of War*, p. 318

2. Geoffrey P. Megargee, *Inside Hitler's High Command*, (Lawrence, KS: University Press of Kansas, 2000.

3. Haffner, *The Meaning of Hitler*, p. 116.

trolled the Channel, the North Sea, the Mediterranean Sea and the Atlantic Ocean. Germany had few capital ships to challenge Britain, no landing crafts for an invasion, and few heavy bombers for destroying coastal defense. In the summer of 1941, Germany turned its back on England and the West. Germany turned eastward, invading the Soviet Union; The "Drive to the East" to obtain "Lebensraum" had begun. How is that a threat to England? or America?

During the Battle of the Atlantic in 1941, Hitler gave orders to avoid maritime conflicts with the US Navy. Indeed, his whole foreign policy scheme ignored the United States, as "...there was ... no plan for attacking the United States nor dealing with that country as a military target had Hitler achieved continental fulfillment."[1] In his final tragic days in the bunker in Berlin, as the Soviet Army was closing in, the Fuehrer moaned, "The war with America is a tragedy; illogical, devoid of fundamental reality."[2] America was the wrong enemy.

Following the collapse of the Nazi regime in 1945, American scholars poured through German government records attempting to find evidence of a more ambitious foreign policy plan — an attempt to conquer the word, or at least to invade North America as FDR had repeatedly warned: none was found. "After a lengthy and minute ransacking it transpired that nowhere in these [German documents] was there to be found any evidence of any German plans to attack the United States."[3]

The frightening prospect of Hitler conquering the world was nothing more than FDR's pipe dreams buttressed by bogus maps courtesy of British propagandists. Hitler couldn't conquer the world for he couldn't even conquer London and Moscow. Yet today, six decades after the propaganda battles were fought, the average American still believes that Hitler planned to rampage around the globe and had FDR not led the country into war, we would all be speaking German. It is pure speculation as to what Hitler would have done had he been successful in his quest to defeat Russia. Perhaps such a triumph would have emboldened him and he would have launched a war against the Atlantic powers. But such speculation must first deal with the basic fact that Hitler's Germany was not the Herculean military force of the TV documentaries and history textbooks. And a triumph over the Soviet Union would surely have left the Germans bloodied and depleted. As with all American wars of the 20th century, the President had exaggerated and distorted the enemy's goals and capabilities.

When Great Britain gave Poland a territorial guarantee in 1939 it was contrary to established English policy and against the recommendation of the military. The British Chief of Staff had told the cabinet that with the existing budget Czechoslovakia could not be defended; the same was true of Poland. Historian Paul Kennedy explains one aspect of the British dilemma:

> ...the amount of cash that was needed to rebuild a two-ocean navy, to provide the Royal Air Force with both its fighter defenses and its long-range bombers, and to equip the Army for a European field role — all of which the Chiefs of Staff desired — was well beyond the industrial and financial capacity of the country.[4]

Britain usually refrained from military commitments on the continent, but in 1939 "it began to toss guarantees about with reckless abandon, and with little regard for its ability to

---

1. Compton, *Swastika and the Eagle*, p. 265.
2. Ibid., p. 266.
3. Frederic Sanborn, "Roosevelt is Frustrated in Europe," in Harry Elmer Barnes, ed., *Perpetual War For Perpetual Peace*, p. 191.
4. Paul Kennedy, "Appeasement," *The Origins of the Second World War Reconsidered*, p. 151.

implement these guarantees if they were put to the test."[1] Former Prime Minister Lloyd George fumed about the irresponsibility of the Germanophobe Conservative government of Chamberlain and Churchill. Lloyd George recognized that Britain could not defend Poland without the assistance of Russia. A deal with the communist giant would have to be struck. Lloyd-George complained: "Without Russia our guarantees are the most reckless commitment any country has ever entered into — I say more — they are demented."[2]

Without even attempting to obtain some concession from Stalin in exchange for assistance in defeating Germany in the battle for Eastern Europe, Britain gave a guarantee that it could not provide. Britain and France had two realistic choices — either make a deal with Russia to assist in stopping Germany, or allow the fourth partition of Poland to occur. Instead they declared war, incurred the wrath of Germany, created a war in the West that no one wanted and watched the war in the East unfold — a war they could not win.

The British public was enraged in 1939 over the collapse of Czechoslovakia and the crisis over Danzig, but this was no reason for the cabinet to panic and guarantee the Polish borders. The British had long believed that Germany had been mistreated in the issue of Danzig and the Polish Corridor; the fourth partition of Poland was not significantly different than the first three partitions. And if the issue was simply the illegality and immorality of invading Poland, why not declare war against the Soviet Union as well, for on September 17, Russia annexed the western half of the beleaguered nation. To add to the moral dilemma, Russia soon invaded Finland, Lithuania, Estonia and Latvia as well. Idealists were in a terrible dilemma; there were too many evil men and too many evil acts taking place, and not enough young men to throw into the slaughter.

The British-French declaration of war was one of the most bizarre in modern history. The declaration was issued September 3, but no war followed. Britain and France huddled meekly for months behind the Maginot Line and the English Channel. They declared war but refused to fight. With more military equipment than Germany, with a larger population and economic base, they did nothing. They allowed Germany to attack them at its own convenience; the attack came in May 1940. It was a tragic war for the British, who perhaps were the great losers in the six-year war. In an effort to defeat Hitler over Poland, they had to drain their national wealth; worse for the proud British, they had to abandon their Empire. In retrospect, it would be difficult to justify the tragic loss of the three hundred thousand young Brits in this capricious venture.

When the war was over, one does wonder whether the Poles found the British guarantee worth the paper it was printed on. Warsaw and the other Polish cities were in ruins, six million Poles were dead, and the Polish government was the puppet of Moscow. Colonel Beck, the Polish leader, had been adamant in his refusal to discuss the issues of Danzig and the Corridor with Germany; now he saw the entire nation of Poland submerged under the Red Russian wave.

In contrast, the Czech leadership acquiesced in Germany's demand for the Sudetenland, lost their country temporarily, but preserved their land, their cities and their people. After the war the Czech President Edward Benes stood overlooking the undamaged, beautiful city of

---

1. William Henry Chamberlin, *America's Second Crusade* (Chicago: Henry Regnery, 1950), p. 57.
2. Gene Smith, *The Dark Summer: An Intimate History of the Events That Led to World War II* (New York: Macmillan, 1987) p. 163.

Prague and said, "Is it not beautiful? The only central European city not destroyed, and all my doing."[1]

One of the most memorable facets of the European War is the apparent lesson of appeasement. Nothing has seared itself into the minds of Americans more than the allegedly imprudent concessions made to Germany at Munich in 1938. To the American public and their leaders, the cravenness displayed at Munich merely whetted the appetite of a conqueror. The lesson of Munich is so powerful that no American statesman can negotiate with an adversary, no compromises can be made, and no deals concluded — even sixty years later. The Munich syndrome controls all. But negotiations in international relations necessarily involve deals, compromises and concessions. One side is not always right, the other always wrong. But the "no appeasement" lesson of Munich makes it impossible for America to deal with conflicts on an equal basis with other nations. The Munich lesson has created in the US a sense of arrogance, of never dealing with others, of always making demands. This arrogance has been reinforced by the massive military power and unrivaled economic wealth of the United States. America believes it can and should do anything it wants in world affairs.

The Munich conference didn't represent a cave-in to an aggressor; it was a realistic recognition that the Treaty of Versailles was flawed and adjustments needed to be made. Some diplomatic concessions succeed, some fail. It is the task of diplomacy to make judgments about the possibilities of negotiations. For a variety of reasons — not all involving Hitler — the Munich deal eventually fell apart. But all diplomatic negotiations cannot be abandoned because one deal went sour. Financial institutions loan money to individuals; that is their business. One would not think it an intelligent policy if banks would stop loaning money because one customer went bankrupt.

German foreign policy before the war made no attempt to challenge the West or to acquire a great naval fleet or an overseas empire. It didn't even aspire to reacquire Alsace-Lorraine from France. Had Adolph Hitler never entered the scene, had there been no Nazi Party, German policy would have been essentially the same, perhaps with less intensity, and hopefully, without the evil of the concentration camps. Germany's foe was in the east of Europe; its drive for expansion was directed at the communist giant, Russia, an ambition that the United States during the Cold War could fully understand. Nazi Germany fired the first shots in the Cold War against Soviet communism.

---

1. Taylor, *The Origins of the Second World War*, p. 180.

Chapter 8. World War II: A Soviet Victory

Hiroshima and Terror Bombing

Monday, August 6, 1945 dawned bright and clear over the southern Japanese port city of Hiroshima. The summer sun quickly warmed the city as the 300,000 residents began another day of work and school. At 7:00 AM air raid sirens sounded; a few planes were seen in the distance, but by 8:00 AM the all clear sound was heard. Hiroshima had suffered little damage from US bombing. Located at the confluence of seven rivers that emptied into the Inland Sea, it was surprising that it had not drawn more attention. There was a rumor that a special weapon was being readied to drop on the city. And, the rumor was true.

At 2:45 AM, early Monday morning, Captain Paul Tibbets eased the B-29 superfortress into the air at Tinian Island, 1600 miles south of Hiroshima. Tibbets had nicknamed his bomber 'Enola Gay' after his mother; in the plane rested 'Little Boy,' an atom bomb ten and a half feet long carrying the equivalent of 12,000 tons of TNT. The atomic age would begin that morning over the city of Hiroshima.

The long flight across the western Pacific Ocean brought the 'Enola Gay' near Hiroshima before 8:00 AM. At twelve miles from the city the bombardier sighted through the Norden bombsight at a bridge over one of the rivers. Flying at 31,000 feet all was ready, and at 8:15 AM 'Little Boy' was thrust out into the sky. The awesome weapon was set to burst at 19,000 feet over the city, where it would spread its radiation and blast far and wide. The first atom bomb used in war struck the city with enormous force — the temperature reached 50 million degrees at the center of the inferno. The eyeballs of anyone looking at the blast were melted in their sockets. The entire valley was filled with a luminous light, as though a gigantic photographic camera had snapped a picture. Seconds later the blast hit and windows miles away were blown out and doors were turned inward. Winds much greater than hurricane force demolished all structures within the city center. People near the center were incinerated, the light being so intense that their shadows were etched onto pavement where they were standing. A major hospital in the city that might have attended to the injured was blown away. Children walking to school vanished from the earth. Women spending a little time in their garden, old men out for their morning stroll, pets romping in the yard — all gone in a flash. Those civilians who supported the war and those who harbored reservations — all nowhere to be found.

Initial casualty reports stated that 50,000 people were killed instantly, but such grim totals swelled in the ensuing months as the injured died of their burns, or over many years as victims wasted away from radiation poisoning. The death toll from the Hiroshima and Nagasaki bombings totaled a minimum 200,000, possibly as high as a million. President Harry Truman, belligerent and confident, boasted that the bomb "is the greatest thing in history."[1]

True to his brusque, assertive personal style, Truman made a quick decision to use the new weapon on Japan and never looked back. Later, when the controversy swirled about whether the atom bomb was needed to bring about Japan's surrender, the President said, "I have no regrets and, under the same circumstances, I would do it again."[2] And in Trumanesque manner, he elaborated: "When you deal with a beast you have to treat him as a beast."[3] Just who the "beast" was, Truman didn't give details. Was the "beast" the little child walking to school that morning? The old man taking his morning stroll? The woman in her garden? Perhaps the target was missed and 'Little Boy' was intended for the Japanese Foreign Ministry in Tokyo?

It had been a long, ugly, bloody war with 50,000,000 killed; American leaders felt that a few thousand more enemy deaths would make little difference, especially if the bomb would save American lives. Japan had refused to surrender unconditionally, and an invasion of the Japanese islands was planned for later in the year. It was anticipated that there would be a Japanese defense force of eight million men plus volunteer citizens awaiting the US invasion. Some Allied spokesmen talked of a million American casualties, although Truman spoke more moderately of 500,000. The estimate of the United States military was 46,000 American deaths. That being the picture, "Little Boy" and "Big Boy," which was dropped on Nagasaki on August 9, were heralded as saving American lives. Secretary of War Henry L. Stimson expressed the administration feeling when he said, "I felt that to extract a genuine surrender from the Emperor and his military advisors they must be administered a tremendous shock which would carry convincing proof of our power to destroy the Empire."[4]

When Stimson expressed these feelings to General Dwight Eisenhower, Ike emphatically disagreed. Eisenhower observed that "The Japanese were ready to surrender and it wasn't necessary to hit them with that awful thing."[5] Admiral Frank Leahy, Truman's Chief of Staff, was also opposed to the use of an atomic weapon, saying, "It is my opinion that the use of this barbarous weapon at Hiroshima and Nagasaki was no material success in our war against Japan.... [in using it] we had adopted an ethical standard common to the barbarians of the Dark Ages."[6]

In October 1944, the United States had destroyed the Japanese Navy at the Battle of Leyte Gulf. By January 1945, US submarines had sunk half of the Japanese merchant fleet and two-thirds of its tankers. By the summer of 1945, incendiary bombing had destroyed over half of the sixty largest Japanese cities. American ships and planes were bombarding the nation with

---

1. Andrew, *For the President's Eyes Only*, p. 153.
2. www.rjgeib.com/heroes/truman/truman-atom-bomb.html
3. Walter LaFeber, *America, Russia and The Cold War, 1945-1990* (New York: McGraw-Hill, Inc., 1991), p. 26
4. Keegan, *A History of Warfare*, p. 379.
5. John Denson, "War and American Freedom," in John Denson, ed., *The Costs of War*, p. 47.
6. Ibid., p.46.

impunity. The United States Strategic Bombing Survey of World War II agreed with Eisenhower and Leahy. It reported on the imminent collapse of Japanese resistance:

> Certainly prior to 31 December 1945, and in all probability prior to 1 November 1945, Japan would have surrendered even if the atom bomb had not been dropped, even if Russia had not entered the war, and even if no invasion had been planned or contemplated.[1]

At any rate, no invasion of the Japanese homeland was planned for months, and the government in Tokyo was at that very moment attempting to fashion a surrender plan through three different nations. Truman was aware of these plans. What was the hurry? There were few American troops under fire or being killed by the Japanese at that time. Why not hold the bomb in abeyance awaiting the outcome of the surrender talks? Perhaps there was a time for the use of the bomb, but not in August.

The list of leaders who advised Truman against using the bomb at that time is a Who's Who in the annals of World War II: General Dwight Eisenhower, Admiral William Leahy, Admiral William Halsey, General Douglas MacArthur, British Field Marshal Bernard Montgomery, American diplomats Joseph Grew and John J. McCloy, former president Herbert Hoover, physicists Albert Einstein, Leo Szilard, and others. Nearly all of the five star military leaders advised against the use of the bomb. Harry Truman and the civilian leadership made the fateful decision to use the bomb.

The Allies and the Axis powers had grown accustomed to terror bombing of civilians during the war; Hiroshima and Nagasaki were just piled on top of London, Berlin, Tokyo, Dresden, Hamburg and dozens of other cities. In March 1945, Tokyo was bombed with inflammatory weapons by three hundred B-29s causing a firestorm, roasting over 80,000 Tokyo residents. American pilots flying low over the city after the attack reported smelling the stench of burned, decaying flesh. Over the course of several nights in July 1943, Allied bombers leveled Hamburg, with 80% of the city destroyed and 30,000 residents killed. The list of terror bombed cities by both sides goes on and on.

The most mindless and gratuitous bombing of a city was the Allied attack on the beautiful German town of Dresden, February 13-15, 1945, just weeks prior to the end of the war. Russian and Western armies were closing in on Germany and it was just a matter of time before Germany capitulated. Refugees were fleeing the Soviet Army and tens of thousands of innocent civilians were trapped in the Dresden inferno.

Dresden was the capital of the old Kingdom of Saxony and a necessary stop on the grand tour of great European cities. The old city was a university town and an arts center. Its market square dated from the Middle Ages; its Romanesque churches and great cathedrals were memorable works of architecture containing priceless art. Dresden was bombed merely to spread terror among the doomed residents and refugees, as there was little military or industry located in that area. Allied planes dropped 650,000 incendiaries killing over 35,000 people, and possibly as many as 70,000. There were too few able-bodied people left alive to bury the dead. Refugees, mostly women and children, had crowded into the city to escape the brutality of the advancing Russian Army; tragically they came face to face with the faceless horror of American and British bombers. Allied bombers even attacked the Dresden zoo, and fighter planes strafed people fleeing along railroad tracks to escape the conflagration. Some say this horrific act of brutality

---

1. www.doug-long.com/ga1.htm

was designed to please Joseph Stalin, as he doubted that the West was doing enough in the war effort. But terror bombing, or "area bombing" as it was called by the British Bomber Command, had been well established since 1942.

Allied terror bombing during the war killed as many as 700,000 and injured nearly one million enemy civilians. Allied bombing destroyed 20% of all German homes, leaving over seven million people homeless. German terror attacks on England resulted in 20,000 to 40,000 deaths of civilians. Anglo-American terror bombing caused at least 20 times the civilian destruction as German bombing on England.

For centuries, international law had explicitly forbidden armies from killing civilians; the rules of air war, however, were embryonic. *Draft Rules of Aerial Warfare* had been written for The Hague convention in the 1920s but were never adopted by the world's nations. While many wished to prohibit aerial bombardment of cities, such action was not illegal. The famed British military expert, Captain B. H. Liddell Hart asserts that Hitler attempted early in the war to gain British agreement to jointly forswear bombing anything except strictly military targets; the British refused.[1]

When World War II began, aircraft attacks were confined to factories, utilities, transportation hubs, and military bases — "strategic bombing" it was called. But strategic bombing required clear weather, accurate bombsights and ample and unmolested time over the target, all of which were often lacking. The British were losing half of their planes when daylight raids were conducted against German strategic targets; therefore, a new tactic was thought necessary.

The first use of terror bombing was in February 1942 when Britain bombed the homes of factory workers around the city of Mannheim, Germany. Terror bombing became, thereafter, the accepted tactic by British and American pilots. Bombing operations "should now be focused on the morale of the enemy civilian population," said a British military directive.[2] While Secretary of War Stimson and Prime Minister Churchill publicly denied that civilians were being targeted, Churchill's direction was precise: "All the industrial centers should be attacked in an intense fashion, every effort being made to render them uninhabitable and to terrorize and paralyze the population."[3]

Air Force General Curtis LeMay confided to others that United States bombing of cities during World War II "would get us tried as war criminals if we lost."[4] But few Americans are this candid or well-informed. They shriek with horror and anguish when office workers are killed in "terror" attacks, as on September 11, but shrug off similar wanton, barbaric attacks by the US military on wartime opponents. Nazi Germany and communist Russia exterminated civilians in concentration camps. American and Britain, fighting against tyranny, killed civilians in their own homes. Such is the Folly of War.

---

1. William H. Chamberlin, "The Bankruptcy of a Policy," in Harry Elmer Barnes, ed., *Perpetual War For Perpetual Peace*, p. 531.
2. Keegan, *A History of Warfare*, p. 374.
3. Ralph Raico, "Rethinking Churchill" in John Denson, ed., *The Costs of War*, p. 353-354.
4. *The American Conservative*, July 19, 2004, p. 26.

The unconditional surrender policy was popular in the United States and served to boost war enthusiasm, but it reinvigorated the German war effort. Joseph Goebbels, the Nazi propaganda minister said, "I should never be able to think up so rousing a slogan." General Wilhelm Canaris, the director of German intelligence and a leader of the dissident generals, complained, "Now I cannot see any solution."[1] The unconditional surrender policy was a boon to the Nazis, and a disaster to the generals in revolt against Hitler.

Opposition to the policy of unconditional surrender was common among military leaders. General Eisenhower thought it cost American fighting men's lives and raised German morale and General Albert Wedemeyer felt that the policy served to "weld all the Germans together."[2] General Ira Eaker's opinion was that, "A child knew once you said this to the Germans, they were going to fight to the last man."[3] The British intelligence service thought the policy was disastrous to secret operations in progress and would make the Germans fight "with the despairing ferocity of cornered rats."[4]

But such an idealistic, moralistic policy is typically American. The nation views wars as an abnormal disruption in their lives and the "evil man," the malevolent force that caused the disruption, must be eradicated. Realists fight wars in a calculating manner seeking to correct or manage the problems that provoked the conflict and view discussions at the end of wars as opportunities to rebalance power and redesign spheres of interest. However, idealistic Americans view wars as a means of punishing the perpetrator; postwar settlements offer opportunities for vengeance. US leaders know the people can be aroused to fight if the war is presented as a Manichean struggle between the forces of light and dark. But when the war is fought as a crusade, it is not possible to sit down with the enemy and make peace. The idealist war must end with an execution.

The US goes to war not to obtain some practical advantage, not to occupy territory or secure markets for trade. America goes to war to defeat the enemy — just to win the war. In *American Diplomacy* George F. Kennan points out that:

> the real source of emotional fervor which we Americans are able to put into a war lies less in the objective understanding of the wider issues involved than a profound irritation over the fact that other people have finally provoked us to the point where we had no alternative but to take up arms.[5]

The US concentrates so exclusively on military victory that it pays no heed to the "Aftershocks" that erupt following the war. Wars are to be fought by generals; diplomats deal with negotiations separately after the war. Wars and diplomacy never meet. The old saying, "America wins the war but loses the peace," captures this confusion about military adventures. Americans refuse to recognize that the manner in which a war is fought determines the nature of the peace at war's end. War and peace are not distinctly separate entities, but more like the vine and the fruit. National leaders must deal with them together.

European views on war and peace have been influenced by the realist thinking of men like Karl van Clausewitz, whose book *On War* has been the "Bible" of realists since the mid-19th

---

1. Fleming, *The New Dealers' War*, p. 176.
2. Ibid., p. 175.
3. Ibid.
4. Ibid., p. 174
5. Kennan, *American Diplomacy*, p. 73.

century. To the realist, "war is the continuation of [foreign] policy by other means." Simply stated, wars are fought to obtain some foreign policy goal that could not be obtained through diplomacy. Nothing could be further from the American perception; Americans don't kill to achieve some political goal; Americans kill to destroy evil. The inability of Americans to make shrewd calculations during war can be seen in the fiasco ending the war against Japan.

Early in 1945, Japan began sending out peace feelers to the United States. Two days before leaving for the Yalta Conference in February 1945, FDR received from General Douglas MacArthur a 40-page summary on Japanese peace offers. MacArthur suggested that the United States open negotiations with Japan because Nippon was prepared to allow the occupation of its homeland, remove all troops from occupied nations, surrender all arms, submit to criminal war trials and allow the regulation of its industries. Japan did ask only that their Emperor be retained in some capacity. President Roosevelt, however, dismissed the General's urging, saying, "MacArthur is our greatest general and our poorest politician."[1] In May, Ambassador Joseph Grew counseled the new President, Harry Truman, that surrender could be obtained from Japan if the United States would give assurances that the Emperor would be retained. Nothing came of Grew's suggestion and the war continued.

President Truman continued to spurn Japanese peace offers through the summer, thereby creating a policy dilemma. By prior commitment, Russia was scheduled to enter the war against Japan on August 9, a development which portended trouble for the future in Far Eastern affairs. And the possible use of atomic weapons loomed in the background. Would Truman accept the Japanese terms, or would the United States continue the war, ensuring Russian occupation of Manchuria, as well as the first use of the atom bomb. Truman rejected the Japanese terms. The Japanese "beast" had to pay.

The week of August 6, 1945 was a disastrous week in Japanese history. Hiroshima was bombed on August 6. On August 9, Nagasaki was bombed and the Russian Army began the occupation of Japanese-held Manchuria. The six member Japanese cabinet met following the Nagasaki blast and the Russian declaration of war. The vote on unconditional surrender was 3–3, the same vote that occurred earlier in the year. No cabinet member had changed his mind, even during that awful week! The United States — historians, politicians, and the public — has consistently exaggerated the singular effect of the atom bomb on Japanese decisions.

On August 11, an Imperial conference was held, so named due to the dominating presence of the Emperor. Emperor Hirohito told the expanded cabinet that, "We must bear the unbearable" and surrender.[2] Distraught cabinet members and hardened military leaders wept unashamedly; a few Army leaders even plotted against any capitulation. But the custom of the Imperial conference requires acceptance of the Emperor's request; the Japanese would surrender on America's terms. On August 14, the Japanese government cabled Washington that its peace terms were accepted. And what of the status of the Emperor? Incredibly, the US later agreed to the continuation of Emperor Hirohito's reign, subject only to the supervision of the US military. The peace terms that Japan had requested early in the year were eventually granted to Japan. With a little less idealistic zeal to crush the enemy and a little more realistic calcu-

---

1. William H. Chamberlin, "The Munich Called Yalta," in Richard Fenno, ed., *The Yalta Conference* (Boston: D. C. Heath and Company, 1955), p. 54.

2. Andrews, *For The President's Eyes Only*, p. 154.

lation about political goals, the war in the Pacific could have ended in the spring of 1945. The world, then, would not have heard of Hiroshima and Nagasaki, nor would the Chinese communists have been given a foothold in Russian-occupied Manchuria, courtesy of the Soviet Union. Surely all will see Folly in these decisions.

DIPLOMACY BY FRIENDSHIP — ROOSEVELT AND STALIN

A few days before he left for the Yalta Conference in February 1945, Franklin Roosevelt delivered his fourth inaugural address to the nation. Flushed with apparent success in the war and nearing the end of his life, Roosevelt displayed his abiding sense of idealism. He said, "We have learned to be citizens of the world, members of the human community. We have learned the simple truth, as Emerson said, 'the only way to have a friend is to be one.' "[1]

Roosevelt's conception of the post-war world envisioned the abandonment of all colonial empires, rejection of the realist spheres of interest and elimination of the concept of a balance of power. In the post-war world, Roosevelt regarded the colonial empires of England, France and the Netherlands as a greater menace to peace than the Soviet Union's Empire. France was already attempting to reclaim its colony of Indochina. Roosevelt was disgusted at this action: "France has had the country — thirty million inhabitants — for nearly one hundred years, and the people are worse off than they were at the beginning."[2] The Four Policemen — the US, the Soviet Union, Great Britain, and China — would police the world, ensuring that with these idealistic reforms, international affairs would return to their "natural" harmonious state. There would be no more French, or British or Dutch Empires and no more international power struggles.

There were men around the President who cautioned him about the communist regime in Moscow and about the acquisitiveness of Stalin, but FDR had taken the measure of "Uncle Joe" and believed that Stalin could be charmed. When Soviet expert William Bullitt warned that Stalin was a "bandit whose only thought when he got something for nothing was, the other fellow was an ass,"[3] Roosevelt expressed doubts and retorted, "I just have a hunch that Stalin isn't that kind of man. Harry [Hopkins] tells me he's not and that he doesn't want anything but security for his country. I think that if I give him everything I possibly can and ask for nothing in return, he won't try to annex anything and will work with me for a world of peace and democracy."[4] President Roosevelt saw himself as the replacement of the established diplomatic channels in Britain and the US. He bragged to Churchill: I think I can personally handle Stalin better than either your Foreign Office or my States Department." FDR continued: "Stalin hates the guts of all your top people. He thinks he likes me better, and I hope he continues to do so."[5]

An incident during the Tehran Conference at Thanksgiving time in 1943 illustrates FDR's efforts at "Diplomacy by Friendship." When Roosevelt arrived in the Iranian capital, Stalin

---

1. Chester Wilmot, "Stalin's Greatest Victory," in Richard Fenno, ed., *The Yalta Conference*, p. 75.
2. Hofstadter, *The American Political Tradition*, p. 348.
3. Alex DeJonge, *Stalin* (New York: William Morrow and Company, 1986), p. 398.
4. G. F. Hudson, "The Lessons of Yalta," in Richard Fenno, ed., *The Yalta Conference*, p. 41.
5. Marks, *Wind Over Sand*, p. 172

offered the President the use of a villa in the Soviet Embassy compound, warning that there were assassination plots afoot in the city. Apparently, it never occurred to FDR that Stalin had ulterior motives. The Russians were known to bug offices and dwellings, and in addition, such an arrangement was intended to create tension between the two Western leaders, Roosevelt and Churchill. Roosevelt eagerly accepted Stalin's offer; this unexpected proximity to the Russian leader would facilitate his effort at friendship. FDR told friends that Stalin was "gettable" and he speculated on the source of Stalin's charm: "Do you suppose that [his training for the priesthood during Stalin's youth] made some kind of difference in Stalin? Doesn't that explain part of the sympathetic quality in the nature which we all feel?"[1]

With Winston Churchill out of the way, Roosevelt and Stalin began their "romance." At dinner ceremonies and during after dinner drinks, the Russian and American leaders began making jokes at Churchill's expense. They teased the Prime Minister about his Britishness, about his cigars, about other habits, about John Bull. Stalin and Roosevelt were bonding — at Churchill's expense. Stalin caught the mood and felt "from that time our relations were personal ... we [Stalin and FDR] talked like men and brothers."[2] As the conversation warmed, Stalin suggested that after the war 50,000 German officers should be shot and killed by the Allies. Churchill, uneasy and hurt from the teasing, took umbrage at the thought of such a crime and exclaimed, "I would rather be taken out into the garden here and now and be shot myself than sully my own or my country's honor by such infamy."[3] Roosevelt hoping to deflate the tension quipped that he agreed with Stalin, except he would only kill 49,000 Germans. An angry Churchill immediately left the room. Stalin and Roosevelt's juvenile game of "freeze out" had gone too far.

By all accounts Roosevelt was a charming, affectionate man; he had survived in US politics not by intellect, certainly not by honesty, but by his affability. But in Stalin he was up against a master at bureaucratic struggles and personal ruthlessness. Handshakes, backslaps and nightcaps were not enough in this desperate game of international politics. Stalin had survived in the turbulent, dangerous world of Russian politics since the mid-Twenties. He was intellectually prepared, personally adroit, cunning and determined to pursue Russian interests. FDR may have been able to discern and overwhelm the political bosses of America's cities and his personal aides; in Stalin he was up against one the 20th century's most cold-blooded and capable leader. It was no match.

Roosevelt met with Stalin and Churchill at Tehran and at Yalta early in 1945. Depending solely on his personal charm, FDR was not prepared with an agenda or with any clearly defined foreign policy in mind. He intended just to get along with the Russian leader. The State Department had prepared an extensive file on issues to be decided at Yalta; the file was essentially unused when FDR met Stalin in the Crimea in February 1945. Churchill's personal interpreter, A. H. Birse, commented that, "He [FDR] knew little of Soviet mentality or had been badly advised. It was not enough, as he evidently thought, to clap Russians on the back and say they were good fellows, in order to reach mutually advantageous agreement with them. Something more subtle was required."[4]

---

1. DeJonge, *Stalin*, p. 413.
2. Robert Conquest, *Stalin: Breaker of Nations* (New York: Viking Press, 1991), p. 263.
3. Winston Churchill, *Closing The Ring* (Boston: Houghton-Mifflin, 1951), p. 374.
4. DeJonge, *Stalin*, p. 415-416.

But there was more to America's flirtation with communist Russia than FDR's personal style. Hitler and Nazi Germany had created a worldview that saw "race" as the organizing principle of society. Communists, on the other hand, were guided by a worldview of "economic classes." Germany saw the Jews as the enemy of society; Russia saw the capitalist class as the adversary. The Western world in the 1930s and 1940s was struggling with a severe economic depression, a depression that many felt was caused by the greed and mismanagement of the capitalist class. New Deal Democrats, like Roosevelt, had more sympathy for communism than for Nazism; class warfare made some sense, race war did not. Indeed at mid-century American liberalism was gearing up for a great crusade against racism at home. Nazi Germany was a much more serious threat to Roosevelt and his political party than communists. It was possible to befriend Stalin; it was unthinkable to befriend Hitler. Throughout the Thirties and Forties, the FBI and other government agencies ferreted out suspected Nazi and German sympathizers, while at the same time Russian communist spies were sprinkled throughout government, even in FDR's White House.

Given Franklin Roosevelt's proclivity to meet with and charm people, it is puzzling why he failed to take advantage of his noted charisma before the war began. In August 1941, several weeks before the Pearl Harbor attack and at a critical time in negotiations with Japan, Roosevelt refused to attend a summit meeting with Japanese Prime Minister Konoye. Roosevelt engaged in no personal diplomacy with the leaders of Japan, Germany, or Italy prior to the war, yet Roosevelt met with the dictator Stalin at Tehran and at Yalta. One can only speculate on the diplomatic success of FDR's personal magnetism on Hitler, Mussolini, and Tojo, the Axis leaders.

A few weeks before his death Roosevelt lamented, "I wish someone could tell me about the Russians. I don't know a good Russian from a bad Russian." [1] Ever the liberal idealist, to the end Roosevelt colored the world in white hats and black hats. While Roosevelt was clapping Russians on their backs, bonding with the Russian dictator and speculating on the Russian character, the Russian Army was plunging deep into the heart of Europe. By early 1945, Soviet forces were in command of Poland, Romania, Bulgaria, the Baltic States, much of Austria and Czechoslovakia and a healthy slice of Germany. All this before the US Army had crossed the Rhine River. "[T]he Soviet armies stood with all the capitals of Eastern Europe already in their hands and the three great capitals of Central Europe [Berlin, Prague, and Vienna] within their grasp." [2]

The apogee of the Roosevelt-Stalin friendship was the Tehran Conference in late 1943; by the time the two met again at Yalta in February 1945, tensions already were evident as the Soviet armies raced toward Berlin and the Russian grip tightened on hapless Poland. By the summer of 1945, relations would worsen; FDR died in April and in July the voting public in Great Britain removed Churchill. If there was any chance of a peaceful post-war world, that dream was lost without the two wartime giants of the West.

---

1. Ibid., p. 416.
2. Chester Wilmot, "Stalin's Greatest Victory," in Richard F. Fenno, ed., *The Yalta Conference*, p. 72

APPEASING JOSEPH STALIN

Because of the failure of the Munich Agreement with Germany in 1938, any concession to an "aggressor" was repugnant to the Western world. It was politically dangerous for a statesman to engage in negotiations that resulted in diplomatic concessions. However, in actuality, appeasement didn't end at Munich; throughout World War II the West quietly gave in to the Soviet Union. Consider the following concessions granted to Stalin by 1945:

- the new boundary of Poland (the Curzon Line).
- the new Polish communist government (the Lublin government).
- preponderance of Soviet power in the Balkans.
- reparations from Germany.
- the French occupation zone of Germany taken from the Western zones.
- granting to the Soviets three votes in the United Nations.
- Soviet control of ports, bases and railroads in Chinese Manchuria.
- Soviet control over Mongolia

Poland became the focal point of discussion and eventual disagreement among the Big Three powers in 1945, for issues about Poland — Danzig and the Polish Corridor — had provoked World War II. If Poland could not be kept free and independent, what was the purpose of the long, bloody, destructive war? At the Yalta Conference, it became palpable that Stalin's view and the Western views on Poland diverged. Two issues confounded the conference: the future boundary of Poland and the nature of the new Polish government.

The Curzon Line was a proposed eastern border of the newly created state of Poland in the treaty discussions of 1919. However, the eastern boundary actually settled upon after World War I was 200 miles farther east. In 1945, Stalin demanded that the Curzon Line (so named after a British diplomat, Lord Curzon) be the new border, and that the entire nation of Poland be moved 200 miles westward at the expanse of Germany. Concisely, Russia would expand westward 200 miles and Germany would shrink 200 miles as Poland was shifted westward. Churchill expressed concern about German minorities left in Poland by this change of borders when he said, "It would be a pity to stuff the Polish goose so full of German food that it died of indigestion."[1] To avoid such future bouts of indigestion, it was decided that millions of nationals in the new areas would be moved into a new homeland. Polish nationals living east of the Curzon Line and German nationals along the new German-Polish border would be displaced; there would be a "Moving Day" for four million Poles and eight million Germans. President Roosevelt accepted this new boundary and the displacement of millions of Poles and Germans, only asking that the arrangement not be disclosed until after the next election. FDR discerned that Polish voters in the US, an important part of the Democratic Party, would not accept this manhandling of their native homeland.

There were two rival Polish governments existent in 1945: the London-based Poles whose support in Poland was suspect for they had fled the country, and in Poland the Lublin- based communist government which was dominated by Stalin. Inasmuch as the Russian Army was sprawled across Poland by 1945, the Lublin group was in position to control post-war Poland. Churchill and Roosevelt did extract a pledge from Stalin that there would be "free and unfet-

---

1. Winston Churchill, *Triumph and Tragedy* (Boston: Houghton-Mifflin, 1953), p. 374.

tered elections" in Poland following the war and that the new Polish government would include more than the Lublin group. Why the Western leaders would expect Western style democratic elections in a communist government is difficult to fathom. The last "free and unfettered election" held in Russia was in November 1917, at which time the Lenin and his communists, not liking the unfavorable outcome of the vote, closed the doors of the Russian legislature, arrested some duly-elected lawmakers and ran the nation for the next 28 years without ballots and votes. In 1945, it would be no different in Poland. Throughout the Thirties and during the war, FDR had deluded himself about the nature of communist Russia; the delusion continued at Yalta.

The mood of appeasement toward Russia was dramatically evident in the "Balkans deal" formulated by Churchill and Stalin in October 1944. Churchill tells the story of the deal in *Triumph and Tragedy*:

> The moment was apt for business, so I said, "Let us settle about our affairs in the Balkans. Your armies are in Romania and Bulgaria. We have interests, missions, and agents there. Don't let us get at cross-purposes in small ways. So far as Britain and Russia are concerned, how would it do for you to have ninety per cent predominance in Romania, for us to have ninety per cent of the say in Greece, and go fifty-fifty about Yugoslavia?" While this was being translated I wrote out on a half-sheet of paper:
>
> Romania — Russia 90%, Others 10%
>
> Bulgaria — Russia 75%, Others 25%
>
> Greece — Britain and US 90%, Russia 10%
>
> Yugoslavia — 50-50%
>
> Hungary — 50-50%
>
> I pushed this across to Stalin, who had by then heard the translation. There was a slight pause. Then he took his blue pencil and made a large tick upon it, and passed it back to us. It was all settled in no more time than it takes to set down.[1]

Prior to the war when British Prime Minister Chamberlain was appeasing Germany on the issue of Czechoslovakia, Churchill became incensed about the "softness" displayed by Britain toward Hitler. Churchill's anti-appeasement talk in 1939 soon earned him the prime ministership of Britain, and Churchill declared that there would be no more appeasement of Hitler. But in October 1944, Winston caved in to Stalin. Churchill accepted the slaughter of millions of people during World War II to keep Eastern Europe free from German control, but then meekly acquiesced to Soviet control in that same area when the war was over. Idealists and even realists were dumbfounded at this deal. The concession made to Stalin at the Yalta Conference and the Balkan Deal concluded the Eastern European questions. Stalin was pleasantly appeased.

As the Allied ring tightened on Germany in the spring of 1945, a debate erupted concerning the merit of a proposed American-British military thrust to capture Berlin from the west before the Russians arrived from the east. Germany and Berlin had previously been divided among the Big Three powers (the United States, Britain and the Soviet Union); each nation would have a predetermined occupation zone of Germany and Berlin. So the debate about the US Army thrust into Berlin was not about any permanent occupation, but about prestige and about

---

1. Ibid., p. 227.

using the occupation as a lever against potential Russian misbehavior. General Eisenhower believed that any diplomatic advantage would be diminished by the estimated 100,000 casualties that would be incurred. [The Russians who eventually did occupy the city had 300,000 casualties.] The issue was settled when President Truman said, "I am quite prepared to adhere to the occupational zones...."[1] Stalin's Army would stand alone astride Berlin by April 1945.

The Allies never determined a clear policy about how to treat Germany after the war. Some plans envisioned breaking Germany into four or five nations, thereby reducing its power. Others talked of removing all industry from the nation, returning Germany to a pasture. The three Allied occupation zones (four zones when the United States and Britain reshaped their zones to grant France a zone) would permit the Allies to take reparations from the defeated nations for ten years, a venture which was especially appealing to Russia as it had suffered great physical damage. It was tentatively decided that $20 billion would be removed from German industry and production, half delivered to the Soviet Union. The agreement deteriorated as Russia and the West fell to quarreling over post-war conditions. The Russians eventually helped themselves to whatever they could take out of their German zone (East Germany).

And finally, Stalin received what he wanted in the Far East. Having its hands full with Germany, Russia remained neutral during the Asian war, but Stalin did guarantee that three months after the end of the war in Europe (May 8), Russia would enter the war against Japan (August 8). Roosevelt and the Joint Chiefs of Staff felt that Russian assistance against Japan was necessary to moderate American casualties. As an inducement, Russia was promised the return of all territory and concessions that had been lost in the Russo-Japanese War of 1906. These concessions gave Russia dominance in the rich area of Manchuria and included:

- Leases of the naval base at Port Arthur and the port at Darien.
- Control of the South Manchurian railroad that operates between the Trans-Siberian Railroad and the Darien-Port Arthur area.

It was FDR's view that these concessions were merely returning what was rightfully Russian property, taken in an earlier war by the rapacious, and now out of favor Japan. In an odd twist of fate, these concessions had been won by Japan at the Treaty of Portsmouth (New Hampshire) that was presided over by FDR's cousin, Theodore. It was Teddy Roosevelt who sponsored these Japanese gains in 1906. And had FDR studied the State Department briefs on the Far East, rather than playing "Diplomacy by Friendship," he would have known that these concessions had all expired or had been sold by the Soviet at an earlier time. Apparently Roosevelt did consult with his Executive Assistant in charge of Far Eastern Affairs, Launchin Currie. Currie would certainly have encouraged this appeasement of Stalin for Currie was a paid secret agent of the Soviet espionage system working in the White House.

At no time did Roosevelt consult with the Chinese government of Chiang Kai-shek about disposing of property in Chinese Manchuria, for had he done so, Chiang would have objected. Mao Tse-tung, Chiang's rival for control of China, was poised to take over Manchuria with Stalin's assistance. The appeasement of Stalin in the Far East was a windfall for the Chinese Communists. From Manchuria they would launch their successful drive to oust Chiang and take over the world's largest nation.

---

1. Moskin, *Mr. Truman's War*, p. 54.

In 1941, Roosevelt refused to concede to Japan any further control of mainland China without China's consent. Yet at Yalta, FDR gave away critical areas of China to Stalin without the approval of Chiang Kai-shek. Ostensibly, the war in the Pacific had been fought to prevent rapacious neighbors from carving up China; at Yalta Roosevelt proved that 100,000 US servicemen had died in vain in the Asian war. In *The Lesson of* Yalta, G. F. Hudson states the problem succinctly.

> There can be little doubt that Roosevelt avoided consulting Stettinius [the Secretary of State] about this deal for the same reason that he avoided consulting Churchill or Chiang Kai-shek — because he anticipated that they would object. He did not want to read the State Department memorandum because they might not fit in with his intentions.[1]

Either by appeasement or conquest during the war, Stalin's realm grew by 24 million subjects and 275,000 square miles of territory. World War II had been fought to prevent aggressors from taking foreign lands. But at war's end, Poland, Eastern Europe, China and much of the Far East were not "free." What was the purpose of this war? Germany and Japan had been defeated, but a new "evil" had arrived. Aftershocks — the unintended consequences of war — had degraded the Allied victory. Such is the Folly of War.

The Moral Issues — The Nuremberg War Crimes Trials

Nazi Germany's foreign policy was a rational attempt to rectify problems stemming from the German unification in 1871 and the Treaty of Versailles; this foreign policy charted a policy that would have been pursued, to some degree, by any German regime. But, seldom has there been a government that practiced such hideous racial programs and that engaged in so many human rights abuses. Never before in history have the winners placed the losers on trial for crimes; but never before have the losers deserved some legal reckoning. On April 12, 1945, US forces entered a Nazi concentration camp at Ordure, Germany where 21,000 emaciated survivors existed among a mountain of corpses. General Patton, in tears, became ill and left the camp. General Eisenhower toured the camp with teeth and fists clenched. To a GI standing nearby, Eisenhower snapped, "Still have trouble hating them?"[2]

There were indications as early as September 1, 1939 that this war would be more brutal than most. As an economy move in Germany, 100,000 "Useless Eaters" — invalids, handicapped, mental patients, disabled children — were exterminated. Later the slaughter of the gypsies commenced. As the war against the Poles ensued, they felt the cold fury of Nazi brutality. Between 1939 and 1944, Nazis killed two to three million Polish citizens. The Poles were to be reduced to subservient labor for Germany and limited to four years of education. Poland with "a residual inferior population" was to be a "leaderless working mass" for the Master Race of Germany.[3] In 1941 and 1942, a "war of annihilation" was waged against the Russians. Two million of the five million captured Russian officers were executed.

---

1. G. F. Hudson, "The Lessons of Munich," in Richard Fenno, ed., *The Yalta Conference*, p. 46.
2. Moskin, *Mr. Truman's War*, p. 56.
3. Haffner, *The Meaning of Hitler*, p. 134.

But it was the German Nazi attempt to annihilate the Jews — the Final Solution — that demonstrated the most hideous element of Nazi policy. Until 1941, public knowledge of Nazi murders of Jews and others had been muffled, partly due to Nazi attempts to conceal such activity and partly by the fact that most anti-Jewish action was buried in Eastern Europe, far from the prying eyes of the Western press. But during the week of the Pearl Harbor attack, Hitler's Final Solution was revealed. This fateful decision was prompted by the failure of the German military campaign against Russia.

On December 6, 1941, the Russian Army began a counterattack around Moscow against the invading German Army. The German military offensive into Russia, launched in June, was expected to take a few weeks; the German Army had not made provision for a winter campaign. A war during the Russian winter boded ill for the invaders. The German military machine was not equipped for an extended campaign, nor was its economy geared for a multi-year industrial production battle against Russia and the West. Hitler's dilemma became severe with the attack on Pearl Harbor. The Axis Pact did not obligate Germany to come to Japan's aid after December 7, but in anticipation of an US declaration of war and to curry favor with Japan, Germany declared war on the US December 11. Desperate times called for desperate measures.

The next day, December 12, Hitler ordered the extermination of the Jews. Paul Goebbels diary entry on that date reveals the decision: "With regard to the Jewish question, the Fuehrer decided to make a clean sweep."[1] Two months later, at the Wannsee Conference, the "Final Solution" was formally ordered. Germany had been at war in Europe for over two years and the prospects for a military victory looked bleak; the foreign policy plans of *Mein Kampf* were in tatters. It was manifest to the Nazi leader that the German foreign policy of dominating Europe and establishing puppet regimes in Eastern Europe would fail. Hitler always maintained that World War I was a result of a conspiracy by European Jews. He now saw their conniving causing another war in Europe. The Fuehrer proclaim late in 1942: "If Jewry should imagine that it could bring about an international world war to exterminate the European race, the results will not be the extermination of the European race, but the extermination of Jewry in Europe."[2] Frustrated over the collapse of his plans in Eastern Europe, in anger and spite, Hitler turned the Nazi war machine against European Jews; this was a war Hitler knew he could win. "Hitler the War Leader" now became "Hitler the Exterminator."

By mid-January 1942, millions of Jews were being moved eastward where extermination camps were located. Auschwitz, Sobodor, and Treblinka: the names resound with revulsion. In 1935, there were nine million Jews living in Europe; ten years later three million remained. Of the six million Jews who left Europe or were killed, probably half were executed in the camps.

> To Hitler, during the last three and a half years of war, the war became a kind of race that he was still hoping to win. Who would reach his goal sooner, Hitler with his extermination of the Jews or the Allies with their military overthrow of Germany? It took the Allies three and a half years to reach their goal. And in the meantime Hitler too, had certainly come terrifyingly close to his.[3]

---

1. http//history.acusd.edu/gen/WW2Timeline/holocaust.html
2. Michael Shermer and Alex Grobman, *Denying History* (Berkeley, CA: University of California Press, 2000), p. 196
3. Haffner, *The Meaning of Hitler*, p. 145.

German government and military leaders were placed on trial in Nuremberg, Germany starting in October 1945. Twenty-one defendants, including Hermann Goering and Rudolph Hess, were tried; eighteen were convicted most of whom received the death penalty. The Western allies — the United States, the Soviet Union, Great Britain, and France — conducted the trials and handed down the verdict. The victorious Allies acted as both prosecutor and jury. The German leaders were accused of committing three types of crimes:

Crimes against the Peace — planning, preparing and initiating wars of aggression in violation of various treaties which forbade wars of conquest.

War Crimes — mistreatment of prisoners, murder, using slave labor, holding hostages, plunder of property, wanton destruction of cities and towns.

Crimes against Humanity — extermination and deportation of people due to race, religion, and political views.

Never before in history had the winners of a war sought to place the losers on trial for crimes. At the conclusion of past wars, losers were either participants in a negotiated peace treaty, or suffered the ignominy of being partitioned, broken up into separate nations or in some way made to pay the price for their behavior by loss of territory. However, placing the leaders of one nation in a legal proceeding conducted by other nations was unprecedented. Was this trial nothing but a "kangaroo court?" What was the legal basis for such a trial? What specific crimes were committed and when were those crimes made part of international law? Didn't the prosecuting nations commit the same crimes? Were these crimes essentially *ex post facto* laws — laws created "after the fact" simply to ensnare the losers? Many Western observers, such as Winston Churchill, preferred to simply shoot the worst Nazi leaders rather than enact a "fake trial" and demean the judicial process. Many others worried that placing national leaders on trial after a war would intensify future wars. "To label war a crime, as was attempted at Nuremberg, can only make it more terrible because the loser is then bound to fight not for victory or defeat but for life or death."[1] This perception is especially true of the charge of waging war. All nations have waged war, none of them would ever admit that their wars were "wars of aggression waged for conquest."

World War II began when Germany invaded Poland in 1939; but seventeen days later, by prior agreement, the Soviet Union invaded Poland, and in addition invaded several other Eastern European nations. In this regard, the Nuremberg trial became something of a farce with the "Guilty judging the Guilty." Was Germany condemned because it lost the war? And did Stalin sit in judgment because he won? The moral dilemma thickened as the trials moved along:

- Germans were accused of invading Norway in 1940. Germany offered proof that Britain was preparing to invade, so Germany simply took Norway first. Irrelevant, ruled the court!
- Germans attempted to defend themselves by invoking the Nazi-Soviet Pact of August 1939, showing that Stalin had waged a war of conquest. But such arguments were rejected.
- Germany was accused of sinking vessels on the High Seas without making provisions for crew and passenger safety; Germany replied that the Allies did the same. Rejected!

---

1. Ibid., p. 129.

- Germany was accused of wanton bombing of Allied cities; Germany responded that the Allies had done the same and that Germany had lost many more civilians due to "terror bombing" than the Western allies. Rejected!
- German military leaders, Admirals Jodl and Doenitz, argued that they, as military leaders, should not be tried as they were merely carrying out orders and defending their nation. Rejected!
- Nazi leaders argued that they were merely attempting to rectify the injustices of the Treaty of Versailles. Rejected!
- German leaders maintained that they had no intention of starting a general war; the war over Danzig was created by the foolish policies of Russia, England and France. Rejected!

All such protestations were disallowed. The victorious Allied nations prohibited any defense on the grounds of "You did it too," or "I was just following orders."

The concept of trials at the conclusion of war has added a new dimension to foreign affairs. The 20th century has seen attempts to outlaw war; the Kellogg-Briand Peace pact of the 1920s and the United Nations Charter both disallow wars except for self-defense. The United States had been a major force in support of these efforts to limit the scourge of war. However, developments after the fall of communism have led the United States to engage in "preventive war," as in Iraq in 2003, and to disdain the idea of using the collective security umbrella of the United Nations. Applying the logic of the Nuremberg trials, would the United States president and other leaders stand in the docket and be accused of waging "aggressive war" against Iraq. What else is preventive war?

World War II, from the Western perspective, began as a moral crusade against militarism, tyranny and totalitarianism. But the Western crusade lost its way and the moral issues became blurred at countless "terror bombing" sites. The United States entered the war as an innocent virgin determined to retain its purity and to enforce a strict moral code on the world. But war is ugly and transforming. That moral innocence was lost at Hiroshima and Nagasaki, and in the 1000 degree furnace over Tokyo, Hamburg and Dresden, and in the incarceration of thousands of Japanese-Americans in concentration camps in the United States and in the White House's obsession with unconditional surrender to the exclusion of a short war that would benefit all Europeans, especially the beleaguered Jews.

The spectacle of communist Russia and Joseph Stalin sitting in moral judgment on any other nation or leader is mind-boggling. The government of the Soviet Union in the 20th century has been one of history's worst mass murderer. Between 1917 and 1990, one authority estimates that 62 million citizens of the Soviet Union were killed by their own government. During the Nazi era in Germany (1933—1945, admittedly a much shorter period) 21 million were killed. These figures do not include wartime deaths — just murder by government. In 1929 Stalin began the extermination of the Kulaks, prosperous peasants in the Ukraine. Over 15 million were uprooted and sent to Siberia; millions were killed or died of disease. In the mid-Thirties, Stalin began the infamous purges with his gruesome "show trials" of political opponents, many of whom were part of the Jewish Bolshevik community. As World War II grew to a close, Stalin insisted that those Russians who had fled the nation be returned, even if they preferred to seek asylum in another nation. The West complied, defying the Geneva Conventions and simple human decency. Millions of these repatriated souls, including the Volga Germans, perished in the Siberian camps.

As the Nazi menace was stomped out in the spring of 1945, Allied fighting men and journalists were aghast at the sight of concentration camps across Europe. The stories and vivid images of that tragic epic resound yet today, decades later. Equally tragic was the brutality of the Stalinist regime; but there was no US Army liberation in Russia, no journalists to record the horror, no stories and movies to barrage our senses. Franklin Roosevelt taught us to shield our eyes from the human rights abuses of the Russian Gulag; after all, Stalin was our ally and friend.

The Nuremberg War Crimes trials were courageous efforts to proclaim a civilized standard for national leaders to observe in the future. But the trials went astray by attempting to prosecute Germany and Japan for waging "aggressive war" and for committing "war crimes," actions which the Allies were as guilty of committing as the Axis. These extraneous issues became a distraction from the most grievous crimes of slaughtering innocent civilians in extermination camps. Crimes against humanity are the issue that will long be remembered about these times. The barbarity of the government attacks on innocent people should have been the only issue. And there should have been one more defendant in the docket — Joseph Stalin.

THE FOLLY OF WAR

Reflecting on the generation of young men who lost their lives in World War I, Neville Chamberlain commented: "When I think of the 7 million of young men who were cut off in their prime, the 13 million who were maimed and mutilated, the misery and the suffering of the mothers and fathers...in war there are no winners, but all are losers."[1]

The future prime minister of Britain went on to say that he found the idea incomprehensible that war was the real ordeal of manhood and that nations must occasionally be toughened in war. His Cabinet Secretary, Maurice Hankey, seconded this observation: "Modern war is so beastly, so drab, so devoid of the old 'joie de guerre' that everyone hates it."[2] And that was a common view before World War II.

If a natural catastrophe — a horrendous earthquake, a great flood, a collision with a comet — had carried away 50 million people, the world would mourn such devastation for centuries. But because it was a war, even a "good war," history records that World War II was worth 50 million lives. Fifty million people had to die in order to cleanse the world of evil. That is the price for "winning World War II."

But the United States and its ally, Great Britain, didn't actually win World War II.

World War II was not a war that the West could win in any realistic sense of the word. Yes, it is true that the United States and its allies could defeat Germany militarily; the Nazis could be forced to surrender, its military destroyed and its political system reformed. However, the independence of Poland and Eastern Europe was the political goal, and that was not accomplished by this war. When World War II was over, the armies of the Soviet Union were sprawled across the map of Eastern Europe; Poland, the Baltic States, Romania, Bulgaria, Czechoslovakia and Yugoslavia were in the clutches of Stalin or his confederates. There was no

---

1. Overy and Wheatcraft, *The Road To War*, p. 303.
2. Ibid.

practical way to prevent this from happening. The British and French made a choice of allies in 1939; they decided that the Western democracies would ally with Stalin, thus ensuring that communist Russia would be victorious in Eastern Europe. The die was cast on September 17, 1939 when the Soviet Union armies sliced into Poland from the east. By 1945, Soviet armies, at the cost of 13 million dead, had secured Russia's western borderlands. The Western democracies, by declaring war on Germany, had decided that Eastern Europe should not go to Germany, but to Russia. They would have to live with that decision for nearly half a century. The perceptive American diplomat Joseph Grew observed that World War II was a failure, as it accomplished the "transfer of totalitarian dictatorships and power from Germany and Japan to Soviet Russia."[1]

Neville Chamberlain's diplomatic efforts — his "appeasements" — in 1937 to 1939 were designed to control Germany without war, but at the same time grant any reasonable demands for territorial adjustments. Chamberlain perceived that if war broke out, England would lose control of the situation. But with Winston Churchill yapping at his heels calling for a tough line against Hitler, and the British public inflamed by Hitler's apparent reneging on Czechoslovakian independence, Britain rashly declared war and France meekly followed suit. It was evident after September 1939 that Britain and France could do nothing militarily to stop the German and Russian absorption of Poland, for they sent no troops, airplanes or ships against Germany in 1939 and 1940. Seven hundred thousand young British and French troops died during World War II in order to ensure that communist Russia would have a security belt on its western flank. Such is the terrible Folly of War.

Winston Churchill, recognizing the dilemma in the midst of the war, proposed a solution — armies of the Western democracies should invade Eastern Europe through the Balkans, the "soft underbelly of the continent." In World War I, Churchill had advanced the notion of opening a "second front" in the Balkans against the Central Powers. Eventually Britain launched an invasion into the Gallipoli peninsula near Constantinople; it was a military disaster as the West discovered that the "soft underbelly" was unyielding. Consideration was given during the Second World War to injecting Western forces into the Balkans from Italy or from Greece, but such a venture would have been many times more difficult than the Normandy invasion. Long supply lines, inhospitable terrain, questionable assistance from native forces, all caused this idea to be discarded. President Roosevelt himself eventually rejected the idea. It would be a tricky military maneuver and besides, as FDR said to his aide, Harry Hopkins, the United States doesn't "care whether the countries bordering Russia become communist or not."[2] The Soviet Union would have its way in Eastern Europe. This benign view of Russian communism was not the view of President Harry Truman and the other Cold Warriors.

Some realists, with the cunning of a fox, proposed a solution to the dilemma. They suggested that the Western democracies stand aside during the fight over Eastern Europe. In his book, *Great Mistakes of the War*, Hanson Baldwin advocated such a shrewd policy:

> There is no doubt whatsoever that it would have been in the interests of Britain, the United States, and the world to have allowed and indeed, to have encouraged — the world's two great dictatorships to fight each other to a frazzle. Such a struggle, with its resultant weakening of

---

1. McDougall, *Promised Land, Crusader State*, p. 158.
2. Fleming, *The New Dealers' War*, p. 312.

both communism and Nazis, could not but have aided in the establishment of a more stable peace.[1]

Senator Harry Truman also detected an opportunity to let the European heavyweights fight it out: "If we see that Germany is winning, we ought to help Russia; and if Russia is winning we ought to help Germany and that way let them kill as many as possible."[2] It should be noted that this policy of "standing aside" was exactly the policy that the America First committee — the Isolationists group — was suggesting before the war. Isolationists believed that the US should stay out of these strictly European quarrels for they were not really winnable and would surely devastate the country.

But American Militant Idealists are not cunning, nor do they have the patience and humility to wait on the sidelines. When "evil" rears its head, the US — the avenging angel — must attack, and the "evil" must be completely destroyed, even though the international environment will, in the process, be devastated. Only later, in a more sober state of mind, does America look at the wanton destruction that war has caused and realize that something has gone amiss. Despite the fervent moral crusade that America pursued, the world in 1945 was not a safer or more stable place than before the war. World War II was not the ultimate "good war." The *Militant Idealistic* policy of unconditional surrender magnified the error of US involvement; that policy prolonged the war and every month that went by allowed the Soviet armies to drive deeper into central Europe.

At the Yalta Conference in February 1945, Roosevelt acquiesced to Stalin's demands about Poland. But the simple fact was that, short of going to war in Eastern Europe against the Soviet Union, there was nothing else that FDR could have done. All of the loud cries of Republicans about the "give away at Yalta" were just hollow political posturing. FDR had nothing to give away in Eastern Europe in 1945. Eastern Europe had been "given away" during the course of the war. Republican critics would have been more on the mark had they complained during the war that FDR's wartime strategy was flawed, but no such complaints were heard. When the full reality of this folly became apparent to the Democratic Party in the late Forties, they placed the blame for the strategic loss of Poland and Eastern Europe on the Russian communists and Joseph Stalin. They have continued to maintain that President Roosevelt's wartime decisions were golden — Stalin simply failed to live up to his agreement. And so, in order to protect FDR's reputation, the Cold War attitude flourished.

In the eighteenth century, Poland had ceased to exist as the Great Powers partitioned the hapless nation among themselves. From the time of the American Revolution until the Treaty of Versailles in 1919, there was no nation of Poland. For the first century and a half of America's existence, Poland was not on the map of Europe, and those earlier American leaders pursued no idealistic crusade on behalf of Poland, nor did the American people seem to suffer as the result of such a condition. But, by the mid-twentieth century, American leaders were in a froth over the "loss of Poland." A war had to be fought and young men's lives taken. And eventually, thoughtful Americans would ask — For what?

The *Militant Idealistic* fervor of the unconditional surrender policy prolonged the war in the Far East, prompting the US use of atomic weapons and Russia receiving vast concessions in

---

1. Hanson Baldwin, *Great Mistakes of the War* (New York: Harper, 1949), p. 10.
2. Buchanan, *A Republic, Not An Empire*, p. 277.

northern China. Russian control of Manchuria provided Mao Tse-tung and his band of Asian communists a military base from which they eventually chased their opponents off the mainland. How different would the Far East have been had Truman accepted in May the Japanese offer of surrender with their Emperor's throne intact, rather than the tragedy of August 1945. The United States Far Eastern policy had always been to avoid any commitments on the mainland of Asia. Presidents from McKinley to Hoover had accepted the limits of US power in Asia. By 1940, however, FDR began an aggressive policy of forcing Japan out of China; the Open Door policy that had been verbal window-dressing for earlier presidents, was for Roosevelt a policy for which he would go to war. The product of all this heavy breathing of moral platitudes was to see China fall to communism. With all its vaunted power, the United States could not save China.

The cost of human life for such futility was enormous. No war in history had been so destructive.

WORLD WAR II DEATHS

	Military	Civilian	Total
Soviet Union	13,600,000	7,700,000	21,300,000
China	1,324,000	10,000,000	11,324,000
Germany	3,250,000	3,180,000	7,060,000
Poland	850,000	6,850,000	6,850,000
Japan	1,506,000	300,000	1,806,000
Yugoslavia	300,000	1,400,000	1,700,000
Romania	520,000	465,000	985,000
France	340,000	470,000	810,000
Hungary	NA	NA	750,000
Austria	380,000	145,000	525,000
Greece	NA	NA	520,000
Italy	330,000	80,000	410,000
Czechoslovakia	NA	NA	400,000
Britain	326,000	62,000	388,000
USA	295,000	0	295,000
Others	268,000	323,000	591,000
Total	23,289,000	30,775,000	55,714,000

War came easily to the generations that fought the World Wars. Men who grew to manhood in the late nineteenth century were part of the Victorian, imperial generation who saw war as a necessary part of nationhood and manhood. Theodore Roosevelt in the US and Winston Churchill in England were exponents of the martial arts, the glory of conquest, the unfurled flag and John Phillip Sousa's stirring anthems. Teddy thrilled to American wars in 1898 and 1917 and became deeply involved in the Russo-Japanese War. Churchill was a war correspondent and adventurer in several military campaigns — Cuba in 1895, the Afghan War in 1897, Sudan with General Kitchener in 1898 and the Boer War in 1899. At the beginning of World War I, Winston was the head of the British Navy and an architect of the Q-ship violations and other schemes to entice the US to join the British in war. And it was Churchill who cheered for England to take a belligerent position against Germany in 1939. Sir Winston never seemed to find a war he didn't like.

After the fiascos of World War I and World War II, one would think that Churchill's enthusiasm for battle would have cooled, but no. In 1946, Churchill's alluring rhetoric again sounded the call to arms. Winston had located an "Iron Curtain" that had descended across Europe. Time for another war!

Three times in this century, Churchill was instrumental in pulling the US into European quarrels; three times American presidents accepted the inducement. In 1914 and in 1939 the British reach had exceeded their grasp. America, their powerful and rebellious child, would be expected to bail them out. The prospects for Britain in May 1940 looked bleak as the British pondered the war against Germany and the dilemma in Eastern Europe. Lord Halifax, the British Foreign Minister, an associate of Churchill, suggested an answer: "Our only hope, it seems to me, lies with Roosevelt and the USA." A few days later the British military chiefs encouraged this strategy with a memo that assumed that the United States "is willing to give us full economic and financial support, without which we do not think we could continue the war with any chance of success."[1] There was developing a "special relationship" with the United States, one in which when British diplomacy got in over its head, America could be duped into providing assistance. Wilson, FDR, and Truman all fell victim. If a nation seemed to threaten the imperial interests of Britain, the Dutch, or the French, the US was always there to stop the "aggression," apparently unaware of the aggression that had been committed earlier by those Imperial powers in acquiring their own empire.

Just as in World War I, the British had strong allies in New York City and the Northeast of the nation. The financial, cultural, and political elites in America had felt the "special relationship" ardently and worked tirelessly to defeat the Isolationists. Recent research by Thomas Mahl in his 1998 book, *Desperate Deception*, indicates that British intelligence operations in the United States during 1940 and 1941 were much more extensive than previously thought. The British agent, William Stephenson (*The Man Called Intrepid*), directed an extensive espionage operation from two floors in Rockefeller Center, provided by the Rockefeller family. Using this base, British agents worked to undermine Isolationist sentiment by rigging public opinion polls to show greater support for intervention than actually existed. British espionage created the bogus map of Nazi plans to occupy Latin America, smeared Isolationist leaders with the tag of Nazi sympathizers, established "front organizations" that worked for US intervention and influenced the Republican nomination for president in 1940 to ensure that an Isolationist candidate was not chosen. One story even suggests that Senator Arthur Vandenberg, a key Isolationist Republican figure, was seduced and then blackmailed into supporting interventionist measures. The Senator from Michigan, it seems, had a weakness for the ladies, and his taste was well supplied by British intelligence. What is obvious from Mahl's book and others on the

---

1. David Reynolds, "1940: Fulcrum of the Twentieth Century," in Patrick Finney, ed., *The Origins of the Second World War*, p. 438.

subject is that the British were pulling out all the stops to influence American opinion, and had any other nation gone to such length to influence American policy, the United States public would be outraged. The administration of Franklin Roosevelt was aware of these nefarious British ventures and encouraged the effort. Unfortunately, not one whiff of this scandal has reached the mainstream press or history textbooks. Such is the nature of the "special relationship." The politician and journalist Carl Schurz recognized the game Britain was playing in the late 19th century. Schurz denounced US assistance to and emulation of Britain, saying that it was "a singular delusion [that] has taken hold of the minds of otherwise clear-headed men. It is that our new friendship with England will serve firmly to secure the world's peace."[1]

Sadly, after the horror of World War II, a chastened Winston Churchill began to see the Folly of War. In 1945, he "expressed utter dismay at the outlook of the world," saying "that there were probably more units of suffering among humanity as of this hour... than ever before in history."[2] What had 20th century statesmen wrought? Whereupon the British warrior geared up for one more military struggle— the Cold War.

Winston Churchill was known for his soaring rhetoric, his colorful phrases, and his stirring speeches. But often his words had great emotional effect but lacked seriousness and profundity. Speaking of the moral depravity of Adolf Hitler, Winston once said, "if Hitler invaded hell I would at least make a favorable reference [to the devil] in the House of Commons."[3] Churchill was full of breezy statements of that kind, the suggestion being that the German leader had exceeded the Devil in wickedness. And Churchill was not alone in assigning to Hitler the label of absolute evil; that feeling was in the air during and after World War II. The historian, Ralph Raico, observed this emotional phenomenon:

> A moral postulate of our time is that in pursuit of the destruction of Hitler, all things are permissible. Yet why is it self-evident that morality required a crusade against Hitler in 1939 and 1940, and not against Stalin? At that point Hitler had slain his thousands but Stalin had already slain millions.[4]

It is even plausible to argue that Stalin was Hitler's teacher in moral depravity; Stalin did his dirty work in the Thirties, Hitler began the "Final Solution" in 1942 — after the war began. Stalin's savagery was performed in peacetime; Hitler's was an act of vengeance because the war had gone wrong. Stalin began a campaign against Jewish Bolshevism in the Thirties and continued this anti-Semitic purge until his death in 1953, when it was alleged that Jewish doctors were killing patients. But most of Stalin's victims were non-Jews, people who owned property — the capitalist class. If you were a Jew in Germany in 1942, your life would be in severe danger; if you were a capitalist in Russia in 1932, your life was in peril. How idealists can distinguish between the immorality of these two is beyond comprehension.

Many Americans continue to believe that America entered World War II in Europe to save the Jews from the horror of the extermination camps. This scenario suggests that FDR was a savior of a persecuted minority, and had the Isolationists won the policy battle, the United States would never have come to the aid of the Jews. On all counts, this is sheer fantasy. In

1. Justin Raimondo, "Defenders of the Republic: The Anti-Interventionist Tradition in American Politics," in John Denson, ed., *The Costs of War*, p. 77.
2. G. F. Hudson, "The Lessons of Yalta," in Richard F. Fenno, ed., *The Yalta Conference*, p. 42.
3. Churchill, *The Grand Alliance*, p. 370.
4. Ralph Raico, "Rethinking Churchill," in John Denson, ed., *The Costs of War*, p. 343.

reading the records of FDR's speeches about Nazi Germany before Pearl Harbor, one is struck by the absence of outrage on the issue of human rights; Roosevelt's anger at Hitler is almost entirely directed at the Nazi chieftain's foreign policy — his wars of conquest. This is so partly because the "Final Solution" was not established as policy until early in 1942, and the West was perhaps not aware of the extermination policy until later in the war. Thus, America's entrance into the war was largely unrelated to the human rights issue.

In addition, when Roosevelt was given opportunities to save the Jews, he declined. At no time did he seek revision of immigration laws to provide a refuge for the beleaguered children of Abraham. When in the summer of 1939, the S.S. *St. Louis*, a mercy ship carrying 937 Europeans, mostly Jews, sought haven in the Caribbean, it was rejected. The ship's officers frantically cabled the White House and sent two individuals to personally petition the President for assistance. Roosevelt refused even to acknowledge their statements; the United States Coast Guard was ordered to prevent any escapees from leaving the ship.[1]

FDR's unconditional surrender policy effectively prolonged the war, adding months to the travail of the Jews in the camps. In this connection, it should be remembered that it was FDR who sent Americans of Japanese ancestry to "concentration camps" in the American West, despite the fact that no traitorous activities by these poor souls were ever documented. Taking his cues from President Wilson's attacks on ethnic Americans during World War I, FDR campaigned in 1920 against Irish, Italians and Germans, asserting that they had been disloyal and were "dangerous elements." Franklin Roosevelt is not the President who would save the Jews or any minority group.

Hitler spoke often of Germany being a "world power," and even of "world domination." But such talk was the raving of a single man who was given to flights of fancy. Stalin, on the other hand, spoke of communism taking over the world, and such rhetoric was not merely personal ramblings, but a well-developed Marxist theory that had evolved over one hundred years and was espoused by millions of people. The American-British campaign against Germany's perceived efforts at world "domination" resulted in strengthening the Marxist idea and facilitating the spread of Russian communism into areas of the world where it had never been. The dilemmas created by war are unfathomable. Perhaps the Polish Marshall Smigly-Rydz had the most cogent comment when he said, "With the Germans we risk the loss of our liberty, but with the Russians we lose our soul."[2]

The unintended consequences of war — the Aftershocks — take surprising twists and turns:

- the Soviet Union lost 20 million people and its industrial system in Europe had vanished. Yet, it emerged after the war as one of two great superpowers.
- Germany, having lost 7 million citizens, surrendered unconditionally and was occupied by the Allied powers, yet emerged within a decade as Europe's greatest economic power.
- Great Britain and France entered the war with enormous colonial empires and vast national wealth and prestige. But after their "victory" they both were bankrupt and fought losing battles to retain their empires. Most would call that a "Pyrrhic victory," a loss disguised as a victory.

---

1. *Atlanta Journal Constitution*, Parade Magazine, Dec. 7, 2003, p. 4.
2. Buchanan, *A Republic, Not An Empire*, p. 263.

Franklin Roosevelt's deceitful behavior prior to and during the war lowered the standard of presidential conduct. As orthodox historians applaud FDR, potential presidents observe the scene and learn that dissembling, deceit and conniving earn a high mark for presidential greatness. The lying didn't stop with Pearl Harbor. On February 23, 1942, the President delivered a fireside chat in which he praised the American people in, "Your ability to hear the worst without flinching or losing heart."[1] Reporting on the disaster at Pearl Harbor he said, "We have destroyed considerably more Japanese planes than they have destroyed of ours." He lied! He reported that the US had lost three ships; in fact the loss was 8-10 ships. The US had lost 400 airplanes, the Japanese had lost 26. And the deceit continued for months as the President concealed the reality of war from the public. "During the first twenty-one months of the war, not a single photo of a dead American soldier, sailor, or marine was displayed in any publication on the theory that it might panic the public into calling for a premature peace."[2]

Apparently, the public is supposed to see a war as nothing more than a Boy Scout bivouac. Eventually the mothers, fathers and wives of the 300,000 dead young men would learn of the real, enduring consequences of war; the Gold Star flags in the windows of homes across America would tell the poignant story.

Early in the nation's history, leaders were wiser and more discreet about entering wars that could not be won, or that are clearly not of American concern. Said President Washington: "Europe has a set of primary interests which to us have none or a very remote relation. Hence she must be engaged in frequent controversies, the causes of which are essentially foreign to our concerns."[3]

The Fourth of July oration of John Quincy Adams in 1821 formulates the cautionary doctrine of early America:

> America does not go abroad in search of monsters to destroy. She is the well wisher to the freedom and independence of all. She is the champion only of her own. She will recommend the general cause by the countenance of her voice, and the [benevolent] sympathy of her example. She well knows that by once enlisting under other banners than her own.... She might become the dictatress of the world. She would be no longer the ruler of her own spirit.[4]

---

1. Fleming, *The New Dealers' War*, p. 129.
2. Ibid., p. 128.
3. McDougall, *Promised Land, Crusader State*, p. 46.
4. Ibid., p. 36.

Chapter 9. The Origins of the Cold War — The Longest War

The Cuban Missile Crisis

Saturday night, October 13, 1962, the weather report indicated that the cloud cover over Cuba had cleared; the U-2 flights over the tropical island would resume. At 11:30 p.m. Major Richard Heyser left Edwards Air Force base in the Mojave Desert of southern California headed for a rendezvous with destiny. By Sunday morning, Heyser's U-2 with sophisticated photographic equipment was soaring 14 miles above the western end of Cuba between Havana and San Cristobal where suspicious military activity had been reported. After the overflight of Cuba, Heyser's U-2 landed at McCoy Air Force base near Orlando, Florida. There a military jet flew the undeveloped film to Washington D.C. where the Naval Photographic Intelligence Center developed and analyzed the photos. As the team of experts went over the pictures frame by frame, they noticed more than defensive surface-to-air (SAM) missiles. Some objects were large enough to be medium range ground to ground SS-4 Soviet missiles with a range of 1000 miles, capable of striking Washington D.C., Atlanta, Dallas and other cities throughout the southern United States. As they compared the sites in the photos with pictures of SS-4s, the director said, "This sure looks like it. If there ever was a time I want to be right in my life, this is it."[1] It was 5:30 p.m., Monday October 15, 1962, and telephones in the White House, State and Defense Departments began to ring. The Cuban Missile Crisis had just begun.

On Tuesday morning, October 16, National Security Advisor McGeorge Bundy went to the presidential quarters in the White House to deliver the grim news to President Kennedy. "Mr. President, there is now hard photographic evidence ...that the Russians have offensive missiles in Cuba." Kennedy's cryptic response was, "He can't do that to me."[2] Soviet Premier Khrushchev had promised Kennedy that all newly installed military hardware in Cuba was

---

1. Norman H. Finkelstein, *Thirteen Days/Ninety Miles: the Cuban Missile Crisis* (New York: Julian Messner, 1994), p. 42.

"defensive" in purpose, that is designed to protect only against an invasion. To that end, for months Soviet cargo ships had been transporting SAMs, cruise missiles, Soviet bombers and other military equipment that Fidel Castro could use to repel an anticipated invasion. But now, with the identification of the SS-4s, there was clear evidence that "offensive" missiles were in Cuba — ninety miles off the American shore — and pointed ominously at the national capital and other urban areas. And the SS-4s had nuclear teeth. Each of the forty-two medium range ballistic missiles (MRBM) carried a warhead with a one-megaton nuclear bomb, six times larger than the atom bombs dropped on Japan in 1945. Even more threatening, on October 15, U-2 photos detected telltale signs of Soviet intermediate range ballistic missiles (IRBM) which doubled the range of the MRBM. These missiles (SS-5s) with a range of 2000 miles could reach all of the United States, including the US missile ranges in the northern plains states. The SS-5s could knock out America's own missile force! Because of the proximity of these Cuban missiles, the warning time to the United States of any missile attack was reduced from 15 minutes to five minutes. At completion there would have been 42 MRBMs and 21 IRBMs in place on the northern coast of Cuba. The atomic weapons delivered to Cuba by the Soviet Union totaled many times the explosive power of all the Allied bombs dropped on Germany in World War II.

What was Nikita Khrushchev thinking when he sent such a potent package to Castro? In September, before the discovery of the "offensive" missiles in Cuba, the Soviet leader laid down his justification:

> The whole world knows that the United States of America has ringed the Soviet Union and other Socialist countries with bases. What have they stationed there — tractors? No, they have brought armaments there in their ships, and these armaments [are] stationed along the frontier of the Soviet Union — in Turkey, Iran, Greece, Italy, Britain, Holland, Pakistan, and other countries.... They consider this their right! But to others the US does not permit this, even for defense, and when measures are nevertheless taken to strengthen the defenses of this or that country, the US raises an outcry and declares that an attack, if you please, is being prepared against them.[1]

Soviet government records of meetings in May, 1962 give various motives for the risky venture of Khrushchev:

- "The only way to save Cuba is to put missiles there."
- US missiles in Turkey "are aimed at us and scare us."
- "If missiles are deployed near the US, they will be even more afraid."
- "Give them some of their own medicine."[2]

In Premier Khrushchev's colorful words, "Why not throw a hedgehog at Uncle Sam's pants?"[3]

The US had recently placed Jupiter missiles in Turkey and activated them early in 1962. These missiles, placed along the southern border of the Soviet Union, were closer to the Russian industrial heartland than other older missiles in Western Europe. To the Soviets, the Cuban

2. Graham Allison, *Essence of Decision: Explaining the Cuban Missile Crisis* (Boston: Little Brown and Company, 1971), p. 193.

1. Ibid., p. 43.

2. Aleksandra Fursenko and Timothy Naftali, *"One Hell of a Gamble" Khrushchev, Castro and Kennedy, 1958-1964* (New York: W. W. Norton, 1997), p. 182.

3. Ibid., p. 171.

missiles were the equivalent of the Jupiter's, but the Kennedy administration steadfastly rejected any such equivalency. There would be no "missile swap" with the Russians.

After the failure of the Bay of Pigs invasion of Cuba in April 1961, Fidel Castro awaited the next invasion effort by the US. John Kennedy's presidential campaign in 1960 had promised a more active foreign policy and Cuba had become the main target. In the spring of 1962, US troops simulated an invasion of Cuba with landings on other Caribbean islands with 40,000 troops and 84 ships. Later in the year, the administration had leaked news about a military exercise in the Caribbean to liberate a country from the shackles of a dictator named ORTSAC, which is CASTRO spelled backwards. This not-so-subtle provocation involved 7500 Marines, four aircraft carriers, twenty destroyers and fifteen troop transports. The "invasion" was to occur in the fall 1962.

For a year and a half there had been continuing efforts by the United States to assassinate Fidel Castro — Operation Mongoose — with either CIA operatives or Cuban dissidents. Even after the Missile Crisis, the attempts by Kennedy to take the life of Fidel Castro continued. On November 22, 1963, one year after the Cuban Missile Crisis, CIA agents met a paid assassin in Paris where a hypodermic needle with poison was provided; the assassin asked for a more sophisticated weapon, such as a telescopic rifle with a silencer. On that very day and at that very moment, John Kennedy was visiting Dallas, Texas.[1]

In addition to protecting Cuba from a US invasion, Soviet leaders saw the placement of MRBMs and IRBMs in Cuba as a way of achieving a more equitable balance of nuclear power in the world. Kennedy had campaigned in 1960 charging the Republican administration with allowing a "missile gap" to develop in American defenses. He promised that the United States would, under his guidance, catch up with Russia in missilery; but, the fact is that the United States had eight times more intercontinental ballistic missiles (ICBM) than the Soviet Union. It was Russia that needed to catch up! (Intercontinental ballistic missiles have a range of over 4000 miles and can travel from Siberia to North Dakota, or, hopefully, vice versa. In 1962, the United States had 172 ICBMs; the Soviets had 20, although some CIA estimates gave an inflated figure for the Soviets of 75.[2]) Because ICBMs are expensive and more difficult to manufacture, Khrushchev and company had decided to close the missile gap on the cheap; they would send medium range and intermediate range missiles to their Caribbean ally, using Cuba as a potential launching pad for Soviet rockets.

At 11:45 AM Tuesday, October 16, President Kennedy convened a meeting of the Executive Committee of the National Security Council — or ExCom. The ExCom was composed of fourteen American civilian and military leaders in whose hands the fate of the United States and the world rested. Over the next thirteen days, President Kennedy led these men in discussions, while the human race paused, held its collective breath and pondered its destiny. During each day and far into the night, in small groups and large, the fourteen men deliberated the issues: Why did the Soviet Union take this action? What did they intend to accomplish? What dangers did this pose for the US? What is the appropriate response to sixty ballistic missiles only ninety miles from the southern shore of the country? Perhaps never before in American history did so

---

1. Andrews, *For The President's Eyes Only*, p. 305.
2. Lawrence Freedman, *Kennedy's Wars: Berlin, Cuba, Laos and Vietnam* (New York: Oxford University Press, 2000), p. 172.

much hang in the balance, and perhaps never before did a president perform so capably during a crisis.

What should the United States do about the missiles in Cuba? The thirteen days of intense discussions focused on these choices:

- DO NOTHING — The United States was no more insecure than it had been before the missiles came to Cuba; nothing really had changed. Twenty Soviet ICBM located in the Soviet Union had been targeted at America; now sixty shorter range missiles were targeted from Cuba. As Secretary of Defense Robert McNamara said, "It makes no difference whether you are killed by a missile from the Soviet Union or Cuba."[1] This option was quickly discarded because President Kennedy had publicly warned Khrushchev during the previous month not to install "offensive" weapons on the island. Kennedy felt he had to do something.

- USE DIPLOMATIC PRESSURE — A public appeal to Castro and to the Russian leaders coupled with an agreement to withdraw US naval forces from the large base in Cuba, Guantanamo Bay, might defuse the crisis. But because the troops and equipment were Russian, Castro seemed irrelevant, and any discussions with the Soviets at this time would make Kennedy appear craven; the specter of the "give-away at Munich" hung heavily in the air. The recent summit meeting in Vienna did not enhance Kennedy's image in the world.

- A NAVAL BLOCKADE —The greatest asset the United States had in the Caribbean was its Navy. Why not use it to prevent further equipment from entering Cuba? This option seemed to be a relatively non-confrontational one, for as the President said it did not "bring an adversary to the choice of either a humiliating defeat or a nuclear war."[2] Kennedy was considering giving Khrushchev an "out," rather than demanding unconditional surrender. The obvious problem with a blockade, or quarantine as the president called it, was that it didn't deal with the missiles already in place on the island.

- AN AIR STRIKE AGAINST THE MISSILE SITES — Initially this option seemed the most appealing as it promised to knock out the offending missile sites immediately. However, as the discussion progressed there emerged two types of air strikes; a so-called "surgical strike" in which precision bombing hit only the missiles, and a "general strike" which would destroy the area around the sites, thus causing casualties among Russian and Cuban troops. The military chiefs could not guarantee that a surgical strike would eliminate 100% of the missile sites. With Russian troops taking casualties, the Soviet leaders would be compelled to retaliate. As Undersecretary of State George Ball said, "You go in there with a surprise attack. You put out all the missiles. This isn't the end. This is the beginning, I think."[3] Robert Kennedy, the Attorney General, said, "I know how [Japanese Prime Minister] Tojo felt when he was planning Pearl Harbor."[4] It would be a pre-emptive strike with no warning and Robert Kennedy opposed such action, saying, "For 175 years we had not been that sort of country. A sneak attack was not in our tradition. Thousands of Cubans would be killed without warning and a lot of Russians, too."[5]

---

1. Allison, *Essence of Decision*, p. 195-196.
2. Ibid., p. 61.
3. Freedman, *Kennedy's War*, p. 178.
4. Ibid.
5. Ibid., p. 187.

- AN INVASION OF CUBA — CIA Director John A. McCone saw the crisis as an opportunity to not only rid the area of Russian missiles but to eliminate Castro as well. "Cuba was the key to all of Latin America; if Cuba succeeds, we can expect all of Latin America to fall."[1] An invasion of the island would involve at least 150,000 men, 600 aircraft and 200 ships. Even a brief ten-day war would result in over 18,000 casualties. But for the time being this was discarded because it would surely portend a general war against Cuba and the Soviet Union with untold numbers of dead.

As President Kennedy and the other ExCom members contemplated their choices, they faced the most momentous event in the history of the Earth. The Age of the Dinosaurs had ended when a comet struck the Earth, extinguishing the great beasts and ushering in the Age of Mammals. Now — 65 million years later — in 1962, man came face to face with the possibility of his own extinction. The Thirteen Days tolled ominously:

Tuesday, October 16 — At 11:45 AM the first ExCom meeting takes place, at which time the president orders members to "put all other work aside." Every option is discussed, but soon only a blockade and an air strike remain as choices.

Wednesday, October 17 — The option of a blockade emerges as the prime choice of the members who are closest to the president. U-2 flights over Cuba are increased with the understanding that if a U-2 were shot down, there would be immediate retaliation against a missile site.

Thursday, October 18 — ExCom recommends that a blockade should be imposed around Cuba to prevent any military supplies from entering the country. [Military leaders as well as Dean Acheson and John McCone dissent arguing for a more forceful response.] The Air Force is placed on full alert.

Friday, October 19 — Radio Moscow announces that a United States invasion of Cuba is imminent.

Saturday, October 20 — U-2 photos reveal the presence of storage facilities for nuclear weapons. Two Army divisions are alerted for war.

Sunday, October 21 — President Kennedy decides that a "quarantine" will be imposed on Cuba to force compliance with his directives. [Because a "blockade" is an act of war, the President chooses to rename it a "quarantine."]

Monday, October 22 — President John F. Kennedy speaks to the nation on television in a seventeen-minute address. The President asserts that "unmistakable evidence has established the fact that a series of offensive missile sites is now in preparation on the imprisoned island. The purpose of these bases can be none other than to provide a nuclear strike capability against the Western Hemisphere." [The President fails to mention the American offensive missile bases in Turkey.] Kennedy compares this to Hitler's aggression twenty years before and affirms that he will "secure their withdrawal or elimination from the Western Hemisphere."[2] The means to accomplish this is a blockade around Cuba established by the United States Navy 800 miles off the shores of the island. As he speaks, United States fighter jets roar southward toward Cuba, as though to punctuate the President's strong words. Secretary of State Dean Rusk meets with American diplomats at the time of the speech and intones that "we are in as grave a crisis as mankind has ever been in."[3] When Kennedy meets with congressional leaders, they are nearly unanimous in urging an immediate invasion.

Tuesday, October 23 — The Soviet Union calls the blockade an act of piracy and orders its ships to disregard it. American and Russian delegates to the United Nations exchange insults and opinions about the crisis, with the Soviet delegate insisting that there are no "offensive

---

1. Fursenko and Naftali, *"One Hell of a Gamble,"* p. 204.
2. Finkelstein, *Thirteen Days/ Ninety Miles,* p. 66-68.
3. Ibid., p. 68.

missiles" on the island. President Kennedy redraws the blockade line from 800 miles to 500 miles in order to provide an extra day for Khrushchev to respond. It is emphasized that the blockade is for the sole purpose of stopping the flow of "offensive weapons;" food, oil, and other necessary cargo will not be interrupted. The United States prepares its nuclear arsenal — 156 ICBMs and the nuclear bomber fleet — and sends 180 ships including eight aircraft carriers to enforce the blockade. A quarter of a million troops are readied for an invasion of Cuba.[1] President Kennedy is deadly serious!

Wednesday, October 24 — At 10:00 AM the United States Navy establishes a blockade line 500 miles from the Cuban shores and awaits the eighteen Russian ships that are steaming toward a confrontation. Tension runs high in the White House as President Kennedy anticipates the next move. Robert Kennedy, the President's brother and confidant, describes the President's reaction to the impending confrontation on the High Seas and the potential for nuclear war: "His hands went up to his face and covered his mouth. He opened and closed his fist. His face seemed drawn, his eyes pained, almost gray."[2]

Florida military airfields are packed with planes awaiting orders and naval yards are nearly deserted as all ships are on duty in the Caribbean Sea. The American military is placed on Alert level #2 — the highest alert in history except in wartime. The alert message is sent *uncoded* around the world to all American troops — American commanders want Soviet leaders to read the alert message.

(A terrifying but little noted nuclear incident occurred at the height of the crisis. A sentry at a military base in Minnesota mistook a bear climbing the fence for a saboteur and sounded the alarm. The alarm was transmitted to an Air Force base in Wisconsin where mistakenly the alarm for nuclear war sounded, causing the pilots to prepare to scramble. Nuclear war had begun and in minutes airmen would be on their way in aircraft carrying nuclear weapons. Fortunately, the base commander discovered the error and raced to the runways flashing his lights to deter the pilots who were taking off.)[3]

At 10:25 AM on Wednesday, just 25 minutes after the establishment of the blockade, a crucial message is received in the White House: "Mr. President — we have a preliminary report which seems to indicate that some of the Russian ships have stopped dead in the water." Secretary Rusk at this point utters the now famous phrase: "We're eyeball to eyeball, and I think the other guy just blinked."[4]

Thursday, October 25 — Walter Lippmann, the eminent journalist, suggests in his column that a missile swap would resolve the crisis — the United States would remove its Jupiter missiles in Turkey in exchange for the Soviet removal of missiles in Cuba. Citizens are besieging civil defense offices asking how to protect themselves. Where is the nearest bomb shelter? What should I do in case of an atomic attack? The public is moving toward panic!

Friday, October 26 — The first Soviet ship reaching the blockade line is boarded, then allowed to proceed. United States invasion plans continue as Castro asks the Soviets to launch a preemptive nuclear strike against the United States. Khrushchev declines. Plans for the evacuation of main government offices in Washington D.C. go forward. Television correspondent John Scalli is contacted by a Russian KGB agent in Washington who presents a "peace offer." Late Friday night a personal letter is received at the White House from Nikita Khrushchev offering to remove the missiles in exchange for a United States pledge not to invade Cuba. The Scalli-KGB conversations are along the same lines.

Saturday, October 27 — A second letter from the Soviet leadership arrives, this one upping the ante and asking not only for a "no invasion" pledge, but an agreement to remove the American Jupiter missiles in Turkey. An American U-2 spy plane is shot down over Cuba, but the President orders no reprisals. Instead, an "ultimatum" is sent to the Soviets, affirming that America will take the missiles out by force if they are not removed by Tuesday, October 30. The world

1. Lawrence Wittner, *Cold War America: From Hiroshima to Watergate* (New York: Praeger, 1974), p. 220.

2. Finkelstein, *Thirteen Days/Ninety Miles*, p. 76.

3. Beth Fisher, *The Reagan Reversal: Foreign Policy and the End of the Cold War* (Columbia, MO: University of Missouri Press, 1997), p. 132.

4. Andrews, *For The President's Eyes Only*, p. 296.

draws closer to the abyss. Robert Kennedy meets privately with the Soviet Ambassador and discusses a secret deal — the United States would remove its Turkish missiles after the crisis has passed, but this missile swap will never be publicly acknowledged.

Sunday, October 28 — Premier Khrushchev announces over Radio Moscow that the Soviet Union will accept the latest American offer. America will give a "no invasion" pledge and the Soviets will remove their missiles. No mention is made of the Jupiter missiles in Turkey. The Cuban Missile Crisis is over. True to his charm, wit, and grace President Kennedy comments: "This is the night to go to the theater, like Abraham Lincoln."[1]

FROM APPEASEMENT TO CONFRONTATION: 1945-1946

When the Cuban Missile Crisis was over, National Security Director McGeorge Bundy said solemnly, "[h]aving come so close to the edge, we must make it our business not to pass this way again."[2] The Cuban Missile Crisis occurred seventeen years after the end of World War II and by that time the Cold War was well under way. How did the Cold War develop? How did the US and Russia become fervent adversaries after having fought a military struggle against a common foe during World War II? What are the ORIGINS OF THE COLD WAR?

The United States emerged from the World Wars as the only major nation that was not invaded and whose economy was vibrant and thriving. The other Allied victors had only won a Pyrrhic victory, for France had been occupied and crushed by Germany, and Great Britain was destitute and in the early stages of dismantling its empire. *Pax Britannia* was over; *Pax Americana* had arrived. The US presidents would now replace the British Prime Minister as the man to consult when diplomatic problems arose and when questions of war and peace came up.

The wartime "shotgun marriage" between the US and Russia continued to thrive into 1945; Roosevelt's "appeasement" of Stalin on Eastern European questions had pacified the scene. The Soviet Union had been granted a *cordon sanitaire* — a security belt — in Eastern Europe; essentially the West accepted Stalin's wartime gains. There had been no military race between the Russians and the Americans into Germany or Berlin or Prague in the spring 1945, nor any subsequent attempt to oust the Russians from Poland. American leaders gave respect to Russia for their 21 million dead in the war against Germany. Joseph Stalin, who FDR had befriended, was now the leader of a superpower. A State Department memo to President Truman in June 1945 emphasized that the Russians "are not too greatly concerned about developments in Western Europe so long as the Western European countries do not show signs of ganging up on them."[3] Winston Churchill still saw Stalin as a worthy ally and recognized that Russia had obtained legitimate fruits of victory. Thus, Churchill stated: "The principles of the Atlantic Charter ought not to be construed so as to deny to Russia the frontiers which she occupied when Germany attacked her."[4]

1. Arthur M. Schlesinger, Jr., *A Thousand Days: John F. Kennedy in the White House*, (Boston: Houghton-Mifflin, 1965), p. 830.
2. James Nathan, *Anatomy of the Cuban Missile Crisis* (Westport, Ct.: Greenwood Press, 2001), p. 8.
3. LaFeber, *America, Russia and the Cold War, 1945-1990*, p. 27.
4. Lloyd Gardner, Arthur Schlesinger, Jr., Hans J. Morganthau, *The Origins of the Cold War* (Waltham, Mass.: Ginn and Company, 1970), p.12.

Complaints from Republicans began to be heard in the summer 1945 about the "give away" at the Yalta Conference, but most leaders saw that conference's decision as vague and flexible. Admiral William Leahy, the President's Chief of Staff, expressed the common view that the Yalta Agreements were "so elastic that the Russians can stretch it all the way from Yalta to Washington without technically breaking it."[1] The President's personal aide, Harry Hopkins, expressed the administration view after Yalta when he said, "The Russians had proved that they could be reasonable and far seeing, and there wasn't any doubt in the minds of the President or any of us that we could live with them and get along with them peacefully...."[2]

President Roosevelt envisioned Russia joining the United States, Great Britain and China as the "Four Policemen" supervising the world. FDR warned that "The rest of the world would have to disarm" and any nation that was in violation "would be threatened first with a quarantine and if the quarantine did not work they would be bombed."[3] Roosevelt's idea of the Great Powers supervising the world was merely a vision; there were never any specific details.

Was this to be an old-fashioned sphere of influence arrangement whereby each of the powers took responsibility for its area of the world? Stalin saw such an idea as authorization to dominate the traditional Russian security zones in Eastern Europe. Indeed, at Tehran in 1944, FDR seemed to be writing off the area of Eastern Europe. Historian David Fromkin says that Roosevelt "told the Russians they could take over and control completely as their sphere.... so completely that the United States could from this moment on have no further polices with regard to them"[4]

Or was the Four Policemen concept to be more idealistic with a joint world rulership by the Four Policemen? Roosevelt never clarified, and perhaps it was never clear in his own mind. Some remnant of the Four Policemen seemed to have emerged in the Great Powers on the United Nations Security Council with their veto power over peacekeeping matters.

This loose management style of Roosevelt would soon begin to haunt US-Russian relations. FDR spoke out of both sides of his mouth; he told Stalin one thing and he told the American people another. When face-to-face with Stalin, Roosevelt played the realist, agreeing to a Russian sphere of interest in Eastern Europe. But at home, FDR posed as the idealist, promising freedom and independence for Eastern Europe — a world that wasn't to be. Upon his return from Yalta, Roosevelt told the people what they wanted to hear. The Yalta Agreements, he said: "ought to spell the end of the system of unilateral actions, exclusive alliances, the spheres of influence, the balance of power, and all the other expedients that have been tried for centuries — and have always failed."[5]

The Yalta Agreement actually confirmed what Churchill and Roosevelt had done throughout World War Two: respect the Soviet sphere of influence in Eastern Europe. But Franklin Roosevelt — President Moonbeams, the Juggler, the Deceiver — didn't level with the public about the deals made with Stalin. Roosevelt led the country into World War II with fabrications; at the end of the war he deceived the people about the post-war settlements. Death

---

1. LaFeber, *America, Russia and The Cold War*, p. 14.
2. John Spanier, "American Foreign Policy since World War II," in Jerald Combs, *Three Views of America Diplomacy*, p. 431.
3. McDougall, *Promised Land, Crusader State*, p. 154.
4. Fromkin, *In the Time of the Americans*, p. 469.
5. Ibid., p. 485.

took the aging President in April 1945. The next president would have to reconcile all the acts of juggling and deceiving. But Harry S. Truman was no juggler or deceiver. Now the piper would be paid.

When Harry Truman took the oath of office April 12, 1945, he had been Vice-president for less than three months, and he had never been taken into the confidence of Roosevelt. The awesome responsibilities fell heavily upon the simple man from Missouri. Truman expressed his own personal insecurities when he said, "I felt like the moon, the stars and all the planets had fallen on me." He worried that he might be "the last man fitted to handle it [the presidency]."[1] His personal style was vastly different than FDR's: Roosevelt was a chameleon, never presenting the same view to his audience; Truman was a porcupine in his brusque, no-nonsense manner. Representative Samuel Rayburn (D, TX) believed Truman was making decisions before he had adequate information and former Vice president Henry Wallace said he seemed to "decide [questions] in advance of thinking."[2] Overwhelmed by the job, Truman overcompensated by quick, decisive decisions. The buck stopped abruptly, but not thoughtfully, at Harry Truman's' desk.

Within twenty-four hours of taking office, Truman put his associates on notice that there would be no "deals" with Stalin. The new president asserted that appeasement never worked and "We must stand up to the Russians. We had been too easy."[3] Diplomacy under the new president would be sharp, emotional and confrontational. Truman confided that "Diplomacy has always been too much for me."[4]

Two weeks into his presidency, Truman had the opportunity to confront the Russians about alleged reneging on the Yalta agreements; the President berated Soviet Foreign Minister V. M. Molotov with earthy language. A stunned Molotov protested, "I have never been talked to like that in my life." Truman spat back, "Carry out your agreements and you won't get talked to like that."[5] Truman later boasted, "I gave it to him straight, one-two to the jaw."[6] (Truman may have embellished this confrontation after the fact to burnish his image with other plainspoken Americans, but some type of verbal bombast occurred at this early date in the Truman presidency. More about the personal style of Truman and his cultural ancestry in the following chapter.)

For a short period of time in April 1945 there was a tug-of-war for the mind of Harry Truman on the question of relations with Russia. Secretary of War Henry Stimson, an experienced diplomat whose career spanned the era from Teddy Roosevelt to Truman, weighed in to defend the appeasing of Stalin. Stimson, no shrinking violet as he had urged a military confrontation with Japan in the 1930s, now urged a soft line towards Stalin, for he was "not likely to yield... in substance" on the issue of Poland.[7] Stimson, in his old age after a half-century of service to the nation, returned to his Theodore Roosevelt roots and urged a realistic sphere of

---

1. Arnold Offner, *Another Such Victory: President Truman and the Cold War, 1945-1953* (Stanford, CA: Stanford University Press, 2002), p. 46.
2. Ibid., p. 23.
3. LaFeber, *America, Russia and the Cold War*, p.16.
4. Offner, *Another Such Victory*, p. 18.
5. Moskin, *Mr. Truman's War*, p. 83.
6. Stoessinger, *Crusaders and Pragmatists*, p. 60.
7. LaFeber, *America, Russia and the Cold War*, p. 16-17.

influence view. He chided those who were "anxious to hang on to exaggerated views of the Monroe Doctrine and at the same time butt into every question that comes up in Central Europe."[1] Stimson perceptively cautioned Truman about being realistic at home but idealistic in Europe. If US "gunboat diplomacy" is appropriate in the Gulf of Mexico, why is it not acceptable for Russian troops to stand astride Poland and other areas of the Russian *cordon sanitaire*?

But the cantankerous, novice president was much more in tune with the hard-line Militant Idealists around him. The US Ambassador to the Soviet Union, Averill Harriman, counseled that "our objective and the Kremlin's objectives were irreconcilable; they wanted to communize the world, and we wanted a free world."[2] Harriman further asserted that Stalin should not be allowed to establish "totalitarian" governments "unless we are prepared to live in a Soviet-dominated world...."[3] Truman sent Harry Hopkins to Moscow in May to discuss America's concern about European conflicts. For his farewell, Truman informed Hopkins that "he could use diplomatic language, or he could use a baseball bat if he thought that was the proper approach."[4] Truman had been in the White House less than three months, admitted his lack of knowledge in international affairs and had never talked directly with the Soviet leader in his life. Yet, he was already talking to the Russians like a Boy Scout leader to recalcitrant youngsters.

Late in July, Truman had an opportunity to meet directly with Joseph Stalin at the Potsdam Conference near Berlin and the baptismal meeting between the two leaders did not go well. Being unaccustomed to the intense give-and-take of diplomacy, President Truman became highly agitated at one point and his temper flared as he snapped that he had not come to the conference "to hold a police court hearing." He bluntly told Stalin and Churchill, "If they were not going to stick to the main issue, he would pack up and go home." He wrote to his wife that "I reared up on my hind legs and told them where to get off and they got off."[5]

As the months rolled by in 1945, it became obvious that the US under Truman was going to deal differently with Russia. Lend-lease shipments to Russia were abruptly cancelled six days after V-E Day, even though the Soviets were committed to enter the war against Japan in a few weeks. While President Roosevelt had promised that Stalin would have oil concessions in nearby Iran, Truman voided the deal, saying that the Soviets intended to "sweep unimpeded across Turkey...into the Mediterranean and across Iran...into the Indian Ocean." [6] Truman proposed that the European waterways – the Rhine, the Danube, the Turkish Straits – be open to all nations, but he did not include the Suez and Panama Canals. In his *Memoirs*, Truman contends that the Soviets were not really interested in free navigation, but were "planning world conquest."[7] Even though FDR had given Stalin the green light in Eastern Europe, Truman attempted to push the Russian forces back to their pre-war border. A particularly sore spot was Romania as the States Department asserted that "It is our intention to attain positions of

1. Ibid., p. 23.
2. Moskin, *Mr. Truman's War*, p. 146.
3. LaFeber, *America, Russia and the Cold War*, p. 15.
4. Moskin, *Mr. Truman's War*, p. 164.
5. Ibid., p. 214.
6. LaFeber, *America, Russia and the Cold War*, p.35.
7. Garnber, et al., *The Origins of the Cold War*, p. 24.

equality with the Russians."[1] But the harder Truman pushed, the more the Russians dug in their heels. In 1945 when Soviet diplomat Litvinov was discussing the emerging Cold War with American journalist Edgar Snow, Litvinov queried, "Why did you Americans wait till right now to begin opposing us in the Balkans and Eastern Europe? You should have done this three years ago. Now it's too late and your complaints only arouse suspicion."[2]

Lurking in the background of this growing feud was the US policy of an Open Door. At the turn of the century, American leaders had enunciated the Open Door for China, a policy proposing that all nations should have equal access to the riches of the Orient. By the 1940s the Open Door concept was being applied to the rest of the world. The Atlantic Charter called for all nations to provide "access, on equal terms, to the trade and to the raw materials of the world which are needed for prosperity."[3] As one government official emphasized: "The capitalist system is essentially an international system....If it cannot function internationally, it will break down."[4] Earlier in the century President Woodrow Wilson had asserted that the world had to be made safe for democracy; to this, now, was added the idea that the world had to be made safe for capitalism. To US policy makers, the world was to be remade in the image of America. It was not only the Russian Bear that envisioned world-domination; the American Eagle sought to spread its wings across the globe also.

By the late 1940s, it was standard thinking among US leaders that their way of life must be forced upon the world or the nation would collapse — economically and politically. This was an astounding display of insecurity for leaders to conclude that their system had to be replicated all over the globe or the US would not survive. And on the other hand, it was an amazing demonstration of arrogance to think that such a global task could be accomplished. While the Founding Fathers held that the US should remain aloof from the quarrels of Europe, Truman, Acheson, and other Militant Idealists asserted the need to intrude into every nook and cranny on Earth. America had become a nation that Washington, Jefferson, Adams, and the Founders would not recognize.

This rambunctious globalism did face resistance in some domestic quarters. Former Vice-president Henry Wallace by 1946 was complaining about the Truman grasp for world power. Frustrated at Truman's headlong thrust into the world, Wallace ran a third party presidential campaign in 1948 against Truman's Militant Idealism. Wallace appealed to the public's sense of fairness and the recognition that the US must live with other cultures. America can't run the world, Wallace cautioned:

> On our part we shall recognize that we have not more business in the political affairs of Eastern Europe than Russia has in the political affairs of Latin America, Western Europe and the United States.... Whether we like it or not, the Russians will try to socialize their sphere of influence just as we try to democratize [and capitalize] our sphere of influence.[5]

---

1. LaFeber, *America, Russia and the Cold War*, p. 24.
2. Eric Alterman, *When Presidents Lie: A History of Official Deception and Its Consequences*, (New York: Viking, 2004), P. 36.
3. LaFeber, p. 10.
4. Ibid., p. 9.
5. Henry H. Berger, "A Conservative Critique of Containment," in David Horowitz, ed., *Containment and Revolution* (Boston: Beacon Press, 1967), p. 129.

In 1948, Henry Wallace, a farm boy from Iowa, was reviled by the foreign policy elites as a communist fellow traveler. Just as FDR labeled Charles Lindbergh and the America First committee as Nazis, so Wallace and friends were depicted as communists. It is tragic what happens to the democratic debate when war casts its ugly shadow over the land.

Senator Robert Taft, the son of President Howard Taft, attempted to use the Republican Party to oppose the "imperialist" aims of Truman; the effort was generally a failure, as the GOP was quickly frightened into a war stance. When the Truman administration asked Congress to approve a defense pact with a dozen European countries (NATO) in 1949, Taft voted No. "I cannot vote for a treaty," Taft retorted, "which in my opinion, will do far more to bring about a third world war than it will ever maintain the peace of the world."[1] The conservative Senator believed that NATO represented a hostile action against a nonexistent threat, which will only serve to confirm Soviet fears of being encircled. Further, he lamented that American military, economic, and political intrusions overseas are

> likely to build up hostility to us rather than any genuine friendship. It is easy to slip into an attitude of imperialism and to entertain the idea that we know what is good for other people better than they know themselves. From there is an easy step to the point where war becomes an instrument of public policy rather than the last resort to maintain our liberties.[2]

Senator Taft's comments are prescient as the US finds it acceptable policy to wage preemptive war in 2003 simply because Iraq might at some future time attempt to harm the United States. Robert Kennedy's deeply felt aversion to waging pre-emptive war on Cuba in 1962 seems old-fashioned and appealing at this time. Faced with the reality of sixty nuclear tipped missiles ninety miles off the coast, President Kennedy found a way to finesse the issue, allowing the Russians to save face but still securing removal of the threat. Truman's personality showed no finesse like that of the Kennedys, no sense of accommodation like Taft and Wallace, and none of the dissimulation of FDR. His single modus operandi was "to rear up on his hind legs" and talk tough.

CHURCHILL AND GREAT BRITAIN — FLAWED MODELS FOR AMERICA

On May 5, 1946, a perplexing and significant event took place in Fulton, Missouri. Former British Prime Minister Winston Churchill made an address that became known as the "Iron Curtain" speech. Churchill's soaring rhetoric was combined with somber warnings about World War III. "From Stettin in the Baltic to Trieste in the Adriatic, an iron curtain has descended across the Continent" and a "police government" is ruling Eastern Europe. The Soviet Union wants "the indefinite expansion of their power and doctrines." Fortunately, "God has willed" the United States to have atomic weapons. Churchill urged that the Atlantic partners form a "fraternal association of the English-speaking peoples" to combat this insidious threat.[3]

---

1. Ibid., p. 133.
2. Ibid., p. 132
3. LaFeber, *America, Russia and the Cold War*, p. 38.

This speech is indeed strange as it was Churchill who in October 1944 made the "Balkan Deal" with Stalin, a deal in which the British leader awarded much of Eastern Europe to the Russians. At Churchill's initiative, Russia was to control 90% of Romania, 75% of Bulgaria, 50% of Hungary, 50% of Yugoslavia, and in separate arrangements, 100% of Poland. But in March 1946 at Fulton, Missouri, Churchill sounds the alarm — the Russians are coming! Winston had found one more war to fight! As First Lord of the Admiralty during World War I, Churchill had maneuvered the United States into war. Then he ousted Neville Chamberlain in 1940 on a war platform, becoming Prime Minister. From that position he could again design to involve the United States in another dubious, unwinnable British venture — World War II. Now again in 1946, Churchill plays the watchman at the gate for the emerging Cold War.

Winston Churchill has become something of an icon as the man who stood up to the Kaiser, then to Hitler and Tojo, then to Stalin. He is the consummate war hero who never saw a war he didn't like. As a child he had a collection of 1500 toy soldiers; then after his sandbox days, he enrolled at Britain's Sandhurst Military School. Winston first saw military action in Cuba in 1895 while covering the civil war as a journalist. But his heart was really in the uniform of a soldier. Churchill describes his dreams of martial glory: "From early youth I had brooded about soldiers and war and often I had imagined in dreams and day dreams the sensations attendant upon being for the first time under fire!" He confessed that it thrilled his mind "to hear whistle of bullets all around and to play at hazard from moment to moment with death and wounds."[1] Engaged in a real war in his early Twenties, he proudly informed his mother that he "rode up to individuals firing my pistol in their faces and killing several."[2] Winston, usually a dour man, seemed elated to be killing other human beings.

Upon becoming a journalist in the 1890s, he showed up at numerous military campaign: with General Kitchener in Africa, in the Caribbean at the Cuban civil war, at the Boer War in Africa, directing the British Navy in World War I, leading the British into World War II, finding an Iron Curtain draped across the European landscape in 1946. War was not to be shunned, but to be sought after and praised. To Sir Winston, "The story of the human race is war."[3] War "is the normal occupation of man."[4] In this he was a compatriot of Theodore Roosevelt who asserted that "All the great races have been fighting races."

And Churchill always coupled his rousing call to arms with an overstatement of the military capabilities of his perceived enemy. In World War I, the German Navy, it was claimed, presented a dreadful threat to Britain. But during the war the Kaiser's fleet never ventured far from its home waters. In 1940, Churchill (with the help of radio correspondent Edward R. Murrow) told a sobering, frightening tale of Britain besieged by Germany — "we shall fight them on the beaches... we shall fight them in the fields and in the streets...." — never admitting that Hitler had abandoned the Battle of Britain, and with that Germany's hopes of invading England.

Churchill was not only a warmonger but also a slick phrasemaker. The Australian Prime Minister, Robert Menzies, discerned the core of the man when he said, "His real tyrant is the glittering phrase — so attractive to his mind that awkward facts have to give way." And another

---

1. Walker, *The Boys of '98*, p. 28.
2. Ruben, *Forty Ways to Look at Churchill*, p. 93.
3. Ralph Raico, "Rethinking Churchill," in John Denson, ed., *The Costs of War*, p. 325.
4. Ruben, *Forty Ways to Look At Churchill*, p. 93.

friend asserted: "He is the slave of the words which his mind forms about ideas.... And he can convince himself of almost every truth if it is once allowed thus to start on its wild career through his rhetorical machinery."[1] If these judgments sound harsh, consider Churchill's own confession about his weakness: "I do not care so much for the principles I advocate as for the impression which my words produce and the reputation they give me."[2]

Sir Winston Churchill, America's favorite Englishman, is the archetypical Man of the 20th Century, for this "great" leader had a shallow mind and was a lover of war. It is sad that "the American century" is known for just these characteristics.

(The inadequacies and iniquities of the father should not be visited upon the son, but it seems appropriate to relate this charming story about the Churchill family. Late in the 19th century, Winston's father was appointed Chancellor of the Exchequer of the British government, that is, the Secretary of the Treasury. This appointment was made despite the fact that he had no training in accounting or mathematics. And the job did create problems. When shown the government accounting books, he expressed puzzlement over the decimals. "What are those damned dots!"[3])

It is a singular tragedy of US history that Woodrow Wilson, Franklin Roosevelt and Harry Truman chose to come to the defense of England and then to follow a model established by the British, for it is a flawed system. The British record in international relations over the last two centuries is a bloody, treacherous one:

- an Opium War (1839-1842) against the Chinese, forcing China to allow British "drug dealers" to sell opium at Chinese ports. Little is heard of this sorry episode in history books. Most Americans have the naive view that the Opium War was fought to curtail the drug traffic in China.
- the barbaric use of "concentration camps" to incarcerate the Dutch during the Boer War (1899-1902).
- the conquest of 20% of the world's surface by force of arms while acquiring the British Empire. Hitler, Tojo, Mussolini and the Kaiser's aggressions are insignificant compared to Britain's conquest and repression in India, the Middle East, the Far East, Africa and the Americas.
- the sorry spectacle of Churchill manipulating the laws of the high seas to "set up" the Lusitania and other passenger vessels, thereby creating a condition of war between Germany and America in World War I.
- the false stories about German atrocities during the invasion of Belgium in 1914, thereby besmirching Germany falsely and unfairly.
- the false and unfair allegations about Nazi Germany's "wanton" invasion of Norway in 1940, without admitting that Britain was in the process of invading Norway; Germany simply took the Norwegian fjords before the British got there.
- the cruel insistence in repatriating thousands of dissidents Russians (the Cossacks and others) who had fought against Stalin and desperately wanted to stay in the West after World War II.
- the cynical Balkan Deal by Churchill, followed by the inflammatory "Iron Curtain" speech, all designed to ignite an idealistic and misbegotten fire in the belly of Americans.

---

1. Ralph Raico, "Rethinking Churchill," in John Denson, ed., *The Costs of War*, p. 324-325.
2. Ibid., p. 321.
3. Ibid., p. 333

- the awful diplomatic blundering in 1914 and 1939 of the British diplomats, contributing mightily to the instigation of both World War I and World War II.
- and finally, after repeatedly getting in over their heads in 1914 and again in 1939, the unconscionable and deceitful campaigns to involve the US in these British diplomatic blunders — "pulling the British chestnuts from the fire."

From the days of the American Revolution to early in the 20th century, the foreign policy of the United States had followed its own designs. Aversion to European wars and a policy of neutrality with determined independence was well established when Washington, Jefferson and John Quincy Adams laid down their dictum about non-involvement in world affairs. But, with the World Wars in the 20th century, the US began to follow the British model with its large intrusive navy, bases of power around the world and military involvement on every continent. America forsook George Washington, adopting instead the imperial program of Britain and Winston Churchill. It was a flawed model to follow.

THE STALIN YOU NEVER KNEW

It is tragic that a major nation, such as Russia, was encumbered with a leader like Joseph Stalin through much of the 20th century. Shortly before his death, V. I. Lenin, the first Soviet leader, discerned the flaws in Stalin's character and in his own last will and testament Lenin urged that Stalin be removed from his leadership post. On January 4, 1923 Lenin dictated the following note:

> Stalin is too rude, and this fault, entirely acceptable in relations between us communists, becomes completely unacceptable in the office of General Secretary. Therefore I propose to the comrades that a way be found to remove Stalin from that post and replace him with someone else who differs from Stalin in all respects, someone more patient, more loyal, more polite, more considerate to comrades, less headstrong.[1]

Lenin was insightful in his observations about Stalin; his "rudeness" would result in millions of Soviet citizens being killed, maimed or banished to the harshness of Siberia.

In the Twenties, Stalin quarreled with communist leaders, notably Leon Trotsky, about the nature of the communist revolution. Trotsky was one of a group of communist "internationalists" who believed that the communist revolution was destined to spread immediately and inevitably into every nation, Russia simply being the first nation to embrace the new ideology. Stalin, however, conceived of the notion of "socialism in one country," thus suggesting that the revolution could, at least for a short time, be confined to "mother Russia." Trotsky was the international revolutionary who schemed of using Russia as the base for spreading a new socialist world order. Stalin was the nationalist who cautiously dreamed of building a communist world only if the Russian nation was secure and survived.

During a radio broadcast in October 1939, Winston Churchill uttered the now-famous phrase that Soviet foreign policy was "a riddle wrapped in a mystery inside an enigma," thereby suggesting that Stalin's approach to foreign policy was impossible to fathom. Churchill's con-

---

1. DeJonge, *Stalin,* p. 162.

cluding statement is, unfortunately, omitted from the quote. Churchill added: "But perhaps there is a key. That key is Russian national interest."[1]

To Joseph Stalin, the Soviet Union was not "a conspiracy disguised as a state;" its interests were the same as Russian interests under the Czars. Stalin interpreted the holy writ of Marx and Lenin in such a way as to insure that the Russian State was attended to first; the communist world revolution would develop later. The Truman White House accused Stalin of having "expansionist tendencies," and this was correct — the same tendencies as Czar Peter the Great in attempting to secure more Russian lands along the German border, and the same fears as all the Czars in guarding against Prussian-German military threats. Stalin exhibited the same territorial ambition as the Czars in wanting to obtain access to the Mediterranean Sea through the Turkish Straits and to thrust Russian power into Central Asia — toward Iran and Afghanistan. Czarist and communist Russian foreign policy displayed similar inclinations and ambitions.

Even in his dealings with communist parties around the world, Stalin demonstrated more concern for "mother Russia" and "socialism in one country" than for the furtherance of world communism. In the years immediately after World War II, Stalin advised the powerful French and Italian Communist Parties to cooperate with the other national political parties, even suggesting they work together in coalition governments. He advised Mao Tse-tung to support the non-communist government of Chiang Kai-shek in China. (Chiang's military education in the 1920s had been provided courtesy of Stalin.) And when it seemed that President Truman would establish an American foothold on the Asian continent in 1950 during the Korean War, Stalin told Mao, "So What? Let the United States of America be our neighbor in the Far East."[2] Contrary to American mythology, Stalin did not order the invasion of South Korea, although he did grant approval for the attack. In fact, he showed amazing self-discipline during the Korean War. As American aircraft flitted in and around Russian territory, Stalin never allowed Russian planes to retaliate or penetrate Korean air space.

Eastern Europe was an especially sensitive area to Russia as two horrible wars had been fought there in the 20th century. Following World War II, Stalin would accept no anti-Russian government in Poland; in Stalin's eyes the Poles who had fled their native land establishing a Polish government-in-exile in London were disqualified from serving in the new Polish government. But in other areas of the borderlands, Stalin was not quick to create puppet governments following the war. In Finland, Soviet troops withdrew and the Finns ran a free and open election, electing a non-communist government on the doorstep of Russia. Similarly, in Hungary, Czechoslovakia, Romania and Bulgaria, despite the presence of Soviet troops, elections were held and governments functioned immediately after the war without significant interference from Moscow. In Yugoslavia, Stalin urged Marshall Tito to reinstall the old monarchy and create a coalition government, suggestions that Tito eventually disregarded. In Greece, the anti-German resistance movement during the war was heavily dominated by Greek communists, but by 1944 Stalin abandoned them in an effort to cooperate with the British Army

---

1. Winston Churchill, *The Gathering Storm*, (Boston: Houghton Mifflin Company, 1949), p. 449.
2. Stanley Sandler, *The Korean War: No Victors, No Vanquished* (Lexington, KY: University of Kentucky Press, 1999), p. 109.

that was busy cracking Greek communists' skulls. Stalin was prepared to observe the Balkan's sphere of influence deal made with Churchill in 1944.

As World War II ended, Stalin and his Russian compatriots were in need of "licking their wounds" rather than "pouncing on new prey." The war in the Russian homeland had been a catastrophe, destroying over 20 million people, 1700 towns, 70,000 villages, 30,000 factories, 90,000 bridges and 10,000 utility stations. There were over 25 million Soviets who were homeless and millions more without food. The Russian economy was operating at 58% of its 1940 level. No Western nation had been so thoroughly devastated during the war.

The Soviet military was rapidly dismantled after the war, reduced from 11 million troops to 4 million by 1948. The Russian Navy consisted of 300 submarines with only a skeletal surface fleet. Russian insecurity is evidenced by their action in tearing up the main railroad line traversing Poland, a rail line that connected Russia and Germany. This is not an action taken by a nation preparing to launch an invasion into Central Europe. The Russian defense budget was only 20% the size of US defense spending; additionally, the US had a monopoly of atomic weapons. Even the war hawk Dean Acheson acknowledged that with all its troubles, Russia would not attack the West "unless they are absolutely out of their minds."[1] A United States intelligence report in November 1945 recounted the assessment of Russian weakness; it would be 10 to 20 years before the Soviet Union could repair its economy or rebuild its military sufficiently to consider a war against the West.[2] The State Department advisor and future Republican Secretary of State, John Foster Dulles, counseled that war is "one thing which Soviet leadership does not want and would not consciously risk." The Russians would be, he added, "completely outclassed by the mechanized weapons — particularly the atomic weapons — available to the United States."[3] There were few US leaders in 1945, in 1946 or in 1947 who seriously believed that Russia was planning a war on the West.

The failure of the Western democracies to promptly open a Second Front in Europe during World War II caused tension with Stalin. The West had promised the Russians that there would be a military front opened in Western Europe by 1942 in order to relieve the pressure on Russia in the East; the promise was not kept. Later in 1942, the United States and Britain did invade Africa, then in 1943, Italy. But no significant Second Front was opened until June 1944 at Normandy — a mere eleven months before the end of the war! For three years the Russians had to battle the German war machine essentially alone. As British statesman Anthony Eden pointed out, "American have a much exaggerated conception of the military contribution they are making in this war."[4] The casualty figures of World War II in Europe tell the story of the enormous damage done to the Russian military:

MILITARY DEATHS — EASTERN FRONT

Soviet Union	13,000,000
Germany	3,000,000

---

1. LaFeber, *America, Russia and the Cold War*, p. 50.
2. Ibid., p. 28.
3. Wittner, *Cold War America*, p. 9.
4. Marks, *Wind Over Sand*, p. 199.

MILITARY DEATHS — WESTERN AND MEDITERRANEAN FRONTS

Germany	300,000
France	345,000
Britain	326,000
USA	295,000

Between 1941 and 1944 the United States and the forces of the British Empire faced from two to eight German divisions in Western Europe, while in the East the Soviet Union faced 180 German divisions. The German Army suffered 90% of its military deaths in the Eastern Front. The gigantic struggle in Eastern Europe between Germany and Russia took forty-seven months to unfold; the Western Allied attack at Normandy against Germany lasted only eleven months. The Western Allies had spent three years dilly-dallying, picking at the edges of the German occupation of Europe. A legitimate question is raised by this policy of delay: "Was it the real aim of the capitalist powers to misuse their communist ally as their sword on the continent, to let it bleed to exhaustion...?"[1]

There were 17 million military deaths in the European war; 16 million of those deaths were in the Eastern Front. Of those 17 million deaths, 13 million were Russian. Slightly more than one million deaths on both sides occurred in all other fronts — Africa, Italy, and France. Seldom do Western historians reveal that the Western Allies played a relatively small role in the defeat of Nazi Germany. To Russia, a secure and reliable Poland was paramount for their safety. With blood and treasure the Russians had won the right to a secure border in Eastern Europe.

> The refusal to invade Europe in 1942, and the constant postponement of a second front thereafter, consolidated the feeling in Moscow that it was through the Soviet effort alone that Germany had been defeated, and that the security of the Soviet borders, the erection of barriers to future invasion by the Germans would depend on what the Soviet Union might unilaterally perform.[2]

THE TRUMAN DOCTRINE: "SCARING HELL OUT OF THE AMERICAN PEOPLE"

Early Saturday morning, February 21, 1947, an official from the British Embassy in Washington D.C. arrived at a nearly deserted State Department building to convey momentous news. The British government had decided that it would be unable to continue financing its involvement in the civil war in Greece, as the $250 million loan that was needed was beyond the British ability to pay. After two costly, "victorious" World Wars in this century, Great Britain was broke; Britain planned to remove its troops and Navy from Greece within the month. Secretary of State George Marshall affirmed that this news "was tantamount to British abdication from the Middle East with obvious implications as to their successor."[3] British Embassy offi-

---

1. Gerhard Ritter, *The German Resistance: Carl Goerdelier's Struggle Against Tyranny* (Freeport, NY: Books for Libraries Press, 1970), p. 257-258.
2. John Bagguley, "The World War and the Cold War," in David Horowitz, ed., *Containment and Revolution*, p. 96.

cials inquired as to whether the United States would like to take up the British burden in Greece. The British Empire was crumbling; the United States was invited to pick up the pieces.

President Truman and Secretary Marshall were well informed about the deteriorating British military situation in Greece and were eager to assume London's role. But the newly-elected Republican Congress was determined to slash the budget and reduce commitments overseas. On Friday, February 27, an historic meeting was held in the White House attended by Truman, Marshall, Undersecretary of State Dean Acheson, and key congressional leaders, including Arthur Vandenberg (R, MI), chairman of the Senate Foreign Relations Committee. Truman and his advisers wanted to replace the British military with American troops and support the British-imposed Greek government. As the meeting progressed, it became apparent that a routine recitation of British imperial woes in Greece was not motivating Senator Vandenberg and his Republican colleagues.

Dean Acheson, sensing that the Republicans were not receptive to American intervention, interjected his thoughts on world affairs, painting a dramatic and fanciful picture of a modern day battle of Armageddon taking place in the Mediterranean basin. Acheson delivered a powerful sermon about Militant Idealism: "Only two great powers remained in the world, the United States and the Soviet Union. We have arrived at a situation unparalleled since ancient times. Not since Rome and Carthage has there been such a polarization of power on this earth." Acheson continued his performance, proclaiming that the two powers are "divided by an unbridgeable ideological chasm," a struggle between liberty and tyranny. Instead of seeing the Greek Civil War as a local struggle with British imperial overtones, Acheson asserted that the Soviet Union was "committing aggression" and if they were successful it would "open up three continents to Soviet penetration."[1] Stalin, with his power asserted in Europe, Asia and Africa, was bent on world conquest. The freedom of the Greeks was directly linked to the freedom of every American. "The Soviet Union was playing one of the greatest gambles in history at minimal costs. We and we alone are in a position to break up the play."[2]

The participants at the White House meeting were stunned by this dramatic vision presented by Acheson. Senator Vandenberg emotionally astounded by such a view gave assurance to the president that Congress would go along with an aid package for the area if it were presented in such an apocalyptic manner. The Republican leader advised Truman to "scare hell out of the American people."[3] And so Truman did!

The State Department began preparing an aid package for Greece to be presented to Congress, emphasizing the benefits of an Open Door trade policy for American business. But with its emphasis on trade, capital investment and sources of natural resources — especially nearby oil — the program sounded like an investment prospectus rather than an emotional call to arms. Truman and Acheson again "saved" the program as they recognized that the Congress and the people would not embrace the British cause in Greece simply for trade and investment; again the issue of "freedom and tyranny" was woven into the program. Once again, American foreign policy was being presented *not* to aid American business, but ostensibly to protect the liberties of others. Idealism, not greed or self-interest, motivated the public to send money and men to

---

3. LaFeber, *America, Russia and the Cold War*, p. 51-52.
1. Wittner, *Cold War America*, p. 32.
2. LaFeber, *America, Russia and the Cold War*, p. 53.
3. Ibid.

die in foreign lands. Distortions, exaggerations and deceit were all around as the President set about to "scare hell out of the American people" in order to sell his program.

On March 12, President Truman announced his Cold War policy, the Truman Doctrine — a policy that would become the bedrock of United States foreign policy for half a century. The Greek crisis, he asserted, was caused by the "terroristic activities of several thousand armed men, led by Communists." Aggression of this kind was beyond the ability of the United Nations to subdue. Only the United States had the moral fiber, the courage, the vision and the wealth to deal with the disaster. The Truman Doctrine was a sweeping declaration of intent to win the battle for freedom against communism throughout the *world*. Truman concluded:

> I believe that it must be the policy of the United States to support free peoples who are resisting attempted subjugation by armed minorities or by outside pressure.... If we falter in our leadership we may endanger the peace of the world — and we shall surely endanger the welfare of our own Nation.[1]

As seed money, Congress appropriated $400 million for aid to protect Greece and Turkey against Soviet communism. But the facts were contrary to Truman's assertions.

The Greek civil war was an outgrowth of the German wartime occupation of that ancient nation of seven million people. In German-occupied countries, native resistance movements emerged to ambush and sabotage the fascist forces. All resistance organizations were heavily supported by communist and socialist parties, although usually coalitions were formed that included anti-Nazis from all political groups. When the British Army and Navy entered Greece in 1944, they restored to the throne the old, unpopular Greek monarch, despite opposition from 80% of the Greek citizens. Because the anti-German resistance organization (EAM) opposed the monarchy, a civil war broke out between the British-Royalist forces and the resistance movement. After the Truman Doctrine was announced, with American assistance, the civil war ended in 1949 with the EAM subdued, the monarch firmly on the throne and the intimidating presence of British and American military forces. Britain's Navy was reestablished in Greece, thanks to the Truman Doctrine.

The Truman Doctrine raised the specter of not only local communist subversion occurring in Greece, but an effort by the Soviet Union to establish a communist puppet regime in that Mediterranean state. But the Truman Doctrine distorted the history of that region.

The Balkans Deal between Churchill and Stalin in 1944 granted Britain preponderant control in Greece and there was no evidence that Stalin had reneged on the deal. In 1944 Churchill declared that "Stalin...adhered strictly and faithfully to our agreements of October [1944]."[2] In February 1948, Stalin told the Yugoslavs that the Greek revolt by the EAM "should fold up immediately." He further asserted that the revolt had "no prospect of success" as the British and Americans will not permit the rebels to "break their line of communications in the Mediterranean Sea."[3] Stalin was a realist, acknowledging the British-American sphere and respecting the Balkan Deal. The resistance movement was a large, indigenous organization with over two million members and simply ignored Stalin's call to disband. Even though the EAM established a government-in-exile in the mountains of Greece, no communist nation extended

---

1. Nash, *The American People*, p. 860-861.
2. Churchill, *Triumph and Tragedy*, p. 293
3. Todd Gitlin, "Counter-Insurgency: Myth and Reality in Greece," in David Horowitz, ed., *Containment and Revolution*, p. 174.

diplomatic recognition. There is no evidence of military or economic aid flowing directly from the Soviets to the Greek resistance movement, although neighboring states did provide sanctuary to the EAM.

The British interests in Greece were Greek naval ports, not the establishment of "freedom, liberty and elections," as stated by Truman. These idealistic slogans were thrown to the American public as bait to secure public approval of the Truman-Acheson venture.

Turkey was included in the aid package at the last minute as a way of emphasizing the alleged malevolence of Russian conquest; Stalin, like all the Czars, sought some measure of control over the Turkish Straits — the Dardanelles and Bosporus — to facilitate Russian commerce. Russia is landlocked in the south and has always looked for some influence over the Straits. This centuries old aspiration has nothing whatsoever to do with "world communism on the march." As one administration official said, "Turkey was slipped into the oven with Greece because that seemed the surest way to cook a tough bird."[1] It is interesting to note that in October 1944, Churchill, with FDR's concurrence, assured Stalin that Russia was "justified" in seeking control of the Straits. Later, however, Truman rejected this thinking. A shared control of the Straits with Turkey was "justified" in 1944 for FDR; in 1947, to Harry Truman, it was evidence of Stalin's wicked quest to communize the world. Such is the world as seen by Truman and Acheson. "Scaring hell out of the American people" was essentially the game of crying falsely "The Russians are coming."

The exuberant anti-communism and the universality of the message in the Truman Doctrine caused trouble in the State Department, where Secretary Marshall and Soviet experts George Kennan and Charles Bohlen protested that "there was a little too much flamboyant anti-communism in the speech." The Secretary of State warned the President that he was overstating the case a bit.[2] Truman retorted that such rhetoric was necessary to obtain congressional approval of the aid package. It is significant that Harry Truman did not respond by saying that the charges were true — only that they were necessary.

"Mr. Republican", Senator Robert Taft, was one of the most severe critics of the Truman Doctrine. He supported economic aid to the stricken land, but he cautioned that military aid would only serve to entangle the United States in a distant area. He accused Truman of "Manichean thinking" and pointed out that such an attempt to "secure a special domination over the affairs of these countries" was similar to Russian efforts in Eastern Europe. Taft continued: "If we assume a special position in Greece and Turkey, we can hardly...reasonably object to the Russians continuing their domination in Poland, Yugoslavia, Romania, and Bulgaria."[3] Exasperated, Senator Taft exclaimed, "I do not want war with Russia."[4]

President Truman later affirmed that the crisis over Greece "was the turning point in American foreign policy."[5] Up until March 1947, there had been hope of avoiding a protracted conflict with the Soviet Union. But the ideological stridency of the Truman Doctrine, the universal thrust of the message, the intense moralism of the themes, all made it impossible there-

---

1. LaFeber, *America, Russia and the Cold War*, p. 53-54.
2. Ibid., p. 54.
3. Henry H. Berger, "A Conservative Critique of Containment," in David Horowitz, ed., *Containment and Revolution*, p. 129.
4. LaFeber, *America, Russia and the Cold War*, p. 55.
5. Wittner, *Cold War America*, p. 34.

after for the two superpowers to reach any agreement on disputes. All indigenous national revolts were, henceforth, seen as inspired by Moscow; all must be met with American military forces. National revolutions around the globe that had no roots in communist ideology or marginal commitment to Marxism were, henceforth, regarded in America as part of the communist crusade for world revolution. All such revolts were said to be organized, directed and financed by Moscow. National conflicts that were battles among local disputants — Korea, Vietnam, Iran, Guatemala, Laos — would draw in thousands of American troops and see over 100,000 young Americans die in the next few decades. All these tragic wars trace their ancestry to the messianic distortions of the Truman Doctrine. Truman successfully, but foolishly "scared hell out of the American people."

The *Militant Idealistic* policy as conceived by Truman, Acheson, and others now had sharp teeth, a determined nerve and a self-righteous moralism.

- Three months after the Truman Doctrine was proclaimed, the President and Congress applied the lessons of Greek foreign aid to Europe in the Marshall Plan. Even that foreign aid program carried messianic, idealistic threads, as no "government, political parties or groups which seek to perpetuate human misery..." would be eligible for monetary assistance.[1]
- In July 1947, the Cold War policy of "containment" was introduced. As expressed by the Truman administration, it would be "a policy of firm military containment, designed to confront the Russians with unalterable counterforce at every point where they show signs of encroaching upon the interests of a peaceful and stable world."[2] the US would meet the Russians at every point on the globe; the Russians would be greeted with a gun.
- In 1949, the United States created its first military alliance since the American-French alliance of 1778. The North Atlantic Treaty Organization (NATO) was an outgrowth of the Greek military experience in which the United States committed itself to the defense of nations who were supposedly threatened by Russian attack. The phantom military attacks into Europe from Russia would absorb the blood and treasure of the American people for several decades.

THE SOVIET ESPIONAGE THREAT

While the Truman administration was forming tank brigades in Germany, a navy to swarm the Seven Seas and a nuclear force second to none, a different threat was flourishing under the noses of White House officials. Stalin's communist espionage agents were burrowing inside the United States governmental machinery. As Lend-lease equipment flooded into the Soviet Union from the United States — $9 billion between 1942 and 1945 — the Soviets "returned the favor" by sending to the US a legion of spies to steal secrets from their American benefactor. Every Russian ship in American docks arriving to load Lend-lease material was laced with espionage agents working hand in glove with the Communist Party in the US (CPUSA), and allied with highly-placed officials in the government. The American Communist

---

1. Kissinger, *Diplomacy*, p. 453.
2. Ibid., p. 454-455.

Party actively spied on their own government, though the party and their Leftist sympathizers consistently denied any such activities. "While not every American Communist was a spy, hundreds were. The CPUSA itself worked closely with Soviet intelligence agencies to facilitate their espionage."[1]

When the Berlin Wall and the Iron Curtain came tumbling down in 1990, historians obtained access to Soviet government files and found evidence of extensive Russian espionage in the United States. Actually, an American government project had recorded the extent of Soviet espionage over the past fifty years, however, never revealing this incriminating information until 1995. The Venona Project, a program of the National Security Agency, disclosed that there were 329 Soviet agents inside the United States conducting espionage during World War II. These agents remained in place during the late 1940s as the Cold War heated up. Soviet agents boasted that, "We have agents at the very center of government, influencing policy."[2]

Britain and the United States had no agents within the Kremlin, while there were hundreds of Soviet agents operating in the United States, even in the White House:

- Launchin Currie, a senior White House advisor to FDR and Truman.
- Harry Dexter White, the #2 man at the Treasury Department.
- Alger Hiss, senior official in the State Department.
- Duncan Lee, senior official in the US intelligence office (OSS). Imagine!

The Venona Project disclosed the existence in United States government files of nearly 3000 cables that passed between Moscow and Soviet agents in the United States.[3] "On November 8, 1945, FBI Director J. Edgar Hoover began sending Truman a series of reports informing the president that "a number of persons employed by the Government" had been passing information to Soviet intelligence.[4] Incredibly, President Truman disregarded the caution:

- Judith Coplon, Justice Department official with access to FBI counterespionage files.
- Maurice Halpern in Bill Donovan's Office of Strategic Services, US spy operation.

Great Britain's vaunted spy system was a leaky sieve during World War II and the Cold War with three prominent diplomats serving the Soviet Union from Washington D.C. "With this unlikely trio ensconced in the very heart of Washington intelligence and nuclear establishment, it is difficult to imagine what critical information about America's war effort and policies would *not* have been forwarded to Moscow."[5]

- David MacLean, UK Foreign Service official in Washington privy to US military secrets and confidential nuclear files from the Atomic Energy Commission.
- Guy Burgess, Second Secretary of UK Embassy in Washington D.C.
- Kim Philby, UK Intelligence official in Washington D.C.

America's atomic secrets were funneled immediately to Moscow from the atomic laboratories in Los Alamos and elsewhere:

1. John Earl Haynes and Harvey Klehr, *Venona: Decoding Soviet Espionage in America* (New Haven, CT: Yale University Press, 1999), p 21.
2. Fleming, *The New Dealers' War*, p. 322.
3. Harvey and Klehr, *Verona*, p. 1.
4. Andrews, *For The President's Eyes Only*, p. 167.
5. Sandler, *The Korean War*, p 111.

- Klaus Fuchs, British physicist working at Los Alamos on the atom bomb project.
- Theodore Hall, a physicist working on the Manhattan Project.
- David Greenglass, a technician working on the atom bomb at Los Alamos.
- Julius Rosenberg, a Soviet agent who passed along atomic secrets to Moscow.
- William Perl, an aeronautical engineer who relayed critical information about jet engines and aircraft to the Soviets.

Intelligence experts had concluded that the Soviets would not have an atomic bomb until the mid-1950s, but due to the work of Fuchs, Hall, Greenglass and Rosenberg, Moscow exploded its first atom bomb in August 1949, some five years early. Due to his involvement in stealing atomic secrets, Julius Rosenberg was executed for espionage in 1953. The political Left always proclaimed his innocence; the Venona files prove his guilt. Ethel Rosenberg, Julius wife, was executed also, although the Venona Project confirmed that she played only a minor role in atomic espionage. Because of the secret nature of the Venona Project, the United States officials allowed Ethel to go to her death knowing of her essential innocence.

In President Truman's lengthy memoirs, he makes no mention of Soviet espionage — nothing of Alger Hiss, Harry Dexter White, Fuchs, Hall or the Rosenbergs; the issue of Soviet espionage remained a "red herring" and "a lot of baloney" to Truman throughout his life. He established a loyalty program for investigating security risks in 1947, but did so only because Republicans were raising the issue.[1] The only threat to American security that Truman saw was the phantom of Soviet tanks crashing across the Iron Curtain in Europe and fomenting revolution in third World nations.

Senator Joseph McCarthy, a Republican from Wisconsin, has an unsavory reputation because of his vituperative, and at times irresponsible campaign about internal security problems in the Truman administration. It is not my intention to clean up the Senator's image, but he did raise the legitimate issue of internal security at a time when the White House was fixated on Russian military advances in Europe, Korea and elsewhere. To the extent that the Soviets posed a threat to the US, that threat was in the form of 349 agents in suits and ties working in the government of the United States, not in Russian, Korean or Vietnamese military garb on the battlefield.

Two scholars researching Russian communist espionage reveal the true nature of the Russian menace to the US:

> The Soviet Union's unrestrained espionage against the United States from 1942 to 1945 was of the type that a nation directs at an enemy state. By the late 1940s the evidence provided by Venona of the massive size and intense hostility of Soviet intelligence operations caused both American counterintelligence professionals and high level policy makers to conclude that Stalin had already launched a covert attack on the United States. In their minds, the Soviet espionage offensive indicated that the Cold War had begun not after World War II but many years earlier.[2]

---

1. Andrews, *For The President's Eyes Only*, p. 168, 176.
2. Harvey and Klehr, *Venona*, p. 22.

THE FOLLY OF WAR

John Kennedy campaigned for the presidency in 1960 as an energetic, youthful candidate who promised to enhance the image and strengthen the security of the United States. He challenged the nation to "pay any price, bear any burden, meet any hardship, support any friend, oppose any foe" in the cause of freedom around the world. His campaign was in some ways one of fear — fear that America had done too little in defense, fear that there was a "missile gap," and fear that the Republican Party under Eisenhower and Nixon was inattentive, stodgy and flaccid. JFK would provide vigor, movement and action. Executing the CIA-sponsored Bays of Pigs venture, and then implementing Operation Mongoose, a program designed to assassinate Fidel Castro, fit well with the new robust image. Even when he learned that there was no missile gap, the President relentlessly pressed for more nuclear-tipped missiles. Kennedy escalated the arms race, yet all the while expressing concern about nuclear proliferation and atmospheric pollution.

On the eve of the Cuban Missile Crisis, President Kennedy had painted himself into a corner. His rash Churchillian campaign promises forced him to publicly warn the Russians in the fall of 1962 not to place "offensive" missiles in Cuba; the warning carried with it the implicit threat that America would take out the missiles. Later, the young President had second thoughts about the threat when he ruefully commented during the crisis, "I should have said that we don't care" if Khrushchev put missiles there. But, rhetorical discretion was not a part of the young Kennedy's repertoire. The President's imprudent language had raised expectations and by mid-October he had to find a way to wiggle out of the dilemma and remove the missiles. Both Khrushchev and Kennedy had engaged in indiscreet actions and used provocative rhetoric.

There was an atmosphere of hysteria in the US when Castro came to power in Cuba in 1959, with many American leaders vowing to remove the bearded dictator. Castro and communism were deemed a grave threat as the Marxist contagion, it was assumed, would spread throughout the Americas. With the passage of years, the threat seems exaggerated; Castro has been in power for over forty-four years, only ninety miles from the Florida coast, sustained through most of that time by the Soviet Union. The United States survived and even thrived.

But, the missile crisis presented a serious threat and it was dealt with in a calm, rational manner. Robert Kennedy, the President's brother and Attorney General, presented soothing, reasoned leadership during the ExCom deliberations, while all around the conference table hysteria reigned. After the crisis, Robert Kennedy made this observation about the personalities on the ExCom: "The fourteen people involved were very significant — bright, able, dedicated people, all of whom had the greatest affection for the US... If six of them had been president of the US, I think that the world might have been blown up."[1]

The ExCom group of fourteen was bitterly and closely divided on the proper United States response to the Russian missiles. Six of the members were ready to go to war with Russia, even if it meant a general nuclear war. The Joint Chiefs of Staff pressed vigorously for air strikes and invasion. Air Force Chief Curtis LeMay said if we don't strike Cuba the world will see that "they've got us on the run," for "a blockade is almost as bad as the appeasement at

---

1. Allison, *Essence of Decision*, p. 185

Munich."[1] Army General David Shoup was angry and near panic due to the President's efforts to obtain a diplomatic settlement. General Shoup's intemperate outburst included these incoherent thoughts: "Somebody's got to keep them from doing the goddamn thing piecemeal. That's our problem.... You're screwed, screwed, screwed. Some goddamn thing, someway that they either do the son of a bitch and do it right and quit frigging around."[2] Considering this guttural outburst by America's top general, the genius of the idea of civilian control of the military is surely appreciated.

The panic and fury of the military chiefs of the United States is seen in a little-known incident. In March 1962, the Joint Chiefs had proposed conducting acts of terrorism against American citizens, property and institutions in order to provoke an incident that would justify an invasion of Cuba. Targeted in these incredible plans were "US citizens, the US space program and internationally bound air travel..."[3] The highest US military officials were suggesting that the United States kill its own citizens surreptitiously, then blame the incident on Castro and communism. With this gambit the nation had sunk to a new low.

Dean Acheson, former Secretary of State, also presented a visceral analysis of the dilemma. Acheson agreed with the military leaders that an air strike and invasion were essential, as the missiles armed and targeted at America "were in the hands of a madman." Acheson dropped out of the meetings when he saw that Kennedy was going to use the blockade, and then hurled some acerbic words at the beleaguered President. Kennedy was, Acheson fumed, "like a cow with seven stomachs constantly ruminating and incapable of culminating in a digested decision."[4] Dean Acheson, a major architect of the American Cold War policy in the late 1940s, much preferred the bellicose, instinctive and angry responses of Harry Truman. Kennedy, unlike Truman, didn't "talk tough" and "rear up on his hind legs" when confronted with a foreign crisis. It is frightening to consider the outcome of the Cuban Missile Crisis, had Truman and Acheson been in the White House, rather than John and Bobby Kennedy.

When President Kennedy informed the congressional leadership of his decision to blockade the island, they raised objections and recommended an air strike or invasion. The blockade was considered a "weak step" for a superpower.[5] Theodore Sorenson, the President's aide and speechwriter, was, like Robert Kennedy, amazed at the casual attitude toward nuclear war. If the United States attacked the missile sites, the ExCom speculated, "the local Soviet commanders, under attack, might order the missiles fired on the assumption that war was on." Sorenson, in his book entitled, *Kennedy*, continues:

> The air-strike advocates did not shrink from the fact that a Soviet military riposte was likely. "What will the Soviets do in response?" one consultant favoring this course was asked. "I know the Soviets pretty well," he replied. "I think they'll knock out our missile bases in Turkey." "What do we do then?" "Under our NATO Treaty, we are obligated to knock out a base inside the Soviet Union." "What will they do then?" "Why, then we hope everyone will cool down and want to talk." It seemed rather cool in the conference room as he spoke.[6]

1. Freedman, *Kennedy's Wars*, p. 186
2. Ibid.
3. Alterman, *When Presidents Lie*, p. 112
4. Freedman, p. 186-187.
5. Allison, *Essence of Decision*, p. 195.
6. Theodore, Sorenson, *Kennedy* (New York: Harper & Row, 1965), p. 685.

One year after the Cuban Missile Crisis, President Kennedy was dead, and two years later, Premier Khrushchev was removed from office due to his wanton adventurism. These two world leaders had created a nuclear crisis, taken the world to the brink of nuclear war and then both paid the price for their risky behavior. With the publication of Khrushchev's memoirs and the opening of Soviet government files after 1990, we now know much more about Russian motives in the missile venture.

America had a huge lead in ICBM's, Kennedy was exerting enormous diplomatic pressure in Berlin and in Cuba, and United States defense spending was soaring and nuclear testing was being resumed. In Cuba, Castro was being influenced by fanatical revolutionaries, like his brother, Raul, and Che Guevara. This radical Marxist movement was prepared to sacrifice the Cuban revolution on the altar of a hemispheric revolt. Khrushchev felt that Russia was losing control of the Cuban revolution and that it would turn into a Trotskyite movement rather than the more cautious notion of "socialism in one country." And, the Russians were obviously concerned about the United States Jupiter missiles in Turkey as they had made a secret offer to the Turks of $500 million to remove the missiles.

Khrushchev eventually agreed to remove the missiles in Cuba when Kennedy pledged not to invade that island. But at the same time, Kennedy gave secret assurances to Russia that Operation Mongoose (the Castro assassination gambit) would be disbanded, and — most significantly — that the Jupiter missiles in Turkey would be removed. The Jupiter missiles were quietly taken out of Turkey in April 1963, but the public were not told of this missile swap until decades later. The missile swap — Cuban missiles for Turkish missiles — had be kept quiet to forestall protests over any consideration of equivalency. *Time* magazine captured the public mood in an article entitled, "Their Bases and Ours," arguing that "the Russian bases were intended for further conquest and domination while US bases were erected to preserve freedom. The difference should be obvious to all."[1] American diplomacy is so traumatized by the "Munich syndrome" — the fear of making any deal — that US leaders cannot conduct normal negotiations; neither can they be candid with the public about any diplomatic trades. The American sense of exceptionalism disallows normal diplomatic exchanges and concessions. The concept of missile equivalence — that the Turkish and the Cuban missiles represent the same threat to each side — is impossible for the United States public to comprehend. Politically, it would have been disastrous had President Kennedy admitted publicly that there was a missile swap and so he concealed the swap from the public.

As a consequence of this deceit, people are confused about how international problems are solved. Essentially, Kennedy made a diplomatic deal with the Russians, but the America public saw only Kennedy's threat to use military force. Future presidents, learning well, instinctively resort to military force, even when diplomacy would be more appropriate. As Eric Alterman comments, "To the alleged lessons of Munich and Yalta were now added those of the unreported missile crisis. Together the formed the intellectual DNA of US foreign policy and the American people's understanding of the world."[2] Problems are solved only when the United States "muscles up" on nations.

---

1. Quoted in Alterman, *When Presidents Lie*, p. 97.
2. Alterman, *When Presidents Lie*, p. 146.

The Greek Civil War of 1947 was not the first time the US was tempted to intervene in Greek internal affairs. In the 1820s, the Greeks rose up against their Turkish masters, sought independence and called for aid from the US. Some members of Congress, stirred by the Greek revolt that paralleled the American Revolution, suggested sending a mission to the area. But, John Randolph of Virginia rose in the House of Representatives to oppose such folly, saying: "For my part I would rather put the shirt of Nessus [a legendary bloody poisonous garment] on my back, than sanction these doctrines...." If America sends forces into this conflict, Randolph continued, "every bulwark and barrier of the Constitution is broken down; it is become a *tabula rasa* — a *carte blanche* for everyone to scribble on it what he pleases."[1] Randolph and a majority of Congressmen recognized the foolishness of America riding to the rescue of every democratic or national movement in the world. America wished the Greeks well in their struggle but declined to send troops. The Greeks would have to resolve their own internal struggle.

But, 120 years later when Dean Acheson distorted and embellished the Greek condition (he later confessed: "we made our points clearer than truth") and when President Truman called on the Congress to send money and military forces to Greece so that "all nations and all peoples are free to govern themselves...," there was no John Randolph to throw down the gauntlet, and little wisdom emanating from the members of Congress. The contrived international crisis of 1947 in Greece caused the Cold War to be etched firmly on the American mind. President Truman and Secretary Acheson spawned the Cold War by propounding the idea that Stalin was out to communize the world by using military means. The Truman administration presented a picture of the Russian military forces with nuclear weapons poised to invade Western Europe, the Middle East, Asia — anywhere on the globe where the "forces of freedom" did not confront them. The containment policy enunciated by Russian expert George Kennan laid out the blue print for a decades long, relentless struggle against Russian communism. Wherever communists raised their head, American forces must be there to contain and confront.

When Russian agents and their allies overthrew the freely elected non-communist government of Czechoslovakia in 1948, the intensity of the incipient Cold War heated up. The disaster of the Czech coup d'état seemed to confirm the narrative told from the White House. Few at that time agreed with the calm assessment by Senator Robert Taft when he said:

> I know of no indication of Russian intention to undertake military aggression beyond the sphere of influence which was originally assigned to them. The situation in Czechoslovakia was indeed a tragic one but Russian influence has dominated there since the end of the war.[2]

In public, government leaders preached fear and alarm, but in private many discussed a contrary view — the limited nature of Russian policy. Truman government officials told the public that every communist group and leader was linked to the Kremlin, but when speaking confidentially, they acknowledged the complex nature of the Marxist movement; communists wore many different stripes and served many masters. There was no "communist monolith — no world Marxist movement bound together in a tightly-knit web of conspiracy. The author of the containment policy, George Kennan, recognized the danger in the Truman exaggerations:

---

1. McDougall, *Promised Land, Crusader State*, p. 74-75.
2. Henry H. Berger, "A Conservative Critique of Containment," in David Horowitz, ed., *Containment and Revolution*, p. 133.

It was perfectly clear to anyone with even a rudimentary knowledge of the Russia of that day, that the Soviet leaders had no intention of attempting to advance their cause by launching military attacks with their own forces across frontiers.[1]

In his massive study of the Truman years, *Another Such Victory*, Arnold Offner paints a rather benign picture of Soviet military intentions. "But there is no evidence that he [Stalin] intended to march his Red Army westward beyond its agreed-upon European occupation zones, and he put Soviet state interests ahead of desire to spread Communist ideology."[2]

Simply put and as tragic as it seems, the $4 trillion in defense spending and the 100,000 American lives sacrificed in military battle during the Cold War were all done chasing a mirage. There was no external military threat from the Soviet Union as presented by the early Cold Warriors.

Choosing war over peace is ultimately a policy choice exercised by presidents alone; thus the question of which man is in the White House becomes critical. It is interesting to speculate what would have happened had Harry Truman NOT been president at this perilous time after World War II. Had FDR survived into the post war years (he was only 63 at the time of his death) would he have been able to finesse the issues and avoid a confrontation with his "friend" Joseph Stalin? Or, had Henry Wallace, the Vice-president from 1941 to 1945, been selected to run again instead of Truman, would the US have been better off with Wallace's "soft" view of Soviet behavior? Or, had a Republican been in the White House, perhaps Senator Robert Taft, an opponent of NATO and the Truman Doctrine, one could easily imagine fewer confrontations with Stalin and a more accommodating attitude toward Russian power in Eastern Europe.

During the later years of World War II, FDR formed a strong bond with Stalin, even to the exclusion of Churchill; an alliance of Russia and the US had been established. Personality makes policy, whether tax policy or foreign policy. Harry Truman reversed this alliance system; the US rejected Russia in 1946 and 1947, forming an Atlantic partnership with Great Britain, thereby alienating the Soviet Union. A diplomatic *ménage à trois* is an explosive relationship; one party can easily be left out and hurt. In 1943-1945, Britain was on the outside; after 1946, Russia was ostracized. Thus the Cold War came to be.

For over fifty years the standard American view of Cold War history has been to blame Stalin for failing to live up to his Yalta obligations and for his incessant military efforts to spread communism around the globe. Thus, according to the standard view, had Stalin abided by the wartime agreements and tamed his universalist urges, there would have been no Cold War. But, this standard view is not in accordance with the facts. Stalin DID do as expected; he did carry out the agreements. Russian power was present throughout Eastern Europe at the end of World War II and Churchill and Roosevelt accepted that as an inevitable consequence of the nature of that war. There were "communist" activities around the globe, but Stalin did not organize them nor did he order them to wage war on America and its allies.

The Cold War flared when a pugnacious President Truman refused to recognize the power realities in Eastern Europe and challenged Russia's *cordon sanitaire*. FDR befriended and flattered Stalin, accepting the presence of Russian power in Europe; Truman invoked the idealist message of moral condemnation, "reared up on his hind legs" and told them "where to get off."

---

1. Horowitz, *Containment and Revolution*, p. 11.
2. Offner, *Another Such Victory*, p. 456.

Franklin Roosevelt's decision in 1941 to fight an impossible and unwinnable war against Germany over the issue of Eastern Europe, along with Harry Truman's belligerent attitude toward Russia, combined to spawn a fifty-year Cold War, and sometimes a Hot War. For governmental leaders and court historians it became convenient to blame Joseph Stalin for the horrors of the decades long nuclear conflict. The issues of patriotism (FDR and Truman were considered American heroes) and political advantage (FDR and Truman were prominent Democrat Party leaders) caused historians to take the easy way — Stalin, not FDR and Truman, became the villain who caused the Cold War.

Chapter 10. The Korean War: The Great Reversal

War Breaks Out in Korea

After spending a relaxing Saturday gardening at his Maryland farmhouse, Secretary of State Dean Acheson was reading in bed when the direct telephone line from the State Department rang. The Secretary was informed that military units of communist North Korea had invaded South Korea, an American ally. The attack appeared to be an invasion in force, not simply another foray in the continuing civil war between the broken halves of Korea. Acheson immediately called President Harry Truman who was spending the weekend at his home in Independence, Missouri, after having officiated at the opening ceremony of the newly constructed Washington National Airport. Upon hearing news of the invasion of South Korea, the President responded in a surprising, yet typically Trumanesque manner: "Dean, we've got to stop the sons of bitches."[1]

The President flew back to Washington D.C. the next day and scheduled high level meetings to discuss the American response. Newsmen intercepted him as he walked to Blair House for a conference and queried him about US plans. Truman asserted that he was not going to let the North Korean attack succeed and that he was going to "hit them hard."[2] It was Sunday, June 25, 1950, and the first major military conflict of the Cold War was underway.

President Truman's response was surprising because the United States had deliberately rejected plans for the military defense of South Korea. The State Department, the Joint Chiefs of Staff and the President's office had given extensive and serious consideration to the eventuality that Korea might become the scene of a conflict between the United States and the Soviet Union. The decision had been made that the United States would not fight for the defense of the Republic of Korea. This judgment arose from several sources:

---

1. Andrews, *For The President's Eyes Only*, p. 184.
2. Stoessinger, *Crusaders and Pragmatists*, p. 75.

- As early as 1947, the Joint Chiefs of Staff had concluded that "from the standpoint of military security, the United States has little strategic interest in maintaining troops and bases in Korea."[1]
- The Defense Department had compiled a list of nations listed by strategic importance and Korea was at the bottom of the list.
- The Joint Chiefs had determined that the 45,000 men stationed in South Korea, following the partition of that nation in 1945, were a liability and should be withdrawn before a military attack made it necessary to withdraw them under fire.
- The author, diplomat and strategic thinker, George Kennan, was of the opinion that Korea was "not of decisive strategic importance."
- The Joint Chiefs had reported that the "eventual domination of Korea by the USSR will have to be accepted as a probability if troops are withdrawn."[2]
- General MacArthur agreed with the Joint Chiefs that American troops should not be sent to aid South Korea in the event of a war.

The most dramatic evidence of US policy toward Korea was a major policy speech at the National Press Club in Washington D.C. on January 12, 1950 by Secretary of State Acheson. The Secretary emphasized that Korea was *outside* the United States defense perimeter, a perimeter that lay off the coast of the Asian mainland running from the Aleutian Islands in the north, through the Japanese homeland, to Okinawa and the Philippine Islands to the south. Acheson's speech was an echo of a newspaper interview that General MacArthur had given in March 1949. As Commander of American Pacific forces, he excluded Korea from the protective mantel:

> ...our line of defense runs through the chain of islands fringing the coast of Asia.
>
> It starts from the Philippines and continues through the Ryukyu Archipelago, which includes its main bastion, Okinawa. Then bends back through Japan and the Aleutian Island chain to Alaska.[3]

In a more informal moment, the General contemptuously said that "anyone who commits the American Army on the mainland of Asia ought to have his head examined."[4]

In a calculated manner, US leaders had discarded Militant Idealism for strategic prudence. The "abandonment" of Korea was entirely consistent with traditional United States strategic assessments throughout the 20th century. American strategists were heavily influenced by the book *The Influence of Sea Power on History* by Alfred Thayer Mahan published in 1890. This seminal work, mainly about how England utilized its navy to control key points on the globe, caused the United States to focus on the acquisitions of islands in the Pacific — Hawaii, Wake, Guam, the Philippines — rather than the Asian mainland. During World War II, the United States employed this concept to defeat Japan by hopping from island to island using sea and air power. American casualties in the Pacific during World War II were much lower than in Europe because the United States avoided bloody continental land battles.

Confirming this decades long strategic policy, by the summer of 1949, the United States removed all of its 45,000 military fighting men from Korea.

---

1. Wittner, *Cold War America* (New York: Praeger, 1974), p. 73.
2. Stanley Sandler, *The Korean War: No Victors, No Vanquished*, p. 35.
3. Kissinger, *Diplomacy*, p. 475.
4. Leland Baldwin, *Recent American History* (New York: American Book Company, 1954), p. 771.

THE PLIGHT OF A DIVIDED KOREA

Korea is an ancient land founded about 2000 BC. Because of its location, tucked in among China, Russia and Japan, it has been the scene of hundreds of foreign invasions. Often in the past, it sought protection from its sometimes-benevolent neighbor China. The 20th century was unkind to the people of the Korean peninsula as the Japanese took advantage of political turmoil in China and extended Nippon's power over Korea. Korea was no longer the "Hermit Kingdom," as a century ago it became a vassal state of Japan, a protectorate in the parlance of the era, following the Japanese victory in the Russo-Japanese War of 1904-5.

The United States, on several occasions early in the century, gave Japan the "green light" to dominate the Korean peninsula. Recognizing that a scramble for empire was in the winds and aware of its own limits of power in the Far East, Washington acquiesced in the Japanese annexation of Korea in 1910. Some say a trade was made: Japan asserted its authority over Korea and, in exchange, the United States controlled the Philippine Islands. An informal sphere of influence had evolved in many parts of the world as the great powers attempted to dominate their "natural domains." During the presidencies of Teddy Roosevelt and Woodrow Wilson before World War I, the United States acknowledged Japanese interests on the Asian continent. President Roosevelt's thoughts on the Korea situation are illuminating:

> Korea is absolutely Japan's. To be sure, by treaty it was solemnly covenanted that Korea should remain independent. But Korea was itself helpless to enforce the treaty, and it was out of the question to suppose that any other nation ... would attempt to do for Korea what they were utterly unable to do for themselves.[1]

President Theodore Roosevelt, often a realist in international affairs, wisely asserted that, due to limitations of power, there are some endeavors that must be forgone. Roosevelt was not going to tangle with the Japanese Navy in its home waters. That cautionary lesson, applied to the June 1950 invasion, should have given President Truman pause. The Chinese under Mao Tse-tung were the closest allies of North Korea; their massive army lay just over the border.

At the wartime Cairo Conference in 1943, FDR and the other Allied leaders made a commitment that "Korea shall become free and independent" at the conclusion of the war.[2] However, at later conferences, the United States reluctantly deferred to Russian interests and power in the area, agreeing to a temporary joint military occupation of the Korean peninsula. Temporary military occupations of nations by the victorious powers were no stranger to post-World War II settlements. The Allied forces divided Germany, Berlin, Austria and later Vietnam.

In anticipation of occupying a nation, the Soviet Union prepared meticulously by recruiting young communist leaders and preparing them for eventual rulership with a long apprenticeship in Moscow. Assuming somewhat naively that the joint occupation would last only a few months, the administration of Franklin Roosevelt failed to grant diplomatic recognition to any Korean exile groups or to recruit and train leaders for the new government. The woeful condition of American knowledge in the area and the subsequent plight of Korea is illustrated by the story told of a meeting in the State Department during 1945 when Secretary of

---

1. Kissinger, *Diplomacy*, p. 41.
2. Don Oberdorfer, *The Two Korea's: A Contemporary History* (Reading, MA: Addison-Wesley, 1997), p.5.

State Edward Stettinius asked if someone could point out on a map where Korea was located![1] This from the Secretary of State! Even as late as August 1945 when the US dropped the atom bomb on Hiroshima, the United States had made no specific plans for Korea, nor had it put together a staff of experts for planning. This lack of preparedness testifies to the American disinterest in the area as well as its continued innocence in dealing with the Soviet Union.

On August 9, 1945, Russia declared war on Japan and prepared to occupy Japanese-held Korea. In a near panic, the State Department held an all-night meeting August 10 to decide on the temporary division of Korea. Using a map from a National Geographic magazine (apparently the State Department had no maps of Korea), Army Lieutenant Colonel Dean Rusk (later a Secretary of State) drew a line at the 38th parallel indicating a temporary boundary of the divided nation, separating the north, a Soviet zone, from the south, an American zone. The partition was arbitrary, having no antecedent in history and severely disruptive of economic life, as the large population centers and food supply were in the south, but the utilities and mineral resources were in the north. Further it was militarily difficult to defend, as the new border followed no natural boundaries. The partition of Korea was completed without consulting the native people, and violated the aspirations of independence sought by Korean nationalists, such as Syngman Rhee and Kim Il Sung, the eventual leaders of the divided land. There were no experts in Korean history or culture present at the all-night meeting and the last minute nature of the conclave gave an aura of desperation and "Wheel of Fortune" amateurishness to the episode.

Frustrated in their hopes for independence and unity and weakened by partition and military occupation at the hands of the big powers, the two Koreas soon turned to their only alternative — guerrilla raids on each other across the open border at the 38th parallel. A United Nations commission dealing with Korean unification attempted to conduct unification elections early in 1948, but the communist north, noting the much larger population in the South, refused to allow elections in their zone. A civil war in the late 1940s was in full array as each half of Korea attempted to unify the nation by conquest. The civil war was fought along classic ideological lines, with Leftist (communists and non-communists) mostly located in the north and led by Kim Il Sung, against Rightists, located mostly in the South and led by Syngman Rhee. Between 1946 and 1950 the bloody civil war took 100,000 lives; Koreans killing Koreans with enthusiasm, all before the formal start of the "Korean War" in June 1950.

The Rightist forces in the South had a larger population and military force; the North was more heavily armed, the Russians being more generous with equipment before their military forces departed North Korea in 1948. The United State was reluctant to arm the South Koreans, in part because of its own ambivalence about defending Korea, but also due to its concerns with how Rhee was using his Army. He frequently used the military against his own citizens in the South, with mass arrests of political opponents, press censorship, essentially establishing a military dictatorship, all offending American sensibilities. North Korean leader Kim Il Sung had been urging his mentor and benefactor, Joseph Stalin, to unleash the North Korean Army on the South in a unification campaign. Throughout 1949 Stalin refused to allow a unification war. Only if the Republic of Korea (South Korea) launched the attack first could

---

1. Ibid., p. 5.

there be a full counterattack. "Then your move will be understood and supported by everyone," cautioned Stalin.[1]

The unification campaign began to obsess Kim, and in January 1950 he complained to the Soviet ambassador that "Lately I do not sleep at night because I am thinking about how to resolve the question of the unification of the whole country."[2] Kim spent the entire month of April 1950 in Moscow lobbying the Soviet leader for permission to invade the South. Stalin, hoping to impede the headstrong Kim, told the Korean leader to consult with Mao Tse-tung. When Mao gave grudging assent, Stalin finally relented. In addition to China's approval, the venture became acceptable to the Russian leader, as it seemed Washington had given sufficient signals that South Korea would not be defended. Further, Syngman Rhee's political party in the South had suffered a serious electoral defeat in May, losing control of the national legislature. The Soviets had recently detonated their first atom bomb and communist China had just concluded a successful civil war. The ever-cautious Stalin saw the tide of history moving in his direction. It was time to unleash the Korean forces, but the Russian leader made it clear that North Korea was on its own. The Soviet Army would not come to his rescue if military success escaped Kim. There would be aid and advice, but no troops.

AMERICA REVERSE ITS ASIAN POLICY

After a half century of foreign policy that avoided military commitments on the continent of Asia, why did the Truman administration reverse course? Historian Henry Kissinger praises Truman for his actions in coming to the defense of South Korea, saying that Truman "rose to the occasion," and noted that "Few foreign policy decisions are more difficult than to improvise military actions which have never been foreseen."[3] But contrary to the Kissinger assertion and to other historians who shield Truman by suggesting that the June 25 attack was a surprise, the invasion was not unexpected. Indeed the White House, the State Department and the Joint Chiefs of Staff had all discussed the possibility — even the probability — that Korea would be unified under the Red banner. The United States decision had been to cut its losses — remove the troops and limit aid to South Korea.

In 1949, General Dwight David Eisenhower, the Army Chief of Staff, persuaded the other members of the Joint Chiefs of Staff to endorse a memorandum to the National Security Council recommending that our troops "mount out" at the earliest practicable opportunity. After extended discussions, the military chiefs, President Truman and the National Security Council endorsed the idea that there was an unacceptable risk involved in maintaining troops on the Asian continent and recognized the military danger inherent in the Korean situation. In April 1948 they reported, "The United States should not become so irrevocably involved in the Korean situation that an action taken by... any other power in Korea could be considered a *casus belli* for the United States."[4]

---

1. www.historybookshop.com/articles/commentary/korean-war-who-started-ht.asp
2. Oberdorfer, *The Two Korea's*, p. 9.
3. Kissinger, *Diplomacy*, p. 477.
4. Fromkin, *In The Time Of The Americans*, p. 510.

The United States Central Intelligence Agency provided a dismal assessment of the future of the Republic of Korea in July 1949. The Rhee government was authoritarian and offensive to many citizens. This "inefficiency and shortsighted authoritarianism" would eventually result in "a public reaction favoring communism. While economic aid and military training might ameliorate these adverse conditions; it is not expected that these factors can prevent ultimate Communist control of the whole of Korea."[1]

United States military intelligence reported to the White House that an invasion by North Korea into South Korea could be expected by March or April 1950. This report was available to government officials in late December 1949. One intelligence report in March 1950 predicted a full-scale invasion in June 1950. Amazingly, Soviet plans for the invasion seemed to have fallen into American or South Korean control prior to the attack. Military intelligence discovered plans by the North Korean forces that gave a date of the third week in June for the attack. (This Russian-language war plan is now in the National Archives.) If the White House did not know of the imminence of an attack, they were derelict in their responsibilities.

(Kissinger and the other apologists for President Truman are correct in one sense. Assistant Secretary of State Dean Rusk appeared before a congressional committee on June 20, five days before the invasion and reported that there was no evidence of an invasion from the north. During those hearings, Secretary Rusk insulted the Chinese by referring to northern China as "Manchucko," the name Japan gave to that area during its occupation. For all his obtuseness, Dean Rusk was rewarded by two presidents by being named Secretary of State. Rusk may be remembered best for his ardent defense of the American foreign policy fiasco — the Vietnam War.)

Shortly after the June invasion, President Truman announced a rationale for going to war: "The attack on Korea makes it plain beyond all doubt that communism has passed beyond the use of subversion to conquer independent nations and will now use armed invasion."[2] Secretary of State Acheson used more colorful language to convey the same message: "In Korea the Russians presented a check which was drawn on the bank account of collective security. The Russians thought the check would bounce.... But to their great surprise the teller paid it."[3]

The Truman administration could have viewed this June invasion as the concluding stages of a long Korean civil war and remained aloof, using Teddy Roosevelt's idea that if you can't help yourself, don't look to the United States. Instead, Truman portrayed the invasion as having apoplectic proportions; it was international communism on the march, directed by the Kremlin. The United States — the *Militant Idealist* — would come to the rescue. The Truman administration's portrayal of this war caused newspaper headlines to be written such as:

INTERNATIONAL COMMUNISM ON THE MARCH!

But the facts of the story would have suggested a different headline:

KOREA INVADES KOREA!

To the men conducting international affairs for the United States in the 1950s, World War II with its searing example of Hitler's Germany invading small, hapless countries was the

---

1. Sandler, *The Korean War*, p. 41.
2. Wittner, *Cold War America*, p. 74.
3. LaFeber, *America, Russia and the Cold War*, p. 103.

watershed experience of their lives. When the invasion of South Korea occurred, in their minds Stalin became Hitler, communists were Nazis, and Korea was Czechoslovakia. Aggression had to be stopped or it would spread and become even more aggressive, like cancer out of control.

There is a more apt parallel between the Korean War and World War II. Just as Truman confounded Moscow and Pyongyang about America's commitments to defend South Korea, so Great Britain and the West had given many assurances that Poland would *not* be defended should Germany move eastward. When, in the summer of 1939, London and Paris changed course coming unexpectedly and futilely to the aid of Poland, World War II began. Such is the perfidy of politics.

Two days after the invasion, June 27, the President ordered the Seventh Fleet to patrol the Straits of Formosa to prevent an invasion of Formosa (Taiwan) by the forces of communist China. Presuming that the invasion of South Korea was part of an aggressive move by international communism, the President ordered the Secretary of the Air Force to prepare for the destruction of all Soviet air and naval bases in the Far East. Military aid to the Philippines was increased and ominously aid began to flow to the French forces fighting in Indochina (Vietnam). The following day, June 28, the President ordered air and naval forces under the command of General Douglas MacArthur stationed in Japan to provide all assistance to South Korea. On June 30, with news of the near collapse of the Republic of Korea forces, Truman authorized the use of ground forces. The United States was in full battle array against the North Korean military.

On July 26, while in the map room of the White House, the President compared this event to the episode in Greece that had spawned the Truman Doctrine. As the President pointed to oil-rich Iran on the map, he said, "Korea is the Greece of the Far East. If we are tough enough now, if we stand up to them like we did in Greece three years ago, they won't take any next step. But if we just stand by, they'll move into Iran and they'll take over the whole Middle East."[1]

To the President and his advisors, Kim Il Sung and Joseph Stalin had just taken another step on the road to world conquest by international communism. Korea itself was not of strategic value, but it was a symbol of international power and prestige. Whoever held that geographic space would gain some psychological advantage. Korea was just a pawn in the great chess game of international politics. America had to checkmate the communists.

A United Nations "Police Action"

In all previous American wars — 1812, 1846, 1898, 1917 and 1941 — the president had asked Congress to declare war prior to committing large numbers of troops into battle. At mid-twentieth century, after one hundred and fifty years of abiding by the Constitutional requirement that Congress, not the president, decided when the nation goes to war, President Truman established a new practice of "presidential war making." Indeed there have been no congressional declarations of war since then — not in the Vietnam War, not in the Gulf War,

---

1. Fromkin, *In The time Of The Americans*, p. 511.

not in the Iraq War. The war declaration clause of the United States Constitution is essentially a "dead letter."

When Truman asked his friend Senator Tom Connally about involving Congress in the decision to go to war in June 1950, Connally assured the President that he had the sole power to act based on the urgency of the events. Connally responded, "If a burglar breaks into your house, you can shoot him without going down to the police station and getting permission."[1] Ignoring the obvious fact that the homeland had not been invaded, the senior Senator from Texas calmly suggested that the President disregard a significant aspect of Constitutional law and historical practice. To further illustrate the intellectual confusion and emotional panic of the leadership during this crisis, just one month previous, in May, Senator Connally had commented about the situation in Korea in a different manner: "I'm afraid it's going to happen, that is, the abandonment of the Republic of Korea, whether we want it or not."[2] When asked if the Republic of Korea was essential to US security, Senator Connally, the Chairman of the Senate Foreign Relations Committee, replied firmly, "No!" But one month later in the midst of confusion and panic at the highest levels of the US government, the "invasion" of an insignificant, newly-divided nation lying at the doorstep of China, 6000 miles from the United States, produced a military emergency so profound that major Constitutional practices were set aside.

Never before had the US gone to war unless it was made to believe its territory or fleet had been attacked. Presidents McKinley, Wilson and Franklin Roosevelt had been careful to avoid direct and overt military action until it was clear to them that American property was attacked and American lives lost. The US response in Korea did not even rise to the level of a "preemptory attack," for there was no evidence that the US was in danger of being attacked by the North Koreans.

Within days, however, the Truman administration had discovered a better "marketing plan" for this war. During a press conference, a reporter asked the President if this was a "police action" by the United Nations. Like a drowning man, President Truman grasped this intellectual life preserver and the idea of the United States supporting a United Nations "police action" was born. This desperate gambit was soon buttressed by the legal argument that when on June 27 the United Nations Security Council had asked member nations to come to the aid of South Korea, the President had no choice but to commit American armed forces.

Such an interpretation belies the facts. Those American leaders who wrote and signed the United Nations Charter had no such interpretation in mind. The relevant section says that the member states will "undertake," that is "will attempt" to provide troops for any collective action. The correct interpretation is that this provision is totally voluntary. The Truman administration was not compelled to provide troops to this United Nations venture, indeed most member states did not provide troops, and those that did provided troops in meager numbers.

The Truman administration gamely tried to buttress the argument about their United Nations obligations. The United States representative to the United Nations, commenting on the North Korean attack, said that "Such an attack defies the interest and authority of the United Nations."[3] President Truman sent a congratulatory note to Secretary Acheson compli-

---

1. Sandler, *The Korean War*, p. 54.

2. Ibid., p. 42.

3. David W. Clinton, *Two Faces of National Interest* (Baton Rouge, LA: University of Louisiana Press, 1994), p. 165.

menting him on his quick initiative in calling for United Nations action. But then the President gave away the argument when he wrote to Acheson: "Had you not acted promptly in that direction we would have had to go into Korea alone."[1] Indeed, the original United Nations resolution had asked only that North Korea withdraw and that member states give assistance to South Korea; there was no reference to military aid. The United State decision to send military forces preceded the United Nations decision to raise an army.[2] Clearly the Truman administration was directing traffic at the UN, then claiming to merely doing the biding of that organization.

Invoking the United Nations Charter was a cunning effort to give multilateral legitimacy to the administration's thoughtless policy reversal about defending Korea. The Unified Command of the United Nations in Korea was an American operation with significant South Korean support, and nearly nothing from the other United Nations member states. Many historians perpetuate the fiction that it was a legitimate United Nations collective security operation, thereby giving credence to the Truman administration facade. One historian says that "thirty governments decided to lend supplementary assistance in the form of field hospitals, blood plasma, rice and soap. Iceland, for example, made a contribution of cod-liver oil for the troops"[3] Soap? Rice? Cod-liver oil? What about troops to fight and die on the battlefield? It is strange what intellectual gyrations a mind can be twisted into if it has been decided to defend the Truman administration policy.

Sixteen member nations contributed troops to the collective action out of a total United Nations membership of about 60 nations. Troop commitment in land, sea, and air and the resulting deaths were as follows:[4]

	USA	S. Korea	UN
Land	50%	40%	10%
Sea	85%	7%	8%
Air	93%	5%	2%
Deaths	50%	47%	3%

Troops of the United States and South Korea incurred 97% of the deaths in the war. Excluding South Korea, over 95% of the deaths were American. The 40,000 troops sent by the United Nations, nearly all from NATO or British Commonwealth nations, were dwarfed by the over half million United States troops. The Asian, African and Latin American nations sent virtually nothing.[5] The military commitment of the other members of the United Nations was irrelevant to the military effort.

General Douglas MacArthur was appointed head of the "United Nations Unified Command" by President Truman, not by the United Nations, and eventually was removed in

---

1. Ibid., p. 166.
2. Richard Whelan, *Drawing the Line: the Korean War, 1950-1953* (Boston: Little, Brown and Company, 1990), p. 145.
3. Stoessinger, *Crusaders and Pragmatists*, p. 81.
4. Ibid., p. 81; *World Book Encyclopedia*, Vol. 11, (Chicago: Field Enterprises, 1974), p. 303.
5. Whelan, *Drawing the Line: The Korean War, 1950-1953*, p. 153.

1951 by the sole action of the American president. General MacArthur acknowledged that he received his orders from Washington D.C., not from United Nations in New York City. The General commented:

> The entire control of my command and everything I did came from our own Chiefs of Staff. Even the reports which were normally made by me to the United Nations were subject to censorship by our State and Defense Departments. I had no direct connection with the United Nations whatsoever.[1]

Decisions about crossing the 38th parallel, invading North Korea and approaching the boundary with China at the Yalu River were all American decisions with the passive acquiescence of the United Nations. The United Nations did create a United Nations Unified Command to direct all forces in Korea, but it was apparent that General MacArthur and the Joint Chiefs of Staff made all the decisions. As historian Stanley Sandler says in his book, *The Korean War: No Victors, No Vanquished*: "Thus all military forces fighting the North Korean invasion were officially under the UN auspices, but in reality under United States military command."[2] The United Nations "police action" story was a "fig leaf" to conceal the fact that the Truman administration was acting unilaterally and that its foreign policy was in confusion and disarray.

Secretary of State Acheson inadvertently approached the truth when he wrote in his book, *The Korean War*, that a debate in Congress about declaring war would have done harm. Indeed harsh, probing questions might have been asked about why the administration had reversed established policy, and why the administration was so unprepared for the invasion in view of repeated warnings by the military intelligence community. The "harm done" would have been to Truman, Acheson and others responsible for the ineptitude and confusion of the Truman foreign policy. It would be the hope of many that during a debate about a war declaration on the floor of Congress some courageous member would have asked the President:

> Sir, why is it that for years it has been settled policy that the United States would not become involved in a land war in Asia, and why, Sir, is it that it was the clear policy of this administrations just one month ago that we would not expend even one American life for the defense of the Republic of Korea, but now, Mr. President, this month, thousands of young Americans must go to Korea and die?

There were a few critics of the President's unilateral actions. In the Republican Party platform two years later (1952), the GOP charged that the Democrats "have plunged us into war in Korea without the consent of our citizens...." This passage was written by John Foster Dulles, an advisor to Secretary of State Acheson who was in Korea in June 1950. When the invasion took place, Dulles cabled the president suggesting that American forces be sent immediately to the beleaguered South Koreans. It was only later, during the presidential election of 1952, that Dulles got "religion" and decided that the Congress should have controlled the question of going to war.

Senator Robert Taft, an Ohio senator who was often considered the Republican party leader and an erstwhile presidential candidate, charged Truman with "a complete usurpation...of authority to use the Armed Forces of the country," and he complained that if the President had complete authority to send armed forces into war, war would occur more often.[3]

---

1. LaFeber, *America, Russia and the Cold War*, p. 105.

2. Sandler, *The Korean War*, p. 151.

3. Ibid., p. 53.

But the President never met with congressional leaders until June 28, and by that time all the critical early decisions had been made. President Truman need not worry, however, because public opinion polls showed an 80% approval rating for Truman and few in Congress were prepared to fight against the tide of public opinion.

TRUMAN, MACARTHUR AND COMMUNIST CHINA

General Douglas MacArthur's tactical brilliance dominated the war almost immediately after being appointed to command the military force. Following the June invasion, in early August, United Nations forces were in danger of being pushed off the Korean peninsula at the southern port city of Pusan. Whereupon General MacArthur staged a brilliant amphibious landing on the western coast of South Korea at Inchon, the port for Seoul. His military forces successfully landed far behind enemy lines, causing a near rout of the North Korean Army.

By late September, the United States and United Nations were in discussion about whether to follow up their military success, invade North Korea and unify the divided nation. The original United Nations Security Council resolution called for merely "restoring the border" between the two countries. Now, emboldened by the success of General MacArthur, the Truman administration decided to expand the original goal.

The communist Chinese government looked with trepidation upon any United States move into North Korea, its acknowledged ally. Chinese Premier Chou En-lai cautioned that "the Chinese people [would] not stand idly by in the war of invasion."[1] When the Indian Ambassador to China cautioned the United States about approaching the Chinese border, the Truman administration dismissed him as a tool of the Chinese communists. Chiang Kai-shek's military intelligence informed the United States that Red Army troops were massing north of the Yalu River and were going "to throw the book at the United Nations forces in Korea."[2] All cautionary statements and requests for negotiations from China went unheeded. The exceptional nation — America — would not be impeded in its mission of mercy.

The United States had entered the war in June to defend South Korea from the clutches of an international communist movement, allegedly directed by Moscow and Peking. The Truman administration had sold the war to the United Nations and to the public as a threat to international peace and stability due to the involvement of the two communist giants. But now, with an interesting twist of logic and defiance of common sense, the Truman administration in the fall of 1950 argued that China and Russia would not enter the war to save North Korea or guard their borders. General MacArthur expressed disdain for the supposed Chinese intervention, saying that: "...if the Chinese tried to get down to Pyongyang [the North Korean capital] there would be the greatest slaughter."[3]

Secretary of State Dean Acheson's words about American-Chinese relations were meant to be reassuring, although not up to the usual eloquence of the Harvard graduate: "Everything in the world is being done to reassure the Chinese their interests were not jeopardized and I

---

1. Stoessinger, p. 85.
2. Sandler, *The Korean War*, p. 100.
3. Ibid., p. 112.

should suppose that there is no country in the world which has been more outstanding in developing the theory of brotherly development of border waters [*sic*] than the United States."[1]

(The obvious problems of syntax that fouled the Secretary's message are reminiscent of similar language problems of President Eisenhower. The conservative publisher, William F. Buckley, relates the story in the 1950s that the Russians were always confounded by Eisenhower's speeches because of his syntax difficulties. Not knowing for sure what he was saying, the Russians decided "to play it safe and lay low." Perhaps verbal confusion is a promising new form of diplomacy.)

President Truman publicly reassured the Chinese on November 16 that the United States "never at any time entertained any intention to carry hostilities into China" and "because of the long-standing American friendship for the people of China, the United States [would] take every honorable step to prevent any extension of the hostilities in the Far East."[2] The Chinese were not impressed with the soothing words of the Militant Idealists, and why should they, for Truman's actions betrayed his words. In the summer and fall of 1950 the United States had:

- Accused Peking (and Moscow) of fomenting the invasion of South Korea.
- Positioned the American Seventh Fleet in the Formosa Straits at China's front door.
- Made a commitment to protect Chiang Kai-shek's forces on Formosa thereby preventing the conclusion of the Chinese revolution.
- Poured military and financial aid to the French in Indochina to sustain their imperialist venture on China's southern doorstep.
- Invaded China's ally, North Korea, and was now poised to establish its Army at the Chinese border.

The illogical statements and dangerous diplomatic moves of the Truman administration give evidence that the administration was flying by the seat of its pants. It had plunged into a war for which it had no plans, then had to improvise at each new eventuality. John G. Stoessinger, in *Crusaders and Pragmatists*, summarizes the dilemma well: "The conviction that China would not intervene represented an emotional rather than an intellectual conclusion, an ascription to the enemy of intentions compatible with the desires of Washington."[3]

US policy was operating on hopes and dreams, but the lives of thousands of young men, drafted into the war were riding on the validity of Truman's policy. For, if China entered the war after a United States invasion of North Korea, the slaughter of American boys would increase significantly. Indeed, we know now that the miscalculation about the Chinese intervention resulted in over 40,000 additional American deaths on the battlefield of North Korea. Of the 54,000 deaths in the war, 80% were after the United States crossed the 38th parallel.

On October 7, 1950, the United Nations General Assembly, with heavy United States lobbying, voted 47 to 5 to authorize the Unified Command to proceed with the "establishment of a unified independent and democratic Government in the sovereign state of Korea." The United Nations forces were told to "invade" North Korea and to proceed to the border with China at the Yalu River.

---

1. LaFeber, *America, Russia and the Cold War*, p. 116.
2. Stoessinger, *Crusaders and Pragmatists*, p. 86.
3. Ibid., p. 87-88.

In the fall of 1950, General MacArthur's usual military brilliance began to escape him. His self-confidence turned into arrogance, his caution became recklessness, his tradition of honor to constitutional principles failed; and MacArthur began walking in the shoes of Napoleon.

As the United Nations troops moved across the 38th parallel into North Korea, Mac-Arthur split his forces, sending one contingent along the west coast and the other along the east coast, leaving a weakened gap in the middle. The General's inadequate intelligence services informed him that there were only 40,000 Chinese troops massed north of the Yalu River, the boundary between Korea and China; he was confident that they would not be sent across the river. In October, there was light fighting between the United States and Chinese forces near the Yalu River, but China quickly withdrew to safe ground. With his troops split and his guard down, MacArthur walked into the Chinese trap. MacArthur pressed toward the Yalu River border, confident that the war would be over before Christmas. But on October 26, "to the accompaniment of fierce bugle calls, shrill whistles, and blasts of shepherd's horns," over 200,000 Chinese troops attacked the unwary American lines, inflicting enormous casualties.[1] It would take months before MacArthur could stabilize the battlefield and he would never regain his intellectual composure. The 80-year-old military hero would degenerate into a caricature of himself. In March 1951, General MacArthur issued a press release that violated government regulations by not having been cleared by superiors in the Truman administration, and more importantly, the statement contradicted Truman's overall international policy. Attempting to recoup his lost prestige from the fiasco of Chinese intervention, the General suggested that the war could be brought to a successful conclusion by a move in force against China itself. He suggested bombing Chinese bases north of the Yalu River, blockading the China coast with the American fleet and then using the remnants of Chiang Kai-shek's forces in a war against the communist giant. The possibility of using nuclear weapons was discussed. MacArthur wanted to have a showdown with China; to the General, the Korean War was just a sideshow.

After spending much of his life in the Pacific area, the General saw Asia as the focal point of US policy. To MacArthur, the future of mankind was in Asia, not "old Europe." His cries for an Asia First policy struck a responsive chord in the Republican Party and he became something of a hero to the Republican Right, which would later be captured by Senator Joseph McCarthy. This faction in the Republican Party disdained aid to and involvement with Europe, continuing the old Isolationist strain in the GOP. However, they argued that China and Asia must be defended against the communist menace at all costs. Some of this fascination with Asia was simply political opportunism, taking advantage of the fact that China had "fallen" to the communists under Truman's watch. But it was historically consistent with the Republican Party's interest in Asia that went back to the days of the Roosevelt-Dewey-Lodge-Mahan group of imperialists in 1898.

There was a certain rational consistency to much of what MacArthur was saying about the war in Korea. If the war did prove the diabolical nature of international communism, and if the war was fomented by China and Russia, why not have a show down? MacArthur, in his clarion call for an Armageddon, was taking Acheson and Truman at their word. The battle had to be fought someplace against the international menace. As General James Van Fleet com-

---

1. Ibid., p. 88.

mented: "Korea has been a blessing. There had to be a Korea either here or someplace in the world."[1] To MacArthur and his followers, Truman was just delaying the inevitable.

But MacArthur's policy disputes with President Truman were only part of the problem. For some reason at this stage in his life, MacArthur began to have dreams of grandeur and he lost his understanding of the United States Constitution. Perhaps because of his long absence from the United States and his sojourn in Japan where he became something of an American Emperor, or perhaps because the General was in his dotage and had lost touch with reality, he began toying with the idea of emerging as a "man on horseback." MacArthur confided to historian Samuel Eliot Morison that generals, when at war, should be allowed to act independently of the president in determining wartime strategy and tactics. MacArthur began expressing this philosophy to others, complaining that political leaders should not direct those who know how to fight. The General was placing himself above the elected President of the United States and outside the boundaries of the Constitution. Morison saw this as an ominous development in the aged hero: "He never crossed the Rubicon, to be sure, but his horse's front hoofs were in the water."[2]

These were dangerous times for the Constitution. In June President Truman discarded the war declaration clause of the Constitution when he took the US into the Korean conflict; then later that year, General MacArthur imagines a military dictatorship in wartime. The urgencies of a phantom attack by "international communism" was blinding America's leadership. Such is the Folly of War.

Another issue troubling General MacArthur was the belief that the American tradition of total victory was about to elude the nation. World War II, with its unconditional surrender terms and the complete subjugation of Japan, caused a skewed view to appear before the General's eyes. The United States had the military might to finish off its opponents, why not secure *victory*? "There is no substitute for victory", he lamented, suggesting that Truman was accepting defeat in Korea.

In the wars fought after the American Revolution and throughout the 19th century, the US had fought limited wars, accepting negotiated settlements. In its wars against Britain between 1760 and 1815, the United States never pursued a policy of annexing Canada, although some frontiersmen talked of the venture. And near mid-century in the Mexican War, the Polk administration tempered its ambition by not launching a campaign to conquer the whole of Mexico. In the 1840s, the United States compromised with Britain over the disputed border in the Oregon territory. During nearly 30 years of military forays in the Caribbean early in the 20th century, the United States never sought territorial annexation after the Canal Zone was taken in 1903. The notion that there should be no compromise, a sort of a "take no prisoners" approach, is associated more with American diplomacy during and after World War II in the age of Militant Idealism.

Over many months President Truman tolerated the obstreperous general; finally in May 1951, Truman's back-country temper flared as he spat: "I'll show that son of a bitch who's boss.

---

1. Wittner, *Cold War America*, p. 79.
2. Morison, *The Oxford History of the American People*, p. 1072.

Who does he think he is — God?"[1] On April 11, 1951, President Truman removed MacArthur from command of the "United Nations" forces.

The United Nations was a fledgling organization in 1950, and much of the support around the world for the American effort to stop "aggression" in Korea was conditioned on the hope of strengthening collective security actions. Nations that would not otherwise have given support to interfering in a Korean civil war did join this United States directed effort. But, unfortunately, as a result of the United States domination of the organization, the United Nations came to be perceived in the 1960s and after as a tool of the US. The United Nations was no longer seen as an impartial policeman of the world, but rather an organization bent to the will of the United States. It became a politicized body, and it remains so today. When the winds of change blew across the planet in the 1960s, the United Nations fell under the sway of Third World Nations. The noble idea of a collective security force able to thwart aggression and maintain the peace fell victim to the vicissitudes of national struggles. The United Nations never lived up to its promise, because the United States first, then other nations as well, used it for their own narrow purposes.

THE COSTS OF WAR

More than any other governmental endeavor, war changes our lives and our culture. War is expensive, destructive and disruptive. It distorts and even destroys personal, business and governmental plans. War sets in motion new trends and causes the abandonment of established ways. And most of all, war destroys human lives. In this "unexpected war," the United States lost 54,246 young men; 100,000 men came home wounded, disabled and disfigured. Totaling all deaths, civilian and military, there were over one million people who lost their lives in the struggle over Korea; 84% were civilians caught in the horror of modern warfare. Large swaths of the Korean landscape were obliterated; cities were leveled and factories and utilities disappeared. "At the end of the war, Korea lay in smoldering ruins, occupied by foreign armies [China and the United States], oppressed by rival dictatorships, and divided more hopelessly than ever before."[2] Much of the reconstruction costs were paid for, of course, by the US.

Napalm, a jellied explosive made of palm oil and acid, was devastating when brought in contact with human skin. Napalm had been used in World War II and now in Korea often with tragic consequences — on civilians. It is too easy to forget the human tragedies of these military conflicts. A journalist tells this poignant story of a scene in Korea:

> In front of us a curious figure was standing a little crouched, legs straddled, arms held out from his side. He had no eyes, and the whole of his body, nearly all of which was visible through tatters of burnt rags, was covered with a hard black crust speckled with yellow pus.... He had to stand because he was no longer covered with skin, but with a crust-like crackling which broke easily.[3]

---

1. Stoessinger, *Crusaders and Pragmatists*, p. 94.
2. Wittner, *Cold War America*, p. 79.
3. Nash, *The American People*, p. 868

In the midst of the conflict, the National Security Council produced a document known as NSC 68 that provided a *Militant Idealist* blueprint for future Cold War foreign policy. The document presented a wide-ranging analysis of world affairs, emphasizing the growth of the two super powers, the United States and the Soviet Union, and suggested that over the next few decades there would be an inevitable clash between the two. This clash would be unlike great power battles of early times, in that the Soviet Union represented the forces of evil in the world. The struggle was not simply about power, trade and influence, but was a moralistic clash between good and evil. Negotiations were worthless because the enemy had no concept of right and wrong, and one does not compromise with evil. Therefore, the American emphasis will move from the diplomats in the State Department to the military in the Pentagon. Negotiations were out; military conflict was in. The Soviet Union was motivated by a new fanaticism and it "seeks to impose its absolute authority...." upon the world. The document continued: "In the minds of the Soviet leaders, however, achievement of this design requires the dynamic extension of their authority and the ultimate elimination of any effective opposition to their authority.... To that end Soviet efforts are now directed toward the domination of the Eurasian landmass."[1] The only thing preventing communist success was US military might.

The Korean War cost over $54 billion, an immense amount considering that the defense budget at the start of the war had been only $14 billion. By 1952 the Defense Department budget had ballooned to over $50 billion annually and had risen from 5% of the total federal budget to 20%. By 1953 defense spending as a percentage of gross national product reached a peak for peacetime years. Income tax rates were raised to the top rate of 91% — defense was not cheap!

The number of air force groups was increased to 95 and new bases were acquired in Morocco, Libya and Saudi Arabia. The United States military forces were increased to the Cold War high of over 3 million men and to secure that number of recruits the draft was re-instituted. In other words, the government created a lottery system for all 18 year old males that determined how they would spend the next few years of their lives, and ultimately, whether they lived or died. Prior to the war, the US kept 80,000 troops on watch in Europe. After the invasion this was raised to over 250,000. Such is the price of a secure homeland. Such is the price for a war that was never to have been fought.

All this policy change was charting new ground for the United States. For a nation bred on the ideas of small government, low taxes, low government debt and ample room for personal freedom, it was a veritable revolution. Now the nation had a large standing army, reminiscent of European monarchies, with heavy taxation, a burgeoning federal debt and conscription. For the Republican Party it was a heavy blow, for the GOP deemed itself to be the repository of the traditional American values. Senator Robert Taft complained about Truman picking a fight with Joseph Stalin, but Taft's caution was overwhelmed by the voices of alarm and opportunism.

For the Democratic Party, the war and subsequent military build-up was a fatal blow to the party's Fair Deal plans to institute a national medical system. National medical systems were being created all over Europe as modern expensive, life-saving medicine was evolving. Because of the military emergency perceived by the national leaders, America has since limped along with a patch work health care system. Generally, employees receive medical coverage from their employers, a troublesome system for a nation that has the highest job migration rates

---

1. LaFeber, *America, Russia and the Cold War*, p. 96-97.

in the industrialized world and one of the world's highest business bankruptcy and merger rates. Too often this employer-based medical system is not available when it is needed. The price for defending the world against international communism was costly: it deprived the US of a first rate medical delivery system. So, while the US was providing a defense around the world and generously granting foreign aid to Germany, France and other war-racked nations, the Europeans were creating a national health care system. Of course, such contrasts were never drawn for public consideration, and even today the American public seems oblivious to the priorities chosen by the leaders of the early Cold War days and the implications for our daily lives. "Millions for defense, but not one cent for health care", seemed to be the motto of American leaders. It was a time when both political parties sold their souls on the altar of defense against a phantom — militant international communism.

THE FOLLY OF WAR

To paraphrase Army Chief of Staff General Omar Bradley, Truman was the wrong president, at the wrong war, with the wrong enemy. (Bradley's comment was expressed in opposition to a general war in Asia, for he said that would be "the wrong war, at the wrong place, at the wrong time, with the wrong enemy.") The century-old policy of the United States had been to avoid war on the Asian continent and, further, the United States military was going through a "downsizing" and was in no conditions to wage effective war in the Far East. The American Eighth Army in Japan was seriously under normal strength, as were most units. "In 1950 of the ten combat divisions in the United States Army, only one the 82nd Airborne, was considered combat-ready."[1] But the distinctive personality of Harry Truman turned this cautious foreign policy upside down. A reversal of policy was set in motion immediately when the President responded to Dean Acheson about news of the North Korean attack: "Dean, we've got to stop the sons of bitches." In this case, personality trumped policy, for Harry Truman's celebrated anger swept all before it.

The ancestral home of the Truman family was in the British north borderland, a formerly disputed area between England and Scotland. For centuries the English and Scottish kings battled in the borderland and "incessant violence shaped the border regions," says historian David Hackett Fischer in *Albion's Seed*. The culture of the people was "profoundly xenophobic," "suspicious of foreigners," and succeeded in developing individuals who were filled with "pride, stubborn independence and a warrior's courage." Fischer adds that they were "incapable of restraining their rage against anyone who stood in their way, and they felt it necessary to punish the wrongdoer himself by an act of retribution that restored order and justice in the world."[2]

The people of the borderlands migrated to the US in the 18th century and moved in great numbers into the backcountry, populating the hills of Appalachia from Pennsylvania to Georgia before moving on to the West. America's most famous president with ancestry from the

---

1. Sandler, *The Korean War*, p. 36.
2. David Hackett Fischer, *Albion's Seed: Four British Folkways in America* (New York: Oxford University Press, 1989), Borderlands To The Backcountry.

English-Scottish border regions was Andrew Jackson, who served in the presidency over one century before Truman. Jackson's forebears settled in Tennessee, while Truman's ancestor moved on to Missouri. Andrew Jackson became a folk hero in the US for his military exploits against Indians on the frontier and the British in the War of 1812. Old Hickory, as he was called fondly, carried a lead shot in his shoulder throughout his life as a result of one of the many duels in which he engaged. Like the people of the border, Jackson was easily angered, quick to take arms and determined in his ways.

Harry Truman was also noted for his quick temper, most notably when he took great exception to a music critic's complaints about his daughter's singing ability. The President threatened to punch the critic in the nose, blacken his eyes and wound him in the groin. Fortunately, dueling had fallen out of favor by the time Margaret Truman sang her song. At the end of World War II, Truman's personal sense of retribution reached new heights when he decided to drop two atom bombs on a prostrate Japan in the summer of 1945. Apparently his borderland anger and need for retribution overcame any sense of compassion for the 40,000 school children who were killed at Hiroshima and Nagasaki, not to speak of the 100,000 others who also died in the blasts.

Truman's parents were blunt, outspoken people who counseled young Harry to deal with recalcitrant opponents by "talking tough." Truman had a meager education, being the only president in the 20th century that did not attend college. Surrounded while growing up with other high-spirited people who lacked sophistication, Truman never mastered the smooth urbanity of men around him who had immersed themselves in higher education, acquiring restraint in thought and action. Truman always remained an earthy passionate man of the back-country.

The future president tells of an early experience he had in leading other men. Near the end of World War I, Truman was promoted to captain and lead a contingent of soldiers in the battles of St. Mihiel and the Meuse-Argonne campaigns:

> When I first took command of the battery, I called all the sergeants and corporals together. I told them I knew they had been making trouble for the previous commanders. I said, "I didn't come over here to get along with you. You've got to get along with me. And if I hear there are any of you who can't, speak up right now and I'll bust you right back ...." We got along.[1]

Harry Truman's pugnaciousness was his constant companion, even in the White House when dealing with world leaders and delicate issues. There were times when a more genteel style would have been more appropriate. But Harry Truman, true to the lessons of his boyhood, talked tough and hit 'em hard.

For months after his inauguration in 1945, President Truman, like his predecessors, gave support to the policy of abstaining from a war on the continent of Asia. Meetings were held; papers were prepared, discussed and read, the President approving all. But the meetings and papers were imaginary — unreal. The policy of non-involvement was good in theory, but not in practice. When the actual invasion took place, the temper of the President flamed — and new policy was set. The enemy forces were "sons of bitches" and "they" (international communists) were on the march. Truman would show them by talking tough and hitting them hard. His cul-

---

1. Stoessinger, *Crusaders and Pragmatists*, p. 55-56.

tural xenophobia, his sense of retribution, his visceral instincts took over, and America went to war. It is tragic that on such personal whims, nations go to war.

> The evidence is overwhelming that Truman, and no other person, committed the United States to intervene in Korea and that he made this decision suddenly and without reflection. The reason was not to save the Rhee regime, but to strike at a suddenly suspected Soviet conspiracy of conquest, with the same sort of blind instinct and fury that a cowboy strikes at a rattlesnake unexpectedly found curled at his feet.[1]

But how can it happen that an American president could so recklessly, so thoughtlessly, change established American policy? What happened to the famous caution of the Department of State, and where is the power of the Congress to intercede? Or of the Cabinet? Where are the other leaders of the Democratic Party? Or the opposition party?

As the historian Arthur Schlesinger points out in his book, *The Imperial Presidency*, the president now resembles an imperial potentate who has no rivals. An anecdote from the days of President Abraham Lincoln serves to illustrate the power of the president. Lincoln had introduced a controversial matter to the six members attending a cabinet meeting. Following a heated discussion in which Lincoln found no support, the vote was taken. Lincoln announced the voting tally: "One Aye, Six Nays, the Ayes have it!" The president has no rival in his cabinet or in his administration. He is the winner of a presidential election, whether or not his party wins control of the Congress. America has individualized elections, not party or team elections. The presidency is, therefore, an individual office, belonging to the man, not the party. If the president decides on war, war it is.

In Europe, on the other hand, Cabinet government has been shared governance. The Prime Minister is "first among equals;" others share in the decision. In the European system, the Prime Minister is elected as part of a team, not in a separate election as the American president, thus he generally does not stray far from the party's views. In addition, in the European system, there is a competing cabinet from the opposing party, often called a "shadow cabinet," which is active in presenting alternatives to executive action.

America has no competing cabinet or "president in waiting." The party "out of power" in the US is disorganized and leaderless. Concisely, there is no countervailing power to compete with the president, either within his administration or in the other party in the current American system. The Founding Fathers feared a system in which one man could make decisions for war. But now, a once modest presidential office has grown into an Imperial Presidency and along the way has destroyed the vital power given to Congress and to the people — the power to decide on matters of war and peace.

By June 1950, President Truman began to position himself and his party for the congressional elections in November. Truman had won an upset election in November 1948, but since then several international disasters had occurred. In August 1949, the Soviets had detonated their first atomic weapon, breaking the United States monopoly of weapons of mass destruction. And ominously, in December 1949, the communist Chinese under Mao Tse-tung had been victorious in the long Chinese civil war and Chiang Kai-shek had fled with the remnants of his Nationalist Army to the island of Formosa. The China Lobby, an element within the Republican Party, had already begun to blame the Truman administration for "losing China."

---

1. Bevin Alexander, *Korea: The First War We Lost* (New York: Hippocene Books, 1986), p. 24.

Added to the shrill attacks from the GOP was the element around Sen. Joseph McCarthy, which was making stinging charges that the Truman administration was "soft on communism" both in the nation and abroad. Thus, domestic political consideration began to erode the carefully crafted foreign policy in Asia. Truman calculated that he could not afford to be blamed for losing both China and Korea. By coming to the defense of South Korea, President Truman was able to defuse the charges from the Republican Party. In the fall election of 1950, the Democrats lost five Senate seats and 29 House seats, but still retained control of both houses of Congress. One wonders what is the price in dead American soldiers for an electoral victory.

But as the United States lurched from one foreign crisis to another in the 20th century there was less and less opposition to a belligerent America foreign policy. As the Cold War fastened itself on the American people, the only groups opposing Truman were those who wanted MORE military and GREATER confrontations. Truman never had to worry about slowing down the rush to militarize. Republicans promised if they were elected they would hit the enemy harder. The problem was not simply that leaders were militarizing events for political purposes; the public — the chosen people — demanded it.

When the North Koreans attacked across the 38th parallel, Truman could have recognized it as the concluding chapter in a four year Korean civil war. It had all the earmarks of an indigenous struggle to unite the peninsula — a long unified history, a broken nation, and rival national leaders. Walter LaFeber asserts that Truman "was involving America not in a conflict against Stalin but in a Korean civil war that had long been waged between Rhee and Kim."[1] Instead the administration focused on the bogus international communist story. The public was told that "international communism" was on the march and, like Nazi Germany, had to be stopped. Historian David Fromkin comments in his book, *In the Time of the Americans*, "Yet inflamed by an act of communist aggression, Truman and his advisers forgot their prudence and their strategy. Maddened by the waving Red flag, they charged blindly at the wrong place: a spot chosen by the matador."[2]

Had American leaders foreseen the disaster of this hastily-planned war — the heavy casualties incurred, especially as a result of crossing the 38th parallel, the Aftershocks of war, and the deterioration of the United Nations authority — would they have counseled against American forces being deployed in Korea? So a national civil war was turned into an international incident, a nationalist battle became international communism on the move, a nation that had been partitioned by the Great Powers after World War II was now denied the satisfaction of determining its own fate. The alleged masterminds, Stalin and Mao Tse-tung, who ultimately brought China into the war, became the international bogeymen for the US. Cold Warriors in both camps were settling down for a long armed and dangerous struggle.

By mid-century the US had several decades of experience with its *Militant Idealist* foreign policy, and as can be seen in the Korean War episode, it continued to struggle with its new role of "world leader." As the Koreans saw it, twice since 1900 the US had "betrayed" Korea; once early in the century when the United States gave tacit approval to Japan's annexation of Korea, and then again after World War II when the United States sliced the nation in two, granting half to Russia. And the Americans were so disorganized that there had been no planning for the

---

1. LaFeber, *America, Russia and the Cold War*, p. 100.
2. Fromkin, *In The Time Of The Americans*, p. 515.

end of the war, no preparation for conversion to a domestic economy and governmental system. Gregory Henderson, a former United States Foreign Service officer and Korean scholar, sums up the tragedy of American involvement in Korea.

> No division of a nation in the present world is so astonishing in its origin as the division of Korea; none is so unrelated to condition or sentiments within the nation itself at the time the division was effected; none is to this day so unexplained; in none does blunder and planning oversight appear to have played so large a role. Finally, there is no division for which the US government bears so heavy a share of the responsibility as it bears for the division of Korea.[1]

Undoubtedly, the United States intervention saved Korea from being unified under the banner of the communist Kim Il Sung. A "victory" over the forces of aggression was intended to be an example to international communism that military tactics would not succeed. But such lessons were futile, for the United States had to fight these same battles against "communist aggression" time and time again — in Vietnam, in Cambodia, in Laos, in the Philippines, in Indonesia, across the Middle East, throughout Central America — for the next forty years. These were battles that the US could never stamp out, for presidents never understood that these were primarily indigenous revolutionary struggles, very much like the Korean civil war. Instead of looking to Moscow for the origins, the United States should have looked at the native people and their aspirations for national independence. Communism had become, for most Third World leaders, a useful protest movement, a convenient set of ideas for rallying natives against Western imperial masters. The communist movement was, for restive nations like Korea, at the minimum, an attention-getting device, and at most, a false god which, because of its own intellectual hollowness, was destined to collapse.

The United States continues to maintain troops in South Korea. Fifty years after the "great reversal" and the unhappiness of the Korean War, there remain 23,000 American troops guarding the ramparts against a debilitated, destitute, but heavily-armed North Korea. Will the American superpower remain on guard even after the patient dies, as is the case with NATO in Europe, where long after the disappearance of the communist Soviet Union, NATO is thriving and even expanding into Eastern Europe? One wonders what it will take to once again reverse the American policy, bring the troops home and write the closing chapter of that ill-considered, tragic war.

---

1. Oberdorfer, *The Two Korea's*, p. 7.

Chapter 11. The Vietnam War: The Great Tragedy

The Gulf of Tonkin Incident

The US destroyer *Maddox* does not claim the illustrious place in history as the battleship *Maine* from the Spanish-American War, or the *Lusitania* from World War I, and not even the destroyer *Greer* of pre-World War II fame. But the *Maddox* does stand alongside its more famous sisters in playing a significant role in an incident on the high seas that propelled the US into another tragic military conflict.

The *Maddox* left its port in Taiwan on July 27, 1964 heading into the Tonkin Gulf on a DeSoto patrol. The DeSoto patrols had been conducted sporadically since 1963 and were intended, in the words of Secretary of State Dean Rusk, "to gather information on North Vietnam coastal defenses that would be useful to the OPLAN 34A raids against the coast."[1] Because of this, the *Maddox* was more of a "spy ship" than a warship. Moreover, during this period of international tension, the United States Navy wanted to "show the flag" in the waters off the coast of North Vietnam. The *Maddox* had orders to go no closer than 8 miles off the Vietnamese coast and no closer than 4 miles off any Vietnamese islands. These orders were deliberately provocative as most Asian nations, including North Vietnam, claimed 12 miles off the coast as their national waters. Most Western nations, however, claimed only 3 miles. It is interesting to note that American orders to its destroyers patrolling off the coast of nearby communist China were to stay 15 miles off its coast, obviously clear of the disputed 12 mile limit. China's 12-mile limit was respected; North Vietnam's was not. The United States was looking for a fight.

For many months South Vietnamese raiders, with clandestine assistance from the CIA and the military, had been conducting raids against North Vietnamese facilities along the coast, knocking out radar sites, fuel storage facilities, utilities, roads and bridges. These raids, dubbed OPLAN 34A, were conducted at the instigation of the United States in order to "convince the

---

1. Edwin E. Moise, *Tonkin Gulf and the Escalation of the Vietnam War* (Chapel Hill, NC: The University of North Carolina Press, 1996), p 50.

DRV [Democratic Republic of Vietnam, or North Vietnam] leadership that its current support and direction of war in the Republic of Vietnam [South Vietnam] and its aggression in Laos should be reexamined and stopped."[1]

The *Maddox* reached the Gulf of Tonkin on July 31 and patrolled along the North Vietnamese coast on August 1 and August 2. The *Maddox* patrol coincided with an OPLAN 34A raid along that coast, thereby giving the impression that the *Maddox* was providing cover for the South Vietnamese raid. In fact, the South Vietnamese raiding vessels came within sight of the *Maddox* as they returned to their home base.

North Vietnam, stung by the coastal raids, sent three PT boats into the Gulf of Tonkin in search of the enemy raiders; on August 2 the *Maddox* radar picked up three North Vietnam PT boats closing rapidly on its stern. When the PT boats closed to within 6 miles, the *Maddox* began firing warning shots. As the "attacking" vessels continued their pursuit, the *Maddox* fired repeatedly, striking the advancing crafts just as they launched torpedoes at the *Maddox*. The torpedoes missed their target, but one of the North Vietnamese PT boats was damaged and four of its crew were killed by the *Maddox* fire. All three vessels turned for their home port with the *Maddox* in pursuit, which was broken off when American aircraft arrived. That was the extent of the Gulf of Tonkin incident on August 2. No Americans were killed or injured; one bullet hole was found in the *Maddox*.

Captain John Herrick of the *Maddox* suggested that the DeSoto patrols be suspended for a time, but, instead, the decision was made in Washington D.C. to reinforce the *Maddox* with another destroyer, the *Turner Joy*. The United States Navy did not want to give the appearance that the Seventh Fleet was driven from the Gulf by three PT boats; to that end the two destroyers were told to take up patrol "11 miles, repeat, 11 miles" off the coast of North Vietnam.[2] The White House was aware that North Vietnam claimed 12 miles off its coast as national waters, but an official of the United States said defiantly, "We do not admit this claim and the theory is to show this by penetrating to the extent of one mile."[3] The *Turner Joy* was a full-fledged warship and the United States Navy was looking for a fight. With another OPLAN 34A raid on August 3, the likelihood of a naval battle was great.

The night of August 4 was stormy in the Gulf of Tonkin; far out to sea the glare of star shells lit up the night and gunfire was heard. The Chinese military along the coast had seen and heard the signs of battle and asked the North Vietnamese whether they were fighting the Americans. The Vietnamese made the same inquiry of the Chinese; the answer in both cases was "No." The American destroyers had launched torpedoes and fired their guns at apparent attacking ships; but this second attack was a phantom! What actually happened that night now seems clear.

When in the dark of night on August 4, the two American destroyers had "detected" enemy crafts on radar and "spotted" enemy torpedoes swirling through the waters, they had responded vigorously. But Captain Herrick concluded shortly that "Freak weather effects and overeager sonar man may have accounted for many reports. No actual visual sightings by *Maddox*."[4] Commander James Stockdale (Ross Perot's Vice-presidential running mate in 1992),

---

1. Ibid., p. 5.
2. Ibid., p. 95.
3. Ibid.
4. Anthony O. Edmunds, *The War in Vietnam* (Westport, CT: Greenwood Press, 1998), p. 41.

pilot of a jet aircraft on the scene that night, said he saw no enemy crafts: "Not a one. No boats, no wakes, no ricochets [sic] off boats, no boat impacts, no torpedo wake — nothing but black sea and American firepower."[1]

But the Navy had hastily notified Washington D.C. that its vessels were under attack, presumably a repeat of the August 2 incident; the White House was ready and sprang immediately into action. Operation *Pierce Arrow* was the American response: sixty-four sorties from nearby aircraft carriers pounded North Vietnam that evening. Near midnight when the retaliatory attack was concluded, President Johnson appeared on American television to announce that "gunboats and certain supporting facilities in North Vietnam" had been attacked by American aircraft. A few days later a somber and better-informed Lyndon Johnson privately expressed disgust at the August 4 phantom attack: "Hell, those dumb, stupid sailors were just shooting at flying fish."[2] But the deed had been done: the US had attacked and killed North Vietnamese over a nonexistent attack on the Gulf of Tonkin. With that, the war began to escalate.

Although the Johnson administration always maintained that the President spoke on American television after the raids, it now appears that this is untrue. Johnson's speech was delivered at 11:36 p.m. and the first American plane did not reach its target over North Vietnam until 1:15 AM — all times EDT. The North Vietnam Foreign Ministry was monitoring American television and alerted local military commanders that an attack was imminent. The Red Vietnamese shot down two planes, killing one pilot and capturing a second injured airman, who was held in captivity for over eight years. It cannot be determined with certainty whether the hasty, ill-advised television appearance of LBJ resulted in these tragedies, but what is certain is that the United States government was dishonest about this situation and rash in pursuing its propaganda campaign to the American public that evening.

In his midnight speech to the public, the President made the most of his opportunity. Johnson's hyperbole against the communists resembled Franklin Roosevelt's harsh and reckless verbal attacks on Germany in 1941 and Truman's exaggerated charges in the Greek crisis and the Korean War. Johnson's report to the nation also distorted the events. It was classic Militant Idealism: "Aggression by terror against peaceful villages of South Vietnam has now been joined by open aggression on the high seas against the United States of America.... We Americans know — although others appear to forget — the risk of spreading conflict. We still seek no wider war."[3]

On August 6, in testimony before Congress, Secretary of Defense Robert McNamara denied that there was any connection between the Saigon raids on North Vietnam and the destroyer's mission: "Our Navy played absolutely no part in, was not associated with, was not aware of, any South Vietnam actions, if there were any."[4]

Prompted by the North Vietnamese attacks on United States ships, on August 7, Congress approved by an overwhelming vote (416-0 in the House and 88-2 in the Senate) the Gulf of

1. Thomas Paterson, J. Gary Clifford, Kenneth Hagan, *American Foreign Relations: A History Since 1895* (Lexington, Kt.: D. C. Heath and Co., 1995), p. 410

2. Edmunds, *The War in Vietnam*, p 42.

3. Bruce Russett, *No Clear And Present Danger: A Skeptical View of U.S. Entry into World War II* (New York: Harper & Row, 1972), p. 81.

4. LaFeber, *America, Russia and the Cold War*, p. 240.

Tonkin Resolution granting the President power to respond to North Vietnam's alleged aggression. For several months administration officials had been looking for an incident that would justify a previously prepared war resolution. The fabricated incident in the Gulf of Tonkin suited Johnson's needs, as had the *Maine*, the *Lusitania*, and the *Greer* episodes for earlier presidents. The Gulf of Tonkin Resolution proclaimed:

> That the Congress approves and supports the determination of the President as Commander in Chief, to take all necessary measures to repel any armed attack against the forces of the United States and to prevent further aggression.[1]

There was only cursory debate on the resolution in Congress, but questions were raised as to whether the resolution was the equivalent of a declaration of war. A leader in the House of Representatives declared that the resolution was "definitely not an advance declaration of war,"[2] and Senator William Fulbright assured the Senate that President Johnson had no intention of using it as a declaration of war. White House papers show that executive officials believed that "the resolution will indeed permit selective use of force, but hostilities on a larger scale are not envisaged...."[3] But, Lyndon Johnson saw the matter as more than a mere reprisal. The President assumed it was "like grandma's nightshirt — it covered everything."[4] Later, when congressional opposition to the war grew, the President complained that members of Congress "gave us this authority...in August 1964, to do whatever may be necessary."[5] It turned out that Congress had given the President a "blank check" in Southeast Asia. Once granted, it could not easily be retrieved.

The presidential election was only three months away and both parties were jockeying for position. Senator Fulbright admitted that politics played a part in his efforts to secure passage of the Gulf of Tonkin Resolution, as he saw it as undermining the candidacy of the Republican nominee.[6] Senator Barry Goldwater was already talking about escalation of the war with an aggressive five-point program to militarize the area:

- Order Hanoi to stop its aggression in South Vietnam.
- American reconnaissance flights over North Vietnam to show the flag.
- Aerial interdiction of the Ho Chi Minh Trails leading into South Vietnam.
- Naval patrols in the Gulf of Tonkin showing the flag and blockading the North Vietnamese ports.
- Reconnaissance flights over the Vietnam-China border to threaten China.[7]

Countering Goldwater's belligerent military scheme, President Johnson posed as the moderate man of peace, pledging that "we are not about to send American boys nine or ten thousand miles away from home to do what Asian boys ought to be doing for themselves."[8] The United States would be the arsenal of democracy; the fighting — and dying — would be done by others. President Johnson was overwhelmingly elected president in November on a platform

---

1. Edmunds, *The War in Vietnam*, p. 138.
2. Moise, *Tonkin Gulf and the Escalation of the Vietnam War*, p 227.
3. Ibid.
4. Edmunds, *The War in Vietnam*, p. 43.
5. Moise, *Tonkin Gulf and the Escalation of the Vietnam War*, p 226.
6. J. William Fulbright, *The Arrogance of Power*, p. 52.
7. Richard J. Barnet, *The Roots of War*, p 313-314.
8. Edmunds, *The War in Vietnam War*, p. 43.

of peace and non-involvement. Presidents Wilson in 1916 and FDR in 1940 had also been elected on a peace platform, and in both cases within two years those presidents had led the nation into war. Johnson learned well from his predecessors how to manipulate the electorate. LBJ had pursued an aggressive policy in south East Asia, provoked a response from the enemy and launched a reprisal. When the Republicans urged a sharp military response, Johnson posed falsely as the war of peace.

The Johnson administration had already made plans for extensive air attacks on North Vietnam beginning in February 1965, and the secret DeSoto patrols were being intensified. Johnson was criticizing Goldwater for his hawkish statements, but at the same time LBJ planned even greater use of American air and sea power than Goldwater espoused. A story about the 1964 presidential election has often been repeated: a voter noted that the Democrats told him that if he voted for Goldwater, there would be war in Vietnam. He voted for Goldwater, and sure enough, there was war in Southeast Asia. Electoral politics had become the art of illusion.

The Johnson administration was eager to put the Gulf of Tonkin Resolution to work; within nine hours of its passage a message was sent to American Ambassador Maxwell Taylor in Saigon to make recommendations about increasing the US response to North Vietnamese activities. On August 5, the United States notified Thailand that it was considering injecting ground troops into that neutral nation. And most ominously, on August 14 the Johnson administration set January 1, 1965 as the date for the beginning of an air campaign against North Vietnam. Although the public was unaware of these behind the scene maneuvers by President Johnson, public opinion polls showed a wide approval for the President. Eighty-five percent supported his handling of the Gulf of Tonkin Incident, and acceptance of a military response against North Vietnam increased from 31% to 50%. Johnson's distortion of events had galvanized public opinion.

The Johnson administration presented a genuinely benign picture of the US destroyer's presence in the Gulf of Tonkin. To the public and to Congress, Johnson conveyed the following story:

- American destroyers were conducting a routine patrol in the international waters of the Gulf of Tonkin approximately thirty miles off the coast of North Vietnam, when they were wantonly and deliberately attacked by PT boats of the Democratic Republic of Vietnam on two separate occasions. The North Vietnamese boats initiated hostile action and the American ships merely returned fire in order to defend themselves. The United States government and the ships in the Gulf had absolutely no knowledge of any raid against North Vietnamese installations that may have been occurring at that time. This action by North Vietnam was a systematic and calculated attack on US ships and military personnel on the high seas.

However, a candid, informed, and honest observer of the incident would relate an entirely different story:

- The Johnson administration instigated the entire series of events that came to be known as the Gulf of Tonkin Incident. The coastal raids against North Vietnam (OPLAN 34A) were "Made in America," and the DeSoto patrols were intelligence gathering operations associated with the raids. (Secretary McNamara later acknowledged that he was untruthful before Congress on August 6 when he denied that the Navy had any knowledge of the raids against North Vietnam.) The *Maddox* and *Turner Joy* were *not* on routine patrols, but were part of offensive operations against the nation of North Vietnam. Further, the destroyers had been operating in the coastal waters of North Vietnam, having received orders to penetrate inside the 12-mile limit. After suffering an attack by Saigon raiders on the night of August 2, North Vietnam sent PT boats into its coastal waters to intercept the raiding party, and while investigating, was suddenly and for no reason attacked by the *Maddox*. The *Maddox* shot first! The North Vietnamese PT boats eventually fired back in self-defense. The alleged August 4 attack on the destroyers never happened; LBJ deliberately distorted the events. Prior to the August incidents, President Johnson had prepared a resolution asking Congress for authority to escalate the war against the North Vietnamese. The Gulf of Tonkin incident was a sinister ploy to create an incident justifying military action against North Vietnam and to inflame American public opinion. It served, also, to undermine the Republican Party on the eve of the November election.

In 1964 there were few that would have disputed the President's dishonest story of this incident. But a decade later, former Undersecretary of State George Ball, refuted the President's account:

> At that time there's no question that many of the people who were associated with the war...were looking for any excuse to initiate bombing [of North Vietnam].... [I]t was the "deSoto" patrols, the sending of a destroyer up the Gulf of Tonkin was primarily a provocation.... I think there was a feeling that if the destroyer got into some trouble, that would provide the provocation we needed.[1]

Today we know that George Ball was correct; the Johnson administration orchestrated the episode, stimulated the pubic emotions for war, unfairly undermined the candidacy of Republican Barry Goldwater and falsely accused North Vietnam of crimes on the high seas. The next month, September 1964, despairing of any negotiated settlement with the United States, North Vietnam began sending its first combat units into South Vietnam to assist the ongoing rebellion against the Saigon government. The Vietnam War had begun and there would be no turning back.

Ho Chi Minh and the View from Hanoi

The centuries-old dilemma of the Vietnamese people is captured in an ancient proverb: "Vietnam is too close to China, too far from heaven."[2] Vietnam hangs off the southern coast of China in the shape of a giant S-curve. Traditionally, Vietnam was divided into three regions:

- Tonkin in the north, dominated by the Red River valley and delta around the city of Hanoi and its port of Haiphong.
- Cochinchina in the south, situated on the Mekong River and delta near the principal city of Saigon, the most diverse area of Vietnam with its thousands of Chinese merchants.
- Annam, the narrow strip of coast in the center, a rebellious area of great poverty, yet boasting creative, artistic, and politically astute people.

---

1. Moise, *Tonkin Gulf and the Escalation of the Vietnam War*, p. 99-100.
2. James S. Olson and Randy Roberts, *Where The Domino Fell: America and Vietnam 1945-1990* (New York: St. Martin's Press, 1991), p. 2.

For two thousand years these areas were controlled or influenced by China, and being a tributary of China, the Vietnamese absorbed the Mandarin culture with its paternalistic elites, submissiveness of the people, high sense of morality and fair play and a belief that truth and reality are obtained only by deep personal study. The attributes of a democratic society with its open public debates, disputatious nature and frequent change of governmental leadership were foreign to Mandarin culture. While the people of Vietnam plotted and schemed to rid themselves of Chinese influence, they became a cultural reflection of their subjugator. The democratic ideas that America attempted to introduce there fell on stony ground.

During the 19th century, the Vietnamese faced a new conqueror as the French sought control of the area of Indochina — Vietnam, Laos, and Cambodia. By 1890, the French had completed their conquest and were busy "uplifting" and exploiting the people of Indochina. The French converted thousands of native souls to Catholicism and established numerous schools and colleges for the young. Roads, utilities and ports were expanded, creating jobs and income for the native population. It was during the early 20th century that over six hundred rubber plantations were established in Vietnam, mostly in the south. But during the process of westernizing, the natives often suffered. The French retained a monopoly of the profitable opium trade, as did the British in coastal areas of China proper, always making sure that native demand for the drug was supplied. The French considered rice to be a cash crop for export, frequently leaving peasants hungry from insufficient food. As wealthy landlords acquired land, peasants sank into near serfdom. Native schools and languages were replaced by French language and French schools. The French even forbade the use of the term Vietnam, instead decreeing that the area was to be known as French Indochina. Gradually two levels of society evolved: a small group of prosperous Vietnamese Catholic converts living off the new French economy and colonial administration, and at the bottom, a large group of Vietnamese Buddhist peasants and urban laborers who suffered. Vietnamese revolutionaries bitterly condemned French occupation: "The French treat our people like garbage.... The meek are made into slaves; the strong-minded are thrown into jail. The physically powerful are forced into the army, while the old and weak are left to die.... The common people see the blade and block [the guillotine] before them and are paralyzed with fear."[1] The French contemptuously referred to the Vietnamese as "les jaunes" — the yellows. For Americans twenty years later, they were "raggedy little bastards in black pajamas."[2]

For two thousand years the Vietnamese people had fought against conquerors and invaders. The Vietnamese experienced little relief when, during World War II, the Japanese supplanted the French. Chinese warlords, French missionaries and merchants, then Japanese armies had taken liberties with the people of Tonkin, Annam and Cochinchina. Late in World War II, when Japan lacked food because of the allied blockade, the Japanese military confiscated the Vietnamese rice crop and sent it to their own homeland. The result of this heartless action was a severe famine resulting in nearly two million deaths in Vietnam.

The alluring song of nationalism always whispered to the Vietnamese patriots, especially in the rebellious area of Annam in central Vietnam. This spirit of rebellion was never more evident than in the soul of Nguyen Sinh Cung, born in 1890 in Annam; Nguyen later in life

---

1. Ibid., p. 7,8.
2. Marvin Gettleman, ed., *Vietnam* (Greenwich, CT: Fawcett Publishing, 1965), p. 62-63.

became known as Ho Chi Minh. Young Ho was regaled at his father's knee with tales of French and Chinese treachery and Vietnamese heroism. Their home was a hotbed of activity against the French and their sycophant allies — Vietnamese Catholics and the Mandarin ruling class.

Ho Chi Minh at age five was running messages in the nationalist underground. After completing his schooling, he left the French province at age 22 and sailed the world, even spending some time working in New York City. And, at age 29 in 1919, he was in Paris when the Big Four allies met at Versailles to determine the shape of the post-war world. Believing the scintillating rhetoric of President Wilson's words about "national self-determination," the young Vietnamese nationalist sought a meeting with the Wilson to plead his case for the overthrow of French imperialism and self-determination for his people. Ho Chi Minh's Eight Point Plan for his nation included basic American ideas: no taxation without representation, free speech and press and fair and equitable treatment of all. Donning the best Western formal wear of the time for an interview with President Wilson, Ho Chi Minh waited in vain to plead his case. Wilson would not see him; there would be no new Vietnamese nation sponsored by the US.

Spurned by the West, Ho Chi Minh turned to the Soviet Union and Leninism for succor. Ho helped form a communist party for the Vietnamese and spent time in Moscow exploring the writings of Karl Marx and the Soviet leader Vladimir Lenin. While there, Ho became a convert to the Leninist notion that imperialism was a result of capitalist oppression. Lenin had "liberated" his own nation of Russia; Ho would use Lenin's thoughts to free Vietnam. Ho Chi Minh explains his fascination with Lenin: "I loved and admired Lenin because he was a great patriot who liberated his compatriots; until then I had read none of his books.... At first patriotism, not yet communism led me to have confidence in Lenin...."[1]

President Wilson's rejection in 1919 of Ho Chi Minh's appeal had thrown the Vietnamese revolutionary into the arms of the communist Lenin. With his hopes dashed by the West, Ho Chi Minh's revolutionary aspirations were validated by Marxist-Leninist theories. It is significant to note that Ho was first a nationalist, only later did he become a Marxist. There seems no reason to doubt Ho's eventual commitment to Marxist ideas, but there is every reason to believe that his dedication to Vietnamese nationalism superseded all. Ho and his compatriots would surely have resisted being incorporated into the Chinese or Russian orbits of power, just as he passionately resisted French and American domination.

Ho Chi Minh died in 1969, still a dedicated nationalist-communist. But, Ho never succumbed to the cult of personality, like Mao Tse-tung, nor did he use the savage power of the state to slaughter millions, as did Stalin. Ho never lost touch with the common people and wore the garb of the peasant throughout his life. In Vietnam, there were no opulent palaces, no sinister prisons, no mammoth staged parades and no strutting praetorian guards. Just a simple little Asian man who relentlessly pursued his father's dream — a nation of, by and for the Vietnamese people.

When World War II ended in 1945, the Vietnamese people anticipated that independence and self-government would soon bless their land. To this end in 1945, Ho formed the Viet Minh — the League for Vietnamese Independence. At that time the United States began assisting the Viet Minh to oust the Japanese and their French collaborators. President

---

1. Ibid., p. 31,32.

Roosevelt expressed disdain for the French occupiers: "France has had the country — thirty million inhabitants — for nearly one hundred years, and the people are worse off than they were at the beginning...The people of Indochina are entitled to something better than that."[1]

To thwart a French re-occupation, the Potsdam Conference of July 1945 decreed that Chinese forces would temporarily occupy the Tonkin area south to the 16th parallel, and the British would occupy the Cochinchina region. Emboldened by the removal of the French and Japanese, Ho Chi Minh declared the existence of the Democratic Republic of Vietnam in September 1945. And in honor of the tacit support provided by the Americans and recalling America's own revolutionary past, the Viet Minh announced their own declaration of independence: "We hold these truths that all men are created equal, that they are endowed by their Creator with certain unalienable Rights, among these are Life, Liberty and the pursuit of Happiness...."[2] Jefferson, Washington and Adams might have been impressed, but the World War II allies were not. Great Britain, China, France, and eventually the United States, all combined to subvert the Vietnamese independence effort.

The Viet Minh was the strongest native political force in Vietnam, but with 200,000 troops in the north, the Chinese quickly established a government in Hanoi that was compatible with their interests. In the south, the British gradually relinquished control to French Legionnaires and other adventurers who dreamed of the old days of empire. By the spring of 1946, French generals in the field, however, came to the realization that retaining control of Indochina was a thankless task. General Jacques Leclerc, head of the French forces in Vietnam, declared: "Fighting the Viet Minh will be like ridding a dog of its fleas. We can pick them, drown them, and poison them, but they will be back in a few days."[3]

To that end, the French and Vietnamese negotiated the French-Vietminh Accords in March, 1946, with France recognizing Vietnam as a "free state" within the French Union, much like the British Commonwealth of Nations. The French decree announced that:

> The French Government recognizes the Republic of Vietnam as a free state, having its Government, its Parliament, its army, and its finances, and forming part of the Indochinese Federation and the French Union.[4]

The only question was the status of Cochinchina in the south, whose fate was to be determined in a future election. But within weeks of forming this accord, the French government began to renege, declaring the Republic of Cochinchina to be an autonomous state within the French Union. The Viet Minh dream of a united independent Vietnam was subverted. This setback was more than sentimental; the Cochinchina region was rich in food, having the fertile Mekong River delta as a granary for the nation. Without the food of the south, the north would not survive as an economic unit. When support from the Soviet Union and China was not forthcoming, the Vietnamese were left to their own devices. Desperately, Ho turned to Washington D.C. but was rebuffed again. Ho declared despairingly: "We ...stand quite alone; we shall have to depend on ourselves."[5]

---

1. Olson and Roberts, *Where The Domino Fell*, p. 21.
2. Ibid., p. 20.
3. Ibid., p. 25
4. Gettleman, *Vietnam*, p. 61.
5. Ibid., p. 55.

The First Indochina War, between the French and the Vietnamese (Viet Minh), began in November 1946 and lasted until the spring of 1954, at which time the French Army was defeated at Dienbienphu in northern Vietnam. Ho Chi Minh resolutely declared to French Premier Georges Bidault: "If we must, we will fight. You will kill ten of our men, and we will kill one of yours. Yet, in the end, it is you who will tire."[1] The same determined words could have been said to American presidents a decade later.

In the early stages of the First Indochina War, the US pursued a policy of benign neu-trality, a residue of the Roosevelt pro-Viet Minh position, moderated with a concern for but-tressing France as a European ally. In 1950, however, the American sympathy for Ho Chi Minh was dramatically transformed as the Korean War erupted and the National Security Council issued its famous NSC 68. NSC 68 proclaimed that "the threat of Communist aggression against Indochina is only one phase of anticipated Communist plans to seize all of Southeast Asia."[2] By the summer of 1950, money and military equipment were flowing into Indochina to aid the French effort to re-capture their lost colony. By the end of the year, President Truman had sent $200 million to the French and by 1954, the year of the French defeat, over $1 billion had been sent to the imperial army of France in Vietnam. America was paying over 75% of the cost of the French imperial venture, ostensibly to fight international communism.

In 1945, American leaders had regarded the Viet Minh as a nationalist organization, fer-vently trying to create its own nation. By 1950, Washington was painting the North Vietnamese as ferocious communists, intent on spreading an evil, dangerous doctrine throughout Asia. Ho Chi Minh had been a nationalist during World War II; by 1950 Ho was the epitome of a com-munist agent of Moscow and Peking. In actuality, Ho and his dreams of national independence had not changed; it was the American perception of world events that had become distorted. The Truman administration, overwrought by the Korean War, had become obsessed with inter-national communism.

After eight years of the Indochinese War, the French were staggering against the ropes. Three generals and nearly 1500 officers had been killed in the eight years of fighting. Tens of thousand of French soldiers were either dead or missing, with over 100,000 injured. Most of Vietnam was under the control of the Viet Minh with the French bottled up in the large cities. With support at home crumbling, the French Army decided to make a stand at a remote valley in Tonkin near the Laotian border; Dienbienphu would be the final stand — for one side or the other. The French "trap" to snare the Viet Minh Army was set in a high mountain valley; an air-field was constructed to supply the French bastion. Unanticipated was the Viet Minh's ability to haul disassembled cannons up the mountains; the airfield was useless and the garrison was trapped under the hail of bombardment from the cannons placed in the hills overlooking the garrison. By March 1954, the French troops were doomed if aid was not provided. The United States was asked to come to the rescue.

President Eisenhower received divided counsel on the question of intervention. Vice-president Richard Nixon, Secretary of State John Foster Dulles and Admiral Arthur Radford, Chairman of the Joint Chiefs of Staff, led the hawks. Dulles and Radford talked of "massive retaliation" against the Viet Minh, and Vice-president Nixon spoke about not letting "the Com-

---

1. Olson and Roberts, *Where The Domino Fell*, p. 26.
2. Edmunds, *The War in Vietnam*, p. 38.

munists nibble us to death all over the world in little wars." Nixon held that there "is no reason why the French forces should not remain in Indochina and win."[1] However, when the White House sought advice from a select group of congressmen, it was advised to find some allies before undertaking such a venture. Dulles hastened to London to plead with the British Cabinet to join an allied invasion, but the British demurred.

President Eisenhower and Army Chief General Matthew Ridgeway — two old soldiers from World War II — understood that the French could not be saved with B-52's and massive retaliation; only ground troops could relieve the French dilemma. On March 31, Eisenhower announced that he "could conceive of no greater tragedy than for the United States to become involved in an all-out war in Indochina."[2] On May 7, 1954 the Vietnamese overran the French garrison at Dienbienphu. French colonial rule was over; the independence of Vietnam was assured. Or so thought Ho Chi Minh.

The Geneva Conference was convened in the summer of 1954 to determine the exact fate of Indochina. It was a complex conference: "Nine countries gathered at the conference and produced six unilateral declarations, three bilateral cease-fire agreements and one unsigned declaration."[3] The conference convened during the siege at Dienbienphu; tensions were high and patience was low among the delegates. The French and the Viet Minh found discussions difficult. The Viet Minh leaders ignored the French-created puppet Vietnam emperor, Bao Dai. Hearing rumors of Chinese intervention, Eisenhower geared up the military for an invasion of Indochina. Secretary of State Dulles refused to shake hands with China's Chou En-lai and snubbed nearly everyone, acting like "a Puritan in a house of ill repute." But with all the contentiousness, the conference did bring forth a settlement for Vietnam. The main ingredients were:

- Vietnam was to be temporarily divided at the 17th parallel in central Vietnam for purposes of a ceasefire; French troops were to withdraw to the south and Viet Minh forces to the north.
- National elections to unify the country were to be held within two years, by 1956.
- No new foreign troops were to be brought into the country — essentially, troop strength and weaponry were to be frozen at current levels.
- The three nations of Indochina were forbidden to join any military alliance.

The United States refused to sign the document, although its representative vowed to support it. Inasmuch as the United States was not a direct participant in the war, Dulles' curious personal disdain for communist leaders was not a serious impediment. But, something of the bizarre American circumstances was expressed later by Henry Kissinger, who said: "I know of no other instance in diplomatic history of a nation guaranteeing a settlement it has refused to sign and about which it has expressed such strong reservations."[4] The reservations Kissinger referred to were displayed when the United States formed the Southeast Asia Treaty Organization (SEATO) designed to present a military bulwark against further communist encroachment in Southeast Asia. Vietnam was forbidden by the Geneva Treaty from being a participant in SEATO, but Secretary Dulles and friends decreed that Vietnam was covered by the military clauses anyway.

---

1. Olson and Roberts, *Where The Domino Fell, p* 41.
2. Ibid., p. 42.
3. Kissinger, *Diplomacy*, p. 634.
4. Ibid., p. 636.

The Indochina War came to an end with the signing of the Geneva Treaty July 21, 1954. After eight bloody years of fighting, 95,000 French deaths and 300,000 Viet Minh deaths, peace broke out in the jungle land of Tonkin, Annam, and Cochinchina. Within two years, according to the Agreements, Vietnam would be a functioning independent nation. Had Ho Chi Minh finally succeeded?

NGO DINH DIEM AND THE VIEW FROM SAIGON

The Geneva Agreements established an independent and unified Vietnam, but Militant Idealists in the United States opposed this development believing that a communist nation would emerge. The ink was hardly dry on the Agreements before Secretary Dulles created SEATO to frustrate Vietnamese national unity. There was little that the United States could do about communist North Vietnam, but the Eisenhower administration was determined to prevent the Viet Minh from dominating the south.

And so, in the mid-1950s, for the first time the United States undertook an experiment in "nation building." Washington D.C. exported its ingenuity, resources, technology and ideology to the colonial land of South Vietnam. American-style democracy with its tumultuous elections would be infused into this Mandarin culture in the midst of a national civil war; an ample dose of the American military would be imposed to control the growing insurgency. American troops poured into the nation along with diplomats and political missionaries. The capital of the new nation would be Saigon; the US was accepting applications for a new South Vietnamese leader.

The "ideal" candidate was soon found; he was in exile from Vietnam, residing in a Catholic seminary in the United States. His name was Jean Baptiste Ngo Dinh Diem. A bipartisan "Vietnam Lobby" had grown up in the 1950s led by Cardinal Richard Spellman, Senator John Kennedy, Senator Lyndon Johnson and Supreme Court Justice William O. Douglas. These friends of Vietnam immediately put forth Ngo Dinh Diem's candidacy as Prime Minister under the French-tinged Emperor Bao Dai.

In a gesture of disdain for Ho Chi Minh and his Viet Minh insurgents, Diem had fled Vietnam and was living in exile in America since 1950. But the Ngo family had strong roots in Vietnamese history, having served briefly as Royalty centuries before, then later, as Mandarins in the Imperial court. Showing their adaptability to new circumstances, the Ngos converted to Catholicism when the French occupied Vietnam. Thus in the 20th century, the Ngos were known for being supplicants of the Chinese Mandarin class, the Catholic Jesuits and the French imperial administrators. All these attributes were despised by Ho Chi Minh and a majority of the Vietnamese peasantry. Ho and Diem had little in common; they would become bitter rivals in this divided land over the next ten years.

On July 7, 1954, with the blessing of the United States, Emperor Bao Dai appointed Ngo Dinh Diem Prime Minister of the new state of South Vietnam. Diem was asked to be the "George Washington" of Vietnam, but his personality was singularly unsuited for such a task, as he followed a strict monkish regime each day, scrupulously avoiding contact with others. Rising before dawn for prayer, Diem underwent a daily physical examination, spent ample time in solitary study and conducted occasional afternoon interviews, some running for hours as he delivered the "mandate from heaven" in long monologues to visitors. Diem found it impossible to engage in the give and take of Western democracy. His job, as he saw it, was to deliver edicts, much like tenth century Popes. His workdays ran 14-15 hours, and often he fell asleep in his sparsely furnished bedroom while reading arcane documents. True to the ethic of the Mandarin, Diem sought insight into virtue by prolonged and persistent solitary study.

In many ways Diem was a stranger in the land. The Vietnam Lobby had selected him because he was a confirmed anti-communist and devout Catholic. Yet Vietnam was a land of Buddhists; of the 15 million people living in South Vietnam, ten million were Buddhists, but only one and a half million practiced Catholicism. Diem appointed Catholics to lead the Army and to staff government jobs. His inner circle was composed of his own Catholic extended family; his brother, Ngo Dinh Nhu, was his assistant and other brothers filled critical governmental posts. Besieged all around by enemies, Diem used the Army as his personal bodyguard, rather than an instrument for preserving the new nation. Hoping to bolster the Catholic population of Cochinchina, the word went out to Catholics in North Vietnam that they would be safer in the South; rumors spread that the Virgin Mary was alive in Saigon! Some 600,000 Catholics made the trek southward in the mid-1950s, giving Diem a small army of supporters who were settled strategically in lands belonging to groups whose support for Diem was suspect.

South Vietnam was a diverse land with numerous ethnic and religious groups, presenting an intractable dilemma for a resolute Mandarin and dogmatic Catholic. For a consummate western politician, forming a nation out of the polyglot of Cochinchina would have been difficult. For Diem it was impossible. Consider these disparate groups:

- Chinese living in and around Saigon numbered around one million. They were bitter foes of the communist Viet Minh, as the Chinese were dedicated capitalist traders, yet they fumed at the restrictions imposed on their life by the pious Diem Catholic clan. The Vietnamese Mafia, dominated by Chinese, had its own army to protect its investments in the vices — gambling, prostitution and drugs.
- Khmers, some half a million strong, were remnants of a Cambodian nation that once ruled the Mekong delta area.
- Montagnards, mountain people of the central highlands, despised all outsiders, but were forced to accept thousands of re-settled northern Catholics.
- Religious sects: These groups numbering in the millions presented a formidable opposition as they controlled strategic trade routes and each possessed a sizeable army.

During 1954 and 1955, the Catholic regime of Diem waged a civil war against the Saigon-based Chinese Mafia, resulting in the deaths of thousands of innocent civilians, but successfully rooting out the evils of the vice lords and the Mafia's army. Using CIA money, Diem bribed the leaders of the religious sects and chased away the remaining leadership. By the spring of 1956, Diem felt secure enough to overthrow the Emperor Bao Dai and to eject the small remaining French forces. After holding a rigged election in which he received 98% of the vote, Ngo Dinh Diem proclaimed the Republic of Vietnam in the South. The flawed election and Diem's autocratic ways should have raised concern in Washington, for as a veteran diplomat observed, "The campaign was conducted with such cynical disregard for decency and democratic principles that even the Viet Minh professed to be shocked."[1] However, all that American leaders saw was

---

1. Bernard Fall, *The Two Viet-Nams* (New York: Praeger, 1963), p. 257.

that their "nation building" project was working. And it was only costing $250 million a year to sustain Diem, his family of court followers and his Catholic army.

National unification elections, as required by the Geneva Agreements, were scheduled for summer 1956, and most unbiased observers expected that Ho Chi Minh and the Viet Minh would win. In his memoirs, President Eisenhower made the following candid observation: "I have never talked with a person knowledgeable in Indochina affairs who did not agree that had elections been held at the time of the fighting, possibly 80% of the population would have voted for the communist, Ho Chi Minh, as their leader."[1]

When in 1956, Secretary of State Dulles proclaimed that the US had no responsibility for abiding by the election requirements of the Geneva Agreements as it was not a signatory nation, the duplicity of the US was revealed. The Geneva Agreements were part of international law, as are all treaties entered into by sovereign nations. All non-signatory nations have a legal obligation to give them respect, and certainly not to subvert them. The hypocritical stance of the United States is exposed in this episode: America poses as a "law-abiding" nation — except when its purpose is served by disregarding the law.

America eventually abandoning the pretense of supporting democracy and self-government for the South Vietnamese, and instead assisting Diem in thwarting national elections. Pursuing the goal of stopping international communism was the American lodestar, and its was pursued without regard to the rule of law or concern for its allies. Secretary Dulles was completely candid when he complained of the diplomatic isolation of the United States on this issue: "We are confronted by an unfortunate fact — most of the countries of the world do not share our view that communist control of any government anywhere is in itself a danger and a threat."[2]

American violations of the 1954 Geneva Agreements were numerous and severe. They included the following:

- Refusal to conduct national unification elections by 1956.
- Subverting the stipulation that the two zones of Vietnam were to be "temporary" zones. (The exact relevant clause specified that the two zones were "provisional and should not in any way be interpreted as consisting a political or territorial boundary.")[3]
- Creating SEATO and including Vietnam as a corollary state, thereby violating the provision against military alliances.
- Violating the treaty clause that limited the introduction of new military troops and weapons.

Once again, Ho Chi Minh and the Vietnamese were denied their goal of Vietnam unity and had to "go it alone," this time against the Saigon government of Diem, assisted by the United States. Initially the novel effort at "nation building" went well. A formidable national leader, Ngo Dinh Diem, was in power and had established a Catholic base of power. The US was shoveling money into Saigon, and the CIA and the military were providing advisors and equipment. In the North, Ho Chi Minh was fuming about Treaty violations, but the American public was content.

---

1. Wittner, *Cold War America*, p. 164.
2. LaFeber, *America, Russia and the Cold War*, p. 167.
3. Wittner, *Cold War America*, p. 163.

However, by 1958, through the dim mists of jungle life, signs of discontent could be seen; by the early 1960s, a full-scale civil war had erupted in South Vietnam. The first sign of any serious misstep was the Diem-American policy toward the peasants in the villages. Emboldened by his early success, Diem set about to control village life. But, such an effort ran counter to Vietnamese history, as even in the time of the Viet Empire the royals accepted their limits. "The empire stops at the village gate" was a saying of traditional Vietnam. Peasants had always elected village leaders, but Diem abolished that centuries-old practice and instead appointed village chiefs, usually Catholic allies. As Vietnam expert and author Bernard Fall has said: "When Diem ended the 400- to 500-year tradition of the democratic election of village chiefs...he made...probably his most crucial mistake." [1]

Villagers were stirred to revolt against this oppression, sometimes taking the extreme measure of killing Diem's appointees, thereby joining other rebels against Diem's government. The communist-dominated Viet Minh quickly saw their opportunity and joined the slaughter of village chiefs. In 1958, there were over 1000 village chiefs murdered — three a day, on average. By the early 1960s, thousands of Buddhists in Vietnamese villages were in open revolt against the Catholic, US-led Saigon government.

It was in this context that Saigon and Washington hatched the idea known as the Strategic Hamlet program. Because the emerging civil war was most evident in the villages and hardest to control there, it was decided that villagers would be moved into armed encampments — strategic hamlets — where, surrounded by barbed wire and Diem's military forces, the revolt could be quelled. By 1962, over 3,000 hamlets with 4 million residents had been established, and in the process villages that had existed for centuries were destroyed and ancestral lands abandoned.

Reinforcing this brutality to the rural people was a "peasant urbanization" program of forcibly removing them to urban settings, thereby taking away the "fodder" of the Viet Minh revolt. According to Harvard social scientist Samuel P. Huntington, this would elevate the peasantry to a "higher level" of economic development. The problem was, however, the peasants didn't want to go to a "higher level." And such a forced removal of people against their will was forbidden by the human rights principles established by the Nuremberg War Crimes Trials after World War II. People could not be herded around, Hitler-like and Stalin-like, against their will.

This peasant urbanization scheme is American do-goodism at its worst. One is reminded of the tale of the Boy Scout leader who advised his group they must do a good deed daily. Soon three Boy Scouts reported to their Scoutmaster that they had done their deed; they had helped an old lady across the street. When the Scoutmaster inquired why it took three boys to do the good deed, they replied that the old lady actually didn't want to go across the street, so they had to force her to go.

The peasant-Buddhist revolt deepened and eventually linked up with the Viet Minh rebels. Now, Diem had a tiger by the tail. The Mandarin elitism of Diem, reinforced by his indomitable personal and religious beliefs, prevented him from engaging in any compromise with the insurgents. And, his American benefactors were unwilling to back down from their hard-line anti-communism. There would be a military showdown in South Vietnam.

---

1. Bernard Fall, *Last Reflections On A War* (New York: Doubleday, 1967), p. 233,234

Indeed, the Kennedy administration seemed to relish a fight in the jungles of Vietnam or elsewhere in the Third World. President Kennedy's Secretary of State, Dean Rusk, was full of Wilsonian moral talk about the "gangster war...of terror and aggression,"[1] and John Kennedy had brought General Maxwell Taylor to the White House to launch a drive against the jungle guerrillas. Taylor had resigned from the Army command under President Eisenhower because Ike discouraged heavy defense spending and rejected adventurous talk of "counter-insurgency." With their jaunty Green Berets, the Kennedy men were ready to do battle in the old Imperial enclaves, in much the same way as the young, exuberant Teddy Roosevelt stirred American imagination over Cuba and the Philippines sixty years before. "Elite counterinsurgency forces — paratroopers and rangers — were the chosen agents, supported by electronic gadgetry and helicopter gunships. Cuba and Indochina, trouble spots inherited from the outgoing administration, were the battlefields they selected."[2] The Kennedy defense budget skyrocketed upward and the Eisenhower worries about a "military-industrial complex" faded from view.

Diem had militarized the scene with his brutal and successful repression of all opponents after 1954. Such successes emboldened him to use the Army against all opponents. A legislative election in 1959 saw the secret police operating the polling places, suppressing all media coverage of Diem's opponents and placing limits on the right to assemble. Diem was arresting thousands of opponents, incarcerating them and using torture to obtain confessions. Vietnamese nationalism was emerging and communism was halted, but freedom and democracy were smothered.

In December 1960, opponents of the Saigon government coalesced into the National Liberation Front (NLF), determined to overthrow, by any means, the government of Diem. Prime Minister Diem labeled them "Viet Cong," meaning Vietnamese Communists, but the group included many that were never Marxists and never part of the Viet Minh. The militant orientation of the group, in fact, stirred opposition in Hanoi, as Ho Chi Minh preferred that the conflict be resolved on the diplomatic level with conferences held and notes exchanged. Philippe Devillers, a French scholar and authority on Vietnamese history, describes the origins of the NLF:

> It was in such a climate of feeling that, in 1959, responsible elements of the Communist Resistance in Indochina came to the conclusion that they had to act, whether Hanoi wanted them to or not. They could no longer continue to stand by while their supporters were arrested, thrown in prison, and tortured, without giving some lead to the people in the struggle in which it was to be involved. Hanoi preferred diplomatic notes, but it was to find that its hand had been forced.[3]

Contrary to the fiction disseminated from Saigon and Washington, the military revolt against Diem was initiated by his own subjects — the people of South Vietnam. The French chronicler, Jean Lacouture, writes that the "Vietcong" movement was from the grass roots and was "impossible to avoid." The peasantry essentially told the guerrilla leadership: "If you do not enter the struggle we will turn away from you."[4] The Pentagon Papers, a confidential

---

1. Gettleman, *Vietnam*, p. 36.
2. Fromkin, *In The Time Of The Americans*, p. 6.
3. Gettleman, *Vietnam*, p. 226.
4. Jean Lacouture, *Vietnam: Between Two Truces* (New York: Random House, 1966), p. 176.

assessment of the situation in Vietnam prepared by the United States government, was forced to admit that:

> Enough evidence has now been accumulated to establish that peasant resentment against Diem was extensive and well founded. Moreover, it is clear that the dislike of the Diem government was coupled with resentment toward Americans. For many peasants the War of Resistance against French-Bao Dai rule never ended; France was merely replaced by the US...".[1]

The NLF was an immediate success. "In the space of two years the Liberation Front of the South gained control of the greater part of the countryside in Cochin China and also of a large zone between the Fourteenth and Seventeenth Parallels."[2] But, despite their accomplishments, the NLF laid low. The advice of General Giap, the military leader of the Viet Minh, was precise: "Establish yourself in the Central Highlands...the Americans and their puppet Diem will stay in the cities."[3] The guerrillas would be elusive and never confront the superior power of the American guns. Le Duan, the NLF founder, advised: "When the enemy masses we disperse. When the enemy passes we harass. When the enemy withdraws we advance. When the enemy disperses, we mass."[4]

As Diem began losing the civil war to the NLF, he created the fiction that South Vietnam was being invaded by North Vietnam; the National Liberation Front, it was said, represented an invading force of communists carrying weapons made in China and the Soviet Union. In 1961, the United States State Department caught the spirit of this canard when it issued its White Paper, "A Threat to Peace." The document asserted that there was an "elaborate program of subversion, terror and armed infiltration carried out under the direction of ...Hanoi," and "agents, military personnel, weapons, and supplies" were being sent into South Vietnam.[5]

These bogus assertions were for public consumption only: US government documents from the early 1960s show that the anti-Diem movement was an indigenous revolt. President Kennedy was informed in the fall of 1963 that the problems were caused by Diem's intractable polices, as "the basic elements of communist strength in South Vietnam remain indigenous South Vietnam grievances...."[6] The State Department Director of Intelligence conceded in 1964 that "by far the greater part of the Vietcong forces in South Vietnam are South Vietnamese, the preponderance of Vietcong weapons come not from Communist countries but from capture, purchase, and local manufacture."[7] The prestigious International Institute for Strategic Studies found that between 1965 and 1971 the United States sent $99 billion in aid to South Vietnam; the Soviet Union in the same period sent less than $2 billion to North Vietnam.[8] Other government sources admitted the same: "Throughout this time no one has ever found one Chinese rifle or one Soviet weapon used by the VC."[9] Undersecretary of State George Ball confessed in

---

1. William Griffen and John Marciano, *Lessons of the Vietnam War* (Kotawa, NJ.: Rowman and Allenheld, 1979), p. 71.
2. Gettleman, *Vietnam*, p. 229.
3. Olson and Roberts, *Where The Domino Fell*, p. 70.
4. Ibid., p. 71.
5. Griffen and Marciano, *Lessons of the Vietnam War*, p. 82.
6. Barnet, *The Roots of War*, p. 105.
7. LaFeber, *America, Russia and the Cold War*, p. 239.
8. John Lewis Gaddis, *Russia, the Soviet Union and the United States* (2nd. Ed.) (New York: McGraw-Hill Publishing Company, 1990), p. 263.
9. Barnet, *The Roots of War*, p. 275.

1965 that the anti-Diem guerrillas were "largely an indigenous movement" and that the conflict was "essentially a civil war within that country."[1] The military forces of the Saigon government were notorious for losing, or even selling weapons, most of which found their way into the hands of the Vietcong. Diem's Army posts were often dubbed "Vietcong PX's" due to their carelessness with American-provided weapons.

The end of the Diem regime was quick and bloody. The death march began May 8, 1963 when, for reason of state security, Diem forbade a parade honoring the Great Buddha's 2587th birthday in the Buddhist center of Hue. This was an especially grievous decision because only two weeks before in the same city of Hue in Annam, the Diem government had conducted massive parades honoring some Catholic appointments. Thousands of Buddhists demonstrated against the restrictions; predictably government troops fired into the crowd killing several — and the final revolt began. Rioting spread to other cities and into colleges and schools; Buddhist pagodas became staging grounds for dissidents and Army units invaded the sacred grounds. A particularly memorable scene occurred in June when an elderly Buddhist monk, Thich Quang Duc, sat cross-legged like a Buddha in a city thoroughfare, poured gasoline on himself, and lit a match. The horrid scene was caught on film and the world watched the self-emulation of a little Asian man, distraught about his own government's policies. Ngo Dinh Diem's sister-in-law, Madame Nhu, crassly referred to this heroic act as a "Buddhist barbecue."

By August, the Kennedy administration saw the handwriting on the wall and cabled Ambassador Henry Cabot Lodge in Saigon that, "There is no possibility that the war can be won under a Diem administration."[2] The word was passed to Buddhist military leaders that a coup d'état against Diem would be accepted by Washington. On Friday November 1, the generals struck; Diem and his brother, Ngo Dinh Nhu, were captured while hiding in a church in the suburbs of Saigon. Their lifeless bodies were turned over to the Buddhist generals later that day. The bloody work of assassins was in the air. Three weeks later, Friday, November 22, President John Kennedy traveled to Dallas for his own rendezvous with destiny.

LYNDON JOHNSON AND THE VIEW FROM AMERICA

United States foreign policy continued to be obsessed with its military prowess, inconsiderate of its allies, hypocritically idealistic and unable to discern its own limited national interests. Arrogance to others and deceitfulness to the nation remained its hallmark. Militant Idealism was becoming a permanent part of the landscape

At the height of the Vietnam War — 1965 to 1968 — the personality of President, Lyndon Baines Johnson carried this flawed policy to ridiculous extremes. The ego of Lyndon Johnson had to be satisfied; the Vietnam War became Lyndon's War. One day as the President prepared to board an Army helicopter, a soldier wanting to be helpful said, "This is your helicopter, sir." Johnson arrogantly retorted, "They are all my helicopters, son." The illustrious French monarch, Louis XIV, is said to have boasted, "I am the State." And so, "King Johnson" asserted that all military equipment was his and the Vietnam War was his also:

---

1. Ibid. p. 276.
2. Olson and Roberts, *Where The Domino Fell*, p. 103.

I am not going to lose Vietnam. I am not going to be the President who saw Southeast Asia go the way China went.[1]

I've had enough of this. This is just like the Alamo.[2]

I didn't just screw Ho Chi Minh; I cut his pecker off[3] [following the initial bombing of North Vietnam in 1964]

The Texan president saw his foreign policy in earthy, masculine, sexual tones:

If I left the woman I really loved, the Great Society, in order to get involved with that bitch of a war on the other side of the world, then I would lose everything at home. All my programs. All my hopes and all my dreams.[4]

If you let a bully come into your front yard one day, the next day he will be on your porch and the day after that he'll rape your wife in your own bed.[5]

His crudity knew no bounds. When journalists asked why he prevailed in Vietnam, LBJ "unzipped his fly, drew out his substantial organ, and declared, 'This is why.' "[6]

Johnson's towering ego eclipsed even those around him — the "Best and the Brightest" in David Halberstam's incisive phrase. The President's advisers, men of vast experience in government, academia and business, provided guidance, but they quickly learned that the game was to tell the President what he wanted to hear. Dissent was not a welcome companion in the councils of the White House. The President's press secretary testified that, "No White House assistant could stay in the President's graces for any considerable period without renouncing his own ego."[7] A "Caligula Syndrome" haunted the Executive Mansion as Lyndon Johnson overwhelmed all advisers. Chester Cooper, a member of the National Security Council staff, relates his unreal, dream-like experience in NSC meetings:

During the process I would frequently fall into a Walter Mitty-like fantasy: When my turn came, I would rise to my feet slowly, look around the room and then directly look at the President, and say very quietly and emphatically, 'Mr. President, gentlemen, I most definitely do *not* agree.' But I was removed from my trance when I heard the President's voice saying, 'Mr. Cooper, do you agree?' And out would come a 'Yes, Mr. President, I agree.' [8]

Advisers degenerated into sycophants as the Johnson ego swept all before it. Jack Valenti, an old Texas friend, suffered humiliation as the President used Valenti's lap as a footstool in the presence of dignitaries. The National Security Advisor, McGeorge Bundy, a Dean at Harvard University, was mortified when the President of the United States demanded that Bundy deliver papers to him in the toilet stall while he was emptying his bowels!! The President demanded slavish behavior from his assistants. When discussing a candidate for a position in the White House, LBJ explained the job requirements: "I want LOYALTY! I want him to kiss my ass in Macy's window at high noon and tell me it smells like roses. I want his pecker in my pocket."[9]

1. James D. Barber, *The Presidential Character* (Englewood Cliffs, NJ: Prentice-Hall, 1972), p. 51.
2. Ibid., p. 51-52.
3. David Halberstam, *The Best and the Brightest* (New York: Random House, 1969), p. 414.
4. Doris Kearns, *Lyndon Johnson and the American Dream* (New York: Holt, Rinehart and Winston, 1976), p. 263.
5. Kearns, *Lyndon Johnson and the American Dream*, p. 270.
6. Alterman, *When Presidents Lie*, p. 181.
7. Stoessinger, *Crusaders and Pragmatists*, p. 186.
8. Chester Cooper, *The Lost Crusade* (New York: Dodd, Mead, 1970), p. 223.
9. Halberstam, *The Best and the Brightest*, p. 434.

LBJ had manipulated, bribed, cajoled, persuaded, pressured and threatened political bosses and congressional colleagues in the United States Congress for years, and now he descended on Vietnam in the same pompous, overbearing manner. When bombs and bullets did not phase the Asian leaders, Johnson tried bribery in the form of money to turn the Mekong River system into an Asian Tennessee Valley Authority. President Johnson believed that American "foreign policy must always be an extension of our domestic policy," and he hoped to realize "the dream of the Great Society in the great area of Asia, not just here at home."[1] Ho Chi Minh thought the offer of money and technology sounded like Western imperialism and said "No Thanks." Johnson discovered, to his chagrin, that foreign policy was not just like domestic politics. The Indochinese leaders were unimpressed by either the American military or the American treasury. President Johnson tried first being Dr. Strangelove, then Mother Teresa; he found no success with either.

Johnson's Vietnam policy was driven by Texas-sized braggadocios rather than a deep knowledge of Vietnamese history and culture. "We are the number one nation and we are going to stay the number one nation,"[2] boasted the President, yet he had never read a book about Southeast Asia. By his own admission he had read just six books since he left college in 1930! He confessed that he remembered only one. None of his principal advisers had specific knowledge about Southeast Asia, displaying no awareness of the Vietnamese drive for national unity and independence, nor the Vietnamese traditional hatred and fear of the Chinese. American policy was framed exclusively in terms of the universal Cold War and the existence of a monolithic communist organization. Johnson and company were oblivious to the growing split between China and the Soviets, a schism that was manifest in their disagreement over how to deal with the Vietnam question.

The energizing force behind America's Vietnam policy was the "domino theory." President Eisenhower first used the phrase "domino theory" in April 1954 during a press conference. He likened the nations of Southeast Asia to a row of dominoes, and painted a picture of the first domino [Vietnam] being pushed over by the communists, with succeeding nations automatically falling behind the "bamboo curtain." Should Vietnam fall, the President warned, "the possible consequences of the loss are just incalculable to the free world...."[3]

Later, President Kennedy professed belief in the domino theory as he said, "if South Viet-Nam went, it would not only give them an improved geographic position for a guerrilla assault on Malay, but would also give the impression that the wave of the future in southeast Asia was China and the Communists...."[4] Kennedy could wax poetic about such matters — Vietnam was the "cornerstone of the Free World in Southeast Asia, the keystone to the arch, the finger in the dike...."[5] President Johnson saw even more dire consequences, for "an Asia so threatened by Communist domination would certainly imperil the security of the United States itself."[6] For the beleaguered Johnson, the domino theory became a cry of desperation as he grappled with

---

1. Fulbright, *The Arrogance of Power*, p. 53.
2. Barnet, *The Roots of War*, p. 3.
3. Dwight Eisenhower, "Falling Dominoes," in Jeffrey P. Kimball, *To Reason Why: The Debate About the Causes of U.S. Involvement in the Vietnam War*, p. 31.
4. John F. Kennedy, "Chinese Dominoes," in Jeffrey Kimball, *To Reason Why*, p. 37.
5. Goran Rystad, "Images of the Past," in Jeffrey Kimball, *To Reason Why*, p. 57.
6. Lyndon Johnson, "Still Fighting Against the Munich Analogy," in Jeffrey Kimball, *To Reason Why*, p. 43.

the anti-war movement: "We fight in Vietnam today so that we will not have to fight in San Francisco tomorrow."[1]

The domino theory was an amalgam of a sizzling new 20th century idea called "geopolitics," combined with a residue of the "lessons" of the Munich conference in 1938. Early in the 20th century a British geographer, Sir Halford Mackinder, advanced the idea that national power could be understood according to geographic space. Whichever nation controlled the "Heartland" would control the world. Mackinder suggested that the "Heartland" was an area stretching from Germany into Russia, with the "Rimlands" of the Americas being less important. American writers, such as Alfred Mahan, chose, in contrast, to emphasize the merits of acquiring crucial chokepoints on the seas — Panama, Hawaii, etc. Mahan's model was Great Britain and its Navy; Mackinder's was Germany, Russia and land forces. In the hands of opportunistic politicians and fear-obsessed leaders, geopolitics was a delightful method to galvanize the public into believing that the United States must be everywhere — or it would be nowhere.

This emphasis on geography was combined with the so-called "lessons" of Munich, which to American leaders meant no negotiations with an adversary. By the 1950s, the domino theory dictated to the United States that all "hot spots" anywhere on the globe were to be dealt with by the generals not the diplomats, as each nation was vital to American interests and each incident must be won. In the hot world of the Cold War, there was no room for error. Any successful aggression by the communists and any subversion that ended in a communist victory would diminish the realm of freedom. Freedom, a universal value, was indivisible.

The notion that geography was destiny had occurred to American leaders earlier. The proximity of Cuba to the shores of America had given importance to the Spanish-American War, as did the hope that the Philippine Islands would afford the new American imperialism an opportunity for the trade of China. In World War I and World War II, the fear of German presence on the fringes of the Atlantic gave urgency to the American war effort. When in 1947, President Truman announced his Truman Doctrine, he argued that allowing communists to win the Greek civil war would permit the enemy to take over three continents. The roots of the domino theory ran deep in America's hyperactive recent history. The fate of geography, in an exaggerated form, was always lurking in the halls of the White House.

Critics of the Vietnam War and the domino theory were rare. Only two members of Congress voted against the Gulf of Tonkin Resolution. Senator Wayne Morse condemned the resolution on Constitutional grounds:

> I believe that history will record that we have made a great mistake in subverting the Constitution of the United States...by means of this resolution. We are in affect giving the President... warmaking powers in the absence of a declaration of war. I believe that to be a historic mistake.[2] [Sen. Morse introduced a bill in 1966 to repeal the Gulf of Tonkin Resolution. It received five votes in the Senate.]

A few brave souls stood against the tidal wave of Cold War thinking. The diplomat Averill Harriman opined that "the United States should not stake its prestige in Vietnam." And another diplomat, Chester Bowles, thought that we were "headed full blast up a dead end street." The Asian scholar and United States Senator, Mike Mansfield, thought the venture could involve the "expenditure of lives and resources that would bear little relationship to the

---

1. Barnet, *The Roots of War*, p. 258.
2. Stoessinger, *Crusaders and Pragmatists*, p. 181.

interests of the United States."[1] And most significantly, General Douglas MacArthur, learning his lesson from the experience in Korea, reverted to his earlier aversion to Asian wars, and stated "we would be foolish to fight on the Asiatic continent and that the future of Southeast Asia should be determined at the diplomatic table."[2]

George Ball, the Undersecretary of State and a member of the inner circle advising LBJ, persistently registered his concern about US policy, but Dean Rusk, Robert McNamara, McGeorge Bundy, Maxwell Taylor, and most of all, Lyndon Johnson failed to take criticism seriously. The discussions in the Oval Office took on the form of ritual — war plans were broached, hawks would make their case, George Ball or someone would dissent, and all would be satisfied that a "debate" had occurred. The war plans would be approved.

"Rolling Thunder," the American bombing campaign against North Vietnam, was unleashed in February 1965, and with that event, the war became Lyndon's War. And, it would become America's longest military struggle, concluding only when US troops left the war-torn nation nearly ten years later. On the night of February 7, 1965, Viet Cong guerrilla forces attacked the American military base at Pleiku, killing seven Americans. Using the attack as a pretext for the bombing campaign that had been planned the previous year, General Curtis LeMay, the Air Force Chief of Staff, was soon sending over 200 sorties a day to reign terror on the North. At war's end the United States had dropped three times as much tonnage of bombs on Vietnam as it had on all the Axis powers during World War II. Carpet-bombing became *de rigueur* because precise targeting was impossible with small jungle targets. Ton after ton of explosives were dropped until Vietnam looked like a denuded moonscape, with over 20 million craters left on the ground. One of every thirty persons living in Indochina was killed, one in twelve were wounded, and one in five became homeless. America was bound and determined to preserve "freedom" in Southeast Asia. Lyndon Johnson had to destroy Vietnam in order to save it.

The bombing campaign had been launched for the purpose of forcing Ho Chi Minh and the communist guerrillas to stop committing aggression in the South. The thought was that if the US killed enough North Vietnamese peasants and urban workers, Ho would call off the Viet Cong guerrilla force, a tactic which assumed that Ho controlled the guerrilla movement in the South. It is unfortunate that every American school child had been taught that American bombing during World War II had brought the Axis powers to their knees and that the atom bomb on Hiroshima had ended that war in a day. These lessons suggested that victory could be achieved even without ground forces. American technology alone would defeat the foe. However, there were fallacies with this idea:

- *The United States Strategic Bombing Studies* of World War II did not prove that aerial bombardment was a panacea, although those studies did suggest that modern nations could be devastated from the air. The extensive terror bombing of Germany and Japan only marginally reduced their industrial output and actually stiffened the resolve of the people to fight. Undersecretary of State George Ball worked on those World War II studies and conveyed this message to the president — to no avail.
- As for the Hiroshima and Nagasaki lessons, it is not at all clear that the atom bombs forced a precipitous Japanese surrender. The Japanese leaders may have been more

---

1. Olson and Roberts, *Where The Domino Fell*, p. 96.
2. Ibid., p. 88.

distraught over the prospect of a Russian invasion into Korea and adjacent areas; in addition peace feelers had been floating around for months before the atomic attacks.

- As for stopping the flow of men and material from North Vietnam down the Ho Chi Minh Trails and into South Vietnam, the United States own records show that the Viet Cong movement was indigenous. US intelligence groups calculated that "80-90% of the estimated 17,000 VC had been locally recruited, and that there was little evidence that the VC relied on external supplies." Less than 5% of all VC weapons were communist made. The Pentagon Papers note that "the primary sources of Communist strength in South Vietnam are indigenous."[1] Bombing North Vietnam would have little affect on the civil war in the south.

Intelligence studies done for Walt Rostow of the National Security Council in 1964 told the same story; bombing the North would not diminish the revolt in the South and would eventually trap the United States into greater and greater commitments. After a year and a half of bombing, Secretary of Defense McNamara informed the president that "Rolling Thunder" had "no significant impact on the war in the South," and more troops sent to fight in the South would provide "no evidence" that the war is turning around.[2]

The European governments who were on the front line of the war against Russian communism remained unconvinced that a military struggle in the jungles of Southeast Asia was critical to the survival of the free world. In 1954, when Secretary of State John Foster Dulles beseeched Great Britain to join in the defense of French Indochina, Foreign Minister Anthony Eden declared the domino theory invalid and privately told friends that Dulles is the only case of a bull carrying around a china closet with him. A decade later, French President Charles DeGaulle advised that the United States "cannot win this war," and Prime Minister Harold Wilson of Britain told the Americans that it was "a dead end war."[3] These cautions fell on deaf ears: America is, after all, the exceptional nation. The French couldn't do it, but America could.

To protect its air bases, United States Army troops were sent into Vietnam in February 1965 — 3,500 to begin, then by summer over 100,000 more. As the killing intensified and more troops were sent in to justify the previous action, American involvement in Vietnam reached the "point of no return." By 1966, there were 400,000 United States troops at war in the jungles and plateaus of Indochina. The dominoes that were falling were American boys — first 3,500 to protect the air base, then 10,000 more to protect those sent to protect the air bases. Then more! And more! In 1966, the Joint Chiefs of Staff told the President that the war would take another 200,000 ground troops and five more years of heavy fighting. Johnson stood up, told the generals they were crazy, and walked out. In March 1968, with over 500,000 troops caught in the crossfire of the Vietnam civil war, Johnson announced that he was not a candidate for reelection.

The "Best and the Brightest" were constantly reassuring themselves that victory was around the corner: "We are making progress. Every quantitative measurement we have shows we're winning this war." The numbers were on the side of an American victory — the body counts, the tonnage of bombs, the rounds of ammunition, the number of troops, the planes, the defense budget, the American industrial production. But, in April 1975, when the North Viet-

---

1. Griffen and Marciano, *Lessons of the Vietnam War*, p. 115.
2. Wittner, *Cold War America*, p. 254.
3. Olson and Roberts, *Where The Domino Fell*, p. 136.

namese-Viet Cong Army occupied Saigon, the awful facts had to be recognized. The full force of the great American delusion was apparent for the world to see —

> Of course we're making progress. We're always making progress. It's just that sometimes the other side makes progress faster than we do.[1]

NIXON, DE-ESCALATION AND THE END OF THE WAR

The massive communist Tet Offensive fell on the sleeping cities of South Vietnam and the American military encampments in the middle of the night. It was January 31, 1968, and it was the beginning of the end of the American travail in Vietnam. The Vietcong guerrillas and the North Vietnamese military struck every town and military base in South Vietnam on Tet, the anniversary of the Vietnamese New Year, hoping to overthrow the Saigon government. Enemy troops even stormed into the US embassy in Saigon killing several Marines and causing havoc in numerous United States strongholds, but ultimately failed to bring down the South Vietnam government In the multi-day effort, the communist forces lost over 40,000 men; the combined South Vietnam and American losses were less than 4,000. By almost any measure, it was a stunning defeat for the communist forces. And yet, Tet began the concluding chapter of American involvement. A verbal exchange after the war between a US officer and a North Vietnam colonel is revealing:

> American — "You know, you never defeated us on the battlefield."
>
> Vietnamese — "That may be so, but it is also irrelevant."[2]

The war in Vietnam was more important to the Vietnamese than to Americans, despite the bravado of US leaders. To Ho Chi Minh and his countrymen, the outcome of the war determined their very existence, but if the US lost, it would live to fight another day, somewhere. For Kennedy and Johnson, the war was a "limited" venture; to Hanoi, it was a death struggle. These simple facts baffled American leaders, causing them to underestimate the willingness of the Vietnamese to accept deaths and hardships in order to defeat their new imperial opponents. For the communists, Tet was a brief foray on their quest for national unity; for America it exposed the false optimism emanating from Washington.

To the ordinary American watching film footage of the US embassy being invaded, the deceptive assertions of Washington finally sounded hollow. Walter Cronkite, the dean of American television journalists, while watching the Viet Cong surge into the embassy, is said to have gasped, "And I thought we were winning this damn war." The enemy was defeated on the field of battle, but for the war had been lost in the minds of the US citizenry. Following Tet, President Johnson convened a council of elder statesmen, nearly all of whom had been hawks. When the military chiefs asked for more troops and equipment, Dean Acheson, an architect of the Cold War policy, sniffed: "With all due respect, Mr. President, the Joint Chiefs don't know what they are talking about."[3] The hawks, now transformed to doves, advised the President to

---

1. Frances Fitzgerald, "How Does America Avoid Future Vietnams," in Harrison Salisbury, ed., *Vietnam Reconsidered: Lessons from a War* (New York: Harper & Row, 1984), p. 303.
2. Edmunds, *The War In Vietnam*, p. 49.

find a diplomatic solution. The lessons of Munich and the domino theory would have to be set aside, temporarily.

With anti-war protestors swirling across the country and a presidential election looming in November, Lyndon Johnson decided to surrender his own personal arms. On March 31, 1968, the President stunned the nation by announcing that he would not run for reelection. In November, the electorate turned to Richard Nixon to extract the nation from the Vietnam quagmire. The newly elected President had declared that he had a plan to end the war, but failed to divulge the nature of that plan to the electorate. Later, Nixon proclaimed he would "Vietnamize" the war, a program reminiscent of the Diem period from 1954-1963. President Nixon intended to replace US troops with Vietnamese forces, supplied with an abundance of American weapons. But in the midst of this effort, Nixon secretly began carpet-bombing the nominally neutral nation of Cambodia in an effort to destroy the rebel sanctuaries at the terminus of the Ho Chi Minh Trails. When a coup overthrew the neutralist leadership, President Nixon ordered an invasion of Cambodia. Vietnamization had given way to retribution on a neighboring nation. The resulting turmoil in Cambodia produced an immense slaughter of the natives by communist rulers, all memorialized in the book, *The Killing Fields*.

Richard Nixon was a complex man. He was an intense politician but a confirmed loner, truly a political chameleon. Who was the REAL Nixon? The leader of Militant Idealism, always ready to unleash bombs and bullets on the evil international communist menace? Or the prudent realist who extended the hand of friendship to China and talked warmly with Russians about disarmament. During the 1968 election, Nixon promised to wind down the war, but instead bombed and invaded Cambodia creating a wider war. He talked of letting Asian boys fight their own war, then kept the war going four more years. During that time, another 20,000 young American men died — fully 40% of all deaths during that long war occurred during the four years of the Nixon presidency.

He was candid with his aides about the war, telling them, "I've come to the conclusion that there is no way to win the war. But we can't say that, of course."[1] Always on the search for "peace with honor," he struggled to find either. Presenting himself as a man dedicated to disarmament, he supervised the greatest arms build-up in US history as arms sales to the world soared ten-fold since the mid-1960s.

As Nixon's search for "peace with honor" continued month after month, criticism pounded the President. Clark Clifford, a Washington insider, complained that our policies "once had validity but were now obsolete." Even Henry Kissinger opined that our reasons for involvement "were no longer as compelling...."[2] To the diplomat-scholar, George Kennan, Nixon was making withdrawal far too complicated. Kennan argued that "there is more respect to be won in the opinion of the world by a resolute and courageous liquidation of unsound policies than in the most stubborn pursuit of extravagant or unpromising objectives."[3]

National Security Adviser Henry Kissinger announced just before the presidential election in November 1972 that "peace was at hand. We believe that an agreement is within

3. Barnet, *The Roots of War*, p. 114.

1. LaFeber, *America, Russia and the Cold War*, p. 258.

2. John Mueller, "Reassessment of American Policy," in Harrison Salisbury, ed., *Vietnam Reconsidered: Lessons From A War*, p. 52.

3. Fulbright, *Arrogance of Power*, p. 17-18.

sight."[1] Then, oddly after the election, peace slipped from his grasp, raising the question of whether Kissinger engaged in cheap electioneering. Following his successful re-election, President Nixon resumed the attack on North Vietnam with the notorious month-long "Christmas bombing." North Vietnamese negotiator, Le Duc Tho called the raids "the most barbarous and inhuman ones ever seen in the history of warfare," and testified the bombers were "attacking indiscriminately, hospitals, schools, factories, and dwelling-houses — all considered military targets."[2] It was reminiscent of the terror bombing against the citizens of Germany and Japan during World War II. The bombing of North Vietnam, as the peace talks failed, is baffling, for it was President Thieu of South Vietnam who had rejected the peace terms — not Hanoi. It is fair to ask President Nixon — Why do you punish and kill the citizens of North Vietnam for the intransigence of the South Vietnamese government? Would it not have been more appropriate to remove President Thieu than to slaughter innocent men, women and children north of the 17th parallel?

Early in January 1973, President Nixon finally sent a "threat and a promise" to President Thieu, warning that the "Gravest consequences would ensue if [you]...reject the agreement," then Nixon promised "continued assistance in the post-settlement period...."[3] The merciful end to the long nightmare finally came on January 27, 1973. The Paris Peace Accords stipulated no formal winners and no losers in the nearly twenty years of armed conflict. Its terms were:

- A cessation of all military activities on the ground.
- The United States would immediately cease all naval and air bombardment of the North.
- American forces would be withdrawn within 60 days of the signing of the document.
- The US would refrain from introducing new weapons and would dismantle all military bases.
- All Vietnamese troops — both communist and South Vietnamese — would remain in place pending a decision of the Vietnamese government.

It is significant to note that these terms are nearly identical to the terms which were offered by the National Liberation Front (the Viet Cong) in 1969 — and rejected by the Nixon administration. Twenty thousand American deaths later, the document was accepted!

The reluctant South Vietnamese leadership was given numerous secret promises about America's future commitments — promises that went begging when Nixon resigned from office and when Congress refused to provide money for more South Vietnam misadventures. President Nguyen Van Thieu realized that without American troops, weapons, and money his government in Saigon could not survive. Twenty-eight months later, America's first effort at nation-building collapsed. Today, Saigon is named Ho Chi Minh City, and the ancient land of Ho Chi Minh is united at last.

---

1. Olson and Roberts, *Where The Domino Fell, p.* 252.
2. Larry Berman, *No Peace, No Honor: Nixon, Kissinger and Betrayal in Vietnam* (New York: The Free Press, 2001), p. 223.
3. Olson and Roberts, Where The Domino Fell, p. 253-254.

THE FOLLY OF WAR

Although the decisions about the Vietnam War were made in Hanoi, Saigon and Washington, the bleeding and dying were done in the jungles by "lesser" men. The letters of soldier written to their loved ones describe the horror and futility of battle:

> What I didn't like was when we burned the village down. The women and kids were crying and begging you not to burn them down. A lot of them stay inside and you have to drag them out. Ma, that's not good to see. I look back at what was once a village and the people crying, but as the sergeant told me, that's war. I guess he was right.[1]

> Our guys were falling everywhere.... We were pinned down, all day and all night. It was raining something pitiful.... So we just lay there...hearing our partners dying and crying for their mothers. It was total chaos.

> We were watching bullets kick dirt of the parapet.... I didn't know how badly I was hurt, only that I couldn't stand up.... the enemy had penetrated to within hand grenade range of my command post.... We were dry-mouthed and our bowels churned with fear, and still the enemy came in waves.[2]

During eight years of intense warfare (1965-1973), the United States suffered over 50,000 deaths — 550 Americans died every month for eight years. Even those surviving veterans found the war continued to hound them; their suicide rates and deaths rates were much higher than normal and between 20% and 30% were addicted to drugs. Every day for six years the United States spent $90 million keeping the war machine going. Because the enemy was hard to locate, chemicals were used to defoliate the jungle. Millions of gallons of herbicide — Agents Orange, White, Purple and Blue as they were disarmingly called — were dumped on forests, streams, crops, villages and people. One third of the hardwood forests and one half of the beautiful mangrove forests were destroyed. "Some 325,000 peasants by 1967 saw their crops destroyed through defoliation."[3] This indiscriminate use of toxic poisons produced havoc into the next generation — cancers, diabetes and birth defects claimed their children. Saddam Hussein's use of chemical weapons was modest compared to this. But then, apparently when your country is "doing good" that doesn't count against you.

Beginning with the terror bombing of World War II and culminating in Hiroshima and Nagasaki, the United States has used its weaponry with such abandon as to bear little relation to any useful purpose. After destroying the village of Ben Tre, an Army colonel justified the purge by saying, "We had to destroy it in order to save it." Thus, in the process of "saving" South Vietnam, we had to destroy it. American leaders — humane, rational men — must find a more productive response than to defoliate, incinerate, firebomb, atomize and kill.

It was the misfortune of the United States to have two presidents during this period — Johnson and Nixon — who were emotionally unstable. Both men displayed dark recesses of personality — deceit, dishonesty, conniving, duplicitous. Both men had matured in a climate of deception fostered by Franklin Roosevelt in the 1930s and 1940s. Both men thought first of how to win, how to be elected, how to defeat the enemy; neither seemed to have a strong sense of right and wrong, neither were guided by the fixed star of principle. Politics to each was a street

---

1. Griffen and Marciano, *Lessons of the Vietnam War*, p. 139.
2. Edmunds, *The War in Vietnam*, p. 54-56.
3. McDougall, *Promised Land, Crusader State*, p. 192.

fight with no holds barred. LBJ lied about the Gulf of Tonkin Incident, deceived the Congress about the subsequent resolution, concealed his plans for war and painted a picture of international communism on the march when, in fact, the struggle in Vietnam was an indigenous civil war. He and his minions talked optimistically about a "light at the end of the tunnel" when all that could be seen was a black hole. Nixon dissembled on his withdrawal plans, secretly spread the war into Cambodia, then fashioned a phony peace in January 1973 which, with new evidence, it now appears he had planned to subvert, allowing him to escalate the war.[1]

President Eisenhower offers an appealing contrast to these two volatile, unsteady leaders. As a general in World War II, Ike displayed prudence and good judgment, arguing against the unconditional surrender policy and the use of the atom bomb on Japan. Perhaps his German Mennonite ancestry with its streak of pacifism nurtured this prudence. And while Army Chief of Staff in the late 1940s, Ike initiated a policy of abstaining from war on the Asian continent, a policy abruptly trashed by Harry Truman in June 1950 as the Missourian took the US into the Korean civil war. Ike was elected on a promise of ending that war, and having accomplished that, "Eisenhower spent the rest of his term seeking to calm the American people on the issues of war and peace even as his predecessor had felt the need to stir them up."[2] And again, it was President Eisenhower who made the decision not to enter the Indochinese War to aid France in 1954. The situation in Southeast Asia deteriorated rapidly after he left office in 1961. Personality does make policy. The disaster we call the Vietnam War was caused by the choices of Presidents Kennedy, Johnson and Nixon.

It is true that Eisenhower had a certain fascination with "spooks and spies," allowing the CIA to run wild, overthrowing national leaders in Iran, Guatemala and elsewhere. And he did tolerate the bombasts of self-righteous Secretary of State John Foster Dulles, who was especially fond of moral condemnations of "atheistic communism," and inclined to hurl atomic thunderbolts at the Kremlin — massive retaliation was his favorite threat. But, Eisenhower often played "good cop and bad cop," using Dulles to frighten, while he soothed the angry spirits. It was Ike who warned solemnly about the "military-industrial complex" and cautioned about excessive defense spending. He had seen enough war to be wary of warmongers and foresaw a more peaceful future: "People want peace so much that some day government had better get out of the way and let them have it."[3]

Eisenhower was able to keep the Republican militarists under control, as did a successor president, Ronald Reagan in his own way. Said Ike to the flame-throwing GOP militants: "Look, I am tired...of just plain indictment of the Soviet regime. I think it would be wrong — in fact, asinine — for me to get up before the world now to make another one of those indictments.... What are we ready to do to improve the chances for peace?" Continuing, Eisenhower talked of the high costs of defense and the treadmill of the arms race. The President saw such spending as an unproductive drain on the economy: "Now there could be another road before us — the road of disarmament. What does this mean? It means for everybody in the world: bread, butter, clothes, home, hospital, schools — all the good and necessary things for decent living."[4]

---

1. Berman, *No Peace, No Honor*, chapter. 13.
2. Barnet, *The Roots of War*, p. 286.
3. Ibid., p. 242.
4. Ibid., p. 287.

It is not too much of a stretch of the imagination to envision an Eisenhower-like presidency in the 60s — and no Vietnam War.

Alternatives to the intransigent rule of Ngo Dinh Diem were available in the 1950s. It is interesting to note that the United States did accept a neutralist Laos in the early 1960s, one that was not aligned with either Cold War power. There were opportunities to neutralize South Vietnam at the time the French left in the mid-50s. One such prospect centered on Prince Buu Hoi, a respected cancer specialist and the cousin of Emperor Bao Dai. Prince Buu Hoi had the support of the religious sects and the Army; further he was a Buddhist and did not carry the difficult personal baggage of Diem or his links to Washington. But Buu Hoi was not a fervent anti-communist and strongly supported the Geneva Agreements, even favoring travel and trade across the 17th parallel and unification elections. After the fall of Diem in 1963, other Saigon politicians occasionally talked of neutralizing South Vietnam and dealing with the National Liberation Front. All such neutralist talk was rejected by Militant Idealists. Nation building by Washington would be on its own terms and no neutralists need apply.

Another diplomatic tactic was available had the American leaders been flexible of mind. The great enemy of Vietnam had always been China, which had just gone through a disruptive civil war. What better time to offer friendship and aid to the new nation of Vietnam, both North and South, and build a buffer at the Vietnam-China border against future Chinese attacks? Ho Chi Minh could have become the "Tito" of Southeast Asia, a leader who would put the lie to the notion of a communist monolith in Asia. In fact, we know that Hanoi was never a puppet of Peking or Moscow; Russia sent little aid to Hanoi until 1965 when LBJ escalated the war, and Moscow failed to grant diplomatic recognition to North Vietnam until 1950, five years after its inception. "[T]he likelihood in view of past history that a Vietnam united under the Communists would be more apt to serve as an impediment than an aid to Chinese expansion was never considered by US experts."[1] The Militant Idealism of America would not allow dealing with "evil;" there would be no deal with Hanoi.

It had become nearly impossible for American leaders to engage in diplomatic negotiations and compromise. The lessons of Munich — the failed compromise over Czechoslovakia — overwhelmed their better judgment. The "lessons of history" are always a tempting treat for the mind and Mark Twain expressed his concern about the wrong lessons from history:

> We should be careful to get out of an experience only the wisdom that is in it — and stop there; lest we be like the cat that sits down on a hot stove-lid. She will never sit down on a hot stove- lid again — and that is well; but also she will never sit down on a cold one anymore.[2]

The half loaf in Vietnam was not enough; all compromises were shunted aside. Like an incantation, the US beat the drums of war: "aggression was occurring" — "communism was on the march" — "the responsibilities of power" — "doing good for others." America had to have it exactly its way. In the end, America's all or nothing policy failed. And over 50,000 of its sons were in jungle graves and thousands of others came home with limbs blown off and brains racked with drugs.

The domino theory became, like the Ten Commandments, something to obey but never to question or to fully understand. More incantations! American leaders could never explain

---

1. Goran Rystad, "Images of the Past," in Jeffrey Kimball, ed., *To Reason Why*, p.70
2. Fulbright, *Arrogance of Power*, p. 32.

why Vietnam itself was vital to American interest, but in linking that nation in sequence to all other nations, Vietnam became a part of an unbroken and inviolate chain. Thus, logically, all nations were vital to the US; none of the dominoes could fall behind the communist curtains without great danger. the US must be everywhere, doing all things, for all people.

The ridiculous conclusion to this exaggerated notion was the issue of Quemoy and Matsu, two insignificant islands 5 miles off the coast of communist China. Quemoy, with a population of 50,000 and 68 square miles in size, is the largest island in a small group of islands in the Formosa Strait. In 1958, John Foster Dulles invoked the domino theory warning China that the US would defend the islands to its death. If the US lost these two "flyspecks" it would threaten America's position all across the Pacific Ocean and the Asian continent. To show that such silliness is a bipartisan affair, Nixon and Kennedy fell to arguing during the presidential debates in 1960 about which candidate would do a better job of defending Quemoy and Matsu. Five miles off the coast of China, and eight thousand miles from the shores of North America! Dots on the map! This isn't mature foreign policy; it is a childish sandbox dispute!

In an effort to justify the war in Vietnam, presidents resorted to inane psychobabble. Presidential speeches often became studies in psychology rather than international relations:

- the "psychological impact...on the countries of the world."
- to "avoid humiliation."
- to shore up "the confidence factor."
- to prevent "defeat and humiliation."
- to demonstrate "will and character."
- to avoid being seen as a "pitiful, helpless giant."
- to maintain "respect for the office of the President of the United States."
- to win an "honorable peace."[1]

The Vietnam War was not an aberration, but rather part of a line of foreign policy decisions reaching back over half a century. The wars against Spain, Germany and Japan — in 1898, 1917, 1941 — had seen American leaders misleading the public and deceiving themselves. With Asia First Republicans hounding them about losing China and then Korea, Democrat presidents plunged ever deeper in the Asian swamps. The Munich lessons blocked all attempts at compromise. The domino theory offered a near-scientific explanation for involvement. Our bases need protection. Soon, American credibility was on the line. The machismo of presidents is called into question. Eventually — as in all wars — the death of 200, then 1200, then 12,000 men in battle is justification enough. The validation is complete: We are there because boys are dying. We are there because we are there!

In 1962, over 100 American fighting men died in Vietnam, making a small down payment on the future tragedy there. Prompted by this early mindless bloodletting, Ambassador John K. Galbraith asked President John Kennedy a sharp question:

> Incidentally, who is the man in your administration who decides what countries are strategic? I would like to have his name and address and ask him what is so important about this real estate in the space age. What strength do we gain from alliance with an incompetent government and a people who are largely indifferent to their own salvation?[2]

---

1. Jonathan Schell, "Credibility and Limiter War," in Jeffrey Kimball, ed., *To Reason Why*, p. 122
2. Thomas G. Paterson, J Garry Clifford, and Kenneth J. Hagan, "JFK: A 'Can-Do' President," in Jeffrey Kimball, ed., *To Reason Why*, p. 185.

In his memoirs, *In Retrospect*, former Secretary of Defense Robert McNamara reveals the decision-making process used to decide on the war. McNamara confesses that there was little or no thought given to strategic goals and processes. "War planning" was all extemporaneous, sort of a fit of absentmindedness: "But we never carefully debated what US force would ultimately be required, what our chances of success would be, or what the political, military, financial, and human costs would be if we provided it. Indeed these basic questions went unexamined."[1]

America had entered all its wars in an emotional fit rather than with a cool, calculated plan. Never did McKinley, Wilson, FDR or Truman weigh costs and benefits in a rational process. But because the US appeared to "win" each of the previous wars, few observers had the courage to point out the flaws in its war making. Vietnam was different, only in that the US clearly lost that war, and with that the agony of re-evaluation began.

One group in America — those around President George W. Bush — has concluded that the "lessons of Vietnam" were that the US failed to assert its power quickly and massively. Complicating this misguided effort, they assert that the news media carped about every minor thing undermining the task. The cause in Vietnam was right, but the leaders in the White House chose the wrong path to military victory. This group, known generally as "neoconservatives," began pursuing military glory in Iraq in 2003.

Others, more prudent of mind and modest of spirit, perceive a different lesson from Vietnam. To this group, Vietnam was a foolish, horrid war; a war pursued by men who had learned false lessons at the feet of Woodrow Wilson, Franklin Roosevelt, and Harry Truman; lessons that failed to recognize the limits of American power, interests and public support. They acknowledge that the US does not have to defend Quemoy and Matsu, Saigon or Timbuktu. That there is greater power in America's example at home than in its bombs dropped on Hanoi or Baghdad.

Presidents during the Vietnam War told the nation that if the dominoes fell, the US would have to retreat to the shores of California. Saigon is now called Ho Chi Minh City; Vietnam is a communist nation. The dominoes fell — and America survived just fine. The presidents did not tell the truth! Sadly 54,000 young Americans died for nothing!

---

1. Moise, *Tonkin Gulf and the Escalation of the Vietnam War*, p.2.

CHAPTER 12. THE PERSIAN GULF WAR: PUNISHMENT OF AGGRESSION

IRAQ INVADES KUWAIT

At 2:00 AM, August 2, 1990, 1800 tanks of the Iraqi Army rumbled across the Iraq-Kuwait border heading southward towards Kuwait City sixty miles away, surprising the few motorists who were now sharing the six-lane superhighway with an invading army. By 7:00 AM all resistance in the city had disappeared, and at noon the occupation of the nation of 7450 square miles was complete; in a few hours the Iraqi blitzkrieg had done its deed, incurring 100 deaths on both sides. When the invasion began, the Emir of Kuwait, Sheik Jabir al-Ahmed al-Sabah, fled with his extended family in a fleet of Mercedes limousines into Saudi Arabia. The only casualty in the royal family was the Emir's brother who was killed defending the palace.

At the time of the invasion, the White House medical staff was attending to President George Bush. The President describes hearing the news of the invasion:

> At about 8:20 in the evening on Wednesday, August 1, 1990, a troubled Brent [Scowcroft, the National Security Advisor] appeared at the basement White House Medical Office with Richard Haass, the NSC's Middle East expert, in tow. I was sitting on the edge of an exam table in a T-shirt getting deep heat treatment to relieve my sore shoulder, the result of hitting a bucket's worth of golf balls earlier in the day. As I buttoned up my shirt, the three of us stepped out into the brightly-lit hall. "Mr. President," Brent said gravely, "it looks very bad. Iraq may be about to invade Kuwait." This was the first news I had heard confirming our worst fears.[1]

The United States issued the obligatory public condemnation and called for the withdrawal of all Iraqi forces. However, the Pentagon did not stir from its nighttime slumber. The Defense Department issued a statement saying that the situation was being watched but Secretary of Defense Dick Cheney had no plans to come to work. A Pentagon spokesman said tersely: "There is no decision for him to make. This ain't our show."[2]

---

1. George H. W. Bush and Brent Scowcroft, *A World Transformed* (New York: Alfred A. Knopf, 1998), p. 302.
2. Jean Edward Smith, *George Bush's War*, p. 17.

The United States had been warned by Arab leaders not to become involved in the crisis. On July 23, Saudi Arabia put its military forces on alert and told the United States that the Arabs were resolving the matter. The next day, July 24, King Hussein of Jordan emphasized caution, saying that "President [Saddam] Hussein [Iraq's President] was receptive and responsive," and Egypt's President Hosni Mubarak was "confident that accommodations can be worked out without delay." Arab leaders asked that the United States avoid "any provocative action that is liable to add fuel to the fire and render the easing of tensions more difficult."[1] It appeared that Jordan, Egypt and Saudi Arabia were managing this inter-Arab spat.

The initial reaction elsewhere in Washington D.C. was surprise mixed with caution. One staffer on the National Security Council quipped, "Hey, too bad about Kuwait, but it's just a gas station."[2] Admiral William Crowe, recently retired Chairman of the Joint Chiefs of Staff, commented on *Nightline* that the United States could control the air and sea in the Persian Gulf, "But the question of ground troops in the vast desert, that's another matter altogether."[3] Others in the military talked of putting "the economic screws to Iraq," but the idea of military action was not raised. Senator Sam Nunn, the influential senator from Georgia, said, "I don't think we have a military obligation at this moment."[4] Half way around the world in Siberia, Secretary of State James Baker was meeting with his Russian counterpart, Eduard Shevardnadze. They issued a joint statement condemning "the brutal and illegal invasion of Kuwait," but called only for an international arms boycott of Iraq.[5] On August 3, as he left for a conference in Colorado, President Bush responded to a journalist's question about the use of the United States military saying, "I am not contemplating such action."[6] The invasion was unfortunate, but apparently not a crisis that would cause one of America's 20th-century wars.

Tension between the two Arab neighbors was caused by a number of problems: a border conflict which originated when Great Britain created the two nations early in the 20th century, disputes over oil production quotas and pricing, and most urgently, Iraqi anger at Kuwait for not forgiving loan obligations incurred during the nightmare war that Iraq fought against Iran.

An OPEC meeting on July 10 had resulted in a tacit agreement to abide by production quotas, but Kuwait's unreliability in fulfilling such promises caused Iraqi concern. On July 17, President Hussein demanded that Kuwait return $2.4 billion in "stolen oil" and forgive the wartime debt. Complaining about his nation's financial troubles and declining oil revenues, Saddam exclaimed, "We have warned them [Kuwait]. It is a conspiracy to make us live in famine."[7] Over one hundred thousand Iraqi troops, including the famed Republican Guard, had massed at the Iraq-Kuwait border by late July.

Then, in the midst of the crisis, President Saddam Hussein summoned American Ambassador April Glaspie to his palace for a conference. Glaspie was an experienced diplomat having served in seven different Arab nations and had handled many crises before. Glaspie had been on the job in Iraq since 1987 but had never met the President. President Hussein rarely met with

---

1. Bush and Scowcroft, *A World Transformed*, p. 310.
2. Smith, *George Bush's War*, p. 17.
3. Ibid., p. 18.
4. Ibid.
5. Ibid.
6. Ibid., p. 17.
7. Sandra Mackey, *The Reckoning: Iraq and the Legacy of Saddam Hussein*, p. 279.

diplomats, so there was an air of mystery in this meeting, which took place on July 25, eight days before the eventual invasion of Kuwait. The discussion began with an extended monologue by Saddam about the tumultuous relationship over the years between the United States and Iraq, his hopes for improved relations, the Iraqi monetary debt of $40 billion as a result of the war with Iran from 1980-1988 and the Iraqi need for oil prices to be around $25 per barrel. Towards to end of the conversation this exchange took place:

> GLASPIE — I know you need funds. We understand that and our opinion is that you should have the opportunity to rebuild your country. But we have no opinion on the Arab-Arab conflicts, like your border disagreement with Kuwait. I was in the American Embassy in Kuwait during the late 60s [during another Iraq-Kuwait border conflict]. The instructions we had during this period were that we should express no opinion on this issue and that the issue is not associated with America. James Baker has directed our official spokesman to emphasize this instruction. We hope you can solve this problem using any suitable methods.... All that we hope is that these issues are solved quickly.... Frankly, we can see only that you have deployed massive troops in the south. Normally that would not be any of our business.... I received an instruction to ask you, in the spirit of friendship not in the spirit of confrontation, regarding your intentions.

> SADDAM — It is natural for you as a superpower to be concerned. But what we ask is not to express your concern in a way that would make an aggressor [Kuwait] believe that he is getting support for his aggression. We want to find a just solution which will give us our rights but not deprive others of their rights. But at the same time we want the others to know that our patience is running out....

During the meeting Saddam told Glaspie that he had just talked by telephone to President Mubarak who had called to assure him that there would be meetings between Kuwait and Iraq in Saudi Arabia on July 31 and August 1. "Look, the good news. President Mubarak told us that he's arranged a meeting between us and Kuwait," to which the Ambassador responded, "Congratulations."[1]

Two days after the meeting with Saddam, Ambassador Glaspie left for consultations in the United States. While stopping over in London to visit her mother, the Ambassador received news that Iraq had invaded Kuwait. Later she discovered that the July 31 meeting between Iraq and Kuwait had gone badly. When Saddam pressured the Kuwaitis for financial assistance, the Kuwaiti princes responded by saying that the Iraqis should do what they had done in the past when they needed money — "put its women on the street."[2] This was the ultimate insult to the Muslim leadership of Iraq who are especially sensitive about their women. Angered by the insulting haughtiness of the Kuwaitis, Saddam ordered an invasion of the tiny kingdom. King Hussein of Jordan, who was acting as an intermediary along with Mubarak, explained the collapse of discussions this way:

> They [Iraq] recalled with fury, for example, that after Iranian-backed terrorists had tried to assassinate the Emir [Kuwait's ruler] Iraq had blasted Iran with everything [they] had — ground-to-air missiles, the works. Iran had retaliated causing 1500 civilian casualties, but [now] Kuwait would not write off its debt, or end the border dispute, or stop stealing oil.[3]

---

1. *New York Times*, Sept 23, 1990. The entire conversation between Hussein and Glaspie can be found on various websites. The transcript comes from Baghdad and the US has not acknowledged or denied its authenticity.

2. Joseph Wilson, *The Politics of Truth* (New York: Carroll & Graf Publishers, 2004), p. 124.

3. Smith, *George Bush's War*, p. 22-23.

The ultimate intentions of Saddam Hussein in Kuwait were not clear. Some around President Bush saw the occupation as an attempt by Iraq to absorb the entire country permanently, then to launch an invasion of Saudi Arabia. However, Saddam told King Hussein that he was planning to withdraw his troops from Kuwait once order was restored in a few days, retaining only some disputed border area and an island. When he withdrew, retaining only the oil-rich Rumaila area and Bubiyan Island, he would appear to be generous. As the rich Kuwaitis were resented in the Arab world, there would be no tears shed for this "calculated dismemberment."

THE IRAQ-KUWAIT DISPUTES

Early in the 20th century, Great Britain in its imperial role had served as midwife to the birth of Iraq and Kuwait. The Turkish Ottoman Empire, which had exercised dominion over most of the Arabian area for several centuries, disintegrated after World War I and British military forces had subsequently poured into the region. Disregarding the wishes for independence of the Arab residents, the League of Nations granted to Britain supervision over the area at the head of the Persian Gulf with the authority to create nations. In 1922, British High Commissioner Sir Percy Cox traveled to the Persian Gulf area where he literally drew lines in the desert sand: POOF! There was Iraq, and POOF! And there was Kuwait. Creating nations in the Middle East and Africa was common practice in those days. Colonial offices in Paris and London kept large maps handy, along with rulers and sharp pencils. Seldom were the wishes of native inhabitants consulted.

During the rule of the Ottoman Turks, the area known as Kuwait had been administered from Basra, a city presently in southern Iraq. There had been no nation called Kuwait, but in 1922 the British created Kuwait out of "thin air," more correctly, out of desert sand. Bedouin traders had settled the area in the 18th century as drought forced struggling nomads toward the waters of the Persian Gulf. About the time that the American Benjamin Franklin was establishing a thriving business in Philadelphia, the al-Sabah family was asserting its influence over the area around the Kuwait Gulf. Kut, meaning a fortress near water, became a trading center, specializing in smuggling, trading in pearls and slaves and extracting money from imperial suitors — the British, the Russians, the Turks, or whoever would pay. The Kuwaitis acquired a reputation as "riverboat gamblers," even establishing a stock market in recent years in Kuwait City that operated somewhat like a casino. When oil was discovered in their land early in the century enriching the princes, their risk-taking became exaggerated.

When Britain drew lines in the sand creating the two nations, London had in mind protecting its relationship with the al-Sabah family, always more reliable than the fractious mixture of tribes, clans and religious groups in Iraq. To box in the turbulent Iraqi nation, the British essentially landlocked the troublesome Iraqis, providing only a 36 mile opening to the Persian Gulf. A swampy area known as Shatt al Arab at the delta of the Tigris and Euphrates Rivers leading into the Gulf provides the oil-rich Iraqis with its only harbor area. That waterway is also the shared boundary between Iraq and Iran, providing an additional source of difficulty. Blocking the entrance to the Shatt al Arab is Bubiyan Island, of course, conveniently delivered to Kuwait by the British in the 1920s. Baghdad repeatedly asked Kuwait to sell or lease Bubiyan Island and some of their coastline, but to no avail. Kuwait, a British protectorate, received the deep-water port at Kuwait City and 120 miles of coastline. This, then, is the conflicted border that the US would go to war to defend in 1991.

Further complicating the dispute was the problem of the fabulously rich Rumaila oil field that straddles the Kuwait-Iraq border. This immense field of oil stretches 50 miles across the desert sand, and oil there has been found as deep as 10,000 feet. Estimates are that it contains 30 billion barrels of oil, three times the amount in the Alaskan Prudhoe Bay field. Some 90% of the field lie in Iraqi territory, but modern drilling technology allows slant drilling; Iraq repeatedly accused Kuwait of drilling into the Iraqi side of Rumaila. Thus the Iraqi claim that Kuwait had "stolen" billion of dollars of oil.

Historically, Iraq contained three separate regions: the area around the cities of Mosul in the north, Baghdad in the center, and Basra, including Kuwait, in the south. All governments of Iraq have laid claim to the British protectorate of Kuwait, although occasionally Baghdad tacitly recognized that nation by signing treaties with the Kuwaitis. The Hashemite kings who occupied the Iraqi throne from the 1920s until the 1950s made efforts to correct the territorial injustice. General Qassim, the military governor who followed the Hashemite kings, and the Baath party of President Saddam Hussein also attempted to absorb Kuwait. Periodically Iraq invaded Kuwait — in the 1930s, the 1960s, the 1970s, and finally in 1990. In the earlier times, the British military came to Kuwait's assistance; then in 1991, the United States and its coalition partners. At the time of an invasion in 1961, General Qassim commented that "[t]here is no doubt that Kuwait is part of Iraq. This fact is attested by history and no good purpose is served by imperialism denying and distorting it."[1] British diplomat Sir Anthony Perkins admitted British self-interest in creating a compliant Kuwait and a nearly land-locked Iraq: "We [the British) protected our strategic interests rather successfully. But in doing so we created a situation where the people living there felt they had been wronged."[2]

As this Iraq-Kuwait dispute unfolded in the summer of 1990, the Bush administration never acknowledged the legitimacy of any Iraqi complaints. Secretary of State James Baker's lengthy memoir, *The Politics of Diplomacy*, and President Bush's book, *A World Transformed*, a collaboration with Brent Scowcroft, gives only scant coverage to the underlying issues that provoked the crisis. Bush and Scowcroft briefly mention the Rumaila oil fields and the conflict over oil pricing, but are dismissive of Saddam's complaints. Neither memoir provides adequate coverage of the questionable origins of Kuwait, the decades-long dispute between the two nations and the imperial role of Britain in the origins of the nations. To President Bush and Secretary Baker, Saddam was just another megalomaniacal dictator on the march, like Hitler. The United States — the avenging angel — was clearly justified in flying to the area to deliver heaven-sent justice.

The two Arab nations also had vastly different philosophies about oil production and pricing. Kuwait is a "boutique nation," in the colorful words of columnist George Will. Only 40% of the Kuwait population are native Arab; the remainder are imported workers, many from non-Arab lands. Its per capita income is $14,000 per year, several times that of Iraq. With a population of under 2 million and the third largest oil reserve in the world (20% of the world total), it provides immense monetary benefits to its subjects. Indeed, the annual income the Kuwaiti

---

1. Mackey, *The Reckoning*, p. 273.
2. Smith, *George Bush's War*, p. 28

government derives from its non-oil portfolio is greater than the oil profits generated each year. Thus, Kuwait has an interest in over-producing oil and depressing prices to protect its extensive stock, bond and property holdings from any inflationary influence on oil prices.

But low oil prices are financial suicide to the relatively poor nation of Iraq, who with 20 million people was financially strapped after the disastrous Iran-Iraq War. Oil prices had fallen below $15 a barrel; Saddam Hussein needed oil to be at $25 per barrel to balance his books. Iraq began the war against the Ayatollah Khomeini in 1980 with a budget surplus of $35 billion and ended the conflict eight years later with a deficit of $80-100 billion. Creditors — Japan, Russia, Germany — were circling. Most ignominiously, Iraq owed Kuwait $35 billion as a result of wartime loans, and Kuwait wanted its money back. In demanding debt repayment, Kuwait differed from Saudi Arabia and other Gulf States who had written off these debts as a goodwill investment. To the Saudis this was a reward to Iraq for having protected them from the savagery of Iran. But Kuwait, ever the gambler, asked Saddam to pay up. The Emir of Kuwait was overproducing oil and driving down the price at the same time as he put the arm on Saddam to pay his debts. Concerning this Kuwaiti intransigence and Saddam's foul mood, an American official commented, "When the lion is hungry, you don't tell it there is not going to be any dinner."[1]

Many people watching this struggle between the desperately hungry "lion" and the spoiled "rich kid" saw the "rich kid" as causing the problem. This perception motivated Arab leaders, such as King Hussein, President Mubarak and even King Faud of Saudi Arabia, to work toward a compromise settlement — an Arab solution. The Saudi ruler said simply, "It's all Kuwait's fault... they brought this on themselves."[2] On the eve of the July 31 meeting, King Hussein urged the Emir of Kuwait to become more compliant, but received no commitment. Jordan's King Hussein attempted to warn the United States of the impending military conflict and the troubles created when America shielded Kuwait. It seemed to many Arab leaders that Kuwait was not taking the Iraqi threats seriously. Hussein warned President Bush: "Listen, you must encourage the Kuwaitis to sit down with the Iraqis and the Saudis to resolve the border problems, and the oil overproduction, and any other problems that require negotiations."[3]

The Emir of Kuwait took Saddam's warnings in a light-hearted way, even mocking the Iraqi threat, beckoning Saddam to come down for the summer: "I invited Saddam to visit Kuwait since he had not done so for a long time." To the confident Emir, this "was just a summer cloud that would pass away."[4]

Saddam Hussein regarded these issues as legitimate international disputes requiring compromise, but the Kuwaitis, emboldened by their big brother, the US, refused to negotiate. President Bush took no ameliorative action, nor did he show any interest in the legitimacy of the disputes. To the American President, the adventure was pure melodrama; it was a "Bad guy" threatening a "Good guy," the same tired moralistic perspective used by every president in the 20th century to define their wars. What should have been regarded as a regional nuisance, was

1. Ibid., p. 23.
2. Ibid., p. 61.
3. Queen Noor, *Leap Of Faith: Memoirs of an unexpected life* (New York: Hyperion, 2003), p. 305.
4. Alberto Bin, Richard Hill, and Archer Jones, *Desert Storm: A Forgotten War* (Westport, CN: Praeger, 1998), p. 23

turned into an international threat. What should have been a problem for negotiations and compromise, became a nasty, brutish war. George Bush helped to make it so.

President Saddam Hussein was certainly playing to the millions of poor Arabs who despised the Kuwaitis. The "boutique nation" was able to provide a bounty to their subjects — no income tax, free education through the university, free medical care, subsidies for housing and transportation, family allowances for each child. And for the al-Sabah princes and families, there were luxurious homes on the French Riviera and elsewhere in posh spots around the world. Kuwait symbolized much of what the Arab world despised — a pampered pet of the imperial British, and now the arrogant Americans, using "Arab oil" for their own selfish purposes. The residents of Kuwait were living a luxurious life while most of the Arab world subsisted on $400 or $500 per person each year. Saddam aspired to be the champion of the Arab masses; Kuwait would be his foil.

President Bush failed to recognize that Kuwait was "hiding" behind the skirts of the United States, as it had done for so long with the British. A hint of this brazen Kuwait tactic could be seen in an incident during the Iraq-Iran War in the 1980s. To protect Kuwait oil exports, the United States reflagged Kuwaiti tankers with the American flag, thereby making any Iranian attack upon them a challenge to the United States. When the reflagging of eleven tankers was complete, a Kuwaiti prince commented nonchalantly that "these are now American vessels" and none of Kuwait's worry.[1] This attitude of dependence remained as Iraqi troops massed on their border in July 1990; the Kuwait foreign minister casually said "if the Iraqis attack us, we would call the Americans."[2]

The American attitude of coming to the defense of small nations has strong roots in the Cold War period. Reflexively, the United States responds to aggression anywhere and anytime, failing to recognize extenuating circumstances and legitimate grievances. By giving implicit guarantees to Kuwait, the United States emboldened the Emir, discouraged compromise and prompted him to dismiss Iraq's complaints. The Arab solution, which Egypt, Jordan and Saudi Arabia attempted to achieve, was made impossible by Kuwait's failure to take the threat seriously. With the US playing the "mother hen," the chicks never learned to fend for themselves. Kuwait could have been a leader in forming a Gulf alliance system to be used against Iran or Iraq. But, instead Kuwait let Americans take the lead, organize a defense and die for them. An old American saying seems appropriate here, adapted to the Muslim Middle East:

Allah helps those who help themselves.

"THIS WILL NOT STAND, THIS AGGRESSION AGAINST KUWAIT"

The Arab League, a regional organization of Arab nations, expressed disapproval of the illegal Iraqi invasion, but remained divided about any response, expressing dislike for the rich, arrogant Kuwaitis as well as the militaristic, brutal Iraqis. Even the Gulf Cooperation Council, composed of fellow Persian Gulf nations, seemed unconcerned about the matter, as an "Arab

---

1. Smith, *George Bush's War*, p. 31.
2. Ibid., p. 61.

solution" was being fashioned. President Bush was asked on Friday, August 3 to allow this peace process to take place without vitriol being leveled against the sensitive, mercurial President Hussein. Crammed into the front seat of a C-20 Gulf Stream with three others while flying to Colorado on Friday, two days after the invasion, President Bush telephoned Mubarak and King Hussein, receiving the following caution from the Egyptian President: "I really implore you, sir, to keep calm. We want to deal with this in an Arab context, to find a way that gives us a foundation for a better future.... George, give us two days to find a solution."[1] The excitable President agreed to take no actions for 48 hours, until Sunday afternoon, and to avoid doing or saying anything that would upset these delicate negotiations. Bush did, however, emphasize that he would not accept the permanent occupation of Kuwait.

But the President did not honor his word to refrain from rancorous comment. The next day in talks with British Prime Minister Margaret Thatcher, George Bush had his resolve stiffened, the Prime Minister lecturing him about international affairs. As a British official recalled, "The Prime Minister performed a successful backbone transplant."[2] Later that day, Saturday, Bush and Thatcher, playing their role as Militant Idealists, were spewing moralistic venom into the airways against the Iraqi dictator. Comments such as "naked aggression," and this action was an example of "the evil in human nature," and "an aggressor must never be allowed to get his way," created an atmosphere that made negotiating with the Iraqi leader difficult. Alighting from a helicopter on Sunday, August 5 after a trip to Camp David, the President, finding a memorable sound bite, said firmly, "This would not stand. This will not stand, this aggression against Kuwait."[3]

President Bush and the Prime Minister Thatcher were both children of World War II and they measured actions in the world arena by perceptions formed in dealing with the Axis: Tojo, Mussolini and Hitler. Bush had spent his young adult years as a fighter pilot of some distinction in the Pacific War against Japan. He was, at the time of the invasion of Kuwait, reading a book about World War II and his statements linking Saddam and Hitler reflected his strong conviction about how to deal with aggression. Some weeks later, he commented that in Iraq we face "Hitler revisited, a totalitarianism and brutality that is naked and unprecedented in modern times."[4] In Bush's memoirs, *The World Transformed*, the President discloses his insight into the aggression against Kuwait: "I knew what had happened in the 1930s when a weak and leaderless League of Nations had failed to stand up to the Japanese, Italian and German aggression."[5] And the Iron Lady of England, Margaret Thatcher, added her somber thoughts: "If Iraq wins no small state is safe. They won't stop here. They see a chance to take a major share of oil. It's got to be stopped. We must do everything possible."[6]

However, an "Arab solution" to this problem would have been more acceptable than an imposed remedy from either the United States or the United Nations, for it would have had the imprint of the Arab world rather than representatives of the old imperial nations. But the effort at a regional solution was deliberately torpedoed immediately by President Bush and Brent

1. Bush and Scowcroft, *A World Transformed*, p. 318.
2. Andrews, *For The President's Eyes Only*, p. 519.
3. Smith, *George Bush's War*, p. 89.
4. Steve Yetiv, *The Persian Gulf Crisis* (Westport, CT: Greenwood Press, 1997), p. 68.
5. Bush and Scowcroft, *A World Transformed*, p. 303.
6. Ibid., p. 319.

Scowcroft. In the Bush-Scowcroft book, *A World Transformed*, Scowcroft admits they did *not* want a solution achieved by the Arabs:

> I was wary of an "Arab solution," fearing that it might end up in a compromise with Saddam. It was a real dilemma. If we refused to give time for a possible Arab settlement, we could alienate our best friends when we needed them badly. But if we acquiesced, and the Arabs came out with a compromise, how could we reject it?[1]

This amazing statement reveals the hubris of the Bush administration. A legitimate regional dispute between two Arab states that was being dealt with by interested Arab nations was deliberately undermined by the United States because a peaceful compromise solution might be found (heaven forbid!) and the United States would not be in control. George Bush would rather have a war and kill a few thousand people than have a compromise among the involved parties. The long Cold War, during which the US ran everything, had created a monster — the American nation had run amuck.

When King Hussein of Jordan visited the President in Kennebunkport, Maine the American leadership again displayed its haughty behavior. Fuming about Saddam Hussein's grab of oil-rich Kuwait, Bush said to King Hussein: "I will not allow this little dictator to control 25 percent of the *civilized world's oil*."[2] Hussein's entourage remembered the biting, insulting words: "civilized world's oil." The message from the palatial compound of Kennebunkport was clear. President Bush's use of the phrase "civilized world" indicated that he thought there was no civilization except that of America and the West. As King Hussein and the Arabs knew, in fact, the oil does belong to the Arab states, not the United States and the "civilized world!"

(It may be of some significance that George Bush's personal and financial ties run through Kuwait. In the 1960s, Bush's Zapata Offshore Oil Company had drilled one of the first oil wells in the Persian Gulf just off the coast of Kuwait. Thus, there may have more to Bush's efforts than the Wilsonian moralizing that he trumpeted.[3])

By the weekend of August 4 and 5, George Bush had made his unilateral decision: the United States would reverse the conquest of Kuwait with armed might if necessary. Yet, congressional leaders had not been briefed, the National Security Council's decision-making process had not been utilized and the military had not been consulted. The United States had no formal defense treaty with Kuwait or any clear obligation to intervene. As with President Truman in the Korean War, this would be presidential war-making on the spur of the moment, and war-making with little thought as to its justification, how the task was to be done and with what consequences. To the chagrin of General Colin Powell, Bush's decision to go to war was not "carefully debated and formulated...."The President seemed to fall in love with his own words.[4] He was prepared and confident; he would act alone. It was "High Noon" on the deserts of the Middle East and as Colin Powell commented later: "the President had six-shooters and was blazing away."[5]

---

1. Ibid.
2. Queen Noor, *Leap Of Faith*, p. 310.
3. Smith, *George Bush's War*, p. 77.
4. Bob Woodward, *The Commanders* (New York: Simon and Schuster, 1991), p. 302.
5. Ibid., p. 261.

More than other war presidents, George Bush made this dispute into a personal duel; it seemed as though knights of old had donned their suits of armor, mounted their steeds and gone to jousting. This President saw all politics as personal. In bursts of frenetic activity, Bush sent flurries of notes to friends, arranged social events and developed a "Rolodex" type of presidency. Friends were massaged by the gregarious chief and adversaries were barraged with assaults. Historian Jean Edward Smith describes the Bush onslaught against Saddam:

> For George Bush, it was invariably first person singular. "I've had it"; "I am getting frustrated"; "Consider me provoked"; "I am not ruling out further action"; "I don't want to say what I will or will not do"; "I am more determined than ever in my life"; "I have not ruled out the use of force"; "I have no specific deadline"; "I will never again agree to a halfway effort." It was as if foreign policy had become autobiography.[1]

When King Hussein of Jordan, who was always considered a soothing influence in the Middle East, attempted to secure a negotiated settlement and resisted American truculence, Bush complained that Hussein had committed a "personal betrayal." And, in a display of adolescent behavior, the President even took to deliberately mispronouncing Saddam's name, placing vocal emphasis on the first syllable, as SADdam, which in Arabic means mere "shoeshine boy." This, then, is how we make decisions that lead to the Folly of War. Years later the President reflected on his moralizing about Saddam and using World War II as a guidepost:

> I saw a direct analogy between what was occurring in Kuwait and what the Nazis had done, especially in Poland.... I saw a chilling parallel with what the Iraqi occupiers were doing in Kuwait. I caught hell on this comparison of Saddam to Hitler, with critics accusing me of personalizing the crisis, but I still feel it was an appropriate one.... I did not have a personal grudge against Saddam Hussein, but I had a deep moral objection to what he had done and was doing. It was unprincipled, and we could not permit it to go on.[2]

By the second week of the occupation, angered by President Bush's intrusion into Arab affairs, Iraq dug in for a long stay and proclaimed the former Kuwait to be the 19th province of Iraq. "The Kuwait branch had finally returned to the Iraqi tree."[3] And when the Iraqi leader made one more effort at "compromise" and offered to withdraw from occupied Kuwait in exchange for Israel withdrawing from occupied territories of Palestine, — which interestingly was also a matter of United Nations sanctions, — the President scoffed at this effort of linkage. Negotiations were over unless Iraq capitulated. It was to be "unconditional surrender."

BUILDING AND BUYING A COALITION

Bush saw himself as something of a savant about world affairs, having spent time as Director of the Central Intelligence Agency, Ambassador to the United Nations, Ambassador to China and Vice-president of the United States. In the course of twenty years in these positions, he had developed friendships and acquaintanceships with dozens of governmental leaders. His oil business brought him into contact with all the rulers in the Persian Gulf. Late in August, the President had formed the contours of the coalition that would provide multilateral cover for his

---

1. Smith, *George Bush's War*, p. 2.
2. Bush and Scowcroft, *A World Transformed*, p. 375.
3. Mackey, *The Reckoning*, p. 280.

war against Iraq. President Bush neglected to consult with and involve other elements of the United States government, but he did not neglect to gather allies around him. The entire operation of coalition building was run out of the Oval Office. President Bush's effort at building a *Militant Idealist* coalition was a superb diplomatic effort, effectively disarming his domestic critics. As Pentagon official and war hawk Richard Perle said later, "That coalition — let's be blunt about it — was at least as important in securing 51 votes in the United States Senate as it was in assembling forces capable of dealing with Saddam Hussein's Army."[1]

The international coalition to support Desert Shield, as the protective mantel around Saudi Arabia was called, was composed of 37 nations with half a million troops, 240,000 of which were United States forces. Even states with marginal ties to the United States participated: Syria contributed 15,000 troops and prickly allies, like France, sent 16,000. When the Arab diplomatic solution was scuttled in August, the United States led coalition was the only game in town. The coalition was a rather diverse crew with disparate interests, dominated by the United States. Secretary of State James Baker admitted that the coalition was in reality a phantom: "This was not multilateralism. It was a US operation that received financial support from states as powerful as Japan and Germany to those as small as Malaysia."[2]

Many of the participating nations had ulterior motives, even mercenary purposes for joining the Bush coalition. Egypt received over $7 billion in the form of loan forgiveness as a "prize" for going along with Washington. Surprisingly, Syria, no friend of the United States, sent a military contingent. It was surprising until one learns of the inducement: the Bush administration agreed to give recognition to Syria's conquest in Lebanon — a strange response given the mission of mercy in Kuwait. The Soviet Union, preoccupied with its collapsing communist union, gave support to the effort, although it did not send troops. As with many participating nations, Russia lined up for financial aid as a price for its support of the coalition. During a September trip to Moscow, Secretary Baker was asked, "can you help get some money from the Saudis for us?"[3] The asking price for cooperation was $4 or $5 billion. Even little Romania received $80 million in "humanitarian" aid, and on and on the payoffs went.

And, nations that did not cooperate received the scorn of Uncle Sam. Yemen voted against several United Nations resolutions about Iraq, and upon casting one negative vote a wrathful Secretary James Baker predicted correctly, "Well, this will be the most expensive no vote they ever cast."[4] Coalition building did not necessarily involve everyone agreeing with the Bush rationale for opposing Iraq; nations with vast disagreements with the United States were lining up to receive US dollars. In simple terms, many nations were bribed to go along. Coalition building was the great game of "show me the money." Because of this, the coalition was operated out of Washington. "In reality, the United States directed the political and military policies of these operations, with only secondary involvement by other nations," as one author conceded.[5] As in the Korean War, it only appeared on the surface to be a multinational operation. The coalition was essentially a "cover" for the United States acting like the Lone Ranger.

1. Gilbert Achcar, trans. by Peter Drucker, *The Clash of Barbarians* (New York: Monthly Review Press, 2002), p. 120.
2. Yetiv, *The Persian Gulf Crisis*, p. 23.
3. James Baker, *The Politics of Diplomacy* (New York: G. P. Putnam's Sons, 1995), p. 294.
4. Baker, *The Politics of Diplomacy*, p. 325.
5. Yetiv, *The Persian Gulf Crisis*, p. 55.

The critical link in the coalition chain was the successful effort of Defense Secretary Dick Cheney to convince the rulers of Saudi Arabia to allow United States forces to occupy military bases "temporarily" in Saudi Arabia. This was a momentous decision for the Saudi leadership; never before had tens of thousands of foreign troops — infidels — been stationed for military purposes in the *Land of the Two Shrines*, the Holy Land of Mecca and Medina. In a dramatic two hour conference with the Saudi leadership in Jeddah over the first weekend after the invasion, Secretary Cheney, assisted by Paul Wolfowitz, Under Secretary of Defense for Policy, presented Central Intelligence Agency photos showing Iraqi troops massed along the Kuwait-Saudi border, purportedly in preparation for an invasion of Saudi Arabia. At the time, Iraq had over 100,000 troops in the tiny country, which is about the size of New Jersey. Normal dispersal of troops would naturally leave some along each of Kuwait's borders. Photos could show where troops were located; photos could not discern the Iraqi intentions. No one could point to any Iraqi talk of invading Saudi territory; the grievances that Iraq had were exclusively directed at Kuwait. In fact, United States government reports seemed to contradict Cheney. Iraq had eleven divisions in Kuwait; eight of the divisions were along the Iraqi-Kuwait border, one was in Kuwait City. Only two of the eleven divisions were positioned along the Saudi border.[1] Hardly a distribution of troops preparing to invade Saudi Arabia.

But Secretary of Defense Cheney, ever the hawk, pressed the Saudi King with the argument that the US would be there now to defend the Arabian nation, but it would not lift a finger later to liberate it should Iraq invade. Such a scenario was highly unlikely, but the persistence of Cheney and the looming presence of Saddam's Army were persuasive. Still, there was divided counsel among the Saudi leadership, a group that usually made decisions by consensus. Crown Prince Abdullah opposed admitting "infidel forces" into the Muslim Holy Land, arguing that the threat from Iraq was not credible. Eventually, King Faud cast the deciding vote to comply with Cheney's request, and responded to Abdullah by asking why is the Kuwaiti "royal family living in our hotel rooms?"[2] (Obviously, the fact that the Kuwaitis were living in Arabian hotels says nothing about whether the next Iraqi stop would be Jeddah.) The United States gave several critical assurances to the Saudis to allay their concerns, with Bush promising not to terminate the mission and to leave when asked by the Saudi's.

By Monday morning, August 6, Saudi Arabia was in line and the Bush *Militant Idealist* coalition was forming. There would be an American solution to the conflict, with Arab states playing only a supporting role. In the fall of 1990, American troops came to the *Land of the Two Shrines*; over a decade later they still remained in Saudi Arabia. Great Britain, which had been the protector of the Persian Gulf for many decades, had laid to rest its lines of imperial power at mid-century when it withdrew its fleet and regiments from the Middle East. By century end, the United States was picking up those lines, pouring its fleet, troops and air force into the region and settling in for a long imperial occupation in the Persian Gulf. The Iraqi War of 2003 would ensure the American hegemony in the region.

One week after the invasion, on Wednesday, August 8, the President delivered a speech to the nation in which he explained the first steps taken in defending Arabia. He said in part:

---

1. Bin, *Desert Storm*, p. 27.
2. Yetiv, *The Persian Gulf Crisis*, p. 14.

[T]he Saudi government requested our help, and I have responded to that request by ordering United States ground and air forces to deploy in the kingdom of Saudi Arabia....The mission of our troops is wholly defensive. Hopefully they will not be there long. They will not initiate hostilities.[1]

The entire speech was a masterful display of equivocation and outright dishonesty. The President left his listeners with the impression that the Saudis had, on their own, rushed to Washington, hat in hand, pleading for protection against the brutal dictator who would next overrun their kingdom. President Bush delivered a thoroughly deceitful oration that turned the facts upside down. It was a fantastic re-creation of the recent history of the crisis. Consider the distortions:

- Bush never told the nation about the Arab efforts to mediate the troubles between Iraq and Kuwait or that the US had undermined these efforts.
- He never revealed that Saudi Arabia and others initially blamed the Kuwaitis for the crisis..
- He never explained that the initiative for sending troops into the Middle East came from the White House, not from Saudi Arabia, nor did he mention the pressure Secretary Cheney had applied to the Arab leadership to obtain consent for the incursion of troops into Saudi Arabia
- He failed to explain the nature of the "proof" of Iraq's intention to invade Saudi Arabia, nor did he admit that American intelligence estimates had privately counseled the President that there was no evidence that Iraq intended to invade Saudi Arabia.[2]
- He never leveled with the American people about how many troops would be needed, and later even lied about the matter by saying that there would be no more than 50,000 troops needed. A decision had already been made to send 500,000 to the Gulf.
- He never admitted that his ultimate intentions were not simply to defend Saudi Arabia, but to use the US troops to invade Kuwait and dislodge Iraq, punish and weaken the Iraqi military, invade the nation of Iraq, and remove Saddam from power.
- The United States did initiate hostilities, a fact that he deceitfully concealed.

When the presidential war-making machine gets into gear, truthfulness and candor disappear.

Another critical link in building a successful coalition was obtaining United Nations support for American actions. Beginning the day after the invasion, the United Nations Security Council began adopting sanctions against Iraq's illegal action. The primary sanction, #660, condemns the Iraqi invasion and orders immediate withdrawal. There were other sanctions assessed against Baghdad including an order to stop development of weapons of mass destruction and assigning a United Nations team to inspect Iraq and ensure its compliance.

DESERT SHIELD TO DESERT STORM

Was the President sending troops merely to defend Saudi Arabia – Desert Shield? Or was he going to initiate hostilities, invade Kuwait and remove Iraqi forces – Desert Storm? Or would

---

1. Smith, *George Bush's War*, p. 97, 99.
2. Ibid., p. 79.

he go farther and invade Iraq itself, removing Saddam Hussein from power and create a new nation? What was the purpose of the coalition?

The United States military chiefs expressed caution about plunging into the Middle East cauldron. Colin Powell, speaking for the military chiefs, urged the continued use of economic sanctions, as did General Norman Schwartzkopf, who bluntly asserted that sanctions are working and war is "crazy."[1] Admiral Crowe and General David Jones of the Air Force thought a military venture was moving too fast, was hasty.[2] These and other leaders were content with Desert Shield — the simple defense of Saudi Arabia — hoping to give sanctions a chance to force Iraq out of Kuwait.

But those around the President in the White House urged an immediate war to liberate Kuwait — Desert Storm. President Bush's instincts were on the side of Desert Storm, as he had within three days of the invasion announced that this aggression would not stand. But Bush concealed his hand, always unsure of the public's acceptance of a war; the public would have to be babied along. Like Franklin Roosevelt before World War II, the President suggested if the nation would only defend its ally, war would not be necessary. In both cases the President was deceiving the people and in both cases war came. The public was reeled in with the hopes of no war, but the action of the President ensured that war would occur. The coalition was formed for Desert Shield, only later did the coalition members realize that they were in a war to invade and liberate Kuwait.

The urgency of the situation was heightened by stories describing atrocities committed by Iraqi troops while in Kuwait. Photographs depicted oil well fires deliberately set by the invaders to show contempt for the rich Kuwaitis. There were less well-documented stories of destruction of works of art in Kuwaiti museums, and personal tales of rape and murder, even killing babies for loot! These appeals on behalf of humanity touched the hearts of compassionate Americans, and just as in earlier wars, persuaded many that a war was worth the price.

One Kuwaiti woman, Nayirah by name, found the means to travel to the United States and appear before Congress to testify of the horrors of the Iraqi occupation. Her story, told to the Congressional Human Rights Caucus, was a tale of Iraqi soldiers stealing incubators from hospitals to sell for money, and even dumping the babies along the road to die. The "babies for loot" story was captivating and produced an outpouring of disgust at Iraq; the Bush administration made the most of it. In the US this type of humanitarian appeal always falls on receptive ears, for the public yearns for some gleaning of evidence to justify war — killing as a "good deed." Only later was it discovered that the story was bogus; the refugee woman, Nayirah, was actually the daughter of the Kuwait ambassador to the United States, and the story had been fabricated and even rehearsed in a Washington D.C. public relations office associated with Kuwait. Bush administration officials denied they knew that the story was fallacious, but of course, they made no attempt to look into it before utilizing it for war propaganda, or later to correct the malevolent impression of Iraq.[3] An exceptional, self-righteous nation never needs to say, "I'm sorry, I made a mistake." Just as in World War I, false stories of human rights violations had pushed the American electorate over the edge.

---

1. Yetiv, *The Persian Gulf Crisis*, p. 18.
2. Ibid., p. 19.
3. Ibid.

Deception by the White House should not conceal the truth about the "rape of Kuwait" by Iraqi troops. There was mindless looting and heavy destruction of schools, hospitals, offices, homes and museums. As many as 10,000 Kuwait residents were killed and thousands were taken captive and sent to Iraq as slaves. The brutality presided over by Saddam Hussein made the work of Militant Idealists easier.

Support was building in Congress for a national debate on whether the nation should go to war immediately, or continue to apply economic sanctions against Iraq. The curtailment of Iraqi trade by an American blockade of the Persian Gulf and the freezing of their assets had already taken a heavy toll on Iraq, reports showing that its gross domestic product had been cut in half in less than six months. All Iraqi oil shipments had ceased and its revenues plummeted. Severe rice and wheat rationing was ordered and inflation soared. In the first few months after the invasion, Iraq became a pariah nation, as even its neighbors supported the sanctions. But, the reality is that no one could point to any economic sanction program that had ever quickly derailed a resolute dictator. Economic sanctions, even a throat-strangling blockade, would do great harm to the people, but leave Saddam in place, which is, of course, precisely what happened after the Gulf War over the next decade. And successful sanctions may take years, meanwhile the toll against the people and property in Kuwait was mounting.

As the weeks rolled by and the President moved ever closer to a commitment of troops into battle, leaders in Congress pressed the issue of asking Congress for a declaration of war, or at least a "force resolution," one along the lines of the Gulf of Tonkin Resolution before the Vietnam War. The Bush administration preferred not to take the issue of war to Congress, for as Secretary Cheney and Director Scowcroft argued, the United States was going to go to war with or without the approval of Congress. A "No" vote from either House would only serve to embarrass the President, but not deter him. At a news conference in the White House on January 9, 1991, Bush said, "I don't think I need [a resolution from Congress].... Saddam Hussein should be under no question on this. I feel that I have the authority to fully implement the United Nations resolutions."[1] The President Bush was in a wrathful mood and would brook no interference on his mission of mercy. "For me," Bush retorted, "it boils down to a very moral case of good versus evil, black versus white. If I have to go [to war], it's not going to matter to me if there isn't one congressman who supports this, or what happens to public opinion. If it's right, it's gotta be done."[2] The Korean War President, Harry Truman, had taught the lesson well — a president who is doing a good deed and covers himself with the authority of the United Nations can disregard the war declaration clause in the Constitution.

Despite White House opposition, congressional resolutions both for and against the immediate use of force were introduced in both houses of Congress. However, it should be noted that all members were under the sway of Militant Idealism. The question of the United States remaining neutral on the issues in the Persian Gulf never came up. No support existed for the idea that this was an Arab problem and none of America's concern. All subscribed to the notion of the US "carrying out its responsibilities." The question before the Congress was should the US wage war now, or later. After three days of argumentation, the vote was taken on January 12; the President's course of action — immediate use of force — was sustained by votes

---

1. Ibid., p. 67.
2. Bin, *Desert Storm*, p. 59

of 52-47 in the Senate, and 250-183 in the House of Representatives. Public opinion polls conducted during the month of January indicated that the public believed the President was doing a good job and approved of the prompt use of military action. President Bush was in control of the pace of war, just as with every President who chose the route to war.

On January 9, one week before the air war against Iraq began, Secretary James Baker was sent on a mission to "give peace one last chance." Meeting in Geneva, Switzerland with Iraq Foreign Minister, Tariq Aziz, the Secretary informed Aziz at the outset that he was not there to negotiate; he was there to deliver an "ultimatum." The United Nations had passed Sanction # 660 ordering Iraq out of Kuwait and there would be no other matters discussed until there was compliance. The Iraqis, faced with a certain military hurricane in the next few days, came to the table with an offer. Iraq would leave the nation of Kuwait when the following conditions were met:

- The "United Nations" military force in Saudi Arabia must be replaced with an all-Arab force.
- All United Nations sanctions must end when Iraq withdraws.
- Syrian forces in Lebanon that had been in that beleaguered country for ten years must be withdrawn.
- Israel must withdraw its forces from Lebanon and the occupied territory of Palestine — the West Bank and Gaza — which it had illegally occupied since 1967, actions that had been condemned by United Nations sanctions.

Iraq requested linkage — Iraq's occupation of Kuwait must be dealt with along with similar occupations in Lebanon and Palestine. The Arab world was pleased at this attempt by Iraq to equate Israeli aggression with Iraq's aggression. However, Secretary Baker would hear none of this and the talks went nowhere. Baker emerged from the meeting expressing his disgust: "In over six hours of talks I heard nothing today that suggested to me any Iraqi flexibility whatsoever on complying with the United Nations Security Council resolutions."[1] Secretary Cheney and Director Scowcroft had initially opposed holding the Baker-Aziz meeting and now their view was confirmed. Their concern had been that the image of America might be shown to be weak if, heaven forbid, a compromise was achieved.

It is interesting to analyze the American leaders constant desire to look strong during any crisis. Iraq was a nation of 20 million; the United States a nation of over 250 million, certainly the greatest military power in the history of mankind. Yet, Cheney and Scowcroft were worried about burnishing the nation's image rather than attempting to obtain a satisfactory diplomatic conclusion to the crisis. Also, one wonders about Baker's comment on "flexibility," as it is not usually thought that "ultimatums" display flexibility. If the term "flexibility" means coming to the negotiating table with an open mind and new ideas that offer creative solutions, certainly Aziz was more "flexible" than Baker was. Baker and the United States had sung the same uncompromising song since the weekend of August 4 and 5 six months ago. Baker really didn't mean flexibility; he meant submissiveness.

On a moonless January night Desert Storm came to Baghdad, as the United States air power erupted on that forlorn nation. The American people watched in amazement, and it appears with some delight, as CNN televised the "festivities" into living rooms across the nation. At 7:08 p.m. when the first cruise missile hit its target, Marlin Fitzwater, the press

1. Yetiv, *The Persian Gulf Crisis*, p. 27.

spokesman for the President, announced "the liberation of Kuwait has begun." The avenging angel had arrived.

For the next month, Iraq was pounded mercilessly with "smart bombs" from nowhere and dumb bombs from B-52s, with Tomahawk self-guided cruise missiles and Hornets and Stealth bombers. The air war began January 16, and by the time the war came to an end, the United States had flown over 100,000 sorties, the greatest concentration of air power ever delivered — 98% by American pilots. General Colin Powell had demanded that if the American military was used, it must be applied in massive doses. He was not disappointed. The United States deployed 50% of its total military force in this campaign, even bringing in heavily armored troops from Germany.

Negotiations with Baghdad continued during the air war, primarily through the efforts of Russian leader Mikhail Gorbachev. Secretary of State James Baker and the Russian Foreign Minister issued a joint statement late in January suggesting a deal in which Iraq would withdraw in exchange for a cease fire and the promise that the United States created coalition would "address" the Arab-Israeli question. Baker was embarrassed when President Bush disowned the proposal. There would be no linkage; "unconditional surrender" was the only game.

Two weeks later, Iraq, battered and bloodied, from the incessant bombing was staggering against the ropes. Through the Russian foreign ministry, Saddam floated another deal: an immediate withdrawal if United Nations sanctions would end, plus a promise from President Bush that its retreating troops would not be attacked as they returned to Iraq. To this, George Bush said, "Nyet." There are no negotiations. "The goals have been set out. There will be no concession — not going to give."[1] Militant Idealists do not compromise.

On February 22, another offer, another rejection. Iraq offered to withdraw from Kuwait over a period of three weeks, beginning one day after a cease-fire, in exchange for a United States commitment that all sanctions would be lifted. The President continued his hard line saying there would be no end to the war until Iraq accepted all United Nations resolutions. Since all of the resolutions were a result of Iraq's occupation of Kuwait, one wonders why the key was not resolution # 660, the initial resolution that demanded Iraq's withdrawal. The subsequent resolutions would become irrelevant or inoperative once the withdrawal occurred. One wonders why "irrelevant resolutions" had become so important to President Bush. Perhaps the clue was provided when Brent Scowcroft admitted that the United States objectives were now expanding with the war's success. "The President...saw the danger of an Iraqi withdrawal before its Army had been destroyed."[2] Apparently the real reason Bush would not accept the proffered deals was that there had not been enough damage done to the Iraqi military.

Generals do not like to stop fighting until there is a clear cease-fire, when both sides have agreed to stop shooting. Saddam Hussein's attempts to secure a cease-fire were normal efforts to protect retreating troops, not just a ploy to trick the adversary. President Bush reacted to each request for a cease-fire as though it was a loaded cigar, fit only to be tossed away. The tragic horror of this situation became apparent on the evening of February 25.

On that day Baghdad finally conceded defeat, announcing that its troops were withdrawing from Kuwait immediately with no preconditions. Saddam, ever the showman and

---

1. Ibid., p. 38.
2. Bush and Scowcroft, *A World Transformed*, p. 477,478.

playing to the Arab crowd, bragged that his "forces had proven [their] ability to fight."[1] But, disaster lurked in the skies over the retreating army. At nightfall, to avoid surrendering to the coalition forces, the Iraqi Army along with hundreds of foreign workers climbed into over a 1000 vehicles, and using the cover of darkness, attempted to escape into Iraq along Highway #6 toward Basra. Because President Bush refused several requests for a cease-fire, the war was technically still in progress, and American Apache helicopters, F-15s and F-16s and even B-52s caught the convoy heading home, raining death on the fleeing army and assorted stragglers. An American pilot describes the carnage: "I could see Iraqi trucks from a long distance. I then locked on target and fired away knowing that the hapless Iraqis on the other end never had a chance."[2]

The United States fighter pilots later referred to it as a "turkey shoot." American planes destroyed the lead and the rear vehicles in the five-mile long convoy, effectively blocking their advance to Basra and dooming tens of thousands to a fiery death. "Within hours, Highway #6 had become the 'highway of death' filled with bombed-out vehicles hopelessly stuck in a traffic jam of hellish doom."[3] This action should be seen as cowardly and illegal, as the United States forces were under no fire from the fleeing army. International treaties — and common decency — deal with shooting fleeing troops and non-combatants in the back.

Earlier in the war when cease-fire proposals were discussed and rejected, President Bush did publicly announce that the United States forces would not shoot the Iraqi troops in the back when they retreated. In *The Politics of Diplomacy*, Secretary Baker admits that the United States gave assurances that "withdrawing troops would not be attacked."[4] But war somehow brings out the savagery in people; a promise made and discarded, a commitment broken, human rights violated. Tens of thousands of dead Iraqis fleeing home, shot in the back by American pilots.

In the next two days, Baghdad agreed to rescind the annexation of Kuwait and to comply with all twelve United Nations resolutions. In *A World Transformed*, a triumphant President Bush tells of savoring those moments:

> In what was probably too cute by half, we agreed to end hostilities at midnight, Washington time, for a ground war of exactly 100 hours. Just after 9:00 pm I spoke to the country. "Kuwait is liberated. Iraq's Army is defeated. Our military objectives are met.... No one can claim this victory as its own. It was not only a victory for Kuwait but also a victory for all the coalition partners. This is a victory for the United Nations, for all mankind, for what is right."[5]

The United States war was a devastating example of a blitzkrieg; one that would have made the German generals who invented it proud. In a ground war that had lasted just 100 hours, and an air war of just 6 weeks, the coalition forces had dropped 142,000 tons of explosives on Iraq, killed 100,00 Iraqi troops and 400,000 civilians, losing only 148 of its own. John Hay, Secretary of State during the Spanish-American War, might have deemed it another "splendid little war."

---

1. Yetiv, *The Persian Gulf Crisis*, p. 40.
2. Ibid., p. 41.
3. Ibid.
4. Baker, *The Politics of Diplomacy*, p. 404.
5. Bush and Scowcroft, *A World Transformed*, p. 486.

AMERICAN-STYLE DIPLOMACY

In 1980, when Iraq invaded its neighbor Iran, the United States immediately befriended and rewarded Iraq. National Security Advisor Zbigniew Brzezinski stated publicly that the United States would not object to "an Iraq move against Iran."[1] As James Baker describes in his book, *The Politics of Diplomacy*, United States policy turned on a dime to support Iraq against the Ayatollah's Iran. America provided Iraq with an array of benefits during its war:

- Removed Iraq from the list of terrorist states.
- Extended diplomatic relations after a 17 year hiatus.
- Extended financial credits, eventually amounting to nearly one billion dollars.
- Shared military intelligence from spy satellites for use against Iran.
- Reflagged Iraqi tankers with the Stars and Stripes to provide protection against Iranian attacks.
- Provided Iraq with chemicals for use in poison gas attacks on the Iranian hordes.

However, when in 1990, Iraq invaded Kuwait, with much greater justification than its war on Iran, the United States condemned the attack and organized a massive coalition to thwart Iraq's designs. Headlining the American opposition was the idealist argument that this was "wanton aggression," similar to German aggression under Adolf Hitler, and must be stopped to establish an example to other would-be conquerors. The dismal Iraqi human rights record — use of poison gas, mass execution of citizens, arbitrary punishment of political opponents, sham elections — was always handy to use for beating up on Saddam.

One has to ask — where was this self-righteous posture in the 1980s while the war against Iran was in progress? The human rights record was the same — deplorable. Iraq had invaded Iran in the autumn of 1980 — that was aggression. Chemical warfare was used against Iran. Where were the complaints? Where was the international coalition to stop Hitler-like actions? In 1990, the Bush administration organized a world-wide military coalition against Iraq that was said to be guilty of military aggression, human rights abuses, and using poison gas, all of which Iraq had done with the support of the United States within the last ten years in the war against the Ayatollah.

Any questioning of this revised version of United States policy was rejected out of hand. President François Mitterand of France, ever the rationalist, observed: "Saddam Hussein in Kuwait is no different from Assad [President of Syria] in Lebanon. France sees no difference between what is going on in Kuwait and what is going on in Lebanon."[2] For this unhelpful comment, the Frenchman was condemned by American "irrationalists." It was seldom noted that essentially the Bush administration was calling into question the eight years of Reagan support for Saddam Hussein. Reagan often used scalding rhetoric, but had more deftly dealt with the dictator on the Tigris.

When it suits their fancy, war presidents conduct foreign policy by invoking the moral precepts of idealism, using an emotional message to enlist gullible voters. Then, at other times, turning on a dime, presidents use realism, which allows for a flexible and pragmatic approach: what is in the "national interest" varies from incident to incident, alliances with nations shift,

---

1. Smith, *George Bush's War*, p. 43.
2. Baker, *The Politics of Diplomacy*, p. 314.

"bad behavior" is overlooked. But this is not the case with idealism; principles must be maintained — wrong is wrong and sin is sin. American leaders speak the pious language of idealism, then succumb to the temptations of realism. Presenting no consistency to the world, the nation stands first on one foot, then the other. One year we are the preacher, the next the warrior. One year we are instituting a quarantine of evil, the next year finding common cause with aggressors. US citizens may fail to see this hypocrisy, but other national leaders recognize it. And it confounds the world.

Militant Idealism acts to freeze US diplomacy. This can be seen in the United States refusal to enter into any meaningful negotiations with Iraq at any time from August through January when Desert Storm began. When the United Nations passed resolution #660 condemning Iraq's occupation of Kuwait and ordered withdrawal, the United States disdained all efforts to compromise or to provide an "out" for Saddam. The attempts of Arab leaders to find an Arab solution in August and September were rejected by President Bush. Saddam had cautioned Ambassador Glaspie, "Do not push us into [war],"[1] but Bush would not throw a "bone" to the Iraqi dictator. The Arab world is one in which pride and saving face are important. President Bush was intent on showing American power and resolve; he would not allow Saddam to save face. Those aspects of Middle Eastern culture that emphasize personal image and the give and take of bargaining were rejected by the moralistic superpower.

Again in January and February, when the horror of Desert Storm was unleashed on Iraq, the Russians and the French tried to find a middle ground, one that would remove Iraqi troops from Kuwait, avoid the full effects of the war, but allow Saddam to save face. The Russian foreign minister cautioned Secretary Baker: "If we put him [Saddam] in a corner, we'll have an explosion. Threats of force will never dislodge him." To this suggestion Baker contemptuously retorted, what about real force rather than just the threat?[2] The deal that the Russians and the French broached involved a ceasefire in Kuwait with a withdrawal and linkage of the Arab-Israeli issue to the Iraq-Kuwait conflict. The Russian and French were asking for a ceasefire to protect the retreating troops and a promise to open a conference on the problems between Arab Palestinians and the Israelis. James Baker contemptuously dismissed it saying, "it sounds like a formula Neville Chamberlain might have approved," referring to the "failed" Munich conference in 1938.[3] When United Nations resolutions were passed and sanctions were assessed, as far as the United States was concerned, negotiations ceased; diplomacy was suspended. Any concession was considered a reward for aggression; the Iraq-Kuwait conflict had no legitimacy. The crisis had moved from normal diplomacy to law enforcement. As the police do not treat with the robbers holed up in a bank, so the Bush coalition does not negotiate with aggressors.

But, world affairs are not like the rigid and unchanging granite face of a mountain, but more like a glacier that is relentlessly moving, and sometimes even having the turbulence of an avalanche. US presidents — Militant Idealists — position themselves in front of the avalanche, thinking instead that it is a stable mountain. The last avalanche the US stood in front of was during the 1960s; it was called the Vietnam War. The Aftershocks of the United States involvement in the Persian Gulf have just begun to form.

---

1. *New York Times*, Sept. 23, 1990.
2. Baker, *The Politics of Diplomacy*, p. 398.
3. Ibid., p. 399.

Some of the aversion to compromise is a generational issue, having its strongest supporters in the men and women who fought World War II. President Bush, Secretary Baker,
Prime Minister Margaret Thatcher were of the World War II generation and perceived the
world through the prism of the Munich and Yalta Syndrome. Any compromise or
"appeasement" of Saddam would only reward him and worsen the problem. Toughness, resolution, force were the keys to success. As Prime Minister Thatcher often cautioned, "don't go
wobbly now." The World War II generation will not abandon their Munich Syndrome perception; such a view will be replaced with a more accommodating approach when the next generation comes on the scene. America could have responded differently to the invasion of Kuwait.
"A younger president would have lacked Bush's historical referent of World War II, and it is
reasonable to conjecture, would not have approached the crisis the same way." This observation
by political scientist Steve Yetiv was confirmed by Richard Haass of the National Security
Council, who said, "I can easily imagine that something else would have happened under
another president." Another NSC staffer commented in the same vein: "Had this been four years
earlier or four years later, it may have come out quite differently."[1]

The summer of 1990 saw the political fortunes of George Bush fading. His "no new tax"
pledge was in tatters, the nation was on the edge of a recession, the budget impasse seemed to
overwhelm him, he was increasingly seen as a whiney, lapdog personality. There was nothing
like a foreign crisis to energize Bush. By the spring 1991, the Bush presidency had the highest
voter approval rating in history — over 90%. Timing was crucial. "If Iraq had invaded Kuwait at
the beginning of 1992, and if the US economy had been booming at the time [and if Bush could
have shed his "wimp" image], would the president have been as likely to risk war...."[2]

And so, wars occur when one man — the President — decides for one reason or another
to use the military. There is nothing inevitable about such an undertaking. Going to war is a
policy choice just like raising taxes or reforming welfare. Some Presidents chose to avoid war —
Cleveland, Coolidge, Eisenhower — others, seem to find war more easily —Truman, Johnson,
Bush.

The willingness, even the desire of the United States to take over the leadership in any
international crisis is the result of the long years of fighting the wars of the 20th century, combined with the America sense of its own exceptional character. James Baker saw this as our duty:

> We must stand for American leadership, not because we seek it but simply because no one else
> can do the job. We did not stand united for forty years to bring the Cold War to a peaceful end
> in order to make the world safe for the likes of Saddam Hussein.... [I]t is a choice between
> what's right and what's wrong.... I think that we have the courage and the fortitude to do what
> is right.[3]

Steve Yetiv writing on the Persian Gulf War saw the same situation: "Since no other
country in the world had the capability and stature to stop Iraq, the responsibility devolved to
the United States."[4] Just why the United States is the indispensable nation is never made
entirely clear. Is it because our leaders are wiser? Have better intelligence information? Have

---

1. Yetiv, *The Persian Gulf Crisis*, p. 63.
2. W. Lance Bennett and David L. Paletz, (ed.), *Taken By Storm: The Media, Public Opinion, and U.S. Foreign Policy in the Gulf War*, (Chicago: The University of Chicago Press, 1994), p. 259.
3. Baker, *The Politics of Diplomacy*, p. 340.
4. Yetiv, *The Persian Gulf Crisis*, p. 13.

more schooling? Or perhaps this indispensability is based upon possessing greater weapons? More sophisticated missiles? More nuclear weapons? Or again, might it be due to the wealth of the citizenry and their willingness to spend as much for defense as the rest of the world combined? Or perhaps, just American exceptionalism. Whatever the basis, former Secretary of State Madeleine Albright said it well:

> If we have to use force, it is because we are Americans. We are the indispensable nation. We stand tall. We see further into the future.[1]

The self-proclaimed confidence, even arrogance, projects the US into areas of the world where it has no legitimate concerns, spreading American blood into localized conflicts, and creating ill-will among the world's nations toward the United States. No one likes a haughty busybody.

THE FOLLY OF WAR

American-Iraqi relations had seriously deteriorated *before* the invasion of Kuwait, and in reviewing this relationship one can observe a number of incidents that caused the eventual rupture and war. The early months of 1990 were described by the State Department as Saddam's "Spring of Bad Behavior."(It is significant that there was reference to "bad" behavior, not "dangerous" behavior — America is always the moralist.) Saddam's misdeed during the spring were several:

- He executed an Iraqi-born journalist working for the West who was an alleged spy.
- He angrily denounced a Voice of America editorial that asserted Iraq was a police state.
- He accused the United States of meddling in the Persian Gulf region.
- He placed Scud missiles in western Iraq where they could strike Israeli cities.
- He increased his efforts to obtain weapons of mass destruction and sophisticated missilery that could strike Israel.

Perhaps his greatest "sin" was a provocative speech on April 2, 1990 to his military leaders, at which he confirmed for the first time that Iraq had chemical weapons (dozens of states have them, but don't admit it), and he vowed, under certain conditions, to use them. Saddam boasted to his generals that if Israel ever attacked Iraq again (Israel had destroyed an Iraqi nuclear facility in 1983), "By God, we will make fire eat up half of Israel." Secretary of State James Baker, like the prophets of old, was moved to condemn, with righteous indignation, this "Burn Israel" speech. Said the Prophet-Secretary Baker, such talk is "inflammatory, irresponsible, and outrageous." A review of United States policy toward Iraq was undertaken immediately, and within ten days cables were flying to the Middle East advising diplomats that the US would no longer aid and abet Iraq. "Iraq will be on a collision course with the US..." asserted a cable to the ambassador in Baghdad.[2] The date was April 11, 1990, four months before the invasion of Kuwait.

The "Burn Israel" speech was a trigger that reversed Washington's policy towards Iraq. When the Bush administration showed its sensitivity toward Israel, red flags of alarm were

---

1. Mackey, *The Reckoning*, p. 358.
2. Baker, *The Politics of Diplomacy*, p. 268, 269.

raised in the Arab world. It was customary for Arab leaders to fulminate about Israel. Was the new administration so touchy, so defensive about the Jewish State, so in league with Israel, that Saddam and other leaders were to be muzzled on the issue of Zionism and the Palestinian question?

The United States relationship with Israel is based on the political pressure of powerful Zionist organizations in the United States and on idealistic considerations — Israel is the only democracy in the area, therefore Israel is the cornerstone of United States Mid-east policy. A policy based on realism would dictate that America would nurture greater diplomatic ties with the twenty Arab nations, some of whom have huge pools of petroleum, rather than with one tiny nation having no tangible benefits for the United States. The initial rupture in the United States relations with Iraq came about over Iraq's rough talk toward Israel and America's idealistic sensitivities.

Immediately prior to the August 1st invasion, the United States gave confusing signals to Iraq about its dispute with Kuwait. Ambassador Glaspie's comments to Saddam on July 25 were at least neutral on the Iraq-Kuwait dispute: "We have no opinion on the Arab-Arab conflicts, like your border disagreement with Kuwait." At a Washington D.C. press conference on July 24, a week prior to the invasion, State Department representative Margaret Tutweiler was asked by a journalist whether the United States had sent any note of protest to Iraq about 30,000 troops massed on Kuwait's border. Tutweiler responded that she was unaware of any such protest, then added: "We do not have any defense treaties with Kuwait, and there are no special defense or security commitments to Kuwait."[1]

Five days later, two days before the Iraqi invasion, John Kelly, Assistant Secretary of State for Near Eastern Affairs, when asked by a congressional committee whether the United States had any defense commitments in the Gulf area if fighting broke out over oil or territorial disputes, responded, saying that, "we have no defense treaty relationships with any of the countries. We have historically avoided taking positions on border disputes or on internal OPEC deliberations...." When asked if the United States would come to the aid of any nation that was the victim of an armed invasion, Kelley said he could not answer a hypothetical question. When pressed for a response, he said that the United States did not have a treaty commitment that would obligate us to engage US forces. [2]

There are significant parallels between the Korean War and the Gulf War. Both presidents — Truman and Bush — gave signals to their adversary — North Korea and Iraq — that the United States would "stand aside" if military activities began, then when an invasion occurred, the presidents "sucker punched" their opponents. And both presidents make their decision to send troops into death's door without careful thought or collective discussions, both making personal decisions, based largely on emotion, to stand up to the "bully." Both bypassed the United Nations Security Council peacekeeping apparatus, forming an American-led coalition instead. In the case of Truman, the UN was sidestepped due to the veto power of the Soviet Union. But President Bush had every reason to take the issue to the UN. The Cold War was over and Russia was in a compliant, weakened condition. The time was propitious to use a UN peacekeeping force of Asian, African and Middle Eastern troops to defang Iraq. The UN

---

1. Smith, *George Bush's War*, p.53
2. Ibid., p. 59-60.

nuclear inspection team had found evidence of weapons of mass destruction and in the early 1990s successfully disarmed Iraq. So why not use the United Nations?

George Bush likened himself to Teddy Roosevelt, one of his favorite presidents, and there are indeed many parallels in their lives. They were patricians from the Northeast with strong emotional ties to Europe. Their families had great wealth, were educated at Ivy League schools and used their family connections for political advancement. Both had suffered from reputations as weaklings, as lapdog or wimps, and both moved West to seek their fortunes and redeem their reputations. Both saw their presidency making its greatest mark in foreign affairs, both in the Caribbean and elsewhere — for Teddy in the Far East, for Bush in the Middle East. The two men found the sinews of military power attractive, but both cultivated the aura of personal silence: TR was said to "speak softly" (which he didn't) and Bush confessed that "I just am not one who flamboyantly believes in throwing a lot of words around."[1] Searching for a role to play, Bush said hopefully, "maybe I'll turn out to be a Teddy Roosevelt." Teddy was always on the lookout for petty dictators to unseat, hoping to thrust American power into neglected niches. George Bush found his patsy along the Tigris River.

And what of Kuwait? What is Kuwait thinking of, for the Iraqi "lion is hungry!" How did little Kuwait expect to defend itself against a raging neighbor, especially after Saudi Arabia had set an example of forgiving the Iranian war debts owed to Iraq? There were no regional defense alliances; no one else in the area to come to Kuwait's aid. Oh, but there are always the Americans! Looking through the State Department comments prior to the invasion, one sees statements, such as: We are "strongly committed to supporting the individual and collective self-defense of our friends in the Gulf with whom we have longstanding ties,"[2] and other nebulous bureaucratic-speak that Kuwaitis, ever hopeful, interpreted to mean that America would be there to defend them. The simple fact is that Kuwait had no other defense than to call on the United States. As Senator Daniel Moynihan said in an exasperated manner during the Senate debates on the force resolution: "[T]hose Kuwaitis ... have taken over [the] Sheraton Hotel... and they're sitting there in their white robes and drinking coffee and urging us to go to war."[3] To emphasize that the invasion was not the moral melodrama being spun out by the Bush administration, Moynihan continued: "All that happened is that one nasty little country has invaded a littler but just as nasty little country."[4] And, as previously mentioned, it was the Saudi King's opinion that, "It's all the Kuwaitis' fault. They brought this all on themselves."

But the small Gulf states, including Kuwait, needed protection from the brutal dictator on the Tigris. But, why look to the US and the Western world? Could a regional force have been created that would have been able to defend Kuwait, or other Gulf nations? Knowing the mercurial ways of Saddam Hussein, why hadn't the Gulf States formed an alliance for their own protection? The Gulf Cooperation Council was formed in 1981: it was comprised of six Arab nations bordering the Gulf (Kuwait, Saudi Arabia, Qatar, Bahrain, United Arab Emirates and Oman), all except Iraq and Iran. These states have a combined population of 27 million and a gross domestic product of $600 billion. Had they devoted a reasonable portion of their immense

---

1. Michael Duffy and Dan Goodgame, *Marching In Place: The Status Quo Presidency of George Bush*, (New York: Simon and Schuster, 1992), p. 148
2. Smith, *George Bush's War*, p. 53.
3. Bush and Scowcroft, *A World Transformed*, p. 396.
4. Ibid., p. 445.

wealth to adequate defense, rather than on frivolous living by the princes or on bountiful hand outs to their subjects, they could have dealt with their own defense needs. Iraq's population is 20 million and its economy is one-sixth the size of the combined Gulf Cooperation Council States. The Gulf States failure to arm themselves is reminiscent of a nature film scene from Africa depicting a herd of antelopes, one thousand strong, fleeing a single hunting lion. As the herd flees, the lion targets one straggling antelope, ignoring the herd of a thousand. If the antelopes were bright enough, they would realize that they could band together, turn on the lion and stampede it. But in the case of Kuwait, the Emir and princes knew that it was not necessary for them to spend their own money on defense or to spill their own blood. The United States — its young people in military uniforms and its taxpayers — would do it for them.

Much of the United States rationale for the war centered on idealistic issues: correcting Iraq's human rights abuses, stopping aggression, removing Saddam's war machine, especially the chemical and biological weapons. Certainly, Bush can take satisfaction in stopping Iraq's annexation of Kuwait, but the general issue of world-wide aggression, or human rights, or developing weapons of mass destruction for one's own protection, is a continuing question, and may not be eliminated by any apoplectic action by a guardian angel. Idealists can stop a specific source of sin, but the satisfaction of eliminating evil in all its forms, has eluded even the Highest of Authority. Yet the American campaign against evil continues.

On a more realistic level, the war did reduce Iraq's power in the area, though not nearly enough to satisfy American hawks, Israel or Iraq's Arab neighbors. The world's sixth largest air force was heavily damaged and its Army reduced to half its size. Half of its 5800 tanks were destroyed and over half of its artillery pieces were gone. The incipient Iraqi nuclear weapons program was eliminated, as was most of the chemical and biological weapons development. The "Million-Man Army," so much lauded in the Middle Eastern press, was reduced to a shell. However, the Iraqi Republican Guard remained largely intact, having been pulled back to guard the capital. To its chagrin, the United States learned that the Iraqi troops it had destroyed in the liberation of Kuwait were largely conscripts from the Kurdish north and the Shia Muslim south — young boys in their teens who were sent to the front as "cannon fodder." President Bush's effort to damage the Iraqi Army by refusing an early cease-fire had failed. Civilian casualties were high, some estimates at four hundred thousand, despite efforts by the allies to avoid bombing homes and neighborhoods. With 70% of the bombs going astray, it was understandable that civilians were hit. A United Nations post-war survey commented on the "near apoplectic" damage done, nearly reducing urban areas to pre-industrial levels.

The United States has become a Persian Gulf power with bases in Qatar, Bahrain, Saudi Arabia and Kuwait. The earlier policy of using surrogates for American power, at various times Saudi Arabia, then Iran, later even Iraq, has been replaced by the direct application of American power. American forces will remain in the area on a long-term basis, just as in Europe and the Far East, with estimates of the costs of the venture — maintaining 20,000 troops in the area plus the equipment on land and sea — running over $50 billion yearly.

And why not go to Baghdad and finish off the Saddam regime in 1991? A regime change — the removal of Saddam Hussein and his Baath Party — was always a peripheral goal. Building a UN coalition to reverse the occupation of Kuwait made winning the war on narrow, targeted grounds fairly easy; but if the purpose of the war was extended to creating a new Iraq, the coalition would self-destruct. Arab, French, Russian opposition would have been strident in opposing such a venture and the facade of unity lost. Even locating the President of Iraq, with his many disguises, his doubles, and his numerous hiding places would have been a formidable task extending the war for months. Middle East experts always cautioned against lunging intemperately into the cauldron of Iraq with its various disputatious factions; the nation may not be able to be put together again. The realist geopolitician, Brent Scowcroft expressed appropriate caution: "The trick here was to damage his [Saddam's] offensive capabilities without weakening Iraq to the point that a vacuum was created, destroying the balance between Iraq and Iran, further destabilizing the region for years."[1] However, American hesitation about plunging into the Middle East was cast aside when Bush the Younger answered the terror attacks of September 11, 2001 by going to Baghdad.

"I have an obligation as president to conduct the foreign policy of the country as I see fit," retorted George Bush when questioned about consulting Congress about going to war.[2] The President did not seek advice from Congress until August 28, nearly one month after Iraq invaded Kuwait, and by that time the American response had been set. The President concealed from Congress the critical assessment from the CIA that the Iraqi attack on Kuwait seemed to be limited to that country, and he concealed from the public until after the November congressional elections that he had decided to vastly increase the number of troops sent to the Middle East. The President gave the public the impression that Desert Shield was the American policy, but, in fact, was working silently and steadily to implement Desert Storm.

When in January the nation fell into debate, and resolutions were introduced in Congress, both for and against the use of force, President Bush warned that the debate and vote were irrelevant. "In truth, even had Congress not passed the resolution I would have acted and ordered troops into combat. I was comfortable in my own mind that I had the constitutional authority."[3] But this all leaves Congress in a horrible dilemma. If a President goes forth toward war, spewing inflammatory rhetoric, flashing steel and fire, moving troops, making demands on the adversary, what choice does a member of Congress have? When Congress debates a force resolution or a declaration of war, do they really have an option? Can a member of Congress, in the midst of a military crisis, actually vote "NO?" Presidents can take the country so far down the road to war that a congressional vote becomes nothing but a rubber stamp.

From the 1940s onward, the national leaders of the two major parties had developed a "consensus" on the role of the United States in world affairs. During this time any discussion on foreign policy centered only on management of agreed to policy — which party would do the better job of managing the various wars. Any politician who questioned Militant Idealism was either shunned or rebuked as a "fellow traveler," a neo-fascist or an Isolationist. Under these distorted conditions, gradually a national creed evolved that says, "Politics stops at the water's edge," meaning essentially that one does not question the president's decision on foreign matters. All must fall in line no matter how dangerous or foolish the policy. Republicans might question Truman, Kennedy or Johnson on domestic policy, but they must snap into line on world affairs. As James Baker admits in his memoirs, although the Baker family was a "fervent

---

1. Ibid., p. 383-384.
2. Smith, *George Bush's War*, p.4.
3. Bush and Scowcroft, *A World Transformed*, p. 446.

opponent of the New Deal... it never occurred to my dad — or to me — to question Roosevelt's leadership in the conduct of foreign affairs."[1]

Think of it! James Baker is saying that when FDR made decisions about welfare, jobs, bank regulations and a host of other domestic matters, the President was not only wrong, but he was endangering the soul of the nation. But, when the same man made decisions about our relationship with Britain, Germany and Japan, FDR was the fount of all wisdom and it would be virtually treasonous to question his judgment. This is an incredible assertion by a serious, accomplished public servant, one who reached the pinnacle of service to his country. This notion of blind obedience to presidential authority on foreign policy is indeed a prescription for monarchy or dictatorship; certainly it does not express the noble democratic ideas of rational man engaging in spirited debate on profound questions of public policy. In this we should side with the Vietnam War generation that not only questioned, but also protested a war that was destructive foolishness. To do anything else is to forsake the promise of a democratic society.

What is the price to pay for the liberation of Kuwait? During the Congressional debate on the force resolution in January, Senator George Mitchell had pondered that question:

> Just this morning I heard it said that there may be "only" a few thousand American casualties. But for the families of those few thousand ... the word ["only"] will have no meaning. And the truly haunting question, which no one will ever be able to answer, will be: did they die unnecessarily?[2]

Deaths of coalition troops as a result of Desert Storm were modest. The US lost 148 (25% from friendly fire) and the total coalition deaths numbered 234. It is estimated that 10,000 Kuwaitis died in the incident from August through liberation in February. The country was heavily devastated and rebuilding was a long process, but one that was facilitated by the immense wealth of the state. The financial costs for Desert Shield and Desert Storm were in the neighborhood of $60 billion, with many nations contributing. An enraged and spiteful Iraq had sabotaged the Kuwaiti oil fields as they left in February, causing an immense environmental disaster, not only in the Persian Gulf waters but in the air, as smoke from fires deliberately set in the oil fields, engulfed the planet for weeks. It was estimated that 6 million barrels of oil went up in smoke.

It was by standard definitions a stunning military success for the United States: a short war, few American casualties, an enemy surrender, and a restored Kuwait. But the basic problems remain as intractable as ever: an unstable Persian Gulf area, volatile oil prices, uncertain oil supplies and Saddam's brutal reign in Iraq. The Gulf War solved a few problems and created a new set of difficulties. And so it is with all wars.

The Bush administration has often asserted that one of the triumphs of this war was that the "monkey of Vietnam was finally off our backs." No longer would nations dismiss America's military power as a "paper tiger," nor would they be able to say that the United States was a nation that couldn't accept battlefield casualties. The stunning military success of Desert Storm had lifted the burden. America was back in control again — around the world.

In the short run, the United States was successful in removing the Iraqi from Kuwait and restoring the autocratic al-Sabah princes. But in the long run, the United States tarnished its

---

1. Baker, *The Politics of Diplomacy*, p. 276.
2. Bush and Scowcroft, *A World Transformed*, p. 445.

image in the streets and bazaars of the Arab world, portending difficulties in the future. The United States is seen as the champion of the rich princes, the international oil companies and the hated Zionists. President Bush thrust American military power into the center of a cauldron of turmoil. "The real problem for the Middle East is not the Gulf crisis per se, but the problems we will face after the crisis is 'resolved'," said the United Nations Secretary General, Boutros Boutros Ghali.[1]

The disastrous consequences following this war — the Aftershocks — came to the US in the morning of September 11, 2001 over the skyscrapers of New York City, the blue skies of Washington D.C. and the farm lands of Pennsylvania. Muslim terrorist groups had for many decades seethed at America's support for Israel. After the Gulf War they had another serious grievance against the US superpower: American military forces were stationed in the Holy Land of Saudi Arabia, defiling the *Land of the Two Shrines*. On that terrible September morning, many innocent people paid a heavy price for the liberation of Kuwait and the Folly of War.

---

1. Mackey, *The Reckoning*, p. 30.

CHAPTER 13. THE WAR ON TERROR: THE CONTRIVED WAR

TUESDAY, SEPTEMBER 11, 2001

By Sunday night September 9, all the hijackers were in their assigned places: Mohammed Atta and his crew in Portland, Maine, Marwan al Shehhi and his crew in Boston, Hani Hanjour near Dulles airport, and Ziad Jarriah with his fellow hijackers in the Newark area. The terrorists spent their last hours attending to various personal duties. Some wrote letters to family and friends, even promising attendance at future events. Others called home for a final visit with loved ones. Mohammed Atta, the ringleader, spent several anxious hours in last minute surveillance of Logan Airport in Boston. A few of the religious fanatics, unMuslim-like, gorged on a last sumptuous meal and indulged their carnal needs with "lap dances" at a sex club.

Atta carried in his luggage a Terrorist Primer that had been prepared for the suicide band of brothers. The suicide pilots and their aides were instructed to sever all earthly ties, shower, shave all excess body hair and perfume their bodies as though entering battle — or preparing a corpse for burial. The Terrorist Primer gave instructions to the Muslim extremists about preparations for their momentous journey and provided words of encouragement at their final moment of anguish:

Recite the verses about forgiveness. You will not return to earth and you will plant fear into the hearts of the infidels.

At 5:30 AM Tuesday, September 11, Atta and his traveling companion Alomari checked out of the Portland, Maine Comfort Inn and drove the ten minute trip to the airport. As the sun rose across the eastern seaboard of the United States on that fateful day, Atta and Alomari could see that Allah had favored them with a perfect day — the sky was blue and cloudless. They boarded their 6:00 AM commuter flight to Boston, commencing the first leg of their historic journey.

Fear is indeed an act of worship. Fear them not, but fear me, if you are a believer.

American Airlines Flight #11 from Boston to Los Angeles took off at 7:59 AM with a crew of 11 and 81 passengers, including Atta, Alomari and two other accomplices. Sixteen minutes into the flight — at 8:15 — Flight #11 ignored air traffic controller's directions to climb to 31,000 feet, then inexplicably turned northward away from the normal flight pattern. Air traffic controllers and nervous American Airlines executives watched helplessly as the large Boeing craft soared through the skies without apparent direction. The airline had been hijacked!

Unbeknownst to airline personnel watching the awful sight from air traffic control facilities, two passengers and a member of the crew had been stabbed and their throats cut. The First Class cabin and the cockpit were sealed off from the rest of the plane. The minutes passed ominously:

8:21   Flight #11 ignores dispatcher orders to respond to commands.

8:22   The plane's transponder stops working.

8:23   Flight #11 wanders aimlessly in the sky.

8:27   Flight attendant Betty Ong hysterically reports to air traffic control that acts of violence and even murder have occurred on the airplane.

8:28   The American Airlines plane turns southward following the Hudson River toward New York City.

8:29   Through an open telephone line the words are heard on the ground: "Don't try to make any stupid moves! Just stay quiet and you'll be okay."

8:40   Flight #11, flying at only 900 feet and nearly 400 miles an hour, skims the skyscrapers of New York City.

8:42   Flight attendant Amy Sweeney excitedly tells traffic control, "This plane has been hijacked." She reports that a passenger's throat has been cut and "He appears to be dead."

8:44   Amy Sweeney's final, hysterical words: "I see water and buildings. Oh my God! Oh my God!......."

The last thing to do is to remember God and your last words should be that there is no God but Allah and that Mohammed is His prophet. Angels are calling your name.

* * *

United Airlines Flight #175 left Boston's Logan Airport bound for Los Angles at 8:14 and by 8:42 it too had strayed from its normal flight pattern. Marwan al Shehhi and his accomplices had hijacked the Boeing 767.

The end is near and the heavenly promise is within reach. Women of paradise will be your reward.

Brian Sweeney, a 38-year-old businessman on board Flight #175, left a poignant final cell phone message for his wife:

Hi, Julie, it's Brian. I'm in a plane being hijacked and it does not look good. I just wanted to let you know that I love you and that I hope to see you again. If I don't, please have fun in life and live life the best you can.

At 9:03, Flight #175 with 65 people aboard slammed into the south tower of the World Trade Center.

There is no God but Allah and Mohammed is His prophet. Angels are calling your name.

* * *

For a nation watching incredulously, it was now clear what was happening: one plane crashing into the World Trade Center could be an accident, but two passenger liners into each of the massive towers was by design.

Aboard American Airlines Flight #77 from Dulles International Airport destined for Los Angeles were three elementary school children, recipients of a National Geographic scholastic award. They were flying to the West Coast where they were to explore the Channel Island National Marine Sanctuary near Santa Barbara. Bernard Brown, Asia Cotton, and Rodney Dickens, ages eleven, along with their teachers and other passengers perished as Flight #77 destroyed a wing of the Pentagon building at 9:38.

When the confrontation begins, strike like champions who do not want to go back to this world. Angels are calling your name.

* * *

United Airlines Flight #93 left Newark Airport at 8:42, just three minutes before the first aircraft crashed into the north tower. While cruising over Pennsylvania, Ziad Jarriah and his "kamikaze crew" were confronted by passengers led by Todd Beamer, whose charge into the airline cockpit has been immortalized by the words, "Lets Roll." After a violent struggle the plane crashed at nearly 600 mph into the Pennsylvania countryside. It is now assumed that Flight #93's destination was the national Capitol. Todd Beamer and his valiant band of Americans saved the nation from an even greater horror.

Pray for yourself and your Muslim brothers for the final victory and fear not, for soon you will encounter God. Angels are calling your name.

* * *

Armed only with box cutters and knives, nineteen Muslim terrorists had created devastation in the United States, defacing the skyline of America's most prominent city and killing three thousand people. The vaunted United States military machine lay impotent; the FBI, CIA and other sophisticated high-tech agencies of government watched helplessly.

President George W. Bush was visiting the Emma E. Booker Elementary School in Sarasota, Florida at the time of the attacks. A few minutes after the first crash at 8:45, Presidential advisor Karl Rove whispered in the President's ear that a plane had flown into the World Trade Center. Then, shortly after 9:00 AM, Chief of Staff Andy Card told the startled President even worse news: "A second plane hit the second tower. America is under attack." President Bush, perplexed and in anguish, continued talking to the second graders, emphasizing his theme that was written on the chalkboard: "Reading makes a country great." Bob Woodward describes the scene when the President heard the news: "A photo of that moment is etched for history. The president's hands are folded formally in his lap, his head turned to hear Card's words. His face has a distant sober look, almost frozen, edging on bewilderment."[1]

When the shaken President emerged from the second grade classroom, he spoke briefly to the nation through the television cameras, evidencing a cold fury. Echoing his fathers call to arms against Saddam Hussein in 1990, Bush the Younger stated that, "Terrorism against our nation will not stand." Later in conversation with aides, the President's Texas-size bravado was

---

1. Bob Woodward, *Bush at War* (New York: Simon and Schuster, 2002), p. 15.

heard: 'We're at war.... We're going to take care of this.... And when we find out who did this, they're not going to like me as president. Somebody is going to pay. We're going to find out who did this and kick their asses."[1]

Later in the day, the President began presenting his "In Defense of Freedom" statements. "Freedom itself was attacked this morning by a faceless coward.... We go forward to defend freedom and all that is good and just in the world."[2] President Bush's statements were reminiscent of FDR's accusations and exaggerations about Hitler's Germany and Harry Truman's charges about Stalin's Russia — except that George Bush wasn't exaggerating. America had actually been attacked.

On Tuesday morning between 8:45 AM and 10:06 AM on September 11, 2001 the people of the United States of America were directly attacked for the first time in their history. The blood of civilians was spilled on American soil and the enemy was within the gates. When the human toll was finally tallied months later, it was learned that 3000 people had been killed — in the four commercial jets, in the World Trade Center, and in the Pentagon. These tragic moments are seared into our collective memory; we all remember what we were doing at the instant we learned of the disasters. America will never be quite the same.

What Did We Know and When Did We Know It?

"I don't think anybody could have predicted that these people would take an airplane and slam it into the World Trade Center," said Condoleezza Rice, National Security Advisor to the President.[3] Agencies of the United States government had, in fact, received numerous clues that an attack was coming, but as with the Japanese attack on Pearl Harbor sixty years before, the clues went unheeded. However, unlike President Roosevelt, President Bush failed to appoint a commission immediately to answer the question of whether the September 11 attack could have been prevented. Bush seemed disinterested in the question of "what did we know and when did we know it?" or why US security agencies failed to respond to numerous signs of impending disaster. FDR appointed the Roberts Commission on January 24, 1942 to investigate the Pearl Harbor disaster. The Roberts Commission rendered a grossly unfair judgment that placed the entire blame on the military commanders at Pearl Harbor. But, at least the President made an effort to assess responsibility, flawed as it was. For George Bush, it would be two years before he appointed a commission to study why such a tragedy could have happened.

Terror attacks on American property and personnel had begun after American troops were stationed in Saudi Arabia in 1990 and as the American-British led embargo and blockade devastated Iraq. For nearly a decade it was evident that Islamist Arab groups, seeking revenge, were plotting against the US and its allies:

- 1993. The World Trade Center was bombed by Arab terrorists. Plans were also discovered to blow up the tunnels leading into New York City, the United Nations building and the New York City offices of the FBI.

---

1. Ibid., p.17-18.
2. Noam Chomsky, *9/11* (New York: Seven Stories Press, 2001), p.148, 152.
3. www.underreported.com.

- 1994. Plots were discovered in which Arab terrorists were planning to commandeer twelve commercial jets as they flew across the Pacific Ocean, blowing them up simultaneously.
- 1994. An Arab terrorist plan to hijack an Air France commercial jet and fly it into the Eiffel Tower was foiled.
- 1995. An Arab terrorist plot to fly a small airplane into the CIA building was discovered.
- 1996. The American military barracks, known as the Khobar Towers in Saudi Arabia, were bombed resulting in nineteen deaths and hundreds wounded.
- 1998. American embassies in Kenya and Tanzania were bombed with 263 deaths.
- 1999. An effort to blow up Los Angeles International Airport was thwarted.
- 2000. The American naval vessel, the USS Cole, was heavily damaged by a terrorist bomb in Yemen resulting in seventeen deaths.
- 2001. During a G-8 summit in Genoa, Italy, a plot was discovered to fly a small plane into the host building.

In 1999, a research arm of the Library of Congress prepared a report for US intelligence agencies which stated in part that "Suicide bombers belonging to Al Qaeda's Martyrdom Battalion could crash-land an aircraft packed with high explosives into the Pentagon, the headquarters of the CIA, or the White House."[1]

It wasn't as though the FBI was completely asleep. Robert Mueller, the Director of the FBI, claimed that his agency had 331 potential terrorists on its "watch list." This list had been sent to the airlines with notices that no one on the list should be allowed to fly. Despite this warning, two of the September 11 hijackers were on that list. Certainly the most outrageous security lapse involved Arab terrorist use of aviation training schools in the United States, which for years had been training pilots from all over the world. The four pilots of the hijacked United and American airliners all took flight lessons in aviation schools in Florida, Arizona, Minnesota and Oklahoma. Further, they often took actions that created suspicion, as when they showed interest only in learning how to guide a large jet plane in flight, not in taking off and landing. The FBI received a written warning in July 2001 from counter- terrorism expert Kenneth Williams. The so-called Phoenix memo began: "The purpose of this communication is to advise the bureau and New York of the possibility of a coordinated effort by Osama bin Laden to send students to the United States to attend civil aviation universities and colleges"[2]

In August 2001, on the eve of the terror attacks, the Minneapolis office of the FBI sent a memo to headquarters raising concern about a known Arab terrorist, Zacarias Moussaoui, whose activities during his tenure at a Minneapolis flight school were suspicious. Moussaoui's behavior prompted one flight school instructor to speculate about how much damage a terrorist could do by flying a commercial jet loaded with fuel into a public building. FBI headquarters in Washington D.C. eventually disregarded the warning received from Minneapolis.

Intelligence agencies of the government did send warnings to the airlines about a possible effort to hijack airliners. The following memo was typical: "It is highly likely that a significant al Qaeda attack is in the near future, within several weeks."[3] That memo was sent June 28, 2001.

---

1. *Washington Times*, National Weekly Ed., Dec. 2-8, 2002, p. 33.
2. John Miller and Michael Stone, with Chris Mitchell, *The Cell: Inside the 9/11 Plot, and Why the FBI and CIA Failed to Stop it* (New York: Hyperion Books, 2002), p. 289.
3. *Washington Times*, National Weekly Ed., Dec 2-8, 2002, p. 33.

The Congressional Intelligence Committee investigation of the terror attacks unearthed a "briefing memo" that was circulated in the White House in July 2001. Richard Clarke, the former White House terrorist expert, emphasized the importance of the memo in his testimony before Congress in 2003. The memo warned:

> We believe that Osama bin Laden will launch a significant terrorist attack against the US and/or Israeli interests in the coming weeks. The attacks will be spectacular and designed to inflict mass casualties against the US facilities or interests. Attack preparations have been made. Attack will occur with little or no warning.[1]

Finally, the tragedy turned into farce when visa applications by Mohammed Atta and several other terrorists were reviewed and processed by the Immigration and Naturalization Service. The INS granted visa approval on July 17, 2001. The approval papers were actually received at an American flight school in March 2002 — six months after Atta and the others had done their awful deed.

Most of the terrorists had entered the country with student visas in the summer of 2000. While traveling around the country and taking flying lessons, they left an extensive trail of money. Government banking agencies track money by requiring any transaction over $10,000 to be reported. A total of $500,000 was transferred from overseas banks to the US bank accounts of the infamous 19 terrorists. Repeatedly, amounts in excess of $10,000 were moved, yet no government agencies investigated this money flow.

In July 2003, the Senate and House Intelligence Committees issued a scathing report criticizing the FBI, CIA and other agencies for their lack of diligence in maintaining contact with al-Qaeda agents, and a gross failure to communicate with each other. The committee detailed the weaknesses of the security agencies:
- the FBI failed to identify al-Qaeda cells operating in the United States.
- the CIA failed to follow up on their watch list of terrorists.
- the FBI had knowledge of two hijackers but did not pursue the matter.

Senator Bob Graham (D, FL) summarized the committee attitude: "The attack of September 11 could have been prevented if the right combination of skill, cooperation, creativity and some good luck had been brought to the task."[2]

Condoleezza Rice's assertion that the administration had no warning of an attack, and President Bush's failure to promptly appoint an investigative commission, suggests that the administration was concealing something. It seems clear, however, that the Bush administration did not know the attack was coming — but they should have. The President's sole focus on finding and punishing the perpetrators has served to obscure the fact that the US intelligence community had failed to protect its citizens. But, if this nation is going to pursue an aggressive foreign policy, sending the military into every region of the world and advising all nations on the proper conduct of their foreign policy, the government must employ greater security precautions. One place to begin is guarding the borders more effectively, which includes a reassessment of the student visa program. The United States military is able to defeat the nation of Iraq, but the FBI, INS and other security agencies must be able to protect the homeland. In this endeavor, they have failed.

---

1. David Corn, *The Lies of George W. Bush: Mastering the Politics of Deception* (New York: Crown Publishers, 2003) p. 142
2. *Atlanta Journal Constitution (AJC)*, July 25, 2003, p. A10.

WHY DO THEY HATE US?

A plaintive wail was heard across the land immediately after the tragic attacks — Why Do They Hate Us? On the cover of *Newsweek* magazine, in presidential addresses, at dinner tables, the question was asked and debated. Citizens of the exceptional nation were having trouble understanding why anyone would want to commit such a beastly deed against them. After a century of "doing good," why this? In its anguish to understand their dilemma, Americans neglected to notice that all Muslim governments actually condemned the terror attack, and public opinion polls indicated that a vast majority of people in the Arab world considered such an attack to be contrary to the teachings of the Koran. It should have been apparent that "they" — the Arab world — all didn't hate us.

But nineteen Muslims intent on suicide and murder did hate something about the US, and many more in the Arab world shared their hostility. Over the next few months, Americans would become acquainted with Osama bin Laden and al-Qaeda, with the Taliban and Shiites and Kurds, and a host of other strange sounding names from far away. Suspicion for the terror attacks fell immediately on the Arab Muslim militant of immense personal wealth who had founded a loosely-organized network of terrorists called al-Qaeda: his name is Osama bin Laden. Through interviews with journalists and speeches to Arab television, bin Laden has detailed the reasons for his 1996 "Declaration of Jihad on the Americans Occupying the Country of the Two Sacred Places." Here is a sampling of bin Laden's public comments and complaints about US policy:

- We declared jihad against the US government because the US government ... has committed acts that are extremely unjust, hideous, and criminal whether directly or through its support of the Israeli occupation of [Palestine].
- And we believe the US is directly responsible for those who were killed in Palestine, Lebanon, and Iraq....
- Due to its subordination to the Jews, the arrogance and haughtiness of the US regime has reached to the extent that they occupied [Arabia]....
- By being loyal to the US regime, the Saudi regime has committed an act against Islam. [1]
- The Muslims have realized they are the main targets of the aggression of the coalition of Jews and the Crusaders [the Western nations]. [2]
- In our religion, it is not permissible for any non-Muslim to stay in our country [Saudi Arabia]. Therefore, even though American civilians are not targeted in our plan, they must leave. We do not guarantee their safety. [3]
- We do not differentiate between those dressed in military uniforms and civilians; they are all targets in the fatwa. [4]
- So we tell the Americans that if they value their lives and the lives of their children, to find a nationalistic government that will look after their interests and not the interests of the Jews. [5]

---

1. Peter Bergen, *Holy War, Inc. Inside the Secret World of Osama bin Laden* (New York: Free Press, 2001), p.19 all of the first four quotes.
2. Bergen, *Holy War, Inc.*, p. 95.
3. Ibid., p. 20.
4. Miller, *The Cell*, p. 191.
5. Ibid.

• And to Americans, I say to it and its people this: I swear by God the Great, America will never... taste security unless we feel security and safety in our land and in Palestine.[1]

Osama bin Laden's use of the term "Crusaders" to describe Western governments is a deliberate attempt to link the US to the infamous Christian Crusades of the twelfth and thirteenth centuries, when Christian knights from Europe invaded the Muslim-held Holy Land, looting, killing and desecrating Muslim sites. The two hundred-year long Crusades against Muslim control of the Holy Land left bitter memories in the Arab world. Osama bin Laden sees himself as just one of many Arab Muslim leaders who have struggled against the infidel West over the last fourteen centuries.

Much of the Arab rancor toward the West arose as a result of British duplicity during and after World War I. The British were attempting to carve out new colonies in the Middle East, but the Ottoman Turkish Empire stood in the way. Early in the war, Britain promised Arab chieftains that if the Muslim tribes assisted in the defeat of the Turks, the West would assist in the creation of an independent Arab nation. (Americans know about these hollow commitments to Hussein of Mecca because of the exploits of his English companion, Lawrence of Arabia.) This proposed Arab state would encompass what is today much of the Middle East — Iraq, Syria, Lebanon, Jordan, Palestine, and possibly Saudi Arabia. In November of 1916, Hussein stood in the Great Mosque in Mecca and proclaimed himself "King of the Arab Lands," then threw his considerable military and political forces onto the side of Britain. The Arab leaders provided military aid, the Turks were defeated, but Britain reneged on the deal.

The British promises fell victim to their own greed for a Middle East empire and to conflicting promises to Palestinian Arabs and to European Jews for a "home" in Palestine — promises contained in the Balfour Declaration of 1917. Arab nationalism emerged in the 19th century as the Ottoman Empire began to disintegrate and Arabs from Gibraltar to the Persian Gulf began to regard themselves as a coherent political entity based on their common religion, language and culture. Despite the urgent pleas of Hussein's son, Faisal, at the Versailles conference in 1919, a single unified Arab nation was denied. Instead, faithful to the secret agreements made among the Western nations in 1916, the Middle East was carved up like the proverbial Thanksgiving turkey into the arbitrary jumble of nations on the map today. France took Syria and Lebanon, while Britain helped themselves to Iraq, Jordan and Palestine (later Israel). "In every instance boundaries met the needs of European colonialism."[2]

The fiction existed that these new Arab states were "mandates" of Britain and France; the Western powers were just sponsoring the Arab nations until they were ready for independence. The reality was that the League of Nations mandate system was a "cover" for Western imperialism. From the Arab point of view, after a hiatus of eight centuries, the Western "Crusaders" had returned; puppet rulers were placed on thrones, Western schools, customs and languages were ever present and Western armies patrolled the streets and guarded the borders.

Attending the Versailles conference pleading for national self-determination was not only Faisal of Arabia, but also Ho Chi Minh of Vietnam. The Western powers denied the national aspirations of both the Indochinese and the Arabs; the Aftershocks of this foolish, shortsighted decision to placate the decaying remnants of European imperialist have rever-

---

1. Ibid., p. 320.
2. Sandra Mackey, *The Reckoning: Iraq and the Legacy of Saddam Hussein*, p. 107.

berated down through the 20th century. Injustices abounded in the newly created Western colonies in the Arab world:

- The Kurds, an ancient people scattered through the north of the region, were denied their own state.
- Iraq was formed by melding together Kurds, Sunni Muslims and Shiite Muslims, an unhappy, unruly blend and a recipe for future troubles.
- Iraq was given only a trace of a maritime coast on the Persian Gulf, a testimony to the desire of Britain to rein in the disputatious state and curry favor with neighboring Kuwait.
- A bogus nation of Kuwait was created at the head of the Persian Gulf for the convenience of the British Navy.
- Greater Syria, the perceived dominant nation, was reduced to the truncated state of Syria and left with a small rather inhospitable seacoast on the Mediterranean Sea.
- Lebanon was created out of the coastal area of Greater Syria. France found it advantageous to separate Lebanon from Syria as Lebanon had a large Christian population, a residue of the Crusades and a potential ally of Paris.

During the period of the mandates, native factions formed and occasionally erupted against British or French rule, always remembering the failed promises and treachery of the West. These uprisings of the native population would be met with rifles and cannons until order was restored. And never a whimper of protest came from Washington D.C. about the loss of "liberty" or "repression of the people." It is quite amazing how brain dead American leaders could be when the British were quelling riots and suppressing national aspirations. Perhaps when Saddam Hussein put down Kurdish and Shiite riots in the 1990s, he should have dressed his Republican Guard in British uniforms and flown the Union Jack. It should be noted here that the architect of much of the British Empire in the Persian Gulf area was Winston Churchill.

To add insult to injury, by mid-century the Arab world was stunned when Israel was carved out of a portion of Palestine. The United Nations decision to create two nations in Palestine, one Jewish, the other Arab, was opposed by the Arab world. The Arab position was that there should be a single state in Palestine with Jews and Arabs sharing power — a sort of Middle East multi-cultural nation. Immediately after the birth of Israel in 1947, neighboring Arab nations tried to destroy the infant state, but the Israeli military drove off the Arab armies, and in the process uprooted 750,000 Palestinians. (The official Israeli story is that the Palestinian refugees fled during the war, and therefore have no "right of return." In view of recent Israeli attempts to uproot the remaining Palestinians from the West Bank — or Arab Palestine — the Arab story of forced eviction seems more plausible.)

Palestine, the Holy Land, is the setting of religious shrines of three major religions — Judaism, Christianity and Islam. The city of Jerusalem is a particularly contentious issue, as the Jews cherish the Wailing Wall where, it is said, the ancient Jewish Temple was located. Yet, for Muslims the site is equally sacred, as the Dome of the Rock is the second most holy place in Islam. Sandra Mackey, in *The Reckoning*, describes the significance of Palestine to Arabs:

> The loss of Palestine translated into an intolerable loss of honor for the mythical Arab nation. As a near sacred symbol among Arabs — the site of victory over the European Crusaders in the twelfth century — Palestine crystallized into a tormenting symbol of Arab humiliation at the hands of what they judged the arrogant imperialistic West. To the Arabs, Israel suckled on Western diplomacy and economic support, was the new Crusader State, the insidious surro-

gate of Western imperialism. And the 700,000 Palestinian refugees displaced by the 1948 war for Palestine became the emblem of Arab outrage at forces they could neither overcome nor vie with successfully. Ignoring the levels of their own complicity in the loss of Palestine and the refusal of most Arab states to accept the Palestinians as refugees, the Arabs nursed their feeling of belittlement and humiliation, vowing to never forget or forgive.[1]

For over five decades, Arabs have watched the West, principally the United States, pour money, military aid and political support into the government of Israel. No other nation in the world receives such largesse from the US. When Israel's military struck deep into Arab Palestine in 1967 and then into Lebanon in 1982, the United States remained mute. When Israel developed a nuclear arsenal with missiles to deliver weapons of mass destruction — the only nuclear power in the region — the United States looked the other way. Arabs notice that the same solicitous attitude is not displayed toward Arab states.

The Aftershocks of the war to liberate Kuwait in 1991 spawned another set of issues that poisoned relations between the United States and the Arab world. In the fall of 1990, United States military forces were stationed in Saudi Arabia, where they remained for years. Injecting these forces into the *Land of the Two Shrines* was thought necessary to defeat Saddam Hussein, but fervent Muslims, like Osama bin Laden, took strong exception to this incursion of infidel troops into their sacred domain. To the strict Muslim, placing foreign troops in Saudi Arabia is tantamount to invading and occupying Vatican City, thereby defiling the Roman Catholic Papacy.

Following the successful liberation of Kuwait in 1991, the United States, Great Britain and France established "no-fly" zones in the northern and southern thirds of Iraq, forbidding Iraqi aircraft from entering these zones, ostensibly for the purpose of protecting the minority populations in the areas. In addition, the United Nations established a total embargo on imports into Iraq in an effort to stop the importation of arms and war materials. The embargo not only stopped the flow of weaponry, but also the importation of food, medicine and other necessities. During the twelve years of the embargo and no-fly zones, hundreds of thousands of Iraq civilians died — from bombs and missiles, from starvation or from diseases that went untreated due to the lack of medicine.

There have been a number of Arab figures who have emerged to capture the imagination of the Arab in the street — General Gamal Nasser of Egypt in mid-century, the unstable, ruthless Iraqi dictator Saddam Hussein, and the ghost-like terrorist, Osama bin Laden. Only bin Laden expresses the virulent anti-Americanism that swirls through the Middle East striking terror in the hearts of Americans. Pakistani General Pervez Musharaf comments that bin Laden is "a cult figure among Muslims who resent everything from the decline in moral values as conveyed by Hollywood movies and TV series to America's lack of support for Palestinians killed by Israeli occupation forces...."[2] Americans regard Osama bin Laden as sort of a mad unibomber; the Arabs see him as Robin Hood in a turban.

The collective memory of the Arab world reaches back many centuries to the ignominy of the Crusades and, more recently, to European duplicity and colonialism. Failed promises, harsh imperial rule, military repression, American armies in their Holy Land, and most of all, the "sell-out" to Israel. The question, "Why Do They Hate Us?" seems unfathomable to Americans, but to Arab Muslims the answers are self-evident.

---

1. Ibid., p. 345.
2. Bergen, *Holy War, Inc.*, p. 34.

Bush Goes to Baghdad

President George W. Bush opened the door to National Security Advisor Condoleezza Rice's office while she was meeting with three United States senators and announced:

Fuck Saddam. We're taking him out![1]

In a style more reminiscent of a high school football coach revving up the team before a game in his native Texas, George W. Bush, the most ardent Christian to hold the presidency since Woodrow Wilson, crudely announced his new policy toward Iraq. The date was March 2002. Bush was going to Baghdad.

The United States digression into Iraq was puzzling to many informed observers. In October 2001, the United States had launched its War on Terror with a withering air attack against the Muslim fundamentalist government in Afghanistan, the hideout of al-Qaeda. The fragile Taliban ruling clique quickly disappeared, while American ground troops futilely hunted for Osama bin Laden and his band of terrorists. Most of the al-Qaeda survivors undoubtedly slipped away into neighboring Pakistan where they found refuge in the friendly Muslim communities of mountainous western Pakistan.

On September 12, 2001, the day after the terror attacks on the US, Secretary of Defense Donald Rumsfeld raised the matter of going after Iraq, not just the al-Qaeda organization. Rumsfeld, supported by his second in command Paul Wolfowitz, had been developing plans to target Iraq and President Saddam Hussein well before September 11. Now, with the emotional public uproar over the attacks, it would be easier to launch a full-scale war against Saddam.

(Former Secretary of the Treasury Paul O'Neill says in his recent book that the Bush administration targeted Saddam as early as January 2001. O'Neill comments that "From the beginning there was a conviction that Saddam Hussein was a bad person and that he needed to go."[2])

However, Secretary of State Colin Powell raised a flag of caution about a Baghdad venture, pointing out that any widespread attack in the Middle East would erode an international coalition and provoke angry outbursts in the Arab world. Privately, Powell was aghast at the audacity of the hawks in the Defense Department and their insistence on including Iraq in the War on Terror. "What the hell are these guys thinking about?" he snapped to Army General Hugh Shelton.[3] Wolfowitz and his associates were like chirping birds: "To Iraq! To Iraq! To Iraq!" President Bush remained focused on al-Qaeda in the fall of 2001, but he always gave a wink and a nod to Wolfowitz when the issue of Iraq came up.

A prominent critic of going to Baghdad once made the case for staying out of the *Land of the Two Rivers*. His caution should have tempered the desire by President Bush for revenge:

> Once you've got Baghdad, it's not clear what you do with it. It's not clear what kind of government you would put in place of the one that's currently there... I think to have America military forces engaged in a civil war inside Iraq would fit the definition of quagmire, and we have absolutely no desire to get bogged down in that fashion.[4]

---

1. *Time*, March 31, 2003.
2. *AJC*, Jan. 11, 2004, p. A7.
3. Woodward, *Bush At War*, p. 61.
4. *The Nation*, April 26, 2004, p. 3

Another critic of the Baghdad venture made a similar argument: "We recognize that the seemingly attractive goal of getting rid of Saddam would not solve our problems, or even necessarily serve our interests.... Had we continued the [war to liberate Kuwait] and overthrown Saddam, we might be worse off today...."[1] And still one more critic urged caution before plunging into the thicket along the Tigris and Euphrates Rivers:

> I firmly believe that we should not march into Baghdad.... To occupy Iraq would instantly shatter our coalition, turning the whole Arab world against us.... It would take us way beyond the imprimatur of international law... assigning young soldiers to a fruitless hunt for a securely entrenched dictator and condemning them to fight in what would be an unwinnable guerrilla war. It could only plunge that part of the world into even greater instability and destroy the credibility we were working so hard to reestablish.[2]

These wise criticisms of a military adventure into Iraq were spoken during the Gulf War in 1991. The first critic was Richard Cheney, then Secretary of Defense; the second comment was from Brent Scowcroft, National Security Advisor under the Bush I. The third was President George H. W. Bush, the father of the current president. Scowcroft remains a skeptic about the Baghdad foray; Cheney has reversed himself and caught the war fever. One can only wonder what the two Bushes talk about as the US is now mired in "an unwinnable guerrilla war."

As the months rolled by and the United States forces swept through Afghanistan without any significant trophy of Osama bin Laden or other al-Qaeda leaders, the President edged closer to the Iraq option. Bush began bristling at Powell's cautious multi-lateral approach, saying that he didn't want other nations to dictate American policy. "At some point we may be the only ones left. That's okay with me. We are Americans," the President boasted.[3] Gradually the administration began focusing attention on the erratic behavior of Saddam Hussein: his horrid record on human rights, his wars against neighboring states, his quest for weapons of mass destruction. The Iraqi dictator was an easy target for moralistic Americans. Bush bore down on Saddam's sins and crimes:

- Saddam had aggressively launched two wars in 1982 and 1990 against Gulf States.
- He had allegedly gassed thousands of people in the 1980s during the war with Iran.
- Iraq had flouted more than a dozen United Nations resolutions.
- Saddam was attempting to obtain or develop nuclear, chemical and biological weapons.
- Tragic stories of cruelty to Iraqi subjects abounded.

During the fateful State of the Union Message of January 29, 2002, the President turned the spotlight on Iraq. Mentioning Iraq along with Iran and North Korea, Bush said: "States like these and their terrorist allies constitute an *axis of evil*, aiming to threaten the peace of the world."

It was apparent at that moment that the US was going to invade Iraq, for the President never mentioned the words Osama bin Laden or al-Qaeda in his speech. By using the phrase "axis of evil" the President associated Iraq and Saddam Hussein with the World War Two "axis of evil" — Nazi Germany and Adolf Hitler. For the American people, there is no more potent connection to evil than to bring in the issue of Hitler. The War on Terror would go to Baghdad and Bush was rallying the people for another moral crusade.

---

1. Mackey, *The Reckoning: Iraq and the Legacy of Saddam Hussein*, p. 352
2. Bush and Scowcroft, *A World Transformed*, p. 464.
3. Woodward, *Bush At War*, p. 81.

On the evening of September 11, 2001, the President announced what came to be called the "Bush Doctrine." The President warned: "We will make no distinction between those who planned these acts and those who harbor them."[1] The Bush Doctrine reflected the searing emotions of the moment as the nation cried out for revenge. Thoughtful people, however, immediately gasped at the inclusiveness of the Bush Doctrine. There were al-Qaeda cells in Germany, Britain, the Philippines, Canada and many other locales, even in the United States. Indeed, most of the nineteen hijackers had lived in the United States for over a year. What exactly would be the reprisal for harboring terrorists? How would the US punish Germany, Britain and even itself?

Further, the issue of who the terrorists were demanded definition. Terrorists from the Palestine area had wreaked havoc on Israel for decades — were these Palestinian terrorists to be lumped together with the infamous nineteen of September 11? Was Israel's safety now linked to the United States? Terrorist groups operating in and around Israel had never attacked the United States. Was Bush going after Hamas, Hezbollah and other anti-Israeli organizations, as well as al-Qaeda? The War on Terror began to resemble an emotional tirade rather than a carefully crafted response to a serious security problem. A form of justice out of the old American West suited this man from the plains of Texas. Masculine bravado colored his speeches:

> Wanted dead or alive. That's how I feel.
> We are going to rain holy hell on them.
> You're with us or against us.
> I want to have them quaking in their boots.
> We will export death and violence to the four corners of the earth....
> We're going to kill them. We're going to put their heads on sticks.
> We're going to find out who did this and kick their asses.
> I'm a war President.

Within minutes of the attack on the World Trade Center, the President announced that the nation was "at war." Had the government of another nation launched the attacks, a declaration of war would have been appropriate. But, the shadowy figures of al-Qaeda and elusive Osama bin Laden were more difficult to deal with. Afghanistan was an obvious al-Qaeda base, but then what would the US do next? These Arab terrorists were everywhere — but nowhere. The American military machine was designed to attack an enemy nation's military bases, command structures or cities. American cruise missiles, B-52 bombers, even the infantry was really helpless against an obscure, elusive terrorist figure. Bush inadvertently described the dilemma the US faced when he said: "A faceless enemy has declared war on the United States of America. So we are at war." Faceless enemies are not the natural prey of the Defense Department. Further defining the predicament, Bush warned: "This is an enemy that runs and hides, but it won't be able to hide forever. An enemy that thinks its havens are safe, but won't be safe forever."[2] The enemy monster residing in the palaces of Baghdad was much easier to destroy. Saddam Hussein was available; Osama bin Laden was not. The War on Terror would take a detour through old Baghdad.

---

1. Ibid., p. 30.
2. Ibid., p. 41.

MUSHROOM CLOUDS, ANTHRAX AND TERRORISTS

The Bush administration's public campaign to wage a war against Iraq was in full steam by September 2002. National Security Advisor Condoleezza Rice laid down the opening salvo that stunned the nation: "We don't want the smoking gun to be a mushroom cloud."

The horror of seeing the twin towers in New York City collapse was traumatic enough, but the image of a mushroom cloud forming above Washington D.C., New York City or any other metropolis was sufficient to startle even complacent citizens into a cry for war. Secretary of Defense Rumsfeld graphically reinforced the picture: "Imagine a September eleven with weapons of mass destruction. It's not three thousand — its tens of thousands of innocent men, women, and children."[1] When in October 2001, strains of the deadly biological agent anthrax were received at several locations in the United States, government leaders and the public were near panic. The drumbeat for war against Iraq continued throughout the fall 2002:

- Vice-President Cheney: "We do know, with absolute certainty, that [Saddam] is using his procurement system to acquire the equipment he needs in order to enrich uranium to build a nuclear weapon. We're to the point where time is not on our side."
- Secretary of State Colin Powell: "I just know that time is not on our side."[2]
- Cheney: Armed with an arsenal of these weapons of terror, "Iraq could directly threaten America's friends throughout the region and subject the United States or any other nation to nuclear blackmail."
- President Bush: "The Iraqi dictator must not be permitted to threaten America and the world with horrible poisons and diseases and gasses and atomic weapons."
- Bush: An Iraqi "alliance with terrorists could allow the Iraqi regime to attack America without leaving any fingerprints."[3]
- Secretary of Defense Rumsfeld urgently warned that, "There is no doubt in my mind that they currently have chemical and biological weapons."[4]

In his State of the Union message of January 2003, President Bush specifically accused Saddam of attempting to procure material for nuclear weapons. Bush claimed, "Our intelligence sources tell us that [Saddam] has attempted to purchase high-strength aluminum tubes suitable for nuclear weapons production."[5] The President announced that British sources had confirmed that Iraq had attempted to buy aluminum tubes from the African nation of Niger. Using his normal grave tones and knowing countenance, Richard Cheney warned: "We believe they had, in fact, reconstituted nuclear weapons."[6]

Not only had Saddam Hussein acquired weapons of mass destruction, but the Bush administration also claimed there was clear evidence of Iraq's growing comradeship with Osama bin Laden and al-Qaeda terrorists. During the September "advertising campaign" promoting the war against Iraq, both Bush and Rice warned of the "marriage" between Saddam and bin Laden:

---

1. www.truthout.com, "Selling of the Iraq War," June 30, 2003.
2. Jay Bookman, *AJC*, September 4, 2003, p. A17.
3. www.truthout.com,
4. *Time*, June 9, 2003, p. 29.
5. *The New Republic, TRB*, June 2, 2003, p. 6.
6. *Time*, June 9, 2003, p. 29.

Bush — "Al-Qaeda becomes an extension of Saddam's madness."

Rice — "There clearly are contacts between al-Qaeda and Iraq." [1]

Secretary Powell's influential speech before the United Nations in February 2003 affirmed that an al-Qaeda operative, Abu Musad al-Zarqawi, was living in northern Iraq. As America began marshalling troops on the edges of Iraq, the American public was convinced that Iraq and al-Qaeda were linked in a deadly anti-American embrace. Shortly, the United States would be under attack; the deadly duo of Saddam Hussein and Osama bin Laden could choose from a variety of weapons — anthrax, poison gas and atomic bombs. With these calamitous images in mind, the American public gave consent to a pre-emptive war in the Persian Gulf.

However, as with a long line of fabricated or distorted incidents — the *Maine*, the *Lusitania*, the bogus Nazi maps, the *Greer*, the Greek and Korean civil wars, the Gulf of Tonkin Incident — the story told by administration officials was not accurate. Some of these sensational tales now appear to be outright fabrications, others give evidence of panicky misinterpretation. The allegation that Iraq used chemical warfare on its own citizens is a case in point.

United States government documents allege that between 1983 and 1988, on ten occasions during the Iran-Iraq War, Saddam used poison gas on his own citizens, resulting in the death of over 30,000 people. It is undeniable that both Iran and Iraq were using chemical warfare during that long war. However, the conditions of the alleged Iraqi use of poison gas on its own citizens are disputed. For example, the gas attack on the Iraqi town of Halbjah in March 1988 may have occurred when Iranian helicopters sprayed poison gas on the town, or it may have occurred when Saddam took reprisal on the area because the Kurdish residents had given support to an Iranian incursion into northeastern Iraq. There were vigorous Kurdish separatist efforts taking place during the war with Iran; Saddam did not take kindly to such "traitorous" actions.

As the Iraqi biological and chemical warfare program was being readied for use in 1983, President Ronald Reagan sent a special envoy to Baghdad to discuss US assistance to Saddam during the war. The envoy, Donald Rumsfeld, engineered renewed diplomatic relations with the dictator on the Tigris River, eventually supplying him with biological and chemical weapons — anthrax, botulism and various toxic gases. Senator Robert C. Byrd (D, WV.) claims to have seen government records showing shipments of West Nile virus and dengue fever virus to Iraq in the 1980s. The Senator concludes: "We had in fact transmitted germ warfare to Iraq, a veritable cookbook of ingredients of use only in concocting biological and chemical weapons." [2] These lethal exports were all licensed by the United States Department of Commerce and included extensive shipments of insecticides, some from Dow Chemical Corporation. It is clear that some noxious biological and chemical agents originated in the United States, sent to Iraq with the approval the United States government.[3]

In summary, Iraq did use chemical agents during the war with Iran, but almost entirely on the advancing Iranian troops. If poison gas was used on civilians, it was a reprisal against the treacherous Kurdish alliance with Iranian Kurds. At the time of these incidents, the United

---

1. www.truthout.com.

2. Robert C. Byrd, *Losing America* (New York: W. W. Norton and Company, 2004), p. 150.

3. *Washington Post*, Michael Dobbs, Dec. 30, 2002, p. AO1; Alex Callinicos, *The New Mandarins of America Power*, (Malden, Mass.: Blackwell Publishers, 2003), p. 19

States government was encouraging such chemical usage and even supplying Baghdad with the agents. The Bush administration is aware of the United States complicity in this sorry episode, yet unashamedly blames the illegal and inhumane use of such weapons solely on the treachery of Saddam Hussein.

The story of the Iraqi gambit in Africa to purchase aluminum tubes is equally disappointing to those expecting to hear the "truth" from the White House. The story was totally bogus and known to be bogus by many in the Bush administration when President Bush told the American people of the supposed incident. Prior to the Bush announcement of the quest for uranium by Iraq, the CIA had sent long-time diplomat Joe Wilson to Africa to ascertain the validity of the story. Wilson confirmed that the alleged incident was based on forged documents; all subsequent investigations have corroborated this. Once again the Bush administration was so desperate that it grasped any shred of evidence, no matter how flimsy or flawed.

The spurious nature of the Bush allegations became more evident as the President proclaimed victory in the Iraqi War. The false charges tolled throughout the year 2003:

- "Saddam Hussein has chemical weapons" NONE FOUND!
- Saddam has a secret arsenal of scud missiles. NONE FOUND!
- Iraq has anthrax spores, not "verifiably accounted for." FALSE!
- "Saddam has [never] abandoned his nuclear weapons program." FALSE!
- Bio-weapon trailers and decontamination vehicles have been seen. NONE FOUND!
- "Aircraft suited for dispensing chemical and biological weapons" exist. FALSE![1]

Any connection between Osama bin Laden and Saddam Hussein were trivial, most likely nonexistent. In January 2004, Secretary of State Powell finally admitted that there were no links to al Qaeda in Iraq. The Iraqi Baath party of Saddam Hussein enforced a secular state, severing official support for Islam decades ago. Saddam's regime granted general equality of rights in employment and education to women, and there was no enforcement of the Muslim tradition of females being veiled, shrouded or banned from public places. One could see more women walking freely and driving automobiles in the streets of Baghdad than in any city in Saudi Arabia. Iraq never extended diplomatic relations to the Islamic fundamentalist Taliban regime in Afghanistan that sheltered al-Qaeda. Saddam and bin Laden represent two entirely different Muslim worlds. Saddam operated the type of secular Arab State that bin Laden despised.

On October 3, 2003, David Kay of the United States weapons inspection team reported that 1,200 inspectors had been searching for evidence of weapons of mass destruction since the March invasion; none were found. The United States own inspectors had come up empty. The entire justification for war was as hollow as the Gulf of Tonkin fabrication. But the Bush team was undaunted, for the weapons issue was always just a fig leaf anyway. Donald Rumsfeld admitted as much when he said: "The absence of evidence is not evidence of absence [of weapons]."[2] In other words there is no smoking gun, which proves there is a smoking gun! George Orwell, wherever he is, must be smiling.

---

1. Editors&Publishers.com.
2. *Harper's Magazine*, April 2003.

PAX AMERICANA — AMERICAN WORLD HEGEMONY

The Bush administration had pulled a "bait and switch" on the public; the War on Iraq was unrelated to the War on Terror. All the lurid tales about weapons of mass destruction, gassing Iraqi citizens, mushroom clouds over America, al-Qaeda terrorists using Iraq as a haven, were exaggerations, distortions, even lies. To find the real reason for Bush going to Baghdad, one must look elsewhere.

In September of 2002, President Bush issued his National Security Strategy (NSS) which provoked a furor in the intellectual community. Required by Congress since the 1980s, the NSS is usually a boilerplate recital of the President's foreign policy goals. What made this 2002 document so controversial was the bluntness of its words as well as the substance of its policy. Prompted by the September 11 terrorist attacks and emboldened by President Bush's Texas-sized bravado, this NSS document announced in strident terms that the US would fling its military force across the oceans and continents — for the betterment of mankind, of course. The "New World" order would be run from Washington D.C. Provocative phrases march across the pages of the document:

- We cannot let our enemies strike first.
- Today, our enemies see weapons of mass destruction as weapons of choice.
- The only path to peace and security is the path of action.
- We will not hesitate to act alone.
- Our best defense is a good offense.
- The United States will, if necessary, act preemptively.
- We must deter and defend against the threat before it is unleashed.
- The allies of terror are the enemies of civilization.

American foreign policy, henceforth, would project its power around the globe, maintaining bases on every continent and in every region, anticipating land, sea and air combat with numerous adversaries — a *Pax Americana*. Rejecting the more passive stance of deterrence and containment, the US will assume a more active policy toward its enemies — and supposed enemies. America will act unilaterally, "ignoring international opinion" if necessary. And for the first time in its history, the White House announced that it would strike before it is attacked; war may be preemptive, even preventive.

Major international efforts have been expended during the 20th century by the world's nations to discourage preemptive war and eliminate preventive war, as wars undertaken prior to any clear attack have usually been the province of aggressor states. All countries belonging to the United Nations have foresworn any preemptive or preventive attacks. The relevant section of the United Nations Charter dealing with this matter is Article #51, which states: "Nothing in the present Charter shall impair the inherent right of individual or collective self-defense if an armed attack occurs against a Member of the United Nations." Concisely, a nation (or a group of nations) can use its military force only when an obvious attack has been launched against that nation. All nations are under the legal obligation not to strike first.

The administration of Franklin Roosevelt made determined efforts to ensure that Japan fired first in the Pacific war in the 1940s, accepting thousands of casualties as a result. President John Kennedy anguished over the issue of whether the US should strike first against the Russian missiles in Cuba, finally choosing not to act preemptively. Throughout the Cold War years, when each superpower accumulated thousands of nuclear weapons, both rejected the idea of a first strike. In an effort to ensure that America's intentions are not misunderstood, presidents throughout the 20th century have rejected any first use of weapons. But with George W. Bush, no more.

In typical Texas style, President Bush announced that "the best offense is a good defense," and the world is warned that the United States may be the first to strike. The use of such a trite slogan borrowed from football talk reflects the rather unsophisticated attitude of the Bush administration. (It does, however, fit nicely with Bush announcing, "Fuck, Saddam! We are taking him out," and the Bush comment about North Korean's diminutive President Kim Jong Il being a "pygmy.") All of this locker room talk plays well with Yahoos across the nation, but does not invite confidence among leaders of other nations or the informed public.

For an American president to speak approvingly of preemptive and preventive war invites others to do the same. India may strike first against Pakistan to forestall a Pakistani nuclear launch. China may find it more convenient to strike against Taiwan rather than wait for a later disadvantageous moment. Israel may bomb Syria, Russia may invade Chechnya, just to get in the first licks. There are dozens of nations that may find precipitous attacks more acceptable now that America has shown the way. The century-long effort of international organizations, and of the United States itself, to contain war is placed in jeopardy by the Bush NSS.

The NSS document worries that "rogue states" will use weapons of mass destruction against the US, but when was this ever done? So-called rogue states (Iraq, Iran, Syria, Libya, North Korea and Cuba) have shown remarkable restraint in their weapons policy. None have shown any willingness to make weapons of mass destruction their "weapons of choice." Surely their restraint is, in part, because of the enormous deterrent element in the American nuclear arsenal. The United States endured forty years of Cold War, always rejecting the notion of a "first strike." Containment and deterrence worked against the formidable power of the Soviet Union. Why not continue to use this policy against states having far less military capabilities?

The subtleties of preemptive and preventive war have escaped the writers of the 2002 NSS document. Consider the following scenarios about personal safety that are analogous to international affairs:

As you walk along a darkened street, a hostile-looking stranger approaches and brandishes a knife. Before he slashes, you quickly disarm him.

As you walk along a street, each person who passes you seems suspicious and you quickly frisk him or her to see if each is carrying a weapon that could be used to harm you.

Terrified of being attacked by a random stranger, you break into homes throughout your neighborhood searching for weapons that you fear may be hidden there.

Preemptive war and preventive war can take on many disguises. Preemptive war — taking discreet military action against a threatening adversary before the adversary strikes — has generally been accepted only if the following conditions exist:[1]

- The threat of harm is imminent to the nation.
- There is evidence that an attack is clear and specific.
- Such an attack would do damage to the vital interests of the nation.
- All diplomatic solutions to the dispute have been exhausted.

---

1. Paul W. Schroeder, "The Case Against Preemptive War," *The American Conservative*, Oct. 21, 2002.

In the three scenarios listed above, only #1 is consistent with the rules of international law. A weapon is clearly evident and there is an obvious intent to use it in a way that could do great bodily harm. The law does not require awaiting an attack before responding; a preemptive war is lawful in this scenario. Scenarios #2 and #3, on the other hand, evidence some paranoia and utilize a "dragnet" approach to confiscate weapons — weapons that may not even exist. Scenarios #2 and #3 are called preventive war; each involves making unwarranted assumptions about the existence of weapons and a potential attack. International law and custom prohibit all preventive war.

President Bush made a spirited effort to prove the existence of Iraqi weapons of mass destruction and that Saddam Hussein was poised to use them. Six months after the attack on Iraq was launched, no weapons were found and the docile nature of the Iraqi regime when threatened with American military power suggests that there was no intention to strike the US. Neither preemptive war nor preventive war was justified in this instance. International law, while recognizing the legality of a preemptive strike under certain conditions, does not allow for "regime change" or "nation building." Properly used, preemptive war permits reprisals against a nation in order to disarm and neutralize a pending attack. It does not permit an army of occupation and the imposition of an America-led government. Preemptive war cannot legally be used as a cover for imperial conquest, hegemony or "nation building."

The unilateralism in the NSS document reinforces Bush's abrupt go-it-alone attitude in other areas of foreign policy: rejection of the Kyoto agreement, refusal to join the International Crimes Tribunal, rejection of the ABM treaty, refusal to support the ban on anti-personnel land mines and more. Some of these international agreements have flaws, but Bush has shown little interest in remedying the flaws. The United States has simply said "No," and walked away from the bargaining table "like a sullen, pouting, oblivious and over- muscled teenager."[1]

For some neoconservatives, the NSS of 2002 and the Bush unilateralism suggests that the real agenda is to undermine the United Nations. County and state organizations of the Republican Party are busy passing resolutions demanding that the United States withdraw from the UN. Arch-neoconservative Richard Perle disclosed this goal in an article entitled "Thank God for the Death of the UN." Said the Chairman of Bush's Pentagon's Defense Policy Board:

> Saddam Hussein's reign of terror is about to end. He will go quickly, but not alone: in a parting irony, he will take the UN down with him.... What will die is the fantasy of the UN as the foundation of a New World order. As we sift the debris, it will be important to preserve, the better to understand, the intellectual wreckage of the liberal concept of safety through international law administered by international institutions.[2]

The Bush NSS document, with its emphasis on universal moral values, could have been written by President Woodrow Wilson, who shared George Bush's Protestant evangelical fervor. It asserts that "the United States must defend liberty and justice because these principles are right and true for all people everywhere. These are God-given values. These aren't United States-created values." [3] Then the document sets up a straw man, easily demolished by the Bush team: "No people on earth yearn to be oppressed, aspire to servitude or eagerly await

---

1. www.foreignpolicy.com/issue_novdec_2002/gaddis.html.
2. Joseph Wilson, *The Politics of Truth*, (New York: Carroll & Graf Publishers, 2004), p. 420
3. *International Herald Tribune online*, www.iht.com/articles/77501.html.

the midnight knock of the secret police." In other words, the Iraqis will welcome the American invaders as "liberators" not conquerors.

However, as most Bush critics see the situation, the conflict is not between the "midnight knock on the door" and Western-style liberty, but a question of who dispenses this liberty and how much liberty should be dispensed. As the war in Iraq ended in the summer of 2003 and the American occupation began, it became clear that a significant portion of the Iraqi population opposed the American presence in their land. During 2005 as "pacification" of Iraq continues, the American-led coalition forces are suffering more casualties than during the war itself. It is proving more difficult to conquer the towns and cities than to defeat Saddam's Army. It would seem that the Iraqi people want to dispense their own liberty.

The Bush administration clings to the word "liberty" as though it was a lifesaver, the assumption being that all humans will rally around the Americans if the Stars and Stripes are accompanied by "Miss Liberty." But liberty is only one of a number of political values that guides a society, others, of at least equal importance, are security, social stability and equal treatment. Conservatives since the days of Edmund Burke have argued that man is not "free" unless he has security and stability of society. Burke, an icon of true conservatives, when told that the French revolutionaries were spreading liberty throughout the world, is said to have contemptuously responded that if the revolutionaries really wanted to spread liberty they should open all the prisons and mental institutions. Then all would be "free."

If one takes a serious look at the woes of American society today, it would be easy to conclude that this nation itself suffers from an excess of liberty: fathers flee their families, young men maraud through the streets of cities after dark spreading fear, corporate executives raid the company treasuries for their own opulent lifestyle, young women casually abort fetuses as a means of birth control and corporations flee the United States taking jobs to foreign lands. In comparison to Islamic lands of the Middle East, the American crime rate is high, prisons are overflowing, family life is in disarray and the nation's streets are unsafe to walk at night. With all these social problems, an inferior public school system, increasing disparity in income and an inadequate health delivery system, just who does the US think it is to wander the world looking for nations upon whom to impose "regime change?"

MILITANT IDEALISM DELUXE

But, the US plunges immodestly into every region of the world, warning in the NSS document that "our forces will be strong enough to dissuade potential adversaries from pursuing a military buildup in hopes of surpassing, or equaling the power of the United States." Carrying the banner of liberty and benevolence, President Bush offers to the world the deluxe version of Militant Idealism. Unconcerned with the fact that shadowy terrorists are impervious to the American military, the Bush defense budget has soared to new heights. In the fiscal year 2004, $400 billion will be spent to "defend" America, an amount equal to the combined defense spending of all other nations on earth. With approximately 30% of the world's economic output, the United States produces 50% of the world's armaments. The six notorious "rogue nations" spend a total of $14 billion, about 4% of the United States total.[1] South Korea, an American ally, spends nine times as much as North Korea on defense, Japan more than China,

Israel spends as much on defense as Iraq and Iran combined, yet it is only the "rogue nations" whose expenditures are highlighted and condemned. Each of these American allies — South Korea, Japan, Israel — is deemed to be in dire need of additional military defense, provided, of course, by the United States.

The United States has 300,000 troops scattered around the globe in over 130 foreign countries, but the demands are always for more. There are 41,000 troops in Japan and another 41,000 remain on guard at the Korean War truce line, even though South Korea has a much larger economy and military force than its communist neighbor. The United States keeps nearly 100,000 armed forces personnel in the Far East. Another 120,000 troops are still stationed in Europe, more than a decade after the Cold War ended. The North Atlantic Treaty Organization (NATO), created in 1950 to defend against a supposed armed attack by the communist Soviet Union, has not been disbanded, even though the Soviet Union doesn't exist and "communists" don't march anymore. Indeed NATO is alive, well and growing, as membership will increase to 26 nations in 2004. Continued US control of the military command structure of NATO is protected by the increase in membership of NATO. The new members, all from Eastern Europe, give the United States a margin of safety in NATO votes, as the likes of Lithuania and Bulgaria are easily influenced by foreign aid grants and are grateful to the United States for the infusion of military bases adding dollars to their economy. The seven little sisters from the Baltic region and the Danube basin will counterbalance the votes of France and Germany, countries that frequently see matters differently than the United States. Using Defense Secretary Rumsfeld's callous words — New Europe has been called into being to balance Old Europe.

The United States possesses over 50% of the world's nuclear weapons. It is a major supplier of the world arms trade and its closest ally in the Middle East, Israel, is that region's only nuclear power. The major nuclear powers showing declared and undeclared weapons are:

USA	10,600
Russia	8,600
China	400
France	350
Britain	200
Israel	200
Pakistan	35
India	35
North Korea	2

Iraq's sporadic attempts to develop nuclear weapons have become a major issue for the United States. For several decades the US has attempted to stop the spread of nuclear weapons through the Nuclear Non-proliferation Treaty, which most nations have signed. Significantly, non-signers of the Treaty include the Middle East nations of Iraq, Iran and Israel. The White House points accusing fingers at Iraq and Iran for their quest for nuclear weapons, but seldom does it condemn Israel for the same behavior. Further, Israel has been slapped with more United

---

1. www.thirdworldtraveler.com/Pentagon.

Nations sanctions than Iraq, yet no protest comes from the White House about Israel's sorry record.

If the United States is successful in stopping the spread of nuclear weapons and freezing the "Nuclear Club" at the present numbers, the United States will retain a preponderance of nuclear power. This serves the interest of the Militant Idealists whose armed forces can then be stationed around the world with little fear of nuclear attacks from "rogue states." George Bush told the world that Saddam Hussein was developing nuclear missiles that threatened the nation; he deceived the people. Saddam's short-range missilery threatened Israel and any American troops that the Militant Idealists stationed in and around Iraq. The widespread perception is that the Nuclear Non-proliferation Treaty represents a humane and wise attempt to protect the world from the scourge of nuclear wars. The perception is false. In the hands of the Militant Idealists, it is a tactical effort to disarm their opponents.

If the United States were indeed interested in ridding the world of nuclear peril, it would launch a campaign of general nuclear disarmament; no American administration since the Cold War began has introduced the issue of abandoning nuclear weapons. Obviously, the American position on nuclear weapons is self-serving and hypocritical, not idealistic and humanitarian. Our weapons and those of our allies "keep the peace and spread democracy;" our designated enemies' weapons threaten world order. As historian Paul Schroeder has said about American policy: "To put it bluntly, it declares that there is one law for the United States and other states of which it approves, and another law for the rest. It is Orwellian: all states are equal, but some, especially the United States are vastly more equal than others." [1]

There is, of course, another way to deal with the vulnerability of US troops stationed around the world: bring the troops back to the North American continent, reduce the level of weaponry and reassess US policy towards Israel.

The National Security Strategy document of 2002 says gravely that, "The great strength of this nation must be used to promote a balance of power that favors freedom." The USS Kitty Hawk, one of the carrier battle groups, is a veritable floating city of several thousand. This nuclear powered vessel is 1100 feet long, twenty stories high with a flight deck 250 feet long. A crew of 6,000 operates and maintains the 70 aircraft stored in its belly. But this behemoth of the seas is not alone; surrounding it are Aegis cruisers with the most sophisticated radar system, several destroyers and frigates, submarines and supply vessels. The United States Navy has thirteen such carrier groups: no other country has any.

The neoconservative architects of Bush's foreign policy must be pleased with the military juggernaut that straddles the oceans and continents. Secretary Colin Powell once commented to Congress that he wanted to see a condition in which "there is no future in trying to challenge the armed forces of the United States." Speaking for the US, Powell trumpeted, "I want to be the bully on the block." [2]

John Dryden, the poet laureate of England three centuries ago, had an appropriate comment:

When the chosen people grow too strong

---

1. Paul W. Schroeder, "The Case Against Preemptive War," *The American Conservative*, Oct 21, 2002.

2. Clyde Pestowitz, Rogue *Nation: American Unilateralism and the Failure of Good Intentions* (New York: Basic Books, 2003), p. 23,24.

The rightful cause at length becomes the wrong.

THE NEW CONSERVATIVES — THE BIBLE BELT AND THE BORSCHT BELT

Neoconservatives have recently taken over the Republican Party, where their sojourn began some thirty years ago. In the midst of America's travail over the Vietnam War, war hawks in the Democratic Party left their traditional home and came to reside in the Grand Old Party. Their militant attitude about projecting American power around the world was out of fashion in the party of George McGovern in the early 1970s. They affirmed that the Vietnam War was a worthy cause, poorly managed by Washington. This group's leadership is predominately Jewish and their sentimental attachment to the state of Israel conditioned them to a muscular response in any international crisis. They urged the US to stand stalwart in defense of the "only democracy in the Middle East." Ronald Reagan's election in 1980 brought them to Washington D.C. in large numbers and their influence on Republican politics surged.

(The issue of ethnic-racial influence on United States foreign policy is an unexplored, sensitive and little discussed issue. "Dual loyalty"— a citizen having an allegiance to America and another nation — is spoken about in hushed tones. The Jews and Israel are only one of many such relationships: Cuba, Ireland, Korea, Mexico, Iran and Haiti raise similar dilemmas. Presidential candidates are in peril if they say the wrong thing in Miami about Cuba, or about Mexico in southern California or anywhere in the country against Israel. In dealing with this issue it seems apparent that such divided loyalties create an intractable problem for United States foreign policy. With each ethnic-racial group pulling this way and that, what is "American" foreign policy? Is American policy protecting Tel Aviv, Seoul, and Kuwait City, or New York, Los Angeles and Chicago?)

The ancestry of the present neoconservative group is rooted in liberal and even leftist politics of the 1930s and 1940s. Their orientation was always toward big government, in domestic or international matters. The "nanny state" that organized social welfare programs at home in the 1930s was matched by the *Militant Idealist* State conducting *Pax Americana* around the globe. True conservatives, as opposed to neoconservatives, are discreet in their approach to problems, averse to using the power of government, concerned about the effects of unintended consequences (Aftershocks of war) and thrifty with the people's money. Neoconservatives, or fake conservatives, have radical views about America's role in the world, are devoted to the use of governmental power to accomplish various programs and wasteful with the public's tax dollars (the war in Iraq will cost at least $200 billion). The Republican Party welcomed the newcomers to their fold in the 1970s; by 2003 most of the old guard conservatives had been steamrolled by the Neo-cons.

The *eminence grise* of the neo-con movement is Richard Perle, who as an aide to Senator Henry Jackson (D, WA) worked to secure protection for Jewish émigrés from Russia in the 1970s. From the beginning, the neoconservative movement displayed a solicitous concern for the needs of Israel. Perle is a personal friend of Israeli Prime Minister Ariel Sharon and is on the Board of Directors of the Jerusalem Post; at one time Perle was an official with an Israeli weapons manufacturer. Another influential leader in the movement is William Kristol, former chief of staff for Vice-president Dan Quayle and presently editor of *The Weekly Standard* magazine, the Bible of the neo-con movement — a publication funded by Rupert Murdoch's (Fox) News Corp. George W. Bush's Defense Department is staffed by heavy-hitters from the neoconservative wing of the GOP: Secretary of Defense Donald Rumsfeld, Paul Wolfowitz is Deputy Defense Secretary and Douglas Feith, Assistant Secretary of Defense for Policy. In the State Department, Undersecretary of State John Bolton and an assistant, David Wurmser, hold forth. And always hovering in the shadows, as a modern day Cardinal Richelieu, is Vice-president Richard Cheney a recent convert to the creed.

The neoconservatives have been lobbying in the highest levels of government for over thirty years for the United States to launch its *Pax Americana*. Presidents Ford, Carter and Reagan either rejected or diluted their prescription for American global reach. Emboldened by the elder Bush's foray into the Persian Gulf in 1990, Paul Wolfowitz prepared a Defense Department memo in 1992 that contained phrases similar to the 2002 NSS document: the United States may have to take preemptive action to prevent the development or use of weapons of mass destruction, with Iraq singled out. Alarmed at the strident tone of the memo and the implications of American hegemony, the Bush administration sent it back for "redrafting."

In 1996, five years before the terrorist attack in 2001, Perle, Feith and Wurmser produced a study titled, "A Clean Break: A New Strategy for Securing the Realm," the realm being Israel. It was written with the imprint of the Israeli Institute for Advanced Strategic and Political Studies and became a blueprint for the aggressive policy of the Likud Party of Ariel Sharon. The study urged the overthrow of Saddam Hussein because of his vitriolic statements and support of Palestinian terrorists. The neo-cons argued that with Saddam removed, Syria and Iran would be intimidated and the geo-political dynamics of the Middle East would change. In other words, Israeli-Palestinian peace lay through Baghdad.

In 1998 many leading neoconservatives signed a letter addressed to President Clinton urging that the US adopt the strategy outlined in "A Clean Break." That letter to the White House stated that containment had failed and "removing Saddam Hussein from power...needs to become the aim of American foreign policy." For those in the State Department who were cautious of a unilateral approach, the letter emphasized that "American policy cannot continue to be crippled by a misguided insistence on unanimity in the United Nations Security Council."[1]

Neoconservative strategists have targeted Saddam Hussein for several decades — long before the September 11, 2001 terror attacks on America, and long before there were any serious attempts by Iraq to develop nuclear weapons. The relentless drive of Perle, Wolfowitz, Rumsfeld, Cheney and cohorts finally bore fruit when the inexperienced President George W. Bush panicked after the September 11 attacks and accepted their radical idea of *Pax Americana*. The notion that America's occupation of Iraq was based significantly on concern for Israel's security seems well-establish by 2003. President Bush admitted as much during a May, 2003 meeting in the White House when he said, "I saved [Prime Minister Ariel] Sharon's ass in Iraq. He owe me..."[2]

The neoconservative relationship with Israel is troubling. There are, of course, arguments to be made for *Pax Americana*, apart from the American-Israeli connection. But Perle, Feith and Wurmser working for an Israeli think tank, then working in the highest levels of America's government and presenting the same strategic plan dealing with Israel's security crisis, raises ques-

---

1. *Time*, March 31, 2003, p. 175.
2. *Current History*, Jan. 2004, "The Middle East Entangles America" p. 6.

tions about their national loyalty. Is *Pax Americana* designed to protect the US or Israel? As conservative philosopher Russell Kirk said: "It has seemed as if some eminent neoconservatives mistook Tel Aviv for the capital of the United States."[1] Some in Israel recognize the explosive nature of this problem and are frank in confronting it. The Israeli commentator, Akiva Eldar, recently wrote in an Israeli publication that Perle, Feith and others "are walking a fine line between their loyalty to America's government and Israeli interests."[2]

But allegiance to *Pax Americana* ranges far beyond the Jewish intellectual community of New York City and Washington. The massive public support afforded Bush for his global adventures comes largely from devout evangelical Protestants. These same Protestant pietists first dreamed of crusade a century ago to "Take up the White Man's Burden," and then "To Make the World Safe for Democracy." On Sunday mornings from Protestant pulpits, parishioners are regaled with stories of Armageddon and latter day events. According to some Protestant Biblical scholars, events at the end of the world will occur in the Holy Land, with Israel and Palestine as central players — and God is on the side of the Jews. The Muslim menace must be crushed to make way for the kingdom of God. Anti-Muslim vitriol spews from many Protestant pulpits across the Bible Belt of the South each Sunday:

Jerry Falwell	— the prophet Mohammed was a "terrorist."
Jimmy Swaggert	— "this is not really a war between nations. It is a war with a religion."
Billy Graham	— Islam is "wicked."
Pat Robertson	— Islam is "worse that the Nazis."

The Reverend Pat Robertson, erstwhile GOP presidential candidate, revealed his view of international relations: "The entire world is being convulsed in a religious struggle — the struggle is whether Hubal, the Moon God of Mecca, known as Allah, is supreme, or whether the Judeo-Christian Jehovah is God."[3] The International Fellowship of Christians and Jews is the largest private philanthropic organization contributing to Israel; $20 million was collected in 2002. This Christian solidarity with Israel can draw on 70 million American voters. This relationship is indeed an unlikely marriage that unites the Protestant Bible Belt of the South to the Jewish enclaves around New York's Borscht Belt.

THE FOLLY OF WAR

The weekend of August 4-5, 1990 was one of the most fateful in American history. At some time during those two days, President George Bush made a tragic decision to send American armed forces in massive numbers into Saudi Arabia, ostensibly to reverse Iraq's occupation of Kuwait. The United States, along with its Atlantic ally, Great Britain, has been at war with the nation of Iraq continuously since that period, and American troops remain in and around the Muslim Holy Land of Saudi Arabia yet today. The American-British war on Iraq has traveled through three stages:

1. John Erhman, *The Rise of Neoconservatism: Intellectual and Foreign Affairs -1945-94* (New Haven, CT.: Yale University Press, 1995), p.186.
2. www.thornwalker.com/ditch/snieg_conc/html, Stephan Sniegoski, "The War on Iraq."
3. *AJC*, Craig Nelson, Dec. 25, 2003, p. A16.

1. 1990–1991. The allied coalition forces during January and February, 1991 eject Iraq from Kuwait. After the liberation of Kuwait, American forces remain to guard the ramparts in Saudi Arabia.

2. 1991–2003. The United Nations sanctions — an embargo on imports into Iraq and a boycott on the sale of oil — against Saddam Hussein's regime are enforced by military contingents of the United States, assisted by Britain. In addition, the United States and Britain create and enforce the "no-fly" zones in Iraq.

3. 2003–2004. President George W. Bush decides to perform an "unnatural act" on Saddam Hussein and "take him out."

The Persian Gulf area had been important to the United States since World War II, as this nation consumes vast amounts of oil. But until 1990, American policy always relied on more subtle means than war to affect policy. In 1954, a CIA-engineered coup in Tehran toppled a popular Prime Minister and replaced him with a compliant and unpopular monarch, the Shah of Iran. There were no missiles hurled around, no American flags flying at the head of advancing columns; just a razor-like thrust and the pro-American Shah was on the Peacock throne. In the dark days of recession in the 1970s, Arab leaders, using the OPEC monopoly on oil, forced up the price of a barrel of oil from $2 to $15. In 1973, Saudi Arabia instigated an oil embargo on the US because of its massive military aid to Israel. Despite these serious provocations, the United States did not inject its military into the Arab world. And, when Iranian religious zealots took US embassy officials hostage in 1979, holding them captive for months, still no Stars and Stripes flew in Islamic lands. Using client states, quietly affecting policy with clandestine means, skillfully working the diplomatic lines, the US accomplished its purposes. But in 2003, under the cover of a War on Terror, George W. Bush has launched a War on Iraq, and the American presence in the Gulf region is subtle no more.

The thirteen-year war with Iraq is book-ended by the Bushites 1991 war in Kuwait and the 2003 invasion. Less well known is the fact that from 1991 to 2003 the war continued, as the United States attempted to control Saddam through economic sanctions and the "no-fly" zones. With the economic sanctions — Sanctions of Mass Destruction — Iraq was cut off from the rest of the world — no airlines flew in or out of Baghdad, no goods could be imported, no oil could be sold. (It should be noted that Saddam himself rejected the importation and distribution of food and medicine for some five years, hoping to worsen conditions and undermine the UN sanctions.) Iraq was an economic pariah in the world, the purpose being to force Saddam to disclose and then dismantle his weapons program. It was expected that a few months of such a stranglehold would put Saddam in a "box," but the brutal dictator did not relent, and extreme hardship struck the land. Scarcity forced the cost of basic necessities to soar (the cost of a sack of rice increased 6-fold, eggs 7-fold), unemployment was rampant, infant mortality doubled. A once vibrant economy became a "pawn shop" economy with people selling furniture, clothing, personal mementos, to obtain cash. Even medicine was blocked — diabetics could not obtain insulin, there were no vaccines, no antibiotics, and no chemicals to purify drinking water. Women began gleaning in the fields for scraps of food and men lit oil lamps due to lack of electricity; Iraq had turned back to the conditions of Mesopotamia and the age of Nebuchadnezzar. One expert on the Middle East, commented acidly that, "American policy-makers need to recognize that the only 'box' into which sanctions put Iraqis is coffins."[1]

Even the prestigious establishment journal *Foreign Affairs* carried an article entitled "Sanction of Mass Destruction," emphasizing that "economic sanctions may well have been a necessary cause of the deaths of more people in Iraq that have been slain by all so-called weapons of mass destruction throughout history" (excluding the gas chambers of Nazi Germany).[1] United Nations estimates are that 90,000 people died each year — 40,000 children and 50,000 adults — as a result of the United States inspired sanctions.

Not only did the intransigence of Saddam Hussein subvert the sanctions, but also by the end of the decade the entire venture was costing the US $100 million each year and was tying down thousands of troops. President Clinton had avoided dealing with the problem; George W. Bush would face up to the crisis. The United States had to confront Saddam or relent.

The "no-fly" zones established in 1991 and 1992 were a particularly onerous burden on the United States. After uprisings of Kurds in the north and Shiite Muslims in the south were put down brutally by Baghdad in 1991, the United States, with the support of Britain and France, established areas in the northern and southern thirds of the nation, around the Kurdish and Shiite areas, where Iraqi aircraft were not allowed to fly. These "no-fly" zones were never supported by precise United Nations actions, but were imposed by the United States using adroit legal maneuvering of existing sanctions. The United States and Britain patrolled the skies relentlessly, knocking out any radar, guidance systems and aircraft that were in violation. France withdrew from this program in 1996, joining most of the United Nations members in condemning these overflights as unwarranted violations of Iraq's sovereignty.

At the turn of the 21st century, American planes patrolled the skies of Iraq from their airbases inside Saudi Arabia and American naval vessels blockaded the Persian Gulf, making sure nothing that would sustain the Iraqi people crossed the barrier. Human rights organizations estimated that over 500,000 Iraqi children died as a result of the stringent blockade. Proving that the administration of George W. Bush has no monopoly on obtuseness and cruelty, when President Clinton's Secretary of State, Madeleine Albright was asked about the effect of these American actions on the children of Iraq, she replied: "We think the price was worth it."[2]

And what of Saddam Hussein? Could he not see the wrath of the United States descending upon Baghdad? Recent research by American intelligence reveals that both sides misunderstood the other. Since 1979 when Iran fell to the Islamists, Saddam was regarded as the United States ally in controlling Iran. The friendship and support from the Reagan administration confirmed this. Iraq's weapons program was a clear warning to Iran not to undertake any adventuresome forays in the Persian Gulf. There was that unpleasantness over Kuwait in 1990-91, but the failure of the United States to "go to Baghdad" in 1991, signaled to Saddam that the US-Iraq partnership was still valid. And the vigorous UN inspection and sanctions had caused Iraq to abandon all weapons of mass destruction in the early 1990s. However, if Iraq was to a bulwark against Iran's budding nuclear program, Iraq must appear to still have nuclear weapons. Thus, Saddam never would admit that all weapons had been destroyed. Saddam's weapons were a charade and Baghdad thought the Americans understood this; certainly,

---

1. Lawrence Potter, "The Middle East At the Millennium," *Great Decisions 2000*, Foreign Policy Association, p. 60, quote by Prof. F. Gregory Gause III.

1. John Mueller and Karl Mueller, "Sanctions of Mass Destruction," *Foreign Affairs*, 78, (May/ June 1999), p. 51. Also, Gilbert Achcar, *The Clash of Barbarians*, (New York: Monthly Review Press, 2002), p. 19.

2. Mackey, *The Reckoning*, p. 372.

Saddam thought, Clinton and Bush II had spies in Iraq to confirm the absence of weapons. But there were no American spies and George W. Bush was in the hands of the Neoconservatives who finally found their chance to take him out. The practical realism of the Reagan years flared into Militant Idealism under George W. Bush and Saddam's miscalculation cost him his regime.[1]

George W. Bush is basically a decent man, though clearly limited in his understanding of history. Had the dreadful fangs of terror not struck America on September 11, the Bush presidency may have been remembered as a sober, wholesome time. Bush campaigned during the 2000 presidential election on solid conservative themes:

> If we are an arrogant nation, they [the world] will resent us.... If we are a humble nation, they will respect us as an honorable nation.

> I don't think our troops should be used for what's called nation building.

> I'm going to be judicious as to how to use the military. It needs to be in our vital interests, the mission needs to be clear and the exit strategy obvious.[2]

As images of the smoldering ruins of the World Trade Center burned into the minds of all Americans, George W. Bush panicked and decided to cut the knot of confusion in the Persian Gulf by removing Saddam Hussein's murderous regime. President Clinton had vacillated, but Bush confidently strode into the witch's brew called Baghdad. As the President saw it, he could take this perilous and decisive action because God was on his side. Being a born-again Christian, George W. Bush believes that he is an instrument of God, elected to lead a regeneration of the US and the world. As Norman Podhoretz, the godfather of neoconservatism, has written:

> George W. Bush now knew that the God to whom, as a born again Christian, he had earlier committed himself had put him in the Oval Office for a purpose. He had put him there to lead a war against the evil of terrorism.[3]

President Bush's press conferences sounded as though Jerry Falwell or Pat Robertson had written the script, loaded as they were with references to "evil." Old Testament retribution had come alive in the White House; during one session with reporters Bush referred to "evil" and "evildoers" ten times. The President saw his role as similar to that of the Messiah, cleansing the earth of wrongdoers. In a speech at the National Cathedral shortly after the attacks the President shared his thoughts on a world purged of sin. "Our responsibility is already clear: to answer these attacks and rid the world of evil."[4] Emphasizing his point about the September 11 attacks, the President said: "We haven't seen this kind of barbarism in a long time," then condemned these evil men for "flying US aircraft into buildings full of innocent people and show no remorse."[5] Obviously George Bush was absent from history class on the day the subject of

---

1. *AJC*, Bob Drogin, October 13, 2004, p. A6. This recent information is from CIA agent Charles Duelfer's research mainly over the years of the Iraq War and includes numerous interviews with Iraqi officials, including Saddam Hussein.
2. Presidential debate of October 11, 2000.
3. *Commentary*, Sept. 2002.
4. *Washington Post* online, Charles Bakington, Sept. 14, 2001.
5. Woodward, *Bush At War*, p. 94.

American terror bombing of Dresden, Tokyo, Hiroshima, Nagasaki, Berlin, Hamburg and other cites was discussed.

It is customary in the US for Presidents to invoke the name of God, even suggesting rather formalistically that there is divine blessing for their policies. But somehow George Bush's relationship with God seems more intense, perhaps even providential. Has the President's personal religious belief become a national civil religion? The President enlightened the nation on divine intervention: "Behind all of life and all of history there is a dedication and purpose, set by the hand of a just and faithful God."[1] When asking the public to support a preemptive strike against Iraq, Bush explained that "the call of history had come to the right country. The liberty we prize is not America's gift to the world; it is God's gift to humanity."[2] Woodrow Wilson's idealistic quest to "make the world safe for democracy" has now become a divinely inspired crusade to reveal God's political plan.

Modesty and prudence in foreign policy eludes President Bush for he sees the United States providing world leadership consistent with a divine plan: "the call of history has come to the right country." Presidential speechwriter, Michael Gerson, tells of the following conversation with Bush: "Mr. President, when I saw you on television, I thought — God wanted you there. The President replied, 'He wants us all here'."[3] God's team is in place in the White House.

Bush's fervent devotion to the evangelical creed raises questions about the manner in which policy is set in the Bush White House. Was the decision to go to war made during prayer and Bible study in the family quarters? Did God reveal to the President that it was time to send American emissaries into Baghdad? Did the President weigh all the options — the costs in lives and traumatized bodies? The monetary costs? The effect of America's invasion on our world image? Will "The Battle Hymn of the Republic" replace "America, the Beautiful" in the hearts of Americans?

In the hours immediately following the terrorist attacks on the United States, President Bush proclaimed that freedom was under attack. This "off the cuff" remark has endured and remains the official explanation of why nineteen Arab suicide terrorists took such drastic action. But this "freedom theory" defies common sense, as the September 11 attacks and all those preceding attacks, occurred only after US troops were sent into Saudi Arabia. No terror attacks had taken place prior to 1990, yet American freedom has been around for many decades.

Nor is this "freedom" explanation consistent with Osama bin Laden's publicly stated motives. Several Western journalists have interviewed the terrorist leader and his propaganda tapes have been widely circulated on Arab television. He says nothing about destroying American freedom or anything about overturning American culture, although he doesn't approve of it. He doesn't rant and rave about American pornography, drugs and Hollywood movies. He does talk fervently about United States foreign policy.

Peter Bergen interviewed bin Laden in his mountain redoubt just before the September 11 tragedy. Bergen explains the attack this way:

> What he condemns the United States for is simple: Its policies in the Middle East. Those are...the continued US military presence in Arabia; US support for Israel; its continued bomb-

1. Lee McAuliffe, "Rambo," *AJC*, April 21, 2003.
2. Jim Wallis, "Dangerous Religion," *Sojourner Magazine* online, September-October, 2003.
3. Ibid.

ing of Iraq; and its support for regimes such as Egypt and Saudi Arabia that bin Laden regards as apostates from Islam.[1]

Another American journalist interviewed the leader of al-Qaeda in Afghanistan in 1998 and was given the same story: "Bin Laden told me his first priority was to get the US military bases out of Saudi Arabia, the holiest of lands in Islam."[2] Osama bin Laden sees any terrorist attack on the US as retribution for the brutal sanctions carried out against the Iraqi people as "the American-led sanctions resulted in the deaths of more than one million Iraqi children."[3] One of America's leading scholars on the Middle East, Bernard Lewis, comes to the same conclusion:

> For Usama bin Laden and his circle, the prime and immediate cause of the present phase of the struggle is the American military presence in Arabia — the Holy Land of Muslims, where the Prophet Muhammad was born and lived and died, where the Qur'an [Koran] brought God's final revelation to mankind, and where the first Muslim state was founded and ruled by the Prophet himself.[4]

Osama bin Laden's declaration of jihad against the US states his justification:

> For more than seven years the United States is occupying lands of Islam in the holiest of territories, Arabia, plundering its riches, overwhelming its rulers, humiliating its people, threatening its neighbors, and using its bases in the peninsula as a spearhead to fight against neighboring Islamic peoples.[5]

In a 1998 interview with PBS Frontline, Osama bin Laden made clear what provoked his anger at the US:

> The call to wage war against America was made because America has spearheaded the crusade against the Islamic nation, sending tens of thousands of its troops to the land of the two Holy Mosques over and above its meddling in its affairs and its politics, and its support of the oppressive, corrupt and tyrannical regime that is in the control.[6]

The hate that generated the horrid attacks on New York City and Washington arose from Islamist abhorrence of American foreign policy, not hatred of America or its freedoms. Any resolution of this dispute is not more defense spending, not more bombs thrown at Arabs, not an intrusive search for terrorists, but recognition that US foreign policy has gone out of control. Instead of plotting a War on Terror, the US should engage in a fundamental reassessment of its foreign policy, one that would include removing the offending troops from Saudi Arabia, reducing the American presence in the Persian Gulf, recognition of the desperate plight of the Palestinians, and moderating American aid to Israel.

The Bush administration appears to be determined to pursue this global venture, even if it means imposing a police state on the US. The colored security alerts, the intrusive, time-consuming inspections at airports and other venues, the cancellations of airplanes flights, the veil of suspicion cast upon all people who look Arab, bedevil and distort our lives because the US has chosen to impose a *Pax Americana* on the world. The fact is that ordinary citizens have lost

---

1. Bergen, *Holy War, Inc.*, p. 222.
2. Miller, *The Cell*, p. 190.
3. Ibid., p. 187.
4. Bernard Lewis, *What Went Wrong?* (New York: Harper Collins, 2002), p. 164.
5. Ibid.
6. Achcar, *The Clash of Barbarians*, p. 58.

freedom because of this grasping, overly ambitious policy. Until the US abandons its global reach, we will continue to look over our shoulder, and squirm at every thump in the night.

> The danger to ordinary Americans will remain with us as long as the United States remains committed to an unrestrained projection of her power everywhere in the world. Instead of realizing that the threat to America exists because of the policy of global hegemony, Mr. Bush persists in the view that this hegemony is the divinely inspired, morally obligatory, open- ended, and self-justifying global mandate of the Unites States. As long as that remains so, the terrorist threat to American will be unlimited and permanent."[1]

Conservatives in and out of the Republican Party profess allegiance even devotion to the Founding Fathers' wisdom. It is an article of faith for modern conservatives to seek "original intent" in reading the United States Constitution; to search for what the Revolutionary generation intended. Yet, when the issue of war and foreign policy arises, many conservatives reject the prudent counsel of Washington, Jefferson and others. Where is the modern Republican Party's devotion to modest goals and no entanglements in the world? It was not always so, for through the early years of the 20th century, Republican leaders championed a neutralist policy. It was the Democrat Party that first led the nation, by deceit and exaggeration, into foolish foreign wars.

But by mid-century it was apparent that the "war party" was winning elections — FDR had won four presidential elections — and the Democratic Party was entrenched in power throughout the nation. An expansive foreign policy and the wars which followed won elections for Franklin Roosevelt, Harry Truman and many other lesser men in politics. Learning quickly, the Republican Party by the 1960s was out-muscling the Democrats. Lawrence Korb, an official in the Reagan administration, saw first hand the inclination of neoconservative Republicans to overreach; they were, it seems, congenitally inclined to see threats everywhere. Korb reports: "They came in with a worldview, and they looked for things to fit to it." For a time the militant exuberance of these neo-cons was directed at China — the Tiananmen Square tragedy was highlighted. Then came Donald Rumsfeld's "rogue states" gambit and the "axis of evil" pitch by George Bush targeting much of the Muslim world. As Lawrence Korb says, "If they [the neo-cons] hadn't had 9/11, they would be doing the same thing to China,"[2] or someone else.

The bucolic setting of America as a passive "City on a Hill" has turned into a marauding, rogue superpower, marching to and fro across the globe. The financial costs are beginning to drain the coffers — the Iraqi occupation is costing $4 billion each month. Defenders of the bloated defense budget cry for more; each Stealth bomber costs $2 billion, the equivalent of nearly 40,000 public school teachers' salaries for life. The "indispensable nation" is virtually alone in the world, supported by the public opinion only in Israel. Even our traditional allies in Europe, those nations that we spent so much blood and treasure "defending" in two World Wars, have turned against US foreign policy. The hopes of peace following the Cold War victory have turned into a foreboding that another World War is upon us. It is as amazing as it is tragic that much of the world believes George Bush to be as dangerous as Osama bin Laden and Saddam Hussein. Sadly, for the first time in our nation's history, people across the world fear America.

---

1. *Chronicles, A Magazine of American Culture*, April 2003, p. 47.
2. *Time*, June 9, 2003, p. 32, 33.

Chapter 14. A Presidential Conversation in the West Wing

In the tumultuous days of 2005 with the United States having been under attack from terrorist groups, a remarkable and dramatic scene takes place in the West Wing of the White House. Four 19th century Presidents gather under clouds of war to confer with four chief executives who presided over America's 20th-century wars. The imaginary scene is similar to Walter Lippmann's "Four Dialogues" in his book *American Inquisitors*; those dialogues involved Thomas Jefferson, William Jennings Bryan and Socrates discussing religion and its relationship to government. As with Lippmann's work, an attempt has been made to accurately reflect the beliefs of long departed men as well as the current President; some of the dialogue uses the Presidents' own words.

JUST IMAGINE THE CONVERSATION IN THE WEST WING ——

After a cold, clear winter day in Washington D.C., night has fallen and eight leaders of America — past and present — gather to exchange views about America's 20th century foreign wars and entanglements. The lights are low in the room and the eight distinguished men sit comfortably and casually in cushioned chairs around a warming fire; the congenial and relaxed atmosphere belies the tension across the land known as the United States of America. The "Father of the Country" speaks first:

> GEORGE WASHINGTON — These are perilous times for our nation, but the entire 20th century was one of wars and foreign crises. While the earlier century had only two brief wars, those with foreign opponents in and around the borders of the nation, the more recent century has seen our nation fling itself into conflicts far from its borders, and —

> GEORGE BUSH — If I may interrupt, please. As the current resident of the White House I would like to ask that we begin this meeting with prayer; all meetings in my White House are started with a request of the —

> THOMAS JEFFERSON — Religion is an intensely private matter, Mr. Bush, and while I see nothing wrong with inviting Divine guidance, praying should be an individual matter. Religion and politics are separate and distinct realms.

WOODROW WILSON — Mr. Jefferson, as Christians we know it is impossible to remove God from any segment of our lives. I agree with Mr. Bush. We are all Christian believers here in this room and during such a time of crisis we should turn to our Lord. The Lord was always a guide to me during the crisis of World War I.

WASHINGTON — I must say that this is an extraordinary request. During the Philadelphia convention in 1787 when the present Constitution was drafted, we thought it improper and unnecessary to make a display of our religion. There was no mention of prayer until the convention drew to a close, and it was the feeling of the delegates at that time that we should not ask for "foreign aid." Each of us is free to seek Higher counsel. Gentlemen, shall we discuss the matter at hand? Why has our nation fallen into the habit of war?

RICHARD NIXON — I would like it noted that I oppose wars; I am a man of peace. I attempted valiantly to bring an end to the war in Vietnam, a war I might add, that was begun under the administration of my predecessor, a Democrat.

FRANKLIN DELANO ROOSEVELT — Richard, the implication of your statement is that there are Democrat wars and Republican wars. This is divisive and dangerous poppycock! The wars of our century were fought to defend against militaristic nations and national leaders who were as dangerous as they were mad. Democrats and Republicans alike courageously fought Hitler, Tojo, Mussolini and the Kaiser.

JOHN QUINCY ADAMS — Mr. Roosevelt, you are a student of history and know that each age has its monsters and its madmen. General Washington and his successor, my father John Adams, faced wild, murderous revolutionaries in France and never thought to send —

JEFFERSON — And President Madison and I contended with Napoleon Bonaparte who takes second place to no one in aggressively extending French power across Europe, even touching our continent. Yet we never sent troops to war in Europe to vie with Bonaparte.

ADAMS — Yes indeed, every age has its monsters. The question is how does our nation deal with them? Do we launch crusades around the world to slay the dragons, or do we keep our powder dry and develop our own self-governing society? The counsel of General Washington and others was to be neutral with regards to European quarrels and limited in the scope of our foreign policy.

WASHINGTON — Mr. Jefferson and I are often given credit for America's policy of avoiding entanglements in Europe, our neutrality policy. But it should be noted that this policy was well established in our land long before I delivered my Farewell Address in 1796, thus the neutrality policy bears the approval of history. It was not invented; it evolved over decades of experience.

GROVER CLEVELAND — I too would like to give my assent to the foreign policy of our earliest, and perhaps wisest President. I often spoke approvingly of the wisdom of neutrality during my two terms as President. As I told the nation in 1893, America stands for peace, commerce, and honest friendship with all nations, entangling alliances with none.

ROOSEVELT — That was then and this is now. The dangers America faced during the World Wars demanded our unswerving response. We can't go back to —

ADAMS — Mr. Roosevelt, why do you dismiss the traditions of neutrality with the statement "That was then and this is now?" And "we can't go back?" Please explain what you mean.

ROOSEVELT — I mean to say that times are different and each age must develop its own response to world crisis.

JEFFERSON — Do you mean that whatever decisions you made in the 1930s or that Mr. Bush made in 2003 in the Iraq invasion should not be questioned or —

ADAMS — Or that the wisdom that had evolved for a century and that taught my generation to limit its involvement with foreign intrigues is immediately thereafter irrelevant?

ROOSEVELT — The world is a different place in the 20th century than —

NIXON — Franklin, let me help you out. When we fought the fascist menace in World War II — and I say "we" because I was in the Navy in the Pacific — we had to face the enemy air force, heavy weaponry and eventually atomic weapons during the Cold War. Modern technology is a fearsome thing. The world is interdependent today and we live with the ever-present threat of attack. In 1800 you could relax your guard; in 1960, we could not.

CLEVELAND — My presidency was one hundred years after the Founding Fathers and I still found the idea of a limited foreign policy to be achievable. Decisions about war and the extent of our foreign policy are choices made by presidents. I fail to see how a new century negates the wisdom of the ages. "That was then and this is now" is simply a rhetorical device to avoid dealing with the question.

WASHINGTON — Our nation can trade globally, have extensive contacts with nations of the world, but still remain aloof from their political intrigues, border clashes and civil wars. Modern Germany and Japan are today among the greatest economic powers on earth, yet they do not engage in foreign entanglements, and have never sent troops into other regions to settle quarrels. The Vietnam War, Mr. Nixon, was a useless slaughterhouse for young Americans.

NIXON — As the preeminent nation of the world, we must carry out our international responsibilities. It is our job to defend freedom. Young men fought and died in Vietnam so that their children would never have to fight in a war again.

WILSON — That is exactly what we did in World War I. That was to be a "war to end all wars." We entered that conflict to achieve noble and transcendent goals.

ADAMS — Mr. Wilson, how did that noble effort work out? Can the thousands of young men who died in France rest contentedly for eternity knowing that this grand venture of ending all wars was successful? Tell me please, after World War I, were there anymore wars?

JEFFERSON — Indeed the world is moving faster and is more interdependent than in 1800. That is not the issue. It is not clear to me why such conditions demand that America send troops all around the world today. These modern conditions could just as easily be the prescription for staying home and minding one's own business. There are many nations today that remain neutral and have modest military forces, are there not?

NIXON — Yes, Tom, but they are smaller nations — Switzerland, Sweden, Denmark come to mind. A great nation cannot afford to do that.

ROOSEVELT — I have a different perspective than some of you. In 1941 America saw its friends in trouble. Hostile forces besieged China and England and we came to their assistance. Suppose my neighbor's house catches on fire and I have a length of garden hose that I can lend him. The right thing to do is lend him the hose and help out. That is what we —

ADAMS — Mr. Roosevelt, your simple homespun stories were apparently convincing to the people in mid-century, but they do not impress me. Loaning a garden hose to a neighbor and taking a neutral nation to war are not analogous. War involves death and high taxes, and raises profound questions of legality. And sadly, military efforts often turn sour. Serious public questions are raised in taking a nation to war. None of these profound questions are inherent in the simple act of being neighborly and lending a hose. Is this the way your administration thought through the question of American belligerency in 1941?

ROOSEVELT — These simple truths were an effective way of communicating with millions of people. My administration realized that never since Jamestown and Plymouth Rock has our civilization been in such danger as in the 1940s. The Nazis had sworn to overthrow the democracies and we fought them in Europe to prevent their invasion of the Americas.

ADAMS — Let us be specific about this issue of international menaces. In the years from 1803 to 1812, the British seized 1,000 American ships on the high seas and kidnapped over 9,000 American seamen. In some years they captured a thousand young boys, forcing them to work as "slaves" in their vessels. Yet, through those times we were generally able to maintain our peaceful posture.

WASHINGTON — Conducting a neutralist foreign policy, as I did, requires patience. In 1794 the British, our main tormentor, confiscated 300 American vessels, then, not to be outdone, the French began duplicating these nefarious deeds. Yet we retained our neutral position. During my eight years of presidency, no young men died from the wounds of war.

WILSON — The Germans were not just kidnapping our citizens; they were killing them in the Atlantic Ocean during World War I with their submarines. This was an unacceptable action, threatening and evil. And they were wantonly destroying property of American businesses. The civilized world cannot allow such attacks on civilization.

JEFFERSON —Our patience, sir, runs thin. How many American boys died in the fields of France after you declared war on Germany?

WILSON — We lost 125,000 young men in the year of fighting, and the nation cheered because they knew that the —

ADAMS — You lost 125,000 men to vindicate the deaths of two hundred during the submarine warfare? Why did you allow Americans to enter a war zone? Why didn't you just forbid Americans to travel on the high seas? Wouldn't that have solved the problem?

NIXON — But the nation's honor cannot allow that. A great nation cannot just be punched around by bullies — cannot be dragged through the mud. You have to stand up to them or they will pick you to death.

WILSON — For two and a half years my administration attempted to secure pledges from the Germans to stop their wanton use of the submarine, but to no avail. The Kaiser left me no alternative.

CLEVELAND — Mr. Wilson, alternatives are always available. Mr. Roosevelt, how many American men died at the hands of Germany in the north Atlantic Ocean *before* World War II?

ROOSEVELT — Well, we lost eleven on the USS *Kearney* and 115 on the USS *Reuben James.*

CLEVELAND — To vindicate a little over 100 dead Americans, you went to war in Europe and lost over 300,000? I am troubled by such behavior.

ROOSEVELT — But you must know that Germany declared war on us, we did not —

CLEVELAND — Mr. Roosevelt, I am surprised at you. You are talking to me as though I was an unsophisticated citizen. Are you saying that *you* did *not* want war with Hitler? Were you not relieved that war came? Did you not maneuver to get into that war?

ROOSEVELT — Well, yes, we looked forward to defending law and order and defeating a monster that was attacking our ally, Great Britain.

NIXON — Franklin is correct. Law and order must be upheld in the international arena.

WASHINGTON — Why is it that defending law and order has become the province of America? The 20th century has invested much effort into organizations such as the United Nation. Why is that body not responsible for maintaining law and order?

BUSH — Too often we have found that selfish nations obstruct worthy goals of the United Nations. The United States will not allow others to stop our defense of freedom. Sometimes you have to stand alone. It is hard work but with God's help we will prevail.

WILSON — I do have a concern about current America foreign policy, Mr. Bush. You do seem to be undermining the United Nations. The only hope for the world is international cooperation. Why have you gone off on your own? There is a special place in my heart for these —

BUSH — America must do what it needs to do. We cannot let other nations dictate your policy to us.

WILSON — But America is a signatory power of the United Nations charter and that charter clearly says that nations may not wage war on others unless they have been attacked? America was never attacked by Iraq.

BUSH — What was September 11? Three thousand Americans died that day and it is my —

WASHINGTON — Mr. Bush, aren't you confusing the individual terrorists who struck America on September 11 with the government of Iraq? Iraq had nothing to do with the terror attacks.

BUSH — All I know is we were hit by the Islamic terrorists. And the terrorists could have gotten weapons of mass destruction from Iraq. We didn't want a mushroom cloud to appear over New York. And it is my job to —

ADAMS — But Iraq didn't have such weapons. They had been destroyed years before. President Bush, is it you policy to invade any country that "might" have designs on the United States? If so, your century will be busy with invasion all the time.

JEFFERSON — Perhaps we should move on. You modern presidents speak of "law and order" and of "freedom," but American foreign policy must be designed for more modest goals. For us to attempt by war to reform the world and bring them to accept principles of morality and respect for the equal rights of nations would show us to be maniacs of another character.

BUSH — God has created America for a special purpose and He has given us the strength to accomplish great things. Foreign crises occur for a reason. It is all in a Divine plan. I, for one, will not waffle. Will not shrink form our responsibility.

WILSON — The United States must carry out the teachings of Jesus Christ, for nothing escapes His attention and He is watching to see if we follow His plan.

JEFFERSON — I find this talk of Jesus and His plan very confusing. Has America changed from a government of the people to a government of priests and prophets?

ADAMS — Mr. Bush, Mr. Wilson, this is a republic, not a theocracy. Is policy made in the Congress and the town meetings across the land, or is it made from the pulpit and the prayer circle?

ROOSEVELT — Our chief purpose to humanity rests on our combining power with high purpose. We can be both a policeman and a preacher to the world. My cousin, Theodore, often talked of the noble cause of war and aiding in the betterment of mankind. The world is a better place because of our crusades in Europe in the 20th century.

NIXON — I was privileged to lead the nation through some its darkest hours in the Cold War, under a nuclear cloud. As Franklin has said so eloquently, our task is to combine power and principle. Our nation is unique in that it understands better than the rest of the world that ideals must be the centerpiece of policy, but that military power must always be available in abundance. Power and principle, that's it.

CLEVELAND — In the year 2001, was the United States a safer place for the citizenry than in the year 1901? I dare say it is not. All the wars, all the money spent, all the deaths of valiant young men — and now young women — has not purchased a contented and secure nation.

BUSH — It is a safer place. We are winning the war on terror. As commander-in-chief it is my job to protect the country. I get up every morning thinking of how I can do my job better. After September 11 —

CLEVELAND — Mr. Bush, you seem to think that people are questioning your patriotism or devotion. The question is what is the best manner of serving the interests of America. We think that the 20th century has seen too much inflammatory rhetoric on these issues. I do recall your father, the first President Bush, saying to a world leader that provocative words during presidential elections should be understood as mere electioneering — just "empty rhetoric" he called it. Why do you modern presidents campaign on the graves of dead American soldiers? Is there no limit to your need to get elected?

BUSH — That's just politics. Everyone understands that during the political season we say and do things that are tough.

NIXON — Yes, George, you have to be tough.

BUSH — Let me finish. During one of the primary campaigns my supporters made accusations against my opponent, John McCain. Something about his wife's drug addiction and their adoption of a child who was not white. McCain complained to me, but I told him that this was just politics. Politics is rough and —

JEFFERSON — Did we fight a revolution against England and establish self-government for it to come to this?

NIXON — Tom, you are being quite sanctimonious. I have read that you advised that the blood of patriots would occasionally have to "water the tree of liberty." Rough politics is better than a bloody revolt.

BUSH — We don't want blood in the streets of America so we are carrying the torch of freedom to other lands. America's security is not confined to the coast of America.

WASHINGTON — A major reason for our revolt against England was that being a colony of his Majesty's realm pulled us into every European war. During my presidency we took responsibility for security on our continent. That is all. We hoped with independence to leash the dogs of war, as Mr. Jefferson said.

JEFFERSON — It seems that now the "dogs" are running wild. The less we have to do with the amities and enmities of Europe the better we are.

CLEVELAND — When war in Spanish Cuba threatened to involve the United States in the 1890s, I refused to be drawn in. A war over Cuba with Spain would make thousands of American households dark and leave empty chairs in living rooms across the land. Unfortunately, my successor, President McKinley allowed the war party to run wild. Each president makes choices; these wars are not inevitable.

NIXON — The World Wars and the Cold War have strengthened the forces of freedom. I agree with Franklin — though this pains me to do so — America must use a combination of power and purpose; it is our duty, as no one else can take the responsibility. The world needs leadership and it was my distinct privilege to provide that leadership for many decades.

JEFFERSON — During my presidency we were a beacon to mankind, an example of self-government for the world to behold, but we rejected war. I have the consolation to reflect that during the period of my administration, not a drop of the blood of a fellow citizen was shed by the sword of war. Not one of you in this room who served the nation in the 20th century can make that statement.

WILSON — American soldiers performed brilliantly in the World Wars because they saw that America was coming to the rescue of Europe in defense of those attributes we hold dear. We were the mediating nation, working to heal the wounds of war. Our nation is composed of heroes.

JEFFERSON — Yes, it is true that war confirms the heroic virtues, but what horrid creatures we men are that we cannot be virtuous without murdering one another. Mr. Roosevelt, my anti-war sentiments conflict with your cousin Teddy's view of war. I am aware that he has judged me to be the nation's worst president. Now, when I gaze at Mount Rushmore and see our visages etched in stone together, I am pleased to be cheek by jowl with Theodore, although Theodore may not be pleased with my companionship. America has a bountiful heart in that it can embrace not only a war-loving president but also a peace-loving president.

CLEVELAND — The burden of my political tenure was that a public office is a public trust. When a citizen is elevated to an elective office, he must never misuse the public's confidence; never spend heedlessly, never distort the truth. Self-government must never waste the people's money or debase the public debate. As I read the record of World War II, I find deviations from the truth. Mr. Roosevelt, am I right?

ROOSEVELT — In the heat of battle all sides are inclined to say things —

CLEVELAND — You told the people some inflated stories about Germany and Japan, even talking of a map that was not —

ROOSEVELT — In order to overcome the distortions of my opponents, I did add a bit of spice to the mix, but history confirms that I was on the right side.

ADAMS — How can you say that deceit is *ever* on the right side of self-government? The democratic process is all-important. The fuel of a republican government is truth.

NIXON — Let me get in here and come to the defense of my good friend Franklin. Deceit is no stranger to me, er-ah, I mean, that my opponents always called my things like "Tricky Dick." We lived in a perilous century with the nuclear cloud over our heads. The average citizen does not keep up on things and must be, well, lets say, babied along. That's what we had to do, just baby them along. Just like Franklin, all of us had to cut a few corners with the truth, but that's what politics today is about. I used to tell my fellow politicos that they should campaign as a conservative, then govern as a liberal. Ha. Ha. Politics is like selling any —

WASHINGTON — I find all casual talk of distorting the truth very disagreeable to my soul. In my day such duplicity was performed by scurrilous newspapermen, not by presidents.

CLEVELAND — I was faced in my second administration with a crisis over the attempted annexation of Hawaii. Congress wanted to annex those islands after American revolutionaries had overthrown the native monarch. This action was a perversion of our national mission. We

don't conquer other people! The only honorable thing to do was to undo the wrong and I refused to annex the Hawaiian Islands. Mr. Bush, does your Christian conscience trouble you about your war in Iraq? I am thinking of the allegations about Saddam Hussein that turned out not to be true.

BUSH — Not at all. Overthrowing Saddam Hussein was a righteous act. Our actions have warned other dictators that there is a limit to how much abuse the world will tolerate. I share the view of Mr. Wilson — there is a right and a wrong in the world. I truly believe that the Lord wants us to have democratic societies. He is on the side of freedom. Saddam was evil.

CLEVELAND — And Mr. Bush, it appears that you were less than honest in preparing your nation for the war in Iraq.

BUSH — We had some faulty intelligence information, but the important thing to remember is that Saddam is gone and the Iraqi people will have a better society.

JEFFERSON — Perhaps the American experiment in self-government, is just that — an experiment, and one that failed. I hear catastrophic wars defended as valorous, and now it is said that lying by presidents is acceptable. What has gone wrong in our country?

BUSH — We live in a dangerous age, quite different from those of 1790. Missiles can fly, mushroom clouds can form, anthrax plague can be —

ADAMS — Mr. Bush, we have heard those stories before; they are no better with the retelling. Why is it that 20th century presidents must panic the nation? Why exaggerate problems?

BUSH — The reality is that "rogue nations" are attempting to develop weapons of mass destruction and if given a chance they will use them against the United States. I am not a pacifist. America must be pre —

WASHINGTON — I must ask you a searching question, Mr. Bush. What has America done to the so-called "rogue nations" that would cause them to want to send nuclear weapons to our land?

ROOSEVELT — You gentlemen of the earlier times did not face such devastating weaponry and such instant death. Technology has changed the nature of foreign policy. Our nation cannot any longer remain aloof from these international battles. Republicans and Democrats alike recognize the menace. You men two hundred years ago had to contend with frigates and cannon balls.

BUSH — Today we face ICBM's and chemical warfare. You are judging us unfairly by two hundred-year-old standards.

WASHINGTON — Again my question — What has America done to cause these small nations — Iraq, North Korea — to hate us so? and want to destroy our fair land? Have you provoked them in some way? Do these rogue states hate other nations? Do they threaten Switzerland, Sweden, Canada? Why only America?

ADAMS — The answer is obvious. If America did not go forth across the globe attempting to slay monsters, there would be no "rogue nations." A peaceful life with ample time for self-development is the benefit of neutrality.

JEFFERSON — I believe the four of us from the earlier century are in agreement. You have brought these troubles on yourself. You spend as much on defense as the rest of the world combined, you intrude into every nook and cranny of the globe and then you claim that you are threatened. Do you see any connection?

ROOSEVELT — We are only attempting to preserve the Four Freedoms that I spoke of before World War II — Freedom of speech, freedom of worship, freedom from want, and freedom from fear. We must be the arsenal of democracy.

ADAMS — Mr. Roosevelt, you give us slogans! Meaningless slogans. How does American foreign policy ensure that six billion people have no "fears"? And that every "want" is satisfied? And further, our nation is now an "arsenal of nuclear weapons," not an arsenal of democracy.

WILSON — These are ambitious goals that Franklin has set forth and they cannot be realized in our lifetime, but they must be the polestar of our mission. Mankind has improved his lot with vision, with ideals. These are no just slogans, certainly they are not meaningless. They are noble sentiments.

ADAMS — Let me apologize for my intemperate remarks. Your noble slogans are not meaningless. I become quarrelsome at times; it's a family trait as my father John was also temperamental. What I mean is that your slogans are impossible to —

WASHINGTON — Perhaps I can explain how we feel. When we launched a revolt — a war — against England in the 1770s, our goals were quite exact: independence from the Crown, removal of English troops from the West, new American boundaries to the Mississippi River and fishing rights in the North Atlantic. We strove for nothing abstract and unreachable.

JEFFERSON — And in subsequent wars, the goals were also specific and achievable. One cannot reasonably fight a war for freedom or for democracy. We felt strongly about overthrowing the monarchial rule in the colonies, but we never dreamed of carrying such a crusade to other parts of the world. Your purpose is noble — I have myself been accused of overreaching and dreaming of impossible goals. But I firmly believe that you —

WASHINGTON — I have seen to much war and too many deaths, I must say that a nation's foreign policy must be more concrete, more specific than your Four Freedoms. The successful achievement of such abstractions as "freedom" cannot be measured when the war is over. How do we measure success in war when the goal is so elusive, so ethereal?

NIXON — May I be candid with all of you? The 20th century is basically a different political environment than the 18th or the 19th. Our nation is now more truly a "democracy" than two hundred years ago. In 1790, Mr. Washington, you did not have to deal with a prying and ruthless national press, nor did you have to pay much attention to the wishes of the people. Your decisions were the province of your cabinet — and a splendid one it was. They were, I believe, Mr. Jefferson, Mr. Hamilton, Mr. Knox and Mr. Randolph. I had a fine cabinet too, not as distinguished, but adequate. But we had to justify our policies every day before the press and the public. And the public is a demanding master. If public opinion began to sway against the communists, well, you just had to move with it. Can't fight it. Public opinion has been our master in this age. And public opinion often demands a fight. You see this in Great Britain when public opinion demanded war in 1914 and in 1939, dragging a reluctant leadership with them.

WILSON — Mr. Nixon, you are coming perilously close to saying that democracies are warlike. My own feeling is that democracy is a peaceful system and I spoke often of making the world safe for democracies. Are you telling me that a world of democratic nations would still war on each other? I don't accept such an idea. Democracies are peace loving.

ADAMS — Such academic chatter is a waste of time. Nations fight and quarrel whatever their political system. Wars are caused by clashing power and interest, not abstract political ideas. Presidents in the 20th century have burnished a "special relationship" with what is now called Great Britain. For those of us who were born and raised with the idea of England as the enemy of American, such an enduring Anglo-Saxon alliance is perplexing. Why have you adopted Britain as your special friend? We earlier presidents always considered London to be at least mischievous, if not threatening.

BUSH — Great Britain has been a staunch friend through two World Wars and we owe to the British —

ADAMS — Mr. Bush, we are aware of what has occurred. What we are asking is why. We read outrageous statements from the four of you about fighting for "freedom" with London. We regard London as the fount of oppression in the world, and I'm sure the colonial peoples, held in subjugation by England, agree.

WASHINGTON — And Britain is widely regarded as the nation that promoted the notion of popular rule, yet they retained an extensive empire. Mr. Wilson, how can you believe in the peacefulness of democratic nations when you know that Great Britain has been the world's greatest oppressor?

NIXON — The relationships of nations that develop over time are not altogether rational. For years the United States hid behind the skirts of the British Navy, right Franklin? And when it came time in the 20th century for America to take the lead, it felt comfortable for us to ally with Britain. And then as a politician, what you do is sell the US-British relationship to the press and the people, using any means you can. It may not make sense, but that's the way it is.

BUSH — Prime Minister Tony Blair has been a good friend of America in the war against terror in Iraq. We continue to have a special relationship. My reading of history tells me that we live in a very dangerous age and —

ADAMS — If I might interrupt. I don't want to seem impertinent, but Mr. Bush you speak of your reading of history. Please tell me what books you have read on 18th and 19th century life? How would you know that your own age is more dangerous than another?

BUSH — I confess that I don't read a lot and that I have an aversion to long books. I don't read newspapers either. I get my news directly from my team. I should have said that I have the impression that our age is more dangerous.

JEFFERSON — I believe you were asked during the presidential debates in 2000 what political philosopher you admired most and you replied Jesus Christ. Is that correct? Do you regard Jesus as a political philosopher — in the same nature as John Locke or Baron de Montesquieu?

BUSH — Well, we didn't study those gentlemen, as I remember. But what I meant was that the Bible was the best guide to —

JEFFERSON — The Bible? Guide to tax policy? to defense policy? to issues of federalism and civil rights?

NIXON — We have been on this issue of religion and government before. We need to recognize that the nation is more religious today than in the days of the Founding Fathers. Protestantism has been revitalized and —

WILSON — I know something of both the Bible and of political philosophers and I see no conflict between the two. If we follow the teachings of Jesus, our Savior, we will capture the essence of good government.

WASHINGTON — America's neutralist and limited foreign policy was designed in part to smooth the waters of politics in the nation. Early America was composed of various factions, or what are called interest groups now. Our neutralist policy allowed us to avoid the antagonisms of North vs. South, East against the West, worker against business. Sections and groups would have lined up on each side of a foreign quarrel. Neutrality serves to deflect internal quarrels.

ADAMS — Exactly! In my own time, groups representing Greece and Latin American nations came to us asking for aid in their national revolts. And good-hearted Americans began aligning themselves with each foreign appeal. Such an endeavor threatened the harmony of the nation and served to distract us from our own society. When these factions approached me, I told them that we have objects of distress to relieve at home.

NIXON — We have a large and diverse nation and it is only natural that various groups will attempt to influence foreign policy. There are the Cubans in Florida, the Vietnamese in Southern California, and the Jews across the land. These groups have as much reason to ask for assistance for their ancestral homeland — Cuba, Vietnam and Israel — as any other groups of Americans.

JEFFERSON — If America continues to dabble in every region of the world, raising the hopes of every ethnic group in the land, what will become of an "American" foreign policy? Jews will rush to aid Israel, Cubans will back Cuba, and Africans will come to expect America to attend to that continent. How will you conduct foreign business as you are pulled in every direction?

CLEVELAND — Indeed, this is one of the reasons that I opposed the imperial policy of Theodore Roosevelt and his group. Unlimited immigration and acquiring colonies only confuses America foreign policy.

NIXON — It is the task of a president to meld the conflicting groups together, to mix the stew of politics. You have to cater to the Jews, you have to attend to the Cubans in Florida — or

you will not win Florida's electoral votes, and that's a lot of votes. It's a balancing act and I was quite good at it, so was Franklin — the best.

BUSH — As a Christian nation we have an obligation to carry out the Lord's work. All of humanity is bound together under heaven, I truly believe that. I have proposed a relaxation of our immigration laws and opening our borders to destitute workers in Mexico. They need jobs and we need workers.

ADAMS — Some of your opponents say you need their votes in the next election.

JEFFERSON — Mr. Bush, it is apparent you are guided by a different, and I would say dangerous, set of ideas than we used two hundred years ago. You see nothing wrong with flooding the nation with immigrants from a poor neighboring nation; you find it acceptable that American foreign policy is drained for the benefit of ethnic groups. I fear for my nation.

WASHINGTON — Gentlemen, it is time to draw this meeting to a close. It would be appropriate for each of us to make a closing statement reflecting our most sincere beliefs about American foreign policy. I will begin, and we will close with Mr. Bush. When I left office I said that it is the true interest of America to steer clear of European contentions and to avoid becoming the pawn of the British. Those words of advice are true yet today. We should be the true friend of mankind by making this country an example for the world to see. If instead of the provocations of war, bloodshed and desolation, we should excel in the arts, in industry, in commerce, in philanthropy, how much happier mankind would be.

JEFFERSON — It should continue to be a maxim with us not to entangle ourselves in the affairs of Europe. Europe has a set of interests remote from our own. Through peaceable means we should make it in the interests of aggressors to do what is just. As for America, we should abstain from future wars unless invaded. Presidents should follow the guidance in the Constitution and do nothing to commit the nation to war unless the Congress should give its consent. Wars are the people's business.

ADAMS — The wars of the 20th century have been fought for noble purposes, but the goals of granting freedom to everyone and of eliminating all wars are unreachable. Your wars are not evil; they are folly. We should be the well-wishers to the freedom and independence of all, but the champion only of our own.

CLEVELAND — When members of the "war party" came to me asking for support in the war in Cuba, I said "No." Some of you need to learn to say "No" to war. And all of you need to follow the rule of honesty in government. There is no excuse for distortions and exaggerations — even for a good cause. It is the policy of neutrality to reject any share in foreign broils and ambitions upon other continents or in repelling their intrusion. It is the policy of Monroe and of Washington and Jefferson — alliances with none and friendship to all, even to rogue nations.

WILSON — I am often accused of transforming American foreign policy by infusing it with idealism. To this I proudly plead guilty. As a people, we must be true to our ideals and the world will thank us for our leadership. Unfortunately, my noble purpose has been distorted into a militant crusade. War is the scourge of mankind and must be eliminated. I took the nation into war in 1917, not to secure selfish advantage, but to improve the world system.

Replacing the old system of power politics with a new system of peace and disarmament based on the lessons of His book should be our objective.

ROOSEVELT — Never before in history has civilization been threatened by such monsters as we faced in World War II. Some wars can be avoided; World War II was a just and necessary war. It was a good war. I was criticized for refusing to negotiate with the Japanese, but you cannot tame a tiger into a kitten by stroking it. America must be the arsenal of democracy.

NIXON — No one can say that war is good for the country, economically or socially. But we must not shrink from the challenge of military conflict. Periods of peace are usually periods of stagnation. The United States is best when confronted by a military crisis. It brings out the best in people and causes presidents to rise above their station. Most of our greatest presidents were war presidents.

BUSH — September 11 has presented America with the opportunity to reshape the world, as Wilson did in 1919 and Truman after World War II. America is finally dealing with the terrorist menace and we are beginning to return to normal conditions. We have not seen terrorist bombings in months and the last remaining Muslim cells are being dismantled. During my administration we have increased the size of the military and we have shown the enemy that we will not be intimidated. I am determined to ensure the freedom of every American.

As President Bush concludes his statement, the door opens and Andrew Card, the Chief of Staff, enters and beckons President Bush to the hallway. After several minutes, the president returns, looking grave and shaken. There is bustling outside the room and several Marine guards and Secret Service agents appear agitated. President Bush stands nervously before the seven seated former presidents.

BUSH — I have just been informed that America is under terrorist attack. A bomb has just destroyed the Brooklyn Bridge isolating Manhattan Island from Brooklyn and Long Island. Terrorists are inside Hoover Dam and on the Golden Gate Bridge. It is a coordinated attack. All government buildings in Washington are being evacuated Gentlemen, we must leave the White House.

ADAMS — And I thought we were winning this war!

INDEX